THE ROUGH GUIDE TO

Kent, Sussex & Surrey

written and researched by

Samantha Cook and Claire Saunders

ROUGH GUIDES

roughguides.com

Contents

Introduction to
Kent, Sussex & Surrey

Traditionally, the southeast corner of England was where London went on holiday. Throughout the nineteenth and early twentieth centuries, everyone from royalty to illicit couples enjoyed seaside fun at Brighton – a splash of saucy decadence in the bucolic county of Sussex – while trainloads of Eastenders were shuttled to the hop fields of Kent for a working break from the city and boats ferried people down the Thames to the sands at Margate. Surrey has historically had a lower tourist profile, though its woodlands and hills have long attracted outdoors-lovers.

While many of its old seaside towns floundered in the late twentieth century – barring **Brighton**, which has always been in vogue – this stretch of England's coast is in the throes of an exciting renaissance. It's fashionable once more to enjoy the cheeky charms of the traditional resorts, while quieter seaside towns that have historically depended on fishing or shipbuilding offer a more laidback appeal. The cliff-fringed **coastline** itself provides excellent walking, swimming and watersports, along with heaps of bucket-and-spade fun. Inland, ancient **woodlands** and sleepy **villages** preserve their picturesque charm – there are even pockets of comparative **wilderness**, perhaps surprising in a relatively populous area so close to London. Sandwiched between the lofty chalk escarpments of the North and South Downs, a vast sweep is taken up by the largely rural **Weald** – the name comes from the Saxon "wald", or forest, dating to the days when it was almost entirely covered by woodland.

   This is also a region of huge **historical** significance, with the coast, just a hop away from the Continent, having served as a gateway for an array of invaders. **Roman remains** pepper the region – most spectacularly at **Bignor** and **Fishbourne** in Sussex and **Lullingstone** in Kent – and many roads, including the main A2 London–Dover, follow the arrow-straight tracks laid by the legionaries. Christianity arrived in Britain on the **Isle of Thanet** – the northeast tip of Kent, long since rejoined to the mainland by silting and subsiding sea levels – and in 597 AD, Augustine established a monastery at **Canterbury**,

ABOVE CAMBER SANDS

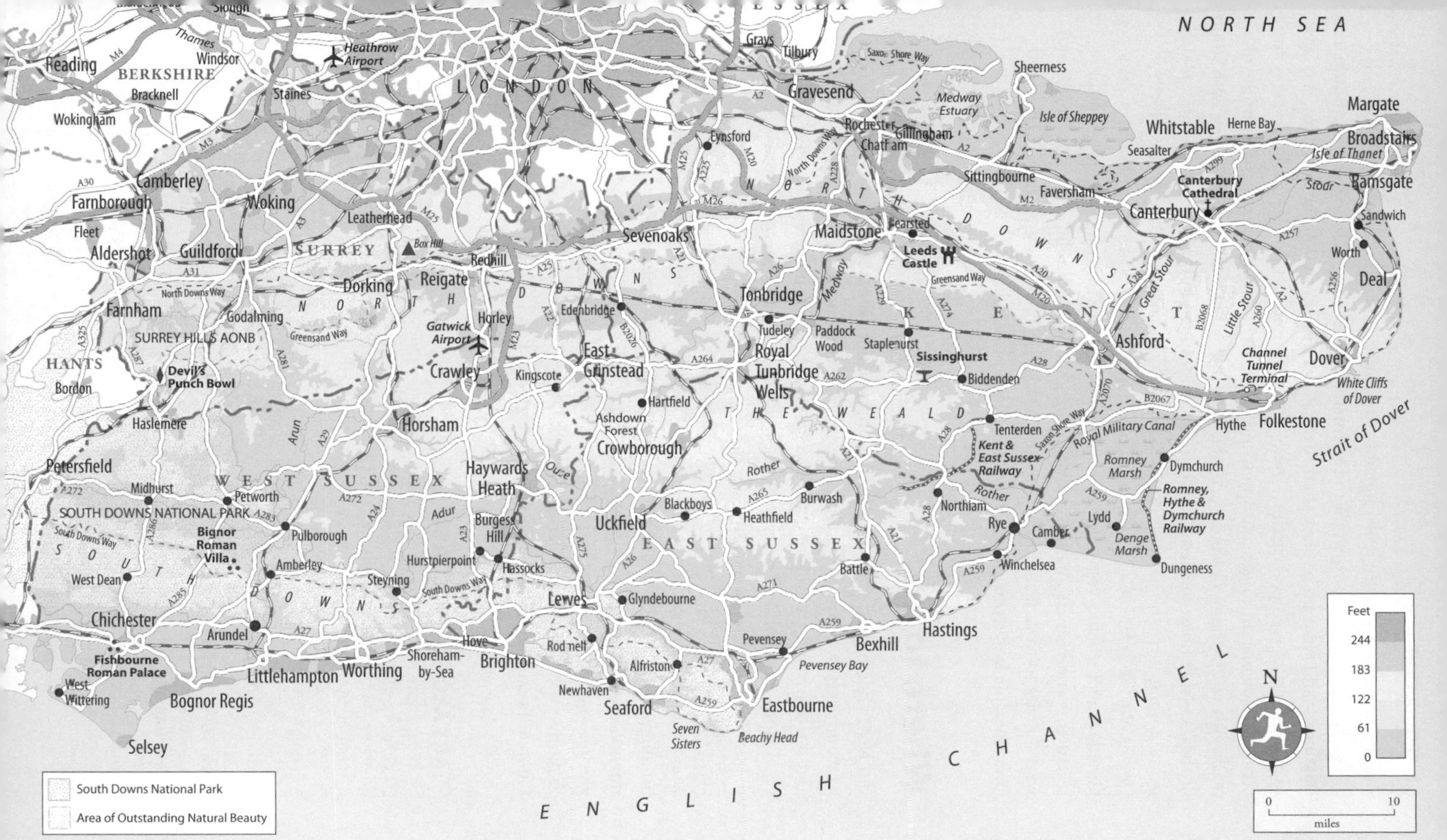

NORTH SEA
ENGLISH CHANNEL
Strait of Dover
LONDON
BERKSHIRE
SURREY
HANTS
WEST SUSSEX
EAST SUSSEX
KENT
NORTH DOWNS
SOUTH DOWNS
THE WEALD
Reading
Windsor
Slough
Thames
Heathrow Airport
Bracknell
Wokingham
Staines
Camberley
Farnborough
Fleet
Aldershot
Woking
Guildford
Leatherhead
Box Hill
Redhill
Reigate
Dorking
Farnham
Godalming
SURREY HILLS AONB
Greensand Way
North Downs Way
Bordon
Devil's Punch Bowl
Haslemere
Petersfield
Midhurst
Petworth
SOUTH DOWNS NATIONAL PARK
South Downs Way
Bignor Roman Villa
Pulborough
Amberley
West Dean
Chichester
Arundel
Fishbourne Roman Palace
West Wittering
Bognor Regis
Selsey
Littlehampton
Worthing
Shoreham-by-Sea
Hove
Brighton
Steyning
Hurstpierpoint
Hassocks
Burgess Hill
Haywards Heath
Horsham
Crawley
Gatwick Airport
Horley
Kingscote
East Grinstead
Edenbridge
Ashdown Forest
Crowborough
Hartfield
Uckfield
Blackboys
Heathfield
Burwash
Lewes
Glyndebourne
Rodmell
Newhaven
Seaford
Alfriston
Seven Sisters
Beachy Head
Eastbourne
Pevensey
Pevensey Bay
Bexhill
Hastings
Battle
Rye
Winchelsea
Camber
Northiam
Tenterden
Kent & East Sussex Railway
Rother
Lydd
Denge Marsh
Dungeness
Romney Marsh
Dymchurch
Romney, Hythe & Dymchurch Railway
Royal Military Canal
Saxon Shore Way
Hythe
Folkestone
Channel Tunnel Terminal
White Cliffs of Dover
Dover
Deal
Worth
Sandwich
Ramsgate
Broadstairs
Isle of Thanet
Margate
Stour
Herne Bay
Whitstable
Seasalter
Canterbury
Canterbury Cathedral
Great Stour
Little Stour
Ashford
Biddenden
Sissinghurst
Staplehurst
Paddock Wood
Tudeley
Royal Tunbridge Wells
Tonbridge
Medway
Leeds Castle
Bearsted
Maidstone
Sevenoaks
Eynsford
Rochester
Chatham
Gillingham
Sittingbourne
Faversham
Isle of Sheppey
Sheerness
Medway Estuary
Gravesend
Tilbury
Grays
Arun
Adur
Ouse
M4
M3
M25
M23
M20
M26
M2
A2
A3
A21
A22
A23
A24
A25
A26
A27
A28
A29
A30
A31
A225
A228
A229
A256
A257
A259
A260
A262
A264
A265
A271
A272
A274
A275
A281
A283
A285
A286
A287
A299
A325
A2070
B2026
B2067
B2068
Feet
244
183
122
61
0
N
0
10
miles
South Downs National Park
Area of Outstanding Natural Beauty

still the home of the Church of England. The last successful invasion of England, in 1066, took place in Sussex, when the **Normans** overran King Harold's army at **Battle** near **Hastings** – and went on to leave their mark all over this corner of the kingdom, not least in a profusion of medieval **castles**. There are other important historic sights at every turn – from **Tudor** manor houses and sprawling Elizabethan and **Jacobean** estates to the old dockyards of **Chatham**, power base of the once invincible British navy – along with some of the country's finest **gardens**. You can also stride along impressive long-distance **walks**, prime among them the glorious **South Downs Way** in Sussex and the gentler **North Downs Way** from Surrey to East Kent. Both Sussex and Kent – a county historically famed for its fruit and veg – are superb **foodie** destinations, with countless gastropubs, restaurants and farmers' markets providing delicious, local produce, from asparagus and wild cherries to fresh seafood and Romney Marsh lamb, and award-winning **vineyards** and venerable **breweries** producing excellent wines and ales.

Where to go

On Kent's north coast the sweet little fishing town of **Whitstable**, famed for its oysters, is a favourite getaway for weekending Londoners. **Margate,** becoming cooler by the day, and the charmingly retro **Broadstairs** make good bases on the Isle of **Thanet**, with its clean sandy bays, while the east coast has the low-key Georgian seaside town of **Deal**, the mighty **Dover Castle**, **Folkestone** – home to the art Triennial – and the strangely compelling shingle headland of **Dungeness**. Inland is the university city of **Canterbury**, where the venerable cathedral dominates a compact old centre packed with medieval buildings, while Kent's Weald boasts a wealth of historic **houses**, among them the mighty estate of **Knole** and **Hever Castle**, Anne Boleyn's childhood home, along with the glorious **gardens** at **Sissinghurst**, a stunning array planted by Vita Sackville-West. Exploring the many other historical attractions in the Weald – such as Winston Churchill's estate at **Chartwell** or Charles Darwin's family home at **Down House** – could

ART ALONG THE COAST

There's something in the air on the Kent and Sussex coast, where a crop of exciting new galleries, with their cutting-edge architecture and top-notch collections, have brought fresh energy and glamour to the faded seaside towns of the Southeast. Regenerating ailing coastal communities with high-profile buildings is no new thing, of course – the **De La Warr Pavilion** (1935), Bexhill's Modernist icon, was built partly for that very reason, although it was originally an entertainment hall and not a gallery. Within a couple of decades it had fallen into decline, but is buzzing again since a gorgeous restoration in 2005. Nearby, in Hastings, the **Jerwood**, whose shimmering black-tiled exterior echoes the look of the local fishing huts, opened in 2012 to display a fabulous modern British collection, while even Eastbourne, more associated with OAPs than YBAs, has the **Towner**, open since the 1920s but moved in 2009 to a gleaming new location. In Kent, much noise has been made about the **Turner Contemporary**, instrumental in having returned a smile to the face of once merry Margate; while Folkestone, if anything, has come even further, with the 2008 staging of the first lively **Triennial** – a major public show that has featured artists from Tracey Emin to Cornelia Parker.

CLOCKWISE FROM TOP LEFT *THE TIGER INN*, EAST DEAN, SUSSEX; CAROUSEL ON BRIGHTON BEACH; DOVER CASTLE

fill a long and happy weekend; the Georgian town of **Royal Tunbridge Wells**, or countless peaceful villages, make appealing bases.

The jewel of **Sussex** is the **South Downs National Park**, a glorious sweep of rolling downland that stretches from Hampshire into Sussex, meeting the sea at the iconic chalk cliffs of **Beachy Head and Seven Sisters**. There's wonderful walking along the Downs, not least along the South Downs Way, but equally rewarding are the less-tramped pockets of countryside, from the gorse-speckled heathland of **Ashdown Forest** on the edge of the sleepy High Weald, to the sandstone cliffs of the **Hastings County Park** on the coast.

Buzzy **Brighton**, a hip university town with a blowsy good-time atmosphere, makes an irresistible weekend destination, while handsome **Lewes**, in the heart of the South Downs, is famed for its Bonfire Night celebrations; **Hastings**, east along the coast, is an up-and-coming seaside community with a pretty old town and the scruffy but hip St Leonards neighbourhood to explore. On the edge of lonely **Romney Marsh**, picturesque **Rye**, with its cobbled streets and medieval buildings, lies within minutes of the family-friendly beach of **Camber Sands**. In West Sussex, the attractive hilltop town of **Arundel**, surrounded by unspoilt countryside, boasts a magnificent castle, while the lovely old cathedral town of **Chichester**, set between the sea and the South Downs, makes a perfect base for exploring the creeks and mudflats of **Chichester Harbour** and dune-backed **West Wittering** beach. Like Kent, Sussex abounds in great landscaped estates and gardens, among them seventeenth-century **Petworth House**, with its vast parkland roamed by deer, the Capability Brown-designed **Sheffield Park**, sprawling **Wakehurst Place** and the informal, imaginative garden at **Great Dixter**.

While **Surrey** boasts some attractive market towns, the chief appeal is in the **Surrey Hills**, in the North Downs, where ramblers and cyclists enjoy bluebell woods, mellow chalk grasslands and unspoiled hamlets like **Shere** or Peaslake. The wild heathlands of the **Devil's Punchbowl** feel very different, but are equally good for walking. The main sights include the **Denbies** vineyard, where you can tour the winery and enjoy tastings, the eccentric Edwardian estate of **Polesden Lacey**, and the great gardens of **RHS Wisley**, with its wonderful giant greenhouse.

When to go

Kent, Sussex and Surrey often feel slightly warmer than the rest of the country, and the Sussex coast in particular sees a lot of sunshine – Eastbourne is officially the sunniest place on the UK mainland. Weather-wise, the **summer** is the best time to head for the coast, though it can get crowded – and more expensive – at this time, and at weekends and during the school holidays. Travel during the week, if you can, or book well in advance. **Spring** can be a lovely season, especially for ramblers and cyclists, with the wildflowers in bloom; given the profusion of woodlands, **autumn** is frequently glorious, with great banks of fiery foliage set off by bright skies and crisp air. **Winter** tends to be quiet, with many of the major attractions closed; this is an ideal time to snuggle up with a pint of real ale in a country pub, or to enjoy the strange allure of an off-season English seaside town.

FROM TOP VINTAGE SHOP, BRIGHTON; ST THOMAS À BECKET, ROMNEY MARSH; ROCHESTER SWEEPS FESTIVAL >

Author picks

Our authors have explored every corner of Kent, Sussex and Surrey, and here they share their favourite experiences.

Glamping We all enjoy a spot of wild camping, and there are plenty of places to do that here, but for a bit more glamour we love *Barefoot Yurts* (see p.170), *Billycan Camping* (see p.241), and *Bloomsburys* (see p.150).

Wacky accommodation B&Bs are all very well, but for the utmost in unusual stays, try Margate's *Walpole Bay Hotel* (see p.93), the Martello Tower near Folkestone (see p.125), the Belle Tout lighthouse at Beachy Head (see p.217) or the *Old Railway Station*, Petworth (see p.248).

Quirky churches There are some real gems in this region. Track down the Marc Chagall windows in Tudeley Church (see p.142), St Thomas à Becket, stranded in Romney Marsh (see p.129), and the beautiful Berwick Church with its Bloomsbury Group murals (see p.221).

Seaside fun Enjoy simple, old-fashioned pleasures at our favourite retro *gelaterias* – *Morelli's* in Broadstairs (see p.97) and *Fusciardis* in Eastbourne (see p.212) – and while away a day crabbing at Whitstable (see p.80), East Head (see p.297) or Bosham (see p.298).

Vintage finds You can grab fabulous retro gladrags and funky vintage furnishings in Margate Old Town (see p.94), along Harbour Street in Whitstable (see p.86) and Norman Street in St Leonards (see p.183), and in the North Laine in Brighton (see p.276).

Funky festivals It's fun to get festive with the Rochester Sweeps (see p.71), at Jack on the Green, Hastings (see p.183), and with the Bognor Birdman (see p.286).

Fab gastropubs The region's bursting with them, but at a push we'd plump for the *Griffin Inn* in Fletching (see p.201) and the Michelin-starred *Sportsman* in Seasalter (see p.85).

> Our author recommendations don't end here. We've flagged up our favourite places – a perfectly sited hotel, an atmospheric café, a special restaurant – throughout the Guide, highlighted with the ★ symbol.

21

things not to miss

It's not possible to see everything that Kent, Sussex and Surrey have to offer in one trip – and we don't suggest you try. What follows, in no particular order, is a selective taste of the region's highlights, including gorgeous beaches, outstanding beauty spots, historic big-hitters and compelling cultural experiences. All highlights have a page reference to take you straight into the Guide, where you can find out more. Coloured numbers refer to chapters in the Guide section.

1

2

3

01 WALK THE SOUTH DOWNS WAY
Page 213
You'll enjoy amazingly scenic walking along this 100-mile long-distance path, which meets the sea at the magnificent Seven Sisters cliffs.

02 CHARTWELL
Page 152
Winston Churchill's country estate offers fascinating insights into the man, along with lovely grounds and local woodlands to explore.

03 THE TURNER CONTEMPORARY
Page 89
The modern art gallery that kick-started Margate's rebirth hosts excellent temporary high-profile exhibitions, and all for free.

04 THE DEVIL'S PUNCHBOWL
Page 304
Wild, raw and a little eerie – this Surrey heath is one of the county's more dramatic beauty spots.

4

5

 RYE
Page 166

Beautifully preserved medieval town packed with good hotels, restaurants and independent shops, with Camber Sands' beachy fun just minutes away.

 WEST WITTERING
Page 296

A delightfully uncommercialized dune-backed beach offering simple seaside pleasures and excellent watersports.

 THE GOODS SHED
Page 57

In a region packed with fabulous farmers' markets, Canterbury's foodie hotspot tops them all.

 PALLANT HOUSE GALLERY
Page 288

Chichester's modern art gallery offers a stupendous British art collection in an elegant Georgian building with an airy, modern extension.

 CYCLING
Page 29

Kent, Sussex and Surrey offer everything from family-friendly lanes to mountain-biking runs, with a number of particularly enjoyable coastal options.

7

8

9

14

10 CHARLESTON FARMHOUSE
Page 221
The country base for the bohemian Bloomsbury Group, Charleston is a riot of ebullient decoration.

11 PROSPECT COTTAGE
Page 130
Derek Jarman's shingle beach garden typifies the strange, unsettling allure of Dungeness.

12 ASHDOWN FOREST
Page 194
A gorse-peppered heath, Ashdown offers great walks and plenty of Pooh Bear fun – A.A. Milne set his stories here.

13 BROADSTAIRS FOLK WEEK
Page 98
A torchlit procession, lively pub gigs all over town and folk and world music bring a spirit of anarchy to this pretty coastal resort.

14 CANTERBURY CATHEDRAL
Page 41
Mother Church of the Church of England, Canterbury Cathedral has an extraordinarily rich history.

15 WHEELERS OYSTER BAR
Pages 85
Exceptional seafood dished up in a pocket-sized place – a contender for the best fish restaurant in the country.

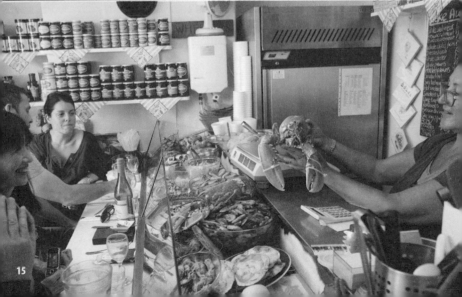

16 BOTANY BAY

With its towering chalk stacks, this is the most dramatic of Thanet's superb sandy beaches.

17 BRIGHTON'S CAFÉ CULTURE

Whether in gay Kemptown, bohemian North Laine or on the seafront, Brighton is the perfect place to while away a few hours with a coffee or a beer.

18 PETWORTH HOUSE

This enormous stately home boasts an astonishing hoard of art treasures and a deer park designed by Capability Brown.

19 DOVER CASTLE

You could spend a long, busy day in this vast fortress, exploring medieval tunnels, an Anglo Saxon church, royal apartments and an underground World War II hospital.

20 SISSINGHURST

Vita Sackville-West's ebullient, romantic garden is a blaze of colour, contrasts and surprising plantings.

21 ALFRISTON

With a glorious setting, this is the picturesque village to end them all, with a village green, cosy smuggling inns and good local walks.

16

17

19

20

21

Itineraries

Kent, Sussex and Surrey are wonderfully diverse, and these suggested itineraries offer a variety of different pleasures – from lively seaside fun in Brighton to a wealth of amazing historical sights and some of England's finest gardens. Mixing the big names with secret gems, they should help you discover some of the richness and diversity of this lovely region.

A WEEKEND IN BRIGHTON

FRIDAY NIGHT

Dinner Start off the weekend in style with champagne and oysters at *Riddle and Finn*. **See p.269**

Komedia Head to the hip *Komedia* theatre to catch some comedy or live music. **See p.275**

SATURDAY

Royal Pavilion Set aside a full morning to take in the splendours of George IV's pleasure palace by the sea. **See p.254**

The seafront Crunch along the pebbles, amble to the end of the tacky Palace Pier and grab a fresh mackerel sandwich from *Jack and Linda's Smokehouse* for lunch. **See p.257**

Shopping Spend the afternoon exploring the independent shops of the Lanes and North Laine. **See p.275**

Dinner Check out the excellent *Terre-à-Terre*, for vegetarian cooking like no other. **See p.269**

Nightlife Head out on the town – Brighton is positively bursting at the seams with über-cool bars and clubs, as well as a great collection of traditional boozers. **See p.272**

SUNDAY

Brunch Try *Bill's* or *Café Coho* for a lazy brunch. **See p.269 & p.271**

Yellowave beach sports venue Burn off the calories with a game of beach volleyball. **See p.259**

Duke of York's cinema If it's raining, hunker down at Brighton's independent cinema, or take in the exhibits at the Brighton and Hove Art Gallery. **See p.275 & p.256**

Lewes If you fancy a complete change of scene, hop on a train to nearby Lewes (15min), where you can wander through the town's ancient twittens and visit an ancient castle. **See p.226**

THE HISTORY TOUR

There are enough historical attractions in Kent, Sussex and Surrey to fill a trip of three weeks or more. Here we cover the biggest hitters on a tour that could easily last a fortnight.

❶ **Chatham Historic Dockyard** Ships, art, and a working Victorian ropery in the colossal dockyard from England's Great Age of Sail. **See p.72**

❷ **Canterbury** With three sights – including the mighty cathedral and the ancient abbey – comprising a UNESCO World Heritage Site, this venerable city is full of historic splendour. **See p.38**

❸ **Dover Castle** The mighty cliffside fortress packs in millennia of history, from its Roman

ABOVE BEACH HUTS ON BRIGHTON SEAFRONT

lighthouse to its claustrophobic World War II bunkers. **See p.112**

❹ Battle Abbey Site of the most famous battle ever fought on English soil, the 1066 Battle of Hastings, which saw the end of Anglo-Saxon England. **See p.186**

❺ Royal Pavilion, Brighton Opulent, quirky and marvellously OTT, George IV's Regency pleasure pavilion is quite unlike any other palace in the country. **See p.254**

❻ Fishbourne Roman Palace The largest and best-preserved Roman dwelling north of the Alps. **See p.292**

❼ Petworth House Seventeenth-century Baroque mansion, built by one of the wealthiest couples in the land, with sweeping parkland landscaped by Capability Brown. **See p.247**

❽ Polesden Lacey Elegant and utterly Edwardian, with wonderful grounds just perfect for picnicking. **See p.309**

❾ Knole The fifteenth-century childhood home of Vita Sackville-West, eulogized in literature and film, is an immense treasure-trove with an irresistible, faded beauty. **See p.151**

THE GARDEN OF ENGLAND

All three counties are heaven for garden fans, with a wide variety, from formal to revolutionary, to inspire even the most tentative of gardeners. The following are the must-sees; there are many more.

❶ Sissinghurst Abundant, romantic, nostalgic, witty – the bohemian cottage garden to end

them all, designed by Vita Sackville-West and her husband. **See p.146**

❷ Prospect Cottage, Dungeness The late Derek Jarman's windswept shingle patch is a poignant, artistic memorial to an extraordinary filmmaker. **See p.130**

❸ Great Dixter The innovative, experimental garden of the late, great Christopher Lloyd features informal garden rooms set around a Wealden hall house, and is still very much living and evolving. **See p.189**

❹ Sheffield Park Beautiful at any time of year but especially famed for its autumn colour, when banks of flaming foliage are reflected in the mirror-like surfaces of the landscaped garden's lakes. **See p.196**

❺ Wakehurst Place The country estate of Kew's Royal Botanic Gardens is a glorious 465-acre site taking in formal gardens, meadows, woodland, lakes and wetlands. **See p.199**

❻ Hannah Peschar Sculpture Garden A magical hideaway, with modern sculptures dotted around wild, lush woodland. **See p.310**

❼ Vann Water Garden One of the few gardens designed by the great Gertrude Jekyll that's open (occasionally) for visits, and a wonderful example of her revolutionary, informal style. **See p.307**

❽ RHS Wisley The RHS flagship offers a huge amount, including a giant glasshouse and all manner of experimental gardens, plus an excellent garden shop. **See p.311**

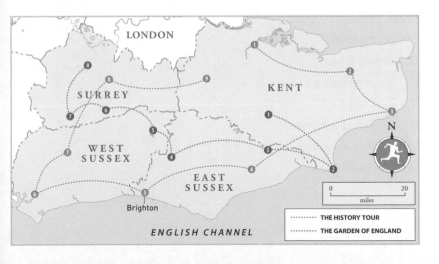

LOCAL FRUIT FOR SALE, *THE GOODS SHED*, CANTERBURY

Basics

Getting there

With **London** on its doorstep, the **Eurotunnel** at its eastern end, and **Gatwick** – Britain's second largest international airport – to the west, the Southeast is easily accessible by air, road or rail, with excellent transport connections that include the country's first high-speed rail line in Kent.

By car

From the M25 London Orbital, several major **roads** strike off south: the A2/M2 to Canterbury and the North Kent coast; the M20 to Folkestone; and the M23/A23 to Brighton. If arriving from the west, the A27 runs west–east across the coast, giving access to coastal towns including Chichester, Brighton, Eastbourne and Hastings, though it can be slow going – the 60-odd miles between Chichester and Hastings can take up to two hours to drive.

By train

Kent and the easternmost part of Sussex around Hastings is served by **Southeastern** trains. By far the quickest way to travel into Kent is on its regular high-speed services: one line (HS1) zips from London St Pancras to Ashford International, taking less than 40 minutes; the other runs along the North Kent coast past Rochester, Faversham, Whitstable, Herne Bay, Margate and Ramsgate, before heading inland to Canterbury, Ashford and then down to Folkestone. There are also regular, slower services into Kent from London Bridge, Charing Cross, London Waterloo and Victoria. Trains to Hastings, Rye, Battle and Pevensey in Sussex leave from Charing Cross and Victoria.

The rest of **Sussex**, and parts of Surrey, are served by **Southern Railways**. The fast service to Brighton from London Victoria takes just 50 minutes, and there are also regular services to Eastbourne, Lewes, Arundel, Littlehampton and Chichester. Brighton is also connected to London King's Cross and London Bridge by First Capital Connect. From the west, there are good connections from Portsmouth and Southampton along the coast to Brighton.

Surrey is predominantly served by **South West Trains**, which run regular services to Farnham, Guildford and Dorking from London Waterloo; Southern also runs a service to Dorking, from London Victoria.

By bus

National Express (@nationalexpress.com) run coaches from London's Victoria Coach Station to Arundel, Ashford, Battle, Bexhill, Bognor, Brighton, Chichester, Deal, Dover, Eastbourne, Folkestone, Hastings, Hythe, Lamberhurst, Littlehampton, Guildford, Maidstone, Shoreham, Tunbridge Wells and Worthing.

By plane

Gatwick Airport, just north of Crawley in Sussex, is Britain's second largest international airport, and has good rail connections on to Brighton and other destinations within Sussex. In North Kent, **Manston International Airport** (@manstonairport.com), twenty minutes from Canterbury, has connections to Jersey, Dubrovnik, Naples, Oporto and Verona. Just west of Brighton, **Shoreham Airport** (@shorehamairport.co.uk) has in the past operated scheduled flights to the Channel Islands and Paris, and at the time of writing is considering starting up some flights again.

By ferry, Eurotunnel and Eurostar

Ferries run from France to Dover and Newhaven (just east of Brighton) on the south coast. P&O Ferries (@poferries.com) and DFDS (@dfdsseaways.co.uk) operate the Calais-to-Dover route (hourly sailings; 1hr 30min), and DFDS also runs a service from Dunkerque to Dover (hourly sailings; 2hr). Transmanche run two daily ferries (4hr) between Dieppe and Newhaven. Consult @directferries.com, @ferrybooker.com or @seaview.co.uk for up-to-date information on who sails where. Fares vary between operators according to the date, time and type of crossing.

Often quicker and more convenient are the drive-on/drive-off shuttle trains operated by **Eurotunnel** (@eurotunnel.com) through the Channel Tunnel from Calais to Folkestone (35min). Book well ahead for the lowest prices, which start from under €70 for a car with all passengers.

The **Eurostar** train service (@eurostar.co.uk) operates through the Channel Tunnel from Calais, Brussels, Lille and Paris to London St Pancras, with some trains stopping off at Ashford International and Ebbsfleet International in Kent.

Getting around

Getting from A to B by public transport is generally pretty straightforward in Kent, Sussex and Surrey, at least when it comes to towns; the problem comes in getting to off-the-beaten-track attractions or villages deep in the countryside, which might only be served by one solitary bus, or involve a long hike from the nearest train station, making travel in anything but a car distinctly challenging.

Fortunately, some of the region's loveliest **countryside** – including Devil's Dyke and Beachy Head and the Seven Sisters in the South Downs National Park – has good public transport connections, and there are a huge range of wonderful long-distance walking and cycling routes (see p.28) if you're happy to ditch transport entirely.

Throughout the Guide we give public transport information for sights and attractions that are served by regular buses or trains.

By train

There are good connections around Kent, Sussex and Surrey with **Southeastern**, which covers Kent and the easternmost part of Sussex around Hastings, and runs the country's only high-speed rail services (see p.21); **Southern Railways**, which serves the rest of Sussex and some of Surrey; and **South West Trains**, which covers Surrey. The essential first call for information on routes, timetables, fares and special offers is **National Rail Enquiries**.

The key to getting the best **fares** is to book early and buy an "**advance**" ticket, which are only valid on the date and time specified; the most expensive tickets are "**anytime**" tickets bought on the day, which permit flexible travel on any train. For any journey, you can buy a ticket in person at any station, or by phone or online from any train operator or simply by using a quick and easy online booking site like ⓦthetrainline.com; the National Rail Enquiries website also offers direct links from its journey planner for purchasing specific fares. Bear in mind that some journeys (for example Hastings to London) are covered by more than one train operator, and an advance ticket bought from one operator will not be valid on the route run by the other. It's worth noting, too, that if you are travelling on one of the high-speed services operated by Southeastern you'll need a high-speed ticket, or else be required to pay a supplement.

There are a couple of **travel passes** that are worth considering: the **Kent Rover** gives you 3 consecutive days of unlimited train travel for £38 per adult (with up to 4 kids at £5 each); and in Sussex the **Downlander Pass** gives you a day's unlimited travel on Southern trains and local buses in the South Downs area (adults £10, kids £2.50, or £12.50/2.50 to include train travel on the whole Southern network).

Finally, it's worth bearing in mind that the region's **heritage railways** can be a useful means of getting to attractions otherwise not easily accessible, as well as being fun trips in their own right; the Romney, Hythe & Dymchurch Railway (see p.127) is a good way of getting to and from Dungeness; the Kent & East Sussex Railway (see p.149) connects Tenterden in Kent to the picture-perfect Bodiam Castle just over the border; and the Bluebell Railway (see p.196) links East Grinstead mainline station in Sussex with Sheffield Park.

By bus

The bus network in **Kent** is split into two: Stagecoach covers the east of the county, including Ashford, the Canterbury, Herne Bay and Whitstable triangle, Dover, Deal, Folkestone and Hythe; and Arriva covers the west, including Ashford, Gravesend, the Isle of Sheppey, Maidstone, Sevenoaks, Tonbridge and the Medway towns.

In **Sussex** and **Surrey**, buses are operated by a variety of operators including Arriva, Brighton and Hove buses (which cover the surrounding area as well as the city itself), Compass Bus, Metro Bus, Southdown PSV and Stagecoach, as well as smaller community operators. East Sussex County Council's website has links to bus timetables and a useful interactive bus map (ⓦeastsussex.gov.uk; search for "bus timetables and maps"); West Sussex County Council (ⓦwestsussex.gov.uk) lists local bus operators; and Surrey County Council's site (ⓦsurreycc.org.uk) has a county-wide map of bus routes plus links to timetables.

In most cases, **timetables** and routes are well integrated. Buses between towns tend to be frequent and regular, but services can be sketchy once you get into the countryside, and on Sundays they sometimes dry up altogether.

Tickets are bought on board the bus, and it's generally cheaper to buy a return ticket (or day pass) than two single fares – check with the driver. Children under 5 travel free, and older children will generally pay two-thirds of the fare. Many bus companies offer **travel passes**, but these are probably only of use if you are travelling in Kent in an area covered exclusively by Stagecoach or Arriva.

The impartial official service **Traveline** has full details and timetable information for every bus route in Kent, Sussex and Surrey.

By car

Once you get away from the main towns and the coast, driving is, inevitably, the easiest way to get around the region -- and in the case of many off-the-beaten track attractions, it's the only practical means of transport.

If you are driving, keep plenty of change handy; some towns do still offer free parking but they're few and far between, and parking machines and meters never offer change. Pay-and-display car parks are generally cheaper than on-street meters. Both Brighton and Canterbury offer **park-and-ride** schemes, which can be a useful way to bypass the stress of parking, especially in Brighton where parking charges have risen through the roof in recent years.

If you want to **rent** a car, the main rental companies have branches all over the region; expect to pay around £30 per day, £50 for a weekend or from £120 per week. The price comparison website ⓦ carrentals.co.uk is a good first port of call. If you'd rather rent something with a bit more personality, several small outfits offer retro **VW campers** (see p.25).

The AA (ⓦ theaa.com), RAC (ⓦ rac.co.uk) and Green Flag (ⓦ greenflag.co.uk) all operate 24-hour **emergency breakdown services**, and offer useful online **route planners**. You can make use of these emergency services if you are not a member of the organization, but you will need to become a member at the roadside and will also incur a hefty surcharge.

PUBLIC TRANSPORT CONTACTS

Arriva ☎ 0844 800 44 11, ⓦ arrivabus.co.uk
First Capital Connect ☎ 0845 026 4700, ⓦ firstcapitalconnect.co.uk
National Express ☎ 08717 818178, ⓦ nationalexpress.com
National Rail Enquiries ☎ 0845 748 4950, ⓦ nationalrail.co.uk
Southeastern ☎ 0845 000 2222, ⓦ southeasternrailway.co.uk
Southern Railways ☎ 0845 127 2920, ⓦ southernrailway.co.uk
South West Trains ☎ 0845 6000 650, ⓦ southwesttrains.co.uk
Stagecoach ☎ 0871 200 2233, ⓦ stagecoachbus.com
Traveline ☎ 0871 200 2233, ⓦ travelinesoutheast.org.uk

Accommodation

Kent, Sussex and Surrey offer a good range of attractive accommodation, from inexpensive guesthouses to cosy village inns, luxurious country retreats and cool boutique hotels. Camping is a good option, with glampers particularly well catered for in Sussex.

It is usually best to **book in advance**, especially in summer, and at certain times it's essential. Accommodation in Brighton, and all the seaside towns, is at a premium on summer weekends, while festivals such as the Whitstable Oyster Festival, Broadstairs Folk Week and the Goodwood events near Chichester fill up their towns very fast. Some places impose a minimum stay of two nights at the weekend and/or in high season – this is practically universal in Brighton and the bigger seaside destinations, but can also be true of some of the more remote guesthouses or glampsites, too – though these conditions can often be waived at the last minute if an establishment has not filled its rooms.

Hotels, inns and B&Bs

Hotels in Kent, Sussex and Surrey run the gamut from opulent country piles to (quite) cheap and (mostly) cheerful seaside guesthouses. The absolute minimum you can expect to pay is around £60 for a reasonable double room in a simple B&B, rising up to at least £200 for something more luxurious, be it a country manor set in its own grounds or a sleek sea-view affair in Brighton. For a good level of comfort, service and atmosphere you're looking at paying between £70–100, though of course there are exceptions.

ACCOMMODATION PRICES

For all accommodation reviewed in this guide we provide **high season** (July–Sept) weekend prices, quoting the lowest price for one night's stay in a double or twin room in a **hotel or B&B**, the price of a dorm bed (and a double room, where available) in a **hostel**, and, unless otherwise stated, the cost of a pitch in a **campsite**. For **self-catering**, we quote the minimum you might pay, for a night or a week, depending on the establishment, in high season. Rates in hotels and B&Bs may well drop between Sunday and Thursday, or if you stay more than one night, and some places, especially the seaside resorts, require a two-night minimum at the weekend and/or in high season.

TOP TEN BOUTIQUE BOLT HOLES

Belvidere Place Broadstairs. See p.97
Elvey Farm Pluckley. See p.161
The Front Rooms Whitstable. See p.82
The George Rye. See p.170
Guest and the City Brighton. See p.267

The Oast in Wittersham See p.150
Reading Rooms Margate. See p.93
Richmond House Chichester. See p.290
Swan House Hastings. See p.180
Wingrove House Alfriston. See p.219

Though we have quoted **prices** in our reviews (see p.23), it is increasingly the case that rates are calculated according to demand, with online booking engines such as Ⓦlastminute.com often offering discounts on last-minute reservations, and establishments raising or lowering their prices according to how busy they predict they might be.

Staying in a **B&B** will generally, but by no means always, be cheaper than a hotel, and will certainly be more personal. While often little more than a couple of rooms in someone's house, B&Bs tend to offer something rather special, and the houses themselves may well be part of the appeal – a converted oast house in Kent, for example, or a Sussex lighthouse. In Surrey, certainly, staying in a country B&B is by far the best accommodation option, allowing you to see the best of the county. B&B facilities have improved drastically in recent years, with tea- and coffee-making facilities, good bathrooms and a hearty breakfast being standard – certainly in the places featured in the Guide – along with all sorts of luxurious added extras like fluffy robes and posh bath products. Most offer en-suite bathrooms, or at least private bathrooms. Rooms that do share bathrooms will be cheaper. In addition, most B&Bs now offer free wi-fi as standard, which is not always the case in hotels.

Another good option, especially for foodies, is to stay in a **"restaurant with rooms"**. In these places the focus is mainly on the meal, which will invariably be good, with the added luxury of an extremely short and easy trip up to bed after a long and enjoyable dinner. Restaurants with rooms often offer meal-plus-bed deals, and a delicious breakfast to boot, which prove good value.

Hostels

Even for those who can't face the idea of bunking up with snoring strangers, **hostel accommodation** is well worth considering. Most hostels nowadays, whether owned by the Youth Hostels Association (YHA) or independently run, have shaken off their institutional boy scouts/backpackers-only image, and offer a mix of dorms – with anything from four

to twelve beds – as well as simple double, triple or family rooms.

There are twelve **YHA** (Ⓦyha.org) hostels in Kent, Sussex and Surrey: three in Kent – in Canterbury, Margate and out in the countryside near Gillingham; five in Sussex – Alfriston, Eastbourne, Littlehampton, Telscombe (near Lewes) and Shoreham; and three in Surrey, two of which are in the Surrey Hills near Dorking, and one is in the Devil's Punchbowl. YHA hostels can offer very good value, especially for families. Many are in glorious rural locations, making great bases for walking or cycling holidays, and the costs (rates vary according to season and demand) are very competitive, with double rooms from as little as £40. Facilities, and atmosphere, vary from hostel to hostel; each has self-catering kitchens and some also have cafés, but all are comfortable, clean and safe. In addition, the YHA has a couple of basic camping barns in Kent and Surrey, which offer simple, communal accommodation, a roof over your head, plus kitchen and washing facilities and communal areas – for around £14 per person per night.

The YHA is a member organization, part of the global HI (Hostelling International) group, but non-members are welcome to stay for an added fee of £3 per night. At around £15 per year for an individual, which includes children travelling with you, £20 for two adults, or £10 if you're under 26, membership is well worth considering.

There are also a handful of **independent hostels** (Ⓦindependenthostelguide.co.uk) in Kent and Sussex. Of these, the *Kipps* hostels, in Brighton and Canterbury, are both highly recommended, offering good inexpensive rooms and dorms, and with a friendly, sociable atmosphere.

Camping

Camping is an excellent option in Kent and Sussex, whether you want a simple, wild camping experience, pitching your own tent in a car-free field, or a more luxurious all-in glamping holiday, snuggling up in a tipi, a quirky shepherd's hut or a vintage Airstream caravan. Smaller, quieter sites

TOP FIVE CAMPSITES
Blackberry Wood Sussex. See p.235
Hidden Spring Sussex. See p.192
The Warren Kent. See p.125
Welsummer Kent. See p.159
WOWO Sussex. See p.201

dominate the scene, with a number of beautifully situated sites in bucolic countryside – in the North and South Downs, say, or on the clifftops along the east coast – though there are larger caravan sites clustered around the more popular seaside destinations like Camber and the Thanet resorts. Sussex in particular has taken up the **glamping** trend with relish, with some of the best-equipped and most enjoyable sites in the country, though there are some excellent choices in Kent, too, including a safari-style option in a wild animal park (see p.128).

Most campsites close in the winter, though exact dates vary according to the weather on any one year; we've included this information in our reviews. **Prices** for pitches start at as little as £5 per person for the most basic site, but you could pay as much as £300 for a couple of nights in your own two-yurt hideaway, warmed by a wood-burner with kitchen and shower.

Several small outfits offer **retro VW campers**, or "glampervans", which cost around £350–500 for a long weekend; check out ⓦvwweekender.co.uk (Henfield, West Sussex); ⓦcjscampers.com (Uckfield, East Sussex); ⓦhiredaisy.com (Hastings, East Sussex); ⓦrentaretrocamper.co.uk (Deal, Kent); and the ⓦtheglampervanhirecompany.com (near Faversham, Kent).

Self-catering

Self-catering, whether in a rural cottage for two, a city-centre apartment or a family house by the sea, invariably proves cheaper than staying in a hotel and offers far more flexibility. Where once a week-long stay was standard, many places nowadays offer breaks of as little as one night, though there will usually be at least a two-night minimum stay at weekends and in the summer. Depending on the season, you can expect to pay around £300 a week for a small, out-of-the-way cottage or maybe three or four times that for a larger property in a popular spot. Note that properties owned by the National Trust and Landmark Trust, which are in historically significant and beautiful buildings, tend to be pricier than other options and often booked up long in advance.

SELF-CATERING AGENCIES

Bramley & Teal ⓦ bramleyandteal.co.uk. Stylish cottages in East Sussex and Kent, with good searches including "eco-friendly" and "dog-friendly".

Cottages4You ⓦ cottages4you.co.uk. Wide range of properties in the region, including some in Surrey.

Freedom Holiday Homes ⓦ freedomholidayhomes.co.uk. Based in Cranbrook in Kent, and with more than 200 holiday homes across Kent and Sussex.

Garden of England Cottages ⓦ gardenofenglandcottages.co.uk. Classy self-catering in Kent and Sussex, with a good choice of traditional buildings in rural settings.

Landmark Trust ⓦ landmarktrust.org.uk. A preservation charity that has converted historically important properties into characterful accommodation – from tiny Tudor cottages to Arts and Crafts mansions.

Mulberry Cottages ⓦ mulberrycottages.com. Upmarket self-catering in the south of England and Scotland, with a good selection in Kent and Sussex.

National Trust ⓦ nationaltrustcottages.co.uk. The NT owns many cottages, houses and farmhouses, most of which are set in the gardens or grounds of their own properties – the dozen or so in Kent, Sussex and Surrey include a garden studio in Virginia Woolf's Monk's House, and a lighthouse keeper's cottage on Dover's White Cliffs.

Rural Retreats ⓦ ruralretreats.co.uk. A nice selection of places in Kent and Sussex, including lighthouse keepers' cottages.

Stilwell Cottages Direct ⓦ cottagesdirect.co.uk. A good choice of properties in Kent and Sussex, with direct booking.

Food and drink

You're never far from somewhere really good to eat in Kent and Sussex, whether you want a simple Ploughman's lunch in a pub garden or a Michelin-starred blowout; the Surrey countryside, too, has a fair share of classy gastropubs and restaurants. Kent and Sussex, in particular, have embraced the local food movement with gusto, with countless gastropubs and restaurants sourcing food locally, naming their suppliers, and even growing their own. Kent, which has long tagged itself "the allotment of England" and is traditionally famed for its fruitgrowing, still produces delicious veg, soft fruits and juices, along with fresh fish and exceptionally tasty lamb fed on the nutrient-rich Romney marshes, along with a variety of good cheeses. Sussex, too, offers plenty of fresh juices, artisan cheeses and Romney lamb, with fresh fish from the Hastings fleet and scallops from Rye Bay. Surrey has yet to attach itself to

slow food principles with such vigour, but most of its best restaurants will list ingredients that have made the quick hop across the border from Kent and Sussex.

This part of the country is also excellent for **real ale** and **wine** – along with a couple of historic local breweries there are scores of local microbreweries and small-scale, award-winning vineyards producing delicious tipples, and no shortage of traditional country pubs or good restaurants where you can enjoy them. For more on local food in Kent, see ⓦ producedinkent.co.uk, and in Sussex, see ⓦ www.sussexfoodawards.biz.

Restaurants and gastropubs

One of the great pleasures of a trip to this region is to head out to a country **gastropub**, filling up on delicious, locally sourced food before or after a bracing walk. The distinction between restaurant and gastropub is becoming fuzzier every day, with the gastropubs tending to lead the way when it comes to innovation and high cuisine principles: the Michelin-starred *Sportsman* (see p.85), in Seasalter near Whitstable, for example, which is one of the best places to eat in the country, despite its unprepossessing pub exterior, or the equally good

Curlew (see p.193), another unpretentious place in a former coaching inn near Bodiam in East Sussex.

Beware, though – most places have caught on to the "gastro" buzzword, and not everywhere that calls itself a gastropub (with the inevitable shabby chic refit that that entails) is going to be good. We've reviewed the very best places in the Guide, but as a rule of thumb it's worth checking to see if an establishment names its suppliers on the menu or online, has a regularly changing menu, and doesn't try to cover too many bases.

As for **restaurants**, most towns of any size that are geared up for tourists will have a few very good options, from veggie cafés to simple bistros and seafood joints – we've reviewed these in the Guide. The most popular seaside towns, including Whitstable, Broadstairs, Ramsgate and Brighton, as well as the countryside surrounding Chichester, and the area around Faversham in North Kent, are to varying degrees foodie hotspots, with fabulous restaurants, gastropubs and on-trend options from tapas bars to Modern European bistros.

Markets and farm shops

Sussex and Kent have a number of thriving **farmers' markets**, selling delicious seasonal produce and

---

LOCAL SPECIALITIES

Cobnuts This tasty Kentish hazelnut, harvested between mid-August and October, can be bought at local farmers' markets and found as an ingredient on menus throughout the county.

Fruit Kent's mild climate and rich soil provide excellent conditions for growing fruit. Wild cherries have been eaten here since prehistoric times, and cherry and apple trees were planted by the Romans and the Normans, but it was Henry VIII who really developed a taste for fruit and veg varieties as we recognize them today. In 1533 he employed the first royal fruiterer to plant orchards in Teynham, a few miles west of Faversham, and the county, "the fruitbowl of England", never looked back.

Hops Though the industry has declined drastically in the last sixty years, Kent in particular still has a strong emotional attachment to the hop, which was such a crucial part of the economy in the nineteenth century (see p.137). Local breweries, including the venerable Shepherd Neame in Kent, and Sussex's Harveys still use local hops in their beers, and you can also buy live plants to

grow, or dried garlands of bines for decoration – as seen in countless pubs and hotels in the Weald. Some artisan food producers also add hops to crackers or biscuits to add a unique, slightly bitter flavour.

Huffkins An old-fashioned Kentish speciality – a soft, flat, small oval loaf with a deep dimple in the centre, occasionally served like a bap, and often served warm.

Lamb Though many of the famed Romney Marsh lambs now live elsewhere (see p.128), the appearance on menus of their prized, deliciously tender meat is the sure sign of a good restaurant; the sweet, succulent meat of Sussex's Southdown lamb is equally prized.

Oysters The old fishing town of Whitstable, on the north coast of Kent, is the place to eat these briny treats (see p.84); they even have an annual festival to give thanks for them.

Rye Bay scallops The season for Rye Bay's prized bivalves –some of the best in the country– lasts from November to the end of April, and reaches its peak in February, when more than 15,000 of them are consumed during Rye's week-long Scallop Festival.

TOP FIVE FOR A TREAT
Apicius Cranbrook. See p.148
The Curlew Bodiam. See p.193
Drake's Ripley. See p.311
The Pass *South Lodge Hotel*. See p.201
Wheelers Whitstable. See p.85

artisan bread, cheese, chutneys, fruit juices and the like from local producers, along with beers and wines produced in the region. These are lively, well-attended affairs, and always worth a visit, even if just to browse. We've reviewed the cream of the crop in the Guide; you can find a comprehensive list of farmers' markets in Kent on ⓦ kfma.org.uk; in Sussex on ⓦ eastsussex.gov.uk and ⓦ westsussex.info /farmers-markets.shtml; and in Surrey on ⓦ surreycc .gov.uk. **Farm shops** are also good places to pick up picnic supplies or foodie treats to take home – many have diversified to sell deli products and produce from other farms as well as from their own, offering a wide choice. We've reviewed some of the best, but it's always worth stopping off to nose around any you may come across on your travels.

Drink

Kent, Sussex and Surrey excel in traditional **country pubs**, often picture-postcard places with oak beams, mullion windows and real fires. The vast majority have local ales on offer, and the best will also list wines from the local vineyards, and fruit juices and ciders from local suppliers. Most serve food, and though many have been "gastrified" to within an inch of their lives, even the fanciest will have a room set aside for drinkers who simply want a quiet pint.

For cutting-edge **bars** and cool **cocktails** you'll do best in Brighton; even Kent's most popular tourist destinations, including Canterbury, Whitstable and the Thanet towns, have quite a low-key drinking scene, preferring quiet pubs and friendly drinking holes over sleek see-and-be-seen joints. One trend that is making quite a stir in Kent in particular is the arrival of the **micropub** – minuscule, independently run and very simple places, often set up in old shops and open for limited hours, where a small crowd of real-ale fans can hunker down to enjoy beer, conversation and – well, nothing much else, really; that's the whole point.

Real ale

Both Kent, the heartland of the old hopping industry, and Sussex, which was also scattered with hop farms, are known for their **real ales**; there are also a handful of good microbreweries in Surrey. The biggest local names are **Shepherd Neame** (ⓦ shepherdneame .co.uk), the nation's oldest brewery, which operates from Faversham in Kent as it has for centuries, producing its characteristically earthy ales – Spitfire and Bishop's Finger among them – and running a huge number of local pubs; **Harveys** in Lewes, Sussex (ⓦ harveys.org.uk), which dates back to 1792 and is known for its traditional cask ales, including the flagship Sussex Best bitter; and the **Dark Star Brewing Co** (ⓦ darkstarbrewing.co.uk), which started out in 1994 in the basement of a Brighton pub and has grown to become Sussex's second largest brewery after Harveys.

There are also an increasing number of **microbreweries**, some of them very small indeed, producing interesting, top-quality ales and porters. These outfits often apply traditional methods and creative innovations – Kent's Ripple Steam Brewery, for example, which makes beer with green hops rather than dried, giving a fresher taste – selling their seasonally changing selections in local pubs, restaurants and farm shops, and occasionally online.

Wine

English wine is fast shucking off its image as somehow inferior to its longer-established European counterparts. And Kent, Sussex and Surrey, where the soil conditions and geology are almost identical to those in France's Champagne region – and where the climate is increasingly similar, due to a helping hand from global warming – are home to some of the country's most highly

---

TEN BEST FARMERS' MARKETS AND FARM SHOPS

Cowdray Estate Farm Shop Sussex.
   See p.245
The Goods Shed Kent. See p.56
Lewes Farmers' Market Sussex. See p.231
Macknade's Farm Shop Kent. See p.78
Middle Farm Shop Sussex. See p.223

Penshurst Farmers' Market Kent. See p.141
Quex Barn Farm Shop Kent. See p.94
Sharnfold Farm Shop Sussex. See p.213
Shipbourne Farmers' Market Kent.
   See p.132
Shoreham Farmers' Market Sussex. See p.283

regarded vineyards. These chiefly produce white and sparkling wines, for which nearly all of them can claim a raft of prestigious awards, but there are some fine rosés and robust reds out there, too.

Most good restaurants in Kent and Sussex in particular will make a point of listing local wines, and you'll be able to buy them in farm shops and at the vineyards themselves. You can also find bottles from the major producers in supermarket aisles: Waitrose, which has stocked English fizz for years, is the main stockist. It's worth checking out a few **vineyards**, joining their guided tours and taking advantage of free tutored tastings: the wines will change from year to year, of course, but rosé and Chardonnay fans especially should check out Kent's **Chapel Down**, which also does superb fizz and excellent whites, while **Biddenden**, also in Kent, also have some fine off-dry sparkling wines and a distinctive, very delicious Ortega. In Sussex **Ridgeview** is renowned for its bubbly, while **Sedlescombe** (ⓦ englishorganic wine.co.uk) adopts innovative biodynamic principles for its wine making, with delicious results, and **Bolney**, unusually, is best known for its reds.

See ⓦ englishwineproducers.com and ⓦ sparkling englishwine.com for details of more vineyards around the Southeast.

A SPARKLING SUCCESS STORY

The **English wine industry** is booming. Around four hundred vineyards across the country produce about four million bottles a year (more than fifty percent of it sparkling), and the best of the harvest more than rivals the more famous names over the Channel. **Sparkling wine** is the biggest success story, with several wines from the Southeast beating the best Champagnes in international blind-tasting competitions. New vineyards are springing up all the time: **Rathfinny Estates**, outside Alfriston, has just started planting vines that will eventually cover 600 acres, making it not only the biggest vineyard in the country – overtaking **Denbies** in Surrey – but also one of the largest in Europe.

Several vineyards in Kent, Sussex and Surrey now offer tours and tastings. Among the best are:

Biddenden Kent. See p.148
Bolney Estate Sussex. See p.197
Carr Taylor Sussex. See p.185
Chapel Down Kent. See p.149
Denbies Surrey. See p.308
Ridgeview Sussex. See p.235

Sports and outdoor activities

Kent, Sussex and Surrey offer a good range of outdoor activities, chiefly walking and cycling, along with excellent sailing, watersports and birdwatching. There are also good opportunities for adrenaline junkies, including rock climbing and paragliding, and the region's home to some of the finest golf courses in the country – including two at the Goodwood Estate in Sussex, and three near Sandwich. As for spectator sports, Surrey boasts the Epsom Downs racecourse, home to the Derby for nearly 250 years, and Sussex is home to Goodwood, site of the UK's major horse and motor races. For something even gentler, cricket is king in this part of England, still played on quiet village greens as well as on the bucolic county ground at Canterbury and at the lovely ground near Firle, near Lewes, home to one of the oldest cricket clubs in the world.

Walking

Perhaps unexpectedly, given how populated this corner of the country is, Kent, Sussex and Surrey are superb **walking** destinations, with plenty of trails, of all lengths and for all abilities, where you can get away from it all within minutes. From blustery seaside hikes atop towering chalk cliffs, to pretty rambles in ancient woodlands and undulating paths following ancient pilgrims' routes, the three counties offer a wide variety, whether you're after a country pub stroll or a long-distance trek.

The chalky hills of the **North Downs** and **Greensand Way** – both of which curve their way through Surrey to East Kent – along with the **High Weald** in Kent and Sussex, and the **South Downs** in Sussex, are all prime walking territory. **Long-distance paths** include the 150-mile-long **North Downs Way** (ⓦ nationaltrail.co.uk/northdowns), which starts at Farnham in west Surrey and heads through the beautiful Surrey Hills, following old pilgrims' paths to Canterbury and Dover along the highest points of the Downs. Further south, and running roughly parallel, the 108-mile **Greensand Way** heads off from Haslemere in Surrey, traversing dramatic heathland, ancient woodlands and the pretty Kent Weald countryside before ending near the border with Romney Marsh.

In Sussex, the **Sussex Downs** – part of the **South Downs National Park** (W southdowns.gov.uk), which spreads into Hampshire and is crisscrossed by nearly 2000 miles of footpaths – provide fantastic walking opportunities, whatever you're after; the website details some good options that start and finish at a bus stop or train station. The jewel of the South Downs is the 100-mile **South Downs Way** (W nationaltrail.co.uk/southdowns), which follows ancient paths and droveways along the chalk escarpment from Winchester all the way to the glorious Beachy Head cliffs. Running north to south through the South Downs, the 38-mile-long **New Lipchis Way** (W newlipchisway.co.uk), from Liphook in Hampshire to West Wittering, affords you the special thrill of arriving in Chichester on foot. In the Weald, the largely rural and heavily wooded area that spreads through both Kent and Sussex, the 95-mile **High Weald Landscape Trail** (W highweald.org), from Horsham to Rye via Groombridge and Cranbrook, takes you from bluebell woods to marshlands, via winding sunken lanes, past some of the area's prettiest villages. The North Downs Way and South Downs Way are linked by the 80-mile **Weald Way** (W kent.gov.uk), a peaceful route that heads south from Gravesend to Eastbourne, spanning chalk downlands and valleys and taking you through Ashford Forest, and by the 40-odd-mile **Downs Link** (W westsussex.gov.uk), which follows the traffic-free course of a disused railway line from near Guildford, winding through woods, heath and open country before linking up with the South Downs Way and following the River Adur down to Shoreham. The 150-mile **Sussex Border Path** (W sussexborderpath .co.uk), meanwhile, loosely follows that county's inland boundary with Hampshire, Surrey and Kent, starting in Thorney Island and ending in the lovely medieval town of Rye.

Long-distance **coastal paths** include the splendid 163-mile **Saxon Shore Way** (W kent.gov.uk), which heads from Gravesend to Hastings, following the coastline as it would have looked 1500 years ago – which, in some parts is now quite far inland – encompassing the bays of Thanet and the White Cliffs of Dover, and taking in the appealing small towns of Faversham, Deal and Rye. Curving a twenty-mile course along the Thanet shore, from Minnis Bay in the west to Pegwell Bay near Sandwich, the **Thanet Coastal Path** (W thanetcoast .org.uk) is an excellent way to experience the lovely beaches in this part of Kent.

We've flagged up especially nice walks throughout the Guide, and recommend some of the best walking books in our Books section (see p.326). There are countless more walks in Kent, Sussex and Surrey; check W visitkent.co.uk, W visitsussex.org and W surreycc.gov.uk. In addition, the **National Trust** (W nationaltrust.org.uk/visit/activities/walking) is a good resource, with downloadable walks of varying lengths from most of their properties.

Cycling

Kent, Sussex and Surrey offer rich pickings for cyclists. From gentle traffic-free woodland trails suitable for family pottering to heart-thumping training routes, from invigorating coastal clifftop paths to sleepy country lanes, the routes are varied and well marked.

Of the **National Cycle Network** routes (W sustrans.org.uk), Route 1, which runs from Dover all the way up to Scotland, takes in the East Kent coast between Dover and Sandwich before heading inland via Canterbury to meet the North Kent coast at Whitstable and Faversham, while Route 2 – also known as the **South Coast Cycle Route** – follows most of the south coast from Dover to Cornwall, dipping inland at various points, with an uninterrupted stretch between Dover and Worthing.

In Kent, the **Crab and Winkle Way** (W craband winkle.org), also a walking path (see p.60), forms part of National Cycle Route 1 and provides a quick and scenic route between Canterbury and Whitstable on the coast. Just east of Whitstable, the eight-mile **Oyster Bay Trail** (W kent.gov.uk) is a family-friendly seaside path that leads to Herne Bay and the beachfront Reculver Country Park; from there you can link up with the 27-mile **Viking Coastal Trail** (W visitthanet.co.uk/Viking), which follows the Thanet coast all the way round to Pegwell Bay, south of Ramsgate, before looping inland through quiet countryside. You can also cycle

---

ACTIVE FUN: A TOP FIVE

Paddle your own canoe along Kent's quiet waterways See p.62
Make like a monkey on a zip-line See p.144 & p.158
Swoop above the South Downs on a paraglider See p.224
Outjump your opponents at Brighton beach volleyball See p.259
Pedal in the wake of Olympic champions at Box Hill See p.309

SEVEN SPLENDID WALKS

The Cuckmere Valley and the Seven Sisters An eight-mile circular walk in one of the most beautiful parts of the South Downs National Park, offering magnificent views of soaring white cliffs and velvety green chalk grassland. See p.216

Ashdown Forest There are lots of good paths through the gorse-speckled heaths of Ashdown Forest, with the added fun for kids of tracking down Pooh Bear's favourite haunts. See p.194

Cocking to West Dean The five-mile Chalk Stones Trail threads through some stunning Downland scenery, following the trail of thirteen chalk sculptures by artist Andy Goldsworthy. See p.246

Whitstable to Seasalter Crunching along the shingle the two miles from the

oyster-loving town of Whitstable to the superb *Sportsman* gastropub is a lovely way to experience this stretch of the North Kent coast. See p.80

Herne Bay to Reculver A splendid stretch of the long-distance Saxon Shore Way, taking you from the old-fashioned seaside resort to the ruined clifftop church towers standing sentinel over the wildlife-rich Reculver Country Park. See p.87

The Crab and Winkle Way Follow the line of a disused steam railway from Canterbury to Whitstable, passing orchards and ancient woodland on your way. See p.60

The Surrey Hills Using a country village like Shere or Peaslake as your base, the Surrey Hills offer countless rambles through Surrey's glorious old woodlands. See p.308

---

from Hythe to Winchelsea in Sussex along the **Royal Military Canal** (W royalmilitarycanal.com), a gratifyingly flat thirty-mile ride through quiet marshes. Shorter rides include the ten-mile **Tudor Trail** (W kent.gov.uk), a largely traffic-free route between some of the Weald's most important historic houses; the flat, marshy lands of the Hoo Peninsula and the Isle of Sheppey are also very good for cycling. If you're after something more active, head to **Bedgebury Forest** (W forestry.gov.uk/bedgebury), which is crossed by National Cycle Route 18 and features challenging off-road mountain bike trails.

In Sussex, the **South Downs Way** (see p.213) is as exhilarating for cyclists as it is for walkers, though bear in mind you'll be sharing the path with horses as well as pedestrians. The **South Downs National Park** website (W southdowns .gov.uk) has a number of downloadable cycle rides that start and finish at a bus stop or train station. The gentle **Downs Link** walking/cycling path (see p.283) and the **New Lipchis Way** (see p.296) are also worth checking out, while the flat **Manhood Peninsula** (W selseycyclenetwork.org.uk) is a great place to cycle, with a good network of canalside towpaths and a couple of routes from Chichester, including the 11-mile **Salterns Way** (W conservancy.co.uk/page/cycling/346/), which leads to East Head via country lanes, roads and designated paths. In the High Weald of Sussex the nine-mile **Forest Way** (W sustrans.org.uk) follows an old railway line from East Grinstead to Groombridge, on the Kent borders, skirting the northern edge of Ashdown Forest as it goes.

In **Surrey**, the steep zigzag road up **Box Hill**, long a popular route for training cyclists, formed part of the road race cycling event in the London 2012 Olympics, and is particularly popular at weekends. A couple of National Cycle Network routes also run through Surrey – the quiet **Route 22** (W sustrans .org.uk), which follows tranquil paths and bridleways between Guildford and Rowledge, south of Farnham, and the stretch between Guildford and Cranleigh on the **Downs Link** (see p.283) are particularly worthwhile.

Watersports

With its long, varied coastline, its marshlands and its rivers, the Kent and Sussex region offers excellent watersports. Sailing, windsurfing and kiteboarding are especially good around **Whitstable** (see p.81), with good jet-skiing, sailing and kayaking in **Herne Bay** (see p.87), windsurfing and kiteboarding at **Margate** (see p.97), and superb surfing in Thanet's **Joss Bay** (see p.97), where there's a top-notch **surf school** (W kentsurfschool.co.uk). The seaside town of Hythe, on Kent's east coast, is also something of a windsurfing centre (see p.126), while the nearby **Action Watersports** (W actionwatersports.co.uk), inland in Lydd, offers waterskiing (including barefoot skiing), wakeboarding and jet-skiing on a purpose-built lake. Further down the coast, just across the border in Sussex, blustery **Camber** is another major centre for wind- and kitesurfing, with local outfitters offering paddleboarding, kitebuggying and paddlesurfing (see p.174); while on the **Manhood**

Peninsula (see p.296), surfing, including stand-up paddlesurfing, power-kiting, paddleboarding and wind- and kitesurfing are also popular. There's **diving** all along the south coast, with some good wrecks to explore; trips run from Eastbourne (see p.211), Brighton (see p.259) and the Manhood Peninsula (see p.296), among others.

Finally, if its buff beach fun you're after, **Brighton** is the place, offering year-round beach volleyball and other sports at the excellent **Yellowave Beach Sports Venue** (Ⓦyellowave.co.uk); local operators also offer scuba diving, paddleboarding, kayaking and wakeboarding, with windsurfing, stand-up paddleboarding and cable wakeboarding on a beachfront lagoon. You can **sail** around Brighton, too; the local sailing school offers courses in dinghy sailing and high-speed powerboat rides.

Birdwatching

Birders are spoilt for choice in Kent and Sussex, with large swathes of lonely marshland, dense, ancient woods, and otherworldly shingle habitats all offering splendid twitching territory.

There are seven major **RSPB reserves** (Ⓦrspb.org.uk) in **Kent**: the Blean Woods near Canterbury (see p.60); Cliffe Pools (see p.74) and Northward Hill (see p.74) on the Hoo Peninsula near Rochester; the headland of Dungeness down toward Sussex (see p.130); the lonely Elmley Marshes on the Isle of Sheppey (see p.75); and Tudeley Woods in the Weald near Tunbridge Wells (see p.142). There are also good sightings to be had in the **nature reserves** at Stodmarsh near Canterbury (see p.61), around the Swale Estuary (see p.77) and at Pegwell Bay near Ramsgate and Sandwich (see p.106). Other good locations include **Reculver Country Park** between Herne Bay and Thanet (see p.87); **Romney Marsh** (see p.128); the **Blean woods** around Canterbury (see p.60); and the **White Cliffs of Dover** (see p.117) – though sadly you categorically won't see bluebirds over those. For more on birdwatching in Kent, check the website of the **Kent Ornithological Society** (Ⓦkentos.org.uk).

In **Sussex**, the **WWT Arundel Wetland Centre**, one of just nine Wildfowl and Wetland Trust (WWT) sites in the UK, is home to endangered waterfowl from around the world as well as a host of native birds (see p.240). You'll also spot birds in the shingle-saltmarsh **Rye Harbour Nature Reserve** (see p.170); in the heathland habitat of **Ashdown Forest** (see p.195), in the **Loder Valley Nature Reserve** (see p.199) at Wakehurst Place in the Western High

Weald; and on the Manhood Peninsula around the beautiful **Chichester Harbour** (see p.297) and at the **RSPB Pagham Harbour Nature Reserve** (see p.295). There are two more **RSPB reserves** in West Sussex – one on the Adur estuary, and another at Pulborough Brooks, near Pulborough – and two in East Sussex, at Broadwater Warren across the border from Tunbridge Wells, and Fore Wood, near Battle. You can find out more about birding in Sussex on Ⓦsos.org.uk, the website of the **Sussex Ornithological Society**.

In the **Surrey Hills**, there's an RSPB reserve at Farnham Heath, an area of restored heathland and bluebell woods abounding in crossbills, nightjars, tree pipits, woodcocks and woodlarks.

Paragliding and rock-climbing

Keen **paragliders** make a beeline for the **South Downs**, where local companies (see p.224) offer lessons that mean you can be up there on your own within just one day, along with – slightly – less daunting dual-control gliding sessions.

Meanwhile, there's superb **climbing** around Eridge Green and Groombridge, on the Sussex–Kent border near Tunbridge Wells. **Eridge Rocks** (Ⓦsussexwildlifetrust.org.uk) and **Harrison's Rocks** (Ⓦthebmc.co.uk) offer challenging climbs for experienced climbers, and outfitters nearby offer lessons (see p.193).

SPECIALIST OPERATORS

Canoe Kent Ⓦcanoekent.com. Guided and self-guided canoe trips along the backwaters of Kent, including the rivers Stour and Medway.
Capital Sport Ⓦcapital-sport.co.uk. Cycling tours through Kent, with gourmet, luxury, arty and historic options.
Contours Ⓦcontours.co.uk. Walking holidays in Kent, Sussex and along the North Downs Way in Surrey.
Experience Sussex Ⓦexperiencesussex.co.uk. Activity and craft holidays in Sussex, including guided walks and cycle rides.
Footpath Holidays Ⓦfootpath-holidays.com. Self-guided and guided walking holidays in the South Downs.
Great Oak Walks Ⓦgreatoakwalks.com. Walking holidays in Kent and Sussex, including a Castles and Gardens trip, a walk through the Sussex Weald to Rye, a 1066 walk and another taking in the best of Kent's historic houses.
Pear Tree Tours Ⓦfootprintsofsussex.co.uk. Self-guided walking holidays and short breaks in the South Downs National Park.
So Sussex Ⓦsosussex.co.uk. Family-run outdoor activities operator, offering everything from cycling tours to canoeing and mushroom hunting; they can also organize tailor-made activity holidays.
Walk Awhile Ⓦwalkawhile.co.uk. Self-led and guided walking holidays in the Kent Downs, through the Weald and along the White Cliffs, with luggage transfers.

Festivals and events

Kent, Sussex and Surrey have a packed festivals calendar, which includes plenty of arts and music events and foodie festivals showcasing and celebrating the region's fantastic local produce. There's no shortage, too, of wonderful, quirky festivals and events that you won't find anywhere else in the country, from Sussex Bonfire Night to the Bognor Birdman.

JANUARY TO MARCH

Wassail Middle Farm, near Lewes, Jan. Traditionally held on Twelfth Night, this winter celebration features a ceilidh, mummers, a torchlit procession and plenty of mulled cider. Ⓦ **middlefarm.com**

Rye Bay Scallop Week Ten days end Feb/early March. Ten days of foodie events dedicated to the noble scallop: scallop tastings, cookery demonstrations and special menus at the towns' restaurants, culminating in a scallop barrow race through the streets of Rye. Ⓦ **ryebayscallops.co.uk**

Sussex Beer Festival Brighton, end Feb/early March. Get stuck in to some of the 240 beers and 60 ciders and perries on offer – many local to the Southeast – at this rollicking annual beerfest. Ⓦ **sussexbeerfestival.co.uk**

APRIL & MAY

Brighton and Hove Food and Drink Festival April & Sept. The largest foodie festival in the Southeast, running for ten days twice a year, and encompassing local produce, workshops, tastings, markets, Sussex cheese bowling and more. Ⓦ **brightonfoodfestival.com**

Eastbourne Festival Begins on Easter Saturday for three weeks. Annual cultural festival of music, comedy, theatre, performance and visual arts, including artists' houses and studios open to the public. Ⓦ **eastbournefestival.co.uk**

Jack-in-the-Green Festival Hastings Old Town, end April/early May. See p.183

Rochester Sweeps Festival Early May. See p.71

Brighton Festival May. See p.263

Brighton Fringe May. See p.263

Great Escape Brighton, mid-May. Three-day festival showcasing new music that sees over 300 bands play the city, both in scheduled performances and impromptu gigs. Ⓦ **escapegreat.com**

Glyndebourne Festival Mid-May to Aug. See p.224.

Charleston Festival End May/early June. A week of author talks and events at Charleston Farmhouse, near Lewes, the former home of Sussex's Bloomsbury Set. Ⓦ **charleston.org.uk**

JUNE

Dickens Festival Rochester, early June. See p.71

South of England Show Ardingly, early June. The annual county show, featuring plenty of livestock, showjumping and motorcycle displays. Ⓦ **seas.org.uk**

Meadowlands Festival Glynde Place, near Lewes, June. Boutique music festival in the grounds of the manor house. Ⓦ **meadowlands festival.com**

AEGON International Tennis Eastbourne, mid-June. International ladies' and men's tennis in the fortnight preceding Wimbledon, in the leafy surrounds of Devonshire Park. Ⓦ **lta.org.uk**

Broadstairs Dickens Festival Mid-June. See p.98

Fuse Medway Festival Mid-June. Free three-day weekend festival hosting all manner of contemporary outdoor performances and installations, from street dance to circus, in Chatham, Gillingham and Rochester. Ⓦ **fusefestival.org.uk**

Wye Food Festival Mid-June. Enjoyable little local week-long food festival with a country fair feel, in a pretty North Downs village. Ⓦ **wyefood.com/wyefoodfestival.html**

Chichester Festivities Two weeks in late June. Annual arts festival featuring music, theatre, opera, film, comedy, talks, community arts and street theatre. Ⓦ **chifest.org.uk**

MedFest West Dean Gardens, late June. Food demos, tastings and talks run along live music and dance at this Mediterranean-themed weekend.

Festival of Speed Goodwood Estate, late June/early July. See p.294

Brighton Kite Festival Date varies, but generally June/July. One of the country's longest-running kite festivals, with arena displays, team flying and kite fighting. Ⓦ **brightonkiteflyers.co.uk**

Deal Festival of Music and the Arts Late June to early July. See p.112

Hop Farm Music Festival Late June to early July. See p.143

JULY

Folkestone Triennial July–Sept. See p.121

Paddle Round the Pier Hove Lawns, Brighton, early July. The paddle round the pier is just one part of this free, mini beach and watersports festival, which also features live music, urban sports, a pier-to-pier race, stand-up paddleboard races, and have-a-go watersports. Ⓦ **paddleroundthepier.com**

Food and English Wine Festival July. Two days of cookery classes, wine tasting and local foodie treats in the grounds of Glynde Place, near Lewes. Ⓦ **glyndefoodfestival.com**

Eastbourne Extreme Mid-July. A weekend of extreme sports action – bike stunts, powerboat races, windsurfing, kitesurfing, skating, parkour and more – with plenty of opportunities to get involved as well as watch. Ⓦ **visiteastbourne.com/extreme**

Guilfest Mid-July. This excellent mid-sized music and arts festival, held as part of Guildford's longer Summer Festival, sees live music from big-name bands – from Bryan Ferry to indie kids – dance tents, acoustic stages and lots of family events. Ⓦ **guilfest.co.uk**

Ramsgate Carnival Third week in July. Old-style one-day carnival with parades, floats and marching bands. Ⓦ **ramsgatecarnival.co.uk**

Lounge on the Farm Canterbury, late July. See p.59

Whitstable Oyster Festival Third week in July. See p.85

Chilli Fiesta West Dean Gardens, late July. A weekend devoted to the chilli features cooking demos, talks, live music and dance. Ⓦ **westdean.org.uk**

Glorious Goodwood Late July. See p.294

Hastings Pirate's Day End of July. See p.183

Petworth Festival End of July. Two weeks of music, theatre, comedy and art. Ⓦ **petworthfestival.org.uk**

Old Town Carnival Week Hastings, end of July/early Aug. Nine days of festivities, which include a free beach concert, walking tours, a grand carnival procession, and the ever-popular annual pram race.
Ⓦ oldtowncarnivalweek.co.uk

AUGUST

Airbourne Eastbourne, early Aug. Eastbourne's pride and joy – four days of historic aircraft and military displays that's the biggest free seafront air show in the world. Ⓦ eastbourneairshow.com

Broadstairs Folk Week Early to mid-Aug. See p.98

Whitstable Regatta Early to mid-Aug. More than 220 years old, Whitstable's hugely popular regatta offers boating fun for all the family, wacky water events and a yacht race, as well as stalls, fireworks and fairground amusements. Ⓦ whitstableregatta.com

Bognor Birdman and Worthing Birdman Aug. See p.286

Chichester International Film Festival Aug. Eighteen days of films, including open-air screenings at Priory Park. Ⓦ chichestercinema.org

Herne Bay Festival Mid- to late Aug. Lively community festival with lots of family events, open-air cinema, live music and talent shows.
Ⓦ hernebayfestival.com

Arundel Festival Ten days in the second half of Aug. This long-established arts festival features everything from open-air theatre to salsa bands, with comedy, hot-air balloon rides and a gallery trail thrown in. Ⓦ arundelfestival.co.uk

Medieval Festival Herstmonceux Castle, Aug bank holiday. Over a thousand costumed knights, men-at-arms, jesters, minstrels and medieval traders descend on the moated castle for three days of jousting, tournaments, falconry and more, the highlights being the reconstructed siege and battle that play out twice a day. Ⓦ englandsmedievalfestival.com

Sandwich Festival Late Aug. Street music, picnics and food stalls along with a motorcycle meet, duck race and barn dance at this enjoyable local affair, held over five days around the August bank holiday.
Ⓦ sandwichevents.org.uk

Faversham Hop Festival End Aug/early Sept. Ebullient family-friendly weekend event, celebrating the heyday of the hop with bands, food, and lots of Shepherd Neame beer.
Ⓦ favershamhopfestival.org

Weyfest End Aug/early Sept. Acclaimed grass-roots/folk music festival at the Rural Life Centre near Farnham, Surrey, with acts the like of 10CC and The Hoosiers. Ⓦ weyfest.co.uk

Lewes Art Wave Late Aug/early Sept. The annual visual arts festival for Lewes and the surrounding area sees artists open up their houses and studios to the public. Ⓦ artwavefestival.org

Shoreham Air Show Late summer. Two days of historic aircraft and aerobatic flying displays at Shoreham's wonderful Art Deco airport.
Ⓦ shorehamairshow.co.uk

Brighton Pride Date varies but generally Aug/Sept. See p.277

SEPTEMBER & OCTOBER

Rye Arts Festival Two weeks in Sept. Long-running arts festival, taking in exhibitions, literary talks, classical and contemporary music, comedy and dance. Ⓦ ryefestival.co.uk

Whitstable Biennale First fortnight in Sept. See p.85

Deal Maritime Folk Festival Mid-Sept. See p.112

Goodwood Revival Mid-Sept. See p.294

Seafood and Wine Festival Hastings, mid-Sept. A weekend of live music, wine and local seafood down at The Stade.

Coastal Currents Visual Arts Festival Hastings and St Leonards, mid-Sept. One of the biggest arts festivals on the south coast, featuring open studios, events, exhibitions and performances by local, regional and national artists. Ⓦ coastalcurrents.org.uk

Art in Romney Marsh End Sept to mid-Oct. Held across four weekends, this site-specific show has modern artists and musicians exhibiting work in five of Romney's most beautiful medieval churches.
Ⓦ artinromneymarsh.org.uk

Food and Drink Festival Canterbury, late Sept. This weekend foodie fest sees local producers, suppliers, farms and restaurants set up in Dane John Gardens, along with arts, crafts and clothing stalls.
Ⓦ canterbury.co.uk

Apple Affair West Dean Gardens, end Sept/early Oct. Walks, talks and apples galore, plus the chance to peek into the normally closed state rooms of West Dean house. Ⓦ westdean.org.uk

Broadstairs Food Festival First week in Oct. See p.98

OctoberFeast Lewes, first week of Oct. Annual food and drink festival featuring pop-up dinners, wine tasting, raw-chocolate-making workshops, fungi foraging excursions and brewery tours.
Ⓦ lewesoctoberfeast.com

Brighton Comedy Festival Oct. Over seventy performances across sixteen days, with both big names and newcomers performing. The Brighton Comedy Fringe overlaps. Ⓦ brightoncomedyfestival.com and Ⓦ brightoncomedyfringe.co.uk.

Arundel Food Festival Ten days in Oct. Ten days of foodie events at this newly established festival, which features tastings, suppers, beer festivals, food quizzes, farm tours, foraging and food-themed poetry and drama. Ⓦ arundelfoodfestival.org.uk

Apple Festival Middle Farm, near Lewes, mid-Oct. Hugely popular weekend featuring bands, morris dancers, funfair, food stalls and all all-important cider bar. Ⓦ www.middlefarm.com

Battle of Hastings reenactment Mid-Oct. Annual re-enactment of the famous 1066 battle in Battle, featuring over 1000 soldiers and living history encampments. Ⓦ english-heritage.org.uk

Folk Festival Lewes, Mid-Oct. A long weekend of folk gigs, talks, workshops and morris dancing displays at various venues and pubs around town. Ⓦ lewesfolkfest.org

Canterbury Festival Mid- to late Oct. See p.59

Brogdale Apple Festival Late Oct. A two-day celebration of Kent's finest fruit at the National Fruit Collection near Faversham. See p.77. Tastings, competitions and cooking demos, along with tours and foodie talks. Ⓦ applefestivalkent.blogspot.co.uk

NOVEMBER & DECEMBER

Folkestone Book Festival First week in Nov. See p.126

London to Brighton Veteran Car Run First Sunday in Nov. See p.263

Bonfire Night Lewes, Nov 5, or the day before if the 5th falls on a Sun. See p.230

Dickensian Christmas Rochester, early Dec. See p.71

Burning the Clocks Brighton, Dec 23. See p.263

Travel essentials

Costs

For the most part Kent, Sussex and Surrey, being generally well-heeled areas close to the capital, have prices on a par with London and the more **expensive** parts of England. There are some exceptions, but, especially when it comes to eating and drinking, you should be prepared to spend quite a bit. Your biggest expense will be **accommodation** (see p.23). If you camp, or stay in hostels, buy your own food from one of the region's excellent farm shops, and walk or cycle from place to place, you could get by on as little as £30 per person per day – more if you factor in sightseeing costs. Staying in a B&B and eating out once a day could easily double that, and above that the sky's the limit.

We have given full adult prices for the **admission prices** in the Guide, and in the case of family attractions have quoted children's rates as well. Some places will have reduced prices for seniors, the unemployed and full-time students, but you will need to show ID.

Many of the region's major historic attractions are under the auspices of the private **National Trust** (Ⓦnationaltrust.org.uk) or the state-run **English Heritage** (Ⓦenglishheritage.org.uk), both of which are membership organizations. Prices can be steep for non-members, especially at the major attractions, but some NT properties offer discounts for people arriving on foot or by bike, and the generally excellent experiences offered by both organizations makes the cost worthwhile. If you're going to visit more than a handful of places run by either, it is well worth looking into membership, which will allow you free entry to all their properties for a year. We've quoted the admission prices for non-members in the Guide, adding "NT" or "EH" as appropriate to indicate that members will not have to pay.

Prices for other attractions vary widely. Local town museums may well be free, while some of the major private attractions can charge as much as £20 per adult. Some of these pricier options, like Leeds Castle or Chatham Historic Dockyard, do allow you to return as many times as you wish in a year, however, which works out good value.

Gay and lesbian travellers

Brighton, of course, is the biggest draw for gay travellers in this region, with the lively Kemptown area offering hotels, restaurants and shops all geared toward the pink pound, and an exceptionally lively and laidback LGBT nightlife scene packed into a compact area; **Brighton Pride** (Ⓦpridebrighton .org) is the big summer event. Countrywide listings, news and links can be found at Ⓦgaytimes.co.uk, Ⓦgaybritain.co.uk and Ⓦgaytravel.co.uk.

Maps

For an **overview** of the whole of Southeast England on one map, the AA's *Road Map to South East England* (1:200,000) is probably your best bet, and includes some town plans. There are also several good **road atlases** available: A–Z publishes a *South East England Regional Road Atlas* (1:158,400); *Road Map Kent* (1:158,400); and *Surrey, East and West Sussex Visitors' Map* (1:158,400). Phillip's Red Books has road atlases to both *Kent and East Sussex* (1:150,000) and *Surrey and Sussex Downs*. OS Explorer maps (1:25,000) are best for **walking**. The tourist bodies Ⓦvisitkent.co.uk and Ⓦvisitsurrey .com have downloadable **town maps**, as do many of the official websites for individual towns.

Opening hours

We've given full **opening hours** for attractions, restaurants, cafés, pubs and shops in the Guide, though these do sometimes change from year to year, so it's always worth calling ahead or checking the website before you set off. Last entry for many attractions is 45min–1hr before the closing time.

Opening hours for most businesses, shops and offices are Monday to Saturday 9am to 5.30 or 6pm, with many shops also open on Sundays, generally 10.30 or 11am until 4.30 or 5pm. Big supermarkets have longer hours (except on Sundays), sometimes round the clock. Banks are usually open Monday to Friday 9am to 4pm, and Saturday 9am to 12.30pm or so. You can usually get fuel any time of the day or night in larger towns and cities. Businesses and most shops close on bank holidays (see box opposite), though large supermarkets, small corner shops and many tourist attractions stay open.

Tourist information

The Southeast's regional tourist body, **Visit Southeast England** (Ⓦvisitsoutheastengland .com), has a comprehensive website, packed with useful tips and ideas. Within the region, **Visit Kent** (Ⓦvisitkent.co.uk), **Visit Sussex** (Ⓦvisitsussex.org) and **Visit Surrey** (Ⓦvisitsurrey.com) each have their own website; and further down the scale, individual cities, towns and groups of towns also have their own tourist information websites, which we list within the relevant destination in the Guide.

Local tourist information centres (TICs) are also listed in the Guide. Most major destinations have a TIC, but in some towns staffed offices have been replaced by unstaffed information points (generally just a collection of leaflets). **Opening hours** tend to be Monday to Saturday 9am to 5pm, plus sometimes Sunday in summer. Hours are curtailed in winter (Nov–Easter). Staff will nearly always be able to book accommodation, reserve space on guided tours, and sell guidebooks, maps and walk leaflets.

The **South Downs National Park** has its own information centres (see p.206), which can provide guidance on local walks and outdoor pursuits.

Travellers with disabilities

Kent, Sussex and Surrey have good facilities for travellers with disabilities. All new public buildings, including museums and cinemas, must provide wheelchair access, train stations are usually accessible, many buses have boarding ramps, while kerbs and signalled crossings have been dropped in many places. The number of accessible hotels and restaurants is growing, and reserved parking bays are available almost everywhere.

The **tourist bodies** for Kent, Sussex and Surrey, and for individual towns, have varying amounts of accessibility information on their websites; some allow you to search for accessible attractions and restaurants in the area. Both the **National Trust** and **English Heritage** produce Access Guides for their properties (Ⓦ nationaltrust.org.uk/accessforall and Ⓦ english-heritage.org.uk/publications/access -guide), and details of accessible walks in the **South Downs National Park** -- covering some of the park's most spectacular beauty spots -- can be found at Ⓦ southdowns.gov.uk/enjoying/outdoor-activities /access-for-all.

A useful point of reference is **Tourism for All** (Ⓦ tourismforall.org.uk), which has general advice and listings. Also worth checking out is **The Rough Guide to Accessible Britain** (Ⓦ accessibleguide .co.uk), which has accounts of a few attractions in the region, reviewed by writers with disabilities.

Travelling with children

Kent, Sussex and Surrey have enough farm parks, castles, steam trains, off-road cycling trails, crabbing spots and beaches to keep even the most exacting of children happy. The best **beaches for families**

are in Kent around the Isle of Thanet (see p.88), where there are fifteen sandy strands, plus plenty of traditional family-friendly entertainment; in Sussex the beaches are mainly pebbly, though there are two glorious exceptions at sand-dune-backed Camber Sands (see p.174) and West Wittering (see p.296).

Excellent **farm parks and zoos** in the region include the Hop Farm Family Park (see p.142) and the wildlife parks of Port Lympne (see p.127) and Howletts (see p.62) in Kent, and Drusillas (see p.220), Spring Barn (see p.233) and Fishers Farm Park (see p.248) in Sussex; there are **steam trains** on the Romney, Hythe & Dymchurch Railway (see p.127), the Bluebell Railway (see p.196), and the Kent & East Sussex Railway (see p.149) – the last of these an excellent way to get to Bodiam Castle (see p.190), one of many fine **castles** in this history-rich corner of the country. In North Kent there is a knot of excellent family attractions around Rochester, where the huge ships of the Chatham Historic Dockyard (see p.72) are just a hop away from the enjoyable Dickens World (see p.73), Diggerland (see p.74) and the Chatham Ski Centre (see p.74).

Child **admission prices** for all children's attractions are listed in the Guide. Attractions that are not geared specifically towards children generally admit under-5s for free, and have reduced prices for 5- to 16-year-olds. Under-5s travel free on **public transport**, and 5- to 16-year-olds at a fifty-percent discount.

Breastfeeding is legal in all public places, including restaurants, cafés and public transport, and **baby-changing** rooms are available widely in shopping centres and train stations, although less reliably in cafés and restaurants. Children aren't allowed in certain licensed (that is, alcohol-serving) premises – though this doesn't apply to restaurants, and many **pubs** have family rooms or beer gardens where children are welcome.

Canterbury and around

CANTERBURY CATHEDRAL

1

Canterbury and around

Canterbury offers a rich slice through two thousand years of English history, with Roman and early Christian remains, a ruined Norman castle and a splendid cathedral that looms over a medieval warren of time-skewed Tudor buildings. It's a rewarding place to spend a couple of days, with important historic sights, peaceful riverside walks and a good number of quirky hotels and excellent restaurants, and its small size makes it easy to get to know. Almost everything you will want to see is concentrated in or just outside the compact old centre, which, partly ringed by ancient walls, is virtually car-free. It's a delight to explore – though if you visit in high summer you should expect to share it with milling crowds. For a university town, things are pretty quiet after dark, which makes for a relaxing and restorative city break.

Canterbury is pretty laidback, but should you want to slow the pace even further, you can do so within minutes. Beyond the city a number of picturesque **villages** make good stop-offs for lunch or an overnight stay; indeed, it would be perfectly possible to base yourself outside Canterbury and make day-trips in, combining a city break with **walking** along the North Downs Way or even a **canoe tour** along the Stour. **South** of town, the Downs offer a couple of appealing family attractions as they begin their inexorable roll south, while to the north and west spreads the ancient, dappled woodland of the **Blean** and its many nature trails and walking paths. From here you're a hop away from North Kent's foodie heartland, with both Faversham (see p.76) and Whitstable (see p.79) within easy reach. To the east, and a possible stop-off on the way to Thanet (see p.88) or the east coast, **Stodmarsh Nature Reserve** is an important birding spot and a lovely place for a stroll.

Canterbury

Most of the things you want to see in Canterbury, including the **cathedral**, are minutes away from each other within the bounds of the walled city. Just a short walk outside the walls are a handful of key historical sights – **St Augustine's Abbey**, **St Martin's Church** and **St Dunstan's Church** – while you may also want to head over to the campus of the **University of Kent** to catch a performance at the Gulbenkian Theatre (see p.59).

Brief history

The city that began as a Belgic settlement, spreading out on either side of the River Stour, was known as **Durovernum Cantiacorum** to the Romans, who established a garrison and supply base here soon after arriving in Britain. Life changed almost immediately for the Cantii locals, who found themselves living in a thriving town with

GREYFRIARS CHAPEL

Highlights

❶ **Canterbury Cathedral** Dominating this historic university town, the ancient cathedral, seat of the Primate of All England – the Archbishop of Canterbury – can't fail but inspire a sense of awe. **See p.41**

❷ **Greyfriars Chapel** This tiny Franciscan chapel, with its own pretty walled gardens, makes a tranquil hideaway just footsteps from the city centre. **See p.48**

❸ **arthouse B&B** Quirky, friendly and inexpensive, this artist-owned B&B is a fabulous place to kick back, and the perfect base for exploring the city. **See p.52**

❹ **The River Stour** Whether you stroll or cycle along its quiet banks, glide upon it in a punt, or leave the city behind on a kayaking adventure, the Stour provides charm in spades. **See p.52 & p.62**

❺ **Crab and Winkle Way** Cycling or walking along the old railway track between Canterbury and the seaside town of Whitstable, just seven miles away, is a lovely way to combine city, countryside and coast. **See p.60**

❻ **Chilham** Just one of the pretty villages in the countryside surrounding Canterbury, this Tudor gem makes a great base for walking or cycling the North Downs Way. **See p.63**

HIGHLIGHTS ARE MARKED ON THE MAPS ON P.40 & P.42

1

good roads, public buildings, and a ring of protective city walls. After the Roman withdrawal from Britain the place fell into decline, before being settled again by the Anglo-Saxons, who renamed it Cantwaraburg. It was a Saxon king, **Ethelbert of Kent**, who in 597 AD welcomed the Italian monk Augustine, despatched by Pope Gregory the Great to reintroduce **Christianity** to the south of England. By the time of his death in 605, Augustine had founded an important monastery outside the city walls, and established Christ Church, raised on the site of the Roman basilica, which was to become the first cathedral in England.

After the Norman invasion, a complex power struggle developed between the archbishops, the abbots from the monastery – now St Augustine's Abbey – and King Henry II. This culminated in the assassination of Archbishop **Thomas à Becket** in the cathedral in 1170 (see box, p.43), a martyrdom that created one of Christendom's greatest shrines, made Canterbury one of the country's richest cities – and effectively established the autonomy of the archbishops. Pilgrims from all over Europe flocked to the cathedral to be cured, forgiven or saved; Geoffrey Chaucer's **Canterbury Tales** (see box, p.47), written towards the end of the fourteenth century, portrays the festive, ribald – and not always very pious – nature of these highly social events.

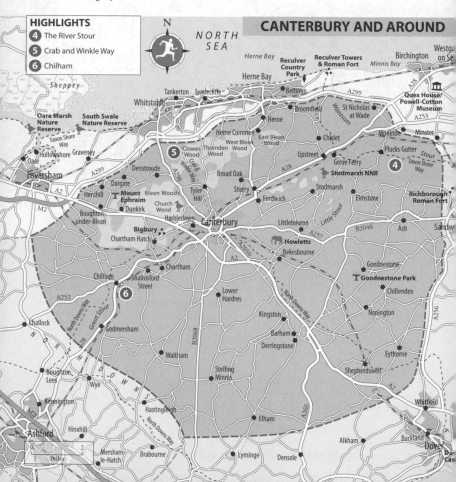

HIGHLIGHTS

4 The River Stour
5 Crab and Winkle Way
6 Chilham

CANTERBURY AND AROUND

Becket's tomb, along with much of the cathedral's treasure, was later destroyed on the orders of Henry VIII, who also ordered the dissolution of St Augustine's Abbey. With its pilgrimage days effectively over, the next couple of centuries saw a downturn in the city's fortunes. However, following a period of calm and prosperity in the wake of the Restoration, in 1830 a pioneering steam passenger railway service was built, linking Canterbury to the seaside at Whitstable, and resulting in another bout of growth. Canterbury suffered extensive damage from German bombing on June 1, 1942, in one of the "**Baedeker Raids**" – a Nazi campaign to wipe out Britain's most treasured historic sites as described in the eponymous German travel guides. Nine hundred buildings were destroyed, and the city smouldered for weeks; the cathedral survived, however, and today, along with St Augustine's Abbey and St Martin's Church, has been designated by UNESCO as a **World Heritage Site**.

Canterbury Cathedral

Buttermarket, CT1 2EH • April–Oct Mon–Sat 9am–5.30pm, Sun 12.30–2.30pm; Nov–March Mon–Sat 9am–5pm, Sun 12.30–2.30pm; last entry 30min before closing; tours Mon–Fri 10.30am, noon & 2/2.30pm, Sat 10.30am, noon & 1.30pm; Quire April–Oct Mon–Fri 9am–4.30pm, Sat & Sun 9am–2.30pm; Nov–March Mon–Fri 9am–4.30pm, Sat & Sun 12.30–2.30pm • £9.50, guided tours £5, audio tours £4 • ☎ 01227 762862, ⓦ canterbury-cathedral.org

Mother Church of the Church of England, **Canterbury Cathedral** may not be the country's most impressive architecturally, but it lords over the city with a befitting sense of authority. A cathedral has stood here since around 600 AD, established by Augustine; it was enlarged by the Saxons, but the building you see today owes most to a Norman archbishop, Lanfranc, who in 1070 rebuilt the place after a huge fire. Already on the medieval pilgrim route to Rome, the cathedral became an enormously important pilgrimage centre in its own right – second only to Rome – after the murder of Archbishop **Thomas à Becket** here in 1170 (see box, p.43). In 1174 it was rebuilt again, and modified over successive centuries; today, with the puritanical lines of the late medieval Perpendicular style dominating, its exterior derives much of its distinctiveness from the upward thrust of its 235ft-high Bell Harry Tower, dating from 1498.

Inside, it is the reminders of earlier days that have the most emotional impact – from the amazing carved columns in the crypt to the steep flights of stone steps worn away by millions of medieval pilgrims – along with a couple of modern sculptures that recall the enormity of the events of 1170. It's well worth taking an audio tour to peel away the many layers of the building's fascinating history. Bear in mind that there's quite a lot of walking, and climbing of stairs, to do if you want to cover all the ground; if you're short of time, concentrate on the **crypt** and **Trinity Chapel**.

The precincts

The cathedral **precincts** are entered through the ornate, early sixteenth-century **Christ Church Gate**, where Burgate and St Margaret's Street meet. (This junction, the city's medieval core, was originally called "Bullstake" – cattle were baited in the street here in order to tenderize their meat – but was renamed **Buttermarket** in the eighteenth century.) Having paid your entrance fee, you pass through the gatehouse to be confronted by one of the finest aspects of the cathedral, foreshortened and crowned with soaring towers and pinnacles.

Note that you can exit the precincts via the large gift shop (see p.59) on Burgate; just next to it, within the grounds, is a little refreshments hut with outdoor tables; the close-up view of the cathedral, and the peace and quiet, make this one of the city's best-kept secrets.

The nave

The fourteenth-century **nave**, the largest space in the cathedral, would have been a bustling arrival point for weary pilgrims. With its soaring Perpendicular pillars and

1

CANTERBURY

■ ACCOMMODATION

ABode	18
arthouse B&B	3
Bluebells	15
Guest House	
Canterbury	7
Cathedral Lodge	13
Cathedral Gate	11
Ebury Hotel	5
Falstaff	4
House of Agnes	13
Kipps	9
Love Lane	2
Millers Arms	1
Neals Place Farm	8
No. 7 Longport	16
Pilgrims Hotel	14
Thanington Hotel	6
White House	12
Wincheap Guesthouse	10
YHA Canterbury	

● CAFÉS & RESTAURANTS

Boho Café	15	The Hutch	6
Browns Coffeehouse	23	Kashmir	4
Café des Amis	8	La Trappiste	13
Café Mauresque	18	Manolis Taverna	16
Café St Pierre	9	Michael Caines at Abode	17
Canteen	14	Moat Tea Rooms	10
Chapman's	7	Old Brewery Tavern	19
City Fish Bar	21	Patrick's Kitchen	2
Cucina Caraccio	5	Posillipo	3
Deeson's	12	Tiny Tim's Tearoom	22
Forge Bistro	11	The Veg Box Café	20
The Goods Shed	1		

● BARS, PUBS, CLUBS & LIVE MUSIC

The Ballroom	4
Bishop's Finger	3
Casey's	6
La Trappiste	5
The Dolphin	1
The Foundry	7
The Parrot	2

HIGHLIGHTS

1	Canterbury Cathedral
2	Greyfriars Chapel
3	arthouse B&B

● SHOPS

Canterbury Cathedral Shop	4
The Chaucer Bookshop	8
Madame Oiseau	1
Steamer Trading Cookshop	5
The Sugar Boy	6
Waterstones	3
Whitefriars	7
Wild Ferment	2

THOMAS À BECKET: THE TURBULENT PRIEST

The son of a wealthy merchant, Royal Chancellor **Thomas à Becket** was appointed Archbishop of Canterbury in 1162 by his good friend and drinking partner Henry II. Becket had no particular experience in the Church, but Henry needed an ally against the bishops and monks who were, as the king saw it, getting far too above themselves and becoming a threat. The friends soon fell out, however, as Henry attempted to impose his jurisdiction over that of the Church and found that Becket seemed to have switched sides. After a six-year exile in France, Becket was reconciled with Henry and was allowed home in 1170 – only to find that his lands were being requisitioned by the king's officers. He incurred the king's wrath once more by refusing to absolve two bishops whom he had previously excommunicated, along with the family who had stripped him of his estates; Henry, in France, was told (untruthfully) that Becket was raising an army, provoking the king to utter the oft-quoted words, "Will no one rid me of this turbulent priest?" (Some sources claim he actually called him "low-born", or "meddlesome", but it is "turbulent" that has tended to stick.)

Hearing this, four knights took it upon themselves to seek out Becket and, on December 29, 1170, finding him in the cathedral, **murdered** him, hacking at him with their swords and slicing off the crown of his head. It was said he was praying when they found him, and was discovered to have been wearing a monk's habit under his robes, and a hair shirt underneath that – held to be proof of his great piety. Within days miracles were said to be occurring at his tomb, and Becket was canonized in 1173. Hundreds of thousands of medieval **pilgrims** from all over Europe, including kings and queens, flocked to the cathedral hoping to be healed or redeemed. Each would be shown the spot where he was murdered, taken to see the bust that contained the piece of skull dislodged by the fatal blow, and, as a grand finale, allowed to watch as a canopy was pulled up to reveal Becket's ornate golden tomb, studded, according to the writer Erasmus in 1513, with jewels as big as goose eggs.

One such pilgrim was Henry himself, who in 1174 walked barefoot and in sackcloth from St Dunstan's Church (see p.51) to the shrine, where he was theatrically beaten by eighty monks and a prior. Whether Henry was driven by a genuine sense of regret, or canny pragmatics – his pilgrimage was a statement to the world that he definitively did not order the murder of Becket, while also being an admission that his words may have inspired it – is open to debate.

vaulted arches, its sweeping views and lofty gilt bosses, it was designed to inspire awe, but was more sociable, and less formal, than the areas beyond. At the eastern end, an elaborate stone screen marks the entrance to the Quire. In the distance beyond, though barely visible from the nave, are the high altar and the Trinity Chapel; in medieval times, obscuring the view of the double ascent up to the holy relics would have added to the sense of expectation as the pilgrimage drew to a close, and even today the screen provides a dramatic pausing point on your journey through the cathedral.

The Martyrdom

The actual spot where Thomas à Becket was murdered, known as the **Martyrdom**, is just off the nave in the northwest transept, marked by a flagstone etched simply with the word "Thomas". Next to it, the **Altar of the Sword's Point** – where, in medieval times, the shattered tip of the sword that hacked into Becket's scalp was displayed as a relic – is today marked by a modern sculpture of the assassins' weapons, suspended on the wall. Taking the form of two swords attached to a jagged cross, and casting sinister shadows, it is a striking image, at once violent and spiritual.

The crypt

From the Martyrdom you can descend to the low, Romanesque **crypt**, one of the few surviving parts of the Norman cathedral and considered the finest of its type in the country. Beneath the Quire and the elevated Trinity Chapel, it is an unusually large space, with a number of chapels branching off from the main area.

1

Becket's original shrine stood down here, before being moved in 1220 to a more resplendent position in the Trinity Chapel. Today, in the main body of the crypt, you can see amazingly well-preserved **carvings** on the capitals of the sturdy Romanesque columns, showing flowers, animals, scallops, sea monsters and winged beasts. There is a fine crop in **St Gabriel's Chapel**, which also boasts some intact, and colourful, twelfth-century Christian wall paintings, uncovered in the 1860s. Among the usual stash of silver plate in the **treasury**, look out for the nineteenth-century brass high altar cross, studded with precious gems.

The Quire

In the main body of the cathedral, the **Quire** is one of the earliest examples of Gothic church architecture in Britain, built between 1175 and 1184 and replete with elegant pointed arches. The thirteenth-century white marble **St Augustine's Chair**, on which all archbishops of Canterbury are enthroned, is located here, at the top of the steps beyond the high altar.

Take time to stop at the decorated stone screen that separates the Quire from the nave and crane your neck upwards to gaze upon the interior of the **Bell Harry Tower**; a vertiginous pattern of arches, pillars and fan vaulting, this is a stunning sight, and all too easily missed.

Trinity Chapel

Beyond the Quire, climbing a steep flight of stone steps, polished and worn wonky by the knees of pilgrims, brings you to the **Trinity Chapel**, the highest point of the cathedral and for centuries its most venerated space. Becket's remains were moved up here from the crypt in 1220; the new tomb, far more ornate than the earlier version, stood in all its marble, gold and jewel-bedecked glory until demolished by Henry VIII's act of ecclesiastical vandalism in 1538. All that remains today is a candle to mark where it once stood. You can get a sense of what it looked like, however, in the beautiful twelfth-century stained-glass **Miracle Windows**, on the north side of the chapel, where along with Becket's life and miraculous works, you can see images of the first shrine, a relatively simple structure, and the second, a more elaborate golden affair.

Also in the Trinity Chapel is the double tomb of **Henry IV** and his wife, **Joan of Navarre**, their heads resting on carved red cushions, and the (somewhat tarnished) gilt

---

MURDER IN THE CATHEDRAL

A rain of blood has blinded my eyes. Where is England? Where is Kent? Where is Canterbury?
O far far far far in the past; and I wander in a land of barren boughs…

The Chorus, *Part 2, Murder in the Cathedral*

The American-born poet T.S. Eliot wrote his play **Murder in the Cathedral** for the 1935 Canterbury Festival, when it was performed in the cathedral itself. After converting to Anglicanism from Unitarianism in 1927 – the same year he took British citizenship – Eliot, a modernist, concerned himself increasingly with spiritual issues in his writing, and went on to become an important voice in the High Anglican Church, characterized by its emphasis on ritual and ceremonial. Written in a mixture of prose, blank verse and rhyme, and with its keening female chorus – who express their beautifully wrought, visceral anguish in lines like "O late late late, late is the time, late too late, and rotten the year" – *Murder in the Cathedral* recalls both Classical Greek drama and medieval morality plays. Though not quite as bleakly existential as Eliot's pre-conversion poems *The Waste Land* (1922) or *The Hollow Men* (1925), it is a profoundly personal work, written in his characteristically lean style. Even for non-believers, the genius he applies to both language and form in exploring vexed issues around faith, temptation, desolation and guilt render it a deeply moving piece of writing – although notoriously difficult to stage.

bronze effigy of Edward III's son, Edward Prince of Wales, or the **Black Prince**. The "achievements" hanging above him – his shield, gauntlets, sword and jerkin – are copies; the originals, which were carried in procession with his funeral in 1376, can be seen in a glass case on the wall south of the Quire.

The Corona
At the far eastern tip of the cathedral, the **Corona** is where, until Henry VIII destroyed it, a silver bust of Becket held the piece of Becket's skull hacked off by his assassin's sword. Today the chapel is dedicated to saints and martyrs of our own time, among them Dr Martin Luther King, Jr and an Anglican archbishop, Janani Luwum of Uganda, murdered by Idi Amin's forces in 1977.

The Great Cloister
On the cathedral's north flank are the fan-vaulted colonnades of the **Great Cloister**, an atmospherically weathered and beautifully peaceful space. Look above you to s ee expressive little faces, bulbous flowers and heraldic symbols carved into the vaulting, and check out the carved graffiti and ancient, crumbling columns. The **Chapter House**, off the cloister, is relatively plain, though it does boast an intricate web of fourteenth-century tracery supporting the roof and two huge stained-glass windows.

The High Street and around
As it cuts a northwest–southeast swathe through the city between Westgate and St George's Gate, Canterbury's **High Street** changes its name three times: the stretch from Westgate roughly to Best Lane is St Peter's Street, followed by the High Street proper from Stour Street to Longmarket, where it turns into St George's Street for the remainder of its length.

Each section of the High Street has its own character; **St Peter's Street** is relatively quiet, with a few quirky restaurants, shops and galleries occupying its hotchpotch of half-timbered, gabled and more modern buildings, while chain stores predominate along the **High Street** proper. Here, though, the side streets offer photogenic medieval vistas – the view up **Mercery Lane** towards Christ Church Gate, for example, a narrow alley of crooked, overhanging shops at the end of which stand the elaborate gatehouse and the cathedral's handsome towers. Much of pedestrianized **St George's Street**, meanwhile, is consumed by the Whitefriars shopping centre (see p.59), before ending up at the edge of the old city walls.

Westgate Gardens
Westgate Grove, CT1 2BQ • Free

The most appealing starting point for a walk along the High Street, **Westgate** is the biggest and most important of Canterbury's six city gates and the only one to have survived intact. With its massive crenellated towers, dating from 1370, it's a handsome structure, lording it over the traffic below. Across the road, and fringing the River Stour, the pretty, flower-filled **Westgate Gardens** make a splendid spot for a picnic or a riverside stroll. Like so many places in Canterbury, they're also historically significant, and have been open to the public since medieval times. You will hardly be able to miss the two-centuries-old Oriental plane tree, with its unfeasibly broad trunk (a whopping 25ft, to be precise); more difficult to spot, however, is the underwater sculpture by the Westgate Bridge. Here, two female statues, one cast in cement and the other in grass resin, float eerily beneath the surface of the clear, shallow water like latter-day Ophelias. This is **Alluvia**, the work of Jason de Caires Taylor, who creates such unsettling and sublimely beautiful underwater sculptures all over the world. It can be easiest to see the statues at night, when they are illuminated.

1

Sidney Cooper Gallery

22–23 St Peter's St, CT1 2BQ • Tues–Fri 10.30am–5pm, Sat 11.30am–5pm • Free • ☎ 01227 453267, ⓦ canterbury.ac.uk/sidney-cooper

An unobtrusive shopfront hides the **Sidney Cooper Gallery**, Canterbury Christ Church University's modern art space. Hosting temporary shows from university staff, students and alumni, along with local and national artists the calibre of Maggi Hambling, Derrick Greaves and Anish Kapoor, it is always worth a look. Most, but not all, works have Kentish associations, and tend towards the cutting edge, featuring anything from sound art to animation to sculpture.

The Old Weavers' House

1–3 St Peter's St, CT1 2AT

The wonky, half-timbered **Old Weavers' House**, standing at the King's Bridge over a branch of the Stour, is one of the most photographed buildings (or rather, three buildings) in Canterbury. Built around 1500, the structure appears to be quintessentially medieval, but is actually a hotchpotch, constructed on twelfth-century foundations and with alterations made between the sixteenth and twentieth centuries. A couple of touristy restaurants now inhabit the place, making much of their picturesque riverside location.

Eastbridge Hospital

25 High St, CT1 2BD • Mon–Sat 10am–5pm • £2 • ☎ 01227 471688, ⓦ eastbridgehospital.org.uk

Tiny **Eastbridge Hospital**, the ancient stone building standing just beyond the King's Bridge, was founded in the twelfth century to provide the poorest pilgrims with shelter (or "hospitality"). Following the Reformation it continued as an almshouse, offering permanent accommodation for people in need; today it is home to a small community of elderly people, and hosts pilgrimage groups from around the world.

Beyond the handsome pointed arch doorway, a couple of steps lead down into the Gothic **undercroft**, the original pilgrims' sleeping quarters; you can see the cubicles they slept in, along with a few exhibition panels recounting the history of the building, and of pilgrimage in Canterbury. Upstairs is the medieval **refectory**, where a striking thirteenth-century wall painting shows Jesus surrounded by the four Evangelists (though only two of them remain), and the light-filled **pilgrims' chapel**, with its beautifully crafted, thirteenth-century oak-beamed roof.

The Beaney House of Art and Knowledge

18 High St, CT1 2RA • Mon–Wed, Fri & Sat 9am–5pm, Thurs 9am–7pm, Sun 10am–5pm • Free • ☎ 01227 378100, ⓦ thebeaney.co.uk

The **Beaney House of Art and Knowledge**, a sturdy terracotta, brick and mock-Tudor ensemble built in 1898, started its days with the aim of improving the masses, and has long been held in fond esteem by the people of Canterbury. Today, despite its modern library and lofty, light-filled rooms, it still has the not unlikeable feel of a Victorian collection, with its stuffed animals, pinned beetles and cases of **antiquities and archeological finds** creating a cabinet-of-curiosities thrill. Look out for the little mummified cat, baring its tiny sharp fangs, the terrifying angled temple sword from eighteenth-century Malabar, and the nineteenth-century face-slapper, used to hit female prisoners in Kashgar – and be sure not to miss the **paintings**, from the seventeenth century onwards. Among the images of Kentish notables, landscapes and historical moments, many of them painted by local artists, perennial favourites include a Van Dyck portrait of Kent MP Sir Basil Dixwell (1638), displaying his long, aristocratic fingers and showing off his expensive black silk robes; the tall, thin and enigmatic *Little Girl at the Door* (1910), by local artist Harriet Halhed; a Reculver scene by Walter Sickert (1937), painted during his four-year stay in Thanet, and the vigorous images of 1930s hop-pickers and gypsies by English Impressionist Dame Laura Knight. In addition, high-profile special exhibitions have featured artists such as Henry Moore.

1

Roman Museum

Butchery Lane, CT1 2JR • Daily 10am–5pm • £6 • ☎ 01227 785575, ⓦ canterbury.co.uk

Following the devastating Canterbury bombings of 1942, excavations of the destroyed Longmarket area, between Burgate and the High Street, exposed the foundations of a Roman townhouse, complete with mosaic floors, now preserved in situ in the city's subterranean **Roman Museum**.

While historical panels give a good introduction to life in Durovernum Cantiacorum, it is the treasure-trove of **artefacts** excavated from the city and sites nearby that really brings it alive. This is a rich hoard: case after case filled with pottery, tiles and amulets (many of them phallus-shaped, a favourite among Roman soldiers), exquisite glass bottles, building tools, fashion accessories – the list goes on. Some are unexpectedly poignant – a commemorative stone for a six-year-old girl, for example, marked with the words "May the earth lie lightly on thee"; the two crumbling military swords, found in a double grave; even the silver spoon marked with the words "I belong to a good man", which was buried for safety when the Romans withdrew in around 410, and which remained hidden underground for 1500 years.

The **remains** themselves, which come at the end of the display, are relatively low-key – protected behind glass in the dark, they amount to the floor supports of an under-heated hypocaust, an undecorated stone corridor, and some stone floor mosaics decorated with geometric and floral patterns. If all this whets your appetite for Roman remains, plan a trip to Lullingstone Roman Villa, in the Weald (see p.153), where you can see some fine mosaics.

The Canterbury Tales

St Margaret's St, CT1 2TG • Daily: March–June, Sept & Oct 10am–5pm; July & Aug 9.30am–5pm; Nov–Feb 10am–4.30pm • £8.25, children £6.25 • ☎ 01227 479227, ⓦ canterburytales.org.uk

Housed in a former stone-built church a few yards off the High Street, **The Canterbury Tales**, based on Geoffrey Chaucer's medieval stories (see box below), is a quasi-educational, and fun, attraction. Equipped with audio guides, visitors set off on a forty-minute wander through atmospheric, odour-enhanced fourteenth-century tableaux, following the progress of a group of pilgrims (or rather, suitably scrofulous mannequins) from the *Tabard Inn* in London to Becket's atmospherically lit, and fabulously ornate, shrine. Each new space provides a setting for one of Chaucer's famous tales – edited down versions of stories from the Knight, the Miller, the Wife of Bath, the Nun's Priest and the Pardoner. Each is told in a slightly different way, using animatronics, shadow play, video, or a combination of the three – and though it's not slick it's all done rather well, with lively lighting, sound effects and tongue-in-cheek

---

THE CANTERBURY TALES

Geoffrey Chaucer's (unfinished) **Canterbury Tales**, written between 1387 and the author's death in 1400, are a collection of stories within a story in which a motley bunch of thirty pilgrims exchange a series of yarns to while away the time as they journey from a tavern in London to the cathedral. The group is a colourful cross-section of medieval society, including a knight, a monk, a miller, a squire and the oft-widowed, rather raunchy, Wife of Bath. Chaucer chose to write their earthy and often ribald tales in English – at a time when French was very much the language of literature – and, although it's a structure that feels entirely natural to modern readers, the fact that each story has a different narrator, with his or her own voice and personality, but that each is linked by their common journey, was entirely new.

The tales themselves are reworked stories, popular at the time, from around the world, ranging from oral folk tales to classic myths – the *Prologue*, however, is entirely Chaucer's work, introducing each character and giving a wonderfully vivid, and humanistic, portrayal of early medieval England. All this, combined with the lively language and universal themes, keep the *Canterbury Tales* as fresh and engaging today as they ever were.

1

dialogue. The bare bum revealed in the scatological Miller's Tale is always a cheeky crowd-pleaser, and it's hard not to get caught up in the bawdy fun of it all.

Canterbury Heritage Museum

Stour St, CT1 2NR • Daily 10am–5pm • £8 • ☎ 01227 475202, ⓦ canterbury.co.uk

The **Canterbury Heritage Museum** provides an illuminating trot through the city's history. Though there are a couple of Iron Age treasures – including a rare, early mirror made from bronze, found buried with the cremated remains of a young woman, and marked with swirling Celtic designs – the story sets off in earnest with the Roman city, displaying a selection of jewellery, pottery and house deities. The **Norman** room features grotesque eleventh-century stone carvings of mythical beasts, and a rather splendid 60ft-long, 1980s wall **frieze** from Canterbury-born Oliver Postgate (he who brought us *Bagpuss* and *The Clangers*). Deftly outlining the complex story of Thomas à Becket and his relationship with the king, the colourful frieze portrays the adversaries as well-matched and largely self-serving, living in brutal times – although as you might expect of Postgate's work, everyone looks pretty affable. The **medieval** pilgrimage souvenirs – tin lead badges portraying Becket's reliquary head (a life-sized bust, which contained the shard of his skull that had been hacked off) – are intriguing, while in the **Tudor** room you can see sections of rose-pink marble capitals that were found on Canterbury's riverbank in 1983 and are believed, by some, to be from Becket's tomb, destroyed by Henry VIII. Highlights from the **Elizabethan** and **Stuart** eras include a beautiful wall painting, alive with roses, carnations, tulips, cherries and acorns, found in a Tudor house nearby. One section covers local-born playwright/poet and alleged spy **Christopher Marlowe**; another is dedicated to novelist **Joseph Conrad**, with a re-creation of his study at the nearby village of Bishopsbourne.

A room at the end pays homage to the beloved **Oliver Postgate**, with nostalgic TV footage and cabinets of real-deal Clangers, while beyond that the tartan-trousered philanthropist **Rupert Bear**, created by local-born Mary Tourtel, practically has a museum all to himself. Here you can see all manner of bear memorabilia, including the very first Rupert book, dating from 1921.

Greyfriars Chapel and Franciscan Gardens

Behind 6 Stour St, CT1 2NR • April–Sept Mon–Sat 2–4pm; Anglican Eucharist held Wed 12.30 • Free; donations welcome • ☎ 01227 471688, ⓦ eastbridgehospital.org.uk

A delightful surprise hidden off Stour Street, literally spanning the river and with pretty, peaceful gardens, the stone-built **Greyfriars Chapel** is the only surviving building from England's oldest Franciscan friary (1267). In the thirteenth century the friary was home to sixty or so friars; it was closed by Henry VIII in 1538 and sold on. This little building was, it is thought, the guesthouse of the friary, and home over the years to both Huguenot and Belgian refugees; one room was also used as a prison in the nineteenth century, as its grim, studded iron door attests. In 2003 a group of Anglican Franciscan friars returned to Canterbury, and they now use Greyfriars as their chapel.

Today you can see a small **exhibition** about Greyfriars and the history of the Franciscans, and can wander through this unadorned building with its original beams and prisoners' graffiti carved into medieval wooden panelling. Upstairs, the whitewashed, vaulted **chapel** still hosts a weekly Eucharist, open to all. Before leaving, take time to wander through the **gardens**, a haven of serenity with the river gurgling past a drift of scattered wildflowers.

Canterbury Castle

Castle St, CT1 2PR • Morning to dusk • Free • ⓦ canterbury.co.uk

Walking down Castle Street, which grows quieter and increasingly residential as it nears the city wall, brings you to the ruins of **Canterbury Castle**. Replacing a simple wooden structure built by William the Conqueror around 1070, this motte-and-bailey affair sitting hard by the Roman town walls was started in around 1086 and considerably altered in subsequent years; by the late twelfth century its importance had dwindled to nothing in the light of Henry II's mighty castle at Dover. For many years it existed as a rather neglected prison, until it fell into ruin in the sixteenth century and was pretty much pulled apart in the eighteenth and early nineteenth centuries.

Today, you can wander around the substantial roofless **keep**, built by Henry I and made of locally quarried flint, Kentish ragstone and Roman bricks. It's an evocative spot, with its sturdy walls silhouetted against the sky and sprouting luxuriant vegetation; most days it is silent but for the wheeling birds tending to their nests, stuffed in the many huge arches and empty windows.

Dane John Gardens

Watling St, CT1 2RN • Free

Dane John Gardens, an attractive and well-used park at the southern tip of the city near the castle, was laid out in the eighteenth century with lawns, flower beds, and a stately avenue of lime trees, along with a bandstand that still hosts concerts in summer. Bordering the southern edge of the gardens are the city walls and the Dane John Mound, a Romano-British burial mound that was incorporated into the city's original castle and now affords good views across the city. There's a small refreshment kiosk, and in late September a **food and drink festival**, with local suppliers and restaurants setting up stalls.

The King's Mile

The **King's Mile** – the stretch from the cathedral up Sun Street and Palace Street, also including Guildhall and the Borough – is a quieter and more characterful place to shop than the High Street, its picturesque historic buildings housing a number of quirky independent shops and cosy small restaurants. Palace Street is the prettiest section; at the top, where it meets the Borough, you can peep through the forbidding stone gate to take a look at the medieval buildings of **King's School**, commonly believed to be the oldest continually operating school in the world, and with an impressive list of alumni, from Elizabethan dramatist Christopher Marlowe to author Somerset Maugham and movie director Michael Powell.

Outside the city walls

From Burgate, it's just a three-minute walk east of the city walls to the vestigial remains of the sixth-century **St Augustine's Abbey**, and then another five minutes to **St Martin's Church**, possibly the oldest church in England still in use. The two, along with the cathedral, comprise UNESCO's **Canterbury World Heritage Site**; for any full account of the city's history, or indeed the history of Christianity in England, they are a must-see. Northwest of town, **St Dunstan's Church**, where Henry II paused on his 1174 pilgrimage to shed his shoes and don his hair shirt, and where the remains of another martyr, Sir Thomas More, are interred, is also worth a look.

St Augustine's Abbey

Monastery St, CT1 1PF • April–June Wed–Sun 10am–5pm; July & Aug daily 10am–6pm; Sept & Oct Sat & Sun 10am–5pm; Nov–March Sat & Sun 10am–4pm • £4.90; EH • ☎ 01227 767345, ⓦ english-heritage.org.uk/daysout/properties/st-augustines-abbey

While Canterbury Cathedral gets most of the attention, the ruined **St Augustine's Abbey**, founded in 598, is just as historically important. Founded as a monastery by the Italian monk Augustine, tasked with re-introducing Christianity to the English, it was vastly altered by the Normans, who replaced it with a much larger abbey; in turn,

1

THE RISE AND FALL OF ST AUGUSTINE'S ABBEY

In 595 Pope Gregory the Great dispatched **Augustine**, a Benedictine monk from Rome, on an evangelical mission to restore Christianity to England after a couple of centuries of Anglo-Saxon paganism had all but wiped it out. The kingdom of Kent seemed like a good place to start: not only was it conveniently close to the continent, but also its king, **Ethelbert**, the most powerful Anglo-Saxon ruler of the time, had a Christian wife, Bertha, and was open to the idea of conversion.

Augustine, reluctantly, fearing he was not up to the task of converting the barbarian Angles, set off with between twenty and forty monks. At one point he turned back, begging the Pope to send someone else; his entreaties went unheard, however, and he finally arrived on the Kentish coast in late 596 or 597. He baptized Ethelbert in 601, an act that effectively rubber-stamped his mission, and immediately set about founding a church within the walled city (today's cathedral), and a **monastery** outside the walls to the east. Following a tradition that forbade burials within city walls, the monastery's first church, dedicated to saints Peter and Paul, became the final resting place of both Augustine (in 605) and Ethelbert (in 616), along with successive archbishops and kings of Kent right up until the middle of the eighth century.

Augustine's monastery continued to thrive after his death. Two more churches, St Mary and St Pancras, were added in the first half of the seventh century, with further extensions being made in the eighth and ninth centuries; by the 900s it was well established as a major seat of learning. The most dramatic changes came in the eleventh century, with the arrival of the **Normans**, who in 1072 established a Benedictine **abbey** here, replacing the relatively simple Anglo-Saxon structures – and moving the holy remains of St Augustine from their original tomb into a far more ornate, jewel-bedecked shrine – with a huge Romanesque church similar in size to today's cathedral. The abbey continued to grow, becoming an important centre of book production, until the **Dissolution**. After being disbanded in 1538, it was converted into a royal palace, with apartments for Anne of Cleves (who never actually stayed here), and following Henry VIII's death it was rented by a string of noble families. In the eighteenth and nineteenth centuries the abbey precinct fell into relative ruin, though it was used variously as a brewery, hospital, jail and pleasure gardens; shocked at such sacrilege, local MP Alexander James Beresford Hope bought the site in 1844 and opened a missionary college four years later. These Victorian buildings are now part of the King's School (see p.49); other buildings in the precinct are owned by Christ Church college, Canterbury prison and English Heritage.

most of this was later destroyed in the Dissolution before falling into ruin. Today, it is an atmospheric site, with more to see than its ruinous state might at first suggest. Its various ground plans, clearly delineated in stone on soft carpets of grass, along with scattered semi-intact chapels, altar slabs and tombstones, evoke the original buildings almost as powerfully as if they were still standing; standouts include the ancient **tombs** of the early archbishops and the remains of the seventh-century **St Pancras Church**, which survived the Norman expansions, and where you can see the Roman brick used in its construction.

Illustrated information panels admirably recount the changing fortunes of the abbey, but to get the most of a visit, complement those with an audio guide from the excellent interpretive centre. These describe not only the more dramatic incidents in the site's history, but also its domestic routines, and really bring the place to life.

St Martin's Church

Corner of North Holmes Rd and St Martin's Lane, CT1 1PW • Easter–Oct Tues, Thurs & Sat 11am–4pm, Sun 9.50am–10.30am; Oct–Easter Tues, Thurs & Sat 11am–3pm, Sun 9.50am–10.30am • Free • ☎ 01227 768072, ⓦ martinpaul.org

In a slightly incongruous location behind the city jail, the lovely **St Martin's Church**, one of England's oldest churches, was built on the site of a Roman villa or temple and used by the earliest Christians. Although medieval additions obscure much of the Saxon structure, this is perhaps the earliest Christian site in Canterbury – it was here that the Frankish Queen Bertha worshipped with her priest Liudhard, welcoming Augustine and his monks after their arrival in England in 597. After King Ethelbert was baptized in St Martin's, Augustine's mission was deemed to be a resounding success, and he was able to go on to build the church and the abbey that dominated Canterbury for centuries.

Entering the church through an ancient shady graveyard, where nearly a thousand gravestones pepper the grassy hills, you'll find a few intriguing vestiges of the building's long history. Beyond the nave – a very early Anglo-Saxon structure of mortared brick and stone, with a fourteenth-century beamed roof – you can see a wall of long, flat Roman bricks in the chancel, dating back to the fourth century, and opposite it a flat-topped Roman doorway. Other highlights include an angled "squint", through which medieval lepers would have watched Mass from a safe distance outside the church.

St Dunstan's Church

80 London Rd, CT2 8LS • Mon–Sat 9am–4pm, Sun 8am–6pm • Free • 🕾 01227 472557

Though many people pass it without a second thought, the tenth-century **St Dunstan's Church** was an important stopping-point for medieval pilgrims on their journey to the city via Westgate – it was from here that King Henry II proceeded barefoot to the cathedral when doing penance in 1174. The church is also remarkable for holding the eternal remains of **Sir Thomas More**, executed upon the orders of Henry VIII in 1535 for refusing to accept the king's desire to split from the Catholic Church. More's head, removed from a spike outside the Tower of London by his daughter, Margaret Roper, is enclosed in a lead casket in the Roper family vault, beneath a stained-glass window portraying scenes from his life. A marble slab marks the spot.

ARRIVAL AND DEPARTURE
CANTERBURY

BY TRAIN
Canterbury East Canterbury East station (in the south) is a 15min walk from the cathedral.
Destinations Bekesbourne (hourly; 5min); Chatham (every 30min; 45min); Dover Priory (Mon–Sat every 30min, Sun hourly; 30min); Faversham (every 20–30min; 15min); London Victoria (every 30min; 1hr 35min); Rochester (every 30–45min; 50min); Selling (Mon–Sat every 30min–1hr, Sun hourly; 10min).
Canterbury West Canterbury West (in the north), a 15min walk from the cathedral, is used by the high-speed train from London St Pancras.
Destinations Ashford (every 10–30min; 15–25min); Broadstairs (hourly; 25min); Chartham (every 35min–1hr; 5min); Chilham (Mon–Sat hourly; 8min; Sun every 30min; 20min); London Bridge (Mon–Sat every 30min; 1hr 40min); London Charing Cross (Mon–Sat every 30min; 1hr 45min); London St Pancras (Mon–Sat hourly; 55min); Margate (hourly; 30min); Ramsgate (hourly; 22min);

Sevenoaks (Mon–Sat every 30min; 1hr 5min–1hr 20min); Sturry (hourly; 5min); Tonbridge (Mon–Sat every 30min; 1hr 5min); Wye (Mon–Sat every 30min; 15min).

BY BUS
National Express services and local Stagecoach East Kent buses use the station just inside the city walls on St George's Lane beside the Whitefriars shopping complex. The travel office sells tickets and has timetables (Mon–Sat 8.15am–5pm; 🕾 08456 002299).
Destinations Broadstairs (every 20–30min; 1hr 30min); Chilham (Mon–Sat hourly; 30min); Deal (Mon–Sat 1–3 hourly, Sun 5 daily; 1hr 5min); Dover (every 30min–6 daily; 35min); Faversham (every 15–40min; 30min); Folkestone (every 30min–2hr; 1hr); London Victoria (hourly; 1hr 50min); Margate (every 20–30min; 50min); Ramsgate (hourly; 45min); Sandwich (every 20min–5 daily; 40min); Whitstable (every 15min; 30min).

GETTING AROUND AND INFORMATION

By car Parking in town can be problematic. There are off-street pay car parks throughout the centre, including on Watling Street, Castle Row, Rosemary Lane, Northgate and Pound Lane.
By bike Canterbury Cycle Hire, based at the *House of Agnes*, 71 St Dunstan's St (see p.53), rents bikes (£16/day, £50 for a family; 🕾 01227 388058, 🌐 canterbury cyclehire.com), with the convenient option of renting from here and dropping off in sister branches in

Herne Bay or Whitstable. They also organize guided cycle tours.
Tourist office In the Beaney Museum, 18 High St (Mon–Sat 9am–5pm, Sun 10am–5pm; 🕾 01227 378100, 🌐 canterbury .co.uk). Ask about Canterbury's Attractions Passport (£26.50), which admits you to the cathedral, Canterbury Tales, and your choice of the city museums, shaving a few pounds off what would ordinarily be the total cost, and gives discounts on other attractions and at some restaurants.

1

CANTERBURY TOURS

Canterbury is small enough to find your own way around very easily, but various **tours** are available should you want a knowledgeable overview. A trip along the **River Stour**, in particular, either on a rowing boat or a chauffeured punt, provides a relaxing and picturesque way to get to know the city. If you are after something a little more active, contact **Canoe Kent** (see box, p.62).

RIVER TOURS

Canterbury Historic River Tours King's Bridge, High St ☎07790 534744, ⍵ canterburyrivertours.co.uk. Informative rowing-boat trips, with lively narration, along the River Stour (March–Oct daily 10am–5pm; every 15–20min; 40min; £8). No reservations necessary; simply turn up at the bridge by the Old Weaver's House.

Canterbury Punting Company Water Lane ☎07786 332666, ⍵ canterburypunting.co.uk. Chauffeured river tours (from March; around 40min) on hand-built wooden punts, with cushions, blankets and rain canopies all provided. Choose from historic tours (£8), candlelit "ghost" tours (£10) and a "romantic" tour for couples (£40). Reservations can be made at their base – *Browns Coffeehouse* on Water Lane (see p.54) – at the tourist office, by phone or online.

Canterbury River Navigation Company/Westgate Punts West Gate Tower ☎07816 760869, ⍵ crnc .co.uk. Chauffeured punting trips (Easter–Oct daily,

weather permitting, 10am till late) along the Stour through the city, and out into the countryside (35min–1hr 5min; £8–14). Call to reserve, or find them outside *Café des Amis* restaurant (see p.56).

WALKING TOURS

The Canterbury Ghost Tour ☎08455 190267, ⍵ canterburyghosttour.com. A tongue-in-cheek mix of supernatural spookery and local folklore, leaving from *Alberry's Wine Bar*, 38 St Margaret's St (Fri & Sat 8pm; 1hr 30min; £9). You can book by phone or online, or simply turn up on the night.

Canterbury Guided Tours ☎01227 459779, ⍵ canterburyguidedtours.com. Informative walking tours of the city and the cathedral precincts, leaving from the Buttermarket (daily: April–Oct 11am & 2pm; Nov–March 11am; 1hr 30min; £6.50). Buy tickets at the tourist office, the Roman Museum or the Canterbury Heritage Museum.

ACCOMMODATION

A crop of fine old **hotels and B&Bs** in the city centre offer all the creaking, authentic antiquity you could ask for, and there's a host of good-value B&Bs just outside the city walls. Prices are reasonable for such a popular city, but if you're driving, check if your accommodation has on-site **parking** – many places in the centre don't, and this will add to the cost. It can be difficult to secure a room in July and August, when prices tend to increase – book well in advance if possible.

HOTELS AND GUESTHOUSES

ABode 30–33 High St, CT1 2RX ☎01227 766266, ⍵ abodehotels.co.uk/canterbury. Your experience at this upscale boutique hotel will depend on how much you can afford: the standard ("Comfortable") rooms are rather ordinary, but the priciest ("Fabulous") suite comes with a rooftop terrace and cathedral views. Many guests make an occasion of it and eat at *Michael Caines'* restaurant (see p.57); various packages, which include a meal in Caines' less expensive on-site tavern (see p.56), make a stay more affordable. __£135__

★ **arthouse B&B** 24 London Rd, CT2 8LN ☎01227 453032, ⍵ arthousebandb.com. Quirky, very comfortable, artist-owned B&B in an old fire station, eight minutes' walk from Westgate. Two stylish double rooms (each with private bathroom), filled with offbeat *objets*, vintage books and witty artworks, some of them by the owners themselves, share a lounge and kitchen where you can make hot drinks. You could also rent both rooms and have the whole house to yourself. The friendly but unobtrusive

owners, who live in a separate studio in the back garden, lay out a fabulous organic continental breakfast in the morning. __£60__

Bluebells Guest House 248 Wincheap, CT1 3TY ☎01227 478842, ⍵ canterburybluebells.com. This cosy Victorian B&B, a 10min walk from Canterbury East station and a 15min walk from the centre, wins lots of repeat custom for its three stylish rooms (two with private bathroom – one of which has a roll-top bath – and one en suite) and thoughtful touches including robes, slippers and fresh flowers. __£75__

Canterbury Cathedral Lodge The Precincts, CT1 2EH ☎01227 865350, ⍵ canterburycathedrallodge.org. Modern hotel, owned by the cathedral and with an unbeatable location within the peaceful precinct grounds; you can eat breakfast outside in good weather. Rooms in the main building are unfussy and contemporary, with something of the feel of conference accommodation. A few cheaper "value" options in an annexe are far more basic, with no views. Rates vary depending on availability, and can be as much as £40 more than quoted here; booking well in advance will bring costs down, as will special offers. Rates include entry to the cathedral. Standard doubles **£90**

Cathedral Gate 36 Burgate, CT1 2HA ☎ 01227 464381, ⓦ cathgate.co.uk. Built in 1438 and with a fantastic location next to the cathedral gate, this ancient pilgrims' hostelry is a warren of a place, all crooked, creaking floors, timber beams, and narrow, steep staircases. It's in no way fancy, but it's comfortable and efficient, with jaw-dropping cathedral views from many of the rooms. They also provide a simple continental breakfast, which you eat in your room. The cheapest rooms share toilets and (tiny) showers, but have basins, and all have tea- and coffee-making facilities. In summer you can get better value for doubles elsewhere, but for singles (who pay around £48) and families (around £150), this is a bargain. **£80**

Ebury Hotel 65–67 New Dover Rd, CT1 3DX ☎ 01227 768433, ⓦ ebury-hotel.co.uk. Comfortable, quiet and rather old-fashioned Victorian hotel, a 15min walk from the cathedral. There's lots of on-site parking, an acre of leafy grounds, and a heated indoor pool with jacuzzi, all of which make up for the slightly out-of-the-way location. **£130**

Falstaff 8–10 St Dunstan's St, CT2 8AF ☎ 01227 462138, ⓦ thefalstaffincanterbury.com. A handsome, good-value fifteenth-century coaching inn by the Westgate. The rooms in the old building have lots of creaky historic atmosphere – some have four-poster beds – while the cheaper, more modern options in the annexe behind (£90) are less interesting, if somewhat quieter. Some singles and family rooms. **£139**

★ **House of Agnes** 71 St Dunstan's St, CT2 8BN ☎ 01227 472185, ⓦ houseofagnes.co.uk. You can't fail but be charmed by the crooked exterior of this B&B near Westgate, and the experience inside is great, too. The main fourteenth-century house (mentioned in *David Copperfield*), has eight stylish rooms, each different, and some sleek modern options are available in the large walled garden at the back. There's a funky little library, and a quirky guest lounge with an honesty bar. There can be street noise from the front, so if that bothers you, or if you want a more spacious room, let them know when you book. **£90**

Love Lane 14 Love Lane, CT1 1TZ ☎ 01227 455367, ⓦ 7longport.co.uk. Three-bedroom early Victorian cottage (sleeps five), backing onto and owned by the same people as *No. 7 Longport* (see below). With a kitchen, conservatory, sitting room and dining room, along with a sweet courtyard garden with barbecue, *Love Lane* can be rented on a self-catering or, if available, B&B basis (min two nights). Breakfasts, included in the price, are delicious. B&B (per room) **£90**, (all 3 bedrooms) **£240**; self-catering (3 nights in high season) **£520**

Millers Arms 2 Mill Lane, CT1 2AW ☎ 01227 456057, ⓦ millerscanterbury.co.uk. One USP at this nineteenth-century Shepherd Neame pub, a 5min walk from the

cathedral, is its location opposite a weir on the Stour – you can hear the rushing water from the rooms at the front. B&B rooms (each named after a character in *The Canterbury Tales*) come in a variety of sizes (including singles), all en suite; each is comfortable, with everything you need, but some are looking a bit tired. **£85**

★ **No. 7 Longport** 7 Longport, CT1 1PE ☎ 01227 455367, ⓦ 7longport.co.uk. This fabulous little hideaway – a tiny, luxuriously decorated fifteenth-century cottage with a double bedroom, wet room and lounge – is tucked away in the courtyard garden of the friendly owners' home, just opposite St Augustine's Abbey. The breakfasts are wonderful, with lots of locally sourced ingredients, and can be eaten in the main house or the courtyard. It gets booked up fast. The same owners run *Love Lane* (see above). **£90**

Pilgrims Hotel 18 The Friars, CT1 2AS ☎ 01227 464531, ⓦ pilgrimshotel.com. B&B rooms above a pub/restaurant just opposite the Marlowe Theatre. It can be noisy at night at the weekends, but the location is hard to beat. There's a two-night minimum stay at weekends, and on occasional summer weeknights too. **£85**

Thanington Hotel 140 Wincheap, CT1 3RY ☎ 01227 453227, ⓦ thanington-hotel.co.uk. An old-school, family-run hotel, about 10min walk from Canterbury East train station. The rooms are comfortable if not luxurious, but it's the suntrap garden and (small) heated indoor pool that give this place the edge. Rates include use of a whisky-stocked bar. **£85**

White House 6 St Peter's Lane, CT1 2BP ☎ 01227 761836, ⓦ whitehousecanterbury.co.uk. If the medieval look doesn't rock your boat, you could try this rather chic B&B, in an elegant Regency townhouse within the city walls. Each of the seven contemporary rooms is different, in both decor and size (there's one single), but all are en suite. The location, just off the High Street and near the Marlowe, is fantastic, and the street, being residential, is relatively quiet. You can't bring the kids, though – it's strictly grown-ups only. **£90**

Wincheap Guesthouse 94 Wincheap, CT1 3RS ☎ 01227 762309, ⓦ wincheapguesthouse.com. A welcoming Victorian B&B on busy Wincheap a few minutes' walk from Canterbury East station. They have a range of en-suite double and family rooms; the nicest is Room 1, a double, which has French doors leading to a small private patio. **£75**

HOSTELS

★ **Kipps** 40 Nunnery Fields, CT1 3JT ☎ 01227 786121, ⓦ kipps-hostel.com. Behind the lumpen exterior of this early twentieth-century house, a 10min walk from Canterbury East station, is an excellent self-catering hostel. It's spruce and clean, with homely touches and a nice walled garden, but above all it's the friendly staff who make *Kipps* special. Along with single-sex and mixed en-suite dorms, they have single, double and triple rooms, and offer discounts

1

on stays of three nights or more in winter. Nightly events mean you can be as sociable as you wish, but it's more a home from home than a party hostel, and quiet after 11pm. No curfew. Breakfast £1.95. Dorms __£20.50__, doubles __£55__

YHA Canterbury 54 New Dover Rd, CT1 3DT ☎0845 371 9010, ⓦyha.org.uk/hostel/canterbury. Half a mile out of town, and 15min on foot from Canterbury East station, this YHA hostel occupies a substantial Victorian villa. Breakfast costs £4.95, but there are self-catering facilities. It's closed during the day, and there's an 11pm curfew. Dorms __£21.40__, doubles __£52__

CAMPSITE

Neals Place Farm Neals Place Rd, CT2 8HX ☎01227 765632. On a working farm off the A290, a mere 20min walk from the city, this is a peaceful and sweetly rural campsite, with just eighteen spacious pitches in an apple orchard, and views towards the cathedral. Facilities include free showers, which are rudimentary but clean. Closed Oct–March. Camping (per tent, plus £2.50 per person) __£10__, caravanning (per caravan, plus £2.50 per person) __£15__

EATING

The combination of a large student population and a lively tourist trade means Canterbury has a good selection of places to eat, with many restaurants in historic settings that add considerably to their atmosphere. **Modern British** and locally sourced food is well represented, and there are a few excellent **ethnic** restaurants, too, along with some quintessentially English **tearooms**. **Prices** tend to be quite high, although many places are raising their game and offering good-value lunch and early-evening menus. Finally, if you have a car, and fancy getting out of town, you have a number of good gastropubs to choose from in the villages around Canterbury (see p.61).

CAFÉS, COFFEE BARS AND TEAROOMS

Boho Café 27 High St, CT1 2AZ ☎01227 458931. This funky, relaxed café-bar, with its quirky decor (paintbox colours, kitschy oilcloths, wonky lampshades and vintage clocks) is a popular spot with a cheerful neighbourhood feel, and quite unlike any other café in the town centre. The menu (around £5–10) offers something for most people, reflecting the mixed clientele, and ranges from full English and veggie breakfasts via tapas and overstuffed speciality sandwiches to home-made burgers (including veggie burgers) and meaty mains. You could also simply pop in for coffee and cake. There's seating on the street, and a pretty suntrap garden at the back. Free wi-fi. Mon–Sat 9am–6pm, Sun 10am–5pm.

★ **Browns Coffeehouse** Water Lane, CT1 2NQ ☎07729 167901. Delightful and very laidback riverside hangout, serving spectacular coffee, with a few pastries, macaroons and cupcakes to go with, and a long menu of Teapigs teas. Relax on a sofa or overstuffed armchair in the light-bathed room, dotted with fresh flowers and old books, or sit out in the garden of the Heritage Museum, which is just next door. Free wi-fi. Cash only. Mon–Fri 7.30am–5.30pm, Sat 9am–6pm, Sun 10am–5pm.

Café St Pierre 41 St Peter's St, CT1 2BG ☎01227 456791. Sweet, spruce little French patisserie and bakery with tables on the pavement and in the small terrace garden at the back. The pastries are divine, from apricot tarts to clafoutis to buttery palmier biscuits, and you can make a light lunch of their *croques monsieur*, quiches and savoury croissants (£3.10–4.20). The excellent baguettes (£4.70), served with salad, include *du jour* specials (smoked herring and red onion, say, or Reblochon with onion chutney). Mon–Sat 8am–6pm, Sun 9am–5.30pm.

Canteen 17 Sun St, CT1 2HX ☎01227 470011, ⓦcanteenfresh.co.uk. While the sugar-crazed schoolkids are swarming around *Shake Shed* next door, the cooler cats head to minimal, health-conscious *Canteen* for fresh juices and smoothies, along with light lunches (from £3) – compose-your-own flatbread wraps and salads, wrapped sandwiches, hot curries or noodle dishes – which you can take away or eat in one of their tranquil little rooms, ranged across three floors. Mon–Sat 9am–7pm, Sun 10am–4pm.

City Fish Bar 30 St Margaret's St, CT1 2TG ☎01227 760873. Sometimes only fish and chips will hit the spot, and this cheery, central chippie is a reliable place to get your fried fish fix. A fish supper costs £6.50, but you can also get your chips with sausage, battered mushrooms or a pastie for around £3.30. There are a couple of tables squeezed into the shopfront, and a few more outside, but it's mostly takeaway. Mon–Sat 10am–7pm.

Cucina Caraccio 15 Palace St, CT1 2DZ ☎01227 472401, ⓦcucina-caraccio.co.uk. It's nothing fancy, but this titchy Italian coffee bar, serving simple breakfasts (cinnamon toast, for example, or sautéed chestnut mushrooms), light lunches (perhaps a warm asparagus, goat's cheese and pancetta salad, a frittata, or antipasto), home-made cakes, and good Italian coffee, makes a handy little pit stop. The tiny front room, with picture windows on to the street, is preferable to the back room, with its open kitchen. Tues–Sat 10am–3.30pm.

La Trappiste 1–2 Sun St, CT1 2HX ☎01227 479111, ⓦlatrappiste.com. Places like this – large, busy café-bars, open all day – are ten a penny on the continent, but *La Trappiste*, despite its best intentions, can feel a little confused. The location, on the King's Mile near the cathedral, is superb, though, and the shabby-chic Art Nouveau

1

THE GOODS SHED

The **Goods Shed farmers' market** (Tues–Sat 9am–7pm, Sun 10am–4pm; ⓦthegoodsshed .co.uk), housed in an old brick goods shed next to Canterbury West train station, is one of the highlights of any foodie's trip to Canterbury. With traders selling local cheeses, breads, charcuterie, fresh produce, herbs and deli items, along with an artisan sandwich stall, a gourmet takeaway stand – *Patrick's Kitchen* (see below) – and a couple of coffee places, it's a fantastic place to pick up picnic food, to stock up before catching a train, or to treat yourself to a delicious meal at the mezzanine restaurant (see opposite).

ambience, along with the outdoor seating (including a roof terrace) is appealing. They serve breakfasts (from £5), "bar dishes" (which, inexplicably, include spag bol and fish and chips; around £10), main courses and Sunday roasts (from £12), and cakes and tarts from the in-store bakery. It's not bad as a quick stop off – pop in for a bowl of mussels (from £7.75) and a Belgian beer, and watch the world go by. Free wi-fi. Daily 8am–11pm.

Moat Tea Rooms 67 Burgate, CT1 2HJ ☎01227 784514, ⓦmoattearooms.co.uk. Endearing, traditional little family-run tearoom in a beamed and mullioned old building with cake stands piled high with scones, cupcakes and home-made sponges. The loose-leaf teas include black, green and jasmine varieties – and although they serve decent breakfasts, light lunches and sandwiches, it's the good-value afternoon tea and cake you should go for. Cream teas from £5.95. Cash only. Mon–Fri 9am–6pm, Sat 8am–6pm, Sun 11am–5pm.

Old Brewery Tavern Stour St, CT1 2NR ☎01227 826682, ⓦmichaelcaines.com/taverns. If you want to eat Michael Caines' food but can't quite stretch to his formal restaurant (see opposite), try this casual tavern, attached to the *ABode* hotel, which serves locally sourced gastropub grub, ales and wines. You could go for a Kentish ploughman's or an Italian platter (both £8.95), or more filling classics (£10–15) including pies, pork belly with faggots, or sausage and mash, or push the boat out for a sirloin steak. There are two- or three-course menus (£9.95/£14.95 at lunch, £10.95/£15.95 at dinner) and a simple kid's menu (children under 5 eat for free). Mon–Fri noon–2.30pm & 5–9.30pm, Sat & Sun noon–9pm.

★ **Patrick's Kitchen** The Goods Shed, Station Rd West, CT2 8AN ☎07843 490944, ⓦthegoodsshed .co.uk. Based in the superb Goods Shed farmers' market (see box above), chef Patrick Williams (*not* he of the Caribbean cookbooks) prepares delicious dishes – from sausage rolls (70p) to savoury tarts (wilted onion and Caerphillly, say; £3), exotic soups, scrumptious puddings, and complete gourmet meals (around £5–8) – all to take away. If you can't wait to tuck in – and if there's space – you can also eat at the tiny three-seat counter. Tues–Sat 9am–7pm, Sun 10am–4pm.

Tiny Tim's Tearoom 34 St Margaret's St, CT1 2TG ☎01227 450793, ⓦtinytimstearoom.com. Surprisingly, there's nothing very Dickensian about this 1930s-style tearoom (complete with piano, palms, fresh flowers and wicker chairs), which offers more than twenty blends of loose-leaf tea, an indulgent choice of hot chocolates, and luxurious afternoon teas (available all day, from £14 per person) with finger sandwiches, scones, pastries and cakes, all made in house. Smaller appetites might prefer the cream teas, breakfasts or lunches – the Kentish huffkins (£7.95), large baps filled with bacon and poached egg, or baked red Leicester and onion, are a tasty local choice. In good weather you can sit in the cute back garden. Tues–Sat 9.30am–5pm, Sun 10.30am–4pm.

RESTAURANTS

★ **Café des Amis** 95 St Dunstan's St, CT2 8AD ☎01227 464390, ⓦcafedez.com. Don't be misled by the name (it's short for *Café des Amis du Mexique*) – this is not a French restaurant, but a lively Mexican/Tex-Mex place. Funky decor, carnival colours and papier mâché artwork set the scene for the vibrant food, which is fresh and full of flavour. From the hot goat's cheese tostadas (£6.50) to the paella (£26.50 for two) or the rich crispy duck burger with a dark, chocolatey *mole* sauce, you can't go wrong; the early-evening weekday menu (5–6pm) gets you two courses plus an alcoholic drink for £13.95. There are also a few children's dishes for £2.95. Mon–Thurs noon–10pm, Fri noon–10.30pm, Sat 11am–10.30pm, Sun 11am–9.30pm.

Café Mauresque 8 Butchery Lane, CT1 2JR ☎01227 464300, ⓦcafemauresque.com. Moroccan-style restaurant, with southern Spanish accents – all tiles, lanterns, scatter cushions and brass candlesticks – near the cathedral. You can go for tasty tapas – anything from tabbouleh to merguez sausages, falafel to lamb meatballs (£3.50–5.50, mixed platters for two from £12.95) – or plump for tagines, couscous or paella. On weekdays the "lunch" deal (actually served noon–5pm, when you can also order sandwiches and soup) gets you a main for £7.95–9.95, while the early-evening menu (5–6pm) costs £13 for two courses. Wash it all down with a jug of sangria or a pot of fresh mint tea, and save room for the sticky date cake to finish. Sun–Fri noon–10pm, Sat noon–10.30pm.

Chapman's 89–90 St Dunstan's St, CT2 8AD ☎01227 780749, ⓦchapmansofsevenoaks.co.uk. A smart, buzzy seafood restaurant offering simple, well-executed food using only the freshest local catch. The menu runs the gamut from chowder with home-made bread (£5.50) to an abundant *fruits de mer* platter for two (£39.50) via salt-and-pepper squid, beer-battered fish and chunky chips or bouillabaisse; and you can wash it all down with a light local wine. The puds are good, too, and there's one meat and one veggie main for non-fish-lovers. Regular themed evenings (all-you-can-eat mussel nights, fish'n'chips nights, live jazz and the like), plus a two-/three-course pre-theatre menu (Tues–Fri 5.30–7pm, Sat until 6pm) for £14.50/£16.50. Tues–Sat noon–10pm, Sun noon–3pm.

Deeson's 25–26 Sun St, CT1 2HX ☏ 01227 767854, ⓦ deesonsrestaurant.co.uk. The interior, with its funky feature wallpaper, linocuts and local art, its mismatched wooden furniture and fresh flowers, is a warm, comfortable setting in which to enjoy creative Modern British cuisine. The quality is not always *quite* as high as the prices might lead you to expect, but if you come for lunch (mains £7–13) or a pre-theatre menu (Mon–Fri 5–7pm; two courses £15, three £20) you'll get your money's worth. Based on local produce (and with a good selection of local wines and ales), the menu changes regularly, but mains such as belly of fruit-fed pork with colcannon and apple butter, or mussels in a local cider, garlic and cream sauce are typical. Mon–Sat noon–3pm & 5–10pm, Sun noon–10pm.

Forge Bistro 61 Dover St, CT1 3HD ☏ 01227 788022, ⓦ facebook.com/forgebistro. Contemporary, relaxed bistro just outside the city walls near the bus station, serving Modern European cuisine in a light, airy space. The food is excellent, Mediterranean with a twist, focused around platters for two (from £7), or nibbles (from £3.50, or four for £12) — you could compose a tasty platter of polenta chips with aioli, aubergine boulettes, *haloumi* with ratatouille, and mini lamb and feta burgers. Mon–Thurs 10.30am–11pm, Fri & Sat 10.30am–midnight.

★ **The Goods Shed** Station Rd West, CT2 8AN ☏ 01227 459153, ⓦ thegoodsshed.co.uk. It doesn't get any more locally sourced than this – a buzzing, shabby-chic restaurant in the excellent Goods Shed farmers' market (see box opposite), where most of the ingredients are provided by the stalls themselves. You can get anything from a light breakfast to a first-class full meal: the regularly changing, Modern British menu might feature dishes such as cauliflower soup with harissa (£6), wild bass for two with anchovies, garlic and capers (£30) and slow-cooked lamb shank with salsa verde (£16). Prices can mount, and it can feel a little subdued in the evening, with the market stalls closed all around you, but the foodie ambience during the day is a delight. Tues–Fri 8–10.30am, noon–2.30pm & 6–9.30pm, Sat 8–10.30am, noon–3pm & 6–9.30pm, Sun 9–10.30am & noon–3pm.

The Hutch 13 Palace St, CT1 2DZ ☏ 01227 766700, ⓦ thehutchcanterbury.co.uk. The unadorned (some might say bland) decor at this modern vegetarian place doesn't do it any favours; get past that, though, to enjoy the fabulous food, especially good value at lunchtime (two/three courses £9.99/£12.50). This is light, fresh and creative cuisine, and while Modern British makes a strong showing (marinated Kentish vegetables with asparagus and pea coulis on a puff pastry base; leek and cheddar tart on a red cabbage ragout), the menu features dishes from around the world – on any one day you might see veggie haggis, spicy kofta and Thai-style tofu. Many are vegan (including all the cheeses) and/or gluten-free. Mon noon–3pm, Tues–Thurs noon–3pm & 6–9pm, Fri noon–3pm & 6–9.30pm, Sat noon–3.30pm & 6–9.30pm, Sun noon–3.30pm.

Kashmir 20 Palace St, CT1 2DZ ☏ 01227 462050, ⓦ kashmirtandoori.co.uk. Though there's no reason to think it from the outside, this is probably the best Indian restaurant in town, a large, friendly, family-run place with a long menu of curries including tandooris, birianis, baltis (with some great Punjabi veg choices) and thalis. Lunchtime sees a two-course deal for £8.95, while on Tuesday nights you can eat as much as you like for £12.95. Mon–Thurs noon–2.30pm & 5.30–11.45, Fri noon–2.30pm & 5.30pm–midnight, Sat noon–2.30pm & 5pm–midnight, Sun noon–2.30pm & 5–11.45pm.

Manolis Taverna 10 Guildhall St, CT1 2JQ ☏ 01227 769189, ⓦ manolistaverna.co.uk. The setting, in a medieval building that was once an old tavern, may feel slightly incongruous at first, but the old-fashioned ambience is perfect for this traditional Greek restaurant, which eschews modern fripperies and concentrates on dishing up authentic, home-cooked food. The menu offers the meaty classics (£11–13) – moussaka, *kleftiko*, *stifado*, *giouvetsi* – veg options (£9–11) including dolmades and feta cheese and spinach parcels, and meze, which you can order as mixed platters from £13.95 per head. Mon noon–2.30pm & 6–10pm, Tues–Sat noon–2.30pm & 6–10.30pm.

Michael Caines at ABode 30–33 High St, CT1 2RX ☏ 01227 766266, ⓦ michaelcaines.com/restaurants /canterbury. Though he isn't based here, Caines' stamp – classic, French-inspired dishes with a contemporary twist – is as strong here as at all his *ABode* restaurants, and the seasonally changing menu in this elegant hotel dining room often features a signature dish or two. Typical choices include tartlet of pigeon with truffle confit onion, alongside creations like cauliflower risotto with nutmeg and parmesan foam from executive chef Jean-Marc Zanetti. Though à la carte can be pricey (starters £10–15; mains £22.50–26.50), and the seven-course sampling menu goes for £72, various special menus (from £14.50 at lunch to £27.50 at dinner) prove good value – as long as you're not famished. Daily noon–2.30pm & 6–10pm.

1

Posillipo 16 The Borough, CT1 2DR ☎01227 761471, ⓦposillipo.co.uk. Long-established, cosy trattoria, a real local favourite, serving robust Neapolitan dishes, crispy wood-fired pizzas (£5.95–11.95), fresh pasta (from £6.50) and splendid fish and seafood specials, including a lipsmacking cod dish with olives, capers, anchovies and oregano (£10.95). The prices are good, for such a classy place, and there's a kids' menu, too (£6.50). Mon–Thurs noon–3pm & 6–10.30pm, Fri–Sun noon–10.30pm.

★ **The Veg Box Café** 1 Jewry Lane, CT1 2NR ☎01227 456654, ⓦthevegboxcafe.co.uk. Above a health-food shop, this is a vegetarian restaurant in the traditional mould, a vaguely hippyish place – colourful walls, green plants, wall hangings, slouchy sofas and pine tables – doing delicious things with alfalfa and tofu. The menu, using organic, local and foraged ingredients, offers huge helpings and plenty of vegan/gluten-free options: the selection changes daily but will feature soup, quiche and salad, and mains (around £7) such as bean burgers with chilli jam, or butternut squash and cumin dahl. They also offer organic coffee and mouthwatering cakes – beetroot chocolate brownie, lemon and almond polenta cupcakes – for around £2.50, fresh fruit and veg juices, and even Prosecco for when you're feeling festive. Free wi-fi. Mon & Tues 10am–4pm, Wed–Sat 10am–10pm; lunch noon–3pm, supper 5–8pm, snacks all day.

DRINKING

Canterbury is a nice place for a drink, with a number of pubs serving **real ales** in cosy, historic buildings. The local Shepherd Neame-owned places are in the majority, but look out, too, for beers from Canterbury's own Wantsum and Canterbury breweries.

Bishop's Finger 13 St Dunstan's St, CT2 8BN ☎01227 76891, ⓦbishopsfingercanterbury.co.uk. Unpretentious, popular old pub, just outside the Westgate, with a fine range of Shepherd Neame and guest ales, large-screen TVs showing the major sports events, a real fire in winter and a patio suntrap at the back. Mon–Thurs & Sun noon–midnight, Fri noon–1am, Sat 11am–1am.

Casey's 5 Butchery Lane, CT1 2JR ☎01227 463252, ⓦpatrickcaseys.co.uk. This Irish pub, in an early sixteenth-century building opposite the Roman Museum, is a good spot in the town centre for a drink. It's a friendly place, serving pies, burgers and other pub grub to a lively crowd, with Shepherd Neame ales and occasional live folk music and quiz nights. Saturday nights see resident DJs spinning dance, reggae, funk and hip-hop. Daily noon–midnight.

★ **The Dolphin** 17 St Radigund's St, CT1 2AA ☎01227 455963, ⓦthedolphincanterbury.co.uk. "Still Canterbury's only 30s-built pub named after a marine mammal", the *Dolphin* is a likeable old pub that's both quite cool, in a shabby way, and very relaxed. With a good selection of local real ales (including Gadds and Hopdaemon), a real fire in winter and a big, grassy beer garden in summer, the emphasis is on chatting and hanging out, with board games and no loud music or TVs to spoil the ambience (though there is a piano player on Sunday nights, and a popular monthly quiz). Tasty food, too, with few pretensions; the Sunday lunch is a local favourite. Free wi-fi. Daily noon–late.

The Foundry White Horse Lane, CT1 2RU ☎01227 455899, ⓦthefoundrycanterbury.co.uk. Good craft beers and lagers from the on-site Canterbury Brewers microbrewery in this big old foundry building; you can watch the whole brewing process as it happens from the bar itself. They offer guest ales and ciders, too, and the food (burgers, sausages, pies and the like, served until 6pm), isn't bad either. Daily noon–11pm.

La Trappiste 1–2 Sun St, CT1 2HX ☎01227 479111, ⓦlatrappiste.com. The best thing about this brilliantly located, European-style café-bar is the long list of Belgian beers – among them Lambic, Trappiste and Abbey, and including wheat, fruit and white varieties – which you can drink with or without food (see p.54). A beer stick (£10) gets you six 1/3-pint glasses of different draft beers; great for a group. Free wi-fi. Daily 8am–11pm.

The Parrot Radigund's Hall, 1–9 Church Lane, CT1 2AG ☎01227 762355, ⓦtheparrotcanterbury.com. Ancient hostelry – the oldest in Canterbury, in a fourteenth-century building groaning with dark-wood beams – in a quiet spot. The interior, of course, has loads of character, and they serve a choice of ales (Shepherd Neame and Hopdaemon, mainly) along with a decent selection of wines by the glass. There's a contemporary beer terrace at the back, and a restaurant (sizzlers, mussels, burgers) upstairs. Daily noon–11pm.

NIGHTLIFE AND ENTERTAINMENT

Nightlife in Canterbury keeps a very low profile – many people are happy to while away their evenings in the cosy pubs, and, with a couple of honourable exceptions, live music venues are few. The city has a rich cultural life, however, with a brace of well-regarded **theatres** and two excellent **festivals** (see box opposite).

CLUBS AND LIVE MUSIC

The Ballroom 15 Orange St, CT1 2JA ☎01227 760801, ⓦtheballroom.co. A rather groovy, decadent-looking club and live music venue, all candles, sexy lighting and mismatched vintage styling. On weeknights they present a mixed bag of live music – blues, open mic, local singer-songwriters, burlesque, cabaret, ska, jazz – with house DJs at the weekends. Days and hours vary.

THEATRES

Gulbenkian Theatre University of Kent, CT2 7NB ☎01227 769075, ⓦkent.ac.uk/gulbenkian. Various cultural events, including contemporary drama, dance, comedy and film, are hosted at this excellent theatre-cum-cinema, which also has gallery space.

Marlowe Theatre The Friars, CT1 2AS ☎01227 787787, ⓦmarlowetheatre.com. This modern new theatre, cutting a bold dash right in the centre of the city, is a popular venue for music, dance and theatre. Shows tend towards the mainstream, with crowd-pleasing touring acts – Jools Holland, Elkie Brooks, the Vagina Monologues and the like – and West End musicals, with the smaller studio space used for more obscure performances and gigs.

SHOPPING

Canterbury Cathedral Shop 25 Burgate, CT1 2HA ☎01227 865300, ⓦcathedral-enterprises.co.uk. You can enter the cathedral shop either from the precincts or from the large storefront on Burgate. It's worth a browse – though the wide range of products tends, naturally, towards the religious or spiritual (Thomas à Becket tree decorations; stained-glass earrings; CDs of choral music), there is also a good selection of books, foodie gifts, mugs, magnets and the like. Mon–Sat 9.30am–5.30pm, Sun 10.30am–4.30pm.

★ **The Chaucer Bookshop** 6–7 Beer Cart Lane, CT1 2NY ☎01227 453912, ⓦchaucer-bookshop.co.uk. A bibliophiles' delight: a friendly, fifty-year-old secondhand bookshop in a crooked old building with two storeys packed to the rafters. You can lose yourself for hours browsing the used, rare and antiquarian titles, ranging from popular literary fiction to *Just William*, via art, travel, food history, local interest and just about anything else you can imagine. Mon–Sat 10am–5pm.

Madame Oiseau 8 The Borough, CT1 2DR ☎01227 452222, ⓦmadame-oiseau.com. A cupboard of a shop on the King's Mile, where they make and sell classy artisan chocolates. The emphasis is on the feminine – the heart-shaped bonbonnière, for example – but there are big chunky bars, too, crammed with fruits and nuts, along with chocolate gingers, chocolate-covered chillies and chocolate teddies for the kids. Mon–Sat 9.30am–5.30pm.

Steamer Trading Cookshop 41–42 Burgate, CT1 2HW ☎01227 768737, ⓦsteamer.co.uk. The Canterbury branch of this upmarket, small chain spreads itself luxuriously across three floors of a fine half-timbered building, chock-a-block with every piece of kitchen kit you could imagine, from copper pans to funky bento boxes. Mon–Sat 9am–5.30pm, Sun 10.30am–4.30pm.

Sugarboy 31 Palace St, CT1 2DZ ☎01227 479545, ⓦsugarboy.co.uk. Step back in time to buy fistfuls of gobstoppers, cola lollies, cough candy and blackjacks, chocolate limes, sherbet lemons and sugar mice. More grown-up palates can enjoy boxes of clotted cream fudge, crystallized ginger, or chocolate-covered coffee beans. Mon–Sat 10am–5pm, Sun 10am–4pm.

★ **Waterstones** 20–21 St Margaret's St, CT1 2TH ☎01227 764051, ⓦwaterstonescanterbury.co.uk. An excellent branch of the bookshop chain, spreading across three floors of a venerable building. The love for books is palpable, with regular big-name author events; a good few staff members (among them novelist David Mitchell and scriptwriter James Henry) have gone on to be famous writers in their own right. There's a nice café upstairs, too, with free wi-fi. Check out the remains of a Roman bathhouse in the basement. Mon–Sat 9am–6pm, Sun 11am–5pm.

Whitefriars Between St George's Lane and St George's, St Margaret's and Watling streets, CT1 2TF ☎01227 826760, ⓦwhitefriars-canterbury.co.uk. Gobbling up a substantial chunk of town between the bus station and the High Street, Canterbury's major mainstream shopping mall has the big high-street names – Fenwick to H&M, Body

---

CANTERBURY FESTIVALS

For three days in early July, a working farm just ten minutes' drive south of town hosts the fantastic **Lounge on the Farm** music festival (ⓦloungeonthefarm.co.uk). Starting low-key and local in 2006, it has grown to become a seriously credible contender on the national circuit, while staying manageable, family-friendly and relatively chilled. With a smart range of old favourites and up-and-coming and local bands, the line-up is always great (previous headliners have included Echo and the Bunnymen, Chic, the Wombats and Spector), and the food, much of it locally sourced, is delicious. You can pitch a tent, and glamping is available in bell tents, tipis and yurts.

The city's second big event, **Canterbury Festival** (ⓦcanterburyfestival.co.uk), takes place in the last two weeks of October and offers an international mix of music, theatre and performance, with poetry, lectures and all sorts of live events thrown in. You'll catch anything from South African gospel choirs to Norwegian jazz, opera to blues, held in a variety of venues including the cathedral, the Marlowe and the Gulbenkian.

1

> ## THE CRAB AND WINKLE WAY
> A **cycling and walking route** that follows the line of the old steam railway from Canterbury to Whitstable (see p.79), and forms part of National Cycle Route 1, the **Crab and Winkle Way** is a delight. Some 7.5 miles long, and largely traffic-free, it starts at Canterbury West train station, heads up to the University of Kent campus, then passes through orchards, ancient woodland, and gentle rolling pastures before ending in Whitstable; the cycling and walking paths do diverge, but meet up again at the midway point at Winding Pond. Whitstable itself, a lovely little seaside town on the north coast, is well worth a stay of a night or two. For more, including a downloadable map of the route, see ⓦcrabandwinkle.org.

Shop to Boots – plus banks, supermarkets and eating places (most of them fast-food, but there is a *Carluccio's* café in Fenwick). Daily; opening hours vary.
Wild Ferment 21 The Borough, CT1 2DR ☎01227 463527, ⓦwildferment.co.uk. This independent off-licence knows its stuff when it comes to wines, and offers a good range from around the world, including Kent, along with a few real and natural varieties, and regular wine-tasting evenings. It also sells Kentish ciders and beers. Mon–Thurs 10am–7pm, Fri & Sat 10am–8pm, Sun 11am–6pm.

North of Canterbury

Covering around eleven square miles between Canterbury and Kent's north coast, the ancient broadleaf woodland of the **Blean** is a wonderful area for walking. Accessible from the North Downs Way – which passes the South Blean – the Saxon Shore Way in the north, the Pilgrims Way from Winchester to Canterbury, and the Crab and Winkle Way between Canterbury and Whitstable (see box above), these dappled and wildlife-rich woodlands feature around 120 miles of footpaths, taking in not only woods but villages, hop gardens, orchards and historical sites. Dominated by oak and sweet chestnut trees, but also featuring silver birch, hazel, beech and ash, among many others, it's an area rich in **birdlife**, with nightingales, nightjars, woodpeckers and tawny owls all making their homes here. With good transport connections, the Blean is an easy place to head for a short day-hike from Canterbury, but there are also plenty of nice spots to stay and eat should you want to enjoy a more leisurely visit.

The area **northeast of Canterbury**, meanwhile, fanning out towards the coast, offers a number of watery pursuits. You can take paddling trips on the **River Stour**, which courses through on its way to the sea at Pegwell Bay; bordering it to the east, the Stodmarsh Nature Reserve is a fabulous birding spot.

Blean Woods RSPB National Nature Reserve

Rough Common, CT2 9DD • Free • Access on foot at all times • ☎07770 68397, ⓦrspb.org.uk/reserves/guide/b/bleanwoods

The 1257-acre **Blean Woods RSPB National Nature Reserve**, near the village of Rough Common a couple of miles northwest of Canterbury, offers some wonderful walking opportunities through the woods; five waymarked paths, the longest of which is eight miles, crisscross this peaceful site. In addition to the nightjars, nightingales and woodpeckers, watch out for the flutter of the Heath Fritillary butterfly, seen in few other places in Britain.

Mount Ephraim Gardens

Hernhill, ME13 9TX • April–Sept Wed–Sun 11am–5pm • £5 • ☎01227 751496, ⓦmountephraimgardens.co.uk

The elegant Edwardian gardens at **Mount Ephraim**, a private estate a couple of miles west of Bossenden Wood in the Blean, provide an appealing contrast with the woodlands around them. Here you can wander ten acres of paths through landscaped, terraced gardens – among them a fragrant rose garden, a Japanese rock garden, and an unusual medieval-style "mizmaze", with soft raised turf paths fringed with wild flowers and swaying grasses. Many people bring picnics, but you can also eat good light lunches and cream teas in their delightful tearoom.

Stodmarsh National Nature Reserve

Stodmarsh, CT3 4BP • Dawn–dusk • Free • ☎ 01233 812525, ⓦ naturalengland.org.uk

Accessible from the village of Stodmarsh, six miles northeast of Canterbury off the A257, the **Stodmarsh National Nature Reserve** encompasses a soggy wetland of reed beds, fens and lagoons in the Stour Valley. It's especially good for **birdwatchers**, with bitterns and marsh harriers, among many others, in residence, but is a peaceful place for anyone to enjoy a short, bracing country walk. Three miles or so of footpaths include a couple of nature trails, with three designated hides.

ACCOMMODATION   **NORTH OF CANTERBURY**

Grove Ferry Inn Upstreet, CT3 4BP ☎ 01227 860302, ⓦ thegroveferry.co.uk. Six quirky boutique-style B&B rooms above this lively contemporary gastropub in a winning setting by the River Stour. A couple of rooms have their own small balconies overlooking the river, and those at the front have views over Stodmarsh. **£75**

★ **The Linen Shed** 104 The Street, Boughton under Blean, ME13 9AP ☎ 01227 752271, ⓦ thelinenshed .com. Shabby chic meets vintage glamour in this beautiful weatherboard home, fronted by lavender gardens and full of home comforts. The guest rooms, two of which have private bathrooms and one of which shares a bathroom

with the owners, are gorgeous, ranging from faded French Provincial to Art Deco in style, and you're made to feel right at home. Gourmet breakfasts are served in a stunning dining room or out in the garden. Minimum two-night stay at weekends. **£90**

Nethergong Nurseries Upstreet, CT3 4DP ☎ 07901 368417, ⓦ nethergongnurseries.co.uk/camping.php. A simple, peaceful and spacious riverside campsite, eight miles northeast of Canterbury, with room for 25 tents in woodland or open fields; there's also a shallow paddling pond. Campfires are allowed, and they sell their own fresh veg at the weekends. Closed Nov–March. **£15**

EATING AND DRINKING

★ **Dove at Dargate** Plumpudding Lane, Dargate, ME13 9HB ☎ 01227 751360, ⓦ doveatdargate.co.uk. This easygoing, intimate country pub achieves standards that far fancier places can only dream of. Dishes, which combine classic French cuisine with Modern European dash, are packed with good local ingredients, many of them grown on their own allotment. Mains, from £10 (more at dinner), might include confit pork belly with black pudding; roasted cod, braised lentils and salsify; or Romney Marsh lamb roasted with black cabbage. Tues–Thurs & Sat noon–3pm & 6pm–midnight or earlier, Fri noon–midnight or earlier, Sun noon–5pm; food served Wed–Sat noon–2pm & 7–9pm, Tues & Sun noon–2pm.

Fordwich Arms King St, Fordwich, CT2 0DB ☎ 01227 710444, ⓦ fordwicharms.co.uk. The attractive ivy-strewn exterior of this unpretentious pub makes a good impression, and the food and drink inside are no less appealing. The daily-changing blackboard menu (starters from £5, mains from £10) offers a welcome variety – with dishes such as spinach and mascarpone lasagne or venison sausages on horseradish mash listed alongside Moroccan lamb with couscous – and there are filling lunchtime sandwiches and ploughman's lunches. There's a riverside garden, and regular live jazz and folk music. Mon–Sat noon–11pm, Sun noon–

5pm; food served Mon–Sat noon–2.30pm & 6.30–9.30pm, Sun noon–3pm.

★ **Gate Inn** Church Inn, Chislet, CT3 4EB ☎ 01227 860498, ⓦ gateinnchislet.co.uk. There's a strong community feel at this friendly pub, which has a riverside garden, shaded by willows and planted with fresh herbs, and a "quiet garden", adults only, overlooking a small lake. Inside, there are church pews or squishy sofas to snuggle up on, log fires, playing cards, board games and an eclectic library. Good cask ales are offered, with a tempting menu of simple, home-made food including pies and chunky black-pudding sandwiches. Occasional live music, from morris dancing to acoustic bands. Mon–Sat noon–3pm & 6–11pm, Sun noon–4pm & 6–11pm; food served noon–2pm & 6–9pm.

Kathton House 6 High St, Sturry, CT2 0BD ☎ 01227 719999, ⓦ kathtonhouse.com. Just a 7min drive from Canterbury, this unassuming-looking restaurant offers special-occasion fine dining in an intimate setting. The food is classic, with lots of rich sauces – pork cheeks in red wine, guinea fowl in Madeira sauce, slow-cooked leg of rabbit in apple brandy – and delectable desserts. Two- and three-course set menus cost £18/£21.50 at lunch, £33.50/£40.50 at dinner. Tues–Sat noon–2pm & 7–9pm.

Old Coach and Horses Church Hill, Harbledown, CT2 9AB ☎ 01227 766609, ⓦ theoldcoachandhorses.co.uk.

> ### PADDLING ABOUT ON THE RIVER
>
> **Canoe Kent** (☎07864 743157, ⓦcanoekent.com) lead off-the-paddled-track guided canoe trips along the River Stour, setting off downstream of Canterbury from the hamlets of **Fordwich** (three miles northeast of town) or **Grove Ferry** (some four miles further on), and including breaks for tea and/or lunch. From Grove Ferry you can take a half- or full-day trip to the nearby **Stodmarsh Lakes** and the nature reserve (half-day £120 for one person, £140 for two; full day £170/£190), while from Fordwich there's the option of a two-day jaunt out to the coast at **Pegwell Bay** or **Deal** (£340/£380). They also offer a full-day Fordwich-to-Grove Ferry return (or vice versa; £170/£190). Pick-ups can be arranged from either of the Canterbury train stations.

Relaxed old pub with a restaurant serving good food at reasonable prices (starters from £5, mains from £9) with a solid menu that changes daily. Typical choices range from roast local Brogdale pork, via asparagus and spinach risotto with goat's cheese and toasted hazelnuts, to pasta with lamb meatballs. Tues–Sat 11.30am–3pm & 5.30–11pm, Sun noon–4.30pm; food served Tues–Sat noon–2pm & 6.30–9pm, Sun noon–2.30pm.

Queens Head 111 The Street, Boughton under Blean, ME13 9BH ☎01227 751369, ⓦqueenspub.co.uk. You can hunker down in this likeable Shepherd Neame tavern to dine on very tasty food (some of it produced on their own farm) from a daily-changing menu. The British basics – sausages, steaks, pies – are all done well, along with some more exotic options including green curry or crispy pork belly and scallop salad with Vietnamese dressing. Starters from £4, mains from £8. Mon–Sat noon–11pm, Sun noon–10pm; food served Tues–Sat noon–9pm, Sun noon–3pm.

Red Lion Crockham Lane, Hernhill, ME13 9JR ☎01227 751207, ⓦtheredlion.org. Set opposite the village green, in a quaint fourteenth-century building with lots of nooks and crannies and a log fire in the beamed interior, this is a classic English village pub, with a garden and play area for kids. Food is served, too, with dishes like baked garlic Camembert and roast vegetable tarts joining the home-made burgers, BBQ ribs and steak-and-kidney puds. Starters from £4, mains from £9. Mon–Sat 11.30am–11pm, Sun noon–10.30pm; food served Mon–Sat noon–2.30pm & 6–9pm, Sun noon–8pm.

South of Canterbury

The area **south of Canterbury**, though often overlooked in the dash from the city to the villages of the Weald or the iconic white cliffs of the coast, holds a couple of places of interest: the well-respected **Howletts Wild Animal Park** and gardens at **Goodnestone** are worthwhile paying attractions, while a number of sleepy little hamlets, including the village of **Chilham**, a handy overnight stop in its own right, make appealing bases for walks along the North Downs Way.

Howletts Wild Animal Park

Bekesbourne, CT4 5EL • Daily: April–Oct 9.30am–6pm, last admission 4.30pm; Nov–March 9.30am–5pm, last admission 3pm • £19.95, children (3–15 years) £17.95; 20 percent reduction if booked online; annual pass £23.95/£18.95; annual pass with Port Lympne (see p.127) £39.95/£29.95; Treetop Challenge £7.50/£6; Animal Adventure £2.50 • ☎0844 842 4647, ⓦaspinallfoundation.org/howletts

Working alongside the Aspinall Foundation conservation charity, which also oversees Port Lympne near Folkestone (see p.127), **Howletts Wild Animal Park** is highly regarded for its conservation efforts, saving and breeding rare species from around the world, and, where possible, returning them to the wild. Spread across the ninety-acre site, the animal enclosures are, in the main, well designed and equipped, with plenty of space for the creatures to retreat if necessary; this is not a zoo, as such, and you are not guaranteed to see all the animals if they are not in the mood to be seen. Though the park is home to black rhinoceros, snow leopards, Siberian tigers and the largest African elephant herd in the UK, along with many other species, the stars here tend to be the primates, including a large number of **gorillas** and some rather lively lemurs. Other diversions include the **Treetop Challenge**, an elevated adventure course with zip-lines, nets and rope-bridges, and the **Animal Adventure Challenge**, a less daunting adventure play area for smaller kids.

Goodnestone Park Gardens

Goodnestone, off the A2 Canterbury to Dover, CT3 1PL • Mid-Feb to March & Oct Sun noon–4pm; April–Sept Tues–Fri 11am–5pm, Sun noon–5pm • £6 • ☎ 01304 840107, ⓦ goodnestoneparkgardens.co.uk

Less than twenty minutes' drive southeast of Canterbury, **Goodnestone Park Gardens** offer a rather romantic ensemble. Covering some eighteen acres, part of an early eighteenth-century estate (which was home for a while to Jane Austen's brother and sister-in-law, and where the novelist was a frequent guest), the gardens began their days in the formal style so fashionable in the 1700s. The high point remains the seventeenth-century **walled garden**, its mellow, centuries-old walls tangled with clematis, wisteria and jasmine, and with deep borders spilling over in a profusion of English country flowers. There's also a **woodland** of old sweet chestnut and oak trees, carpeted with bluebells in spring and alive with vivid blue hydrangeas in autumn, and an **arboretum**, planted with ornamental trees that erupt into blossom in springtime.

Chilham

Kentish villages don't come much prettier than **CHILHAM**, a ten-minute drive southwest of Canterbury in the Stour Valley. This is picture-postcard stuff, a cluster of beamed and tiled fifteenth- and sixteenth-century dwellings centring on a market square – no surprise, then, that it's been used in a number of movies, among them Michael Powell and Emeric Pressburger's delightfully odd *A Canterbury Tale*, and period TV adaptations from Jane Austen to Agatha Christie. It offers more in the way of dozy English charm than actual sights, though **St Mary's Church**, with its looming tower, and **Chilham Castle**, a Jacobean country house whose gardens are occasionally open to the public (ⓦchilham -castle.co.uk), give you something to look at. A tearoom and a couple of pubs do food.

ACCOMMODATION   SOUTH OF CANTERBURY

★ **Castle Cottage** School Hill, Chilham, CT4 8DE ☎ 01227 730330, ⓦ castlecottagechilham.co.uk. Cute B&B in the old gardener's house in Chilham Castle grounds. The three rooms are spruce, clean and airy, with views over the Downs, and the flower-filled garden is an enchanting place to relax. A good option for walkers and cyclists. **£75**

Farthingales Old Court Hill, Nonington, CT15 4LQ ☎ 01304 840174, ⓦ farthingales.co.uk. A peaceful retreat hidden away on an old country lane in the ancient village of Nonington and with extensive gardens to explore. The main house is Elizabethan, but the two en-suite guest rooms occupy a weatherboard Victorian draper's shop in the grounds. **£85**

Woodland Farm Walderchain, Barham, CT4 6NS ☎ 01227 831892. Simple, secluded and sheltered camping spot, a mile or so from the village of Barham and around 20min drive from Canterbury, with great views of the North Downs and space for around twelve tents in an open field and its surrounding woods. It's a friendly place, with basic (but clean) facilities, and allows fires in braziers. Closed Nov–Feb. Camping (per adult) **£5**

EATING AND DRINKING

Chapter Arms New Town St, Chartham Hatch, CT4 7LT ☎ 01227 738340, ⓦ chapterarms.com. Country pub and restaurant, serving traditional British grub, from the simple (honey-roast home-baked ham, pies, suet puddings) to the fancy (beef carpaccio, duck confit). Mains start at around £9 at lunch, £13 in the evening, with a two-course lunch menu (Mon–Sat) at £10. There's a big garden, where you can sip real ales; on sunny days, try to bag a seat on the terrace, which has views of the surrounding orchards. Mon 11am–3pm, Tues–Sat 11am–3pm & 6–11pm, Sun noon–5pm; food served Mon noon–2.30pm, Tues–Sat noon–2.30pm & 6.30–9pm, Sun noon–3pm.

Granville Faussett Hill, Street End, Lower Hardres, CT4 7AL ☎ 01227 700402, ⓦ thegranvillecanterbury.com. Informal Shepherd Neame pub with food brought to you by the same people as the famed *Sportsman* near Whitstable (see p.85). Order from a daily-changing seasonal menu featuring simple classics such as pork belly, mussels or roast leg of lamb (mains £10–16) – good gastropub food, but not in the same league as the *Sportsman*. Tues–Sat noon–3pm & 5.30–11pm, Sun noon–10.30pm; food served Tues–Sat noon–2pm & 6.45–9pm, Sun noon–2.30pm.

★ **Mama Feelgoods** Chalkpit Farm, School Lane, Bekesbourne, CT4 5EU ☎ 01227 830830, ⓦ mama feelgoods.com. Packed with local produce and posh French and Italian goodies, this artisan deli and café, just a 10min drive southeast of the city, is a popular foodie destination for Canterbury locals. The café serves breakfast, good coffee and home-made cakes, and healthy lunches. Mon–Sat 9am–5pm, Sun 10.30am–4pm.

North Kent

TURNER CONTEMPORARY, MARGATE

North Kent

With a coastline that takes in lonely, creek-laced marshlands, shingle and sand beaches and dramatic, sea-lashed chalk cliffs, North Kent offers a splendid variety of attractions. It's perhaps best known for its bucket-and-spade resorts, but anyone with time to spend will uncover medieval castles and lonely bird reserves, ancient festivals and weird museums, cutting-edge galleries and historic villages abounding in excellent places to eat. This coast has traditionally been London's seaside playground, and today, easily accessible on the high-speed train from St Pancras, it still offers blasts of sunny fun within a hop of the capital.

2

Beyond the scruffy edges of London and Essex, the **Medway towns**, clustered around the estuary of the same name at the point where the North Downs fall down to the coast, have two big highlights in **Rochester** and **Chatham**, where a knot of important historic sights and family attractions – chief among them the mighty **Chatham Historic Dockyard**, founded by Henry VIII and for centuries the base of the Royal Navy – are less than an hour from London. From the estuary, the lowlying North Kent marshes creep along the coast to Whitstable, offering excellent **birdwatching**, particularly on the quiet **Hoo Peninsula** and **Isle of Sheppey**. Tucked just inland on the edge of the North Downs, alongside a winding creek, is medieval **Faversham**, a hub of North Kent's burgeoning **foodie scene**. Home to Shepherd Neame brewery and the national fruit collection, it's an underrated base for this part of Kent. Most people are ploughing on to artsy **Whitstable**, a bolt hole for weekending Londoners, famed for its oysters and its lively shops and restaurants. Neighbouring **Herne Bay** is less vibrant, though it offers invigorating clifftop walks all the way to the **Isle of Thanet**, on Kent's northeastern tip – where you'll find an almost uninterrupted sequence of sandy beaches and bays fringed by tall chalk cliffs. The "isle", though not literally cut off from the mainland, has a distinct personality, its trio of appealing historic resorts – brash **Margate**, genteel **Broadstairs** and handsome **Ramsgate** – each offering something different. Since the opening of **Turner Contemporary** in Margate, linking it culturally both with Whitstable and Folkestone further down the east coast, Thanet has grasped with aplomb its mantle as queen of Kent's coastal art scene.

The Medway towns

The estuary towns of the **River Medway**, which stretches seventy miles from West Sussex to the sea, have historically been defined by their naval and shipbuilding industries – a heritage celebrated by the enormous **Chatham Historic Dockyard**, which

BOTANY BAY

Highlights

❶ Rochester With its Dickens connections, cathedral and castle, and enormous Chatham Historic Dockyard on its doorstep, this likeable Medway town makes a rewarding day-trip. **See p.68**

❷ Faversham A neat little creekside town with fabulous restaurants, a historic brewery and an orchard to explore, and lonely marshland walks all around. **See p.76**

❸ Whitstable It's hard not to love laidback, oyster-loving Whitstable, where weekenders rub shoulders with seasalts and artists. **See p.79**

❹ Margate's Old Town Pronounced "romantic, sexy and fucking weird" by local girl Tracey Emin, mad Margate is fast becoming one of south England's hippest destinations. **See p.91**

❺ Botany Bay Thanet's beaches are all superb, but with its huge chalk pillars and its sweep of clean sand, Botany Bay is the most dramatic. **See p.92**

❻ Broadstairs Folk Week Quaint Broadstairs, the prettiest of the Thanet resorts, becomes a lively hotbed of music and street parades during this annual festival. **See p.98**

HIGHLIGHTS ARE MARKED ON THE MAP ON PP.68–69

records more than four hundred years of British maritime history. Of the towns themselves **Rochester** is by far the most appealing, with a clutch of interesting sights and good places to eat. **Dickens World**, near the dockyard, is an unlikely but likeable literary theme park, while the surrounding mudflats and saltmarsh are a big draw for **birdwatchers**, with the depopulated **Hoo Peninsula** and **Isle of Sheppey** boasting a number of important **RSPB reserves**.

2 Rochester

The handsome town of **ROCHESTER** was first settled by the Romans, who built a fortress on the site of the present **castle**; some kind of fortification has remained here ever since. With a Norman **cathedral** and an attractive Victorian high street, the town is probably best known for its connections with **Charles Dickens**, who spent his youth and final years near here, and wrote about it often – mischievously, perhaps, it appears as "Mudfog" in *The Mudfog Papers*, and "Dullborough" in *The Uncommercial Traveller*, as well as featuring in *The Pickwick Papers* and much of his last novel, the unfinished *The Mystery of Edwin Drood*. Many of the buildings he described can be seen today.

Everything you'll want to see is either on or just off the **High Street**, an unspoiled parade of half-timbered, brick and weatherboard buildings that snakes up from the railway station to the River Medway. Lined with independent, old-fashioned shops and coffee houses, it's a great place to wander.

Restoration House

17–19 Crow Lane, ME1 1RF • June–Sept Thurs & Fri 10am–5pm • £6.50; pre-booked tours £7.50; gardens only £3 • ☎ 01634 848520, 🅦 restorationhouse.co.uk

Restoration House is more like a living work of art than your usual stately home. An elegant Elizabethan mansion, given its current name after Charles II stayed here in May 1660 before his restoration, and the inspiration for Miss Havisham's Satis House in

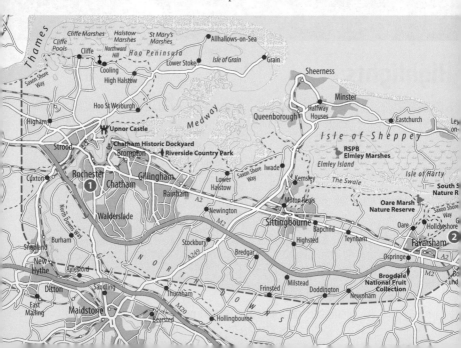

Great Expectations, it was, incongruously enough, owned for a while by Emu-toting entertainer Rod Hull, who saved it from being demolished – it was eventually taken from him by the taxmen, however, and left to dilapidation. The current owners have avoided the manicured restorations of so many old houses; its ragged, crumbling beauty reveals far more about the house's long life and many alterations than something more formal. This is a lived-in house, full of whimsical juxtapositions and evocative details: plaster is cracked and wood is buckled and chipped; mottled Georgian mirrors share space with Renaissance drawings and Gainsborough paintings, while Jacobean furniture sits upon undulating elm floorboards and fresh wild flowers tumble from vintage china. Stop for a cup of tea and a piece of home-made cake in the pantry before wandering around the charming walled gardens, with their fountains, fruit trees and fairytale topiary.

2

Six Poor Travellers House

97 High St, ME1 1LX • March–Oct Wed–Sun 11am–1pm & 2–4pm • Free • ☎ 01634 845609

The **Six Poor Travellers House**, an almshouse founded in 1579 to house impecunious travellers for the night – anyone, from scholars to blacksmiths, on the condition they were neither "rogues nor proctors" – was also used for a while in the eighteenth century as a prison for drunkards and runaway servants, and described by Dickens in his 1854 story *The Seven Poor Travellers*. "A clean white house", as the author put it, "of a staid and venerable air", it is still home to a few permanent residents, but you can wander through six small rooms, including three simple bedrooms with their truckle beds, and a fragrant courtyard herb garden.

Rochester cathedral

Boley Hill, ME1 1SX • Sun–Fri 7.30am–6pm, Sat 7.30am–5pm • Free, audio tours £1 • ☎ 01634 843366, ⓦ rochestercathedral.org

Built on Anglo-Saxon foundations, Rochester's **cathedral**, at the northwest end of the high street, dates back to the eleventh century – though the building has been much modified over the past nine hundred years. Plenty of Norman features remain,

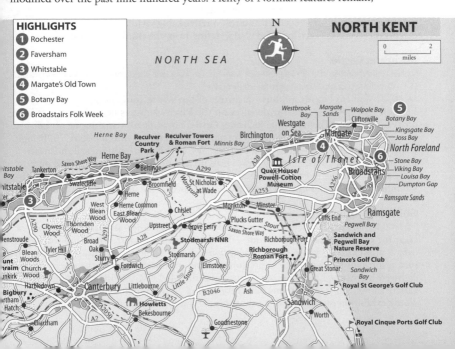

HIGHLIGHTS
1. Rochester
2. Faversham
3. Whitstable
4. Margate's Old Town
5. Botany Bay
6. Broadstairs Folk Week

NORTH KENT

2

ON THE DICKENS TRAIL

Charles Dickens (1812–70) spent many of his formative years in Chatham, and returned to live near Rochester for the last thirteen years of his life with his long-time lover Ellen Ternan, a local actress. They met when she was 18 and he 45, and after his separation from his wife Catherine, lived together until his death.

In addition to the main **sights**, nearly every other building in Rochester has a plaque linking it to the author. The town also hosts two Dickens **festivals** (see box opposite); there's another, along with more Dickens-related sightseeing, in **Broadstairs**, along the coast in Thanet (see box, p.98).

ROCHESTER

Eastgate House High St Now an arts centre, the sixteenth-century Eastgate House features as the Nuns' House in *Edwin Drood*, and Westgate in *Pickwick Papers*. In the garden you can see Dickens' summer study, a large Swiss chalet with gingerbread trimmings, which was moved here from Gad's Hill in the 1960s.

Royal Victoria and Bull Hotel High St. This run-down pub stood in for the *Bull* in *Pickwick Papers* and the *Blue Boar* in *Great Expectations*.

Dickens Rooms, Guildhall Museum See below.

Restoration House See p.68.

Six Poor Travellers House See p.69.

CHATHAM

Chatham Historic Dockyard In 1817 Dickens' family moved to a small house in Chatham, where his father was a clerk in the dockyards, and lived there for six years. Occasional Dickens Dockyard tours (£3.50) illuminate his time here. See p.72.

Dickens World See p.73.

BEYOND ROCHESTER

Gad's Hill Place Higham, ME3 7PA. Now a private school, three miles west of town, this is the Georgian house that Dickens dreamed of owning as a child and bought at the height of his fame in 1856, and where he died in 1870 (a baked potato oven marks the spot). It is not generally open for visits.

St James's Church Cooling. See p.74.

however, particularly in the handsome west front, with its pencil-shaped towers, richly carved portal and tympanum, and in the nave, with its stout Romanesque columns, arches and jagged chevron carving. Look out, too, for the thirteenth-century wall painting (only half survives) in the quire – a remarkably vivid depiction of the Wheel of Fortune – and the star-spangled vestry, dating from the thirteenth century.

Rochester Castle

Northwest end of the High St, ME1 1SW • Daily: April–Sept 10am–6pm; Oct–March 10am–4pm; last entry to keep 45min before closing • £5.65 • Ⓦ english-heritage.org.uk/daysout/properties/rochester-castle

In 1077, William I gave Gundulf – architect of the White Tower at the Tower of London – the job of improving defences on the River Medway's northernmost bridge on Watling Street. The resulting **Rochester Castle**, now ruined, remains one of the best-preserved examples of a Norman fortress in the country, with the stark 100ft-high keep – England's tallest – glowering over the town, while the interior is all the better for having lost its floors, allowing clear views up and down the dank shell. The outer walls and two of the towers retain their corridors and spiral stairwells, allowing you to scramble up rough and uneven damp stone staircases to the uppermost battlements.

Guildhall Museum

High St, ME1 1PY • Tues–Sun 10am–4.30pm; last admission 4pm; Dickens rooms closed 1–2pm • Free • ☎ 01634 848717, Ⓦ medway.gov.uk

Near the river, the **Guildhall Museum** – the old magistrates' court, where Pip was bound over as apprentice to Joe in *Great Expectations* – holds a chilling exhibition on the grim prison ships, or **hulks**, used to house convicts and prisoners of war in the late eighteenth century. Less diverting rooms cover the Medway, Victoriana and local variety shows, while the **Dickens Discovery Rooms**, in the adjoining building, include a wordy exhibition on his life, and a short film about locations that feature in his work.

ARRIVAL AND DEPARTURE ROCHESTER

By train Rochester train station is at the southeastern end of the High St.
Destinations Canterbury (every 30–45min; 50min); Chatham (every 5–25min; 3min); Herne Bay (every 30min–1hr; 48min); London Charing Cross (Mon–Sat every 30min; 1hr 10min); London St Pancras (every 30min–hourly; 35–40min); London Victoria (every 20–40min; 45min–1hr).

By bus Regular local buses to and from Chatham depart from Corporation St, which runs parallel to the High St.

INFORMATION AND TOURS

Tourist office 95 High St (April–Sept Mon–Sat 10am–5pm, Sun 10.30am–5pm; Oct–March Mon–Sat 10am–5pm; ☎01634 338141, ⓦvisitmedway.org).
Kingswear Castle Though most of the cruises on this 1924 paddlesteamer (see box, p.73) set off from Chatham Dockyard, it also offers river tours from below Rochester Castle, including a short trip to view Upnor Castle and afternoon cruises to Darnet Ness.

ACCOMMODATION

North Downs Barn Bush Rd, Cuxton, ME2 1HF ☎01634 296829, ⓦnorthdownsbarn.co.uk. Three luxurious en-suite B&B rooms in a gorgeous barn conversion on the Downs four miles south of Rochester. It's a superb stop-off for walkers on the North Downs Way – they welcome dogs, too – with extensive grounds to explore. **£80**
Salisbury House 29 Watts Ave, ME1 1RX ☎01634 400182. Pleasant Victorian guesthouse with two spotless rooms, friendly owners and a quiet location on a leafy street, just a 5min walk up the hill behind Rochester Castle. **£75**
Ship & Trades Maritime Way, Chatham, ME4 3ER ☎01634 895200, ⓦshipandtradeschatham.co.uk. This lively waterside pub-restaurant near the dockyards offers smart, modern, nautically themed B&B rooms. It can be noisy with deliveries and revelry from the bar downstairs, so ask for a quiet room at the back. **£80**
YHA Medway Hostel 351 Capstone Rd, Gillingham, ME7 3JE ☎0845 371 9649, ⓦyha.org.uk/hostel/medway. Rochester's nearest hostel is four miles southeast, in an old Kent oast house opposite the lovely Capstone Farm Country Park. There's a small kitchen, plus café. Dorms **£22**; doubles **£42**

EATING AND DRINKING

The Deaf Cat 83 High St, ME1 1LX ⓦthedeafcat.com. Opposite the cathedral, this boho coffee shop and gallery, dedicated to the memory of Dickens' deaf cat, serves good coffee, veggie sandwiches and simple home-made cakes to a laidback, unhurried crowd. Daily 9am–5pm.
Garden House Deli 98 High St, ME1 1JT ☎01634 842460. Artisan cheeses and tasty deli items, with gourmet baguettes, quiches and huge salads (from £3), to take away or eat in the wonky old front room or the secluded courtyard. Mon–Sat 10am–4pm.
La Torretta 32 High St, ME1 1LD ☎01634 407402. A slice of Italy in sleepy old Rochester, with fabulous espressos, cannoli (from £1.30), creamy gelato and authentic paninis from £4. Free wi-fi. Daily 8am–6pm.
Topes 60 High St, ME1 1JY ☎01634 845270, ⓦtopesrestaurant.com. Rochester's nicest restaurant, around the corner from the cathedral, serves inventive dishes such as sautéed bass with samphire, crisp pancetta and chorizo jam, or breast of guinea fowl with salsa verde, in a wood-panelled dining room with sloping ceilings. Lunch mains £12.50, with a two-course menu £16; dinner set menus £17.50/£22, with mains from £15 at weekends only. Wed–Sat noon–2.30pm & 6.30–9.30pm, Sun noon–2.30pm.

SHOPPING

Baggins Book Barn 19 High St, ME1 1PY ⓦbaggins books.co.uk. On the High St, look out for the wonderful Baggins Book Barn, England's largest secondhand bookstore. Daily 10am–5.45pm.

ROCHESTER FESTIVALS

So associated is **Charles Dickens** with Rochester that the town hosts not one but two annual festivals in his name (ⓦrochesterdickensfestival.org.uk). Early June sees a weekend of parades, readings and street entertainment, while the Dickensian Christmas is a festive flurry of falling snow and candlelit parades, with much emphasis, of course, on *A Christmas Carol* and Scrooge. Just as much fun is the **Rochester Sweeps Festival**, a May Day bank holiday celebration that re-creates the Victorian sweeps' May Day holiday; a rumbustious street affair featuring a Jack in the Green ceremony, folk music and morris dancing.

Chatham Historic Dockyard

About one mile north of Chatham along Dock Rd, ME4 4TY • Daily: end March to Oct 10am–6pm; mid-Feb to end March & Nov 10am–4pm; HMS *Gannet* 1–6pm; Victorian Ropery and *Ocelot* tours by timed ticket only • £16.50; children (5–15 years) £11; family ticket from £45; tickets last for a year • ☎ 01634 823800, ⓦ thedockyard.co.uk • Bus #140 or #141 from Rochester, or from Chatham train station, which is a 30min walk or a £6 taxi ride from the docks

Two miles east of Rochester, the vast **Chatham Historic Dockyard**, founded by Henry VIII, was by the time of Charles II the major base of the Royal Navy. Britain led the world in ship design and shipbuilding for centuries, and many Royal Navy vessels were built, stationed and victualled here. The dockyards were closed in 1984, with the end of the shipbuilding era, but reopened soon afterwards as a tourist attraction.

Inside the eighty-acre site, you can see an array of fine old ships and some historic buildings. It would take days to explore the whole place, so if pushed for time, concentrate on the **Ocelot sub**, the **Victorian Ropery** and the **No. 1 Smithery**. The main sights are reviewed below, but there are still more buildings and attractions detailed on the website and on the map available at the ticket office.

HMS Gannet

The Victorian sloop **HMS Gannet**, built nearby at Sheerness in 1878, is the most beautiful of Chatham's three historic ships, its elegant rigging and fine teak-planked hull evoking the glorious era of British naval supremacy. Unusually, *Gannet* also has a funnel – steam was not yet a tried and trusted form of naval power, so the ship was designed to be able to use both steam and sails. Nimble and fast, she was typical of the patrol ships used to impose the "gunboat diplomacy" that ensured Britannia ruled the waves then; lively audio tours take you back to 1887, when she set off to capture a group of rebel slave-traders responsible for shooting a ship's officer.

HMS Cavalier

HMS Cavalier, the Royal Navy's last operational World War II destroyer, was built on the Isle of Wight in 1944. In her day she was the fastest in the fleet, equipped with all the latest technology, and she remained active until 1972. You don't need to be a naval buff to get something from walking around this mighty "greyhound", the last of its kind in existence; the ship is kitted out as it would have been in the 1940s, and fascinating audio tours, which include testimony from men who served on destroyers, illuminate just how harsh conditions were on these mighty warships.

Ocelot submarine

Tours of the **Ocelot submarine,** the last Royal Navy warship to be built at Chatham, are not for the claustrophobic. You'll need to climb narrow, steep staircases, squeeze along low-ceilinged, one-person-wide passageways and shoot yourself from room to room through knee-high circular hatches. However, the opportunity to experience close up the astonishingly cramped quarters that housed a crew of 69 men for months at a time, and peer through the periscope at the outside world, make it perennially popular; the fact that *Ocelot* was a Cold War spy ship, and that her movements are shrouded in a certain mystery, only makes it more intriguing.

The Victorian Ropery

The **Victorian Ropery** is one of the surprise hits of the dockyard, its lively guided tours, led by guides in Victorian costume, using the history of rope making to illuminate the history of the docks themselves, and to reflect upon life at sea in the nineteenth century. Rope was made at Chatham from 1618 until the docks closed. During the "Age of Sail", warships would have needed some twenty miles of the stuff for the rigging alone; HMS *Victory* needed thirty miles at least, using it for everything from bucket handles to hammocks to cats-o'-nine-tails.

In 1790, the quarter-mile-long **Ropewalk**, the longest brick building in Europe, was built at Chatham; it is now the only one of its kind left in the world, and still used to make rope for commercial use. Here you get the opportunity to make rope yourself, and during the week can watch ropemakers at work, "walking the rope out" in the lengthy hall upstairs, using traditional machinery dating from 1811.

No. 1 Smithery

Chatham's nineteenth-century brick-built smithy now houses the **No. 1 Smithery**, which, along with temporary art exhibitions, features a splendid **Maritime Treasures** gallery. The highlights are undoubtedly the **ship models**, peaks of artistry and engineering made for a variety of reasons – as part of the design process, as prototypes, or simply as a way for naval POWs to pass the time. Look out for the elegant, fully rigged model of the wrecked HMS *Victory* (1737), carved from bone, a scale model of the Eddystone lighthouse (1865) made by the lighthouse keeper himself, and a model of HMS *Ormonde* (1918), a World War I ship "dazzle painted" with jarring angular designs that, while looking for all the world like Jazz Age modernism, were in fact effective forms of camouflage at sea.

2

Wooden Walls of England

Taking us back to the days of timber-hulled, sail-powered warships – known as "wooden walls" – the **Wooden Walls of England** exhibit, set in seven adjoining timber-framed mast houses, uses a series of scenes populated with mannequins to lead you through a reconstruction of the docks in the eighteenth century. It took around 26 kinds of craftsman to build a wooden-hulled sail-powered warship; you'll encounter joiners, sawyers, shipwrights and smiths, all of them based on people who worked here.

The Big Space

The Big Space is indeed very big, and full of very big things – including a Midget submarine, hulking mine-clearance equipment, a railway carriage used by General Kitchener, a D-Day locomotive and a grim-looking tank. The building, a covered slip built in 1838, is impressive, a colossal wide-span timber structure with a cantilevered frame and an apsidal end that resembles the bow of a ship. From the mezzanine you can take a closer look at the stunning roof, with its exposed timber frame.

Dickens World

Leviathan Way, Chatham Maritime mall, ME4 4LL • Days and hours vary, so check website, but roughly Tues–Fri 10am–4.30pm, Sat & Sun 10am–5.30pm • £13; children (5–15 years) £8; family ticket £40 • ☎ 01634 890421, ⓦ dickensworld.co.uk • Bus #140 or #141 from Rochester, or the same buses from Chatham train station, which is a 30min walk or a £6 taxi ride from Chatham Maritime mall

Despite its unpromising location in the busy Chatham Maritime mall, **Dickens World**, an enjoyable family attraction with literary aspirations, is not at all bad. In this world of dark, crooked old houses, grubby washing strung on lines and shady figures lurking in dank alleys, characters in Victorian costume – Mr Micawber among them – will engage kids in chat, while animatronic dummies in olde-worlde shoppes explain, rather unexpectedly, the intricacies of the Victorian class system.

PUFFING UP THE MEDWAY

Britain's last working coal-fired paddle steamer, **Kingswear Castle**, a handsome open-decked boat built in 1924, offers a variety of river cruises – from 30min jaunts along the Medway to longer Thames Estuary cruises or even day-trips to Southend or Sheerness – from Thunderbolt Pier in Chatham Historic Dockyard. Some trips take you past **Upnor Castle**, an atmospheric sixteenth-century gun fort built on the opposite side of the River Medway. The steamer also offers a couple of trips from Rochester. Tickets can be bought on board or booked in advance (summer only; from £12; ☎ 01634 827648, ⓦ kingswearcastle.co.uk).

2

FAMILY ATTRACTIONS AROUND ROCHESTER

Chatham Historic Dockyard (see p.72) and Dickens World (see p.73) make great family days out, and there are two more excellent family attractions, especially good for active types, nearby.

Chatham Ski Centre Capstone Rd, Gillingham, ME7 3JH ☎ 01634 827979, ⓦ jnlchatham.co.uk. The longest artificial ski slope in the Southeast offers excellent skiing and snowboarding, plus tobogganing and sno-tubing with lessons for kids as young as 4. Prices vary. Mon–Fri 10am–9pm, Sat & Sun 10am–6pm.

Diggerland Roman Way, Medway Valley Leisure Park, Strood, ME2 2NU ☎ 0871 2277007,

ⓦ diggerland.com. Good mucky fun – especially on rainy days – on this small plot, crammed with diggers of every shape and size, with plenty to drive, some to operate, and others mutated into merry-go-rounds and chairoplanes. Children as young as 5 can drive unaccompanied – but check the height restrictions before booking. £17.50; free for anyone less than 90cm tall. Sat & Sun & school hols 10am–5pm; closed winter.

Much is made of the darker side of Dickens, which is great fun, of course, but can sometimes mislead; entering the **Haunted Man**, for example, a cobwebby house full of creepy noises, you might think you're in for a ghost ride. Instead, the dank rooms host holographs playing out scenes from the author's best-known books – intriguing, but not scary. Highlights include the **Great Expectations Boat Ride**, which takes you through the Marshalsea, rat-filled sewers, spooky graveyards and London rooftops (wear waterproofs if you sit at the back), and the film in **Peggotty's Boathouse**, a witty romp that uses 3D and the odd splashy surprise to recount the author's world travels.

The Hoo Peninsula

The marshy **Hoo Peninsula**, jutting out into the Medway and the Thames estuaries north of Rochester, is a lonely area rich in birdlife, attracting migrating and nesting waterfowl. The **Heron Trail** cycling route covers a loop of around seventeen miles, linking the **Cliffe Pools**, **Buckland Lake** and **Northward Hill** reserves, while the **Saxon Shore Way** walking path, which passes through Rochester, is also handy for Cliffe Pools and Northward Hill.

RSPB Cliffe Pools

Cliffe • Daily dawn to dusk • Free • ☎ 01634 222480, ⓦ rspb.org.uk/reserves/guide/c/cliffepools • Bus #133 from Chatham and Rochester stops in Cliffe; by car, park in Cliffe and walk down Pond Lane into the reserve

One of the most important wildlife reserves in the country, the 237-hectare **Cliffe Pools**, a watery landscape of brackish pools and salty lagoons right by the Thames, attracts large flocks of wading birds and waterfowl. Stars include avocets, little egrets, dunin and lapwings, and during migration periods, sandpipers and stints. A number of trails, including the Saxon Shore Way, cross the reserve, giving brilliant views.

Cooling

The village of **COOLING** is an isolated spot, stranded in the Hoo marshes around seven miles north of Rochester. The thirteenth-century **St James's Church** is where Pip meets Magwitch by his brothers' gravestones in *Great Expectations*; you can still see the thirteen sad little lozenge-shaped stone tombs that inspired the scene. The nearby **Cooling Castle**, which was built in the fourteenth century on the edge of marshes to guard the Thames, now sits around two miles inland. Partly ruined and largely used for weddings, it's also a part-time residence for musician Jools Holland.

RSPB Northward Hill

1 mile from High Halstow • Daily dawn–dusk • Free, donations welcome • ☎ 01634 222480, ⓦ rspb.org.uk/reserves/guide/n/northwardhill

Based on a ridge overlooking the marshes, **Northward Hill**, its beautiful bluebell woods filled with nightingale song in spring, boasts the largest **heronry** in the UK, with some

150 pairs of grey heron and around fifty pairs of little egrets. The marshes are a rich breeding ground for lapwing, redshank and avocet, and in winter you can see around ten different kinds of birds of prey. Some 10km of trails offer views of the marshes and the Thames Valley, and lead you to a heronry viewpoint.

Isle of Sheppey

The **Isle of Sheppey**, a flat clump of marshy land measuring just nine miles by four, separated from the mainland by the Medway and the Swale estuary, is often overlooked on a Kent itinerary. That's not to say it hasn't got a certain cut-off appeal: beyond its fifty-odd caravan parks, amusement arcades and industrial estates, beyond the ranks of enormous pylons and its trio of prisons, the island offers an odd, otherworldly sense of isolation and a few quiet attractions, from wide beaches crunching with London Clay **fossils** and empty marshlands rich in **birdlife**. The south of the island is the most appealing, a big-sky landscape where contented cows and fat sheep graze upon the rich salty marshlands of the isolated **Isle of Harty** and the wetland wilderness of **Elmley Marshes**.

Isle of Harty

The **Isle of Harty**, on Sheppey's southeastern tip, may not literally be an island, but separated from the rest of Sheppey by a number of channels it certainly feels cut off. With a few narrow country lanes winding through the watery landscape, this is good walking territory, and a favourite spot for birders; the **RSPB Capel Fleet viewpoint** is one of the best places in England to see birds of prey, including rough-legged buzzards, while the coastal strip between **Shell Ness**, on the island's eastern tip, and Harty's *Ferry House Inn* (see below) is designated as the **Swale National Nature Reserve** (ⓦwww .naturalengland.org.uk), an excellent spot to see waders, waterfowl and birds of prey, along with rare plants and butterflies.

RSPB Elmley Marshes

Kings Hill Farm, ME12 3RW • Daily except Tues 9am–9pm or sunset • Free, donations welcome • ☏ 01795 665969, ⓦ rspb.org.uk /reserves/guide/e/elmleymarshes

The trip out to **Elmley Marshes**, a wilderness area of open grassland, mudflats and saltmarsh on the southwest of the island, famed among birders for its high density of breeding waders, is half the fun: the RSPB sign off the A249 heralds a two-mile drive through lonely wetlands, with big skies stretching out to either side, before you even reach the entrance. From here it's a 1.25-mile walk beside the marshes to the first hide, overlooking a scrape visited by thousands of wading birds. There are five hides in total; the South Fleet hide, further on, affords particularly good views of nesting avocets in spring. In spring and summer you'll see displaying waders, including redshanks and lapwings, along with rare breeding species including grey partridge and yellow wagtail, while in the cooler months you may spot little egrets and wigeon.

ARRIVAL AND INFORMATION   ISLE OF SHEPPEY

By car Sheppey is linked to the mainland by the A249 and the huge Sheppey Crossing bridge. You can also take the smaller road running alongside the A249, which has a small drawbridge and provides faster access to Elmley.

By train There are stations at Sheerness and Queenborough, with connections to Sittingbourne on the mainland.

Tourist information The Bluetown Heritage Centre, 69 High St, Blue Town, Sheerness (Tues–Sat 10am–3pm; £1; ☏ 01795 662981, ⓦ bluetownheritagecentre.com), is a fascinating museum/information centre/music hall/cinema, which concentrates on the history of Sheerness – in particular its historic old Blue Town area – plus a cosy tearoom serving home-made cakes.

Website ⓦ visitsheppey.com.

ACCOMMODATION AND EATING

Ferry House Inn Harty Ferry Rd, Harty, ME12 4BQ ☏ 01795 510214, ⓦ theferryhouseinn.co.uk. A friendly sixteenth-century pub, in a tranquil spot on Sheppey's southern coast. With its sweeping Swale views, the large,

2

flower-bedecked garden is a peaceful place to eat above-average pub grub; the burgers and pies (from £9) are made with beef and lamb from their own farm, while daily specials include savoury tarts and risottos (from £8). They also offer B&B. Tues–Fri 11am–3pm & 6.30–11pm, Sat 11am–11pm, Sun noon–6pm; food served Tues–Fri noon–2.30pm & 6.30–9pm, Sat 12.30–4pm & 6.30–9pm, Sun 12.30–4pm. £85

Flynn's Bee Farm Tea Room Elmley Rd, ME12 3SS ☎01795 874935, ⓦflynnsbeefarm.co.uk. This small, family-owned bee farm, with a shop, also serves delicious cream teas (with honey, naturally) and light home-cooked lunches, which you can eat outside in the garden. Tues–Sat 9am–5pm, Sun 10am–4pm.

The Three Tuns Lower Halstow, ME9 7DY ☎01795 842840, ⓦthethreetunsrestaurant.co.uk. On the way to Sheppey, this sixteenth-century country inn, with a huge streamside beer garden, serves local ales and ciders along with good, seasonal gastropub grub. Tuck into a "Kentish platter" of Scotch egg, pork pie, toasted huffkin and local cheese, or a slow-braised curried lamb shank, or go lighter with the gourmet sandwiches (from £4.50) and interesting veggie choices. Mains from £9. Daily noon–9pm; food served Mon–Sat noon–2pm & 6–9pm, Sun noon–9pm.

Faversham and around

Site of an important medieval abbey (long since gone), the attractive creekside town of **FAVERSHAM** was famed from Elizabethan times for its thriving boat yards, fitting and repairing the wooden barges that worked their way along the estuary to London. Once surrounded by hop gardens, it is still home to the **Shepherd Neame Brewery**, while the importance of fruit-growing hereabouts is celebrated by the **Brogdale National Fruit Collection**. For many years, too, Faversham was at the centre of the nation's explosives industry, with **gunpowder** produced in the nearby marshes for three centuries before fizzling out in the 1930s. On the edge of the North Downs Area of Outstanding Natural Beauty, and separated from the Swale by a web of **marshes** and winding creek inlets, it's a neat, pretty place, its core boasting a well-preserved mix of buildings from medieval via Elizabethan to Victorian. **Market Place** is the hub, fringed with cafés, the independent **Royal Cinema** (ⓦroyalcinema.co.uk) and a handsome sixteenth-century Guildhall elevated on stout columns. From here medieval **Abbey Street** runs down to the peaceful **creek**.

Fleur de Lis Heritage Centre Museum

10 Preston St, ME13 8NS • Mon–Sat 10am–4pm, Sun 10am–1pm • £3 • ☎01795 590726, ⓦfaversham.org/society

The **Fleur de Lis Heritage Centre** should be your first stop; not only does it house the excellent information office and bookshop (see opposite) but also a fabulous local **museum** that punches way above its weight for a town of this size. Packed with lively exhibits on everything from brewing to boat building, agricultural riots to local pirates, the Tardis-like museum also illuminates Faversham's social history with its reconstructed domestic interiors, while offbeat objects, from a mammoth's tooth to a magic lantern, confront you at every turn.

Faversham Creek

Faversham grew up alongside its **creek**, a tidal inlet of the Swale that was used from at least Roman times as a harbour. In the sixteenth century it was crowded with small merchant ships, many of them built locally, and it remained busy until Victorian times, swarming with deft Thames barges. **Standard Quay**, downstream of the swing bridge at the end of Abbey Street, was until 2012 one of just two remaining wooden boat repair yards in Britain; today, however, the cluster of workshops, lopsided timber-framed buildings and weatherboard grain stores house antiques shops, art workshops and a garden centre (with tearoom). There's also a **farmers' market** held here every Saturday. You can walk along the creek to the nearby marshes and a couple of nature reserves (see opposite).

Shepherd Neame Brewery

11 Court St, ME13 7AX • Daily; tour schedule varies, but there is usually a 2pm tour and often another in the morning • £11.50 • ☏ 01795 542016, ⓦ shepherdneame.co.uk/tours-functions/tours

It's rare to find a pub in these parts that isn't owned by the **Shepherd Neame Brewery**, the oldest in Britain, whose Spitfire, Bishop's Finger and Master Brew ales are household names among beer fans. A brewery has stood on this site since at least 1570, drawing water from an artesian well; now this fifth-generation, family-owned business, is best known for their quintessentially Kentish ales, made with hops from local fields. Lively tours take you through the process, from soaking the barley to conditioning the ales and adding special ingredients – oysters, rose petals – for their speciality brews. It's a working facility, thrumming, humid and pungent, and tours are enjoyably interactive: peer into the steaming, churning mash tuns, the oldest in England, and try all the key ingredients, from the burnt toast-tasting chocolate malt, used in stout and porters, to wincingly bitter dried hop pellets and fresh well water. The grand finale is a tutored beer-tasting; you're given three half-pints, and can then choose another half-pint of your favourite, to drink with free snacks.

Brogdale National Fruit Collection

Brogdale Rd, ME13 8XZ • Daily: April–Oct 10am–5pm; Nov–March 10am–4pm; 1hr guided tours April–Oct daily 11am, 1pm & 2.30pm • £10, lasts a year • ☏ 01795 536250, ⓦ brogdalecollections.co.uk

On the southern edge of town, **Brogdale Farm** is home to the largest collection of fruit trees in the world, with thousands of varieties of apple and hundreds of pears, plums, cherries and nuts. It's above all a research facility; you can wander around freely, but you'll get the most from your trip if you join a guided tour or come for one of their regular themed days or festivals. Though spring and autumn are the best seasons to visit, there's something to see all year, plus a café, a nursery stocked with heritage fruit trees and a couple of farm shops – including the excellent **Butchers of Brogdale**.

The Swale

From the sixteenth to the twentieth century gunpowder was manufactured in the marshes northwest of Faversham on the south bank of the Swale; today these tranquil, sheltered mudflats and salt marshes, cut through with fresh and brackish creeks, are prime habitat for migratory, overwintering and breeding birds, among them black-tailed godwit, dunlin, curlew, avocet, redshank and snipe. The **Oare Marsh Nature Reserve** (ⓦwildlifetrusts.org/reserves/oare-marshes), with its headquarters at Harty Ferry, just north of the village of Oare, has a nature trail with hides, and views across the estuary to Sheppey. You can also walk along the creek east of Faversham, following the coast through the **South Swale Nature Reserve** (ⓦwildlifetrusts.org/reserves/south-swale) – rich in wading birds and wildfowl, and flecked with glorious wild flowers – the five miles to Seasalter and its famous gastropub, *The Sportsman* (see p.85).

ARRIVAL AND INFORMATION
FAVERSHAM AND AROUND

By train The station is on Station Rd, a 3min walk up Preston St to Market Place.

Destinations Broadstairs (Mon–Sat every 30min; 35min); Canterbury (every 15–40min; 30min); Dover (every 30min–1hr; 33min); London St Pancras (Mon–Sat every 30min; 65min); London Victoria (every 15–30min; 1hr 10min–1hr 35min); Margate (Mon–Sat every 30min; 30min); Ramsgate (Mon–Sat every 30min; 40min).

By bus Buses stop in the centre of town, on Court St near Market Place.

Destinations Boughton (frequent; 12min); Canterbury (every 15min–2hr; 30min); Whitstable (Mon–Fri 4 daily, Sat 3 daily; 50min).

Fleur de Lis Heritage Centre 10 Preston St, (Mon–Sat 10am–4pm, Sun 10am–1pm; ☏01795 534542, ⓦfaversham.org). Faversham's superb tourist office, with a fantastic local history bookshop and a history museum (see p.76) also organizes 90min walking tours (Sat: April, May, Sept & Oct 10.30am; June–Aug 10.30am & 2.30pm; £3.50; ☎01795 534542).

ACCOMMODATION

★ **Palace Farm** Down Court Rd, Doddington, ME9 0AU ☎01795 886200, ⓦpalacefarm.com. A family farm in a North Downs village six miles southwest of Faversham, with ten comfortable, hostel-style B&B rooms around a courtyard or in a converted granary. They're all en-suite, with bunks and/or double beds, with a communal kitchen, lounge and dining room, plus outdoor eating areas. There's tent camping, in a quiet field with 25 pitches and a couple of tipis; you can rent firepits and bikes. Campsite closed mid-Oct to Easter. Doubles **£40**; camping/adult **£8**; tipis **£60**

★ **Railway Hotel** Preston St, ME13 8PE ☎01795 533173, ⓦrailwayhotelfaversham.co.uk. Opposite the station, this quirky old hotel has been hosting train travellers since Victorian times, and today offers characterful and comfortable B&B in seven en-suite rooms – including a cupboard-sized single and a four-poster

double – with rudimentary showers but lots of personal touches. There's a quiet pub downstairs, along with a recommended restaurant (see below). **£75**

Read's Macknade Manor, Canterbury Rd, ME13 8XF ☎01795 535344, ⓦreads.co.uk. Faversham's Michelin-starred restaurant (see below) has six rooms exuding Georgian country house elegance, from the cut-glass sherry decanters to the opulent floral fabrics, with lovely garden views. Dinner, bed and breakfast deals available. **£165**

Sun Inn 10 West St, ME13 7JE ☎01795 535098, ⓦsunfaversham.co.uk. In the heart of town, in a wonky old building opposite the Guildhall, this sixteenth-century coaching inn, owned by Shepherd Neame, has eight comfortable, if unextraordinary, B&B rooms, and a rather smart food menu. **£75**

EATING AND DRINKING

As the home of Shepherd Neame, Faversham has more than its fair share of irresistible real ale **pubs**, most of them in lovely historic buildings. Many also serve terrific **food**: this is one of Kent's foodiest towns.

★ **The Anchor** 52 Abbey St, ME13 7BP ☎01795 536471, ⓦtheanchorinnfaversham.com. Relaxed old pub in a sixteenth-century building near the creek, all weathered wood, warped beams and dried hops, with no pretension whatsoever. The simple, local food (mains from £9; two-course Mon–Thurs lunch menu £6.95) – perhaps devilled kidneys, fish stew with chorizo, crab on toast, a Kentish cheese ploughman's – is outstanding. Eat in an unadorned dining room or in the cosy bar where locals chat over quiet Shepherd Neame pints and warm themselves by the log fire. Mon–Thurs noon–11pm, Fri & Sat noon–midnight, Sun noon–10.30pm; food served Mon & Tues noon–2.30pm, Wed–Fri noon–2.30pm & 6.30–9pm, Sat noon–3pm & 6.30– 9pm, Sun noon–3pm.

★ **The Carriage** Railway Hotel, Preston St, ME13 8PE ☎01795 531790, ⓦthecarriagerestaurant.com. The unaffectedly stylish room, with its bare floorboards, fresh flowers and mismatched framed prints, is a charming place to settle down to Modern British food, made with local ingredients, from an alumni of Canterbury's superb *Goods Shed* (see p.56). The seasonally changing menu concentrates on simple dishes – try the courgette and gouda tart or lamb cutlets with aubergine purée. Mains around £8 at lunch, £11–17 in the evening. Reservations recommended. Tues 6–9.30pm, Wed–Sat noon–2.30pm & 6–9.30pm, Sun noon–2.30pm.

Jittermugs 18A Preston St, ME13 8NZ ☎01795 533121. Friendly little coffee shop, with distressed wooden

floors, sofas, and bookish bits and bobs scattered around the place. Come for a speedy espresso or tea (the fresh Moroccan mint is delicious) or a light meal (£4–6) of antipasti or salads, toasted sandwiches or stuffed peppers. Mon–Sat 8.30am–6.30pm, Sun 10am–5pm.

★ **Macknades** Selling Rd, ME13 8XF ☎01795 534497, ⓦmacknade.com. Just outside town, *Macknades* is more of a gourmet food hall than a farm shop. They sell the best local produce, with separate concessions for wines, fish, plants and herbs, deli goodies from southern Europe, and a coffee shop serving authentic espresso, cheese and charcuterie plates. There's a smaller branch on West St in town. Food hall: Mon–Sat 9am–6pm, Sun 10am–4pm; café: Mon–Sat 9.30am–5pm, Sun 10am–4pm.

Read's Macknade Manor, Canterbury Rd, ME13 8XE ☎01795 535344, ⓦreads.co.uk. For a dress-up dinner, this Michelin-starred restaurant, in a Georgian manorhouse on the edge of town, is just the ticket. The relaxed elegance extends to the food, which uses local produce, including veg and herbs from the kitchen garden, to create classical dishes with French flair. The menu changes, but foie gras terrine, Montgomery Cheddar soufflé with smoked haddock, and oxtail braised in Madeira are typical. Fixed-price menus only: a good-value £25 at lunch, £58 at dinner. Tues–Sat noon–2pm & 7–9pm.

★ **Shipwrights Arms** Hollowshore, ME13 7TU ☎01795 590088, ⓦtheshipwrightsarmspub.co.uk. Time seems to have stood still in this cluttered old weatherboard pub – peacefully set in the marshes next to a boatyard – where the real ales are very local, as are the regulars. You can walk here, in around 40min, through the marshes from Faversham, after which it's a treat to settle down to a quiet pint in the garden. May–Oct Mon–Fri 11am–3pm & 6pm–close, Sat 11am–4pm & 6pm–close, Sun noon–4pm & 6pm–close; closed Mon afternoon Nov–April.

★ **Three Mariners** 2 Church Rd, Oare, ME13 0QA ☏ 01795 533633, ⓦ thethreemarinersoare.co.uk. An appealing spot, in a creekside village north of Faversham, with a garden and terrace for alfresco dining. Serving good local ales, it excels with its food: simple and perfectly executed dishes such as potato and porcini soup, or garlic-roasted fillet of local cod. Mains start at £14 – you could cut costs with the three-course walkers' menu (Mon–Fri lunch; £11.50), but it's worth splashing out. Mon–Fri noon–3pm & 6–11pm; food served Mon–Fri noon–2.30pm & 6–9pm, Sat & Sun noon–3pm & 6–9pm, Sun noon–3.30pm & 7–9pm.

2

Whitstable and around

The most charming spot along the North Kent coast, and a popular weekend destination for capital-dwellers (known to locals as "DFLs" – "Down From Londoners"), **WHITSTABLE** is a lively, laidback place. Fishermen, artists, yachties and foodies rub along here, and the sense of community, and tradition, is strong. By the Middle Ages this fishing village was celebrated for its seafood, and though it's nowadays more dependent on its commercial harbour and seaside tourism, the **oysters** for which it has been famed since classical times still loom large – you can tuck in at dozens of restaurants, or celebrate them with gusto at the lively annual **Oyster Festival** (see box, p.85).

Sights are few, which is part of the appeal. It's a wonderful place simply to hang out, with a busy little **harbour** and an attractive **High Street** lined with independent restaurants, delis and shops. The **beach**, an uncommercialized shingle stretch backed by flower-filled gardens, weatherboard cottages and colourful beach huts, offers broad empty vistas and blustery walks for miles in each direction, and with its shallow bays and clean, flat waters Whitstable also offers good **watersports**.

The high street

Whitstable's high street runs through town from the railway up to the harbour. Adopting three different names as it goes, it links to parallel streets, and to the sea, via a number of narrow alleys. Starting as **Oxford Street** in the south, it segues into the **High Street** proper beyond the **Whitstable Museum**, then transforms itself again at the **Horsebridge**, once home to the jetty where cargo was loaded and unloaded onto the Thames barges, and now a knot of activity where the town meets the beach. Here marks the start of **Harbour Street**, Whitstable's showpiece shopping stretch, lined with wonky and jauntily painted old buildings housing excellent restaurants and shops.

Whitstable Museum

5 Oxford St, CT5 1DB • Daily 10am–4pm • £3 • ☏ 01227 276998, ⓦ canterbury.gov.uk

The friendly **Whitstable Museum** is full of curiosities. One corner is dedicated to ex-local **Peter Cushing** – the assertion that the man best remembered as Dr Frankenstein was an accomplished model-maker, who also designed scarves for Marks and Spencer, may come as a surprise. Evocative photos recall the days of the **Canterbury & Whitstable Railway**, the world's first scheduled steam passenger service, while local maritime history is covered with figureheads, ships' models, hulking old tools and the odd bit of oyster paraphernalia. The **fossils**, and an **Ice Age mammoth tooth** and tusk, both found nearby, are a hit with kids, while the local "pudding pan pots" are pretty extraordinary, too. Officially known as **Samian ware**, these pottery dishes date back to Roman times, conserved underwater in silt for thousands of years before being hauled up by fishermen and used in local homes.

2

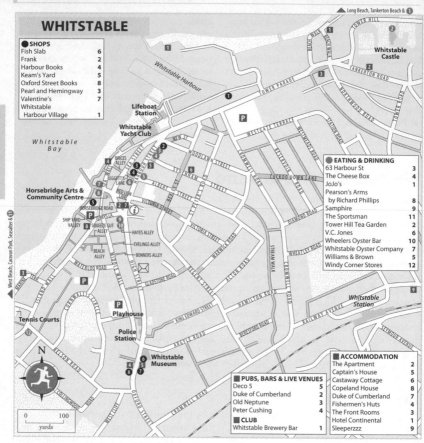

WHITSTABLE

Long Beach, Tankerton Beach & ①

● SHOPS

Fish Slab	6
Frank	2
Harbour Books	4
Keam's Yard	5
Oxford Street Books	8
Pearl and Hemingway	3
Valentine's	7
Whitstable Harbour Village	1

● EATING & DRINKING

63 Harbour St	3
The Cheese Box	4
JoJo's	1
Pearson's Arms by Richard Phillips	8
Samphire	9
The Sportsman	11
Tower Hill Tea Garden	2
V.C. Jones	6
Wheelers Oyster Bar	10
Whitstable Oyster Company	7
Williams & Brown	5
Windy Corner Stores	12

■ PUBS, BARS & LIVE VENUES

Deco 5	5
Duke of Cumberland	2
Old Neptune	3
Peter Cushing	4

■ CLUB

Whitstable Brewery Bar	1

■ ACCOMMODATION

The Apartment	2
Captain's House	5
Castaway Cottage	6
Copeland House	8
Duke of Cumberland	7
Fishermen's Huts	4
The Front Rooms	3
Hotel Continental	1
Sleeperzzz	9

The beaches

A swathe of shingle punctuated by weathered groynes, backed for most of its length by seaside houses and beach huts in varying states of repair, **Whitstable beach** is a glorious place for a stroll, a crabbing expedition or a lazy day's sunbathing, with a gentle slope that makes swimming possible in summer. Just steps away from the high street, it feels a world away, uninterrupted by commerce or cars and bathed in pearly light. Its elemental beauty, brightened by ragged clumps of tough beach plants, splashy wild flowers and peeling, upturned fishing boats, is picturesque without being twee; the skies are huge here, and the sunsets dramatic, with locals and tourists gathering most nights to watch the horizon bleed from orange to purple.

West to Seasalter

You mustn't leave Whitstable without taking a seaside walk **west from the Horsebridge**, where a beachside path takes you past abundant, unruly gardens, weatherbeaten beach huts and covetable seaside cottages on one side with the huge open horizon expanding on the other. The *Old Neptune* pub (see p.86), standing alone on the shingle, marks the start of the town's **West Beach**, a good spot for crabbing and fine for swimming at high tide. Busy with families in summer, the beach gets quieter the further west you go – beyond the caravan park you can either continue by crunching along the pebbles, or keep to the path behind the beach huts. Around two miles from town you arrive at lonely **Seasalter**, marooned between birdlife-rich marshes and a shell-strewn beach with muddy offshore oyster beds. It's an unlikely but lovely spot for the Michelin-starred *Sportsman* (see p.85), one of Britain's best restaurants.

Northeast to Tankerton

Walking **northeast from the Horsebridge**, passing the thicket of clattering masts next to the yacht club, then the lifeboat station and the harbour, and trudging along the shingle beyond, you'll join a broad seaside walkway. On the road above, accessible by a short path, sits **Whitstable Castle** – actually a private manor house and beautiful flower-filled public park, with great sea views, an excellent kids' **playground** and a couple of cafés (see p.85). Well below and sheltered from the road, the path fringes Whitstable's broad, shingle **Long Beach** before emerging at the blue-flag **Tankerton beach**, where there's good swimming and a lifeguard hut. At low tide you can take a stroll along "**the Street**", a half-mile-long clay sandbank that juts out at right angles to the beach and provides sandy bottomed, shallow swimming on either side. Ranks of brightly coloured beach huts sit staggered on the grassy **Tankerton Slopes** rising by the path – Tracey Emin's beach hut installation, *The Last Thing I Said To You Is Don't Leave Me Here*, which was bought by Charles Saatchi for £75,000 in 2000 and later destroyed in a warehouse fire, hailed from here. Scattered with rare hog's fennel, the slopes are classified as a Site of Special Scientific Interest and provide a lovely barrier from the road above. Climbing the steps next to the sailing club brings you up to **Marine Parade**, the road to Herne Bay, and an excellent restaurant, *JoJo's* (see p.84) – about thirty minutes' walk from Whitstable.

Whitstable Harbour

Whitstable's **harbour**, a mix of pretty and gritty that defines the town to a tee, bustles with a fish market, whelk stalls and a couple of seafood restaurants, and offers plenty of places to sit outside and watch the activity. Built in 1832 to serve the **Canterbury & Whitstable Railway**, which carried day-trippers to the beach and back, today it's a mixed-use port, backed by a hulking asphalt plant; the handsome 1892 Thames sailing barge, **Greta** (see p.82), offers boat trips around the estuary.

ARRIVAL AND DEPARTURE

WHITSTABLE AND AROUND

By car Whitstable lies around five miles north of Canterbury on the A290, easily accessible from the M20. Parking is tight: if you can't find a space on the street, try the pay car parks at Keam's Yard or behind the harbour.

By train From the station it's a 15min walk along Cromwell Rd to Harbour St.

Destinations Broadstairs (Mon–Sat every 30min; 25min);

Herne Bay (every 30min–1hr; 7min); London Victoria (every 30min–1hr; 1hr 30min); Margate (Mon–Sat every 30min; 23min); Ramsgate (Mon–Sat every 30min; 35min).

By bus Buses stop on the high street.

Destinations Blean (frequent; 17min); Canterbury (every 15min; 30min); Faversham (3–4 daily Mon–Sat; 50min).

WHITSTABLE WATERSPORTS

Whitstable is an excellent place for **watersports**, with a number of clubs based here and a laidback social scene. There are sailing races most summer weekends, while **windsurfing** and **kitesurfing**, concentrated around Long Beach and the Street, are particularly popular.

Whitstable Yacht Club 3–4 Sea Wall, next to the harbour ☎ 01227 282800, ⊛ wyc.org.uk. Top-class lessons in sailing (from £60 for a taster) and windsurfing (from £50/3hr taster) at this prestigious club.

Oystercoast Long Beach ☎ 01795 536510, ⊛ oyster coastwatersports.org.uk. Tuition in dinghy sailing,

powerboating, canoeing, kitesurfing and windsurfing.

Kent Kitesurfing School ☎ 07709 073697, ⊛ kent kitesurfingschool.com. Kitesurfing (from £100/day) and paddleboarding sessions (£15/hr; lessons £20/1hr) on Whitstable beach and at the Street.

INFORMATION, TOURS AND GETTING AROUND

Tourist information The Whitstable Shop, 34 Harbour St (Mon–Sat 10am–4pm, Sun 11am–2pm; ☎ 01227 770060, ⊚ seewhitstable.com).

Sailing trips The *Greta* (☎ 07711 657919, ⊚ greta1892 .co.uk), a Thames barge moored in the harbour, runs regular 4–6hr trips, including seal- and shipwreck-spotting

(spring–Oct; from £44) around the Swale Estuary.

Bike rental Whitstable Cycle Hire, 56 Harbour St (book in advance; ☎ 01227 388058, ⊚ whitstablecyclehire.com), rent bikes for £16/day or £70/week, with family deals from £50/day. You can pick up here and drop off in Canterbury (see p.38) or Herne Bay (see p.87).

ACCOMMODATION

Though there are some great places to stay in Whitstable, the choice of **hotels** and **B&Bs** is surprisingly limited, and prices aren't low, especially at the weekends (when there may be a two-night minimum). Many people choose self-catering: in addition to the options below you could check ⊚ whitstableholidayhomes.co.uk, ⊚ whitstablecottagecompany.com and ⊚ placestostayinwhitstable.co.uk.

HOTELS AND GUESTHOUSES

⭐ **The Apartment** 3 Tankerton Rd, CT5 2AB ☎ 01227 280151, ⊚ theapartmentwhitstable.com. Covering the top floor of an Edwardian home near Whitstable Castle, this stylish two-room B&B is a peaceful retreat, kitted out with Art Deco and shabby chic furnishings and a gorgeous (shared) bathroom; you can book a massage or beauty treatment in the therapy room downstairs. One room **£130;** both rooms **£150**

Copeland House 4 Island Wall, CT5 1EP ☎ 01227 266207, ⊚ copelandhouse.co.uk. Georgian B&B in a great spot moments from the High Stand with a garden backing onto the beachside walk. The six simple rooms – two with sea views – are bright and comfortable, if a little tired in places. Not all bathrooms are en suite, but gowns are provided. No credit cards. **£80**

Duke of Cumberland High St, CT5 1AP ☎ 01227 280617, ⊚ thedukeinwhitstable.co.uk. Eight en-suite B&B rooms (the larger ones have baths) above this friendly pub (see p.86). It can be noisy on the nights they have live bands, but the music (which is generally very good) usually winds up around midnight. Some discounts if you stay more than one night. **£70**

Fishermen's Huts Near the harbour ☎ 01227 280280, ⊚ hotelcontinental.co.uk/view/fisherhuts. Run by the same people as the *Hotel Continental*, these eleven two-storey weatherboard cockle-farmers' huts (sleeping two to six), offer cute, characterful accommodation by the sea wall near the harbour. Most have sea views, and some have self-catering facilities. Rates include breakfast, served at the *Continental*; weekday rates practically double during school holidays. Sun–Thurs **£70**, Fri & Sat (two-night min) **£150**

The Front Rooms 9 Tower Parade, CT5 2BJ ☎ 01227 282132, ⊚ thefrontrooms.co.uk. There are three guest rooms in this B&B – a Victorian townhouse with art gallery downstairs – decorated with the pale, modern cool of a luxury magazine shoot, and with books and board games giving it a homey feel. One en-suite room

with balcony, and two with shared shower room; you won't have to share with strangers. Sun–Thurs **£120**, Fri & Sat (two-night min) **£110**

Hotel Continental 29 Beach Walk, CT5 2BP ☎ 01227 280280, ⊚ hotelcontinental.co.uk. Though prices are high for what you get, the 1930s *Hotel Continental*, the only formal hotel in town, has a peaceful location overlooking the sea at the start of the path to Tankerton. Don't expect luxury, but do count on a laidback stay, and sunset views from the bar/bistro. Rooms with sea views are almost twice the price of those quoted here. Rates include breakfast. Sun–Thurs **£80**, Fri & Sat (two-night min) **£85**

Sleeperzzz 30 Railway Ave, CT5 1LH ☎ 01227 636975, ⊚ sleeperzzz.net. Though it doesn't look like much from the outside, and the location near the train station has more convenience than wow factor, *Sleeperzzz* B&B offers good value and a friendly welcome, with three large, comfortable, clean en-suite rooms decorated with a dash of seaside style. **£70**

SELF-CATERING

Captain's House 56 Harbour St, CT5 1AQ ☎ 01227 275156, ⊚ thecaptainshouse.org.uk. Charming self-contained loft space (sleeps four), with simple self-catering facilities in a beautiful old house. You have to walk through the owner's home to reach the loft, so if you want more privacy you may prefer the nearby *Polly's Attic*, a bijou apartment owned by the same people, with a similar setup and the same rates but a more scrubbed seaside style. Continental breakfast is delivered each morning to both. **£105**

⭐ **Castaway Cottage** 35 Sydenham St, CT5 1HN ☎ 07973 506104, ⊚ castawaycottagewhitstable.com. Hip self-catering in this terraced fishermen's cottage, just footsteps from Harbour St. With three bedrooms and bags of space, it's comfy, airy and light, with whitewashed floors, quirky artworks and funky furnishings. There's a woodburning stove for the winter, along with DVDs and board games. Two- to four-night stays are available most of the year, and on request in summer. Per week **£700**

2

WHITSTABLE NATIVES: THE WORLD'S YOUR OYSTER

Few molluscs have as much romantic allure as the **oyster**: unadorned, raw food redefined as a delicacy and attributed with aphrodisiac powers. For seafood fans, tucking into a half-dozen oysters is an essential part of any trip to Whitstable – ideally slurped down raw with a dash of Tabasco and a squeeze of lemon, accompanied by a crisp white wine or a hearty local stout – but their resurgence as a local icon is relatively recent. The shallow Swale estuary, fed by nutrient-rich brackish water from the marshy coast, has long been an ideal breeding ground for the bivalves, which are thought to have been eaten around here as far back as Neanderthal times. Certainly the Romans were so taken by their delicate flavour that they towed them by sea back to Italy, and the industry as we know it began in earnest in the Middle Ages. By the mid-nineteenth century Whitstable had close on one hundred oyster dredgers, with the heavy, rocky-shelled "Whitstable Native" oysters being shucked in their millions and sent up the river to Billingsgate. Though for centuries oysters were largely seen as poor man's food, in 1894 the Whitstable Oyster Company received the royal warrant to supply Native oysters to the queen. The twentieth century saw a run of bad luck – disease and overfishing, bad winters and big freezes – and by the 1970s oysters had fallen out of fashion, until the opening of the *Whitstable Oyster Company* restaurant (see opposite) in the 1990s saw the tide turn once more. Note that **Whitstable Natives** are strictly in season from September to March only; outside these months you may find yourself eating the perennial **Pacific oyster** – a larger, prolific breed, some of which are cultivated on the seabed and some of which are dredged wild. Some years, when the crop has been particularly bad, oysters have even been imported in order to meet demand.

EATING

Whitstable is one of the finest places to eat in Kent, especially if you like fresh fish and seafood. Note that many restaurants close surprisingly early – for all its pockets of sophistication, this is a sleepy place at heart – and that opening hours may change during the off-season or at quiet times, when it's an idea to call ahead. A **farmers' market**, with lots of organic produce, is held at St Mary's Hall, on Oxford St, every second and fourth Saturday (9.30am–2pm; ⊚ whitstablefarmersmarket.co.uk).

TAKEAWAY AND PICNIC FOOD

63 Harbour St 63 Harbour St, CT5 1AG ☎ 07767 615458, ⊚ 63harbourstreet.co.uk. Freshly pressed juices (from £2.50) and smoothies (from £3) using the best Kentish fruit and veg, along with great coffee (and hot apple juice in winter) and snacks and deli items from local producers. Takeaway only; no cards. Generally Mon, Tues & Thurs–Sat 9am–5pm, Sun 10am–5pm.

The Cheese Box 60 Harbour St, CT5 1AG ☎ 01227 273711, ⊚ thecheesebox.co.uk. Heaven for turophiles, specializing in British farmhouse and artisan cheeses to take away (buy some sourdough bread, pick up some fresh antipasti from David Brown Deli over the road and a nice bottle from the Wine Room next door, and you'll have the perfect DFL picnic). On Friday night you can eat in, with a glass of local wine, beer or cider. Mon 11am–3pm, Wed 10am–4pm, Thurs 10am–5pm, Fri 10am–10.30pm, Sun 10.30am–4pm.

CAFÉS AND RESTAURANTS

★ **JoJo's** 2 Herne Bay Rd, Tankerton, CT5 2LQ ☎ 01227 274591, ⊚ jojosrestaurant.co.uk. Atop Tankerton slopes, modish *JoJo's* is an unexpected gem in this quiet location. With a sea-view terrace and a deli counter bursting with sun-drenched Mediterranean salads, sandwiches and savoury tarts (from £4.50) – plus fresh smoothies and

tempting cakes – it's a fabulous spot for a light lunch, while the back room buzzes in the evening with happy diners feasting on sharing plates and gazing out at the sea views. Good choices (from £5; up to £27 for a mixed plate) include risotto balls with pea and mint, and mutton and feta koftas. They serve beer, but BYO wine. Reservations recommended in the evening; cash only. Tues 9am–5pm, Wed–Sat 9am–5pm & 6.30–8.30pm, Sun 9am–5pm.

Pearson's Arms by Richard Phillips Horsebridge Rd, 1BT ☎ 01227 733133, ⊚ pearsonsarmsbyrichardphillips .co.uk. In a prime location by the beach, this is more a restaurant that happens to be in a pub than a gastropub per se; local chef Phillips has an excellent reputation for hearty Modern British food, served here in a warmly weatherbeaten first-floor room with sea views. The locally sourced, seasonally changing food – foraged mushrooms with duck egg and brioche or poached haddock with bubble and squeak – is wholesome and good (mains from £14; two-course Mon–Sat lunch menu £10.95). Bag a window table, and watch the sun set over the sea. Mon & Tues noon–2.30pm, Wed–Sat noon–2.30pm & 5.30–9.30pm, Sun noon–9pm.

Samphire 4 High St, CT5 1BQ ☎ 01227 770075, ⊚ letseat.at/samphirewhitstable. Friendly, unfussy and comfy – all timeworn wood, bright cushions, fairy lights and fresh flowers – *Samphire* has won a loyal following for its creative Modern British food, prepared with local ingredients. Mains, from £14, might include nettle and watercress potato cake with Kentish Bluebell cheese, or monkfish with mussel and white bean broth; the veggie choices are great. Breakfast and brunch is on offer, too, and you can pop in for coffee and cake. Mon–Thurs & Sun 10am–9.30pm, Fri & Sat 10am–10pm.

★ **The Sportsman** Faversham Rd, Seasalter, CT5 4BP ☎01227 273370, ⓦthesportsmanseasalter.co.uk. The drab exterior belies the Michelin-starred experience within: *The Sportsman* gastropub, in a lonesome spot between marshes and beach four miles west of Whitstable, serves faultless, deceptively simple food. This is local sourcing to the extreme: fresh seafood, of course, plus lamb from the marshes, meat and veg from farms down the road, seaweed from the beach, bread and butter made right here – even the salt comes from the sea outside. Start, perhaps, with a delectable local slip sole in seaweed butter (£9.95), and follow with crispy duck with smoked chilli salsa and sour cream (mains from £18) – or splash out on the £65 tasting menu (book in advance). Tues–Sat noon–2pm & 7–9pm, Sun noon–2.30pm.

Tower Hill Tea Garden Tower Hill, CT5 2BW ☎01227 281726. A delightful spot on the way out of town towards Tankerton, across the road from but officially part of Whitstable Castle garden. The tearoom in the castle itself, the *Orangery*, may be smarter, but on a sunny day this thatched hut has the edge, offering inexpensive mugs of tea, ice creams, sarnies and snacks, including two hot buttered crumpets for 80p, in a shady, flower-filled, Mediterranean-style garden with glorious sea views. Summer daily, depending on weather.

V.C. Jones 25 Harbour St, CT5 1AH ☎01227 272703, ⓦvcjones.co.uk. Friendly chippie, run by the same family since 1962, with a reassuringly unreconstructed old timers' dining room at the back and takeaway at the front. From around £8 for a huge portion, more if you add mushy peas and all the trimmings, and around half that for takeaway. Cash only. Tues–Sat 11.30am–8pm, Sun noon–8pm (summer), noon–5pm (winter).

★ **Wheelers Oyster Bar** 8 High St, CT5 1BQ ☎01227 273311, ⓦwheelersoysterbar.com. A Whitstable institution, dating back to 1856, and a serious contender for the best restaurant in Kent. It's an informal and friendly old place, with just four tables in a tiny back parlour and a few stools at the (invariably sociable) fish counter at the front.

The inventive, super-fresh seafood is stunning, whether you go for a grilled assortment, "light plates" (Japanese-flaked goujons of Dover sole scented with nori; potted shrimps; spicy squid) for around £9, or more substantial mains like caramelized scallops with Parma ham, pickled cucumber, cauliflower purée and a pea and ham fritter. Mains from £16, half a dozen oysters £6.75. They offer takeaway, too, including crab sandwiches for less than £2. BYO; cash only; reservations recommended. Mon, Tues & Thurs–Sun 11am–close.

Whitstable Oyster Company Horsebridge Rd, CT5 1BU ☎01227 276856, ⓦwhitstableoystercompany .com. With the best location in town, in the Victorian Oyster Stores building by the beach, the "oyster house" opened in 1989 and put Whitstable on the foodie map. Many former fans have moved on, put off by the high prices, but it's not a bad choice, serving simply prepared fish – from wild sea bass with garlic and rosemary to octopus, chorizo and bean stew – in a sun-warmed room with bare brick walls and checked tablecloths. Mains from £17; half a dozen local oysters £9. The same people run the lobster shack on the beach at East Quay, where you can get a whole lobster for £15. Mon–Thurs noon–2.30pm & 6.30–9, Fri noon–2.30pm & 6.30–9.30pm, Sat noon–9.30pm, Sun noon–8.30pm.

Williams & Brown 48 Harbour St, CT5 1AQ ☎01227 273373, ⓦthetapas.co.uk. Modern, light and minimal place serving good tapas (from £4.50) on a seasonally changing menu, along with paella (£16.75; £13.50 for a veggie version with spinach, roast tomatoes, pine nuts and rosemary) and Spanish wines. Takeaway (collection only) available. Mon–Thurs noon–2pm & 6–9pm, Fri noon–2.15pm & 6–9.30pm, Sat noon–2.45pm & 6–9.45pm, Sun noon–2.45pm & 6–9pm.

★ **Windy Corner Stores** 110 Nelson Rd, CT5 1DZ ☎01227 771707. This homely neighbourhood corner store has an excellent food counter, where locals gather to drink good coffee, read the papers and chat; it can be a crush, though there are a couple of outdoor tables, and it's all very informal. The Mediterranean-inspired menu, freshly prepared with local ingredients, changes daily – breakfasts include savoury-topped toasts (try the goat's cheese, tomato and spinach), while later on you could have a fresh salad (from £7) or a delicious home-made cake. Mon–Sat 8am–6pm, Sun 8am–5pm.

WHITSTABLE FESTIVALS

Based on a medieval thanksgiving ritual, the annual **Whitstable Oyster Festival** (ⓦwhitstableoysterfestival.co.uk), held over a week at the end of July, is a high-spirited affair, with food stalls, oyster eating and crabbing competitions, parades, performances and communal oyster picnics, plus art exhibitions and loads of kids' activities. Quite different is the highly regarded **Whitstable Biennale**, a fortnight of experimental art, film, theatre and performance, held in September, and next due in 2014 (ⓦwhitstablebiennale.com).

2

DRINKING AND NIGHTLIFE

Whitstable's nightlife revolves around its **pubs**, with a couple of places, including the local cultural centre, hosting excellent **live music**, and just one **club** out on the beach. Microbrews from the **Whitstable Brewery** (run by the people behind the *Oyster Company* restaurant, but based in a village some miles away) are well worth trying – the oyster stout in particular is good, with a dark, chocolatey taste that goes down very well with the town's most famous snack.

PUBS, BARS AND LIVE MUSIC

Deco 5 15–17 Oxford St, CT5 1DP ☎ 01227 770079, ⓦ deco5.co.uk. Art Deco-themed cocktail bar with regular live music, including gypsy jazz, tango, reggae and flamenco, with food served.

⭐ **Duke of Cumberland** High St, CT5 1AP ☎ 01227 280617, ⓦ thedukeinwhitstable.co.uk. This friendly, comfortable and central pub, with shabby chic decor and a beer garden, has quite a name for live music, encompassing everything from jazz, acoustic and world music to Cajun, big bands and blues. They have rooms, too (see p.82). Mon 11am–10.30pm, Tues–Thurs 11am–11.30pm, Fri & Sat 11am–12.30am, Sun noon–8.30pm.

⭐ **Old Neptune** Marine Terrace, CT5 1EJ ☎ 01227 272262, ⓦ neppy.co.uk. Standing alone in its white weatherboards on the beach, the "Neppy" is the perfect spot to enjoy a sundowner at a picnic table on the shingle, gazing out across the Swale to the Isle of Sheppey, or to hunker down with a pint in the quirky tongue-and-groove interior after a bracing beach walk. Some real ales, plus occasional live music. Mon–Wed & Sun noon–10.30pm, Thurs noon–11pm, Fri & Sat noon–11.30pm.

Peter Cushing 16–18 Oxford St, CT5 1DD ☎ 01227 284100, ⓦ jdwetherspoon.co.uk/home/pubs/the-peter -cushing. Quite extraordinary: a Wetherspoon's pub in a 1930s cinema, with a soaring, opulent Art Deco interior filled with retro movie memorabilia and Cushing paraphernalia. It's popular with locals and old-timers for its inexpensive beer and grub; join them and soak up the old-school glamour. Mon–Thurs & Sun 8am–11pm, Fri & Sat 8am–11.30pm.

CLUB

Whitstable Brewery Bar East Quay, CT5 1AD ☎ 01227 772157, ⓦ hotelcontinental.co.uk. Marooned on the shingle by the harbour, this beachfront barn serves Whitstable Brewery beers to a relaxed crowd during the day before transforming into the town's sole club after dark. DJ nights range from dubstep to funk and reggae, and they host beer festivals, live music and comedy events too. Fri noon to Sun evening; club nights Fri & Sat till 3am.

ARTS AND THEATRE

Horsebridge Arts Centre 11 Horsebridge Rd, CT5 1AF ☎ 01227 281174, ⓦ horsebridge-centre.org.uk. With a gallery and café, and lots of community events, this arts centre also hosts acoustic, blues, jazz and Americana gigs, and stand-up comedy. Mon–Thurs 9am–9pm, Fri & Sat 9am–6pm, Sun 10am–6pm; performances from 7pm.

Whitstable Playhouse 104 High St, CT5 1AZ ☎ 01227 272042, ⓦ playhousewhitstable.co.uk. Comedy, variety, drama and music at this local theatre in a converted church. Tickets from £7.50.

SHOPPING

Whitstable is a great place for shopping, with **Harbour Street** in particular known for its shabby-seaside-chic boutiques and vintage stores. The rest of the high street, while slightly less hip, has far more character than most, with barely a chain to be seen.

Fish Slab 11 Oxford St, CT5 1DB ⓦ fishslabgallery .co.uk. Small, nonprofit gallery in an old fishmonger's, where you can pick up local ceramics, prints and artworks for reasonable prices. This short stretch of the high street is getting artier, with a couple of other galleries nearby. Days and hours vary.

⭐ **Frank** 65 Harbour St, CT5 1AG ☎ 01227 262500, ⓦ frankworks.eu. Colourful, creative and contemporary British graphic design and crafts, with handmade ceramics, prints, jewellery, cards, fabrics and stationery, in a light, airy store. Mon, Thurs & Fri 10.30am–5pm, Sat 10.30am–5.30pm, Sun 11am–5pm.

⭐ **Harbour Books** 21 Harbour St, CT5 1AQ ☎ 01227 264011. Excellent independent bookstore with two floors of novels, local titles, and books on art, politics, travel and photography, many discounted, along with cards and gifts. Mon–Sat 9.30am–5.30pm, Sun 10.30am–5.30pm.

Keam's Yard Near the Horsebridge, CT5 1BU ☎ 07970 633112, ⓦ bwmurals.com/keams_yard_studio_gallery. This freestanding little workshop, facing the sea, hosts a number of artists who exhibit quirky and interesting work in all media, much of it seaside-related, at good prices. Days and hours vary; open most weekends.

Oxford Street Books 20A Oxford St, CT5 1DD ☎ 01227 281727, ⓦ oxfordstreetbooks.com. Wide selection of secondhand and antiquarian books, with out-of-print and rare titles sharing shelves with 95p paperbacks. The history section is especially good. Mon–Sat 9am–5pm, Sun 11am–4pm.

Pearl and Hemingway 14 Harbour St, CT5 1AQ ☎ 01227 770000. Retro clothing, from men's hats to women's underwear, along with funky jewellery and accessories from hip new designers. Mon & Thurs–Sat 10am–6pm Sun 11am–5pm.

CYCLING AROUND WHITSTABLE

The 7.5-mile **Crab and Winkle Way** (ⓦcrabandwinkle.org), following the old steam railway line to Canterbury (see box, p.60), is a popular cycling route from Whitstable (though it's a little easier doing it in reverse), as is the enjoyable **Oyster Bay Trail**, a seaside path that follows the coast round from Swalecliffe, just beyond Tankerton, to Herne Bay (3 miles) and Reculver Country Park (5 miles). From here you can hook up with Thanet's 27-mile-long **Viking Coastal Trail** (see p.29), which takes you along the shore to Birchington, Margate, Broadstairs and Ramsgate.

2

★ **Valentine's** 21 Oxford St, CT5 1DB ☎01227 281224, ⓦvalentines-vintage.com. The perfect vintage furnishings store, friendly and laidback, selling good-looking, high-quality, handpicked homeware, ceramics and glass, from the 1950s to the 1970s, at competitive prices. Mon–Sat 10am–5.30pm, Sun 11am–5pm.

★ **Whitstable Harbour Village** South Quay, Whitstable Harbour, CT5 1AB ⓦwhitstableharbourvillage .co.uk. Weekend market in a colony of fishermen's huts on the harbour, populated by around thirty local retailers and artists, plus local food and drink stalls. March–Dec Sat & Sun 10am–5pm.

Herne Bay and around

The holiday destination of choice for Bertie Wooster's long-suffering butler Jeeves in the P.G. Wodehouse stories, staid **HERNE BAY** keeps a lower profile than the other seaside towns on Kent's north coast. Most of the appeal is on the seafront, where a two-mile prom fringes a typically British combination – cheap caffs, ice-cream parlours, tourist shops and run-down amusements, alongside enormous bow-fronted houses, abundant flower gardens and a bandstand that recall the town's heyday as a Victorian resort. There's a stubby pier, with safe swimming nearby, and in summer the shingly beach is dotted with families. Look out to sea and you'll see the former end of the pier, marooned in the waves since a storm in 1978. Further out still are the menacing outlines of the **Maunsell Forts** – World War II anti-aircraft structures, long since abandoned to the elements. The waters around here are good for **jet-skiing**, and there are clubs in town devoted to dinghy sailing (ⓦwww.hpyc.org.uk) and family-friendly sailing, canoeing and kayaking (ⓦhernebaysailingclub.co.uk). The main reason to come, however, is to take the invigorating walk to the **Reculver towers**.

Reculver Country Park

Visitor centre April Mon & Thurs–Sun 11am–4pm; May–July Mon & Fri–Sun 11am–4pm; Aug Mon & Thurs–Sun 11am–5pm; Sept & Oct Fri–Sun 11am–4pm; Nov–March Sat & Sun 11am–3pm • Free • ☎ 01227 740676

From Herne Bay you can take a glorious coastal walk along the Saxon Shore Way, or a cycle along the Oyster Bay Trail, to the twelfth-century **Reculver towers**, three miles east in **Reculver Country Park**. The park, an area of flat, fossil-flecked beaches and dramatically eroding soft sandstone cliffs topped with velvety meadows, is remarkably peaceful, with only the sound of waves crashing beneath you and wide-open views across to Thanet stretching ahead. A Site of Special Scientific Interest, it attracts many migratory birds; you can check recent sightings at the visitor centre, which also fills you in on local history, in particular Reculver's fame as the testing ground for the bouncing bombs used by the World War II Dam Busters. From the towers it's another appealing walk or cycle of around four miles along the Viking Coastal Trail to **Minnis Bay**, where there's a sandy beach and a popular restaurant (see p.94).

The Reculver towers

Reculver, CT6 6SS • 24hr • Free • ☎ 01227 740676, ⓦ english-heritage.org.uk/daysout/properties/reculver-towers-and-roman-fort

The flat-topped twin **Reculver towers** make a dramatic display on the clifftop, silhouetted against the sky. Built on the site of a Roman fort that protected the

Wantsum Channel, which once separated Thanet from the mainland, the towers are pretty much all that remains of a Saxon monastery that later stood here. Forming the western wall of a church added to the complex in the twelfth century, they were the only part of the structure to escape demolition in 1810 – by which time most of the local village had been abandoned due to drastic coastal erosion – and were kept here as navigational aids. Crouching low behind them are some rather more decrepit remains of the original church, bitten away by centuries of weather.

ARRIVAL AND INFORMATION

By train The station is on Station Rd, on the south side of town; it's a 12min walk up Pier Ave or Station Rd to the sea. Destinations Broadstairs (Mon–Sat every 30min; 22min); Canterbury (every 1hr 10min–2hr; 1hr 10min); Faversham (every 30min–1hr; 15min); London Victoria (every 30min–1hr; 1hr 40min); Margate (Mon–Sat every 30min; 15min); Ramsgate (Mon–Sat every 30min; 26min); Rochester (every 30min–1hr; 48min); Whitstable (every 30min–1hr; 7min).

HERNE BAY AND AROUND

By bus Buses from Canterbury (every 10min); Margate (hourly); Whitstable (every 10min) stop on the high street, a couple of blocks back from the seafront.
Website ⓦ canterbury.co.uk.
Bike rental Le Petit Poisson (see below) is the Herne Bay HQ for the Whitstable Cycle Hire company (see p.82); you can drop off your bike in Whitstable or Canterbury.

EATING AND DRINKING

★ **Butcher's Arms** 29 Herne St, Herne, CT6 7HL ☎ 01227 371000, ⓦ micropub.co.uk. Fantastic micropub in an old butcher's, a few minutes' drive south of Herne Bay. Behind the unassuming shopfront is a 14ft by 12ft cubbyhole crammed with books, dried hops and bric-a-brac, with a crowd of real-ale fans having a good old natter. The weekly changing selection features at least four ales from Britain. Tues–Sat noon–1.30pm & 6–9pm or later.
★ **Le Petit Poisson** Pier Approach, Central Parade, CT6 5JN ☎ 01227 361199, ⓦ lepetitpoisson.co.uk. At the head of the pier, this is a renowned seafood destination on this stretch of coast. Don't be misled by the plain exterior – inside, the wooden-floored and brick-walled dining room is a classy, relaxed setting, particularly appealing at sunset. The menu changes according to what's fresh, but surefire winners include haddock Scotch egg, grilled Dover sole, or rock oysters; wash it all down with a cold dry white from Kent's own Chapel Down vineyard.

Mains from £15. Tues–Fri noon–2.30pm & 6.30–9pm, Sat noon–3pm & 6.30–9.30pm, Sun noon–3.30pm.
Oyster and Chop House 8 High St, CT6 5LH ☎ 01227 749933. Causing quite a stir when it opened in 2012, this small restaurant uses local suppliers to source mostly organic ingredients. The regularly changing menu features lots of free-range meat, with lamb, rabbit and pigeon on the short list, and some delicious, occasionally surprising, desserts. Mains around £15 at dinner, less at lunch. Mon–Sat noon–2pm & 6.15–10pm, Sun 6.15–10pm.
Wallflower The Mall, 116 High St, CT6 5JY ☎ 01227 740392, ⓦ vegetariancaterers.net. The setting isn't inspiring, but the (mainly) veggie food in this casual bistro is good, with strong Mediterranean and Middle Eastern accents served tapas/meze-style. Most ingredients are sourced locally, and it's all home-made and healthy; unusually, they offer lots of vegan and coeliac choices. Takeaway available. Mon–Sat 9am–5pm.

Isle of Thanet

Fringed by low chalk cliffs and sandy bays, the fist of land at Kent's northeastern corner, the **Isle of Thanet** (ⓦ visitthanet.co.uk), may now be attached to the mainland, but still has the feel of a place apart. That's not to say it's inaccessible – it's just ninety minutes from London by train, with regular transport connections to Canterbury and Dover – but taken together, the resorts of **Margate**, **Ramsgate** and **Broadstairs** have a

THE THANET BEACHES

Thanet's chalk coastline, starting with **Minnis Bay** (see p.92) in the west and curving all the way round to **Ramsgate Sands** (see p.98), features more than a dozen fine bays and a string of clean, safe, sandy beaches. We've covered the major beaches in this chapter, but each is worth visiting. All are accessible from the Thanet Coastal Path, or on the Viking Coastal Trail cycling path. For more, see ⓦ thanetcoast.org.uk.

distinct personality of their own. Having developed as seaside getaways in the eighteenth and nineteenth centuries, they still cling to their traditional attractions to varying degrees, and there is a whiff of nostalgia about them all, from Broadstairs' quaint cobbled streets and old wooden pier to Margate's kitschy charms. Turner, who spent much of his time in Margate, said the Thanet skies were "the loveliest … in all Europe", and watching the sun set over the sea from one of its many glorious **beaches** – Thanet has the highest number of blue-flag beaches in Kent – it's hard to disagree.

Brief history

This flat and featureless "Isle" became part of the mainland when the Wantsum Channel began silting up around the time of the first Roman invasion. The Christian evangelist Augustine (see box, p.50) is said to have preached his first sermon three miles west of Ramsgate – a cross marks the location at the village of Ebbsfleet. In the late eighteenth century Margate invented itself as the country's first seaside resort, and by the mid-twentieth century Thanet's sandy beaches had become the favoured bucket-and-spade destinations for Londoners seeking seaside fun. While cheap foreign holidays put paid to its glory days, and Thanet has seen more than its fair share of neglect, it remains a popular holiday spot, with Margate's Turner gallery, opened in 2011, injecting a new spirit of optimism.

Margate and around

"There is something not exactly high class in the name of Margate. Sixpenny teas are suggested, and a vulgar flavour of shrimps floats unbidden in the air."   Marie Corelli, novelist, 1896

While the sixpenny teas and whiff of shrimps may have long gone, there is still something "not exactly high class" about **MARGATE**, a gutsy resort that relishes eccentricity, nostalgia and brash seaside fun. As England's earliest seaside resort – in 1736 the country's first seawater baths were opened here, starting a craze for sea bathing and cures (among them a tasty concoction of seawater mixed with milk) – Margate grew in importance to score a number of firsts, including the first canopied bathing machines in 1750, the first seaside boarding house in 1770, donkey rides in 1790, and the first beach deck-chairs in 1898. At its peak, thousands of London workers were ferried down the Thames every summer to fill the beaches of "merry Margate", and on a fine weekend the place still throngs with day-trippers enjoying fish and chips, candyfloss and sandcastle-building. And while it may not be the prettiest town on the Kent coast, with long years of decline having left their sad legacy in the many boarded-up shopfronts and tatty amusement arcades, the tide has undoubtedly turned. Following the opening of the spectacular **Turner Contemporary** gallery in 2011, a gaggle of hip indie **galleries** have followed in its wake, drawn by the town's faded seaside charm, its glorious skies so beloved of J.M.W. Turner, and its low rents. The artsy buzz – which also fuels a cluster of funky retro shops in the **Old Town** – gives Margate an irresistible energy; that, along with some excellent places to eat and drink, and, not to be forgotten, its clean sandy **beaches**, makes it a must-see once more.

Turner Contemporary

Rendezvous, CT9 1HG • Tues–Sun 10am–6pm • Free • ☎ 01843 233000, Ⓦ turnercontemporary.org

Rearing up on the east side of the harbour, the stunning, opalescent **Turner Contemporary** gallery dominates the seafront. Named for J.M.W. Turner, who went to school in the Old Town in the 1780s, and who returned frequently as an adult to take advantage of the dazzling light, the modern gallery is built on the site of the lodging house where he painted some of his famous seascapes – and had a long love affair with his landlady, Mrs Sophia Booth. Inside, in addition to framing fantastic views of the seascape through its enormous windows, the light-flooded, tranquil space hosts regularly changing exhibitions of high-profile contemporary art.

2

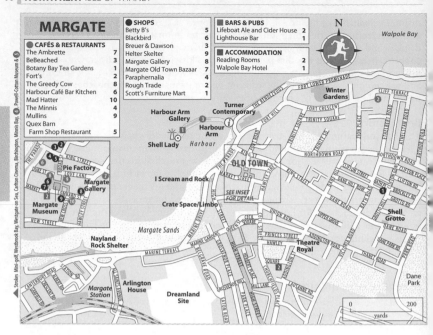

Harbour Arm

ⓦ margateharbourarm.co.uk

Margate's Georgian stone pier, or **Harbour Arm**, crooking out into the sea from next to the Turner gallery, is a funky little enclave, with a parade of old coal stores housing cafés and bars, artists' studios and a gallery. It's de rigueur to walk over to the 85ft-high concrete **lighthouse** at the end, where the views across the little harbour and the broad sweep of Margate's beach are fantastic – especially at sunset. The oxidized bronze **"shell lady"** statue gazing out to sea is a homage both to kitsch seaside ornaments and to Mrs Booth, J.M.W. Turner's beloved landlady.

The seafront

Fronting the beach, Margate's dilapidated **Marine Terrace** isn't pretty, but for nostalgia-lovers it has a rough-and-ready charm. You can sit in the Victorian **Nayland Rock shelter** where T.S. Eliot stared out to sea and drafted his poem *The Wasteland*. "On Margate Sands. / I can connect / Nothing with nothing", he wrote: who knows what existential angst he might have wrought from the seafront today, with its jangling amusement arcades – the flashy **Flamingo** sign has a dash of kitsch pizazz – and the grim **Arlington House**, a brutish concrete 1960s housing block that's regarded as a hideous eyesore or a modernist treasure, depending upon your bent. The seafront is most picturesque when surveyed from the sea, or the Harbour Arm, when the view of low-slung buildings fringing the long beach evoke something of the resort's nineteenth-century heyday.

Dreamland

Marine Terrace/Belgrave Rd, CT9 1XG • ⓦ dreamlandmargate.com

Margate's iconic **Dreamland**, which grew from Victorian pleasure gardens to become a hugely popular theme park in the 1920s, stood derelict and miserable on the seafront for nearly ten years following its closure in 2003. A poignant symbol of the town's decline, it is currently being restored to become a living museum of seaside entertainment and

---

ARTY MARGATE: THE INDIE GALLERIES

While Turner Contemporary rules the roost, Margate has an astonishing number of indie art galleries for a town of its size, most of them artist-led and all of them exhibiting accessible contemporary works in most media. New ones pop up all the time, making use of Margate's interesting abandoned spaces, from butchers' shops to electricity substations, but the following are consistently good. Opening hours and days will vary according to what's on.

Crate Space 1 Bilton Square, High St, CT9 1EE ⓦ cratespace.co.uk

Harbour Arm Gallery Harbour Arm ⓦ margatehar bourarm.co.uk

I Scream and Rock 18 High St, CT9 1DS ☎ 07935 102790, ⓦ iscreamandrock.wordpress.com

Limbo 2 Bilton Square, High St, CT9 1EE ☎ 07812 780984, ⓦ limboarts.co.uk

Margate Gallery 2 Lombard St, Old Town, CT9 1EJ ☎ 01843 292779, ⓦ margategallery.co.uk

Pie Factory 5 Broad St, Old Town, CT9 1EW ☎ 07879 630257, ⓦ piefactorymargate.co.uk

---

popular culture, complete with historic fairground rides – including the UK's oldest surviving roller coaster – classic side-shows and a glorious Art Deco cinema.

The beaches

It's not all about art and vintage shopping: even today most of Margate's visitors come to enjoy the sandy beaches. Though the mass community singsongs that were held here in the late nineteenth century are no more, the town beach, **Margate Sands**, a glorious golden swathe, is a family-friendly delight, with a tidal boating pool, kiddy rides and volleyball nets. Quieter **Westbrook Bay**, to the west, offers shallow water that's great for paddling and watersports, especially windsurfing and kiteboarding, and an eighteen-hole mini-golf course, bowls and tennis nearby.

The Old Town

Margate's burgeoning hipster reputation largely rests on the shoulders of the **Old Town**, a compact area roughly bounded by Hawley Street/Trinity Hill to the east, the waterfront to the west, and the blocks north of New Street up to Northdown Road. This is where Margate began, as a seventeenth-century fishing village, and in its narrow lanes is an energetic concentration of retro shops, galleries and studio spaces, centring on lively little Market Place, lined with outdoor cafés.

Margate Museum

Market Place, CT9 1ER • Sat & Sun 11am–4pm; summer also Wed & bank hols • £1.50 • ☎ 01843 231213, ⓦ margatemuseum.wordpress.com

Secreted away in the old town hall (1820), the volunteer-run **Margate Museum** is easy to miss but worth seeking out, with enjoyable temporary exhibitions on the town's social history. Subjects cover a broad canvas, from Mods and Rockers to Georgian Christmases, but are always enthusiastically and intelligently put together.

Shell Grotto

Grotto Hill, CT9 2BU • Easter–Oct daily 10am–5pm; Nov–Easter Sat & Sun 11am–4pm • £3 • ☎ 01843 220008, ⓦ shellgrotto.co.uk

Discovered, or so the story goes, in 1835, by the children of the Newlove family who were renting the land above it, Margate's mysterious **Shell Grotto** opened as a paying attraction soon after and has been captivating visitors ever since. Resembling a run-down gift shop from the outside, and reached via a short, winding and damp subterranean passageway, the grotto is an extraordinary and rather creepy sight, its hallways and chambers entirely covered with fabulous mosaics made entirely from shells – more than 4.5 million of them, from clams to mussels to oysters, tinted silvery grey and black by the fumes of Victorian gas lamps. The origins and purpose of the grotto, decorated with all manner of symbols and imagery, remain a mystery. Some believe it to be an ancient pagan temple, others a more recent Regency folly, and others

2

are convinced that the Newloves themselves built it, with a canny eye to the tourist trade. Whatever the truth, were it a hoax it was certainly an elaborate one – transporting and storing all the shells alone would have been a superhuman undertaking, not to mention the many years it would have taken to build such a place, and the impossibility of doing so in secret.

Cliftonville

A steep climb from the main town, the clifftop neighbourhood of **Cliftonville** was, in Victorian times, Margate's snooty suburb, and up until the 1930s its fashionable sea-facing hotels hosted such illustrious guests as T.S. Eliot, who recuperated from a nervous breakdown here in 1921. Today it's one of the town's more impoverished areas, much given over to bedsits and hostels, with a deserted 1920s Lido, a clifftop adventure playground and the historic **Walpole Bay Hotel**. The sandy beach, **Walpole Bay**, has good watersports and a tidal swimming pool, while the **bandstand**, on the esplanade, hosts Sunday afternoon concerts. Cliftonville also hosts an excellent **farmers' market** on the last Sunday of the month (10am–1pm).

Botany Bay

Around 2.5 miles east of town, beyond Cliftonville, **Botany Bay** is the flagship Thanet beach and quite different from others in the Southeast. Its towering chalk stacks, sheared off from the cliffs by narrow, winding sand corridors, create dramatic silhouettes, while the caves, shallow rockpools and stepping stones of creamy white boulders, crowned with seaweed moptops, make a veritable seaside playground. There's a very pretty tearoom on the clifftop, too (see p.94).

Powell-Cotton Museum

Quex Park, Birchington, CT7 0BH • April–Oct Tues–Sun: museum & gardens 10am–5pm, house 2–5pm • Museum, house & gardens £7, gardens only £2 • ☎ 01843 842168, ⊕ quexmuseum.org

As if Margate itself didn't hold enough offbeat appeal, the **Powell-Cotton Museum**, in the village of Birchington, five miles west, offers another dose of magnificent eccentricity. Opened in 1896 to house the hunting trophies of Major Percy Powell-Cotton – whose expeditions, made between 1895 and 1939, included such far-flung corners as Abyssinia and Kashmir – this old-fashioned museum is most astonishing for its enormous **wildlife dioramas**. Crammed with staggering numbers of well-preserved and disarmingly expressive creatures, from aardvarks, bongos and dog-faced baboons to snarling tigers and mighty African elephants, these vivid scenes are even more astounding today than when they were made, giving a shocking sense of the abundance of wildlife that humans once took for granted. Colonial collections like this have long been discredited, but as a historical document the museum is unmissable, and today's curators often involve communities from countries the Major visited when preparing new displays. Highlights in the adjoining world-class **ethnographic collection** include bronze casts from Benin, an Angolan initiation costume woven from tree bark, and fabulous sacred and early Christian Abyssinian paintings.

Six rooms of the Powell-Cotton family home, a Regency mansion, are open to visitors, as are the lovely Victorian gardens, with pathways tumbling with abundant plantings and strutting peacocks. It's a great spot for picnics; stock up at the estate's excellent **Quex Barn farm shop** (see p.94).

Minnis Bay

Five miles west of Margate, near **Birchington**, the long, gently shelving sandy beach at **Minnis Bay** often has space when others get full, despite its many obvious charms. It's popular with kitesurfers, windsurfers and sea canoeists, and has good facilities, including showers and a paddling pool, along with kiteboarding lessons and an excellent restaurant-bar on the cliff above (see p.94).

ARRIVAL AND DEPARTURE

By train Margate's station is near the seafront on Station Rd. Destinations Broadstairs (every 5–30min; 5min); Canterbury (hourly; 30min); Faversham (Mon–Sat every 30min; 30min); Herne Bay (Mon–Sat every 30min; 15min); London St Pancras (hourly; 1hr 30min); London Victoria (Mon–Sat every 30min; 1hr 50min); Ramsgate

MARGATE AND AROUND

(every 5–20min; 10min); Whitstable (Mon–Sat every 30min; 23min).
By bus Buses pull in at the Clock Tower on Marine Parade. Destinations Broadstairs (every 5–15min; 25min); Canterbury (every 20–30min; 50min); London Victoria (4 daily; 2hr 30min); Ramsgate (every 5–15min; 30min).

INFORMATION AND GETTING AROUND

Tourist office The Droit House, Harbour Arm, (April–Sept daily 10am–5pm; Oct–March Tues–Sat 10am–5pm, Sun 11am–4pm ☏01843 577577, ⓦvisitthanet.co.uk) is the visitor information centre for all Thanet.
By bike Caitlin's Beach Cruisers, on the Harbour Arm, rents

out all manner of bikes, including Cruisers and Lowriders (£4/hr, £18/day); with 24hr notice and a two-bike minimum they can drop off and pick up at Thanet hotels (Sat, Sun & school holidays 9am–6pm; ☏07956 395896, ⓦcaitlinsbeachcruisers.com).

ACCOMMODATION

★ **Reading Rooms** 31 Hawley Square, CT9 1PH ☏01843 225166, ⓦthereadingroomsmargate.co.uk. Stunning boutique B&B set in a handsome, peaceful Georgian townhouse. The three guest rooms have artfully distressed walls, gorgeous furnishings and huge, luxurious bathrooms; a classy breakfast is served in your room. Two-night minimum at weekends. No children. **£150**

★ **Walpole Bay Hotel** Fifth Ave, Cliftonville, CT9 2JJ ☏01843 221703, ⓦwalpolebayhotel.co.uk. This family-run hotel has changed little since Edwardian times, and

exudes an air of faded gentility from its pot-plant-cluttered dining room to its clanky trellis-gated elevator. Offering a slice of classic Margate eccentricity – the "living museum" and collection of napery art is just one of its quirky charms – it's a favourite of Tracey Emin, who throws parties here and whose art is on show in the dining room. Rooms vary, but most have sea views, many have small balconies, and all are comfy, clean and well equipped, with considerable character. The occasional wear and tear just adds to the allure. **£85**

EATING

OLD TOWN

The Ambrette 44 King St, CT9 1QE ☏01843 231504, ⓦtheambrette.co.uk. Margate's finest restaurant doesn't look like much from the outside, but head through the tatty old pub doors to discover superlative modern Indian food served in a serene dining room. Beautifully presented dishes are light and delicately spiced, featuring ingredients not often seen in Indian restaurants, like oysters, calves' liver, pork and venison, most of them locally sourced. Tues–Thurs 11.30am–2.30pm & 6–9.30pm, Fri–Sun 11.30am–2.30pm & 5.30–10pm.

★ **The Greedy Cow** 3 Market Place, CT9 1ER ☏01843 447557, ⓦfacebook.com/thegreedycowdeli. They keep things simple in this charming deli, from the mismatched retro decor to the menu. The welcome is smiley and food is excellent, healthy and fresh – chunky sandwiches (£4) and creative salads (£7) plus gourmet burgers (£6.20), including a herb and falafel variety, with tasty toppings – black pudding? Tabasco wholegrain mustard? Stilton? Everything's local, of course. Tues–Fri 10am–4pm, Sat 10am–5pm, Sun 11am–5pm.

Mad Hatter 9 Lombard St, CT9 1EJ ☏01843 232626. One-of-a-kind tearoom, in a crooked seventeenth-century building packed with kitsch royal memorabilia, Margate paraphernalia, stodgy Victoriana and year-round tinsel; the lack of irony makes it all the more appealing. The menu

features old-school treats – casseroles, toasties, apple pie with custard – but it's best to concentrate on the cakes and scones. Cash only. Sat 11am–5.30pm, Sun noon–5.30pm.
Mullins 6 Market Place, CT9 1EN ☏01843 295603, ⓦmullinsbrasserie.co.uk. An upscale contemporary Caribbean/Modern European bistro in a converted butcher's. Lunchtime sees ciabatta rolls and rotis (£6.50) alongside Modern European mains from £9; things get spicier, and the setting more romantic, in the evening, when you can enjoy curry goat, jerk pork or Bajan fish cakes from £11. Mon–Sat 11am–3pm & 6–9pm or later.

OUTSIDE THE OLD TOWN

BeBeached Harbour Arm, CT9 1AP ☏01843 226008, ⓦbebeached.co.uk. On a sunny day you can't do better than bag an outside table at this colourful café on the Harbour Arm. Food is locally sourced, and often organic, with lunch options ranging from meatloaf to pancakes, afternoon snacks including cheese on toast or cherry scones, and dinner featuring pastas, tagines and pies. Service can slow down when it's busy, so take your time, relax and drink in the view. Mains £7–9, more in the evening. Wed & Thurs 11am–4pm, Fri & Sat 11am–4pm & 7.30–9.30pm, Sun 11am–4.30pm.

★ **Fort's** 8 Cliff Terrace, CT9 1RU ☏01843 449786, ⓦfortscafe.co.uk. This mellow café on the Cliftonville

2

borders may look like Shoreditch-by-the-Sea, with its formica and leatherette fittings and its classic soul jukebox, but the community feel, unpretentious crowd and excellent locally sourced food back up the style with considerable substance. Breakfasts (from £2) feature *churros con chocolate*, with simple lunches (£3–6) featuring such treats as warm beetroot and goat's cheese on toast or crispy devilled whitebait; prices are amazing, given the quality. Thurs–Sat 9am–11pm, Sun 9am–5pm.

Harbour Café Bar Kitchen 10 The Parade, CT9 1EZ ☎01843 290110. Laidback hangout on the seafront strip, offering breakfasts, relaxed lunches and suppers (handmade burgers, fishcakes, salads, tarts and kebabs; mains from £8) along with top-class jazz nights. Cash only. Tues–Thurs & Sun 9am–6pm, Fri & Sat 9am–11pm.

AROUND MARGATE

Botany Bay Tea Gardens 65 Botany Rd, Botany Bay, CT10 3SD ☎01843 867662. The light lunches, home-made cakes and cream teas are delicious (and inexpensive) at this gloriously pretty little tearoom, but it's the setting that makes it truly special: a flower-filled walled garden near the top of the path to Botany Bay beach. Cash only. April–Sept, in fair weather, Thurs–Sun & bank hol Mon 11.30am–4.30pm.

DRINKING

★ **Lifeboat Ale and Cider House** 1 Market St, CT9 1EU ☎07837 024259, ⓦthelifeboat-margate.com. One of the best pubs anywhere – a cosy tavern in the Old Town with barrels for seats, sawdust floors, and fairy lights twinkling around the door. The drink – local ales, wines and juices, with a fantastic range of ciders and perries – comes from local artisan producers, as do the tasty cheeses, chutneys, sausages and home-made pies. There's occasional live folk

ENTERTAINMENT

Carlton 31 St Mildred's Rd, Westgate on Sea, CT8 8RE ☎01843 834290, ⓦcarltoncinema.com. An independent movie house just west of Margate, family-run and open since 1912, with a little tearoom, *Frederick's*, and a bookstore. **Theatre Royal** Addington St, CT9 1PW ⓦtheatre royalmargate.com. This grand old theatre, built in 1787 (but converted in Victorian times) is the second oldest in England. Crowd-pleasers and stand-up share the schedules with

SHOPPING

Margate's shopping scene is second to none in Kent, with creative little indie shops and pop-ups crowding the Old Town. This is **vintage** heaven, with prices far less than in the big cities, and a friendly, enthusiastic vibe.

Betty B's 12 King St, CT9 1HB ☎07974 533439. You can get crockery, Bakelite, posters and prints here, along with fabulous Swing era and rockabilly clothing, with dresses, coats, accessories and some men's gear. Thurs–Sat

★ **The Minnis** The Parade, Minnis Bay, Birchington, CT7 9QP ☎01843 841844, ⓦtheminnis.com. This relaxed cliffside restaurant, above the beach, offers something for everyone. Local ales and good pub grub can be enjoyed in the beer garden, while the smarter dining room, with its big windows, offers an inventive daily changing set menu (Mon–Thurs noon–9pm, Fri noon–6pm; two courses £12, three £18), light lunches (served till 6pm) and creatively prepared, locally sourced mains (from £10). Good choices abound, from home-cured charcuterie and grilled oysters with chorizo to the delicious pan-fried ribeye of local beef with a wasabi-infused sauce. Daily 10am–11pm; food served till 9pm Mon–Sat, 8pm Sun.

Quex Barn Farm Shop Restaurant Quex Park, Birchington, CT7 0BB ☎01843 846103, ⓦquexbarn .com. A no-fuss café with small garden, linked to the excellent Quex Park farm shop, one of the best in Kent, selling fabulous produce and deli specialities. Food, much of it organic and sourced from the Quex estate, is wholesome and good, whether it's the fresh-baked bread, the farm's sausages, gazpacho, or slow-roast belly pork. Dinner is more elaborate. Mains from £10. Mon–Thurs 9am–3pm, Fri 9am–3pm & 5–8.30pm, Sat 9am–4pm & 6–8.30pm, Sun 9–11.30am & noon–3pm.

music, too. Daily noon–midnight or earlier.

Lighthouse Bar Harbour Arm, CT9 1JD ☎01843 291153. Chilled-out bar at the end of the Harbour Arm, with huge windows overlooking the sea. Sit outside to enjoy the fresh air and the sunsets, or on a comfy sofa inside; in winter the woodburning stove keeps things toasty. Classy snacks include sausages, tapas and good fish specials. Daily noon–midnight.

challenging, contemporary work, dance and circus.

★ **Tom Thumb Theatre** 2A Eastern Esplanade, Cliftonville, CT9 2LB ☎01843 221791, ⓦtomthumb theatre.co.uk. Nostalgic, witty and warm hearted, this is quintessential Margate: a tiny, family-owned rep theatre (just fifty or so seats) in a nineteenth-century coach house, offering music hall nights, magic shows, stand-up, burlesque, spoken word and folk music, along with straight theatre.

11am–1pm & 1.30–4pm.

Blackbird 2 Market Place, CT9 1ER ☎01843 229533, ⓦblackbird-england.com. Gorgeous art and handmade gifts, with an emphasis on textiles and crafts, and a range of make-your-own kits, stationery and letterpress prints. Summer Tues–Fri 11am–5pm, Sat 10.30am–5.30pm, Sun 11.30am–4.30 pm; winter closed Tues & Wed.

★ **Breuer & Dawson** 7 King St, CT9 1DD ☏ 01843 225299, ⊛ breuerdawson.com. The focus here is on impeccably selected men's vintage gear, including sharp 1940s suits and American preppy/military staples, in a beautiful old shop run by Camden Market alumni. Usually Tues–Sun 11am–5pm.

Helter Skelter 13 Market Place, CT9 1ES ☏ 01843 223474, ⊛ helterskelterboutique.com. Reasonably priced, colourful ceramics, clothes, collectibles and furniture from the 1950s to the 1970s, with lots of G Plan and Italian classics. Thurs–Sat noon–5.30pm.

★ **Margate Gallery** 2 Lombard St, CT9 1EJ ☏ 01843 292779, ⊛ margategallery.co.uk. The shop of this sunny art gallery sells a very good, original range of postcards, posters, notebooks and crafts, much of it with a seasidey, Margate-specific bent. Mon–Sat 11am–5pm, Sun noon–4pm.

Margate Old Town Bazaar Market Place, CT9 ☏ 07976 051915, ⊛ margatebazaar.co.uk. Weekly outdoor market, with stalls selling funky crafts, antique jewellery, retro treasures and collectible junk. Sun 11am–4pm.

Paraphernalia 8 King St, CT9 1DA ☏ 07534 707105. Eclectic choice of stuff from around 1800 to 1980, including books, prints, furniture, old cameras and vintage dress patterns – anything you might imagine – in this cut-above junk store. Mon–Fri & Sun 11am–5pm, Sat 10am–6pm.

Rough Trade 5–7 Fort Rd, CT9 1HF ☏ 07976 051915, ⊛ roughtrademargate.co.uk. A ramshackle warehouse in the Old Town, home to vintage, crafts and antiques dealers, and a barbershop. Each stall keeps its own days and opening hours, but there will always be something intriguing here. Daily.

★ **Scott's Furniture Mart** Bath Place, CT9 2BN ☏ 01843 220653, ⊛ scottsmargate.co.uk. Whether you're after a shell-encrusted poodle ornament or an old-school board game, you'll find it in this cheery, family-owned flea market, occupying an old ice factory. Also on the premises – which covers three floors and nearly 17,000ft – are Junk Deluxe (⊛ junkdeluxe.co.uk), specialists in mid-century Modern furniture, and 20th Century Frocks, who sell clothing, including men's gear, from the 1930s to the 1980s. Mon, Tues & Thurs–Sat 9.30am–1pm & 2–5pm. Junk Deluxe and 20th Century Frocks Thurs–Sat 9.30am–1pm & 2–5pm.

Broadstairs and around

The smallest, quietest and most immediately appealing of the Thanet resort towns, unspoiled **BROADSTAIRS** stands on top of the cliff overlooking the golden arc of Viking Bay. At the northern end of the bay, a sixteenth-century wooden **pier** curves out from the picturesque cluster of old flint and clapboard buildings that surround its venerable fishing **harbour**; the sandy **beach** alongside, which can only be reached by foot – or by elevator – feels deliciously sheltered from the town above. Up on the cliffs, the neat gardens, ice-cream parlours and seaview terraces of the large Victorian and Regency buildings give the place a distinctly Mediterranean flavour, while the large **bandstand** hosts concerts of all kinds, and the kitschy **Lillyputt crazy golf** course offers old-fashioned seaside fun and a nice tea garden (⊛ lillyputt.co.uk). Linked to the prom by tiny alleys, sloping **Albion Street** behind is lined with higgledy-piggledy Georgian buildings housing excellent **restaurants**, **bars** and **shops**.

A fishing village turned popular Victorian resort, Broadstairs still benefits from its location within walking distance of several excellent sandy **bays**. Renowned for its excellent **folk festival**, it also has strong connections with **Charles Dickens**: from 1837 until 1859 the author stayed in various hotels here, and eventually rented an "airy nest" overlooking the sea, where he finished writing *David Copperfield*. A festival and a small **museum** play up the associations, and the house he rented is now open as a B&B.

The bays

Broadstairs' town beach, sandy **Viking Bay**, is a lovely golden crescent at the foot of the cliffs, and accessible, in summer, by lift. Fringed with beach huts, Viking Bay has a surf school (see p.97) and a few kiddy rides – and gets crowded on hot days. This is just one of seven sandy coves in the vicinity, however; on the northern edge of Broadstairs, walkable from Viking Bay, you'll find **Stone Bay**, where a staircase winds down the wildflower-tangled cliff-face to a curved beach. Quieter in summer than Viking Bay, it's good for rockpools and for sunny morning swims. Beyond, **Joss Bay**, with its long beach and shallow waters, offers the best surfing in the Southeast, and is home to the **Joss Bay Surf**

School (see opposite). Further north are quiet **Kingsgate Bay**, with its sea caves, and best of all, the stunning **Botany Bay** (see p.92). In the other direction, **Louisa Bay**, easily reached on a sea-level prom from Viking Bay, is a quiet spot beneath cliffs shored up with concrete. It disappears entirely at high tide, but there's a very good beach caff (see opposite).

Dickens House Museum

2 Victoria Parade, CT10 1QS • Daily: Easter–May 2–5pm; June–Oct 10am–5pm • £3.25 • ☎ 01843 863453, ⓦ dickensfellowship.org/branches/broadstairs

One block back from the clifftop prom, the broad balconied cottage that now houses the **Dickens House Museum** was once the home of Miss Mary Pearson Strong, on whom Dickens based the character of Betsey Trotwood in *David Copperfield*. (In the book, this "house on the cliff", outside which the donkey fights that so angered Miss Trotwood took place, was moved to Dover.) Its five small rooms are crammed with memorabilia, including Dickens' letters, illustrations from the original novels, a reconstruction of Betsey Trotwood's parlour, and the author's desk, which he modified to include a rack for six bottles of wine. In addition, Victorian posters, maps, photography and costumes do a splendid job of evoking old Broadstairs.

ARRIVAL AND INFORMATION

By train Broadstairs station is on Lloyd Rd, a 10min walk along the High St to the seafront.

Destinations Canterbury (hourly; 25min); Faversham (Mon–Sat every 30min; 35min); Herne Bay (Mon–Sat every 30min; 22min); London St Pancras (hourly; 1hr 20min); London Victoria (every 30min–hourly; 1hr 55min); Margate (every 5–30min; 5min); Ramsgate (every 20min–hourly; 7min); Whitstable (Mon–Sat every 30min; 25min).

By bus Buses stop along the High St.

Destinations Canterbury (every 20–30min; 1hr 30min);

BROADSTAIRS

BARS & PUBS
Neptune's Hall	1
Salon Bohemia	3
Tartar Frigate	2

ACCOMMODATION
Belvidere Place	4
Bleak House	2
East Horndon Hotel	1
Royal Albion	3

CAFÉS & RESTAURANTS
Albariño	4
Beaches	2
Louisa Bay Café	8
Morelli's	6
Oscar's Festival Café	7
Peen's Gastro Bar	5
Restaurant 54	1
Tartar Frigate	3

0   200
yards

London Victoria (4 daily; 2hr 45min); Margate (every 5–15min; 25min); Ramsgate (every 10–20min; 10min).
Tourist information The nearest tourist office is in Margate (see p.93).
Watersports Joss Bay Surf School (lessons from £35; ⓦ jossbay.co.uk), based at the area's prime surfing beach,

rents out boards, suits and kayaks, and offers lessons for all levels. Kent Surf School, on Viking Bay, is great for beginners; they rent equipment and run bodyboarding, surf skiing, and stand-up paddleboarding sessions, with kids' camps (lessons from £35; ⓦ kentsurfschool.co.uk).

ACCOMMODATION

★ **Belvidere Place** 43 Belvedere Rd, CT10 1PF ☎ 01843 579850, ⓦ belvidereplace.co.uk. This stylish, quirky boutique B&B is in a friendly family home, but manages to be extremely hip, its five rooms featuring sleek bathrooms, cool art and one-off vintage finds. The gourmet breakfasts are superb. **£130**

Bleak House Fort Rd, CT10 1EY ☎ 01843 865338, ⓦ bleak housebroadstairs.co.uk/accommodation.html. An irresistible lure for Dickens fans, who can stay in the castellated house the writer rented for some twenty summers. Four luxurious guest rooms are decorated in slightly stuffy Victorian style – one features a bed in which Queen Victoria slept – and rates include a tour of Dickens' study. **£195**

East Horndon Hotel 4 Eastern Esplanade, CT10 1DP ☎ 01843 868306, ⓦ easthorndonhotel.com. Friendly, comfortable B&B in a large Victorian house overlooking Stone Bay, just a 5min seaside stroll from the centre of Broadstairs. Rooms are large, spruce and well equipped, some with sea views, and there's access to the sandy beach opposite. **£76**

Royal Albion 6–12 Albion St, CT10 1AN ☎ 01843 868071, ⓦ albionbroadstairs.co.uk. Grand eighteenth-century sea-facing hotel, now owned by Shepherd Neame, in a central location and with a sociable terrace bar. Rooms are clean, contemporary and comfortable; the best have sea views and little balconies. **£98**

EATING

Albariño 29 Albion St, CT10 1LX ☎ 01843 600991, ⓦ albarinorestaurant.co.uk. Authentic tapas served in a small, simple room that can get rather full. Cheese or meat platters start at £9.50, while the tasty tapas (£5–7) range from the familiar (tortilla with Manchego; *patatas bravas*) to more unusual choices (salted duck with green olives, butter beans and chorizo; slow-cooked ox cheek), all nicely washed down with the eponymous Galician wine. Tues–Sat noon–3pm & 6–11pm.

Beaches 49 Albion St, CT10 1NE ☎ 01843 600065. With a surfy vibe and friendly crowd, *Beaches* is a sociable place for fresh fruit smoothies (from £3.95) and healthy all-day breakfasts, brunches and lunches. Food ranges from sunny, Mediterranean-influenced snacks such as Spanish tartlets and halloumi, olive and *tzatziki* sandwiches to hearty traditional dishes of pork, caramelized onion and cheddar pie along with burritos or omelettes, all from £4.95. No cards. Daily 8.30am–4pm.

★ **Louisa Bay Café** Louisa Bay, CT10 1QE. It doesn't look like much, but this beach cabin is a local hit for its fabulous bacon butties (from £2.60), made with the best back bacon and delicious fresh bread, and eaten alfresco by the sand; the local sausages and breakfast baguettes are good too, with prime steak burgers, panini and Greek salads for a casual lunch (around £3). March–Oct daily from 10.30am.

Morelli's 14 Victoria Parade, CT10 1QS ☎ 01843 862500 ⓦ morellisgelato.com/stores/broadstairs. Deliciously old-fashioned, very pink, ice-cream parlour, whose 1950s formica, leatherette and wicker decor, including an Italian water fountain, is a vintage lover's dream – as is the free

jukebox, which features Sinatra and Rat Pack classics alongside recent hits. Scoops of home-made gelato cost from £2; order a frothy cappuccino, too, for the all-out retro experience. Mon–Fri 8am–5.30pm, Sat & Sun 8am–6pm.

★ **Oscar's Festival Café** 15 Oscar Rd, CT10 1QJ ☎ 07595 750091, ⓦ oscarsfestivalcafe.co.uk. This pocket-sized café, decked out in fresh pastels, cut flowers and 1950s design classics, extends its impeccable vintage sensibility into the menu, offering such locally sourced delights as potted shrimps, crab sandwiches and traditional pork pies, alongside fabulous cakes and cream teas. Mains from £6. No cards. May–Aug Wed–Sun 10.30am–5pm; Sept–April Thurs–Sun 10.30am–5pm.

Peen's Gastro Bar 8 Victoria Parade, CT10 1QS ☎ 01843 861289. A wide choice of good, seasonal food – superfood salads, gourmet burgers, paella, home-cooked ham with egg and fries – is served in this buzzy bar. Nights can be noisy, with a young, convivial crowd enjoying cocktails and designer beers; brunches (10am–noon) and lunches are more laidback. Mains from £9, with cheaper snacks and tapas. Food served noon–9.30/10pm.

Restaurant 54 54 Albion St, CT10 1NF ☎ 01843 867150, ⓦ restaurant54.co.uk. Modern British cuisine served in a soothing, candlelit dining room. Mains might include watermelon, mint and grilled halloumi salad (£7), roasted butternut squash stuffed with courgette and goat's cheese (£13.50) or tiger prawns, monkfish, plaice and scallops in lemon and coriander batter (£16). Mon–Sat 6–9pm, Sun noon–3pm & 6–9pm.

Tartar Frigate Harbour St, CT10 1EU ☎ 01843 862013, ⓦ tartarfrigate.co.uk. Reserve a window table if you can,

2

BROADSTAIRS FESTIVALS

The town bursts into life each August during **Broadstairs Folk Week** (ⓦbroadstairsfolkweek
.org.uk), one of England's longest-standing folk and roots music events, which features big
names and up-and-coming singers, bands and dancing, with workshops, kids' events and a
spine-tingling torchlight parade. Just slightly less crowded, the **Dickens Festival**
(ⓦbroadstairsdickensfestival.co.uk), held in the third week in June, sees enthusiastic Dickens
fans, many of them dressed in Victorian garb, flock through the town enjoying lectures,
Dickens dramatizations, Bathing Belles contests and traditional music hall. In early October,
Broadstairs Food Festival (ⓦbroadstairsfoodfestival.org.uk) is a weekend foodie event
featuring hundreds of stalls, demos and tastings, all focused on locally sourced produce.

---

and enjoy fresh local seafood and sea views in this popular restaurant above a historic harbourside pub (see below). Classic and classy mains, including skate with capers and black butter, or roast monkfish stuffed with scallops, cost from £16. Mon–Sat noon–1.45pm & 7–9.45pm, Sun seating at 12.30pm & 3.30pm.

DRINKING, NIGHTLIFE AND ENTERTAINMENT

Neptune's Hall 1 Harbour St, CT10 1ET ☎01843 861400, ⓦneptuneshall.co.uk. Old-fashioned Shepherd Neame boozer, all carpets, globe lights and etched glass, where you can join locals at the old mahogany bar, quietly chatting or reading the paper over a pint. Some guest ales from the Whitstable Brewery. Sun–Thurs noon–11pm, Fri & Sat noon–midnight.

Palace Cinema Harbour St, CT10 1ET ☎01843 865726, ⓦthepalacecinema.co.uk. Tiny Grade II-listed indie cinema, down by the harbour in a flint building from 1911; there's even (occasionally) a live cinema organist.

★ **Salon Bohemia** 1 John St, CT10 1LS ☎01843 863033, ⓦfacebook.com/pages/Salon-Bohemia-of-Broadstairs/145418588850642. You're never sure what might happen at this glamorous, boudoir-style bar hidden away behind a pink-painted exterior – cult movies, cool chanteuses, cabaret … or you could just pop in for a glass of bubbly and a quiet chat. Thurs–Sat 7–11pm.

Tartar Frigate Harbour St, CT10 1EU ☎01843 862013, ⓦtartarfrigate.co.uk. By the harbour, with a seafood restaurant (see above) upstairs, this seventeenth-century stone-and-weatherboard pub is a terrific place to spend an evening, especially during one of their friendly folk jam sessions. Mon–Sat 11am–11pm, Sun 11am–10pm.

Ramsgate

RAMSGATE is the largest of the Thanet towns, its robust Victorian redbrick architecture and elegant Georgian squares set high on a cliff linked to the seafront by broad, sweeping ramps. Down by the bustling **harbour** – Britain's only royal harbour, designated after George IV visited in 1821 – a collection of cafés and bars overlooks the bobbing yachts, endowing the place, in summer at least, with a cosmopolitan buzz. The small, busy **Ramsgate Sands**, with its children's rides and jet-ski area, lies just a short stroll away. Other sights include the **Maritime Museum**, in the nineteenth-century Clock House on the quayside, which chronicles local life from Roman times onwards (ⓦramsgatemaritimemuseum.org), and the quirky **Pinball Parlour**, 2 Addington St, where you can see – and demonstrate your flipping skills on – jangling pinball machines from the 1960s onwards (Sat & Sun 1–6pm; ⓦpinballparlour.co.uk).

The Grange

St Augustine's Rd, CT11 9NY • Wed 2–4pm, call (6–8pm) to reserve; also occasional open days • Free • ☎01843 596401, ⓦlandmarktrust.org.uk

If you're in Ramsgate midweek, take a look at **The Grange**, former family home of Augustus Pugin, best known as co-architect of the Houses of Parliament. Designed by Pugin and built in 1843–44, the house is Gothic Revival in style and filled with dark wood, rich wallpapers and decorative tiles – its emphasis on functional interior layouts over exterior symmetry marked a revolution in house design. Only some of the property is open to the tours, but you could stay here; it's owned by the Landmark Trust and rented out as self-catering accommodation. Pugin and his family are buried at **St Augustine's church**, another of his works, next door.

ARRIVAL AND INFORMATION   RAMSGATE

By train Ramsgate's station lies about a mile northwest of the centre, at the end of Wilfred Rd, at the top of the High St. Destinations Broadstairs (every 20min–hourly; 7min); Canterbury (hourly; 22min); Faversham (Mon–Sat every 30min; 40min); London St Pancras (hourly; 1hr 15min); London Charing Cross (every 20–40min; 2hr 15min); London Victoria (Mon–Sat every 30min–hourly; 2hr); Margate (every 5–20min; 10min); Whitstable (Mon–Sat

every 30min; 35min).
By bus Buses pull in at the harbour.
Destinations Broadstairs (every 10–20min; 10min); Canterbury (Mon–Sat hourly; 45min); London Victoria (4 daily; 3hr); Margate (every 5–15min; 30min).
Tourist office Custom House, Harbour Parade, (Mon–Sat 10am–2pm, Sun noon–2pm; ☎01843 598751, ⊕ visitthanet.co.uk).

ACCOMMODATION

Durlock Lodge Minster, 6 miles west, CT12 4HD ☎01843 821219, ⊕www.durlocklodge.co.uk. The pretty old village of Minster offers this good-value, peaceful and friendly B&B in an eighteenth-century house opposite an ancient abbey. Help yourself to a simple continental breakfast and eat it in your room. **£65**
Redcot House 3 Lyndhurst Rd, CT11 8EA ☎01843 595659, ⊕redcot-ramsgate.co.uk. Stylish, relaxed and luxurious B&B in a tall redbrick Victorian house, with three guest rooms, two with en-suite showers

and two with sea views. Thoughtful details include a laptop for guests' use and a welcoming lounge. You'll be plied with home-made cakes, pastries and breads. **£140**
Royal Harbour Hotel 10–12 Nelson Crescent, CT11 9JF ☎01843 591514, ⊕royalharbourhotel.co.uk. Two inter-connecting Georgian townhouses above the harbour house this friendly hotel, with quirky, nautically themed decor, a range of rooms – from tiny "cabins" to larger options with sea views and balconies – a patio and a cosy lounge with fire, newspapers and an honesty bar. **£100**

EATING

Age & Sons Charlotte Court, CT11 8HE ☎01843 851515, ⊕ageandsons.co.uk. Foodie haven in a Victorian warehouse on a shady square, accessed by an alley. The relaxed, kid-friendly ground-floor café, with comfy outdoor seating, serves light bites (£5), including cheese platters or ham hock on bubble and squeak, and cream teas, while the restaurant offers creative Kentish cuisine – steamed local sea trout with salad Niçoise, saltmarsh lamb with samphire and salsify (mains from £11; set lunch £9.95/£12.95 for two/three courses). There's also a basement bar. Café: Tues–Sun 10am–5pm (kitchen closes 3.30pm); restaurant: Tues–Sat noon–3.30pm & 7–9.30pm, Sun noon–3.30pm; bar: Wed–Sat 7pm–late.
Caboose Café and Bar 18 Queen St, CT11 9DR ☎01843 570984, ⊕caboosecafe.co.uk. Bare-bones coffee bar that's both friendly and cool, with gourmet coffee and an inexpensive light menu – sandwiches, salads, Mediterranean-style snacks, all from £3, plus hearty English breakfasts and brunches at the weekend, and wine and cocktails in the evening. Regular live events. Tues

9am–5pm, Wed–Fri 9am–11pm, Sat 10am–11pm, Sun 10am–10.30pm.
★ **Eddie Gilbert's** 32 King St, CT11 8NT ☎01843 852123, ⊕eddiegilberts.com. Above an excellent fishmonger/chippie, this casually elegant restaurant – scrubbed floors, brick walls, exposed rafters – is Thanet's top spot for local seafood, serving everything from fish and chips (from £8) to pan-fried sea bass with chorizo and pea risotto, or crispy smoked-eel soldiers with soft-boiled duck egg. Non-fishy choices – chilled courgette and foraged garlic soup with courgette crisps, say, or home-made pies – are delicious, too. Mains from £12. Mon–Sat 11.30am–2.30pm & 5.30–9.30pm, Sun 11.30am–2.30pm.
Ship Shape Café 3 Military Rd, CT11 9LG ☎01843 597000. Cosy hideaway under the arches by the harbour, full of nautical bits and bobs and favoured by a seasalty crowd tucking into fry-ups, mugs of strong tea and home-made cakes. On a sunny day the outdoor tables make a fantastic vantage point for the activity on the water. Daily 7am–3pm.

DRINKING AND NIGHTLIFE

Belgian Café 98 Royal Parade CT11 8LP ☎01843 587925, ⊕belgiancafe.co.uk. Big, brash brasserie-style place near the seafront, its outside tables usually full with an eclectic crowd enjoying Belgian beers, real ales, and marina views. Inside feels rather continental. Occasional live music. Sun–Thurs 7am–2am, Fri & Sat 7am–3am.
Conqueror Ale House 4C Grange Rd, CT11 9LR ☎07890 203282, ⊕conqueror-alehouse.co.uk. Ramsgate's unassuming, award-winning micropub offers a quiet,

friendly space to sup excellent local ales and ciders, along with apple juice from a nearby orchard. Tues–Sat 11.30am–2.30pm & 5.30–9pm, Sun noon–3pm.
Queen Charlotte 57 Addington St, CT11 9JJ ☎01843 570703, ⊕facebook.com/pages/Queen-Charlotte/14710 2395378044. Cool and quirky little pub with an up-for-it, bohemian crowd, an eclectic playlist, exhibitions, clothes sales, pop-up restaurants and hip live music. Thurs 5.30–11pm, Fri & Sat 5.30pm–midnight, Sun 6–10pm.

2

East Kent

DUNGENESS

East Kent

As the closest part of Britain to the Continent, the east coast of Kent has long been a frontier. Historic evidence of its vulnerability to invasion is at every turn, from stout Tudor castles and Napoleonic fortifications to poignant memorials to World War II, when gunfire in France could be heard from across the sea and entire towns were evacuated. Proximity to the Channel has brought Kent good fortune, too: not least in medieval days, when its Cinque Ports were granted enormous privileges and wealth. In Victorian times tourism entered the fray, with Folkestone in particular attracting the great and the good to its grand seafront hotels. Things are far quieter today. Defined by its iconic White Cliffs and lacking the big tourist towns of Kent's north coast or the Sussex shore, the east coast abounds in quiet bays, rugged headlands and lonely marshes, its low-key seaside towns and villages offering plenty of laidback appeal.

Pretty, medieval **Sandwich**, once an important Cinque Port (see box, p.105) but now no longer even on the coast, makes a charming overnight spot, while further south the former smuggling haven of **Deal** has a certain raffish energy. Its two castles, built by Henry VIII, may be less famous than the mighty complex at Dover, but they're fascinating in their own right: **Deal Castle** reveals the most sophisticated military engineering of its day, while just a seafront walk away, **Walmer Castle** has been home to the Duke of Wellington, among other luminaries. **Dover**, Britain's principal cross-Channel port, a mere 21 miles from mainland Europe, is not immensely appealing but it does provide a springboard for the magnificent **Dover Castle**, and for the stupendous chalk banks of the **White Cliffs**, which offer glorious walks. South of Dover lies **Folkestone**, a down-on-its-luck resort valiantly re-energizing itself as an arts destination, and the **Romney marshes**, with the eerie, arty shingle headland of **Dungeness** at their southernmost tip.

The East Kent coast offers outstanding walking and cycling. The coastal stretch between Folkestone and Dover forms part of the **North Downs Way**, while the section of the **Saxon Shore Way** between Deal and Dover is one of the most picturesque on the entire path. The **Warren**, Folkestone's very own stretch of white cliff, offers dramatic vistas and a broad, fossil-studded beach, while **Samphire Hoe**, an incongruous knob of land created from spoil during construction of the Channel Tunnel, is an intriguing place for a stroll. For a full rundown of walks and cycle rides, from town trails to long-distance jaunts, and a schedule of guided walks and rides, see Ⓦwhitecliffscountryside.org.uk.

Sandwich and around

Tiny **SANDWICH**, on the River Stour six miles north of Deal, is one of the best-preserved medieval towns in England. Hard to believe today, but this was a major commercial port,

SANDWICH

Highlights

① Sandwich With its sleepy quayside and glorious Edwin Lutyens gardens, its nature reserves and its seal-spotting trips, this little medieval gem is a delight. **See p.102**

② Deal The quiet seaside town of Deal boasts a proud maritime history, two Tudor castles, an atmospheric conservation area, great walking, and some superb places to stay and eat. **See p.107**

③ Dover Castle A visit to Dover's mighty castle, which dominates the skyline for miles around and spans Roman remains to World War II bunkers, could fill an entire day. **See p.112**

④ White Cliffs of Dover An exhilarating walk along these imposing white cliffs is an unmissable East Kent experience. **See p.117**

⑤ Wallett's Court Soak up the history and snuggle up in a four-poster in this effortlessly beautiful manor-house hotel. **See p.120**

⑥ The Warren Wildlife-rich and geologically fascinating, the cliffs and beach of the Warren have a rugged, handsome beauty. **See p.124**

⑦ Rocksalt, Folkestone This glamorous harbourside restaurant, right on the water, offers just one excellent reason to visit the up-and-coming town of Folkestone. **See p.125**

⑧ Prospect Cottage, Dungeness Pay tribute to the artistic vision of late filmmaker Derek Jarman at his seaside garden, gazing out from the windswept shingle of Dungeness. **See p.130**

HIGHLIGHTS ARE MARKED ON THE MAP ON P.104

chief among the Cinque Ports (see box opposite), until the Stour started silting up in the 1500s; unlike at other former harbour inlets, however, the **river** hasn't vanished completely and still flows through town, its grassy, willow-lined banks adding to the sleepy charm.

Though the **Secret Gardens** are the biggest formal attraction, it's a pleasure simply to wander around Sandwich, with its crooked half-timbered buildings, narrow lanes, peaceful quayside and riverside path. Shops are few, and very low-key, while historical markers relate fascinating snippets. Just outside town lie a handful of **nature reserves** and the remains of **Richborough Roman Fort**, which you can reach by boat. It's also a major destination for **golfers** – the **Royal St George's** course fringes the coast to the east, with the Prince's Golf Club to the north and the Royal Cinque Ports Club a mile or so south.

Secret Gardens of Sandwich

Knightrider St, CT13 9EW • Daily: April–Sept 10am–5pm; Oct–March 10am–4pm • March–Nov £6.50; Dec & Jan free; Feb two-for-one entry; tours (1hr 30min–2hr; £11) must be booked in advance • ☎ 01304 619919, ⓦ the-secretgardens.co.uk

Designed by Sir Edwin Lutyens and heavily influenced by his famous gardening partner Gertrude Jekyll, the 3.5-acre **Secret Gardens of Sandwich** were restored in 2007 – and given their new name – after being abandoned to the wilderness for 25 years. While they largely retain the design of the original gardens, a few new features,

HIGHLIGHTS

1. Sandwich
2. Deal
3. Dover Castle
4. White Cliffs of Dover
5. Wallett's Court
6. The Warren
7. Rocksalt, Folkestone
8. Prospect Cottage, Dungeness

EAST KENT

THE CINQUE PORTS

In 1278 Dover, Hythe, Sandwich, Romney and Hastings – already part of a long-established but unofficial confederation of defensive coastal settlements – were formalized under a charter by Edward I as the **Cinque Ports** (pronounced "sink", despite the name's French origin). In return for providing England with maritime support, chiefly in the transportation of troops and supplies during times of war, the five ports were granted trading privileges and other liberties – including self-government, exemption from taxes and tolls and "possession of goods thrown overboard" – that enabled them to prosper while neighbouring ports struggled. Some benefitted during peacetime, too, boosting their wealth by such nefarious activities as piracy and smuggling.

Rye, Winchelsea and seven other **"limb" ports** on the southeast coast were later added to the confederation. The ports' privileges were eventually revoked in 1685; their maritime services had become increasingly unnecessary after Henry VIII had founded a professional navy and, due to a shifting coastline, several of their harbours had silted up anyway, stranding some of them miles inland. Today, of all the Cinque Ports only Dover is still a major working port.

3

including a tropical border (we can thank global warming for that), have been added; the lake, with its little island, dates back to the 1970s. Tours detail each area, but it's perfectly nice simply to wander: it's a tranquil place, with plenty of benches and secluded nooks. The informal, country-garden style beautifully offsets the classical lines of the 1911 house (now a private residence), with bold, splashy plantings, unexpected combinations and discrete areas linked by winding brick paths.

The quayside

Sandwich's riverfront **quayside**, peaceful today, was once the heart of a great medieval port, when the wide river estuary known as Sandwich Haven lapped at its banks. While the Haven began silting up in the sixteenth century, and the sea is now miles away, the waterfront gives the place a breezily nautical atmosphere, with small boats moored by the toll bridge, open countryside stretching out across the river, and the cry of seagulls raking the air. **Boat trips** (see p.106) run from the toll bridge over the Stour – note the sixteenth-century **Barbican**, a stone gateway decorated with chequerwork, where tolls were once collected – up to Richborough Roman Fort (see p.106) and down to the estuary to spot seals and birds.

The Guildhall

Cattle Market, CT13 9AH • April–Nov Tues, Wed, Fri & Sat 10.30am–12.30pm & 2–4pm, Thurs & Sun 2–4pm • £1 • ☎ 01304 617197

At the centre of Sandwich, the handsome sixteenth-century **Guildhall** houses the tourist office (see p.106), various venerable council chambers, and displays recounting the history of the town. For centuries, the open square around it hosted a busy cattle market; today there's a small market every Thursday, along with a **farmers' market** on the last Saturday of each month.

Royal St George's Golf Course

1.5 miles east of Sandwich, CT13 9PB • Visitors (Mon–Fri only) need to be introduced by a member, or to email a letter of introduction from their club and to produce evidence of a handicap of 18 or better • ☎ 01304 613090, ⓦ royalstgeorges.com

Sandwich is separated from the sandy beaches of Sandwich Bay by the **Royal St George's Golf Course**, perhaps the finest links course in England. Set in the undulating dunes, and boasting the deepest bunker in championship golf (on its fourth hole), St George's was established in 1887 and has been a frequent venue for the British Open since 1894 – most recently in 2011. Laid out in sympathy with its natural surroundings, it's a stunning spot, with wonderful views of the sea.

THE NOBLE SANDWICH

Perhaps surprisingly, Sandwich makes little of a potential claim to fame: the nation's favourite lunchtime snack, the **sandwich**, was created, so the story goes, in 1762, when a peckish John Montagu, the fourth Earl of Sandwich, absorbed in a game of cards and on a winning streak, ate his beef between two bits of bread so as not to lose concentration. However, as this didn't happen in Sandwich, and as the earl's connections with the place were largely limited to his name, it seems fair enough that the town is happy to sell a few amusing sandwich-related postcards and leave it at that.

Richborough Roman Fort

Richborough Rd, Pegwell Bay, CT13 9JW • April–Sept daily 10am–6pm; Oct–March Sat & Sun 10am–4pm • £4.90; EH • ☎ 01304 612013, ⓦ english-heritage.org.uk/daysout/properties/richborough-roman-fort-and-amphitheatre • The best way to get to the fort is on a riverboat from Sandwich (see below); trips take about 1hr

Marooned in the marshy lands that fringe Pegwell Bay, two miles northwest of Sandwich, stand the remains of **Richborough Roman Fort**, one of the earliest coastal strongholds built by the Romans. Originally a military garrison, the fort developed into first a civilian town and then a major port. Though its sheer size, and its lonely setting, is evocative – the coast that it guarded is now a couple of miles distant – Richborough's historical significance far outshines its appearance. All that can be seen within the huge and well-preserved Roman walls are the remains of an early Saxon church, and a small, but informative museum.

Sandwich and Pegwell Bay Nature Reserve

Three miles north of Sandwich, off the A256, CT12 5JB • Daily 8.30am–7pm • Free • ☎ 01303 266327

The broad expanse of the **Sandwich and Pegwell Bay Nature Reserve**, on the River Stour estuary between Sandwich and Ramsgate, is a superb spot for birdwatchers, boasting a wide variety of seashore habitats including tidal mudflats, saltmarsh, shingle beach, dunes, chalk cliffs and coastal scrubland. The best time to view the wading birds is in winter, or during the spring and autumn migrations, but even in summer you'll spot redshank, shelduck and oystercatchers, along with ringed plovers and little tern. The reserve is on the Viking Coastal cycling trail and the Saxon Shore Way (see p.29).

ARRIVAL AND DEPARTURE

SANDWICH AND AROUND

By train Sandwich station is off St George's Rd, from where it's a 10min walk north to the town centre and the quay. Destinations Deal (every 30min–1hr; 6min); Dover (every 30min–1hr; 25min); Folkestone (every 30min–1hr; 35min); London Charing Cross (hourly; 2hr 20min); Ramsgate (hourly; 15min).

By bus Buses pull in and depart from outside the Guildhall. Destinations Canterbury (every 20min–1hr; 45min); Deal (Mon–Sat every 20min–1hr; 25–35min); Dover (Mon–Sat every 45min–1hr; 45min–1hr); Ramsgate (Mon–Sat hourly; 30min).

INFORMATION AND TOURS

Tourist office The Guildhall (April–Oct Mon–Sat 10am–4pm; ☎ 01304 613565, ⓦ visitsandwich.org or ⓦ whitecliffscountry.org.uk).

River tours Sandwich Riverbus boats, by the toll bridge, head out on seal-spotting jaunts in the estuary (30min–1hr) and on longer wildlife-spotting trips (2hr), and provide

a ferry service to Richborough Roman Fort (see above); you'll need to reserve (roughly April–Aug Thurs–Sun & school hols 11am–6pm; Sept–March Sat, Sun & school hols, dependent on weather; £7–24; ☎ 07958 376183, ⓦ sandwichriverbus.co.uk).

ACCOMMODATION

Bell Hotel The Quay, CT13 9EF ☎ 01304 613388, ⓦ bellhotelsandwich.co.uk. Sandwich's largest hotel is a

rambling hostelry that has stood on this site since Tudor times; the present building dates largely from the nineteenth century. Rooms are comfy, in an uncontroversial, contemporary style; the best (£170) have balconies overlooking the grassy banks of the Stour. The in-house restaurant, with a short menu of locally sourced food, is a good option, too. Minimum two nights at weekends June–Sept. **£110**

Molland Manor House Molland Lane, Ash, CT3 2JB ☎01304 814210, ⊛mollandhouse.co.uk. The history is palpable in this thirteenth-century manor, full of original features, three miles west of Sandwich. It's very family friendly, with accommodating hosts and a big garden with trampoline; if you stay two nights, you'll be welcomed with a delicious cream tea and lots of little luxuries. The five en-suite B&B rooms are spacious and comfortable. **£110**

St Crispin Inn The Street, Worth, CT14 0DF ☎01304 612081, ⊛stcrispininn.com. Attractive fifteenth-century pub in a pretty village a couple of miles southeast of Sandwich. Six B&B rooms are spread between the main building and three "chalets" outside; they're nothing glamorous, but comfortable and clean, and all are en suite. There's decent bar food, along with real ales, in the pub. **£70**

★ **Salutation** Knightrider St, CT13 9EW ☎01304 619 919, ⊛the-salutation.com. Something special – the opportunity to stay in the Secret Gardens of Sandwich, in the peaceful grounds of the Edwin Lutyens-designed 1911 house. Three cottages offer light, luxurious and characterful rooms, with white-painted beams, antique beds and the plumpest bedlinen imaginable. The setup is one of relaxed luxury: each cottage has a well-equipped kitchen and dining area (with complimentary bar), and one has a welcoming living room too, which all guests share. Rates include a rather elegant breakfast in the Lutyens house and free garden admission, including out-of-hours. **£160**

EATING, DRINKING AND ENTERTAINMENT

Elizavet 3–5 Bell Lane, CT13 9EN ☎01304 619899, ⊛greekrestaurantsandwich.co.uk. Greek food may not be terribly fashionable nowadays, but nobody minds here in Sandwich – this convivial restaurant, tucked away in a narrow cobbled lane off the quayside, serves good, old-school Greek food to an appreciative crowd. Mains (£9–14) include all the classics done well, or you can put together a tasty meze platter (£3–7) with souvlaki, halloumi, courgette fritters and the like. And yes, the occasional music nights do feature plate-smashing and dancing. Tues–Sat noon–2pm & 6–11pm, Sun noon–2pm.

George and Dragon 24 Fisher St, CT13 9EJ ☎01304 613106, ⊛georgeanddragon-sandwich.co.uk. A fifteenth-century inn and popular, unpretentious gastro-pub, with good cask ales, roaring real fires in winter and a courtyard garden for alfresco summer dining. The Modern British menu changes regularly: choices might include lamb hash with Puy lentils (£12) or catch of the day with warm potato and olive salad (£15). Booking advised in the evening. Mon–Fri 11am–3pm & 6–11pm, Sat 11am–11pm, Sun 11am–4.30pm; food served Mon–Sat noon–2pm & 6–9pm, Sun noon–2pm.

No Name 1 No Name St, CT13 9AJ ☎01304 612626, ⊛nonameshop.co.uk. For picnic supplies, including hot baguettes, look no further than this excellent French deli opposite the Guildhall. You can also eat in, choosing from a daily-changing blackboard menu of light dishes – tartines, soups, quiche – and heartier mains such as baked mussels,

duck confit and thyme-roasted chicken. Dishes around £5–10. Deli Mon–Sat 8am–5pm, Sun 9am–4pm; bistro Mon–Sat 8am–3pm.

St Mary's Arts Centre St Mary's Church, Strand St, CT13 9HN ⊛stmarysartscentre.org.uk. A friendly little arts centre that punches above its weight, hosting big-name performers (stand-up comedian Rich Hall, vocalist John Williams), along with a solid repertoire of blues, folk, jazz and classical concerts.

St Peter's 10 New St, CT13 9AB ☎01304 612049, ⊛stpeterssandwich.co.uk. Modern British food, locally sourced, in a smart, modern dining room or a courtyard. Mains (around £9.50 at lunch, £12–16 at dinner) are heavily focused on meat and fish – pot-roast shoulder of pork, say, or hake with mussels – but there are always a couple of veggie options. The tapas at lunch (around £4 each) and occasional two- and three-course fixed-price menus prove good value. Wed 7–10pm, Thurs noon–2.30pm & 7–10pm, Fri & Sat noon–2.30pm & 6.30–10pm, Sun noon–2.30pm.

Salutation Tearoom Knightrider St, CT13 9EW ☎01304 612730, ⊛the-secretgardens.co.uk/tea-room. This rather swish tearoom occupies a prime spot at the entrance to the Secret Gardens of Sandwich, and its tea-shaded deck offers a fine outlook over Lutyens' handsome manor house. The home-made cakes are delicious, with a menu of cream teas ranging from a simple two-scone affair up to the indulgent full-chocolate version. Daily 11am–5pm.

Deal and around

The low-key seaside town of **DEAL**, six miles southeast of Sandwich, is an appealing place, with a broad, steeply shelving shingle **beach** backed by a jumble of faded Georgian townhouses, a picturesque **old town** redolent with maritime history, and a

3

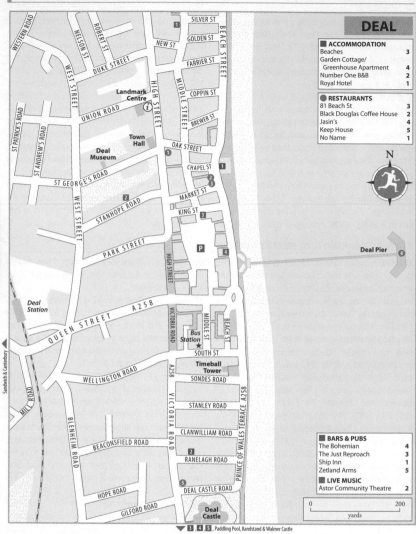

DEAL

■ ACCOMMODATION
Beaches	3
Garden Cottage/	
Greenhouse Apartment	4
Number One B&B	2
Royal Hotel	1

● RESTAURANTS
81 Beach St	3
Black Douglas Coffee House	2
Jasin's	4
Keep House	5
No Name	1

■ BARS & PUBS
The Bohemian	4
The Just Reproach	3
Ship Inn	1
Zetland Arms	5

■ LIVE MUSIC
| Astor Community Theatre | 2 |

0 ————— 200
yards

▼ 3 , 4 , 5 , Paddling Pool, Bandstand & Walmer Castle

striking concrete **pier** lined with hopeful anglers casting their lines. Henry VIII's two seafront **castles**, linked by a seaside path on the Saxon Shore Way, are the main attractions, along with walks and cycle rides along the coast, but above all Deal is a place to simply potter around. A low-key artsy vibe, and a significant gay community, afford it a certain panache; this, along with a small but good selection of restaurants and B&Bs, makes it an increasingly popular weekend destination.

Brief history

It was on this stretch of coast that, in 55 BC, **Julius Caesar**, daunted by the vision of Dover's colossal white cliffs further up the shore, first landed in Britain. **Henry VIII** built three castles in the area, compact coastal fortresses designed to scare off the Spanish and the French; having been named a **limb port** of the Cinque Ports in the thirteenth century (see box, p.105), by Elizabethan times Deal was one of the most important ports in the country. It was renowned for its skilled boatbuilders and courageous sailors – men able to navigate the perilous offshore Goodwin Sands, where countless ships had met their doom, to reach safe harbour in the "**Downs**" anchorage, the sheltered waters closer to land – and by the eighteenth century had become a notorious centre for smuggling. Privateering boosted the local economy until well into the Victorian era.

The seafront

At first glance, Deal's **seafront** promenade may not be the best advertisement for the town. Though handsome, many of its buildings have become a little shabby – on the outside at least – and lack the picture-postcard appeal of the sprucer old-town lanes just inland. That said, it has a likeable, low-key charm, with small independent hotels and restaurants far outnumbering the few amusement arcades and tourist shops; **Beach Street**, the parade of pastel-painted Georgian and Victorian buildings north of the pier, is its prettiest stretch.

Deal beach

The **beach** itself is a long, uninterrupted shingle swathe, almost entirely uncommercialized and perfect for bracing walks. Steeply shelving, it's also a popular spot for sea fishing and even, for the very bold, a circulation-zapping swim. The wide coastal path alongside, suitable for walkers and cyclists, takes you past a picturesque ensemble of fishing boats, tatty lobster pots and chalky white fishing huts via **Walmer Castle**, the largest of Henry's local coastal defences, to the laidback little village of **Kingsdown**, at the edge of the White Cliffs, which is a popular spot for kayaking.

Deal Pier

Built in 1957, **Deal Pier** is almost defiantly unprepossessing, an unlovely concrete affair that replaced a more decorative Victorian iron pleasure pier destroyed by a run-in with a Dutch merchant ship in 1940. You can't leave town without walking its length – all 1026ft of it – however; lacking amusement arcades or end-of-the-pier entertainments, it has its own appeal, offering splendid views back over the town and a good family restaurant, *Jasin's*, at the end (see p.111). It's also a renowned spot for **fishing**, the water yielding bass, ray, smooth hound, dogfish and mackerel in summer, and codling, whiting and flatfish in winter. Channel Angling, at the pier entrance, sells bait and tackle (☏01304 373104).

Timeball Tower

Victoria Parade, corner of Sondes Rd, CT14 7BP • May Sat & Sun noon–4pm; June–Sept Wed–Fri 11am–4pm, Sat & Sun noon–4pm • £2 • ☏ 01304 368255, ⓦ dealtimeball.tripod.com

Deal's **Timeball Tower** was used, in the early nineteenth century, as a semaphore tower in an attempt to monitor local smuggling activity. Abandoned in 1842, the tower was transformed by the addition of a timeball in 1855; the ball dropped down a pole on the roof at exactly 1pm in summer, providing an accurate time check for ships at sea attempting to navigate the offshore Downs. Although the coming of radio put paid to that, the timeball still drops regularly in summer. Inside, a small **museum** displays old clocks, rare timepieces, telescopes and ingenious Victorian telegraph mechanisms.

The old town

Middle Street is the prettiest road in Deal's **old town**, its cute pastel cottages, elegant Georgian houses and narrow alleys making perfect photo opportunities. *Carry On* fans should stop by no. 117, a compact cottage with a blue plaque commemorating Charles Hawtrey, who by all accounts lived out his later years here in eccentric and alcoholic promiscuity. Middle Street's picturesque tranquillity belies the fact that this was the de facto high road for the town's smugglers and pirates – the northern end, marked by the small Alfred Square, was a particularly nefarious stretch, and it's said that a network of secret tunnels still lies beneath the street today.

Deal's **High Street** has a little more character than many of its kind; the shops become more interesting in its old town stretch, with a scattering of independent boutiques, delis, vintage stores and coffee shops north of Broad Street. Off the High Street, at 2 St George's Road, the **Deal Museum** (May, Sept & Oct Sat 11am–5pm; June–Aug Tues–Fri 2–5pm, Sat 11am–5pm; £3; ⓦdealmuseum.co.uk) illustrates the town's social and seafaring history.

Deal Castle

Marine Rd, CT14 7BA • April–Sept daily 10am–6pm; Oct–March Sat & Sun 10am–4pm • £4.80; EH • ☎ 01304 372762, ⓦ english-heritage.org.uk/daysout/properties/deal-castle

Diminutive **Deal Castle**, at the south end of town, is one of the most striking of Henry VIII's forts. Hastily built in 1539–40, along with Sandown Castle (now destroyed) to the north and Walmer Castle (see below) to the south, as part of a chain of coastal defences against potential invaders – and in particular, Henry's French and Spanish Catholic enemies – this was a castle designed to face battle. Its distinctive **shape** – viewed from the air it looks like a Tudor rose – has less to do with aesthetics than to sophisticated military engineering: squat rounded walls were effective at deflecting cannonballs and provided less surface area to be hit. Inside the six outer bastions, themselves mounted with heavy guns, a second set of six semicircular inner bastions protected the cylindrical central keep, its own 14ft-thick walls providing stout defence.

Perhaps disappointingly, after all this effort, the castle never did see serious fighting, though there was a brief skirmish during the Civil War. The castle was garrisoned one last time during the Napoleonic Wars, but again little fighting actually took place.

Self-guided **audio tours** outline every detail of the state-of-the-art military design. Bare rooms reveal how the castle changed over the years and give a good sense of how the soldiers lived; check out the claustrophobic privies with their deep, dark wells. Descending through gloomy cobbled passageways brings you to the basement and the Rounds, a subterranean warren equipped with yet more cannon, facing potential enemies across the dry moat.

Walmer Castle

Kingsdown Rd, one mile south of Deal, CT14 7LJ • March Sat & Sun 10am–4pm; April–Sept daily 10am–6pm; Oct Wed–Sun 10am–4pm • £7.50; EH • ☎ 01304 364288, ⓦ english-heritage.org.uk/daysout/properties/walmer-castle-and-gardens • Hourly buses from Deal; also accessible on foot along the seafront (30min)

The southernmost of Henry VIII's trio of "Castles in the Downs", **Walmer Castle** is another rotund Tudor-rose-shaped affair, built to protect the coast from its enemies across the Channel. Like Sandown Castle (which no longer stands) and its neighbour at Deal, Walmer saw little fighting; unlike those, however, it changed use when it became the official residence of the Lords Warden of the Cinque Ports in 1708 (which it still remains, though the title itself is now strictly ceremonial).

Adapted over the years by its various residents, today the castle resembles a heavily fortified **stately home** more than a military stronghold. All its dozen or so dim rooms – many of them fan-shaped, due to the unusual circular walls – are filled with the memorabilia of previous Lords Warden, including the late Queen Mother and Winston Churchill. Walmer is most associated, however, with the **Duke of Wellington**, who was given the post of Lord Warden in 1828. In his bedroom you can see his simple camp bed, with its original bedding, and the armchair in which he died in 1852. The Iron Duke lay in state in this room for two months before being buried at St Paul's Cathedral; in the two days before his body was taken to London, some nine thousand local mourners trooped past to pay their respects. Other Wellington memorabilia includes his sunken bronze death mask and a pair of original Wellington boots, designed by the Duke after the Battle of Waterloo to be cut lower than the usual boot and thus be easier to wear.

After the gloom of the interior, the castle's terraced **gardens** are a delightful contrast. Begun by Lord Warden William Pitt in 1792 – with help from his famous and eccentric adventuress niece, **Lady Hester Stanhope** – and landscaped in 1865 in an Italianate style, they offer all manner of walks and picnic spots.

ARRIVAL AND INFORMATION
DEAL AND AROUND

By train The station is on Queen St, a 10min walk from the sea.

Destinations Dover (every 30min–1hr; 15min); Folkestone (every 20min–1hr; 30min); London Charing Cross (every 30min–1hr; 2hr 10min); Ramsgate (every 30min–1hr; 20min); Sandwich (every 30min–1hr; 6min); Walmer (every 30min–1hr; 3min).

By bus Buses run from South St in the town centre.

Destinations Canterbury (Mon–Sat 1–3 hourly, Sun 5 daily; 1hr 5min); Dover (every 20min–1hr; 50min); London

Victoria (2 daily; 2hr 35min–3hr 25min); Sandwich (Mon–Sat every 20min–1hr; 25–35min).

By bike There are lots of good cycling paths around Deal. For rental – including tandems, trikes and buggy trailers – try Beach Cycle Hire (from £10/2hr or £25/24hr; weekly rental available; free delivery for rentals of 24hr or more; ☎ 07941 863833, ⓦ beach-cycle-hire.co.uk), on Walmer Beach.

Tourist office Landmark Centre, 129 High St (Mon–Fri 10am–4pm, Sat 10am–2pm; ☎ 01304 369576, ⓦ visitdeal .org or ⓦ whitecliffscountry.org.uk).

ACCOMMODATION

Beaches 34 The Strand, Walmer, CT14 7DX ☎ 01304 369692, ⓦ beaches.uk.com. Just south of town, a hop from the seafront, this is a luxurious, relaxing two-room B&B offering design flair and light-drenched sea views. Breakfasts, with daily specials from eggs Benedict to cinnamon brioche, can be packed up as a picnic to take to the beach, and they offer chairs, loungers and towels for seaside fun. Rates decrease after one night; two-night minimum at weekends. **£110**

Garden Cottage/Greenhouse Apartment Walmer Castle, Walmer, CT14 7LJ ☎ 0870 333 1187, ⓦ english -heritage.org.uk/daysout/properties/walmer-castle-and -gardens/greenhouse-apartment. Breaks of three, four or seven nights in these luxurious self-catering options, both of which sleep four, in the castle grounds. In a gorgeous spot overlooking the eighteenth-century kitchen garden, both are decorated in simple, contemporary style. Three nights:

cottage **£711**, apartment **£611**

Number One B&B 1 Ranelagh Rd, CT14 7BG ☎ 01304 364459, ⓦ numberonebandb.co.uk. This friendly, popular B&B is the nicest place to stay in Deal itself. The handsome Victorian townhouse is in a great spot, near the castle and just a minute from the beach, and its four individually decorated rooms are stylish and contemporary, with luxurious extras including bathrobes, iPod docks and coffee makers. **£85**

Royal Hotel Beach St, CT14 6JD ☎ 01304 375555, ⓦ theroyalhotel.com. Things have quietened down since Admiral Nelson scandalized society by entertaining Lady Hamilton in his bedchamber here, and some of the rooms are looking a bit tired, but there's still a thrill to staying in the only seaward building on Beach Street, especially if you get one of the sea-facing rooms with balconies. Rates include a breakfast buffet, and there's a bar and bistro on site. **£110**

EATING

81 Beach St 81 Beach St, CT14 6JB ☎ 01304 368136, ⓦ 81beachstreet.co.uk. Top-notch contemporary brasserie with a daily-changing menu. Dinner mains might include seafood chowder with a parmesan crust (£15.50) or duck confit with pak choi (£16); lunch is less expensive (two courses for £12.50, three for £15.50). Booking recommended at weekends. Mon–Sat noon–3pm & 6–10pm, Sun noon–4pm.

★ **Black Douglas Coffee House** 82 Beach St, CT14 6JB ☎ 01304 365486, ⓦ blackdouglas.co.uk. Funky bolthole on the blustery seafront, with scrubbed wooden tables, local art on the walls, newspapers and books for browsing, and a focus on good, locally sourced home-made food. It's a great spot for brunch (try the Eggs Douglas, with anchovies and capers; £8) or lunch (maybe Puy lentils with roast beetroot, goat's cheese and pomegranate; £9.50), served on mismatched plates in a cosily informal atmosphere. Friday

evenings see a short menu of home-made pizza and meze. Mon–Thurs 9am–5pm, Fri 9am–5pm & 7–10pm, Sat 9am–5pm, Sun 10am–4pm.

Jasin's Deal Pier, CT14 6HZ ☎ 01304 366820, ⓦ jasins restaurant.com. With its picture windows and pared-down timber decor, perched over the water like a ship's lookout, stylish *Jasin's* looks more expensive than it is. At heart this is a family-friendly caff, serving honest grub – fish and chips, home-made lasagne, toasted wraps – along with smarter specials like crab cakes with sweet potato fries. It's great for breakfast (served till 4pm), when fishermen, laptop-toting hipsters and tourists alike tuck into full Englishes (from £4.50), croissants or chunky bacon sandwiches. There's outdoor seating too, right above the water, and a few takeaway options. Mains £5–10. Free wi-fi. Mon–Fri & Sun 8am–8.15pm, Sat 8am–10pm.

Keep House 1 Deal Castle Rd, CT14 7BB ☎ 01304 368162,

3

DEAL FESTIVALS

The well-regarded **Deal Festival of Music and the Arts** (usually first week of July; ⓦ dealfestival.co.uk) is at the highbrow end of the scale – artistic director is cellist Matthew Sharp. A variety of venues host chamber music, opera, classical and jazz from around the world, with big names, young performers, and a programme of talks and events. Deal's other big music event is the **Maritime Folk Festival** (three days in mid-Sept; ⓦ dealmaritime folkfestival.org.uk), when the town's pubs and streets resound with folk in all its forms, from sea shanties, clogging and morris dancing to nu-folk and world music.

ⓦ keephouse.co.uk. Sweet, sunny tearoom opposite the castle, offering cream teas, high teas – including a savoury option (from £12.95) – and home-made sweet treats (from £3), with lots of loose-leaf teas and unusual tisanes, all grown in England. Thurs–Sat 10am–5pm, Sun 11am–6pm.

No Name 110 High St, CT14 6EE ☎ 01304 375100, ⓦ nonameshop.co.uk. This excellent French deli is a good place to stock up on baguettes, cheese, hams and olives for an upmarket beach picnic. Mon–Thurs 8.30am–5pm, Fri & Sat 8.30am–4.30pm.

DRINKING AND ENTERTAINMENT

Astor Community Theatre 20 Stanhope Rd, CT14 6AB ☎ 01304 370220, ⓦ theastor.org. A lively arts centre in a handsome old Edwardian theatre, hosting live music – local and low-key national bands – literary events, rep theatre, comedy, and the best world movies and classic films.

The Bohemian 47 Beach St, CT14 6HY ☎ 01304 374843, ⓦ facebook.com/TheBohemianResurrection. Following a devastating fire in 2011, the "Boho", which attracted a lively crowd with its mishmash decor – old posters, vintage chandeliers, retro bits and bobs – along with its suntrap beer garden, its real ales and strong cocktails, underwent a massive refit. At the time of writing the resurrection was still under way; check the Facebook page for updates.

★ **The Just Reproach** 14 King St, CT14 6HX ☎ 07432 413226, ⓦ thejustreproach.co.uk. This dinky micropub offers a fabulous range of British microbrews, along with local cider and a few house wines in a snug, bare-bones

room livened up with a scattering of retro memorabilia, and with no TV or music to interrupt the conversation. Food is limited to a few pasties on Saturday lunchtimes. Tues–Thurs noon–2pm & 5–9pm, Fri & Sat noon–2pm & 5–11pm, Sun noon–2pm.

Ship Inn 141 Middle St, CT14 6JZ ☎ 01304 372222. Venerable old-town pub, popular with a local and laidback crowd enjoying a quiet pint, with a really gorgeous early nineteenth-century interior and a garden. Lots of real ales on offer. Daily noon–11pm.

Zetland Arms Wellington Parade, Kingsdown, CT14 8AF ☎ 01304 364888, ⓦ thezetland.co.uk. Around a 45min walk from Deal along the beach, the *Zetland* is a favourite refreshment stop for walkers and cyclists, perched right by the water and with great views of the White Cliffs. The pub grub (from £9), despite its fish specials, is no great shakes. Daily 11am–11.30pm; closed Mon–Fri 3–6pm in winter.

Dover and around

Given its importance as a travel hub – it's the busiest ferry port in Europe – **DOVER** is surprisingly small. Badly bombed during World War II, the town centre is drab and unprepossessing, with a few low-key attractions but little to induce you to stick around; the seafront is equally unassuming, with a marina, a waterside promenade and a couple of boat-tour operators. The main attraction is **Dover Castle**, looming proudly above town and clearly visible from the sea. And few visitors can resist a walk along Dover's legendary **White Cliffs**, inspiration for poets, weary travellers and lonesome soldiers alike.

Dover Castle

Castle Hill, CT16 1HU • April–July & Sept daily 10am–6pm; Aug daily 9.30am–6pm; Oct daily 10am–5pm; Nov to Feb 16 & Feb 25 to end March Sat & Sun 10am–4pm; 17–24 Feb daily 10am–4pm • £16.50; children £9.90; EH • ☎ 0870 333 1181, ⓦ english-heritage.org.uk/daysout /properties/dover-castle

No historical stone goes unturned at **Dover Castle**, an astonishingly imposing defensive complex that has protected the English coast for more than two thousand years. A castle stood here as early as 1068, when **William the Conqueror**, following the Battle of Hastings, built over the earthworks of an Iron Age hillfort; a century later, the **Normans** constructed the handsome keep that now presides over the heart of the complex. The grounds also include a **Roman lighthouse**, a **Saxon church** and all manner of later additions, including tunnels built in the Napoleonic Wars and World War I signal stations. Indeed, the castle was in continuous use as some sort of military installation right up to the 1980s, and its network of **tunnels**, used during World War II, are huge attractions in their own right.

Ideally you should allow a **full day** for a thorough visit, including time for a battlement walk (which takes around 1hr in total); if time is short, head first to Operation Dynamo, where long queues build up as the day proceeds, before making your way to the Great Tower.

Operation Dynamo: Rescue from Dunkirk
Tours (1hr) leave at regular intervals

One of Dover Castle's most popular attractions is its network of **secret wartime tunnels**, dug during the Napoleonic Wars and extended during World War II. It was from these claustrophobic bunkers in 1940 that Vice Admiral Ramsay coordinated **Operation Dynamo**, the evacuation of Dunkirk, which successfully brought back some 285,000 stranded British and Allied troops from the Continent, helped by a flotilla of local fishing and pleasure boats – the "little ships" – sailed by civilians. Defined by J.B. Priestley as "so absurd yet so grand and gallant that you hardly know whether to laugh or cry", Dunkirk marked a turning point in the war. Though "Wars are not won by evacuations," as Churchill put it – and it was clear that the need to evacuate marked a serious defeat – a new determination to win, the so-called "Dunkirk Spirit", was born.

Operation Dynamo tunnel **tours** are lively and affecting affairs, accompanied by the muffled sound of anti-aircraft guns and screaming Spitfires. Guides lead groups through the dark warrens while dramatic vox pops and film footage flickering across crumbling tunnel walls shed light on the build-up to the war and how the evacuation came about. The detail is impeccable, from the genuine graffiti on the walls, scrawled over a period of two hundred years, to the reconstructed chart rooms and repeater stations, eerily alive with the sounds of ringing phones and crackling messages.

The Underground Hospital
Tours (20min) leave every 30min

In 1942, a medical dressing station was set up in the tunnels beneath the castle grounds, where patients, most of them from the castle garrison, were bandaged and stabilized before being transferred to hospitals with better facilities. Billed as a walkthrough experience, tours of the **Underground Hospital** are impressionistic affairs, with rather less hard information than the Operation Dynamo tours next door. Loosely following the journey of a fictitious injured pilot brought to the hospital in 1943, you stride through corridors and wards, mess rooms and dorms, all filled with surgical instruments and the accoutrements of hospital life, as a cacophonous soundtrack booms around you. Dark, stuffy and claustrophobic, the tunnels can feel nightmarish as sirens scream and bombs explode, spectral patients groan and shadowy nurses gossip; eerily, in the operating theatre, as you hear (invisible) doctors talking around their (invisible) patient, the smell of surgical spirit is overpowering.

Dover Secret Wartime Tunnels Uncovered
Though somewhat overshadowed by the high-profile subterranean tours around the corner, the **Dover Secret Wartime Tunnels Uncovered** exhibition shouldn't be overlooked. Lively panels give information on the tunnels themselves, apposite quotes and historical snippets illuminate the Dunkirk expedition, and intriguing exhibits include a case of photos and memorabilia from both a German and a British soldier, following their two very different wars. The **gift shop**, too, is a cut above, with its retro *Dad's Army* mugs and propaganda postcards.

3

The Great Tower

At the heart of Dover Castle is the inner bailey and the amazingly well-preserved **Great Tower**. Built by Henry II as a palace and a residence to welcome important visitors – including those on pilgrimage to Canterbury – this was the last and finest of the enormous rectangular royal towers that had begun with the Tower of London a century earlier. Despite subsequent modernization, notably under Edward IV and in the seventeenth century, it remains one of the best-preserved medieval royal towers in existence.

Inside the tower itself, a series of rooms linked by steep and narrow stone staircases have been painstakingly re-created to look ready to receive Philip, Count of Flanders, in 1186. Everything from the pots and pans in the kitchen to the chess set and richly coloured furniture and wall hangings in the **King's Chamber** has been meticulously reproduced using, where possible, the materials and methods of the time. The chambers in particular reveal a surprising blaze of paint-box colours and jaunty designs – rich blues, reds and gloriously decorative golds designed to flaunt the king's colossal wealth and influence.

Climbing to the **roof** of the tower, passing other visitors huffing and puffing as they descend, rewards you with fabulous views of the castle grounds, the sea, and Dover itself.

The medieval tunnels

Following a nearly disastrous siege by the French Prince Louis and rebel barons in 1216–17, Dover Castle saw a number of improvements in its defence system – not least, a complex set of subterranean **tunnels**, entered from a spot near the Great Tower. These were altered and expanded during the Napoleonic Wars and in the 1850s, but their original plan remains largely intact. There is little to actually see, although a set of lever-controlled doors that could be closed remotely to trap invaders is undeniably impressive, but the dramatically sloping declines, damp, drippy darkness, mysterious nooks and steep staircases are irresistibly atmospheric.

The Roman lighthouse

The Romans put Dover on the map when they chose the harbour – Portus Dubris – as the base for their northern fleet, and, probably in the second century AD, erected a clifftop **lighthouse** (*pharos*) to guide the ships into the river mouth. The remains of the chunky octagonal tower, made from local flint and bricks and refaced in medieval times, still stand – only the four lower stages survive, but you can walk inside the hollow shell.

St Mary-in-Castro

Standing beside the remains of the Roman lighthouse, the **St Mary-in-Castro** church dates back to around 1000 AD. Though subsequently remodelled, it remains a very fine, late Saxon church, with original cruciform layout and soaring internal stone arches. Under Henry III, St Mary's became a church for soldiers – Richard the Lionheart's knights took shelter here before setting out on a crusade, and you can see their graffiti scratched into the wall just above ground level in the original stone arches near the pulpit. Over the next few centuries the church fell into ruin, to be restored by famed Victorian architects Sir George Gilbert Scott and William Butterfield; the latter is responsible for the decorative mosaic tiling that covers the walls.

Roman Painted House

New St, CT17 9AJ • April & June to mid-Sept Tues–Sat 10am–5pm, Sun 1–5pm; May Tues & Sat 10am–5pm; last entry 4.30pm all year; call to check the house is open, as it is staffed solely by volunteers • £3 • ☎ 01304 203279, ⦾ theromanpaintedhouse.co.uk

Built around 200 AD, the **Roman Painted House**, once a rest house for official guests from across the Channel, was demolished around seventy years later. Today, in a purpose-built building near the Market Square, you can see the remains of five rooms, including evidence of the hypocaust, or underground heating system, and various

mosaics, along with – the chief attraction – vibrant Roman wall paintings relating to Bacchus, the god of wine. Roman objects found during the excavation are also on display.

Dover Museum

Market Square, CT16 1PB • April–Aug Mon–Sat 10am–5pm, Sun 10am–3pm; Sept–March Mon–Sat 10am–5pm • £3.50 • ☎ 01304 201066, ⊚ doverdc.co.uk/museum.aspx

Dover Museum is an appealing, slightly old-fashioned place, packed with enthusiastic displays on the town's past. The star attraction, protected behind glass in its own gallery, is a **Bronze Age boat** that was discovered in Dover in 1992, immaculately preserved by river silt for more than 3500 years. The boat – the only one of its kind in Europe – is an astonishing sight, long, dark and sinewy like tough black seaweed; it took ten carpenters one month to build it, using holly, plum, oak, ash, apple, elm and yew, plus dense wodges of moss for waterproofing.

The White Cliffs

Shingly Dover beach may today lack the romance invested in it by Matthew Arnold (see box opposite), but the iconic **cliffs** flanking the town on both sides retain their majesty. Stretching sixteen miles along the coast, a towering 350ft high in places, these vast banks are composed of chalk – plus traces of quartz, shells and flint – and though time and pollution have taken some of the edge off their whiteness, occasional rock falls still shear back the surface to reveal cleaner strata behind, creating new swathes of beach in their wake. Much of the cliffs lie within the Kent Downs Area of Outstanding Natural Beauty, and with their chalk grasslands home to an exceptional number of rare plants, butterflies and migrant birds, have been designated a Site of Special Scientific Interest.

The most dramatic **views** of the cliffs themselves, of course, come from miles out to sea, either from a ferry or on a short tourist cruise from Dover (see p.118). Best of all, though, is to take a **walk** along them, which affords you amazing views of the Straits of Dover – the world's busiest shipping lanes. On a clear day it's even possible to catch a glimpse of France.

Shakespeare Cliff

A mile or so west of Dover • Bus #60, #61 or #61A from Pencester Rd towards Aycliffe

West of Dover, **Shakespeare Cliff**, named for its mention in *King Lear* (see box opposite), is almost ferociously daunting, a towering bastion of chalk leaning backwards as if straining to hold back the sea. The bracing clifftop walk here offers a sweeping panorama – and an excellent, unusual view of Dover and the surrounding cliffs – but anyone with vertigo will want to stay well clear of the edge.

To reach Shakespeare Cliff, you can catch a bus from Dover; alternatively, there's a very steep two-and-a-half-mile climb from North Military Road, off York Street, taking you by the **Western Heights**, a series of defensive battlements built into the cliff throughout the nineteenth century. You'll be glad of the benches at the top.

Samphire Hoe

Below Shakespeare Cliff, off the A20 from Dover to Folkestone • Daily 7am–dusk • Free, parking £1 for up to 2hr

Created from some 175 million cubic feet of chalk marl reclaimed during the building of the Channel Tunnel, **Samphire Hoe**, the nature reserve at the foot of Shakespeare Cliff, is an unsettling spot. Wild and exposed, its chalk meadows, dotted with rock samphire, rye grass and wildflowers, have a raw beauty. On the other hand, this is clearly a man-made landscape, blocked off from the sea by a sea wall and wire fence, and with brutish concrete Tunnel ventilation buildings welcoming you at the entrance. Walking around the Hoe, a total loop of around 45 minutes, does, however, offer invigorating blasts of fresh air, along with splendid views of the sea and of the awe-inspiring Shakespeare Cliff looming above – you may see kestrels, guillemots and kittiwakes swirling overhead.

THE WHITE CLIFFS OF DOVER

There is a cliff whose high and bending head
Looks fearfully in the confinèd deep
Bring me but to the very brim of it,
And I'll repair the misery thou dost bear
With something rich about me. From that place
I shall no leading need.

Earl of Gloucester, *King Lear*, Act 4 Scene 1

The sea is calm tonight,
The tide is full, the moon lies fair
Upon the straits; on the French coast the light
Gleams and is gone; the cliffs of England stand,
Glimmering and vast, out in the tranquil bay.
Come to the window, sweet is the night air!

Dover Beach, Matthew Arnold, 1867

There'll be bluebirds over
The White Cliffs of Dover
Tomorrow, just you wait and see.

(There'll Be Bluebirds Over) The White Cliffs of Dover, sung by Vera Lynn, 1942

As the first and last sight of England for travellers throughout the centuries, the **White Cliffs of Dover** play a complex role in the English psyche. A symbol of national fortitude, independence and pride, they have long represented a barrier for potential invaders; like mighty natural fortresses, they inspire awe and fear. **Julius Caesar** mentions them in his *Commentaries, Book IV*, recounting the Roman invasion of Britain in 55 BC – "steep cliffs came down close to the sea in such a way that it is possible to hurl weapons from them right down to the shore. It seemed to me that the place was altogether unsuitable for landing." Daunted, the invaders sailed further north to Deal and landed there instead.

In Shakespeare's **King Lear** the cliffs represent certain death to the abject and blinded Gloucester, who plans to commit suicide by jumping from them; in a later scene, his son, lying, convinces his father they are at the cliff edge with the words "the murmuring surge/That on the unnumber'd idle pebbles chafes/Cannot be heard so high. I'll look no more/ Lest my brain turn, and the deficient sight /Topple down headlong". Poet Matthew Arnold, meanwhile, gives them a similarly melancholic resonance, invoking their massive grandeur in his famous elegy for lost belief, **Dover Beach**.

Perhaps the most famous mention of the cliffs, however, comes in **Vera Lynn**'s wartime anthem, a rallying call for Britons to keep dreaming of a peaceful future in the wake of the Battle of Britain. It's ostensibly a hopeful song, but the plaintive tune, and the fact that no real bluebird ever flew over the cliffs, imbues the uplifting words with a poignant uncertainty.

To reach Samphire Hoe, pedestrians, cyclists and cars alike enter through a dark single-lane **tunnel** that descends through the cliffs; this was built in the 1880s, an aborted early version of today's Channel Tunnel.

South Foreland Lighthouse

The clifftop, St Margaret's Bay, CT15 6HP • Roughly mid- to end March, mid-April to May & Sept to mid-Oct Fri–Mon 11am–5.30pm; early to mid-April, early to mid-June & mid-July to Aug daily 11am–5.30pm; mid-June to mid-July Thurs–Mon 11am–5.30pm; mid-Oct to Nov Fri–Mon 11am–4pm; guided tours only • £4.50; NT • ☎ 01304 852463, ⊛ nationaltrust.org.uk/south-foreland-lighthouse

Langdon Cliffs, a couple of miles east of Dover, are home to the National Trust White Cliffs Visitor Centre (see p.118), and a popular starting point for **walks** along the clifftop. One enjoyable, undulating four-mile round-trip leads from the visitor centre to **South Foreland Lighthouse**. Following cliff-edge paths and ploughing through chalk downland meadows, it's a fine walk for birdspotters: watch out for kittiwakes in the summer, along with pretty chalkhill blue butterflies fluttering in the wildflowers. Built in 1843 to guide ships past the perilous Goodwin Sands, three miles offshore, the lighthouse itself offers (on clear days) amazing cross-Channel views. This was the site of Marconi's first international radio transmission, and the first lighthouse to be powered by electricity; lively guided tours detail the history, while touchscreens allow you to monitor the comings and goings on the busy Dover Strait. You can **stay** here, too (see opposite).

St Margaret's-at-Cliffe and around

Tucked away off the A258 Dover–Deal road, four miles northeast of Dover and around two miles inland, **St Margaret's-at-Cliffe** (⊛ firstlightcoast.com) was a major smuggling centre in the eighteenth century. There's very little evidence of that today, however; it's a sleepy spot, set on a glorious stretch of the **Saxon Shore Way** (see p.29) and on National Cycle Route 1. The local beach, **St Margaret's Bay**, is charming, and there are some excellent places to stay and eat.

St Margaret's Bay

St Margaret's Bay, a fifteen-minute walk from the village, is the closest point on the British mainland to France, just twenty miles away. A secluded cove of shingle-sand beach with rockpools to explore and the odd fossil to be found, it's a nice spot for a seaside sojourn, with bodyboarding, canoeing and respectable surfing from the wave-cut platform off Ness Point. Both Noël Coward and Ian Fleming rented the house by the beach here (at different times) – Coward, however, who also had a home in Aldington, in Romney Marsh (see p.129), found the seaside presented too many distractions from his work, and moved on in 1951.

If you fancy a break from the beach, pop into the pretty, six-acre **Pines Garden** (daily 10am–5pm; £3; ⊛ pinesgarden.co.uk), with its picnic spots and teahouse, or, if you're feeling more energetic, walk up to South Foreland Lighthouse (see p.117). Follow Lighthouse Road up for a mile or so; the path is poor in places.

ARRIVAL AND DEPARTURE   DOVER AND AROUND

By train Dover Priory station is off Folkestone Rd, a 10min walk west of the centre. For late ferry arrivals, the last train service leaves Dover for London Victoria at 10.45pm.
Destinations Canterbury (every 30min–1hr; 30min); Folkestone (every 15–40min; 12min); London Charing Cross (every 30min–1hr; 1hr 55min); London St Pancras (hourly; 1hr 10min); London Victoria (Mon–Sat every 20–40min; 2hr).
By bus Buses from London run to the ferry terminal, and

then on to the town-centre bus station on Pencester Rd. Destinations Canterbury (every 30min–6 daily; 35min); Deal (every 20min–1hr; 50min); Folkestone (every 20–30min; 15–25min); Hastings (every 1–2hr; 2hr 40min); London Victoria (every 30min–1hr; 2hr 5min–3hr); St Margaret's Bay (every 30min; 20min); Sandwich (Mon–Sat every 45min–1hr; 45min–1hr).
By ferry P&O ferries and SeaFrance run between Dover and Calais, while DFDS offers services to Dunkirk.

INFORMATION AND TOURS

Dover tourist office Dover's helpful and well-stocked tourist office is in the Dover Museum, Market Square (April–Sept Mon–Sat 9.30am–5pm, Sun 10am–3pm; Oct–March Mon–Sat 9.30am–5pm; ⊜ tic@doveruk.com, ⊛ whitecliffscountry.org.uk).
The White Cliffs Visitor Centre Langdon Cliffs, Upper Rd (roughly daily: March–June, Sept & Oct 10am–5pm; July & Aug 9.30am–5.30pm; Nov to mid-Feb 10.30am–4pm; free, parking £3; NT; ⊛ nationaltrust.org .uk/white-cliffs-dover). Displays illuminate the ecology

and history of the local coast and countryside, while the coffee shop, with huge outdoor deck, is the ideal vantage point to watch the port activity below.
Dover Sea Safari Based in the Dover Sea Sports Centre on the beach, Dover Sea Safari (⊛ doverseasafari.co.uk) offer a good selection of high-octane speedboat tours – including harbour and White Cliffs jaunts (1hr 20min; £20), seal-watching trips at Pegwell Bay (2hr; £35) and occasional low-tide trips out to Goodwin Sands, where you are left for an hour to roam free (3hr; £50).

ACCOMMODATION

DOVER

Maison Dieu Guest House 89 Maison Dieu Rd, CT16 1RU ☎01304 204033, ⓦmaisondieu.com. Friendly B&B in a central location, with attractive single, double, twin and family rooms, some with shared facilities, but most en suite. A few have good views over the garden to Dover Castle. There's a laptop for guests' use. **£80**

Marquis at Alkham Alkham Valley Rd, Alkham, 10min west of Dover, CT15 7DF ☎01304 873410, ⓦthemarquisatalkham.co.uk. This swanky restaurant-with-rooms offers ultra-modern boutique-style accommodation hidden behind the exterior of a 200-year-old inn. The ten chic rooms (and two "cottages") have huge windows, many with picture-perfect views across the Downs. Alkham itself, while pretty, is a sleepy place; the award-winning *Marquis* restaurant (see below) is the main draw. Breakfasts, including a rather posh bacon sandwich, can be served in your room. Rates dip to £99 Sun–Thurs, when a room-only rate (£79) is also available. **£149**

Sandown Guest House 229 Folkestone Rd, CT17 9SL ☎01304 226807, ⓦsandownguesthouse.com. The atmosphere is warm at this good-value, comfortable guesthouse, the well-equipped rooms feel homey and welcoming, and there's a lounge for guests' use. A hearty full breakfast costs £5. **£60**

THE WHITE CLIFFS

East Cottage South Foreland Lighthouse, St Margaret's Bay, CT15 6HP ⓦnationaltrustcottages.co.uk/cottage/east-cottage-021003. Luxurious National Trust accommodation – one twin and one double – in a nineteenth-century lighthouse keeper's cottage. Dramatically sited on the edge of the cliffs, it's a magnificently remote spot – though if you stay in high season, or during a public event at the lighthouse, you'll be in the thick of things – and the views over the Channel are fabulous. The TV reception can be dodgy up here, but that's all part of the quirky charm. Three nights: around **£649**

ST MARGARET'S-AT-CLIFFE AND AROUND

★ **Wallett's Court** Westcliffe, CT15 6EW ☎01304 852424, ⓦwallettscourthotelspa.com. Set a little apart from the village, in seven acres of grounds surrounded by rolling countryside, *Wallett's Court* is a gorgeous manor house dating back to the eleventh century, whose residents have included luminaries from Eleanor of Castile to William Pitt. The main house has the best rooms, three splendid affairs with wonky beams, softly plastered walls and venerable four-posters, but the modern options in the converted barns are lovely, too, and there's glamping in two luxurious tipis. The spa boasts a heated indoor pool, and there's a top-notch restaurant (see p.120) – if you take one of their guided foraging tours, dinner will be prepared with the ingredients you find. Doubles **£150**; tipis (per person) **£85**

White Cliffs High St, CT15 6AT ☎01304 852229, ⓦthewhitecliffs.com. The exceptionally friendly *White Cliffs* is *Wallett's Court*'s cooler younger sibling – as luxurious as its classy sister hotel, but with a chilled-out, island resort-style feel. Rooms, in an old Kentish clapboard house, come in all shapes, sizes and styles, from rustic and cosy to airy and contemporary; many have sloping ceilings. Guests can use the spa facilities at *Wallett's Court*, and the restaurant, *The Bay*, is great (see p.120). An excellent buffet breakfast is included; you pay £5 for a full English. **£119**

EATING AND DRINKING

DOVER

★ **Allotment** 9 High St, CT16 1DP ☎01304 214467, ⓦtheallotmentdover.co.uk. A light-filled oasis on Dover's run-down High Street, this is by far the best place to eat in town, serving delicious food in a simple, shabby-chic space. As the name suggests, ingredients are largely sourced from their own and local allotments, and the daily-changing menu concentrates on the best seasonal produce. Breakfasts are simple – eggs Benedict, sourdough pancakes, fresh fruit salads – while lunch or dinner might include pea and halloumi fritters, wasabi-dressed hot beetroot with poached eggs, Dijonnaise lamb, or a goat's cheese tart that is out of this world. Starters around £6.50; mains £8.50–16. Tues–Sat 8.30am–11pm.

Blakes of Dover 52 Castle St, CT16 1PJ ☎01304 202194, ⓦblakesofdover.com. Cosy, wood-panelled basement bar offering real ales and local ciders, with a small beer garden at the back. Food – steaks and pub grub – is served upstairs. Mon–Sat 11am–11pm, Sun noon–10pm.

Hythe Bay Seafood Restaurant at Dover The Esplanade, CT17 9FS ☎01304 207740, ⓦhythebay.co.uk. Sister restaurant to the original in Hythe (see p.128), this has the edge over its older sibling, with a great location on Dover's seafront, and a traditional menu of simply prepared fish and seafood – from scallops to Dover sole, fish pie to lobster – in a bright dining room with broad sea views. There's an outdoor deck for sunny days. Starters from £6, mains from £12. Daily noon–9.30pm; coffee served from 10am.

Marquis at Alkham Alkham Valley Rd, Alkham, CT15 7DF ☎01304 873410, ⓦthemarquisatalkham.co.uk. Awarded a rising Michelin star, the *Marquis* is a destination restaurant with rooms just a 10min drive from Dover. Chef Charlie Dakin uses local produce to create innovative fusion cuisine – typical offerings might include garlic *pannacotta*, breast of Romney Marsh duck with salsify, and Hopdaemon Ale cake (made with Kentish real ale). The à la carte menu will set you back £32.50 for two courses, or £42.50 for three; there's also a good-value lunchtime fixed-price

3

menu at £17.50/£22.50. No children under 8 at dinner. Mon 6.30–9.30pm, Tues–Sat noon–2.30pm & 6.30–9.30pm, Sun noon–3pm & 7–8.30pm.

White Horse Inn Corner St James St and Castle Hill Rd, CT16 1QD ☎ 01304 202911. At the foot of the road leading down from the castle, this friendly local pub – built in 1365, it has been a tavern on and off since the sixteenth century – is the *de rigueur* Dover hangout for cross-Channel swimmers, who traditionally sign their names on the wall after a successful crossing. Daily noon–11pm.

ST MARGARET'S-AT-CLIFFE AND AROUND

★ **The Bay Restaurant** White Cliffs Hotel, High St, CT15 6AT ☎ 01304 852229, ⓦ thewhitecliffs.com. Don't be misled by the cheery, midpriced menu – which includes Goan fish curry, fish and chips and heartfelt pronouncements about "peace and love" – or the weatherbeaten dining room, lined with the owner's photographs and local art. While informal, this lovely restaurant serves gourmet-standard food, from huge bowls of plump mussels in garlicky broth to fresh fish specials and a seriously classy bangers and mash – Kentish wild boar sausages, with hot ham-hock hash, steamed beets and chard. Starters from £5, mains £12.50–17, less at lunchtime. Tues–Sat noon–2pm & 6.30–9pm, Sun noon–3pm & 6.30–9pm.

The Coastguard St Margaret's Bay, CT15 6DY ☎ 01304 853176, ⓦ thecoastguard.co.uk. This family-run beachside pub is a brilliant spot for a summer lunch, with a large terrace (separated from the beach by a car park) and small beer garden that stretches practically down to the shingle. Kent cask ales are served, along with good local food featuring lots of fresh fish and seafood. Menus change regularly, but smoked haddock roasted with a mussel and saffron cider cream, Hoegaarden-battered fresh cod, or roast aubergine soup with coriander and cumin are typical. Starters from £4.50; mains £10–20. Booking advised at weekends. Daily 10.30am–11pm; food served noon–2.45pm, 3–6pm & 6.30–8.45pm.

Wallett's Court Westcliffe, CT15 6EW ☎ 01304 852424, ⓦ wallettscourthotelspa.com. The deliciously cosy setting, in an ancient wood-beamed dining room, is just part of the charm at this hotel restaurant – the outstanding food, locally sourced and full of hearty flavours, features dishes such as Kentish venison, pan-roasted local pheasant and rabbit terrine, with usually one option for veggies and a fresh fish of the day. Two/three courses £34.95/£39.95; Sunday lunch £16.95/£21.95; afternoon tea £16.95. Booking advised. Mon–Sat noon–5.30pm (afternoon tea) & 7–9pm, Sun noon–2.30pm (lunch), 2.30–5.30pm (afternoon tea) & 7–9pm.

Folkestone and around

In the early 2000s, depressed after the demise of its tourist industry and the loss of its ferry link to France, **FOLKESTONE** was a doleful place. Like all the settlements on the east coast, it had long been defined by its relationship to the sea: starting out as a fishing village, it thrived as a smuggling centre in the seventeenth century, then grew in Victorian times to become a busy cross-Channel ferry port and upmarket **resort**. The ravages of two World Wars, followed by a rash of rebuilding, did the place no aesthetic favours, however, and the rise of cheap foreign travel hit hard. With the **Channel Tunnel**, west of town, whisking passengers direct from the M20 to the Continent, and the curtailment of the ferry service to Boulogne in 2000, reasons to stop in Folkestone were diminishing.

Thus began a concerted effort to start again, with many hopes pinned on the arts and the creative industries. Cue Folkestone's **Triennial** art show, which premiered in 2008 to some acclaim. Spearheaded by the multimillionaire Roger de Haan (owner of Saga holidays, which is based here) and his Creative Foundation charity, the event brings considerable attention in festival years, but at other times Folkestone still has the air of a place in limbo. Some parts of town – the neglected seafront alongside Marine Parade in particular – are bleak and shabby, but with the regenerating **Creative Quarter** and the salty little fishing **harbour** (both owned by de Haan), the glorious **Lower Leas Coastal Park**, a sandy town **beach**, and the wild **Warren** cliffs and beach nearby, Folkestone has plenty to offer. Less than an hour from the capital by train, and with some stylish places to eat and stay, it's making waves as a seaside weekender.

The Creative Quarter

Occupying a small corner of town down by the harbour, Folkestone's **Creative Quarter** is a redeveloping slum area now owned by the Creative Foundation, who rent out the workspaces, commercial units and flats to artists. The steep and cobbled **Old High Street**, lined with brightly painted higgledy-piggledy seventeenth- and eighteenth-century buildings, holds most of the independent shops, cafés and galleries; it snakes its narrow way up to **Rendezvous Street**, another appealing little enclave. In Triennial years the Creative Quarter is Folkestone's beating heart; things are far quieter at other times, with many shabby buildings boarded up or empty, but tantalizing pop-ups come and go and the community vibe is tangible, with flyers for local events and fundraisers plastered on windows everywhere.

Lower Leas Coastal Park and around

Folkestone exists on two levels – down by the sea and up on the cliffs, with steep hills and zigzag steps linking the two. Taking up a large, long swathe below the clifftop **Leas** promenade and above the beach, the **Lower Leas Coastal Park** is a glorious expanse of lush plantings, winding paths and pretty footbridges, all accompanied by sea views that on a sunny day have a distinctly Mediterranean flavour.

A man-made creation, made possible following a massive landslide in the eighteenth century, the park – which stretches west of the Leas Lift practically as far as the neighbouring village of Sandgate – was the talk of Victorian and Edwardian Folkestone, its landscaped promenades prime attractions of this genteel resort. Today it also features wildflower meadows and shady woodlands; behind the grassy outdoor

3

THE FOLKESTONE TRIENNIAL

With just two events under their belt so far, the Folkestone Triennial (ⓦfolkestonetriennial.org .uk), a public art project first held in 2008, has played a major part in changing the town's image. Attracting big British names from Tracey Emin to Cornelia Parker and Martin Creed, as well as artists from around the world, the energy of the Triennial, and its importance to Folkestone as a confidence boost, is inestimable. The theme of the first event, brainchild of the Creative Foundation (see opposite), was "Tales of Time and Space", with most works linked explicitly to Folkestone itself, and bringing 170,000 visitors to town; the 2011 show, "A Million Miles From Home", focused more on dislocation and transience, with artists from as far afield as Algeria and Brazil. Aiming for accessibility over elitism, much of the art is also location-specific, with soundscapes, performance art pieces and mobile installations encouraging visitors to roam around and discover Folkestone itself. Talks, tours, workshops and live events keep energy levels high, with eminent critics and curators rubbing shoulders with curious locals.

FIVE INSTALLATIONS

A selection of the art pieces have been made permanent; the following are particularly striking, but you can find a full list on the website.

18 Holes Richard Wilson (2008). Look twice and you'll see that the three concrete-and-green-felt beach huts on the coastal promenade, around 500yd west of the Leas Lift, are actually made from a crazy-golf course, the last remaining part of Folkestone's last remaining amusement park, finally demolished in 2007 after promises to redevelop and regenerate went by the wayside.

Baby Things Tracey Emin (2008). Blink and you'd miss them; these seven small bronzes from Kent-born YBA Emin – baby mittens, tiny cardies, teddies and lone bootees discarded on benches, railings and pavements – comment on the high teenage pregnancy rate in Folkestone and towns like it. Ostensibly ephemeral scraps of jetsam, they pack a surprisingly poignant punch.

FOLKESTONE Patrick Tuttofuoco (2008). These 10ft-high colourful steel letters on the abandoned harbour arm look like graffiti from afar but have come to be a local landmark.

The Folkestone Mermaid Cornelia Parker (2011). Parker's naturalistic version of Copenhagen's idealized Little Mermaid, a bronze life-cast sculpture modelled on a Folkestone woman, sits on a boulder by the harbour, overlooking Sunny Sands beach.

Out of Tune A K Dolven (2011). Norwegian-born artist Dolven has strung a discarded sixteenth-century church bell from a steel cable 65ft high, suspended between two posts on a lonely spot near the Leas Lift, where Folkestone's last amusement park once stood.

amphitheatre, a dramatic zigzag path scales the rockface, complete with mysterious grottoes, up to the bandstand on the Leas. At the park's heart, thrillingly hidden in the woods, is an outstanding **children's playground**, with tube slides, zip-lines and all manner of adventure equipment for all ages. Beyond the point at which steps descend to the seafront *Mermaid Café* the park becomes wilder and less landscaped; it all culminates with a staircase leading up to the *Grand* and *Metropole* hotels on the Leas, relics of the resort's Edwardian heyday.

Leas Lift

Lower Sandgate Rd, CT20 1PR • Daily 9.30am–5.20pm; shorter hours in winter • £1 • ⓦ leasliftfolkestone.co.uk

The last of Folkestone's four Victorian lifts, and one of only three water-powered funicular lifts remaining in England, the 1885 **Leas Lift** chugs up between the Leas seafront parade, with its lawns, formal flowerbeds and bandstand, down to the seafront at the end of Marine Parade, which is somewhat neglected at this spot.

Mermaid beach

The shingle beaches below the coastal park are not bad for swimming, though you should watch out for rocks; the area around the *Mermaid Café*, unofficially called **Mermaid Beach**, is the best, a gently shelving slope with a rough sand bottom. The beach huts here – large concrete and hardboard boxes, painted in bright ice-cream

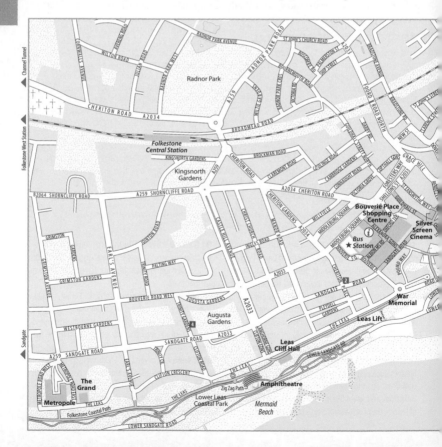

colours – have a poignant, quintessentially Folkestone feel, being at once jaunty, pretty and a little rough.

The harbour and around

Split in two by the now defunct railway viaduct, Folkestone's **harbour** was crowded in Victorian days with ships and pleasure vessels, and with fishermen hauling in their huge catches. Today, quietly awaiting redevelopment, it's an atmospheric spot, fishing boats bobbing in the tidal waters and wild flowers sprouting from its rocky walls, the cobbled **Stade** (or "landing place") studded with black weatherboard fishermen's huts. Small-scale fishing still goes on here, with a weekly fish market, a couple of seafood stalls (the local whelks are delicious), plus a brace of excellent restaurants (see p.125) joining the chip shop, caff and two pubs. It's a peaceful spot, if you don't count the giant seagulls – though you'd do best to try and ignore the hideous 1980s *Grand Burstin* hotel, an outrageous eyesore looming over the far end like a half-built cruise liner.

Sunny Sands beach

It may not always be sunny at **Sunny Sands**, the little beach by the fishing harbour, but it's undeniably sandy, which is a rarity along this shingly shore. The golden stuff is

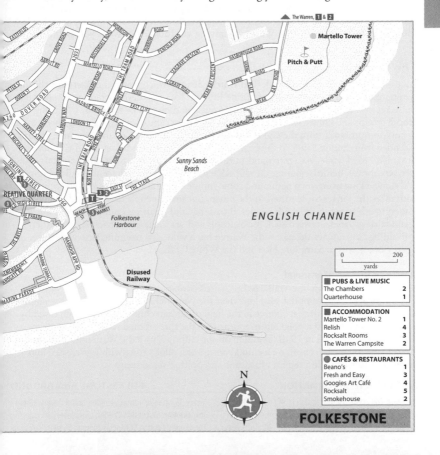

THE MARTELLO TOWERS

Built during the Napoleonic Wars, and based on a Corsican design that had thwarted British troops in 1794, Kent's clumpy Martello towers formed part of a chain of more than one hundred such defences that ran along the coastline from Sussex to Suffolk. Resembling giant – and malevolent – upturned flowerpots, around 30ft or 40ft high, with walls some 8ft thick on the landward side and 13ft thick seaward, the towers were designed to house more than twenty men in cramped quarters above the ground-floor arsenal and below the rooftop gun platform. The predicted French invasion never came, but the towers were handy for keeping an eye on local **smuggling**, and some served as observation decks during **World War II** before being left, as a rule, to rack and ruin.

Some forty or so towers survive in England, many of them listed, and are becoming desirable as property conversions; Folkestone boasts four of them. Walk along the clifftop to the Warren and you will first encounter **Martello No. 3**, which acquired its ugly rooftop accretion in World War II. You can climb the rickety external staircase to the entrance (well above ground level, to confound attackers) for a bird's-eye view of the town and the Strait. There's another tower, available to rent (see opposite) nearby, with more in Sandgate, Hythe and Dymchurch, in varying states of decay, and still more along the Sussex coast from Rye to Seaford.

celebrated every summer with a popular annual sandcastle competition, a cheery affair watched over by the *Folkestone Mermaid* (see box, p.121), and on fine weekends it can get packed. From here you can climb a zigzag staircase and walk along the East Cliff to the very different beach at the Warren, enjoying glorious sea views as you go.

The Warren

Accessible only on foot, fossil-bedecked **Warren Beach**, which fronts the **Warren**, a clifftop nature reserve and Site of Special Scientific Interest, feels wonderfully remote (though it's no secret in these parts, and when the tide is out you may well be joined by fossicking school groups and chilled-out families from the nearby campground). Getting there, a twenty-minute stroll from the end of Sunny Sands, is something of an adventure. Having ascended from Sunny Sands to the East Cliff clifftop, recent landslides mean you have to dip inland for a while, via a pitch-and-putt course, passing a Martello tower on your way (see box above), before rejoining the cliff-edge path. The gradual descent entails a bit of up and down along overgrown paths, and some minor scrambling over rocks – the official path takes the longer route round to the beach, but many people head down through the undergrowth to get to the sands sooner. Broad, flat and gleaming, punctuated by dilapidated groynes, seaweed-slick rocks, fossils and sea shells – and backed by a rather forbidding concrete sea defence – the Warren has a wild, raw magnificence, with huge, open views across to Samphire Hoe and the White Cliffs.

Battle of Britain Memorial

New Dover Rd, Capel le Ferne • Daily • Free • ☎ 01303 249292, ⓦ battleofbritainmemorial.org

The **Battle of Britain Memorial**, also known as the National Memorial to the Few – alluding to Churchill's comment that "Never in the field of human conflict was so much owed by so many to so few" – is a poignant monument to the three thousand Allied pilots who defeated the Luftwaffe in 1940. Standing on the clifftop above the Warren just off the B2011, the memorial centres on a chunky statue of a pilot sitting with legs crossed and gazing out to sea, while a replica Hurricane and Spitfire stand nearby.

ARRIVAL AND INFORMATION
FOLKESTONE AND AROUND

By train Folkestone Central station is off Cheriton Rd, just under a mile northwest of the Cultural Quarter.
Destinations Deal (every 20min–1hr; 30min); Dover (every 15–40min; 12min); London Bridge (every 30min–1hr; 1hr 40min); London Charing Cross (every 30min–1hr; 1hr 45min); London St Pancras (hourly; 55min); Ramsgate

(hourly; 50min); Sandwich (every 30min–1hr; 35min).
By bus National Express coaches from London Victoria (two direct services daily; 2hr 30min–3hr) stop at the bus station in the centre of town near Bouverie Place.

Tourist office 20 Bouverie Place Shopping Centre (Mon–Fri 9am–5pm; ☎ 01303 258594, ⊛ discoverfolkestone.co.uk).

ACCOMMODATION

Martello Tower No. 2 Martello Tower Drive, off Wear Bay Rd, CT19 6PX ☎ 01303 256729, ⊛ martellotower .co.uk. Accommodation doesn't get much quirkier than in this early nineteenth-century round tower (see box opposite), forbidding from outside but packed with atmosphere within. It sleeps six; the top-floor space, with its panoramic views, is a stunner. There's a mature garden, too. Rates drop considerably out of season. Closed Sept–Dec. Per night (2-night minimum): **£225**

Relish 4 Augusta Gardens, CT20 2RR ☎ 01303 850952, ⊛ hotelrelish.co.uk. An attractive Regency building next to the green Augusta Gardens and not far from the Leas, with ten quiet, comfortable boutique-style rooms (one single) and an outdoor terrace where you can eat your cooked breakfast. Little extras include complimentary home-made cake, juices and wine. **£95**

Rocksalt Rooms 1–3 Back St, CT19 6NN ☎ 01303 212070, ⊛ rocksaltfolkestone.co.uk. Four "boutique bolt holes" (they're small) in an unbeatable harbourside location above the *Smokehouse* restaurant, and brought to you by the *Rocksalt* crew. Those at the front are the best, with French windows and water views – those at the back can get stuffy – but they're all very chic and super-comfy, with scrubbed bare-brick walls, plump duvets, espresso-makers and tiny wet-rooms; a tasty continental breakfast is delivered to your room in a hamper. Seaside Sunday offers – £120 for room and a three-course *Rocksalt* Sunday lunch for two – are a bargain. **£85**

★ **The Warren Campsite** The Warren, CT19 6NQ ☎ 01303 255093 (no calls after 8pm), ⊛ campingand caravanningclub.co.uk. Eighty generally sheltered pitches in an unbeatable cliffside location by the Warren nature reserve and beach, walkable from both Folkestone and (at a push) Dover. The views are glorious, but watch out for the poor, pothole-scarred approach road. Non-members pay £7.10 extra per night. Closed Nov–Easter. **£11.70**

EATING AND DRINKING

Beano's 43 Tontine St, CT20 1JT ☎ 01303 211817. Chirpy little veggie restaurant in the Creative Quarter, which covers most bases – come for Mediterranean-inspired breakfasts, veggie sausage toasties or fancy sandwiches, or fill up on quinoa burgers, sweet potato curry, macaroni cheese and nut roasts. They also serve coffee and cake, and there's a courtyard garden for when the weather's good. Mains £5–7. Mon–Fri 8.30am–5.30pm, Sat 9am–5.30pm.

Fresh and Easy 17 Old High St, CT20 1RL ☎ 01303 489506. This lime-green, white and blonde-wood space is a Creative Quarter stalwart – a bright, contemporary spot serving sumptuous home-made French patisserie, croissants, quiches and savoury brioche sandwiches, along with good coffee, fresh-squeezed juices and indulgent hot chocolates (including a Mexican spiced blend and fondant-thick Spanish style). Tues–Fri 9am–6pm, Sat 9am–7pm, Sun 10am–3pm.

Googies Art Café 15 Rendezvous St, CT20 1EY ☎ 01303 246188, ⊛ googies.co.uk. Exhibiting inexpensive local art and hosting regular acoustic and indie gigs in the basement, bohemian *Googies* offers a cheery home-made menu that runs the gamut from American-style breakfasts and eggy brunches (from £7) via snacks and soups (from £3) to home-made burgers and Tex-Mex/Mediterranean mains (from £6). The coffee is good, too, making this a laidback haunt to linger with a newspaper or a laptop by the big picture windows. Mon–Thurs & Sun 10am–6pm, Fri & Sat 10am–11pm.

★ **Rocksalt** 4–5 Fishmarket, CT19 6AA ☎ 01303 212070, ⊛ rocksaltfolkestone.co.uk. A beautiful canti-levered glass-and-wood restaurant with an outdoor deck right on the harbour, a whelk's throw from the fishing boats, *Rocksalt* is a glorious setting for flawless food from Gordon Ramsay's former head chef. Fresh local fish is a winner, of course, from plump mussels via baked mackerel to succulent grilled bream, but the local meat (Romney Marsh lamb, Monkshill Farm pork) and veggie choices, with herbs and salad grown on their own farm, are delicious too. Prices (starters from £7, mains from £11) are reasonable, given the calibre, and the three-course Sunday lunch is great value at £25. The glamorous upstairs bar, with its own deck, is open during the day for coffee. Mon–Sat noon–3pm & 7–10.30pm, Sun noon–3pm.

Smokehouse 1–3 Back St, CT19 6NN ☎ 01303 884718, ⊛ thesmokehousefolkestone.co.uk. *Rocksalt's* sister restaurant, a modern, minimal, brick-and-glass affair on the harbour, serves fantastic fish and chips (from £6.50) to eat in or take away. Though portions are unceremoniously heaped in cardboard boxes, this is no run-of-the-mill chippie – along with cod and haddock, and all the usual accompaniments, you could go for Folkestone flounder, bream, scallops or skate cheeks, and there's always a catch of the day. The toughest choice is whether to have the fish healthily baked – deliciously juicy – or in *Smokehouse's* fabulous, crackly-crisp batter. Tues–Sun noon–4pm & 5–9pm.

3

NIGHTLIFE AND ENTERTAINMENT

The Chambers Radnor Chambers, Cheriton Place, CT20 2BB ☎01303 223333, ⓦpubfolkestone.co.uk. The location, in the shopping streets some way from the seafront, isn't inspiring, but this friendly, laidback basement café-bar is a popular spot for local ales and ciders, with good food (not Fri), and lively events including quizzes, DJ nights and live music, from bluegrass to Hot Chip. Mon–Thurs noon–11pm, Fri & Sat noon–1am.

Quarterhouse Tontine St, CT20 1JR ☎01303 858500, ⓦquarterhouse.co.uk. The anchor of the Creative Quarter, the Quarterhouse hosts a variety of relatively mainstream live music, comedy and theatre, along with festival events and film screenings, in a striking modern building.

Silver Screen Cinema Guildhall St, CT20 1DY ☎01303 221230, ⓦfolkestone.silverscreencinemas.co.uk. Dinky two-screen cinema in the old town hall, showing the latest mainstream and arthouse releases in an unselfconsciously retro setting. Tickets from £5.50; no cards.

Hythe and around

Just five miles south of Folkestone, at the northeastern edge of Romney Marsh, the ancient town of **HYTHE** was a Cinque Port (see box, p.105), and an important entry point for pilgrims crossing the Channel to visit Becket's tomb in Canterbury. Today it's an attractive little seaside town, the northern terminus of the **Romney, Hythe & Dymchurch Railway** (see box opposite), with a broad pebbly beach. During Hythe's heyday and before the silting up of the harbour, the High Street was at the sea's edge; today it lies north of the A259 and the Royal Military Canal, which runs prettily through town on its thirty-mile journey to Sussex. The beach here is good for **watersports**, especially windsurfing; contact the Hythe and Saltwood Sailing Club (HSSC; ☎01303 265178, ⓦHSSC.net) on the waterfront, or the sports-equipment store Activ, 145 Sandgate Rd in Folkestone (☎01303 240110, ⓦactivfolkestone.com).

The Royal Military Canal

ⓦroyalmilitarycanal.com

Fringed on both sides by tree-lined banks, the **Royal Military Canal** was built, like the Martello towers (see box, p.124) – of which Hythe has five – to defend the coast from potential attack from Napoleonic troops. Today it runs for nearly thirty miles from Seabrook, just east of town, through the marshes to a point south of Winchelsea in Sussex; you can walk or cycle its entire length. Cutting through town, the canal gives Hythe its distinctive character, its grassy banks dotted with sculptures and making a splendid place for a shady picnic. **Rowing boats** can be rented from next to Ladies' Walk Bridge (Easter–Sept; £10/hr; ☎07718 761236), and every other year in August the canal hosts a **Venetian Fete**, with assorted bigwigs, bands, schools and community groups taking part in a floating costume parade. Further out of town, the canal becomes increasingly peaceful, with swans gliding on the water, herons and kingfishers in the trees, and bright-yellow water lilies and irises in the shallows.

St Leonard's Church

Oak Walk, CT21 5DN • Ossuary May–Sept 10.30am–noon & 2.30–4pm • Free, charge for ossuary • ☎ 01303 262370,
Ⓦ stleonardschurchhythekent.org

The Norman church of **St Leonard's**, high on a hill on the north side of town, is a handsome building, with a soaring thirteenth-century chancel boasting some fine stone carving, but its main appeal is of a more eerie kind. Step into the ambulatory, where an **ossuary** confronts you with a startling pile of thousands of thigh bones and shelves of grinning jawbones and skulls, neatly packed as if on some ghoulish supermarket shelf. Dating back to medieval times and earlier, they're thought to be the remains of locals buried in the churchyard and moved when the church was expanded in the thirteenth century – some show signs of being descended from Roman settlers. Medieval church officials immediately saw the potential of such a gruesome tourist attraction, and charged pilgrims on their way to Becket's shrine in Canterbury for the privilege of a peep.

Port Lympne Wild Animal Park

3

Lympne, CT21 4LR • Daily: April–Oct 9.30am–6.30pm (last admission 3pm); Nov–March 9.30am–5pm (last admission 2.30pm); dusk safaris July & Aug Wed & Thurs • £19.95, children (3–15 years) £17.95; 20 percent discount if booked online; annual pass £23.95/£18.95; annual pass with Howletts (see p.62) £39.95/£29.95 • ☎ 0844 842 4647, Ⓦ aspinallfoundation.org/port-lympne

Set in around six hundred acres five miles west of Hythe, **Port Lympne Wild Animal Park**, along with Howletts near Canterbury (see p.62), works with the charitable Aspinall Foundation on a conservation and breeding programme for wild and endangered species. The park is home to more than six hundred animals, many of them rare – along with the lovable lemurs and baby gorillas, it has the largest herd of endangered black rhino outside Africa and is the only place in England that's home to rusty-spotted cats and brown hyenas. Port Lympne isn't a zoo, so you're not guaranteed a view of all the animals – and visits are safari-style, with bone-rattling trucks taking you past the hundred-acre "African Experience" (elephants, giraffes, zebras, rhinos), "Carnivore Territory" (big and rare cats, including Barbary lions, now extinct in the wild) and the ever-popular primate enclosure. The Serengeti it isn't – stop-offs are made at a number of cafés, with little time for photography, and the vision of exotic creatures, should you be lucky enough to see them, roaming through the gentle Kent countryside, with views over Romney Marsh to the Channel, is incongruous to say the least – but it's a commendable enterprise, and quite an adventure in this quiet corner of Kent, especially on a sunny day.

The best way to see the park can be outside opening hours: **dusk safaris** including dinner are available, while **accommodation** options range from overnight safaris (see p.128) and glamping to self-catering in a luxurious cottage that sleeps eight.

ROMNEY, HYTHE & DYMCHURCH RAILWAY

The **Romney, Hythe & Dymchurch Railway** (RH&DR; April–Oct daily; Nov–March Sat & Sun, plus special events and tours; £15 Hythe–Dungeness return, less for shorter journeys; ☎ 01797 362353, Ⓦ rhdr.org.uk), a fifteen-inch-gauge line running between Hythe and Dungeness, offers a hugely enjoyable way to travel through this quirky corner of Kent. Built in 1927 as a tourist attraction, its fleet of steam locomotives are mainly one-third-scale models made during the 1920s and 1930s – the hour-or-so-long, 13.5-mile ride (which also stops at Dymchurch, St Mary's Bay, New Romney and Romney Sands, named for the nearby holiday camp, near Greatstone Beach) may feel a little cramped, but if Laurel and Hardy – who reopened the line from New Romney to Dungeness after the war in 1947 – could do it, then anyone can. Hythe station is a 15min walk west of the town centre, on the south bank of the canal by Station Bridge, while the end of the line, in Dungeness, is near the Old Lighthouse (see p.130). New Romney, the original station, is the railway headquarters, with a children's playground and a model railway exhibition (£2).

Hythe Bay Seafood Restaurant Marine Parade, CT21 6AW ☎ 01303 233844, ⓦ hythebay.co.uk. With a nice setting on Hythe's seafront, this once-smart but now slightly tired dining room has a breezy front terrace. It's less upmarket than the newer branch, in Dover (see p.119), but the menu is largely the same, and the fish – simple, traditional dishes including lobster, mussels, grilled sole, fish pie – is good, especially if you choose the local catch. Starters from £6, mains from £12. Daily noon–9.30pm.

Livingstone Lodge Port Lympne Wild Animal Park, Lympne, CT21 4LR ☎ 01303 264647, ⓦ aspinallfoundation .org/short-breaks/livingstone-lodge or ⓦ aspinall founda tion.org/elephant-lodge/elephant-lodge. A safari in Kent may not be the most obvious of holidays, but this wildlife park offers fun overnight breaks (April to mid-Oct Wed–Sun), with game drives led by Zimbabwean rangers, and accommodation and meals in a luxurious tented lodge (some "tents" have four-poster beds; all have shared showers and toilet facilities) overlooking a watering hole. Meanwhile, the *Elephant Lodge* offers three-, four- or seven-night glamping in luxury tents, with evening walking tours and safaris available. Rates drop considerably out of season. Safaris (per person) from **£200**; *Elephant Lodge* (3 nights) **£771.43**

Romney Marsh

In Roman times, what is now the southernmost chunk of Kent was submerged beneath the English Channel. The lowering of sea levels in the Middle Ages, however, along with later reclamation, eventually created a hundred-square-mile area of shingle and marshland now known as **ROMNEY MARSH**. Once home to important Cinque and limb ports (see box, p.105), along with villages made wealthy from the wool trade, this now rather forlorn expanse, stretching inland for around ten miles from Hythe and skimming the eastern edges of the Weald before curving around to meet Rye in Sussex, is in fact made up of three marshes – Romney proper extends as far south as the road from Appledore to New Romney, Walland lies to the south and west, and Denge spreads east of Lydd. Together they present a melancholy aspect, much given over to agriculture and with few sights as such, unless you count the **sheep** (see box below), the birdlife and several curious medieval **churches** (see box opposite). While this flat, depopulated area makes grand walking and cycling country, its salt-speckled, big-skied beauty can also be appreciated on the **Romney, Hythe & Dymchurch Railway** (see box, p.127). The little train is in particular an excellent way to reach lonely **Dungeness**, the shingle promontory, presided over by two colossal nuclear power stations, that is so beloved of artists.

ROMNEY SHEEP

The salty, mineral-packed Romney marshes are famed among foodies for their indigenous breed of **sheep**, a hardy, independent and low-maintenance creature with a stout body and stubby legs. In addition to producing excellent meat, Romney sheep have heavy, dense and long-woolled fleeces; the local woolmaking industry, which started in medieval times, was hugely profitable, spinning off a flourishing smuggling trade that lasted into the nineteenth century. In the nineteenth century nearly a quarter of a million Romneys roamed this waterlogged landscape, and in 1872 the first of them were exported to Australia. Itinerant shepherds, or "**lookers**", followed the flocks as they wandered, shacking up in small brick huts (just a few of these shed-like structures remain today, identifiable by their rusty iron roofs and squat chimneys). There are fewer genuine Romneys around the marsh nowadays – you'd see more in New Zealand – and, as improved drainage has seen much of the land turned over to agriculture, many are bred on farms elsewhere. You may spot a few as you explore, however, foraging in the lush grasses and samphire.

Much **Romney lamb**, which is juicy, tender and sweet (not, surprisingly enough, salty), is exported to France, but it's also a regular on the menus of good Kent and Sussex restaurants, and you can buy it at some of the better farm shops. Vegetarians can enjoy the bounty of the marshes at **Romney Marsh Wools**, a sheep farm near Aldington, which sells luxurious Romney wool products including throws, moccasins and wool-fat soaps (ⓦ romneymarshwools.co.uk).

3

FIVE ROMNEY MARSH CHURCHES

The dozen or so medieval **churches** of the Romney marshes are atmospheric and often isolated places whose largely unrestored interiors provide evocative reminders of the days when the area thrived on the lucrative wool trade and wealth from its ports. The following are the pick of the bunch.

St Augustine's Brookland. Decidedly odd thirteenth-century church, with its conical wooden belfry standing beside it rather than on top of it. Inside, note the wall painting on the south wall, showing the murder of Thomas à Becket, and the unusual lead font marked with signs of the zodiac.

St Clement's Old Romney. Filmmaker Derek Jarman has his simple gravestone in the churchyard of this lovely Norman church. The restful whitewashed interior, with its Georgian minstrel gallery and rose-pink box pews, can be seen in the 1962 Disney movie *Dr Syn, Alias the Scarecrow*, which starred Patrick McGoohan of *The Prisoner* fame.

St Dunstan's Snargate. The terracotta wall painting of a ship (c.1500) on the north wall of this thirteenth-century church (complete with a leaning tower) is said to have been a secret signal to smugglers that this was a safe haven.

St Mary the Virgin St Mary in the Marsh. Author E. Nesbit is buried in the churchyard of this ancient church, parts of which date back to 1133. Her grave is marked by a simple wooden sign.

St Thomas à Becket Fairfield. The iconic Romney church, standing like a lonely sentinel upon the Walland Marsh, is all that survives of the lost village of Fairfield. Its largely Georgian interior, with herringbone floor and exposed beams, is beautifully tranquil.

Dymchurch and around

Five miles from Hythe, **Dymchurch** is torn between defining itself as a cheery family resort – the town sign welcomes you to "children's paradise" – and playing up its smuggling associations, particularly its location as a base for the marvellously named Dr Syn, the smuggling, swashbuckling vicar featured in the early twentieth-century novels of Russell Thorndike. There's little to actually see here, though the sandy beach, with its donkey rides and old-fashioned amusement park, is pleasant enough. There's another nice beach at **St Mary's Bay**, the next stop down on the Romney, Hythe & Dymchurch Railway; just a hop away is the hamlet of **St Mary in the Marsh**, a scrap of a place with a couple of literary associations – Noël Coward lived in a cottage next door to the *Star Inn* pub before moving to Aldington nearby, while his friend, Edith Nesbit, who also lived nearby, is buried in the twelfth-century churchyard (see box above). Once a busy Cinque Port at the mouth of the River Rother, **New Romney** lost its importance after a series of dramatic storms in the thirteenth century silted up its harbour and changed the course of the river, sending it out to the sea at Rye; today it's the hub of the RH&DR (see box, p.127), with an interesting Norman church whose western door is sunk beneath ground level.

Dungeness

An end-of-the-earth feel pervades **DUNGENESS**, the windlashed headland at the southern extremities of Romney Marsh. The largest expanse of shingle in Europe, presided over by two hulking nuclear power stations (one of them disused), "the Ness" is not conventionally pretty, but there's a strange beauty to this lost-in-time spot with its landmark lighthouses and its clanking miniature railway (see box, p.127). Many of the little cottages standing higgledy-piggledy on the golden shingle date back to when this entire area was owned by Southern Railway, and train workers converted old carriages into simple homes; today they're joined by high-concept architectural conversions, fishing boats both dilapidated and jaunty, forbidding watchtowers, rusting winches and decrepit concrete bunkers, with stubborn wildflowers, grasses and lichens clinging to the pebbles like splashes of bright paint. Many artists – most famously the late filmmaker Derek Jarman, whose **Prospect Cottage** continues to draw garden lovers and movie fans alike – have been inspired by the area's extraordinary light, its colossal skies and its quiet weirdness, setting up home in the ramshackle cottages and fashioning gardens from beachcombed treasures.

With its steep beach and fierce current, Dungeness Point is no place for a swim, although you can do so further north towards Lydd, if you take great care with the tides, and it's possible to fish from the beach. The headland has been designated a **National Nature Reserve** and Site of Special Scientific Interest, with no new development allowed. Its unique and fragile ecology supports a huge variety of vegetation, from wild red poppies and deep-pink sea peas to inky-blue sea kale, and animal life – including large populations of the endangered great crested newt – and it's renowned for superb **birdwatching**.

RSPB Dungeness Reserve

Off the Lydd road, three miles from Dungeness, TN29 9PN • Daily: reserve 9am–dusk; visitor centre March–Oct 10am–5pm; Nov–Feb 10am–4pm • £3; visitor centre free • ☏ 01797 320588, ⓦ rspb.org.uk/reserves/guide/d/Dungeness

The marshy Dungeness promontory, poking out vigorously into the Channel, attracts huge colonies of gulls and terns, as well as smew, wheatear and gadwall; you can see them, and all manner of water birds, waders and wildfowl, from the huge picture windows at the excellent **RSPB visitor centre** and from half a dozen hides in the reserve itself, accessible by three easy trails.

The Old Lighthouse

Next to the RH&DR station, Dungeness, TN29 9NB • May & June Thurs & Fri 10.30am–4pm; July to mid-Sept daily 10am–4.30pm; March, April & mid-Sept to Oct Sat & Sun 10.30am–4pm • £3.50 • ☏ 01797 321300, ⓦ dungenesslighthouse.com

Decommissioned since the erection in 1961 of its smaller successor nearby (the "New Lighthouse"), the 143ft-high **Old Lighthouse**, built in 1904 and painted the same velvety black as many of the beach cottages, displays navigational equipment and information panels on its four floors and affords sweeping views from the top. It's nearly two hundred steps up, with an extremely steep final stretch, and can be dramatically windy – vertigo sufferers should beware. The large, round structure next to the Old Lighthouse is the base of the oldest lighthouse of all, built in the eighteenth century and long since gone. It is now a private residence.

Prospect Cottage

Dungeness Rd, TN29 9NE • Roughly a 20min walk from the RH&DR station

The late **Derek Jarman** (1942–94), artist and avant-garde filmmaker, made his home at **Prospect Cottage**, a black weatherboard cottage with sunshine-yellow window frames, and the shingle garden he created in his final years from stones, rusty sea treasures and tough little plants remains a poignant memorial. The flowers may not bloom quite as brightly today, without Jarman's guiding hand, but the poetry of his vision lingers, not least on the side of the house, where a long quote from John Donne's poem *The Sunne Rising* is carved black on black.

As everywhere in Dungeness, there is no fence, and the current resident, Jarman's friend Keith Collins, is used to people nosing around – but do bear in mind that both the garden and the house are private.

ARRIVAL AND INFORMATION
ROMNEY MARSH

By train There's a mainline train station at Appledore, on the Ashford-to-Hastings line, while Dymchurch, St Mary's Bay, New Romney, Romney Sands and Dungeness are all on the miniature RH&DR (see box, p.127).
Romney Marsh Visitor Centre Dymchurch Rd, on the A259 between Dymchurch and New Romney (Easter–Sept Thurs–Tues 9am–5pm; Oct–Easter Fri–Mon 10am–4pm;

ⓦ wildlifetrusts.org/reserves/romney-marsh-visitor-centre). This ecofriendly centre is packed with information on the wildlife of the marsh, with marked trails and organic gardens.
Romney Marsh Countryside Project RMCP organize guided walks and cycles through the marshes, have lots of information on the Dungeness Nature Reserve, and sell handy self-guided walking maps (ⓦ rmcp.co.uk).

ACCOMMODATION, EATING AND DRINKING

Beach Sun Retreat 21 Sycamore Gardens, Dymchurch, TN29 0LA ☎07830 182380, ⓦbeachsunretreat.com. This self-catering house is perfect if you're sick of the British weather – its "sun room", complete with tropical mural, fake palms, DJ decks and gurgling waterfall, is bathed in replica natural sunlight. Though undeniably kitsch, it's more hip than tacky – on the ground floor of an old, timber-clad hotel, the property has a luxurious, airy feel with three opulent double bedrooms, a movie-screening room, and extensive grounds with access to Dymchurch's sandy beach. Some weekend stays available. Per week: **£1800**

★ **Red Lion** Snargate, TN29 9UQ ☎01797 344648. Take a trip back in time at this gem of a pub, which has been in the same family for a century and changed little since the 1940s. World War II memorabilia fills the place, Kentish cask ales and ciders are served at a cluttered marble bar, and they've even got a selection of vintage pub games. The little back garden, quiet but for the clucking chickens, is a delight, too. Daily; hours vary.

Romney Bay House Hotel Coast Rd, Littlestone, TN28 8QY ☎01797 364747, ⓦromneybayhousehotel.co.uk. Accessed down a private drive and presiding alone over the lonesome shingle like a haughty, fading *grande dame*, this 1920s beauty was built by Sir Clough Williams-Ellis, who also designed Portmeirion in Wales, for the Hollywood gossip columnist Hedda Hopper. Today it's a quirky hotel, with ten en-suite double/twins, some with sea views, a cosy drawing room, and a light-filled lounge overlooking the sea, which is just footsteps away. The restaurant (Tues, Wed, Fri & Sat) serves a locally sourced four-course set dinner for £45. No children under 14. **£130**

Royal Oak Brookland, TN29 9QR ☎01797 344215, ⓦroyaloakbrookland.co.uk. This tastefully modernized eighteenth-century tavern – in a sixteenth-century building – has more going for it than royal associations (it's run by the Countess of Wessex's brother). With its huge inglenook fireplace, it's a welcoming place for a drink, but it's the home-made food that really pulls the (well-heeled) crowds, with modern and traditional Brit dishes composed from locally sourced ingredients – potted Kent shrimps, plump Rye scallops, local pheasant, and of course, Romney lamb (mains from £13). They also offer five large, unfussy B&B rooms. Tues–Sat noon–3pm & 6–11pm, Sun noon–3pm; food

served Tues–Thurs noon–2pm & 6.30–9pm, Fri noon–2pm & 6.30–9.30pm, Sat noon–2.30pm & 6.30–9.30pm, Sun noon–2.30pm. **£80**

DUNGENESS

Britannia Inn Dungeness Rd, TN29 9ND ☎01797 321959, ⓦbritanniadungeness.co.uk. At Dungeness Point, right by the RH&DR station and squatting beneath two fluttering Union and St George's flags, this simple pub-restaurant serves Shepherd Neame ales and satisfying grub – fish and chips, sausage and mash, and very good meat pies. Takeaway available. Mon–Sat 11am–10pm, Sun noon–10pm; food served Mon–Sat noon–8.30pm, Sun noon–8pm.

Pilot Inn Battery Rd, TN29 9NJ ☎01797 320314, ⓦthepilot.uk.com. The convivial *Pilot*, just north of Dungeness lifeboat station, is the local favourite for fish and chips (from £8.25), with some fancier daily fish specials and pub grub also on offer. Richardson's, opposite, sells superb smoked and fresh fish. Mon–Sat 11am–10pm, Sun 11am–9pm; food served Mon–Thurs & Sun noon–8pm, Fri & Sat noon–9pm.

Shingle House Dungeness Beach, TN29 9NE ⓦliving-architecture.co.uk. A breathtaking modern self-catering house, offered by Alain de Botton's Living Architecture programme, blending in beautifully with its surroundings. Behind the tarry black timber exterior it's designed to the very last inch – all white tongue-and-groove, stained wood, warm concrete and vast glass walls opening out onto the shingle – and offers seriously luxurious accommodation for up to eight people. It books up very fast and very far in advance; three nights in low season will cost around a quarter of the weekly high-season rate. Per week in high season: **£2840**

★ **The Watch Tower** Dungeness Rd, TN29 9NF ☎01797 321773, ⓦwatchtowerdungeness.com. Originally a lookout post built in the Napoleonic Wars, this is a peaceful and very welcoming B&B on the northern edge of the Ness. A private guest entrance leads through the arty back garden, via your own light, plant-filled private conservatory – where a splendid breakfast is served – into the comfortable twin room with its cheerily Dungeness-themed bathroom. Thoughtful touches are everywhere – there's even an art studio that guests can use for free. **£70**

3

ACTION WATERSPORTS

The coast around Camber in Sussex is renowned for its watersports (see box, p.174); just six miles away in Lydd, **Action Watersports** (☎01797 321885, ⓦactionwatersports.co.uk) is a top-notch facility offering sheltered waterskiing (including high-adrenalin barefoot skiing), wakeboarding and jet-skiing on a purpose-built, 22-acre freshwater lake. Lessons and equipment hire are available, with packages from £23 for a 15min waterski or wakeboard session to a £230 jet-ski package. There's a huge pro shop and showers on site, along with a relaxation area and kids' playground.

The Kent Weald

OAST HOUSES, SISSINGHURST

The Kent Weald

The Kentish Weald, wedged between the North Downs and the High Weald of Sussex, is defined by its gentle hills and country lanes, shallow valleys and tangled broadleaf woodlands. It's a landscape at once quintessentially English, and, with its historic orchards and old brick oast houses – testament to the days when the Weald dominated England's hopping industry – has also come to symbolize Kent as a whole. The western Weald, in particular, is an easy journey from London, and the entire region, packed full of historic sites, royal estates, fairy-tale moated manor houses and some of England's loveliest gardens, makes splendid day-trip territory.

It's perfectly feasible to plan a longer break, too, basing yourself in or around any one of numerous villages – **Cranbrook**, say – or in Georgian **Tunbridge Wells**, by far the nicest of the Weald's large towns. Both sit in the beautiful **High Weald**, scattered with gorgeous little hamlets, with lots of country walking, peaceful places to stay and more gastropubs than you can shake a pint of real ale at. Some of England's finest **vineyards** are scattered around the east of the region, where the chalky soil yields dry whites and sparkling wines as good as any from France.

The commuter towns of Sevenoaks and Maidstone, on the fringes of the Weald, provide little of tourist interest, but are surrounded by a wealth of attractions. Big hitters include **Leeds Castle** and **Hever Castle** – Anne Boleyn's family home – Winston Churchill's estate at **Chartwell**, and the jaw-dropping treasure house of **Knole**, the childhood home of Vita Sackville-West, who went on to create the sublime gardens at **Sissinghurst**. Less known, but with big appeal, are the Roman villa at **Lullingstone**; the fascinating **Down House**, where Charles Darwin lived and worked for forty years; and the delightful Elizabethan manor and gardens at **Penshurst**, along with a host of smaller historic houses and gardens. The Kentish Weald is renowned for its **bluebells**, which carpet the woodlands with a shimmer of mauve each spring – you'll find stunning woods around Chartwell and Sissinghurst, as well as near **Ightham Mote**, a charming Tudor manor house, and at the Edwardian **Emmetts Garden**.

Much of the Weald is commuter territory, so public transport to the main towns is good, but you'll need to drive – or even better, walk or cycle – to explore the countryside in depth. Long-distance **walking routes** include the **Greensand Way** from Surrey, which runs through the Weald before ending at Hamstreet, on the border with Romney Marsh, and many shorter loops and trails link the area's heritage sights. The **North Downs**, easily accessed from the North Weald, offer excellent walking opportunities, with peaceful villages just a hop away from the busy Eurostar hub of **Ashford**.

Royal Tunbridge Wells

It seems unfair that **ROYAL TUNBRIDGE WELLS** is still associated, in many minds, with the fictional letter-writer known as "Disgusted of Tunbridge Wells", a curmudgeonly

Hopping mad p.137
Cycling the Tudor Trail p.141
The Hop Farm Music Festival p.143
The Kent & East Sussex Railway p.149

Shipbourne Farmers' Market p.152
Walks around Chartwell p.152
Castle Farm Hop Shop p.154

Highlights

❶ Sissinghurst Breathtaking garden created by Vita Sackville-West – who defined her planting style as "cram, cram, cram, every chink and cranny" – and her husband. **See p.146**

❷ Apicius Relaxed Michelin-starred dining in Cranbrook, one of Kent's prettiest small towns. **See p.148**

❸ Vineyard tours Learning about English viniculture, and tasting the excellent, award-winning wines, is a wonderful way to spend a sunny Kent afternoon. **See p.148 & p.149**

❹ Smallhythe Place Picture-postcard Tudor cottage, once home to the glamorous Victorian actress Ellen Terry. **See p.149**

❺ Knole This magnificent old estate, with its glorious grounds, is a classic English beauty gone slightly to seed, and all the more lovely for it. **See p.151**

❻ Chartwell Along with beautiful gardens and countryside walks, Winston Churchill's family home reveals the personal side of this gruff statesman. **See p.152**

❼ Hever Castle Gardens Laid out between 1904 and 1908 by Waldorf-Astor, these showpiece gardens include gorgeous Italianate statuary, rose gardens and trees planted in the time of Anne Boleyn, who spent her childhood here. **See p.155**

HIGHLIGHTS ARE MARKED ON THE MAP ON P.136

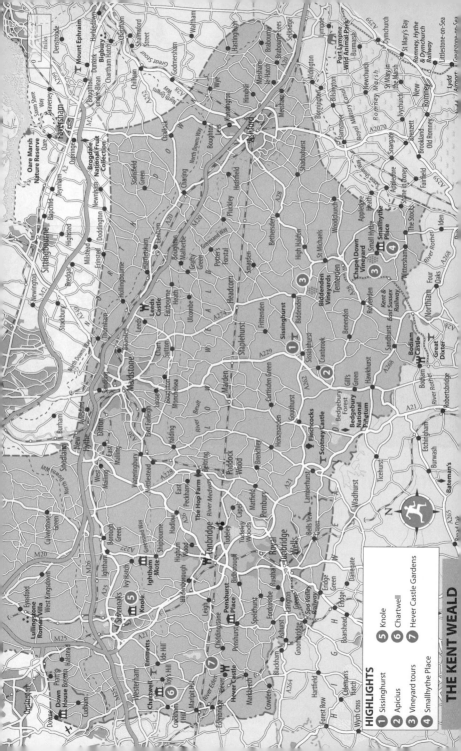

HIGHLIGHTS

1. Sissinghurst
2. Apicius
3. Vineyard tours
4. Smallhythe Place
5. Knole
6. Chartwell
7. Hever Castle Gardens

THE KENT WEALD

HOPPING MAD

Unlike their neighbours on the Continent, medieval Brits preferred their ale syrupy sweet, made with malt and flavoured with spices. Tastes changed in the fifteenth century, however, after Flemish merchants introduced them to beer made with **hops** – which, quite apart from their distinctive flavour, have strong preservative qualities. In 1520 the first hop garden opened, near Canterbury – the Kentish soil provided perfect growing conditions, and the local woodlands supplied essential poles, for training the vines, and charcoal, for drying the hops. Just as significant, however, was the wealth of medieval Kentish farmers, who could invest in new, labour-intensive and untried agricultural ventures. Almost immediately English beer was being exported to the Continent, much to the concern of the Dutch growers, and the industry boomed so dramatically that laws were passed preventing farmers rejecting all other forms of agriculture in favour of hop-growing. By the 1650s, hops were grown in fourteen English counties, with Kent producing one third of the total, and by the 1870s, around 72,000 acres, most of them in Kent, were devoted to the industry. The round **oast houses**, topped with their tiptilted white cowls, soon became as familiar a feature on the Wealden landscape as its woods and orchards.

The harvest required **casual labour** almost from the start. After the coming of the railway, thousands of "**hoppers**", generations of families and entire neighbourhoods, mainly from London's East End, were migrating to the fields of Kent for six weeks every autumn. Taking special "hopper trains", or piling into trucks and buses, joined by gypsy families in their caravans and itinerant workers chancing their luck, the hoppers originally lived in rough tents, but by the early twentieth century these had been upgraded to tiny "huts" – tin shacks, or stables. Some would bring bedding and curtains from home, covering unglazed windows and lining walls with newspapers; others would simply shack up in the straw, wrapping themselves in sacks. Everyone cooked and ate outside on faggot fires, sharing rudimentary washing and toilet facilities.

Days were strictly regulated, with hoppers working in teams or "drifts", tearing down the climbing vines ("bines"), stripping them of their cones, and filling their baskets as fast as they could. Pay was calculated per bushel, and often settled at the end of the season (by which time the rate had often plummeted); more skilled jobs, paid by the day, included that of the stiltmen, balanced on high stilts, who cared for the wires at the top of the wooden hop poles. **George Orwell**, who went hopping near Maidstone in 1931, stated that "as far as wages go, no worse employment exists" – and it was tiring, often painful, work, with hands ripped by prickly stems and covered in rashes from hop resin; but the chance to escape the cramped, polluted East End, the health benefits of fresh air, and the opportunity to meet up with old friends, seemed to override all that. Each farm effectively became its own community, with parties, dances and a Hop Queen crowned; temperance workers, the Salvation Army and the Red Cross would set up camp nearby to provide spiritual and medical care. In local villages, meanwhile, there was much mistrust of these rough Cockney incomers: shops battened down the hatches, and pubs, if they served them at all, consigned hoppers to special areas. Following mechanization in the 1950s the need for hoppers dwindled to almost nothing, and the majority of the oast houses that remain have been converted into private homes.

4

Little Englander renowned for whingeing and umbrage. Don't be misled – this handsome spa town, established after a bubbling spring was discovered here in 1606, and peaking during the Regency period, is actually rather appealing, surrounded by gorgeous High Weald countryside. There are a couple of low-key sights, but above all it's a nice place simply to stroll around, with a chichi Victorian **high street** leading down to the pedestrianized **Pantiles**, some excellent **restaurants** and pubs, and three urban parks: the **Grove** and, to the north, **Calverley Grounds** offer formal gardens, paths and splendid views, while the wilder **Common**, spreading out to the west, is laced with historic pathways.

The Pantiles

Tucked off the southernmost end of the High Street, the colonnaded **Pantiles** – named for the clay tiles, shaped in wooden pans, that paved the street in the

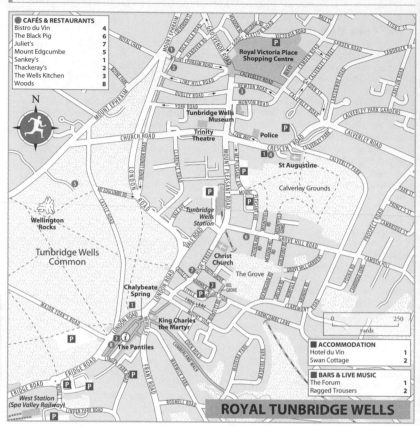

CAFÉS & RESTAURANTS
Bistro du Vin	4
The Black Pig	6
Juliet's	7
Mount Edgcumbe	5
Sankey's	1
Thackeray's	2
The Wells Kitchen	3
Woods	8

ACCOMMODATION
Hotel du Vin	1
Swan Cottage	2

BARS & LIVE MUSIC
The Forum	1
Ragged Trousers	2

ROYAL TUNBRIDGE WELLS

seventeenth century – is a pedestrianized parade of independent shops, delis and cafés that exudes a faded, almost raffish elegance. In Georgian times the fashionable set would gather here to promenade and take the waters, and it remains a lively stretch, especially in sunny weather, when the alfresco restaurant tables are buzzing with people-watching crowds. Hub of the Pantiles is the original **Chalybeate Spring**, in the 1804 Bath House. For 50p, a costumed "dipper" will serve you a cup of the ferrous waters (Easter–Sept daily 10am–5pm), a tradition that dates back to the eighteenth century.

Tunbridge Wells Museum

Mount Pleasant Rd, TN1 1JN • Mon–Sat 9.30am–5pm, Sun 10am–4pm • Free • ☎ 01892 554171, ⓦ tunbridgewellsmuseum.org

A Tardis of a place above the library, **Tunbridge Wells Museum** offers an intriguing mishmash of local history, its old glass cabinets filled with everything from fossils to dandy Georgian glad rags, fading maps and scruffy stuffed animals. With an offbeat section on local cricket-ball manufacture and a spooky cabinet of Victorian dolls, it's particularly worth a look for its exquisite collection of "Tunbridge Ware", the finely crafted wooden marquetry, dating from the late eighteenth century and popular until the 1920s, that was applied to everything from boxes to book covers to furniture, and created a wealth of Tunbridge Wells souvenirs.

King Charles the Martyr

Chapel Place, TN1 1YX • Mon–Sat 11am–3pm • Free • ⓦ kcmtw.org

The first permanent building in Tunbridge Wells, the Restoration church of **King Charles the Martyr** (1649) was the brainchild of Thomas Neale, the entrepreneur who, having built the Pantiles to exploit the tourist potential of the spring, went on to provide a place of worship and an assembly room for visitors. Behind the forbidding exterior lies a beautiful space. Its exquisite domed ceilings, their plasterwork emblazoned with flowers, grapes, cherubs and foliage, remain amazingly intact, while in the north gallery you can perch on the young Queen (then Princess) Victoria's very own pew. Other highlights include hand-written lists of early congregations, including Samuel Pepys, and, as you might expect from its name, a few pieces of memorabilia relating to Charles I.

ROYAL TUNBRIDGE WELLS

ARRIVAL AND DEPARTURE

By train The train station stands where the High St becomes Mount Pleasant Rd.

Destinations Hastings via Battle (every 30min–1hr; 40–50min); London Charing Cross (every 15–30min; 55min); London Bridge (every 15–30min; 45min); Sevenoaks (every 10–30min; 20–25min); Tonbridge (every 10–30min; 10–15min).

By bus Buses set down and pick up along the High St and Mount Pleasant Rd.

Destinations Brighton (every 30min–1hr; 1hr 40min); Edenbridge (Mon–Sat 2 daily; 50min); Hever (Mon–Sat 2 daily; 35–45min); Lewes (every 30min–1hr; 1hr 10min); London Victoria (1 daily; 1hr 40min); Sevenoaks (every 30min– 2hr; 40–50min); Tonbridge (every 20min–1hr; 20–30min).

INFORMATION AND TOURS

Tourist office The Old Fish Market, The Pantiles (Mon–Sat 9.30am–5pm, Sun 10am–3pm; Oct–Easter closed Sun; ☎ 01892 515675, ⓦ visittunbridgewells.com). Guided walking tours of the Pantiles and the Old High Street set off from here (March–Dec Thurs & Sat 11.30am; 1hr; £4).
Spa Valley Railway Based at West Station, a few

minutes' walk southwest of The Pantiles, this historic railroad, with steam and diesel locos, runs short trips via Groombridge to Eridge in Sussex, passing lovely Weald countryside (£10 return Tunbridge Wells–Eridge; ☎ 01892 537715, ⓦ spavalleyrailway.co.uk).

ACCOMMODATION

Forgewood Camping Sham Farm Rd, Danegate, TN3 9JD ☎ 0772 029 0229, ⓦ forgewoodcamping.co.uk. Yes, it's owned by the dad of Florence, of Florence and the Machine, but this tent-only site, set in hundreds of acres of ancient woodland just over the Sussex border five miles south of town, has far more going for it than celebrity connections. Relaxed, friendly and quiet, it has no defined pitches, but you get lots of space, campfires are allowed (with grills, logs – and marshmallows – available on site) and facilities include flushing toilets, showers and a café – all of which are portable, and pack up and move on over the winter. The surrounding Eridge Park Estate offers nice walks and there are regular bushcraft and art courses. Closed Nov–March. Camping (per adult) **£12.50**

★ **Hotel du Vin** Crescent Rd, TN1 2LY ☎ 01892 526455, ⓦ hotelduvin.com. Elegantly set in a Georgian mansion overlooking Calverley Grounds, this member of the *Hotel du Vin* chain is the best place to stay in town, mellow and quietly classy with a cosy bar and lounge and an atmospherically sloping old staircase leading up to the rooms. These are contemporary and comfortable,

with lovely bathrooms, espresso machines and fluffy robes – the best are at the back, with views of the lavender-filled grounds, the hotel vineyard and the park beyond. **£140**
Sunninglye Farm Bells Yew Green, TN3 9HF ☎ 01420 80804, ⓦ featherdown.co.uk. Four miles southeast of town, across the border on a hilltop copse in Sussex, this glampsite – one of the boutique Feather Down Farms chain – offers seven opulent tents (sleeping six), with beds, cooking stoves and flushing loos, on a family farm. The surroundings are bucolic, with a little nature-spotting area and a pond with rowing boats and materials for raft making, and campfires are permitted – you collect firewood yourself from the local woods. Camping (three nights in high season, per tent) **£465**
Swan Cottage 17 Warwick Rd, TN1 1YL ☎ 01892 525910. Artist-owned B&B in a handsome townhouse on a cobbled street near the High Street. The two rooms – an en-suite twin/double and a single with private bathroom – are spacious, quiet and tasteful, with fresh flowers and thoughtful extras including fresh fruit. In fine weather you can eat a delicious breakfast on the shady patio. **£95**

4

EATING AND DRINKING

Bistro du Vin Crescent Rd, TN1 2LY ☎01892 526455, ⓦhotelduvin.com. Romantic candlelit restaurant with a relaxed, French provincial elegance – wooden floors, sepia-tinted walls, cast-iron tables – and lots of tasteful wine memorabilia. The French classics, including steaks, chicken Dijon and lemon sole Meunière are done well, and the wine list, naturally, is superb. Mains from £13, with one- to three-course lunch menus at £9.95/£12.95/£14.95. Mon–Thurs noon–2pm & 7–10pm, Fri noon–2pm & 6–10.30pm, Sat 12.30–2.30pm & 6–10.30pm, Sun 12.30–2.30pm & 7–10pm.

The Black Pig 18 Grove Hill Rd, TN1 1RZ ☎01892 523030, ⓦtheblackpig.net. Pig out without guilt at this excellent gastropub, where locally sourced, free-range and organic dishes might include slow-roast pork belly, venison bresaola or pan-seared sea bass – or simply settle down with a cheese board or a "pigsty" selection (home-made Scotch egg, pork pie, ham terrine) and a glass of wine on the sunny terrace. Daily 11am–11pm; food served Mon–Fri noon–2.30pm & 7–10pm, Sat noon–10pm, Sun noon–9pm.

Juliet's 54 High St, TN1 1XF ☎01892 522931, ⓦjulietstunbridgewells.co.uk. A favourite High Street pit stop for yummy Tunny mummies, with pavement seating and a warm, brick-walled interior replete with splashy paintings and kitschy candlesticks. The home-made food includes all-day brunches, healthy colourful salads, Mediterranean dishes, good Italian coffee, tea and cakes, all served on cheery, mismatched crockery. Mains from £6. Tues–Sat 7am–6pm, Sun 9am–4pm.

★ **Mount Edgcumbe** The Common, TN4 8BX ☎01892 618854, ⓦmountedgcumbe.com. An offbeat place for a drink, a coffee or a bite to eat. Hidden away on the Common, it has a deliciously rural feel, with a garden and its own ancient cave to drink in. Mon–Wed 11am–11pm, Thurs–Sat 11am–11.30pm, Sun noon–10.30pm; food served Mon–Thurs noon–3pm & 6–9.30pm, Fri & Sat noon–9.30pm, Sun bar menu noon–8pm.

★ **Sankey's** 39 Mount Ephraim, TN4 8AA ☎01892 511422, ⓦsankeys.co.uk. Cosy brasserie and oyster bar serving top-notch seafood (Malaysian fish stew, fishcakes, dressed crab) from £9, along with fish and chips. You can

also get simple food – salads, burgers, *moules* – in the pub upstairs, decked out with enamel signs and brewery mirrors, with comfy chairs around an open fire, a sunny deck and large selection of (quite pricey) specialist beers. Restaurant: Tues–Sat noon–3pm & 6–10pm; pub: Mon–Wed & Sun noon–midnight, Thurs noon–1am, Fri & Sat noon–3am; food served Mon–Thurs noon–3pm & 6–8pm, Fri noon–3pm, Sat noon–5pm, Sun noon–4pm & 6–8pm.

Thackeray's 85 London Rd, TN1 1EA ☎01892 511921, ⓣthackerays-restaurant.co.uk. One-time home of the novelist, this weatherboard building offers fine Modern French dining in a smart, contemporary room. Richard Phillips creates dishes such as risotto of truffled sweetcorn, steamed crab and skate ballotine or roast sloe-encrusted venison from fresh market produce, with fine wines to match. Mains start at £22, and the seven-course tasting menu is £69, but various deals, including two- or three-course lunch menus (Tues–Sat; £16.95/£18.95), cut costs; there's also a daily vegetarian menu with mains at around £16.50. Tues–Sun noon–2.30pm & 6.30–10.30pm.

The Wells Kitchen 2–6 Newton Rd, TN1 1RU ☎01892 520342, ⓦthewellskitchen.co.uk. Lively local bar/restaurant serving good Modern European food, with lots of locally sourced meat and fish. Snack on the meze and charcuterie boards or gourmet burgers, or tuck into lamb and pearl barley summer broth, wild rabbit and salt beef terrine, or beetroot risotto, and wash it all down with a local ale. Mains from £10, plus two- and three-course menus (Mon–Fri noon–3pm £13.95/£15.95; Sun noon–7pm £13.95/£19.95). Mon–Wed & Sun noon–11pm, Thurs noon–midnight, Sat noon–2am; food served Mon–Wed noon–3pm & 5–9pm, Thurs & Fri noon–3pm & 5–9.30pm, Sat noon–9.30pm, Sun noon–7pm.

Woods 62 & 64 The Pantiles, TN2 5TN ☎01892 614411, ⓦwoodsrestaurant.co.uk. Probably the best thing about this large, airy bistro-bar – vaguely bohemian, slightly scruffy, and sometimes chaotic – is its location on The Pantiles. The simple food, from Kent rarebit to *moules*, is tasty enough; sit outside for prime people-watching. Starters from £5, mains from £9. Mon–Thurs & Sun 8am–6pm (kitchen closes 5pm), Fri & Sat 8am–midnight (kitchen closes 10pm).

NIGHTLIFE AND ENTERTAINMENT

The Forum Fonthill, The Common, TN4 8YU ☎08712 777101, ⓦtwforum.co.uk. Run by the same people as the *Ragged Trousers* pub, this 250-capacity music venue, right in the centre of town, pulls a young crowd for its lively programme of indie and up-and-coming bands.

Ragged Trousers 44 The Pantiles, TN2 5TN ☎01892 542715, ⓦraggedtrousers.co.uk. This popular, relaxed bar, in the eighteenth-century Assembly Rooms, sees a high-spirited crowd enjoying real ales and occasional live

music, with decent pub grub from £8. Daily noon–11pm; food served Mon–Wed noon–3pm & 6–8.30pm, Thurs & Fri noon–3pm, Sat noon–4pm, Sun 10am–4pm.

★ **Trinity Theatre** Church Rd, TN1 1JP ☎01892 678678, ⓦtrinitytheatre.net. You'll catch art movies, world cinema and cult classics in the excellent Trinity, which also stages quality rep theatre, dance and stand-up in an atmospherically converted church.

Around Royal Tunbridge Wells

Set in the High Weald, **Tunbridge Wells** is moments away from Sussex; the historic **Spa Valley Railway** (see p.139) chugs through lovely countryside from here to Eridge. This area is particularly good for **climbing**, with Nuts 4 Climbing in nearby Groombridge offering taster sessions and lessons (see p.193). To the north is the Elizabethan estate at **Penshurst**, with its glorious grounds, and **Tonbridge**, a quiet town long overshadowed by its upstart neighbour, where you can tour the gatehouse of the once-mighty medieval castle. The tiny hamlet of **Tudeley** nearby offers a surprise in its local church, while the big, brash **Hop Farm** can be worth a stop if you have kids in tow.

Penshurst Place

Penshurst, TN11 8DG • House April–Oct daily noon–4pm; mid-Feb to April Sat & Sun only; gardens April–Oct 10.30am–6pm (last entry 1hr before closing); mid-Feb to April Sat & Sun only; grounds all year • £9.80, grounds & gardens only £7.80; £1 discount if arriving by bike • ☎ 01892 870307, ⓦ penshurstplace.com • Bus #231 or #233 from Tunbridge Wells (Mon–Sat)

Tudor timber-framed houses and shops line the main street of **Penshurst**, set in countryside five miles northwest of Tunbridge Wells. Presiding over it all is **Penshurst Place**, a magnificent fourteenth-century manor house that has been home to the Sidney family since 1552 and was birthplace of Sir Philip Sidney, the Elizabethan soldier, poet and all-round Renaissance Man. The jaw-dropping **Barons Hall**, dating from 1341, is the glory of the interior, with its 60ft-high chestnut-beamed roof still in place; it's all the more stunning for being largely unadorned, with amazingly well preserved life-sized carved wooden figures – satirical representations of local peasants and manor workers – still supporting its vast arched braces. Elsewhere, the formal staterooms are packed with furniture and art, featuring important Elizabethan portraits, some fabulous tapestries and a fine room of armour with some savage-looking halberds; curiosities in the small **toy museum** include a painting on a cobweb and a Noah's Ark made from straw.

The 48 acres of grounds offer good parkland walks, while the eleven-acre walled **garden** is a beautiful example of Elizabethan garden design, with formal, yew-edged "rooms" ablaze with tulips, peonies, roses and lavender. There's also an adventure playground, and an excellent **farmers' market** on the first Saturday of the month (9.30am–noon).

Tonbridge and around

With its prime location and its good road and river connections, **TONBRIDGE** was for centuries far larger and more important than Tunbridge Wells. It's much quieter today – though Jane Austen's father was born here, and fans can pick up a self-guided walking-tour leaflet in the tourist office to follow in the family footsteps – and of chief interest for the mighty gatehouse of its medieval **castle**.

CYCLING THE TUDOR TRAIL

The 10-mile, mostly traffic-free **Tudor Trail**, which runs along Regional Cycle Route 12, allows you to combine a cycle ride with three of the Weald's most popular sights. Starting from **Tonbridge**, which has a train station (see p.143), the six-mile route west to **Penshurst Place** (see above) takes you along the Medway, through broadleaf woodlands, and past wildflower meadows and lakes. From Penshurst continue to **Hever Castle** (see p.155) along country lanes and peaceful bridleways, perhaps stopping off for a drink or meal at the pretty village of **Chiddingstone** (see p.155). It's just a mile to Hever train station, or three miles to Edenbridge station, from Hever Castle.

Tonbridge Castle

Castle St, TN9 1BG • Mon–Sat 9am–4pm, Sun 10.30am–4.30pm; last tour 1hr before closing • 1hr audio tours £7, children £4 • ☎ 01732 770929, ⓦ www.tonbridgecastle.org

A huge motte-and-bailey affair, later home to a large, self-sufficient feudal community, **Tonbridge Castle** was built in 1068 and heavily fortified over the following centuries. Controlling the bridge across the Medway, in a key position between London and the coastal ports, it remained effective as a fortress until the Civil War, using the most advanced design to repel attackers. Today, audio tours lead you around its impressively intact four-storey **gatehouse**, which in size and might is almost a castle in itself. Imparting lots of lively information on the castle's preparations for battle, it's all enjoyably interactive, with re-creations of thirteenth-century life including subterranean storerooms where disconcertingly life-like mannequins lurk in the half-light, and supper tables where rumbustious guards joke and banter. You might even come across the odd poor soldier taking a moment for himself in one of the gloomy privy chambers.

All Saints' Church

Tudeley Lane, Tudeley, TN11 0NZ • Summer Mon–Sat 9am–6pm, Sun noon–6pm; rest of year closes 4pm • Free • ⓦ tudeley.org/allsaintstudeley.htm

It would be easy to drive through **Tudeley**, a scrap of a hamlet on the outskirts of Tonbridge, were it not for **All Saints' Church**. In this simple stone-and-brick structure, peacefully overlooking fields at the edge of the village, you'll find an unexpected surprise: twelve stained-glass windows designed between the 1960s and 1980s by the Russian artist **Marc Chagall** (1887–1985). Commissioned to create a memorial window by the parents of a local woman who died young, Chagall was so taken with the spot that he decided to design the rest of the windows too. They are an extraordinary sight, set low in the walls and easy to approach – the artist's marks are clear to see, while the dreamy golds, turquoises, rose pinks and inky violets wash over each other to create folkloric, almost abstract ensembles of birds, animals and deft floral motifs. It's undeniably moving to see the artist's humanistic and spiritual vision on such a grand, close-up scale, especially when the sunbeams stream through and flood the church with washes of jewel-like colour.

Tudeley Woods RSPB Reserve

Between Tunbridge Wells and Tonbridge on the A21 • Free • ☎ 01273 775333, ⓦ rspb.org.uk

An invigorating mix of woods and heathland, **Tudeley Woods RSPB Reserve** is a haven not only for birds – lesser spotted woodpeckers, nightjars, woodlarks and willow tits among them – but also butterflies and woodland flowers, including bluebells and rare orchids. It's especially interesting during the autumn migration season, and a profusion of **fungi** – more than a thousand species at last count, including the endearingly named Puffballs, Deceivers, and Chickens of the Woods – sprouts along the woodland floor. You can follow three nature trails, between one and three miles in length.

Hop Farm Family Park

Maidstone Rd, Paddock Wood, TN12 6PY • Feb & March Sat & Sun 10am–5pm; April–Aug daily (except during Hop Farm Music Festival) 10am–5pm; last admission 4pm • £14.95, £11.95 online/advance, children £12.95/£10.35; family ticket from £44.95 • ☎ 01622 872068, ⓦ thehopfarm.co.uk • Arriva bus #6 runs to the farm from Tunbridge Wells, Tonbridge and Maidstone (Mon–Sat hourly)

Set in a quintessentially Kentish landscape of Victorian oast houses and fruit orchards, in the Low Weald six miles east of Tonbridge, the **Hop Farm Family Park**, once a thriving hop garden for the Whitbread brewery, has reworked itself into a sprawling family attraction. The attractions are variable, and most of it is relentlessly low-tech, but there's something to please most people.

For kids, the **Magic Factory** offers good, old-fashioned carnival fun with its optical illusions, holograms and oddities – watching yourself fade away into a spider's web never fails to entertain – while the **animal enclosures**, with their contented miniature

---

THE HOP FARM MUSIC FESTIVAL

Held over three days at the end of June and start of July, the **Hop Farm Music Festival** (ⓦhopfarmfestival.com) has grown from a one-day folk and indie event in 2008 to a big deal on the UK's summer festival circuit, with a refreshingly low-key, unpretentious vibe. There's a retro feel to this intimate event: headliners have included Bob Dylan, Neil Young and Prince, with others running the gamut from Bruce Forsyth and Tinie Tempah via Iggy and the Stooges to Patti Smith. There are plenty of up-and-comers and flavours of the month, too, plus acoustic and comedy stages and an indie disco tent.

---

horses, goats, pigs, llamas, sheep and ferrets, are charming. Don't miss the **Hop Story**, which, arranged across a set of old oast houses, uses film footage, mannequins, on-screen actors and written panels to tell the story of the "hoppers", the crowds of Londoners who would decamp to the farms of Kent every year to work on the harvest (see box, p.137). This version of events presents hopping as a kind of bucolic working holiday camp, a cheery Cockney knees-up migrated to the countryside – perhaps forgivably, as this was one of the best-equipped and -organized farms in Kent.

Regular fairs and trade shows are held at the farm – not least the **Hop Farm Music Festival** (see box above) – and events scheduled throughout the day, from **dray and tractor rides** to magic shows; pick up a timetable at the ticket office.

ARRIVAL AND INFORMATION

By train Tonbridge train station is a 10min walk to the castle along the High Street.
Destinations Ashford (every 30min; 35min); Canterbury West (Mon–Sat every 30min; 1hr 5min); Edenbridge (every 30min–1hr; 15min); Hastings (every 30min; 50min–1hr);

AROUND ROYAL TUNBRIDGE WELLS

London Bridge (every 10min; 30min–1hr); London Charing Cross (every 10min; 50min); Penshurst (every 20min–1hr; 8min); Tunbridge Wells (every 10–20min; 10–15min).
Tourist office Castle grounds, Castle St, Tonbridge (Mon–Sat 9am–5pm, Sun 10am–4pm; ☎01732 770929).

EATING AND DRINKING

The Dovecote Alders Rd, Capel, TN12 6SU ☎01892 835966. Two miles southeast of Tudeley, this is definitively not a gastropub – just a quiet, friendly country pub with real ales, a nice beer garden and kids' play area. It's usually buzzing with a cheery, laidback local crowd. Tues–Sun noon–11pm.
Fir House Tearoom Penshurst, TN11 8DB ☎01892 870382. A quaint Tudor tearoom, right outside Penshurst Place and once part of the estate, with a flower-filled cottage garden and a cosy open fire in winter, serving home-made cakes, afternoon teas and high teas, along with soups and light snacks. April–Oct: Tues–Sun 2.30–6pm.
George and Dragon Speldhurst Hill, Speldhurst, TN3 0NN ☎01892 863125, ⓦspeldhurst.com. Though service can be slow, and some dishes disappoint, when the food is good it is very good indeed at this upmarket gastropub, converted from a medieval inn in a tiny village three miles southeast of Penshurst. The menu focuses on local, seasonal, organic ingredients – mains such as seared scallops with sea purslane or Gressingham duck confit start at £12, but there are cheaper options, like steak sandwiches, from £8. Once you've eaten, pop into St Mary's Church across the road to see the Pre-Raphaelite Burne-Jones windows. Daily noon–11pm; food served Mon–Fri noon–2.30pm & 7–9.30pm, Sat noon–2.30pm & 6.30–9.30pm, Sun noon–3.30pm.

The Hare Langton Rd, Langton Green, TN3 0JA ☎01892 862419, ⓦbrunningandprice.co.uk/hare. A couple of miles west of Tunbridge Wells, the family- and dog-friendly *Hare* offers good food in upmarket country pub surroundings, with a nice garden out back. The lovely high-ceilinged bar offers a huge range of single malts, while in the quirky dining room you can eat the occasional exotic treat – Moroccan lamb, apricot and feta salad; bouillabaisse; aubergine, chickpea and squash tagine – along with gastropub favourites. Mains from £10. Mon–Thurs noon–11pm, Fri & Sat noon–midnight, Sun noon–10.30pm; food served Mon–Thurs noon–9.30pm, Fri & Sat noon–10pm, Sun noon–9pm.
★ **The Spotted Dog** Smarts Hill, Penshurst, TN11 8EP ☎01892 870253, ⓦspotteddogpub.co.uk. With its charming, old spotty dog sign, flower-bedecked weather-board exterior and wonky tiled roof, this looks like the perfect country pub. Inside is just as attractive (if you ignore the background music), a fifteenth-century burrow of sloping floors, low, beamed ceilings and open fires, and a back garden with uninterrupted views down over the Weald. Local and guest ales are on offer, and the menu runs the gamut from home-made houmous to Thai green curry. The trad English favourites – ham hock, venison sausages,

game casserole – are the winners, using locally sourced, seasonal and home-grown produce (starters from £5, mains from £10). Mon 11.30am–3pm, Tues–Sat 11.30am–11pm, Sun noon–9pm; food served Mon noon–2.30pm, Tues–Fri noon–2.30pm & 6–9pm, Sat 11.30am–11pm, Sun noon–9pm.

Kent's eastern High Weald

As you head further east into Kent's High Weald from Tunbridge Wells, things get sleepier. This is the domain of one-street villages and tidy market towns; the largest, like **Cranbrook** or **Tenterden** – their quaint, well-heeled high streets lined with antiques shops and upmarket restaurants – feel positively metropolitan compared with the rural hamlets hereabouts. Star attractions include the ravishing gardens at **Sissinghurst**, the award-winning vineyard at **Chapel Down**, and **Bedgebury forest**, with its excellent cycling and walking opportunities, but you should seek out some quirkier destinations, too – Victorian actress Ellen Terry's Tudor cottage at **Smallhythe**, the idyllic **Scotney Castle** gardens and the delightful **Finchcocks Musical Museum** among them.

Goudhurst and around

Surrounded by orchards, woods and hop fields, and offering uninterrupted views across the Weald, the hamlet of **GOUDHURST** has just one main street, its array of weatherboard, half-timbered and tile-hung buildings tumbling down from a sturdy ragstone church towards a tranquil duck pond. With some good places to eat and stay nearby, it's a handy base for a stay in this part of Kent.

Finchcocks Musical Museum

Two miles west of Goudhurst , TN17 1HH • April–July & Sept Sun & bank hols 2–6pm; Aug Wed, Thurs, Sun & bank hols 2–6pm; gardens from 12.30pm • £11, gardens only £3 • ☎ 01580 211702, ⓦ finchcocks.co.uk

A lofty Georgian manor house set in sweeping parkland makes the perfect setting for the unusual **Finchcocks Musical Museum**, a collection of one hundred or so period keyboard instruments, including clavichords, organs and exquisite handpainted eighteenth-century pianos – around half of which still work – along with barrel organs, musical boxes and antique music stands. It's a must for pianists and music lovers, with regular informal **recitals** – if you fancy a play yourself, simply ask at the entrance – but the friendly enthusiasm of the team, and the sheer beauty of the craftsmanship, can't fail but enchant even the most tone-deaf of visitors. A café serves light lunches and home-made cakes.

Bedgebury National Pinetum and Forest

Bedgebury Rd, Goudhurst, TN17 2SJ • Daily: Jan & Dec 8am–4pm, Feb & Nov 8am–5pm; March & Oct 8am–6pm; April & Sept 8am–7pm; May–Aug 8am–8pm • Free, parking £8.50 • ☎ 01580 879820, ⓦ forestry.gov.uk/bedgebury

A glorious two thousand-acre spread of broadleaf woodland and **conifers** – there are more here than anywhere in the world, including rare and endangered species – the Forestry Commission-owned **Bedgebury National Pinetum and Forest** is brilliantly set up for outdoor activities, whether you fancy a woodland stroll and a lakeside picnic, a scoot with the kids around tree-dappled play areas, a vigorous hike, or a high-adrenalin zip-line adventure at the adjoining **Go Ape** treetop park (ⓦgoape.co.uk). It's very popular with **cyclists** – National Cycle Route 18 runs through on its way between Goudhurst and Cranbrook, and there are good off-road **mountain-bike trails** for all abilities, with bike rental and showers on site. Stunning in spring when carpeted with drifts of bluebells, and a lovely place to spot wildlife, from goldcrests to wild boar, Bedgebury looks even more dramatic when sparkling with frost in winter.

Scotney Castle

Lamberhurst, TN3 8JN • Mid-Feb to Oct Wed–Sun 11am–4pm; Nov & Dec Sat & Sun 11am–2pm • House & garden £12.60, garden only £8.10; NT • ☎ 01892 893820, ⓦ nationaltrust.org.uk/scotney-castle

Ruined **Scotney Castle**, a moated fourteenth-century manor house set in 750 gorgeous acres, presents a breathtakingly romantic vision, particularly in spring when wisteria and old roses tangle across the honey-coloured sandstone, and the informal **gardens** blaze with enormous clouds of rhododendrons and azaleas. The gardens are the main attraction, but you can also visit the mock-Tudor **"new house"**, an architecturally important Victorian pile, inherited by Christopher Hussey, architectural writer and editor of *Country Life* magazine, and inhabited until 2006 by his wife, Betty. Rooms have been set up to look as they did when the Husseys lived here – complete with house cat padding around – and you can even take a rest on one of the beds in the Bamboo Room. The estate itself is impressive, with three designated **trails** (30–45min) taking in bluebell woods, a working hop farm and rolling parkland.

ACCOMMODATION AND EATING
GOUDHURST AND AROUND

Chequers Inn The Broadway, Lamberhurst, TN3 8DB ☎ 01892 890 260, ⓦ thechequersinnlamberhurst .co.uk. Nothing fancy at this fifteenth-century coaching house near Scotney Castle: just five clean, comfy B&B rooms above a decent pub and restaurant (rack of lamb, sea trout and the like, from £12) with a riverside garden and an open fire for chilly nights. Jane Austen stayed here, or so they say, which explains the room names. **£90**

★ **Goudhurst Inn** Cranbrook Rd, Goudhurst, TN17 1DX ☎ 01580 212605, ⓦ thegoudhurstinn.com. A gussied-up country pub offering locally sourced gastro grub, lovely Downs views from the garden, and a family- and dog-friendly vibe. Changing menus (mains £12–25) feature British classics with a modern twist – slow-cooked local rabbit with roasted garlic and vanilla creamed potatoes; open ravioli of wild mushrooms – and a cheaper lunchtime menu (wild boar sausages, Welsh rarebit, pies) from £5. There are two- or three-course menus (£19.95/£24.95), and a kids' menu at £6.75. Mon 9am–10.30pm, Tues–Thurs 9am–11.30pm, Fri & Sat 9am–midnight, Sun 11am–10.30pm; food served Mon noon–2.30pm, Tues–Sat noon–2.30pm & 6.30–9.30pm, Sun noon–4pm.

Green Cross Inn Station Rd, Goudhurst, TN17 1HA ☎ 01580 211200, ⓦ greencrossinn.co.uk. Though you wouldn't guess it from the outside, this ordinary little red-brick pub serves delicious fish and seafood – dressed crabs and fresh oysters, lobster spaghetti, *cataplana* (a hearty mussel and chorizo stew), fish pie – which you can eat in the bar with its crackling open fire. Mains from £10. Mon–Sat noon–3pm & 6–10pm, Sun noon–3pm.

★ **Halfway House** Horsmonden Rd, Brenchley, TN12 7AX ☎ 01892 722526, ⓦ thehalfwayhousepub.co.uk. Lovely old pub about five miles southeast of Goudhurst, popular with walkers for its warm welcome, families for its huge garden and play area, and beer lovers for its real ale selection – at least ten at any time, with local cider, too. Crammed with old farm implements and dried hops, the interior is deliciously rustic, if a little hokey, and they serve simple, filling pub grub from around £7. Daily noon–11.30pm; food served Mon–Sat noon–2.30pm & 6–9pm, Sun noon–3pm.

★ **Three Chimneys Farm** Goudhurst, TN17 2RA ☎ 01580 212175, ⓦ threechimneysfarm.co.uk. Hidden in rolling countryside south of Goudhurst, and within walking distance of Bedgebury, this large working farm, once a hop farm, offers two peaceful en-suite B&B rooms in an old oast house, with tennis, badminton and woodland walks, plus lots of friendly horses to bond with on the grounds. Self-catering also available. B&B **£68**, self-catering (per week) **£575**

Cranbrook and around

Kent's smallest town, **CRANBROOK** (ⓦ cranbrook.org), was at the heart of the Weald's thriving medieval cloth industry, and home to a group of Victorian painters, the Cranbrook Colony, who enjoyed a brief spurt of popularity with wealthy London art collectors for their romanticized renditions of English country life. Today the place has the nostalgic and well-heeled air of a Sunday evening BBC TV drama: Stone Street, along with the busy little high street, offer a Wealden hotchpotch of medieval, Tudor and Georgian buildings, and lots of spruce, white weatherboard weavers' cottages, all watched over by the handsome 1814 **Union Windmill**, still grinding corn today (Easter to mid-July & Sept Sat 2.30–5pm; mid-July to Aug Sat & Sun 2.30–5pm; free;

ⓦunionmill.org.uk). With excellent places to eat in town and nearby, it's an ideal base for the fabulous Sissinghurst gardens.

Sissinghurst

Biddenden Rd, off the A262, two miles northeast of Cranbrook, TN17 2AB • **Estate** dawn–dusk; **gardens** mid-March to Oct Fri–Tues 10.30am–5.30pm; last admission 45min before closing; timed tickets may be issued during busy summer periods • £10.40; NT • ☎01580 710700, ⓦnationaltrust.org.uk/sissinghurst

When she and her husband, Sir Harold Nicolson, took it over in 1930, **Vita Sackville-West** described **Sissinghurst** as "a garden crying out for rescue". Over the following thirty years they transformed the neglected five-acre plot into one of England's greatest and most popular country gardens, a romantic and breathtaking display that continues to inspire gardeners today. Spread over the site of an Elizabethan estate, which generations of neglect had left in a dismal condition (only parts of the old house remain), the gardens were designed to evoke the history not only of the ruined site itself, but also of Vita's and Harold's beloved Kent – a heartfelt endeavour that was to absorb them for the rest of their days: the anchor at the heart of their unconventional and open marriage.

The garden is in fact a set of gardens, each occupying different "rooms" within Tudor walls; the classic lines of the design are beautifully offset by the luxuriance of the planting, the flowers and foliage allowed to spill over onto the narrow pathways. Perhaps most famous is the **rose garden**, stunning in late June and early July, when it's at its lush, overblown richest, and the fragrance, described by Vita as reminiscent of "those dusky mysterious hours in an Oriental storehouse", is heavy in the air. The exquisite abundance of tumbling old roses is set off by Japanese anemones, peonies, alliums and irises, among others, and vines, figs and clematis creep over the crumbling brick walls. The **cottage garden**, meanwhile, blazes in shades of orange, yellow and red – a fiery "sunset" scheme at its finest in late summer and autumn. Sissinghurst has two areas that feel entirely unique: the **nuttery**, a heartbreakingly lovely glade of gnarled old Kentish cobnuts above a carpet of woodland flowers, and the magical **White Garden**, with its pale blooms and silvery grey-green foliage.

Focal point of the estate is the tall, brick Tudor **tower** that Vita restored and used as her quarters. You can climb 78 steep wooden stairs to the top, from where you get a bird's-eye view of the gardens, the estate and the ancient surrounding woodlands; halfway up, peep through the iron grille into Vita's **writing room**, which feels intensely personal still, with faded rugs on the floor and a photo of her lover, Virginia Woolf, on her desk. There are a number of **trails** in the woods around Sissinghurst; pick up a guide at reception or online.

ARRIVAL AND DEPARTURE CRANBROOK AND AROUND

By bus Local buses stop on the High St near Stone St. Destinations Ashford (4 daily Mon–Sat; 1hr 12min); Tenterden (7 daily Mon–Sat, 2 on Sun; 25min); Tunbridge Wells (7 daily Mon–Sat, 2 on Sun; 1hr).

ACCOMMODATION

★ **Church Gates** Stone St, Cranbrook, TN17 3HA ☎01580 713521, ⓦchurchgates.com. With a lively location at the heart of Cranbrook, this lovely B&B sits in a creaky sixteenth-century manor house above an upmarket boutique. The two rooms are beamed and a little bohemian, with vibrant colours and wooden floors; best is the double overlooking the churchyard at the back, with its funky bathroom. The owners lead local garden tours. **£65**

★ **Hallwood Farm** Hawkhurst Rd, Cranbrook, TN17 2SP ☎01580 712416, ⓦhallwoodfarm.co.uk. Two

spacious and very pretty B&B rooms – rustic beams, fresh flowers, your own fridge, large bathrooms – in an oast house conversion surrounded by 200 acres of farmland, bluebell woods, blackcurrant fields and apple orchards. You can sample their produce at the huge farmhouse breakfasts. No children. Closed Dec & Jan. Minimum stay two nights. **£100**

Sissinghurst Castle Farmhouse Sissinghurst, TN17 2AB ☎01580 720992, ⓦsissinghurstcastlefarmhouse .com. Stunningly located on the estate, less than 100m from

the gardens, Sissinghurst's Victorian farmhouse building – a huge, spacious affair, rich in old wood – offers seven luxurious, comfortable and tasteful B&B rooms. You can wander around their own pretty gardens, or curl up in the comfy living room, where the placid old house dog may well join you. **£150**
Waters End Iden Green, Cranbrook, TN17 4LA ☎ 01580

850731, ⓦ watersendfarm.co.uk. The open Weald views are amazing from this tranquil 43-acre estate, with waddling ducks and kingfishers darting around the lakes – where you can swim in summer. Elegantly converted barns hold five airy, light en-suite B&B doubles, two of which are very luxurious; all are comfortable, clean and tasteful. **£95**

EATING AND DRINKING

⭐ **Apicius** 23 Stone St, Cranbrook, TN17 3HF ☎ 01580 714666, ⓦ restaurant-apicius.co.uk. This relaxed little place in the centre of Cranbrook has a well-deserved Michelin star, but they don't make too much fuss about it – the welcome is friendly, the ambience easy, and the focus on the food. Prices are astonishingly good value, with two or three courses costing £26 or £30 at lunch, £33/£38 at dinner – the complex flavours and perfect combinations make it almost impossible to resist having three courses. Typical dishes might include celeriac and truffle velouté with foie gras tortellini and baby spinach, or rump of Romney Marsh lamb with sweet and sour onions. Wed–Fri noon–2pm & 7–9pm, Sat 7–9pm, Sun noon–2pm.

⭐ **Black Pig** Moor Hill, Hawkhurst, TN18 4PF ☎ 01580 752306, ⓦ theblackpigathawkhurst.co.uk. Local ales, local wine and local food at this bustling country pub, offering simple mains (from £12) such as pan-fried pork loin or leg of lamb, along with meat, fish or veggie platters to share (from £15), and doorstep sandwiches and smaller dishes, with good veggie options, at lunchtime. There's a sweet garden too. Reservations recommended at

weekends. Daily noon–11.30pm; food served noon–2.30pm & 6.30–9pm.

The Bull The Street, Benenden, TN17 4DE ☎ 01580 240054, ⓦ thebullatbenenden.co.uk. Though it can get hectic, especially during the Sunday lunch carvery, this is a popular rustic pub in a charming hamlet. They serve excellent home-made pub grub – pies, fish and chips, ploughman's and juicy burgers – from £8, plus a handful of Modern European mains (from £12) and local ales, ciders and perries. Daily noon–midnight; food served Mon–Sat noon–2.15pm & 6.30–9.15pm, Sun 12.15–3pm.

The Great House Gill's Green, Hawkhurst, TN18 5EJ ☎ 01580 753119, ⓦ elitepubs.com/the_greathouse. Modern European food served in a smart, sixteenth-century weatherboard pub with a cosy but contemporary interior, a sunny terrace and pretty garden. The regularly changing menu lists such treats as goat's cheese pannacotta, pea and broad bean risotto or venison Wellington, with mains from £12, or lunchtime dishes from £5. Daily 11.30am–11pm; food served Mon–Fri noon–3pm & 6–9.45pm, Sat & Sun noon–9.30pm.

Tenterden and around

The well-to-do little town of **TENTERDEN** (ⓘ tenterdentown.co.uk) – once a major weaving centre and a limb port (see box, p.105) for Rye on the River Rother, but now lodged ten miles inland on the borders of the High Weald – is a handsome place. Its broad, tree-shaded high street, fringed with bow-windowed weatherboard and tile-hung buildings, and bustling with upmarket boutiques, tearooms and antiques shops, is good for a wander before hopping on a **steam train** to Bodiam, and the surrounding area is bursting with relaxing, picturesque places to stay. The south-facing, chalky slopes around here, very similar to those in the Champagne region of France, make perfect conditions for grape-growing – you can stock up on award-winning wines at **Chapel Down** and **Biddenden**.

Biddenden vineyards

Gribble Bridge Lane, Biddenden, TN27 8DF • Mon–Sat 10am–5pm, Sun 11am–5pm (closed Sun in Jan & Feb) • Free; occasional free guided tours • ☎ 01580 291726, ⓦ biddendenvineyards.com

Spread across 23 acres on a gentle, sheltered south-facing slope, five miles northwest of Tenterden and just outside the half-timbered village of Biddenden, the family-owned **Biddenden vineyards** have been established here since 1969. With an endless scroll of awards, they set the bar high for England's wine-making efforts, growing eleven varieties – mostly German, including Ortega, Schönburger, Huxelrebe and Dornfelder – from which they produce single-variety white, red and sparkling wines, plus rosés, ciders and juices. The crispy, fruity Ortega is particularly fine; it's worth trying the smoky, aperitif-style, Special Reserve cider, too. The vineyards are free to visit – either

---

THE KENT & EAST SUSSEX RAILWAY

From Tenterden you can take a nostalgic train excursion on the **Kent & East Sussex Railway** (April–Sept, with some special services at other times, up to 5 services daily in Aug, fewer days in other months; unlimited all-day travel £15, children £10; ☏ 01580 765155, ⓦ kesr.org.uk), a network of vintage steam and diesel trains that trundle their way 10.5 miles to the medieval Bodiam Castle in Sussex (see p.190). Following the contours of the land, the fifty-minute trip is a scenic, up-and-down affair, passing through the Rother Valley and the marshy, sheep-speckled Rother Levels; stops include Rolvenden (two miles from the village of the same name) – where buffs can take a look at the old loco yard – and Northiam (a mile from the village) near Great Dixter (see p.189).

---

wander along two **trails**, finishing with free **tastings** in the farm shop, or book one of the occasional free tours. These peak during harvest time, but might also focus on other important events in the vineyard's calendar.

Chapel Down vineyards

Small Hythe, Tenterden, TN30 7NG • Guided tours & tastings June–Sept 3 daily; May & Oct 3 daily Sat & Sun, call to reserve; shop daily 10am–5pm • Tours £9 • ☏ 01580 763033, ⓦ chapeldown.com

Chapel Down, established in 1977, is a multi-award-winning winemaker, growing eight varieties – chiefly Bacchus, Chardonnay, Pinot Blanc, Pinot Noir and the complex Rondo, as well as the Siegerrebe, which goes to make Chapel Down Nectar, their delicious and non-syrupy dessert wine. The country's biggest producer of English wine, using grapes grown here and around the country, they supply Jamie Oliver and Gordon Ramsay, among others, and have recently branched out into brewing lager, too, using the same Champagne yeast as in their sparkling wines to create a zingy, refreshing and award-winning brew. The enjoyable **tours** are brisk and informative, following the wine-making process from vine to bottle and outlining the traditional methods used to create sparkling wines. A tutored **tasting** at the end gives you generous glugs of around seven or eight wines – and with no compunction to spit them out. You can buy bottles (and taste more) at the shop, or order yourself a glass or two at the on-site **restaurant** (see p.150).

Smallhythe Place

Small Hythe, Tenterden, TN30 7NG • March–Oct Mon–Wed, Sat & Sun 11am–5pm; last admission 4.30pm • £6.60; NT • 01580 762334, ⓦ nationaltrust.org.uk/smallhythe-place

An unfeasibly picturesque early sixteenth-century cottage, all beams, time-worn wood and warped mullioned windows, the rambling-rose-tangled **Smallhythe Place** is particularly interesting for having been home to the unconventional, charismatic actress **Ellen Terry** (1847–1928). The house was opened to the public after Terry's death by her daughter, Edith Craig, and thus it remains, packed with her belongings and all manner of theatrical memorabilia. (Edith was herself a fascinating character: theatre director, actress, costume designer and suffragette, she lived in a lesbian ménage à trois – the "three trouts", near-neighbour Vita Sackville-West called them – in a house on the grounds for thirty years until her death in 1947. But that's another story.)

Wandering through this crooked little dwelling, with its wonky floors and creaking staircases, is like following a treasure trail. Display cases are crammed with mementoes, relics, letters and **costumes**, the walls cluttered with theatrical posters and illustrations. It's a dynamic and intimate exhibit, shedding light on the woman who, born into a family of travelling players, became a child actor and model, married three times, had two illegitimate children, lit up the stage with her naturalistic performances and became the toast of the theatrical, literary and artistic world.

Don't leave without a stroll around the **garden**: plays are staged in the rustic, thatched seventeenth-century **barn**, opened by Edith in 1929, and the informal **tearoom**, with tables beside the reed-fringed pond, is a treat.

4

ACCOMMODATION

Bloomsburys Sissinghurst Rd, Biddenden, TN27 8DQ ☎ 01580 292992, ⓦ bloomsburysbiddenden.com. Friendly, not over-manicured glamping in tipis, yurts, and an en-suite Airstream caravan in the grounds of an artsy garden centre. Good home-made food is served in the pretty flower-filled café, and there's a farm shop/deli on site, along with rather luxurious showers and hot tubs, plus massage, yoga and various therapies on offer. They even host occasional (low-key) acoustic live gigs. You can cook on a fire pit or barbecue, but rates for one-night stays include breakfast. For two: tipis **£145**, yurts and Airstream **£195**

Brook Farm Brook St, Woodchurch, TN26 3SR ☎ 01233 860444, ⓦ brookfarmbandb.co.uk. This seventeenth-century farmhouse, set in five acres three miles east of Tenterden, offers spacious and friendly B&B in a smartly converted barn. The three en-suite rooms are comfortable, un-chintzy and feature lots of warm oak – all have great views, and the largely organic breakfast, taken in the farmhouse, is something special. There's a heated outdoor swimming pool and pond. No under-12s. **£90**

Little Dane Court 1 Ashford Rd, Tenterden, TN30 6AB ☎ 01580 763389, ⓦ littledanecourt.co.uk. Though this fifteenth-century house near the centre of Tenterden offers comfortable, bright, oak-beamed B&B rooms, it's the Japanese-themed cottage in the back garden, complete with futon, Shoji window screens and Japanese DVDs, that gives it the edge. The East-meets-medieval Kent combo can feel a little incongruous, but it's different, and nicely done – you could even order a Japanese-style breakfast, and eat it in the sunny courtyard garden. Doubles **£80**, cottage **£130**

★ **The Oast in Wittersham** The Street, Wittersham, TN30 7EA ☎ 01797 270181, ⓦ theoastinwittersham .co.uk. Gorgeous B&B in a converted oast house at the eastern end of the High Weald. The three romantic rooms are beamed, bright and inviting, kitted out with luxurious extras including mini bottles of wine, and with beautiful bathrooms. The suites, in the roundels, are brilliant value at just £100–120; one has a copper bath and the other a balcony. After breakfast, for which many ingredients are grown right here, you can wander the peaceful gardens and drink in the uninterrupted views – in spring you can even help feed the lambs. **£80**

EATING AND DRINKING

The Lemon Tree 29–33 High St, Tenterden, TN30 6BJ ☎ 01580 763381, ⓦ lemontreetenterden.co.uk. This traditional tearoom/restaurant, in a fourteenth-century timber-framed building, is great for afternoon tea, with home-made cakes and scones, crumpets and teacakes, but also offers cooked breakfasts and old-school comfort food, including pan-fried liver, pies, and sausage and chips (mains £7–9), with lots of local ingredients. Mon–Sat 9am–5pm, Sun 10am–5pm.

Nutmeg Deli 3 Sayers Lane, Tenterden, TN30 6BW ☎ 01580 764125. You'll get the best espresso in town at this snug, buzzing little deli, tucked away on a pedestrianized lane off the north side of the High Street. There are also cakes, healthy organic sandwiches (£4.50), savoury tarts with salad (£7.50) and gluten-free dishes, along with local cheeses and deli goods. With just three tables, and limited counter seating, you may have to wait. Mon–Sat 9am–5pm, Sun 10am–4pm.

The Swan at Chapel Down Small Hythe Rd, Tenterden, TN30 7NG ☎ 01580 761616, ⓦ loveswan.co.uk/chapel down. It's a great place to try Chapel Down wines, of course, but this smart vineyard restaurant is worth a trip on its own account, with a light, flavoursome Modern British menu assembled from locally sourced ingredients. Come for lunch, when you can sit on the terrace overlooking the vineyards, feasting on the likes of lemon sole in a caper and tomato dressing or open ravioli of artichoke, aubergine and broad beans – luckily, the deliciousness overrides the piped muzak. Starters from £8, mains from £10; weekday lunch menu £14.95/£16.95 (two/three courses). Mon–Wed &

Sun 10am–5pm, Thurs–Sat 10am–11pm.

Three Chimneys Hareplain Rd, Biddenden, TN27 8LW ☎ 01580 291472, ⓦ thethreechimneys.co.uk. Dating from 1420, this shabby-chic free house – blistered plaster and exposed bricks, dried hops tumbling over wonky beams – is a nice place to stop for a pint of real ale. The locally sourced food is mainly very good; mains can get pricey (£14–20), but chalkboard menus list smaller dishes (£6.50–8). Try the smoked mackerel salad with pancetta and horseradish dressing, or baked mushrooms with caramelized onion and goat's cheese, and eat in the pub (candlelit in the evening), in the restaurant, in a light-bathed conservatory, or on the terrace. Mon–Fri 11am–3pm & 5.30–11pm, Sat 11am–4pm & 5.30–11pm, Sun noon–4pm & 6–10.30pm; food served Mon–Thurs noon–2pm & 6.30–9pm, Fri noon–2pm & 6.30–9.30pm, Sat noon–2.30pm & 6.30–9.30pm, Sun noon–2.30pm & 6.30–9pm.

West House 28 High St, Biddenden, TN27 8AH ☎ 01580 291341, ⓦ thewesthouserestaurant.co.uk. Michelin-starred Nouvelle British dining in a beamed fifteenth-century cottage. Befitting the warm, rustic atmosphere, flavours are umami-packed and gutsy, with lots of meaty fish, pork, foie gras and game, and though the set up is simple, the compositions are complex and innovative, with intense combinations – try the lamb rasher with egg, salsa verde and anchovy. Two-/three-course menus £25/£35 (£40 on Sun) at lunch; £35/£40 at dinner; five-course tasting menu £50. Tues–Fri noon–1.45pm & 7–9.30pm, Sat 7–9.30pm, Sun noon–2.30pm.

Sevenoaks and around

Set among the greensand ridges of west Kent, 28 miles from London, **SEVENOAKS** is a thriving, well-heeled commuter town. Dating back to Saxon times, and with several historic buildings, mostly from the seventeenth and eighteenth centuries, it is not an unattractive place; its real appeal for visitors, though, is as a jumping-off point for the immense baronial estate of **Knole**, which is entered just off the High Street. Other day-trip attractions nearby include the mosaics at **Lullingstone Roman Villa**, Winston Churchill's home at **Chartwell**, and the ravishing Elizabethan estate of **Ightham Mote**.

Knole

Entered from the south end of Sevenoaks High St, TN15 0RP • **House** Mid-March to Oct Wed–Sun noon–4pm **Orangery/Visitor Centre** Mid- to end March & Oct Wed–Sun 10.30am–5pm; April–Sept Tues–Sun 10.30am–5pm; Nov & Dec Wed–Sun 11am–4pm **Garden** April–Sept Tues 11am–4pm **Park** Daily dawn–dusk • £10.40 house, garden, Orangery & park; £5 garden only; park free; NT • ☎ 01732 462100, Ⓦ nationaltrust.org.uk/knole

Covering a whopping four acres and designed to echo the calendar – with 365 rooms, 52 staircases, twelve entrances and seven courtyards – **Knole** is an astonishingly handsome ensemble, with an endlessly fascinating history. Built in 1456 as a residence for the archbishops of Canterbury, it was appropriated in 1538 by Henry VIII, who lavished further expense on it and hunted in its thousand acres of **parkland**, still home to several hundred wild deer. Elizabeth I passed the estate on to her Lord Treasurer, Thomas Sackville, who remodelled the house in Renaissance style in 1605; it has remained in the family's hands ever since.

The house is given extra dash from being the childhood home of Bloomsbury Group writer and gardener **Vita Sackville-West**, whose bohemian tendencies, by all accounts, ran in the family; one of the great sadnesses of her life was the fact that as a girl, despite being an only child, she was not able to inherit the house she loved with an "atavistic passion". She wrote about it often, and in great detail in her loosely autobiographical novel, *The Edwardians* (see p.323); her one-time lover, Virginia Woolf, made it a fairy-tale castle in her novel *Orlando*, a flight-of-fancy love letter to West herself.

The house

Quite apart from the building itself, which, unusually for an English country estate, largely retains its Jacobean appearance, Knole is famed for its enormous collection of **Stuart furniture**. Much of this was acquired at the end of the seventeenth century, by Charles Sackville, Royal Chamberlain to William III, whose "perquisites" – or "perks" – of the job meant he could keep any unwanted royal furniture. Only a dozen or so rooms can be viewed; many of them, and their contents, are slowly fading or deteriorating, and can feel dim, chilly and a little damp, but this only adds to the air of decaying grandeur.

Beyond the **Great Hall**, it's in the showpiece **Great Staircase** that Knole's wow factor really kicks in: a Renaissance Revival delight with dashes of Rococo, it's alive with decoration and flamboyant murals. Upstairs, long galleries and apartments are packed with Jacobean portraits, eighteenth-century pictures of Tudor notables, Renaissance sculpture and fine old furniture. A small **Museum Room** includes some of the rarest and most fragile pieces. Other highlights include the **Spangled Bedroom**, with its amazing bed, draped in a crimson silk canopy stitched with once-glittering sequins; the **King's Room**, gleaming with silver furniture and gold brocade; and, perhaps most evocative of all, the lustrous **Venetian Ambassador's Room**. This eighteenth-century beauty – described by Woolf in *Orlando* as shining "like a shell that has lain at the bottom of the sea for centuries" – boasts another staggering carved and gilded bed, once belonging to James II; it, and its hangings of sea-green, blue and gold velvet, are literally crumbling away due to a poor restoration job in the 1960s.

4

> **SHIPBOURNE FARMERS' MARKET**
>
> A couple of miles south of Ightham, **Shipbourne Farmers' Market** is consistently rated as one of the best in England, with excellent local produce, a very friendly, sociable vibe, and a real focus on the community. Held every Thursday from 9am to 11am, in and around St Giles' Church, on Stumble Hill, it has some twenty stalls piled high with the freshest local fruit, veg, meat, cheese and bread; profits go to agricultural charities in the UK and in Africa.

Ightham Mote

Mote Rd, Ivy Hatch, TN15 0NT • Feb to mid-March garden Sat & Sun 11am–3pm; mid-March to mid-June, Sept & Oct house Mon & Thurs–Sun 11am–5pm, garden opens 10.30am; mid-June to Aug Mon & Wed–Sun house 11am–5pm, garden opens 10.30am; Nov house & garden Thurs–Sun 11am–3pm; estate daily dawn–dusk • £10.40; NT • ☎ 01732 810378, ⓦ nationaltrust.org.uk/ightham-mote

Hidden in a pretty wooded valley around seven miles east of Sevenoaks, **Ightham Mote** – when you eventually find it – is a magical sight, a fourteenth-century, half-timbered beauty sitting on its own moated island, fringed with a soft stone wall spilling over with colourful wild flowers. There's plenty to see in its twenty-plus rooms, though as it has been much adapted over the centuries by its various owners, from Tudor courtiers to a wealthy American businessman, it is a bit of a mishmash. Every room is different, from the medieval Great Hall to the Victorian servants' quarters to the 1930s Oriel Room, where you can settle down on the sofa and listen to the old wireless; for anyone interested in architecture, or conservation, it's a treat. Highlights include the fifteenth-century **chapel**, with its stunning mid-sixteenth-century painted oak ceiling, and the **drawing room**, dominated by an elaborate Jacobean fireplace and lined with exquisite hand-painted eighteenth-century Chinese wallpaper. The **gardens** offer pretty walks in summer, with an ancient orchard, while the 500-acre estate, waymarked with trails, includes natural springs and bluebell woods to explore.

Chartwell

Mapleton Rd, Westerham, TN16 1PS • **House** Mid-March to June, Sept & Oct Wed–Sun 11am–5pm; July & Aug Tues–Sun 11am–5pm; timed tickets every 15min **Studio** daily: March–Dec noon–4pm **Garden & exhibition** daily: March–Oct 10am–5pm; Nov & Dec 10.30am–4pm • £11.50; garden, studio & exhibition only £5.80 in summer, £4.40 in winter; NT • ☎ 01732 868381, ⓦ nationaltrust.org.uk/chartwell

Packed with the wartime Prime Minister's possessions – including his rather contemplative paintings – there is something touchingly intimate about **Chartwell**, the country residence of **Winston Churchill** from 1924 until his death in 1965. Churchill bought the house in 1922, bowled over by the expansive Weald views; his wife Clementine always had her doubts, however, fearing it would be too expensive to maintain. Indeed, Chartwell had to be put on the market in 1946, when it was bought by a consortium of the Churchills' supporters; the family then had the right to live there until they died, after which it was left to the nation.

Built on the site of a sixteenth-century dwelling, the house was extended greatly in the eighteenth and nineteenth centuries; the imposing 1920s exterior dates from Churchill's era. Filled with fresh flowers and personal effects, Chartwell is set up to

> **WALKS AROUND CHARTWELL**
>
> Chartwell makes a good starting point for a couple of appealing waymarked **walks**; pick up guide sheets from the visitor centre. The shortest option starts at the car park, leading you on a figure of eight through the **woodland** surrounding the estate. Allow forty minutes, and be prepared for a couple of steep stretches; the views are superb. If you have more time (about three hours round-trip), you can walk from Chartwell's main entrance gate to the National Trust garden of **Emmetts** (see opposite), a five-mile loop that passes through a lovely stretch of mature woods.

look largely as it would have in the 1920s and 1930s, revealing the personal side of this gruff statesman – and Clementine's superb eye for design. A Monet hangs in the light-filled **drawing room**, with its colour scheme of soft primrose, lavender and rose, while the **dining room** features fashionable custom-designed Heals furniture. Cabinets of **memorabilia** include a medal given to Lady Churchill by Josef Stalin for her charitable work during World War II, Churchill's 1953 Nobel Prize for Literature, and a Wanted poster offering £25 for his capture, dead or alive, following his escape in 1899 from a Boer POW camp. His flamboyant side is not forgotten, not least in his jaunty velvet **"siren suit"** – a self-designed boiler suit to be pulled on over pyjamas in the event of an Air Raid. An **exhibition** at the end – open when the house is closed – includes a sweet series of notes between him and Clementine, and an illuminating letter from his father written when he was a young man, expressing his fears that he was to become "a social wastrel" and a "public school failure".

Chartwell's delightful rolling **grounds**, bobbing with flowers, dotted with lakes and ponds and shaded by mature fruit trees, are perfect for a picnic. Take a stroll around the romantic English cottage garden filled with old English roses, and look out for three small stones by a path – these are the **graves** of Churchill's beloved brown poodles, and his cat, Jock.

The studio
Churchill defined himself as a have-a-go artist, and admitted to painting to combat the "black dog" – he coined the term – of his depression. His **studio**, lined ceiling to floor with more than one hundred canvases and including his easel, brushes and palette, reveals him to be an enthusiastic and not untalented painter; the works are of varying quality, however, and some of the best can be seen in the house itself. Of these, standouts include an effervescent black-and-white 1955 portrait of Clementine at the launch of HMS *Indomitable* in 1940, and a rather lovely, delicate *Magnolia* (1930).

Emmetts Garden
Ide Hill, around 5 miles from Sevenoaks, TN14 6BA • Mid-March to Oct Mon–Wed, Sat & Sun 10am–5pm • £6.20; NT • ☎ 01732 868381, Ⓦ nationaltrust.org.uk/emmetts-garden

Kent's ancient woodlands hold a good share of England's **bluebell woods**, and some of the very best are to be seen at the Edwardian **Emmetts Garden**. Sitting at the top of the Weald, one of the highest points in Kent – and with wonderful views over the grasslands of the North Downs – the five-acre garden is fringed with woodland whose slopes are carpeted with a violet haze in springtime. In the formal garden itself you can see some surprisingly exotic plantings, many from the Far East, along with a rose garden and rock garden, and there's plenty of space to stroll on hillside paths or picnic in the meadows.

Lullingstone Roman Villa
Lullingstone Lane, Eynsford, DA4 0JA • April–Sept daily 10am–6pm; Oct daily 10am–4pm; Nov–March Sat & Sun 10am–4pm • £6; EH • ☎ 01322 863467, Ⓦ english-heritage.org.uk/daysout/properties/lullingstone-roman-villa

The remains of **Lullingstone Roman Villa**, excavated in the 1950s and protected in a purpose-built building by a trickle of the River Darent, reveal much about how the Romans lived in Britain. Peacefully located in a rural spot, Lullingstone was typical of many houses in this area – indeed, the Darent Valley had the highest density of Roman villas in the country. Believed to have started as a farm around 100 AD, it grew to become a large estate, home to eminent Romans (including, it is thought, Pertinax, governor of Britain in 185–6 and, for just three months, emperor) and was occupied until the fifth century.

CASTLE FARM HOP SHOP

The **Castle Farm Hop Shop** (Mon–Sat 9am–5pm, Sun 10am–5pm; ☎01959 523219, ⓦhopshop.co.uk) sits between the villages of Eynsford and Shoreham, a couple of miles south of Lullingstone. It sells seasonal produce grown or raised right here, including beef, apples, pumpkins, apple juice, hop plants and honey, along with local sausages, ham and deli goodies, but the biggest draw is the lavender products – not only fresh and dried flowers, soaps and essential oils but also teas, jams, chutneys and biscuits, and culinary oils. The farm is particularly lovely in June and July, when the lavender fields (more than eighty acres of them) fill the air with scent, and you can tour their distillery or sign up for an aromatherapy massage; from mid-September to mid-October you can pick your own apples, pears and cobnuts.

The site is known for its brilliantly preserved Roman **mosaics**, but excavations also unearthed rare evidence of early **Christian** practices – the so-called **Orantes paintings**, showing six large standing figures with their hands raised, and the Chi-Rho, an early Christian symbol. These unique finds are now held by the British Museum, but you can see reproductions here, along with replicas of fine marble **busts** found on the site.

The first-floor balcony is the best place from which to view the **mosaic floor** which depicts Bellerophon riding Pegasus and slaying the Chimera, a fire-breathing she-beast, but displays throughout give lively glimpses into Roman domestic life – from decorated glass gaming counters to impossibly delicate bone needles and stunning bronze jewellery, with recipes for such dishes as mussels with lentils and peppered sweet cake revealing the Romans to have eaten very well indeed. Clay slabs marked with the imprints of paws, hooves or the maker's fingerprints have a poignant immediacy, as do a couple of **human skeletons** – one of a young man in a lead coffin decorated with scallops, the other of a tiny baby, one of four found at the villa.

Down House

Luxted Rd, Downe, ten miles northwest of Sevenoaks, BR6 7JT • April–June, Sept & Oct Wed–Sun & bank hols 11am–5pm; July & Aug daily 11am–5pm; Nov–March Sat & Sun 10am–4pm • £9.90, children £5.90; EH • ☎01689 859119, ⓦenglish-heritage.org.uk/daysout/properties/home-of-charles-darwin-down-house

Down House, where Charles Darwin lived and worked most of his life, is a treat, revealing a wealth of snippets about an extraordinary man and an extraordinary age. Darwin moved here from London in 1842 with his wife Emma and their first two children (they went on to have eight more), and remained until his death in 1882. This unremarkable family home – an "oldish, ugly" Georgian house, according to Darwin – provided sanctuary from the social demands of the capital, and was itself a living laboratory. All the family were involved in his work – his children would collect and label specimens from the garden, help look after his pigeons and map the flight path of local bees – as were his butler, the governess and even the local vicar.

Exhibition rooms offer an overview of Darwin's life and times, including a replica of his tiny cabin on the HMS **Beagle**, the ship that housed him on the five-year voyage that he called "by far the most important event in my life". The scrawled **list** of his father's objections to his *Beagle* trip – including it being a "wild scheme" and "disreputable to my character" – is just one of many lists on display. Darwin was an inveterate list-maker; they make fascinating reading, exposing a thoughtful, meticulous and somewhat anxious individual. Downstairs, domestic rooms reveal a comfortable, well-worn upper-class Victorian family home, filled with pictures, mementoes and memorabilia, but above all dominated by Darwin's work. In the **drawing room**, for example, look beyond the bourgeois trappings and you'll see a terracotta jar on Emma's beloved piano. This would have been filled with earthworms, as part of an experiment to see if they could hear or sense music. Darwin's cluttered **study** perhaps tells us most. In the centre sits his battered old horsehair armchair and writing board; in the corner, a screened-off privy. Darwin suffered from regular vomiting, painful wind, dizzy spells and headaches, along with eczema and skin complaints. Some have attributed his symptoms to Chagas disease, caught after being bitten by a bloodsucking South American bug during his *Beagle* journey; others believe that his illness was aggravated by stress.

Don't miss the **garden** – Darwin's outdoor laboratory, where he could observe the natural world in situ, as well as cultivate plants for investigation. A gate opens onto the **Sandwalk**, the path through the meadows that he followed three times a day without fail on what he called his "thinking walks".

Hever Castle

Hever, near Edenbridge, TN8 7NG • April–Oct daily noon–6pm; Nov & Dec Wed–Sun 11am–4pm; last entry 1hr before closing; gardens open 10.30am • £14, gardens only £12 • ☏ 01732 865224, ☒ hevercastle.co.uk

A fortified manor house surrounded by a rectangular moat, **Hever Castle,** built in the thirteenth century, was the childhood home of Anne Boleyn, second wife of Henry VIII, and where Anne of Cleves, Henry's fourth wife, lived after their divorce. In 1903, having fallen into disrepair, it was bought by William Waldorf-Astor, American millionaire-owner of *The Observer*, who had it assiduously restored, panelling the rooms with elaborate reproductions of Tudor woodcarvings. Surprisingly small, Hever has an intimate feel, and perhaps tells you more about the tastes and lifestyle of American plutocrats than Tudor nobles. Some original artworks and features are on display, however, along with pieces belonging to other owners, including Elizabethan portraits and a rare Jacobite sword, carved with verse claiming loyalty to Bonnie Prince Charlie.

Anne Boleyn's room is the most affecting, small and bare other than a huge wooden chest carved with the words "Anne Bullen" and a hulking piece of dark wood from her childhood bed. Next door you can see the book of prayers she carried with her to the executioner's block, inscribed in her own writing and with references to the Pope crossed out. Perhaps even more interesting than the house are the magnificent grounds. Star of the show is Waldorf-Astor's exquisite **Italian Garden**, decorated with statuary, some more than two thousand years old, but there's also a traditional yew hedge maze, an adventure playground and a splashy water maze, along with ponds and weeping-willow-shaded lakes with rowing boats for hire – you could even try your hand at archery.

Chiddingstone

Some nine miles south of Sevenoaks, **Chiddingstone**, surrounded by soft rolling hills, ancient woodlands, and hedge-tangled country lanes, is ridiculously picturesque. "Village" is too grand a name for this tiny place; the one street comprises just a handful of half-timbered Tudor gems and sixteenth- and seventeenth-century buildings, including **St Mary's Church**, a general store (former residence of Thomas Bullen, Anne Boleyn's father), a pub and a school, all owned by the National Trust. Things were not always so quiet; by the early sixteenth century this was a prosperous place, at the centre of the local wool and iron industries. Unsurprisingly, it has often been used as a movie location, standing in for the fictional village of Summer Street in Merchant and Ivory's *A Room With a View*, and with a good pub and **Chiddingstone Castle** on the doorstep, makes an excellent stop off.

Chiddingstone Castle

Hill Hoath Rd, TN8 7AD **House** April–Oct Mon–Wed & Sun 11am–5pm • £8 **Grounds** Daily 11am–5pm • Free • ☏ 01892 870347, ☒ chiddingstonecastle.org.uk

Chiddingstone Castle is in fact a large country house, built in the sixteenth century and castellated in the early 1800s. It's an unusual place, half country manor and half museum, displaying the eclectic collection of the eccentric banker-cum-antiquarian **Denys Eyre Bower**, who bought it in 1955. The grounds are appealing, with patches of woodland, a lake and a rose garden, and the **tearoom**, with comfy old armchairs and a sunny cobbled courtyard, is lovely.

The best of the collection is in the **Japanese Room**, though Bower, who claimed to be the reincarnation of Bonnie Prince Charlie, also collected an excellent hoard of **Stuart and Jacobite** artefacts; note the snuff box with a hidden portrait of James III, the "Old Pretender", inside the lid, and the letter from James's son, the Bonnie Prince himself. Don't miss **Bower's study**, where an overwrought letter from a fiancée, chastising him for dreadful cruelty, sits beside news clippings about his conviction in 1957 for the attempted murder of a girlfriend. Bower always professed his innocence, and was released from prison after four years when his conviction was proved to be a miscarriage of justice.

ARRIVAL AND INFORMATION   SEVENOAKS AND AROUND

By train Sevenoaks train station is off London Rd, about a 15min walk north of the tourist office, or 20min to the Knole entrance.
Destinations Ashford (every 30min; 45min); Eynsford (every 30min; 15min); Hastings (every 30min; 1hr–1hr 15min); London Bridge (every 5–10min; 25–50min); London Charing Cross (every 5–20min; 35–50min); Ramsgate (every 30min–1hr; 1hr 30min–2hr); Shoreham (every 30min; 15min); Tunbridge Wells (every 10–30min; 20–25min).

By bus Buses to Sevenoaks stop on Buckhurst Lane, in the town centre, off the High St.
Destinations Eynsford (4 weekly; 20min); Royal Tunbridge Wells (every 30min–2hr; 40–50min); Westerham (every 1–2hr; 20min).
Tourist office Stag Theatre, London Rd, Sevenoaks (April–Sept Wed–Sun 10am–4pm; Oct–March Tues–Sat 10am–4pm; ☎ 01732 450305, ⓦ sevenoakstown.gov.uk).

ACCOMMODATION

Becketts B&B Hartfield Rd, Cowden, near Edenbridge, TN8 7HE ☎ 01342 850514, ⓦ becketts-bandb.co.uk. Characterful B&B in a beautifully appointed eighteenth-century barn five miles south of Hever near the Sussex border. There are three en-suite bedrooms – one with an antique four-poster, another with its own small garden area, and another under the eaves – with a cosy drawing room, and a flower-filled garden where you can eat breakfast in summer. Country walks head off practically from the doorstep. **£90**

Cabbages and Kings The Old Post Office, Church Rd, Halstead, TN14 7HE ☎ 01959 533054, ⓦ cabbages-and-kings.co.uk. Not quite as Alice in Wonderlandish as its name suggests, this is a comfortable B&B in a Georgian flint post office building a 15min drive east of Downe. The three well-equipped en-suite rooms are just the right side of chintzy, and you can relax in the bijou flower-filled garden or by the open fire. They also own the tearoom downstairs (closed Tues), where breakfast – and, later, home-made cakes – is served. **£85**

Charcott Farmhouse Leigh, TN11 8LG ☎ 01892 870024, ⓦ charcottfarmhouse.com. This pretty sixteenth-century red-tile-hung farmhouse, around four miles east of Chiddingstone, is a relaxing B&B with a wild garden, a terrace and rolling fields outside the front door, a few friendly cats and a laidback dog. The three twin rooms are simple, and the home-made food, from the welcome brownies to the communal breakfasts, is delicious. **£80**

Hever Castle B&B Hever, TN8 7NG ☎ 01732 865224, ⓦ hevercastle.co.uk. If you want to live like a queen, or perhaps, more accurately, like an American hotel magnate, this opulent B&B, in the Tudor-style wing that Astor added in 1903 next to the castle (see p.155), should fit the bill. The 21 luxurious en-suite rooms are each different, but all decorated in impeccable taste – some have four-posters. You can eat breakfast in the wood-panelled dining room, play billiards in the lounge, and best of all, wander the gardens at leisure after hours. **£150**

Ightham B&B Hope Farm, Sandy Lane, Ightham, TN15 9BA ☎ 01732 884359 (no calls after 8pm), ⓦ ighthambedandbreakfast.co.uk. Stunning modern barn, tucked away in perfect tranquility – in the garden of your hosts' house but surrounded by greenery, flowers and trees, and with lovely country walks from the front door. There's one twin and one double, plus an enormous living room and secluded terrace. The tasty, creative breakfast is brought over to you to enjoy at your leisure. No credit cards. **£95**

Old Timbertop Cottage Bethel Rd, Sevenoaks, TN13 3UE ☎ 01732 460506, ⓦ timbertopcottage.co.uk. On a residential road a 10min walk from the town centre, this little white timber-clad cottage offers simple, light, flexible accommodation (a twin bedroom and a sofa-bed in the living room) with basic self-catering facilities. You can have continental breakfast served in your kitchen, or, for £6 extra, a full English next door, in the home of your hosts. **£75**

EATING AND DRINKING

★ **Castle Inn** Chiddingstone, TN8 7AH ☎ 01892 870247, ⓦ castleinn-kent.co.uk. A fifteenth-century pub with a low-slung, beamed interior kept cosy with log fires in winter, and a sunny, flower-filled garden. The unpretentious menu offers good basics (try the ploughman's, with a home-made Scotch egg, cooked ham and Kentish cheese), locally sourced gastro favourites (shoulder of pork, fishcakes, sausage and mash) and fancier options (seared foie gras with brioche) – or simply order a plate of British cheeses, perfect with a local hoppy ale. Starters from £5, mains £10–20; three-course Sunday lunch £22.50. Mon–Sat 10am–11pm, Sun noon–10.30pm; food served Mon–Fri noon–2pm & 7–9.30pm, Sat noon–4pm & 7–9.30pm, Sun noon–4pm.

Food for Thought 19 The Green, Westerham, TN16 1AX ☎ 01959 569888, ⓦ fft-westerham.co.uk. This unassuming tearoom, well placed for Chartwell on Westerham Green, is popular for its simple, home-made food. The light lunches are tasty – salads, omelettes, soups – but it's really a place to stop off for afternoon tea (£9), or a cuppa and a slab of cake or apple pie. Mon–Fri 9am–5pm, Sat 8.30am–6pm, Sun 9am–6pm.

House on the Hill 115 London Rd, Sevenoaks, TN13 1BH ☎ 01732 450120, ⓦ houseonthehillsevenoaks.co.uk. Relaxed restaurant serving Modern British and Mediterranean cuisine (mains £10–12 at lunch, £16–20 at dinner; weekday two-course lunch £15). Food and wine are largely locally sourced, and the menu changes regularly; typical dishes include crab and crayfish risotto, Kent sardines, or roasted saddle of Romney Marsh lamb stuffed with sour cherries, garlic and rosemary. Eat in the bar surrounding the open kitchen, or in the more formal (but still lively) dining room upstairs. Sunday lunch (two courses £17.95) offers a nice variety, with some interesting veggie choices. Tues–Thurs noon–2.30pm & 6.30–9.30pm, Fri & Sat noon–2.30pm & 6–9.30pm, Sun noon–2.30pm.

King Henry VIII Hever Rd, Hever, TN8 7NG ☎ 01732 862457, ⓦ kinghenryviiihever.co.uk. Opposite the entrance to Hever Castle, this handsome tile-hung and half-timbered Tudor inn, now a Shepherd Neame pub, is an atmospheric place for a drink, with its mullioned windows and wood panelling, and its lovely garden with duck pond. Hearty pub grub includes pies, sausages and steaks, with mains from £8. Mon–Thurs & Sun noon–11.30pm, Fri & Sat noon–midnight.

The Plough High Cross Rd, Ivy Hatch, TN15 0NL ☎ 01732 810100, ⓦ theploughivyhatch.co.uk. Friendly gastropub, a few minutes north of Ightham Mote, with daily-changing menus (mains from £10) and a lighter bar menu. There's usually the odd surprise on offer – carrot and coriander fritters, for example – and a good range of fish, with crevettes, squid and scallops making an appearance; to fill up on a budget, go for the creative, very tasty, filled pancakes (£4.95). Mon–Fri 10am–3pm & 6–11pm, Sat 10am–11pm, Sun 10am–6pm; food served Mon–Fri 10am–2.45pm & 6–9.30pm, Sat noon–2.45pm & 6–9.30pm, Sun noon–5.30pm.

4

Maidstone and around

With so many of Kent's most popular day-trip attractions, a handful of lovely villages – **Aylesford** among them – and great North Downs walking all within easy reach, there is little need to linger in the county town of **MAIDSTONE**, though its old centre boasts some attractive buildings dating from its seventeenth- and eighteenth-century heyday. Along with the rather good **Maidstone Museum and Bentlif Art Gallery** on St Faith's St (Mon–Sat 10am–5pm, Sun noon–4pm; closed Sun Nov–March; free; ⓦmuseum. maidstone.gov.uk), with its impressive Anglo-Saxon hoard, important Japanese prints and decorative arts, and ghoulish Egyptian mummy, there are some attractive riverside walks along the Medway, which runs along the western edge of town. You could also take the **Allington Belle Paddle Boat** for a six-mile trip down the river to the **Kent Life** family attraction.

Kent Life

Lock Lane, Sandling, ME14 3AU • Mon–Fri 10am–5pm, Sat & Sun 10am–6pm; last admission 1hr before closing • £8.95, children (3–15) £7.75 • ☎ 01622 763936, ⓦ kentlife.org.uk • Accessible by *Allington Belle Paddle Boat* from the Archbishop's Palace in Maidstone (hourly 11.30am–3.30pm: March & April Sat & Sun; May–Sept daily; 30min; £6 return; ☎ 01622 661064, ⓦ allingtonbelle.co.uk)

Though it offers more than a nod to Kent's agricultural history – leaning farm buildings, a working oast house, authentic hoppers' huts, a re-creation of Ma Larkin's kitchen from TV series *The Darling Buds of May* – the 28-acre **Kent Life**, which occupies an old farm estate on the banks of the Medway, is actually more of a giant outdoor playground than a museum of rural life, and very popular with small kids. Along with seasonal events from lamb feeding to piglet racing to hop picking, star attractions include the (indoor and outdoor) play areas, farmyard pens where you can cuddle a guinea pig or stroke a cockerel, bone-rattling tractor rides, and donkey rides for the very little ones; it's also entirely dog-friendly.

Leeds Castle

Near Leeds, 7 miles east of Maidstone, ME17 1PL • Castle daily: April–Sept 10.30am–6pm, last admission 4.30pm; Oct–March 10.30am– 5pm, last admission 3pm; grounds daily 10am–6pm, last admission 4.30pm; gardens, play areas, maze & grotto daily 10am–5pm • £19.75, children (4–15) £12.50; tickets valid for a year • ☎ 01622 765400, ⓦ leeds-castle.com

Its reflection shimmering in a placid lake, the enormous **Leeds Castle** – it's named after the local village – resembles a fairy-tale palace. Beginning life around 1119, it has had a chequered history, and is now run as a commercial concern, hosting conferences and events, and with a range of paying attractions including golf, hot-air ballooning, Segway tours and jousting, with a branch of the zip-lining treetop adventure park **Go Ape** on site (ⓦgoape.co.uk). The castle's interior, though interesting, fails to match the stunning exterior and the grounds, and twentieth-century renovations have tended to quash its historical charm; if you're happy to forego the paying attractions, you could simply cross the grounds for free on one of the **public footpaths**, while if you **stay the night** (see opposite), admission to the castle and attractions (though not Go Ape) is included.

The castle

Having started its days as a Saxon manor house, the castle was converted into a royal palace by Henry VIII. It is unusual in having been owned by six medieval queens, starting with Eleanor of Castile (wife of Edward I) and ending with Henry V's widow, Catherine de Valois; it was also home to Queen Joan of Navarre (c.1370–1437), wife of Henry IV, who was accused of being a witch. In 1926 it caught the eye of Anglo-American heiress Lady Baillie, who lived here for fifty years, entertaining guests from Charlie Chaplin to Noël Coward. Baillie upgraded many of the rooms in the 1920s and 30s, which makes it difficult to tell the originals from the reproductions – panels clarify what it is you are actually looking at. In the Gloriette, the keep, which housed the royal apartments, the **Queen's Room**, originally Eleanor's, is set up to look as it might have in 1422, while in the **Queen's Gallery** you can see a fireplace installed during Henry VIII's day, and a set of sixteenth-century busts portraying a morose Henry with three of his children. The largest room is the **Henry VIII Banqueting Hall**, with its colossal bay window; most of the decor, though it looks far older, dates from Baillie's time, when she threw cocktail parties here.

The remaining rooms look exactly as they did in Baillie's day. Of most interest are her **dressing room and bathroom**, which were the last word in Deco chic, and the glorious **library**, flooded with golden light.

The grounds

With five hundred acres of beautifully landscaped grounds, crisscrossed with paths and streams, and with peacocks and black swans adding their elegant presence, Leeds Castle is a joy to walk around (note, though, that dogs are not allowed). The **aviary**, introduced by Baillie to house her exotic birds, is filled with unusual and colourful specimens, from chubby kookaburras to violet plantain eaters. Nearby, the **yew hedge maze** can be surprisingly tricky; the kitschy **grotto** beneath it, full of eerie, howling sound effects and glowing-eyed sea monsters, is a little baffling. Other offbeat attractions include a **dog-collar museum** – should you yearn to see the collar worn by Sooty's squeaky sidekick Sweep, or a jagged medieval brass collar used for bear-baiting, this is the place to come.

ARRIVAL AND INFORMATION

By train Maidstone has two mainline stations, both of them central; Maidstone East, on the east side of the river, is a 15min walk from Maidstone West, which lies across the river to the southwest.

Destinations Ashford (every 30min, hourly on Sun; 30min); Aylesford (every 5–30min, hourly on Sun; 6min); Hollingbourne (every 30min, hourly on Sun; 8min); London

St Pancras (4 daily Mon–Fri; 45min); London Victoria (every 25min; 1hr); Tonbridge (hourly, 1 daily on Sun; 27min).

Tourist office In the Maidstone Museum & Bentlif Art Gallery (see p.157), on St Faith's St (Mon–Sat 10am–5pm, plus Sun 10am–4pm in summer; ☎01622 602169, ⓦ visitmaidstone.com).

ACCOMMODATION

Black Horse Inn Pilgrims Way, Thurnham, ME14 3LD ☎01622 737185, ⓦ wellieboot.net. B&B accommodation in garden chalets behind an eighteenth-century country pub/restaurant, three miles from Maidstone, on the southern slopes of the North Downs (dogs are welcome). The simple, well-equipped rooms vary – ask for a lighter one – but all are comfy and clean, and the olde-worlde pub, where you can eat locally sourced dishes like roasted rump of Romney Marsh lamb (mains from £12), is cosy. **£90**

Leeds Castle Leeds Castle, Maidstone, ME17 1PL ☎01622 767823, ⓦ leeds-castle.com. *Stable Courtyard* offers comfortable, good-value B&B on the Leeds Castle estate; the five classy, contemporary rooms in the sixteenth-century *Maiden's Tower* are even more luxurious. There are also six self-catering properties, ranging from a two-person hideaway to the gamekeeper's house, which sleeps ten. Stable Courtyard **£100**, Maiden's Tower **£260**,

self-catering (per week) from **£400**

★ **Welsummer Camping** Lenham Rd, Harrietsham, ME17 1NQ ☎01622 844048, ⓦ welsummercamping .com. Well-run, almost-wild camping in a quiet spot on the slopes of the North Downs, with walking trails all around. A tent-only site, with plenty of space for the kids to romp around, it offers twenty pitches across two car-free meadows and a small woodland area (which also has three pre-erected tents). A small shop sells home-grown and local produce. Campfires allowed; dogs permitted on leads; curfew 10.30pm. Closed Oct–March. Pitches (plus £3 per adult) **£12**, pre-erected tents (plus £3 per adult) **£45**

Wickham Lodge 3 High St, The Quay, Aylesford, ME20 7AY ☎01622 717267, ⓦ wickhamlodge.co.uk. In an extremely pretty village a couple of miles north of Maidstone, this riverside B&B offers three light and stylish en-suite rooms in a Tudor–Georgian house with ravishing gardens. **£90**

EATING AND DRINKING

The Dirty Habit Upper St, Hollingbourne, ME17 1UW ☎01622 880880, ⓦ elitepubs.com/the_dirtyhabit. Dating from the eleventh century, this village pub at the foot of the North Downs is rather smart with its rich oak panelling, gleaming flagstones and plump leather chairs. The menu has a touch of the exotic, with dishes like seared Black Pearl scallops, crispy duck salad or sticky lemon corn-fed chicken listed alongside home-made burgers, fish specials and gastropub staples (mains from £12). There's excellent walking hereabouts; ask for their guide to the best local options. Daily 11.30am–11pm; food served Mon–Fri noon–3pm & 6–9.45pm, Sat noon–9.45pm, Sun noon–9.30pm.

Fortify Café 32 High St, Maidstone, ME14 1JF ☎01622 670533, ⓦ fortifycafe.co.uk. If gastropubs get your goat, you could do worse than head to this excellent veggie restaurant near the river in Maidstone, which serves everything from houmous salad via cheese sandwiches to moussaka, with simple all-day breakfasts that hit the spot. Everything is fresh and tasty, and from as little as £2, the prices are great. Takeaway available. Mon–Thurs 8am–5pm, Fri 8am–6pm, Sat 9am–6pm, Sun 11am–5pm.

Hengist 7–9 High St, Aylesford, ME20 7AX ☎01622 719273, ⓦ hengistrestaurant.co.uk. Helmed by Michelin-starred chef Richard Phillips, this glamorous restaurant offers fine Modern European dining in the quaint riverside

village of Aylesford. Dress up, and enjoy complex, delicate flavours in *nouvelle*-inspired dishes like confit skate wing or foie gras *ballotine*. Prices can mount (starters from £8, mains from £17), but there's a two- or three-course set lunch menu (Fri & Sat £12.95/£14.95), and on Tuesdays you can BYOB to drink with the simple three-course Market Menu (£25.50). Tues–Thurs 6.30–10pm, Fri & Sat noon–2.30pm & 6.30–10pm, Sun noon–5pm.

Mulberry Tree Hermitage Lane, Boughton Monchelsea, ME17 4DA ☎01622 749082, ⓦ themulberrytreekent .co.uk. Six miles southwest of Leeds Castle, this popular restaurant scores high for contemporary, locally sourced food – some of it grown in their own garden – served in a smart dining room or sunny back garden. Mains, from £16, might include Romney Marsh lamb's liver or south coast black bream, with interesting starters (from £7) like smoked eel with salt-baked beetroot or ham-hock *ballotine* with goat's curd. The two- and three-course menus (Tues–Fri all day & Sat lunch £14.50/£17.50) are extremely good value. Tues–Thurs noon–2pm & 6.30–9pm, Fri & Sat noon–2pm & 6.30–9.30pm, Sun noon–2.15pm.

Pepperbox Inn Windmill Hill, Fairbourne Heath, near Ulcombe, ME17 1LP ☎01622 842558, ⓦ thepepper boxinn.co.uk. You get gorgeous country views from the beer garden of this nice old pub, on the edge of a tiny hamlet three miles south of Leeds Castle. If your appetite isn't up to the hearty à la carte dishes – slow-roast pork filled with sausage meat; veal schnitzel stuffed with Gruyère and Serrano ham (mains from £12) – go for the bar menu (from £5), and wash it all down with a pint of real ale. April–Sept Mon–Fri 11am–3.30pm & 6–11pm, Sat 11am–11pm, Sun noon–5pm; Oct–March same hours but closed Sat 3.30–6pm; food served Mon–Sat noon–2.15pm & 6.45–9.45pm, Sun noon–3pm.

Ashford and around

The ever-expanding market town of **ASHFORD** is of most interest as a public transport hub and a jumping-off point for the Eurostar. Despite the tangle of historic narrow alleyways at its core, its handsome Norman church and scores of malls and designer outlets, there is little to keep you here – head out instead to the scatter of nearby villages in the North Downs and Low Weald, **Pluckley** and **Wye** among them, which make good bases for walking.

Pluckley

Owned from the seventeenth century until 1928 by the wealthy Dering family, who left their legacy in the village's many double-arched "Dering" windows, sleepy old **Pluckley**, five miles west of Ashford, distinguishes itself from countless other local villages by being where the phenomenally successful 1990s TV series **The Darling Buds of May**, based on the novels by H.E. Bates, was filmed. Though the tourist buzz has shifted in recent years away from the rumbustious Larkins and towards spooky ghost tours (it is said to be "the most haunted village in England"), Pluckley still trades on the fame brought it by David Jason, Catherine Zeta-Jones et al; a booklet, available in local tourist offices, details the locations in the show, along with other, loosely associated attractions. The Larkins' **Home Farm** itself, actually Buss Farm, on Pluckley Road about 1.5 miles south of the railway station, is only open during the **Darling Buds Classic Car Show** (⊕darlingbudsclassiccarshow.co.uk), a charity event in which Pop Larkin's yellow Roller lords it over various other vintage bangers, in a country fair-style atmosphere complete with morris dancing, cake stalls and kiddy rides.

Wye

Wye, about five miles northeast of Ashford, is a quiet North Downs village that makes a good base for walks along the North Downs Way; head out to the **Devil's Kneading Trough**, one of a network of narrow dry valleys cut into the North Downs, or follow the 2.5-mile nature trail through the **Wye National Nature Reserve**, an area of chalky grassland, woods and steep hills offering superb views out to Romney Marsh and the Weald. Look out for an unusual **white chalk crown** set into the grassy slopes to the east of the village, created in 1902 to commemorate the coronation of Edward VII. Wye hosts a **farmers' market** (⊕wyefarmersmarket.co.uk) on the first and third Saturday of the month, and a local **food festival** in June.

ARRIVAL AND DEPARTURE

ASHFORD AND AROUND

By train Eurostar services to Paris and Brussels leave from Ashford International train station, while the domestic station, linked to it by a foot tunnel, sees regular services to London, the North Weald, East Sussex and the coast. Both are around a 10min drive from junction 10 of the M20.
Destinations Brighton (hourly; 1hr 50min); Canterbury (every 10–30min; 15–20min); Dover (every 10–30min; 30min); Folkestone (every 10–30min; 15–20min);

Hastings (hourly; 40–50min); London Bridge (every 20min; 1hr 10min–1hr 20min); London Charing Cross (every 30min; 1hr 20min); London St Pancras (every 30min; 39min); Maidstone (every 15–30min; 23–30min); Margate (hourly; 50min); Pluckley (every 10–30min; 6min); Sevenoaks (every 30min; 45min); Tonbridge (every 30min; 35min); Wye (every 30min; 6min).

ACCOMMODATION AND EATING

Dering Arms The Grove, Pluckley, TN27 0RR ☎01233 840371, ⓦderingarms.com. This creeper-covered hunting lodge, by Pluckley station, now houses a handsome pub and seafood restaurant. It's the fish you should go for, and especially the daily specials – pan-fried scallops with basil spaghetti and saffron sauce, say, or fillet of black bream with marsh samphire – but they also serve elegant game and meat dishes (starters from £6, mains from £12) along with a more relaxed bistro menu focusing on comforting pies and stews. They have a few cosy and welcoming B&B rooms. Mon–Fri 11.30am–3pm & 6–11pm, Sat 11am–3pm & 6–11pm, Sun noon–4.30pm; food served Mon–Fri noon–2.30pm & 6.30–9pm, Sat noon–3pm & 6.30–9pm, Sun noon–3pm. **£70**

★ **Elvey Farm** Elvey Lane, Pluckley, TN27 0SU ☎01233 840442, ⓦelveyfarm.co.uk. Surrounded by undulating fields, this relaxing boutique hotel offers ten rooms – in an oast house, a barn, a granary or stables – which are rustic without being twee, with stripped beams, exposed walls, funky detailing and modern bathrooms. Most are suites – the light-flooded Canterbury Suite (£250), with its own outdoor hot tub, is a stunner, and there's a thrilling round room in the oast house, but even the cheaper rooms are excellent value. The restaurant serves good, locally sourced food, with mains from £14, and there are plenty of places to sit and relax with a glass of Kentish wine from the bar. **£105**

★ **Five Bells** The Street, East Brabourne, TN25 5LP ☎01303 813334, ⓦfivebellsinnbrabourne.com. All log fires, dried hops and vintage paperbacks, this comfortable, stylish sixteenth-century inn on the Pilgrim's Way, five miles southwest of Wye, serves real ales, good wines and Modern British/European mains (from £9), many of them roasted in a wood-fired oven, plus snacks (from £6) including home-made Scotch hen's eggs and goat's cheese risotto balls. Upstairs are five fabulous, colourful B&B rooms – none has TV or tea-/coffee-making facilities (though they will bring drinks to your room), but two have real log fires. Live acoustic music every Tues. Mon–Thurs 9am–11pm, Fri & Sat 9am–11.30pm, Sun 9am–10.30pm. **£100**

★ **The Plough at Stalisfield Green** Stalisfield Green, ME13 0HY ☎01795 890256, ⓦstalisfieldgreen.co.uk. Lovely country pub in a North Downs village six miles northeast of Pluckley, serving superior food on monthly-changing menus with many ingredients sourced from local farms. The setting may be rustic, but the food is inventive – dishes like Kentish asparagus and crispy duck egg, or grilled plaice with anchovy butter, are joined by such surprises as preserved tomato and smoked Applewood custard tart with nettles, while some obscure craft beers sit alongside the local ales, stouts and cider. Mains from £12; two- or three-course lunch menu £12.95/£15.95. Tues–Fri noon–3pm & 6–11pm, Sat noon–11.30pm, Sun noon–8pm; food served Tues–Sat noon–2pm & 6.30–9.30pm, Sun noon–3.30pm.

The Secret Garden Mersham Le Hatch, Hythe Rd, TN25 5NH ☎01233 501586, ⓦsecretgardenkent.co.uk. Four miles southeast of Wye, this is an enterprising restaurant, with its own garden growing fruit, veg and herbs. They're best known for their generous afternoon teas (booking necessary; £14.75), which you can eat on the terrace in fine weather, but also offer lunch and dinner featuring the likes of Romney Marsh lamb, local sea bass and Wittersham pork. Sun & Mon 10am–4pm, Tues–Sat 10am–5pm & 6.30–9pm.

Wife of Bath 4 Upper Bridge St, Wye, TN25 5AF ☎01233 812232, ⓦthewifeofbath.com. An elegant restaurant – with B&B rooms and good dine-and-sleep deals – offering creative, seasonal dishes like hake with harissa on a butterbean and cucumber salad, pork belly with grilled pickled pear, or pancetta and wild garlic tagliatelle. Two-/three-course lunch menus (Mon–Sat) £17/£20; evening mains start at around £16. Tues 6–10pm, Wed–Sat noon–2.30pm & 6–10pm, Sun noon–5.30pm. **£95**

4

The Sussex Weald

NET SHOPS, HASTINGS

5

The Sussex Weald

Sandwiched between the lofty chalk escarpments of the North and South Downs, the Sussex Weald has a sleepy beauty all of its own: this is an unspoilt landscape of narrow, sunken lanes, scattered villages and farms, ancient woodland, rolling sandstone hills and patchworks of wonky, hedgerow-lined fields. Most of this chapter – bar the towns of Hastings and Rye on the coast – lies within the central High Weald AONB (Area of Outstanding Natural Beauty); there are no large towns to speak of in this tranquil pocket of Sussex countryside, and the landscape seems almost suspended in time. Steam trains puff through bluebell woods, crumbling castles guard against long-forgotten enemies, and venerable country estates gaze serenely over the glorious gardens that are one of the Weald's defining features.

Best-known of the great gardens are **Wakehurst Place**, **Sheffield Park**, **Nymans** and **Great Dixter**, the last of these just a short hop from a romantic castle at **Bodiam** and **Rudyard Kipling**'s country retreat at Bateman's. Kipling was one of many writers and artists who made their home in the area: you can also visit **Henry James**'s townhouse at Rye, and **Farley Farm House**, where Surrealist painter Roland Penrose and photographer Lee Miller entertained Picasso, Miró and Man Ray. **A.A. Milne**, creator of much-loved fictional bear Winnie-the-Pooh, had his weekend home at Hartfield in the heart of **Ashdown Forest**, at the northern edge of the High Weald. The landscape changes dramatically here, with hedgerow-fringed fields giving way to beautiful gorse-speckled heathland crisscrossed with trails – a great place to strike off and get lost.

Down on the coast, the Weald meets the sea around Hastings. This is 1066 country, where the most famous battle in British history was fought in nearby **Battle**, marking the end of Anglo-Saxon England. **Hastings** itself is a vibrant, rough-around-the-edges seaside town with a picturesque old core and an atmospheric fishing quarter, while further east along the coast the perfectly preserved medieval town of **Rye** is one of the highlights of Sussex, even without the added draw of dune-backed **Camber Sands** beach on its doorstep. Both towns are crammed with stylish boutique hotels, and excellent restaurants making the most of fantastic local ingredients – fish from the Hastings fleet, scallops and shrimps from Rye, lamb from Romney Marsh and sparkling wine from local vineyards. Inland, it's much the same story: you're never far away from a gastropub or foodie restaurant, and there are plenty of boutique glamping sites and opulent country-house hotels to splash out on, as well as some lovely back-to-nature campsites at the other end of the scale.

GREAT DIXTER

Highlights

①Rye A medieval gem, with cobbled streets and ancient inns, and plenty of excellent places to eat, shop and sleep. **See p.166**

②Camber Sands In a county of pebbly beaches Camber is a star: miles of soft, fine sand offer bucket-and-spade fun for families or kitesurfing thrills for adrenaline junkies. **See p.174**

③Hastings With a pretty Old Town, a still-working fishermen's quarter, a sleek new art gallery and miles of glorious coastline on its doorstep, Hastings makes the perfect seaside getaway. **See p.174**

④De La Warr Pavilion Bexhill-on-Sea's seaside pavilion is an unmissable Modernist masterpiece

and a vibrant centre for contemporary arts. **See p.184**

⑤Battle Abbey Soak up the atmosphere at the site of the battle that changed the course of British history. **See p.186**

⑥Great Dixter One of the country's greatest gardens, with innovative, imaginative planting that can't fail to inspire. **See p.189**

⑦Bodiam Castle A classic picture-book castle, complete with moat and battlements, that's best reached by river boat or steam train. **See p.190**

⑧Ashdown Forest Hunt for heffalumps in the footsteps of Winnie-the-Pooh, the world's best-loved bear. **See p.194**

HIGHLIGHTS ARE MARKED ON THE MAP ON PP.166–167

5

Rye and around

It's no mystery why **RYE** is one of the most popular destinations in Sussex: this ancient, pocket-sized, hilltop town – half-timbered, skew-roofed and quintessentially English – claims to have retained more of its original buildings than any other town in Britain, and has a street plan virtually unchanged since medieval times.

Rye lies perched on a hill overlooking the Romney Marshes, at the confluence of three rivers – the Rother, the Brede and the Tillingham, the first of which flows south to Rye Harbour and then out to sea. Though the town sees more than its fair share of tourists, especially in the summer months, it has managed – just – to avoid being too chocolate-boxy. There are plenty of good independent shops, a heartening absence of high-street chains, and you're positively spoilt for choice when it comes to great restaurants and places to stay. The main appeal of the town is simply to wander round and soak up the atmosphere: the jostling boats and screeching gulls down at **Strand Quay**; ancient **Landgate** – the town's only surviving medieval gate, once Rye's only connection to the mainland at high tide; and sloping, cobbled **Mermaid Street**, the town's main thoroughfare in the sixteenth century and today its most picturesque street.

Rye also makes a great base for the surrounding area. Within a couple of miles there's one of the finest beaches in Sussex, dune-backed **Camber Sands**, and in the other direction the once-mighty hilltop town of **Winchelsea**.

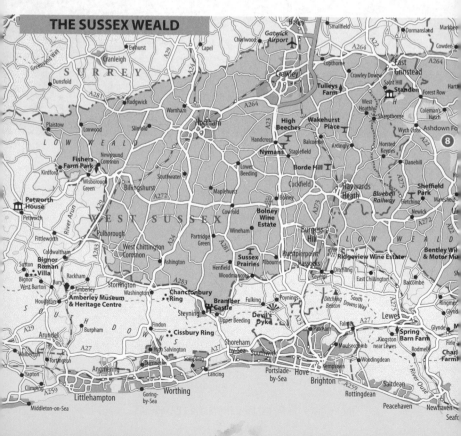

THE SUSSEX WEALD

Brief history

Rye was added as a "limb" to the original Cinque Ports (see box, p.105) in the thirteenth century, and under this royal protection it grew to become an important **port**; it's hard to believe today, with the sea a distant smudge on the horizon, but back then the town was virtually an island at high tide. Over time, the retreat of the sea and the silting-up of the River Rother marooned Rye two miles inland, and the loss of its port inevitably led to its decline; **smuggling** as a source of income became widespread (see box, p.218), with the brutal Hawkhurst Gang making the town one of their haunts in the eighteenth century.

St Mary's Church

Church Square, TN31 7HF • April–Oct 9.15am–5.30pm; Nov–March 9.15am–4.30pm • Church free; bell tower £2.50 • ☎ 01797 224935, Ⓦ ryeparishchurch.org.uk

The top end of town is crowned by the turret of the twelfth-century **St Mary's Church**, one of the oldest buildings in Rye, which dominates Church Square, a peaceful, shady oasis bordered by old tile-hung buildings.

   Inside the church, you can't fail to notice the massive 17ft pendulum beating time in front of you; St Mary's **clock** is the oldest working church-tower clock in the country, installed in 1561, though the pendulum, the clock face and the quarterboys (so named because they strike the quarter hours) are all later additions. The ascent of

HIGHLIGHTS

1. Rye
2. Camber Sands
3. Hastings
4. De La Warr Pavilion
5. Battle Abbey
6. Great Dixter
7. Bodiam Castle
8. Ashdown Forest

ENGLISH CHANNEL

0   2
miles

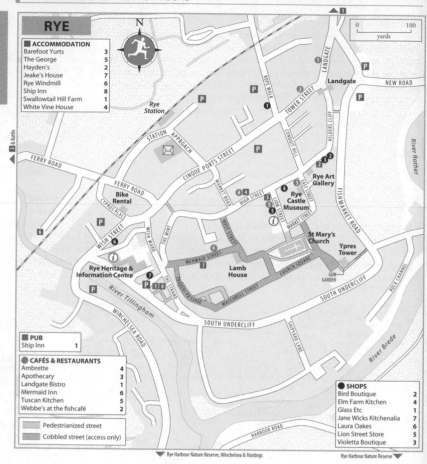

the **bell tower** is a must, involving a fun squeeze through a 16-inch-wide passage and then a scramble up steep, narrow steps past the huge eighteenth-century bells to the rooftop, where there are fabulous views over the clay-tiled roofs and grid of narrow lanes below.

Rye Castle Museum

Ypres Tower Church Square, TN31 7HH • Daily: April–Oct 10.30am–5pm; Nov–March 10.30am–3.30pm • £3, joint ticket with East Street Museum £4 **East Street Museum** 3 East Street, TN31 7JY • Normally April–Oct Sat, Sun & bank hols 10.30am–5pm, but call ahead to check • £1.50, joint ticket with Ypres Tower £4 • ☎ 01797 227798, ⓦ ryemuseum.co.uk

Rye Castle Museum is spread over two sites: the Ypres Tower (Rye's "castle") in the far corner of Church Square; and the volunteer-run museum at 3 East Street. The **Ypres** (pronounced "Wipers") **Tower** was built, probably in the thirteenth century, to keep watch for cross-Channel invaders, though it didn't do a very good job of repelling the French raiding parties that struck in 1339 and 1377; the second attack virtually razed the town to the ground. The raids persuaded Edward III to open his purse and fund the construction of the town's walls and gates. In 1494 the tower became a prison, with the guardrooms in the turrets converted into cells, and it remained so for almost four hundred years, before setting up shop as a mortuary and finally becoming the town museum.

There's not a huge amount to see **inside**: some pottery and a mocked-up cell on the ground floor, helmets and mail for kids to try on in the basement, and up the narrow stone staircase – with its "trick" steps, some deep and some shallow, to send intruders off-balance – there's a small exhibition on Rye's smuggling history. Out front, the **Gun Garden** (open access) looks out over Romney Marsh; it's hard to believe that everything you see in front of you would once have been sea. Maps of Rye's changing coastline are on display at the **East Street** museum site, which also contains an eclectic selection of relics from Rye's past.

Lamb House

West St, TN31 7ES • End March–Oct Tues & Sat 2–6pm • £4.60; NT • ☎ 01580 762334, ⓦ nationaltrust.org.uk/lamb-house

A stone's throw from Church Square, the elegant, redbrick Georgian **Lamb House** was the one-time home of author **Henry James** (1843–1916), who moved to Rye in 1897 after 22 years in London and fell in love with both the town and the house: "I have been to the South, the far end of Florida", he wrote in 1905, "but prefer the far end of Sussex! In the heart of golden orange groves I yearned for the shade of the old Lamb House mulberry tree."

James wrote three of his best-known novels at Lamb House – *The Wings of the Dove*, *The Ambassadors* and *The Golden Bowl* – and entertained a wide circle of literary friends, including fellow Sussex writers H. G. Wells, Rudyard Kipling and Hilaire Belloc. You can still see some of his manuscripts and photos in the house, and stroll in the beautiful walled garden.

A few years after James's death, the writer **E.F. Benson** moved in, giving the house a starring role in his comic *Mapp and Lucia* novels (see p.322) Rye was thinly disguised as "Tilling", while Lamb House became "Mallards". **Tours** of Mapp and Lucia's Rye run in the summer (June to mid-Sept Wed plus first & third Sat of the month; 1hr 30min; £6.75; ⓦ efbensonsociety.org).

Rye Art Gallery

107 High St, TN31 7JE • **Stormont Studio** Thurs–Sat 10.30am–1pm & 2–5pm, Sun & bank hols noon–4pm **Easton Rooms** Mon & Wed–Sat 10.30am–1pm & 2–5pm, Sun & bank hols noon–4pm • Free • ☎ 01797 222433, ⓦ ryeartgallery.co.uk

The small **Rye Art Gallery** comes in two parts: the Stormont Studio houses a rotating permanent collection of over 450 paintings, prints and photographs which includes works by artists associated with Rye – such as Edward Burra, Paul Nash and John Piper, who all lived in the town – and other artists including Vanessa Bell, Duncan Grant, Eric Gill and Edward Ardizzone; while the Easton Rooms hold exhibitions of contemporary art.

Rye Heritage and Information Centre

Strand Quay, TN31 7AY • Daily: April–Oct 10am–5pm; Nov–March 10am–4pm; 20min sound-and-light show every 30min • Sound-and-light show £3.50; audio guides £4; ghost walks £12 • ☎ 01797 226696, ⓦ ryeheritage.co.uk

Down by Strand Quay, it's well worth popping into the privately-run **Rye Heritage and Information Centre** for its excellent **sound-and-light show**, which gives you a potted history of Rye using a model of the town as it would have looked in the early nineteenth century; it's fascinating to see how little its appearance has changed since then. The centre also hires out **walking tour** audio guides and offers occasional **ghost walks**. Upstairs there's a room of wonderfully clunky **penny arcade** machines, some dating back to the 1930s.

5

Rye Harbour Nature Reserve

Lime Kiln Cottage Information Centre, Rye Harbour Rd, Rye Harbour, TN31 7TU • Nature Reserve: open access; Information Centre: open most days 10am–4/5pm • ☎ 01797 227784, ⓦ wildrye.info • Free car park at Rye Harbour

Until the late sixteenth century, most of the land that now makes up the **Rye Harbour Nature Reserve** – a triangle of land between Rye and the sea, bordered to the east by the River Rother and to the west by the River Brede – was a shallow harbour, but the silting-up of the land over the centuries has transformed it into a rare shingle habitat. By turns both bleak and beautiful, the reserve is at its most colourful in late spring, when the beach is speckled with spears of purple viper's bugloss, carpets of pink sea pea, and clumps of sea kale and yellow horned poppy. Miles of footpaths meander around the shingle ridges and saltmarsh, with five **birdwatching hides** set up overlooking lagoons and reed beds; you can download circular walks from the website, which also has details of **special events**, everything from bird watching for beginners to pond-dipping.

Camber Castle

Tours July–Sept first Sat of month at 2pm • £3

The reserve runs occasional guided tours of **Camber Castle**, which was built by Henry VIII as part of a chain of coastal fortifications that also included nearby Deal and Walmer (see p.110). The castle was completed in 1544, costing a princely £23,000, only to be abandoned less than a hundred years later after the build-up of shingle rendered its defensive position useless. Its crumbling walls now lie more than a mile inland, looking out over nothing more dangerous than munching sheep.

ARRIVAL AND GETTING AROUND

RYE AND AROUND

By car The car park at the station charges £2.50 per day; if you're staying overnight you'll need to buy two tickets.

By train Rye's train station is at the bottom of Station Approach, off Cinque Ports Street; it's a five-minute walk up to the High Street. There are services from here to Ashford (hourly; 20min), Hastings (hourly; 20min) and London St Pancras (hourly; 1hr 10min).

By bus Bus #100 runs into the centre of town from Hastings (Mon–Sat hourly, Sun every 2hr; 40min).

By bike You can rent bicycles from Rye Hire, 1 Cyprus Place (Mon–Fri 8am–5pm, Sat 8am–noon; £10/half-day, £15/day; ☎ 01797 223033, ⓦ ryehire.co.uk). The *Rye Rides* booklet can be downloaded from ⓦ eastsussex.gov.uk.

INFORMATION

Tourist offices The official tourist information centre is at 4–5 Lion St (daily: April–Sept 10am–5pm; Oct–March 10am–4pm; ☎ 01797 229049, ⓦ visitrye.co.uk). Rye Heritage and Information Centre, Strand Quay (daily: April–Oct 10am–5pm; Nov–March 10am–4pm; ☎ 01797

226696, ⓦ ryeheritage.co.uk), is privately run, offering audio guides, ghost tour bookings and a sound-and-light town model (see p.169).

Website ⓦ ryeguide.co.uk (also available as a free app, *Visit Rye*).

ACCOMMODATION

★ **Barefoot Yurts** Stubb Lane, Brede, TN31 6BN ☎ 01424 883057, ⓦ barefoot-yurts.co.uk. As soon as you arrive at this magical spot, a ten-minute drive from Rye, you know you're on to a winner: there are just two beautiful yurts (hired together), nestled in their own tranquil clearing. One yurt is the bedroom, the other a stylish sitting room (complete with sofa bed), and there's a separate hut containing a bijou kitchen and shower room, with a small veranda for sitting and watching the world go by. Everything's been thought through beautifully, even down to the herbs growing by the kitchen, and with wood-burning stoves in both yurts you could even brave a (cheaper) stay in winter. 2 nights (Fri & Sat) in summer **£280**

★ **The George** 98 High St, TN31 7JT ☎ 01797 222144,

ⓦ thegeorgeinrye.com. Justifiably popular, this luxurious hotel – Rye's oldest coaching inn – manages to get everything just right, from the wood-panelled snug that greets you as you walk in, to the mellow wood-beamed bar and effortlessly tasteful bedrooms, each individually furnished. You can't really go wrong whichever of the 41 rooms you choose, whether it's the suite styled as a Hamptons-style beachside hangout, the boudoir featuring riotous hummingbird wallpaper and mirrored furniture, or the calm, cosy room lined with vintage Penguin paperbacks. **£135**

Hayden's 108 High St, TN31 7JE ☎ 01797 224501, ⓦ haydensinrye.co.uk. Friendly, family-run and green-thinking, this popular B&B has seven impeccably elegant, contemporary rooms set above a coffee shop in the heart of town. Rooms come with smart bathrooms, bathrobes and iPod docks, and those at the back have lovely views out over Romney Marsh. The locally sourced, organic breakfasts are excellent, and on a sunny day you can tuck into your eggs and bacon on the small terrace out the back. **£115**

Jeake's House Mermaid St, TN31 7ET ☏ 01797 222828, ⓦ jeakeshouse.com. This ivy-clad seventeenth-century guesthouse has an enviable location on Rye's most picturesque street, and inside oozes character, with sagging beams, sloping floors and a warren of creaky corridors. The 11 rooms – most with en-suite bathroom – are traditional in style, with antique furniture, floral wallpaper and quilts on the beds (many four-poster), while downstairs there's a cosy parlour and bar with leather chairs and board games. Breakfast is served in an extraordinary high-ceilinged Baptist chapel, with such treats as devilled kidneys and boiled eggs with Marmite soldiers on the menu. **£90**

Rye Windmill Off Ferry Rd, TN31 7DW ☏ 01797 224027, ⓦ ryewindmill.co.uk. This 300-year-old white smock windmill, just a couple of minutes' walk from Strand Quay, is one of Rye's most famous landmarks. Inside are ten excellent-value, contemporary rooms, including two suites: the one to go for is the Windmill Suite (£150), set over the top two floors of the mill, with a sleigh bed, huge bathroom and a balcony giving fabulous views over the river and rooftops. **£80**

Ship Inn The Strand, TN31 7DB ☏ 01797 222233, ⓦ theshipinnrye.co.uk. The ten fab little rooms above this pub are fresh, colourful and quirky, with bright wallpapered feature walls and funky furnishings. Each is slightly different, so you might get painted wooden floorboards, Union Jack pillows or a bath panelled with a Cath Kidston floral print. None are huge, but there's always the great pub downstairs (see p.172) to hang out in. **£90**

Swallowtail Hill Farm Hobbs Lane, Beckley, TN31 6TT ☏ 0845 337 2948, ⓦ swallowtailhill.com. This lovely family-run site has just two bell tents and two quirky "cottages on wheels". The tents lie at the bottom of a field near a small pond, with a rowing boat on hand. Each comes with deckchairs and its own fire pit, and is simply but stylishly decked out with a wooden bed, rugs and bedside tables made from upturned apple crates. With animal feeding and nature walks thrown in, bikes available to borrow and a small honesty shop stocking fresh farm eggs and the owner's home-made goodies, it's a real gem. April–Sept. 3 nights (Thurs–Sun) in peak season: tents **£280**, cottages **£330**

★ **White Vine House** 24 High St, TN31 7JF ☏ 01797 224748, ⓦ whitevinehouse.co.uk. Where this small, classy boutique B&B excels is the personal touch – nothing is too much trouble. You're surrounded by history, too: behind the vine-covered Georgian frontage the building is Elizabethan, and it still boasts plenty of original features including a stunning French oak-panelled dining room, used for breakfast and then later in the day by the excellent in-house restaurant, the *Ambrette* (see below). The rooms themselves are immaculate, and come with iPod docking stations and sleek, modern bathrooms. **£140**

EATING AND DRINKING

There's no shortage of excellent places to eat in Rye; in addition to the places listed below, both the restaurant at *The George* (see opposite) and the coffee shop at *Hayden's* (see opposite) are recommended. Rye Farmers' Market takes place every Wednesday on Strand Quay (10am–noon/1pm; ⓦ farmersmarketrye.co.uk).

★ **Ambrette** In the White Vine House hotel, 24 High St, TN31 7JF ☏ 01797 222043, ⓦ theambrette.co.uk. Like its award-winning sister restaurant in Margate (see p.93), the *Ambrette* is pretty special: the inventive, contemporary Indian dishes on offer (mains £9–16) include pan-grilled Kentish pork crusted with cinnamon and fennel, and Ramsgate crabs flavoured with mustard oil and cardamom, punctuated with wonderful palate-cleansers that include a popping-candy granita. Desserts are equally sublime, and the setting – the elegant dining rooms of *White Vine House* – more than matches up to the food. Tues–Thurs 11.30am–2.30pm & 6–9.30pm, Fri–Sun 11.30am–2.30pm & 5.30–10pm.

Apothecary 1 East St, TN31 7JY ☏ 01797 229157, ⓦ apothecaryrye.co.uk. Leather armchairs, book-lined walls, scrubbed wooden tables and a wealth of original features – including gold leaf-labelled pharmaceutical drawers from the building's past life as the town's apothecary – make this atmospheric coffee shop the perfect spot to watch the world go by. Daily 9am–5pm.

Landgate Bistro 5–6 Landgate, TN31 7LH ☏ 01797 222829, ⓦ landgatebistro.co.uk. One of the best restaurants in Rye, this small, intimate place – housed in two interconnected Georgian cottages just outside the medieval Landgate – is known for its traditionally British food: there's plenty of fish from the local fishing fleet, Romney Marsh lamb and game in season, and a fondness for English puds such as lemon tart, elderflower jelly, spotted dick and trifle made with syllabub. The three-course set menu is excellent value: £16.80 at lunch, £19.80 at dinner. Wed–Fri 7–11pm, Sat noon–3pm & 7–11pm, Sun noon–3pm.

Mermaid Inn Mermaid St, TN31 7EY ☏ 01797 223065, ⓦ mermaidinn.com. A meal at the restaurant of this creakily historic fifteenth-century hotel is an excellent way to soak up the atmosphere without breaking the bank. Start off with a drink in the bar – where the infamous Hawkhurst Gang of smugglers once drank – before moving on to the low-lit panelled restaurant, where three courses will set you back £25 at lunch, £37.50 at dinner: a meal

5

might start with Rye Bay scallops, followed by black bream with saffron mash, with ginger pannacotta for dessert. Daily noon–2.30pm & 7–9.30pm (Sat from 6.30pm).

⭐ **Ship Inn** The Strand, TN31 7DB ☎ 01797 222233, ⊕ theshipinnrye.co.uk. There's a lovely, laidback vibe at this great quayside pub, the perfect hangout for leisurely Sunday lunches, lazy weekend paper-reading, or a pint of Harveys by the fire after a blowy winter's day walk. The decor is bright, eclectic and cheerful, with mismatched furniture, patterned formica tables, plastic chandeliers and quirky art on the walls, and there are plenty of board games – including a Rye-themed Monopoly – for rainy days. The food is equally good, both seasonal and local, with burgers, ploughman's and the like at lunch, and dishes such as roasted sea bream with samphire (£15.50) at dinner. Daily 11am–11pm; food served Mon–Fri noon–3pm & 6.30–10pm, Sat & Sun noon–3.30pm & 6.30–10.30pm.

Tuscan Kitchen 8 Lion St, TN31 7LB ☎ 01797 223269, ⊕ tuscankitchenrye.co.uk. You'll need to book well ahead to guarantee a table at this very popular restaurant. It doesn't look anything out of the ordinary, with its unassuming rustic decor, but it delivers fantastic, authentic Tuscan food – the likes of tortelloni filled with truffle porcini, or veal shank braised Florentine-style with saffron, all cooked with olive oil from the chef's own olive groves in Tuscany. Thurs 6–9.30pm, Fri–Sun noon–3pm & 6–9.30pm.

Webbe's at thefishcafé 17 Tower St, TN31 7AT ☎ 01797 222226, ⊕ webbesrestaurants.co.uk. Lobsters on ice greet you at the counter as you walk into this smart four-storey, brick-walled building, with arched windows, leather seats and an open kitchen. Get things started with three native oysters washed down with a glass of prosecco (£8.50), before moving on to the mains (£10–16), which might feature bouillabaisse, or a steamed panache of fish in saffron sauce. Upstairs there's a cookery school, offering regular day courses (£95) throughout the year. Daily noon–2.30pm & 6–9.30pm.

SHOPPING

Bird Boutique 113 High St, TN31 7JE ☎ 01797 229927, ⊕ boutiquebird.co.uk. Bringing a little bit of London to Rye, this small boutique stocks womenswear by Humanoid, emilyandfin, Charlotte Taylor, LnA and more. Mon–Fri 10am–5pm, Sat 10am–5.30pm, Sun 11am–4pm.

Elm Farm Kitchen 100 High St, TN31 7JE ☎ 01797 223303. Part of the same outfit as the excellent *Winchelsea Farm Kitchen* (see opposite), this produce store and deli stocks cheeses, wine and bread from the Lighthouse Bakery and Judges in Hastings, and has an excellent deli counter. Mon–Sat 9am–5.30pm.

Glass Etc 18–22 Rope Walk, TN31 7NA ☎ 01797 226600, ⊕ decanterman.com. A treasure-trove of antique and twentieth-century glass, run by Andy McConnell, one of the country's leading authorities on glassware. Mon–Sat 10.30am–5pm, Sun noon–5pm.

Jane Wicks Kitchenalia Strand Quay, TN31 7DB ☎ 01424 713635. Vintage kitchen equipment, crockery and kitchen textiles, inside the Countryways shop down on Strand Quay. Daily 10am–5pm.

Laura Oakes 24 Wish St, TN31 7DA ☎ 01797 229060, ⊕ lauraoakes.co.uk. Bespoke furniture, Perspex wall panels, cushions, lampshades, mugs and bunting are all on sale at this hip store showcasing the work of up-and-coming British-born artist, photographer and pattern designer Laura Oakes, whose pieces are created using digital decoupage. Mon & Wed–Sat noon–4pm.

Lion Street Store 6 Lion St, TN31 7LB ☎ 01797 224007, ⊕ lionstreetstore.com. The best of British arts and crafts are on offer at this fab little store tucked just off the High Street, which celebrates "the useful and the beautiful" – homewares, textiles, stationery, toys, vintage pieces, and original artwork and prints. Mon & Wed–Sun 11am–5pm.

Violetta Boutique 110 High St, TN31 7JY ☎ 01797 227232, ⊕ violetta-boutique.co.uk. Run by an ex-magazine beauty editor, this chic independent beauty apothecary and perfumery stocks Miller Harris cosmetics, fragrance and candles, This Works skincare, Serge Lutens perfume and Paul and Joe cosmetics. Beauty treatments also available. Mon & Wed–Fri 10.30am–3pm, Sat 11am–5.30pm, Sun 11am–4pm.

Winchelsea

Perched on top of Iham Hill two miles southwest of Rye, sleepy **WINCHELSEA** receives a fraction of the visitors of its neighbour, and is probably heartily thankful for it. There are no streams of camera-toting tourists here, just quiet, pretty streets of white weatherboard and tile-hung buildings, a deli-café, post office and church. The tiny town – a neat grid of less than a dozen blocks – is no bigger than a village really but, like Rye, it was once one of the most important ports in the country.

Winchelsea was founded in the late thirteenth century by Edward I, after its predecessor, Old Winchelsea – an important member of the Cinque Ports confederation (see box, p.105) – was washed away by a series of violent storms.

New Winchelsea was built on higher ground, and for a brief period it flourished until, ironically, the sea which had provided its wealth once again delivered its ruin, gradually retreating, silting up the harbour and leaving the town high and dry.

Church of St Thomas à Becket

High St, TN36 4EB • Daily 9am–6pm, closes 4pm in winter.

Perhaps the most obvious reminder of Winchelsea's illustrious past is the **Church of St Thomas à Becket**, the cathedral-like proportions of which seem strikingly out of place in pocket-sized Winchelsea. The magnificent Gothic church was erected by Edward I in 1288, with no expense spared, and would originally have covered most of the square in which it now sits – what you see now is only the chancel and side chapels, and remnants of the ruined transepts. Inside, the first thing that strikes you are the glorious, glowing **stained-glass windows**, the work of Douglas Strachan in the early 1930s. To your left, in the north aisle, are three beautiful **effigies** carved from West Sussex black marble that were brought from Old Winchelsea church before the sea submerged it.

Winchelsea Museum

High St, TN36 4EN • May–Sept Tues–Sat 10.30am–4.30pm, Sun 2–5pm • £1.50 • ☎ 01342 714559

Winchelsea Museum is housed in the old courthouse, one of the oldest buildings in town, and contains maps, models, local pottery and other local memorabilia, as well as a display on past residents of Winchelsea, which have included the actress Ellen Terry, artist John Everett Millais and comedy legend Spike Milligan, who is buried in the churchyard opposite under a gravestone inscribed (in Gaelic) with the immortal words "I told you I was ill".

Winchelsea Beach

Head south for a mile and a half from Winchelsea and you get to **Winchelsea Beach**, a straggle of bungalows and holiday parks backing onto a long expanse of shingle beach, with sand at low tide. The beach, which abuts the Rye Harbour Nature Reserve (see p.170), lacks the wow factor of dune-backed, sandy Camber, but is a good place to escape the crowds.

ARRIVAL AND INFORMATION WINCHELSEA

By car There's free street parking in Winchelsea.

By bus Bus #100 from Rye runs into the centre of town

(Mon–Sat hourly, Sun every 2hr; 5min).

Website ⓦ winchelsea.net.

ACCOMMODATION AND EATING

★ **The Ship** Sea Rd, Winchelsea Beach, TN36 4LH ☎ 01797 226767, ⓦ shipwinchelseabeach.com. This great little place is tucked away from the tourist hordes near quiet Winchelsea Beach: one half is a small but excellent produce store, deli and butcher's; the other is a smart and glossy café-bar and restaurant, serving up burgers, bangers and slow-cooked ribs from the butcher's, as well as smoked haddock toasties, Winchelsea Beach chowder and Rye Bay fish casserole (mains £9–18). Inside, the decor is cool and quirky, with red leather sofas and a funky mosaic bar, while outside there's a beautiful shingle garden decorated with driftwood, cockle shells and fishermen's nets. Deli daily 8am–5pm (8pm on Tues); café-bar and restaurant daily 8am–11pm.

Strand House Tanyards Lane, Winchelsea, TN36 4JT ☎ 01797 226276, ⓦ thestrandhouse.co.uk. This fourteenth-century B&B at the foot of the cliff below

Strand Gate features oak-beamed ceilings, inglenook fireplaces, leaded windows and doorways you have to duck your head to get through, as well as a tranquil two-acre woodland garden which links the hotel with Winchelsea above. Decor is traditional, though there are some slightly more modern rooms in a cottage in the garden, where you get the added bonus of a picnic breakfast delivered to your door in the morning. **£120**

Winchelsea Farm Kitchen High St, Winchelsea, TN36 4EA ☎ 01797 226287, ⓦ winchelseafarmkitchen.co.uk. Excellent deli, wine cellar and coffee shop on Winchelsea's main street. The deli stocks bread from the Lighthouse Bakery in Bodiam, cheese from small producers in Sussex and Kent, cured meats and chutneys, while the coffee shop out the back offers up home-made quiches, soups, cakes and antipasti platters, and has some courtyard seating in summer. Mon–Sat 8am–5pm.

5

WATERSPORTS AT CAMBER

Anyone who's ever struggled to put up a windbreak at Camber won't be surprised to learn that it's a renowned centre of wind-based **watersports**: you'll often see windsurfers or kitesurfers scudding along the waves. If you fancy having a go yourself there are two local outfits to try, as well as nearby Action Watersports (see box, p.131).

The Kitesurf Centre On the beach in Broomhill Sands car park, ☎07563 763046, ⓦthekitesurfcentre.com. Lessons and courses in kitesurfing (£99/day) and kitebuggying (£49/2hr, £89/4hr) on Camber Sands, plus stand-up paddleboarding lessons and trips on the rivers around Rye (£48/2hr).

Rye Watersports Northpoint Water, New Lydd Rd ☎01797 225238, ⓦryewatersports.co.uk. Offers windsurfing (£79/day) and paddleboarding (£48/2hr) lessons on its own coastal lake, plus kitesurfing (£99/day) and paddlesurfing (£48/2hr) on Camber Sands.

Camber Sands

Three miles east of Rye, on the other side of the River Rother estuary, **CAMBER SANDS** is a two-mile stretch of sandy beach that's the stuff of childhood nostalgia: soft, fine sand backed by tufty dunes, with gently shelving shallows stretching for half a mile when the sea retreats at low tide. Along with West Wittering (see p.296), Camber is the only sandy beach in Sussex, and the secret's been out for some time: Camber Village is awash with holiday camps and caravan parks – and the odd chic beach house – and in summer you can find yourself bumper-to-bumper in traffic on the approach road from Rye. The quieter end of the beach is to the west: park at the Western Car Park (the first one you'll come to if arriving from Rye), and scramble up one of the footpaths weaving through the scrubby dunes for your first magnificent view of the beach.

ARRIVAL AND DEPARTURE
CAMBER SANDS

By car There are three car parks: Western, Central and Old Lydd Rd, which are pay-on-entry in summer, pay-and-display in winter. On sunny weekends in summer the car parks can be full by mid-morning, so get there early.

By bus Buses #711 and #100 (Mon–Sat hourly, Sun every 2hr; 15min) run from Rye station.
By bike A three-mile cycle path connects Rye and Camber; bike rental is available in Rye (see p.170).

ACCOMMODATION AND EATING

The Gallivant Hotel New Lydd Road, Camber, TN31 7RB ☎01797 225057, ⓦthegallivanthotel.com. This stylishly renovated motel set just back from the beach has a cool beach-house vibe: rooms are styled with driftwood furniture, white wooden blinds and nautical striped cushions, with wooden boats and shells adding to the seaside feel. The restaurant sources most of its ingredients from within a thirty-mile radius; mains (£15–19) might include roast Dungeness cod with a white bean cassoulet, or roast Pett Level lamb – or you could go all out for the Romney Marsh tasting menu (£40). Mon–Thurs 7.30–9.30am, noon–2pm & 6.30–9pm, Fri 7.30–9.30am, noon–2pm & 6–10pm, Sat 7.30–9.30am, noon–3pm & 6–10pm, Sun 7.30–9.30am, noon–3pm & 6.30–9pm. Midweek <u>£135</u>; Fri & Sat dinner, bed and breakfast <u>£195</u>

Hastings and around

HASTINGS is a curious mixture of unpretentious fishing town, tatty seaside resort and bohemian retreat – it's often remarked that it has the feel of Brighton twenty years ago. Hastings is a town of several distinct neighbourhoods: to the east of West Hill lies the **Old Town**, a picturesque enclave of handsome mossy-roofed houses, meandering twittens (passageways), antiques shops and cafés, with a sleek new art gallery overlooking the still-working fishing quarter; on the other side of West Hill is the **town centre**, very much the poor relation, where you'll find the station and the scruffy main shopping precinct; and further west still is shabby-chic **St Leonards-on-Sea**, once a separate town but now more or less absorbed into Hastings.

5

Five miles west, the small seaside town of Bexhill-on-Sea is home to the **De La Warr Pavilion**, a peerless piece of Modernist architecture, and further along the coast you can visit **Pevensey Castle**, where William's troops encamped before marching on to Battle. Inland there's star-gazing and hands-on science at **Herstmonceux Castle and Observatory**, and wine tasting at **Carr Taylor Vineyard**, while right on the town's doorstep, rugged **Hastings Country Park** stretches all the way east along the cliffs to Fairlight, three miles away.

Brief history

Hastings is perhaps best known for the eponymous **battle** of 1066 which in fact took place six miles away at Battle (see p.186); the victorious William I designated Hastings as one of the six Rapes (districts) of Sussex, and ordered that a castle be built to defend his newly conquered land. In the years that followed, the town became an important **Cinque Port** (see box, p.105), but French raids and destructive storms in the thirteenth century saw the start of its decline as a port, though fishing remained the main industry. After a lucrative dalliance with **smuggling** in the eighteenth century, the town got a second lease of life as the fashion for **sea bathing** took off: in 1800 Hastings' population stood at around 3000, but by 1900 it was over 65,000, thanks in large part to the arrival of the railway.

Old Town

Most of Hasting's sights – and tourists – can be found in the pretty **Old Town**. **All Saints Street** is by far the most evocative thoroughfare, punctuated with the odd rickety, timber-framed dwelling from the fifteenth century. Running parallel to All Saints Street, and separated from it by The Bourne – the town's busy main through-road – is the narrow **High Street**, lined with antiques shops, upmarket homeware shops, galleries, pubs and restaurants. Pedestrianized **George Street** – chock-a-block with shops and restaurants – strikes off to the west; midway along, the West Hill Cliff Railway (see p.178) ascends West Hill.

Down at the southern end of the High Street, the view of the beach is obscured by amusement arcades and fairground rides – the easternmost end of a long line of traditional seaside tat that stretches west as far as Pelham Crescent, underneath West Hill.

Old Town Hall Museum

High St, TN34 3ES • April–Sept Mon–Sat 10am–5pm, Sun noon–5pm; Oct–March Mon–Sat 10am–4pm, Sun noon–4pm • Free • ☎ 01424 451166, ⓦ hmag.org.uk

It's well worth a potter around the **Old Town Hall Museum** to get a succinct, well-presented history of Hastings Old Town, from pre-Roman times, through its heyday as a Cinque Port to the rise of the Victorian resort and the 1930s housing clearance schemes.

Shirley Leaf and Petal Co

58A High St • Mon–Fri 9am–5pm, Sat 10am–5pm • Museum £1

The tiny **Shirley Leaf and Petal Co** has been making artificial flowers and leaves for theatre, film and television sets around the world for over a hundred years; descend the stairs into the cluttered workshop-cum-museum to see the original Victorian tools and moulds that are still in use today. Cloth flowers are for sale in the shop above.

The Stade

At the eastern end of the seafront, tucked below East Hill, the area known as **The Stade** ("landing place") is home to Hastings' still-working fishing fleet – the largest beach-launched fleet in Europe – and is characterized by its unique **net shops**, tall, black

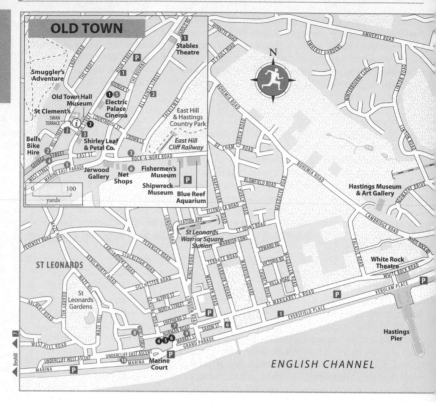

weatherboard sheds built in the mid-nineteenth century to store nets, and still in use today. The beach behind the net shops is a jumble of nets, winches and other fishing paraphernalia, with boats pulled up onto the shingle; several of the net shops sell fresh and smoked fish. There are some good seafood and fish-and-chip **restaurants** along this stretch, of which *Maggie's* (see p.182) is the undisputed queen.

East Hill Cliff Railway

Rock-a-Nore Rd, TN34 3DW • March–Sept daily 10am–5.30pm; Oct–Feb Sat & Sun 11am–4pm • £2.50

Facing the net shops on seafront Rock-a-Nore Road, the **East Hill Cliff Railway**, the steepest cliff railway in the country, ascends to the clifftop Hastings Country Park (see p.184), from where there are wonderful views back over town.

Fishermen's Museum

Rock-a-Nore Rd, TN34 3DW • Daily: April–Oct 10am–5pm; Nov–March 11am–4pm • Free • ☎ 01424 461446

Just past the net shops on Rock-a-Nore Road, a converted seaman's chapel is now the **Fishermen's Museum**. The centrepiece is *The Enterprise*, one of Hastings' last clinker-built luggers (1912) – exceptionally stout trawlers able to withstand being winched up and down the shingle beach. Surrounding it is a wealth of photos, models, fishing nets, stuffed sea birds and other nautical paraphernalia, including one of the original horse-driven capstans used to hoist the boats up onto the beach until they were replaced with motor-driven winches in the 1930s.

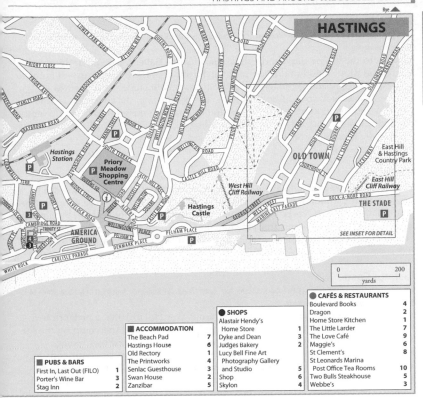

■ PUBS & BARS

First In, Last Out (FILO)	1
Porter's Wine Bar	3
Stag Inn	2

■ ACCOMMODATION

The Beach Pad	7
Hastings House	6
Old Rectory	1
The Printworks	4
Senlac Guesthouse	3
Swan House	2
Zanzibar	5

● SHOPS

Alastair Hendy's Home Store	1
Dyke and Dean	3
Judges Bakery	2
Lucy Bell Fine Art Photography Gallery and Studio	5
Shop	6
Skylon	4

● CAFÉS & RESTAURANTS

Boulevard Books	4
Dragon	2
Home Store Kitchen	1
The Little Larder	7
The Love Café	9
Maggie's	6
St Clement's	8
St Leonards Marina Post Office Tea Rooms	10
Two Bulls Steakhouse	5
Webbe's	3

Shipwreck Museum

Rock-a-Nore Rd, TN34 3DW • April–Oct daily 10am–5pm; Nov–March Sat & Sun 11am–4pm; tours of wreck site roughly monthly, coinciding with the lowest spring tides • Museum free, tours £6 • ☎ 01424 437452, ⓦ shipwreckmuseum.co.uk

The **Shipwreck Museum** details the dramas of unfortunate mariners, focusing on two wrecks: the Restoration 70-gun warship *Anne*, which ran ashore in 1690 when it was damaged by the French in the Battle of Beachy Head; and the Dutch East Indiaman *Amsterdam*, beached in 1749. The latter was carrying textiles, wine and 27 chests of silver bullion when she ran aground, worth several million pounds in today's money; some of it was swiftly liberated by local smugglers before the rest was removed by the authorities. The wreck is now embedded in the sand three miles west of town, with much of its cargo buried with it; only the tops of the ship's ribs show above the sand at low tide. The centre runs **guided tours** to the site of the wreck; see the website for details.

Blue Reef Aquarium

Rock-a-Nore Rd, TN34 3DW • Daily: March–Sept 10am–5pm; Oct–Feb 10am–4pm • £8.20, joint ticket with Smugglers Adventure £14.35 • ☎ 01424 718776, ⓦ bluereefaquarium.co.uk

The **Blue Reef Aquarium** is a well-presented if pricey family attraction, with both tropical and native sea life on display, from giant crabs to rays and seahorses. A small walk-through underwater tunnel brings you face-to-fin with tropical fish, and hourly talks and feeding sessions take place throughout the day.

5

Jerwood Gallery

Rock-a-Nore Rd, TN34 3DW • Tues–Fri 11am–4pm, Sat & Sun 11am–6pm; first Tues of month open until 8pm • £7 • ☎ 01424 425809,
Ⓦ jerwoodgallery.org

Adjacent to the fishing quarter, the sleek new **Jerwood Gallery**, covered in shimmering dark-glazed tiles – a nod to the vernacular architecture of the fishing huts – is home to the Jerwood Foundation's modern art collection, which includes works by Stanley Spencer, Walter Sickert and Augustus John. The paintings in the collection are rotated regularly, and there's also a temporary exhibition space on the ground floor. Up on the first floor there's an airy café with floor-to-ceiling windows and a small terrace looking out over the fishermen's boats on the beach below.

West Hill

West Hill, separating the Old Town from the less interesting modern quarter, can be ascended by the wonderful old **West Hill Cliff Railway** from George Street (March–Sept daily 10am–5.30pm; Oct–Feb Sat & Sun 11am–4pm; £2.50), or on foot, by climbing up through the steep twittens from the junction of Croft Road and Swan Terrace, by St Clement's Church. From the top you'll be rewarded by brilliant views back over the Old Town.

Hastings Castle

West Hill • The 1066 Story: mid-Feb to Easter Sat & Sun 10am–4pm; Easter–Aug daily 10am–5pm; Sept & Oct daily 10am–4pm • £4.35 •
☎ 01424 422964, Ⓦ smugglersadventure.co.uk

William the Conqueror erected his first castle on West Hill in 1066, a prefabricated wooden structure brought over from Normandy in sections and then built on the site of an existing fort, probably of Saxon origins. It was soon replaced by a more permanent stone structure, but in the thirteenth century storms caused the cliffs to subside, tipping most of the castle into the sea. Today **Hastings Castle** is little more than a shell, but the ruins that do survive offer a great view over the town. The castle is home to **The 1066 Story**, an audiovisual show in which the events of the last successful invasion of the British mainland are described inside a mocked-up siege tent, though for the real deal you're better off visiting Battle (see p.186).

Smugglers Adventure

West Hill, TN34 3HY • Daily: April–Sept 10am–5pm; Oct–March 10am–4pm • £7.50, joint ticket with Blue Reef Aquarium £14.35 •
☎ 01424 422964, Ⓦ smugglersadventure.co.uk

Re-creating the eighteenth-century heyday of smuggling (see box, p.218), **Smugglers Adventure** is set in the winding subterranean passageways and caverns of St Clements Caves, which burrow their way into West Hill. The interactive displays, eerie sound effects and narration by "Hairy Jack the Smuggler" offer a fun introduction to the town's long history of duty-dodging. As well as being used by smugglers to store their contraband, the caves have also served variously as a military hospital, a Victorian tourist attraction and a World War II air-raid shelter.

Town centre

Hastings **town centre** lacks the charm of the Old Town or the buzz of St Leonards to the west, and for the most part it's eminently missable. One spot that's worth investigating is the triangle of land known as **the America Ground**, an up-and-coming enclave with a fascinating history (see box opposite), a couple of galleries and some quirky shops (see p.183).

A few hundred yards west, the blackened skeleton of **Hastings Pier** juts out into the sea, burnt down in an arson attack in 2010. Ambitious redevelopment plans for the pier, with a visitor centre, restaurant and open-air cinema, may see it re-open by the end of 2014.

THE AMERICA GROUND

There is a small corner of Hastings that shall remain forever star-spangled, in name at least. The **America Ground** (ⓦamericaground.co.uk), the area of town bordered by Robertson, Claremont and Trinity streets, gained its name almost two hundred years ago. When huge storms in the thirteenth century altered the coastline, over a long period of time creating land where once there was sea, canny locals saw an opportunity to claim the newly created no-man's-land for themselves and escape tax and rent. A ramshackle but thriving settlement gradually developed, of warehouses, farm holdings, lodging houses, even a school, and by the 1820s around a thousand people lived there. When the Corporation of Hastings attempted to seize control of the area, the inhabitants rioted, and raised the American flag, declaring themselves the 24th state of America, and independent from Hastings. Unsurprisingly the powers-that-be weren't having any of it, and in 1828 the site was claimed for the Crown; it was cleared seven years later, and stood empty until Patrick Robinson started the construction of the Crown Estate in 1850, the buildings of which still stand today.

A huge mural on Robertson Passage, on the corner of Trinity and Robinson streets, commemorates the original America Ground, while the annual **America Ground Independence Day** in early July celebrates the area's attempted American citizenship with live music and market stalls.

Hastings Museum and Art Gallery

John's Place, Bohemia Rd, TN34 1ET • April–Sept Tues–Sat 10am–5pm, Sun noon–5pm; Oct–March Tues–Sat 10am–4pm, Sun noon–4pm • Free • ☏ 01424 451052, ⓦhmag.org.uk

As well as hosting temporary art exhibitions, the eclectic **Hastings Museum and Art Gallery** contains permanent displays on the local area and further afield, with exhibits on everything from iguanodons and Hastings smugglers to Native Americans and the Indian subcontinent, the last of these housed in the ornately carved **Durbar Hall**, created for the Colonial and Indian Exhibition held in South Kensington in 1886. There are also exhibits on one-time local residents **Robert Tressell**, who wrote the classic socialist tome *The Ragged Trousered Philanthropists* between 1906 and 1910 while working in the town as a signwriter and decorator, and **John Logie Baird**, whose experiments at his lodgings in Linton Crescent led him to transmit the first television image in 1925.

St Leonards-on-Sea

Not so long ago, **St Leonards** was more than a little down-at-heel, but a recent sprouting of cool cafés and shops has led it to be dubbed "Portobello Road-on-Sea" in the national press, to the evident amusement of the locals. The accolade is rather far-fetched, it's true, but the area does have a bit of a buzz about it, especially along the main drag, **Norman Road**. It's definitely worth spending a morning or afternoon here checking out the galleries and shops (see p.183), and stopping for lunch at one of the great cafés (see p.182), which are more than a match for anything you'll find in the Old Town.

ST LEONARDS ARCHITECTURE

The area of St Leonards west of Norman Road contains some of its finest **architecture**. St Leonards was planned and built by the late-Georgian developer **James Burton** (1761–1837) and son, **Decimus Burton** (1800–1881), and was the first ever planned Regency seaside town. The resort was centred on a private park, now St Leonards Gardens, and the streets around it today contain some of the best examples of the Burtons' architecture. A leaflet from the tourist office describes a **walking tour** around some of the highlights.

5

ARRIVAL AND DEPARTURE

By car The most convenient place to park for the Old Town is the 450-space Rock-a-Nore car park, accessed via Rock-a-Nore Rd.

By train The train station is a ten-minute walk from the seafront along Havelock Road.

Destinations Ashford (hourly; 40min); Battle (every 30min; 15min); Brighton (every 30min; 1hr 5min); Eastbourne (every 20min; 25min); Lewes (every 20min; 55min); London Victoria (hourly; 2hr–2hr 15min); Rye (hourly; 20min);

Tunbridge Wells (every 30min; 35–50min).

By bus Bus services operate from the station at the junction of Havelock and Queen's roads.

Destinations Battle (Mon–Sat hourly, Sun every 2–3 hours; 15min); Dover (hourly; 2hr 50min); Eastbourne (Mon–Sat every 20–30min, Sun hourly; 1hr 15min); London Victoria (1 daily; 2hr 35min); Rye (Mon–Sat hourly, Sun every 2hr; 40min).

GETTING AROUND AND INFORMATION

By bike Rent bikes at Bells Bicycles, 4 George St (☎01424 716541, ⓦbellsbicycles.co.uk; £20/day).

By taxi Hastings Taxis (☎01424 236272).

Tourist offices Within the Town Hall on Queen's Square

(Mon–Fri 8.30am–6.15pm, Sat 9am–5pm, Sun 10.30am–4pm; ☎01424 451111, ⓦvisit1066country.com). Another office in Old Town, within the Old Town Hall Museum (Mon–Sat 10am–5pm, Sun noon–5pm; Oct–March closes 4pm).

ACCOMMODATION

OLD TOWN

Old Rectory Harold Rd, TN35 5ND ☎01424 422410, ⓦtheoldrectoryhastings.co.uk. Elegant, double-fronted Georgian pad next to All Saints Church, with nine luxurious, quirkily styled rooms (one has a feature wall of Wedgwood plates, another a toilet hidden behind a false bookcase); those at the front are grander and light-flooded, though do suffer a bit from traffic noise, while the smaller rooms at the back look out over the tranquil walled garden. Downstairs there's a lovely lounge, with fresh flowers, an honesty bar, plenty of squishy sofas and a real fire in winter. **£100**

★ **Swan House** 1 Hill St, TN34 3HU ☎01892 430014, ⓦswanhousehastings.co.uk. This beautiful boutique B&B – one of Hastings' first – still ticks all the boxes. It couldn't have a more perfect setting, in a lovely half-timbered fifteenth-century building on one of the Old Town's most picturesque streets. Rooms are luxurious and tasteful, with muted paintwork, wooden floors and luxurious bed linen, and there's a pretty decked patio garden for sunny breakfasts (locally sourced where possible, including kippers from the Hastings fishing fleet). **£115**

TOWN CENTRE

The Printworks 14 Claremont, America Ground, TN34 1HA ☎01424 425532, ⓦ14claremont.com. This hip B&B in the old *Observer* building offers loft-style living in the America Ground, with vaulted ceilings, wooden floors, and bare plaster and brick walls, jazzed up with eclectic vintage furnishings. The two bedrooms have plenty of character, with original features from the building's days as a newspaper office: it's worth paying the extra for the suite (£130), which comes with a fabulous bathroom with black-painted boards, fireplace and freestanding bath. **£100**

Senlac Guesthouse 46–47 Cambridge Gardens, TN34 1EN ☎01424 430080, ⓦsenlacguesthouse.co.uk.

Stylish yet affordable, this friendly B&B near the station is fantastic value for money – rooms are bright and contemporary, and bathrooms gleaming. The cheapest rooms share bathrooms; self-contained apartments are also available next door. Breakfast is an additional £8.50. **£50**

ST LEONARDS

The Beach Pad 2 Lorimer Court, 33–35 West Hill Road, TN38 0NA ☎01424 390042, ⓦthebeachpad.com. For something completely different check out this basement garden flat, with just one room sleeping up to 5 (double bunk and 3 singles), which can be rented out as individual bunks or as one unit (both self-catering and B&B). The big selling point is the outside space: a palm-fringed, landscaped deck juts out over the cliff with an uninterrupted 180-degree view of azure-blue sea. The owner can arrange a variety of activities, from bodyboarding to boot-camp breaks. Bunks **£30**, B&B for up to 4 people **£125**, self-catering (3 nights) **£450**

Hastings House 9 Warrior Square, TN37 6BA ☎01424 422709, ⓦhastingshouse.co.uk. Friendly boutique B&B in a Victorian house overlooking a garden square, close to the beach. Each of the modern, luxurious rooms sports a different look, some more eye-popping than others (think pink leather headboard and matching chairs); those at the front boast lovely views over Warrior Square gardens to the sea. **£99**

Zanzibar 9 Everfield Place, TN37 6BY ☎01424 460109, ⓦzanzibarhotel.co.uk. Boutique hotel with rooms themed around the owner's travels, set in a beautifully styled Victorian townhouse overlooking St Leonards' seafront. Cheaper rooms are at the back of the house, with more opulent suites – including a fabulous Manhattan-styled penthouse – facing the sea. The *Pier Nine* restaurant has a lush decked courtyard garden for alfresco dining and excellent, though pricey, food. **£145**

5

EATING

OLD TOWN

Boulevard Books 32 George St, TN34 3EA ☎ 01424 436521, ⓦ thaicafeandbookshop.com. The town's most unique eating experience, this tiny second hand bookshop serves up fantastic home-cooked Thai food in the evenings, with half a dozen tables nestled among the bookshelves. Two courses £13; BYO (corkage £2 per person). Wed–Sun 6–9.30pm, Mon/Tues by arrangement.

Dragon 71 George St, TN34 3EE ☎ 01424 423688. Part restaurant, part bar, this hip, buzzy little hangout – candlelit even in the daytime – has good music, scuffed wooden floors, squishy leather sofas and dark-painted walls hung with art. The menu changes almost daily, but might include dishes such as pan-fried Hastings sea bass on curried puy lentils (£15.50), or duck leg and mulberry apple sauce (£16.50). Mon–Sat noon–11pm, Sun noon–10.30pm.

★ **Home Store Kitchen** 36 High St, TN34 3ER ☎ 01424 447171, ⓦ homestore-hastings.co.uk. This tiny seafood kitchen, tucked away behind Alastair Hendy's Home Store (see opposite), only opens up for lunch at weekends, when food writer and photographer Hendy steps behind the stove to prepare simple plates of fish and seafood, anything from sprats with parsley and vinegar (£8.50) to fish stew (£16.50) or shellfish on ice (£38 for two). There are only a few tables – one in the kitchen itself – plus a few in the courtyard, so book well ahead. Sat & Sun noon–4.30pm.

Maggie's Above Hastings fish market, Rock-a-Nore Rd, TN34 3DW ☎ 01424 430205. The best fish and chips in town can be found at this unpretentious first-floor café, right on the beach. A bit of a Hastings institution, it's very popular, so you'll need to book ahead. Mon–Sat noon–2pm.

Two Bulls Steakhouse 61C High St, TN34 3EJ ☎ 01424 436443, ⓦ twobulls.co.uk. This steakhouse has taken the town by storm since it opened: it's informal and relaxed, with an open kitchen cooking up 45-day hung steaks imported from Ireland, which are grilled over charcoal and served with home-made chips and a choice of sauces and butters. Set lunches (steak or equally good burgers) are great value at £8. Book ahead. Thurs & Fri noon–3pm & 7–11pm, Sat 12.30–4pm & 7–11pm, Sun 12.30–4pm & 6.30–10pm.

Webbe's 1 Rock-a-Nore Rd, TN34 3DW ☎ 01424 721650, ⓦ webbesrestaurants.co.uk. This top-notch seafood restaurant is slap-bang opposite the Jerwood Gallery, a literal stone's throw from the fishing huts, making your lunch's journey from boat to plate about as short as you can

get. Mains such as steamed panache of fish cost around £14, or you can pick and choose from tasting dishes at £3.50 each. There's plenty of outside seating in summer. Mon–Fri noon–2pm & 6–9.30pm, Sat & Sun noon–9pm.

ST LEONARDS

★ **The Little Larder** 39 Norman Rd, TN38 0EG ☎ 01424 424364, ⓦ thelittlelarder.co.uk. Friendly, cosy café with just half a dozen tables, good coffee and a great menu of home-made dishes, including the café's trademark potato scones. The small courtyard garden changes each summer – in the last few years it's been styled as a kitchen, a bathroom and Mr McGregor's garden. Tues–Fri 9am–4pm, Sat 10am–4pm.

The Love Café 28 Norman Rd, TN37 6AE ⓦ thelovecafe .me. Quirky, laidback café, a fabulous hotchpotch of mismatched furniture, recycled lampshades, tartan armchairs, local art on the walls, and a papier-mâché trapeze artist with a nipple on show swinging from the ceiling. Outside, the café hosts popular summer-weekend markets under the watchful gaze of Prince Charles, whose pixelated face is captured in a striking twenty-foot-high mural by street artist Ben Eine (local arts and crafts market last Sat of month; French cheese market every second Fri). Fridays see the café open late for themed food-and-film nights. Mon–Thurs, Sat & Sun 10am–6pm, Fri 10am–11pm.

St Clement's 3 Mercatoria, TN38 0EB ☎ 01424 200355, ⓦ stclementsrestaurant.co.uk. Fish is the thing at this small, intimate restaurant: ninety percent of it comes from the Hastings fleet's daily catch, and dishes on the constantly changing menu might include fillet of cod with bubble and squeak, or Spanish fish stew (both £16.50). Puds are excellent, too: expect crowd-pleasers such as date and fig sticky toffee pudding. A range of good-value set lunches and evening meal menus are also available. Tues–Sat noon–3pm & 6.30–9pm, Sun noon–3pm.

★ **St Leonards Marina Post Office Tea Rooms** 40A Marina, TN38 0BU ☎ 01424 718985, ⓦ postofficetea rooms.com. The floral bunting and knitted cakes in the window set the scene at this lovely, eccentric seafront tearoom, which celebrates proper coffee, manners and cake forks, and bans iPods, laptops and lapdogs. Alongside the cream tea and cakes there are sandwiches, all-day breakfasts and Sunday roasts. The tearoom also hosts weekly knitting nights (Thurs 6.30–8.30pm; £3.50) and monthly pop-up dinners (£20 for 3 courses; BYO). Wed–Sun 10.30am–4pm.

DRINKING AND ENTERTAINMENT

Lots of musicians live in Hastings, and there's a thriving live music scene; pick up the *Ultimate Alternative* listings magazine (ⓦ ua1066.co.uk), available in pubs and clubs throughout town, for a comprehensive guide to what's on.

The Electric Palace 39 High St, TN34 3ER ☎ 01424 720393, ⓦ electricpalacecinema.com. Tiny independent

cinema showing arthouse and world cinema, with a licensed bar. Screenings Wed–Sun at 8pm; £6.

PARADES AND PIRATES: HASTINGS FESTIVALS

Hastings has some great (and uniquely bonkers) festivals, two of which are well worth making a special visit for. The **Jack-in-the-Green Festival** (ⓦhastingsjack.co.uk) sees a weekend of festivities over May Day culminating in a riotous parade of dancers, drummers and leaf-bedecked revellers through the streets of the Old Town up to Hastings' hilltop castle, where "the Jack" – a garlanded leaf-covered figure whose origins date back to the eighteenth century – is ritually slain and the spirit of summer released.

At the end of July, thousands of buccaneers descend on the town for **Hastings Pirate Day** (ⓦhastingspirateday.org.uk), a phenomenally popular day of swashbuckling fun, including shanties, sword-fighting and an attempt on the world record for the Largest Gathering of Pirates – a title occasionally snatched by the scurvy pirates in Penzance.

First In, Last Out (FILO) 15 High St, TN34 3EY ⓣ01424 425079, ⓦthefilo.co.uk. Tiny, ever-popular traditional pub with snug booths, a huge roaring fire in winter, no jukeboxes or fruit machines, and its own microbrewery. Tasty food is served Tues–Sat lunchtimes, and there are occasional live music nights – check the website for details. Mon–Sat 11am–midnight, Sun noon–midnight.

Porter's Wine Bar 56 High St, TN34 3EN ⓣ01424 427000, ⓦporterswinebar.com. Friendly, family-run wine bar, with jazz and acoustic music on Wednesday and Thursday nights and Sunday afternoons, including a regular spot by acclaimed jazz pianist and local resident Liane Carroll. Good, home-cooked, bistro-style food is on offer too. Mon–Fri noon–3pm & 7pm–midnight, Sat noon–midnight, Sun 12.30–11pm.

Stables Theatre The Bourne, TN34 3BD ⓣ01424 423221, ⓦstables-theatre.co.uk. Small theatre hosting amateur and touring productions.

Stag Inn 14 All Saints St, TN34 3BJ ⓣ01424/425734, ⓦstaghastings.co.uk. Friendly, traditional pub that dates back to 1547, with beams, inglenook fireplaces, a secret passage once used by smugglers, and a pair of mummified cats. There's a nice tiered garden out the back, and live music several nights a week: folk on Tuesdays, bluegrass on Wednesdays and shanty singing on Thursdays. Good pub food (mains £6–8) is served every lunchtime and until 9pm Mon–Sat; the Sunday roasts are very popular. Daily noon–midnight.

White Rock Theatre White Rock, TN34 1JX ⓣ01424 462280, ⓦwhiterocktheatre.org.uk. The town's main venue, putting on comedy, bands, theatre, ballet, shows and the annual panto.

SHOPPING

In Old Town, **High Street** and **George Street** are the main shopping streets, with plenty of antiques shops, boutiques and galleries. Also worth exploring are the quirky shops around the **America Ground** in the town centre, which cover everything from dog accessories (Collared at 37 Robertson St) to street art (Inspire Artwork at 34 Robertson St). Finally, don't miss the hip galleries and shops along **Norman Road** in St Leonards; there are a couple more galleries nearby in the colonnades underneath **Marine Court**.

Alastair Hendy's Home Store 36 High St, TN34 3ER ⓣ01424 447171, ⓦhomestore-hastings.co.uk. Step back in time in this extraordinary store that's part shop, part museum. The building has been pared back to its original Georgian framework – all bare plaster and stripped wood – and the rooms over three floors stock simple utilitarian essentials, including brooms, brushes, vintage linen, woollen bedsocks, enamelware, hand-forged scissors, reclaimed furniture and bathroom fittings. Out the back a small seafood kitchen opens up at weekends (see opposite). Tues–Sun & bank hols Mon 10am–5.30pm.

Dyke and Dean The Printworks, 14 Claremont, TN34 1HA ⓣ01424 429202, ⓦdykeanddean.com. Hip interiors and homewares store in the America Ground, selling everything from Plumen light bulbs and enamelware to Welsh throws and soap from Oregon, displayed with utilitarian panache on subway-tiled shelving and wooden display cases held together with clamps. Thurs & Fri 10am–6pm, Sat 10am–7pm, Mon–Wed by appointment.

Judges Bakery 51 High St, Old Town, TN34 3EN ⓣ01424 722588, ⓦjudgesbakery.com. Owned by Green & Blacks founders Craig Sams and Josephine Fairley, Judges has been baking its own bread since 1826, and now offers organic artisan breads, coffee from Monmouth Coffee Shop, cheeses and meats, and lots of other goodies. Mon–Thurs 8.15am–5.30pm, Fri & Sat 8.15am–6pm, Sun 9am–5pm.

Lucy Bell Fine Art Photography Gallery and Studio 46 Norman Rd, TN38 0EJ ⓣ01424 434828, ⓦlucy-bell .com. This excellent small gallery exhibits and sells fine art photography, regularly attracting top-class photographers as well as new talent. Opening days and times vary; check website for details.

Shop 32–34 Norman Rd, TN38 0EJ. Great little shop, run by a collective, that sells everything from fashion and

5

accessories – both vintage and new – to homeware and recycled furniture, with a small section at the back serving up tea and cakes. Wed–Sat 10am–5pm, Sun 11am–4pm. **Skylon** 65 Norman Rd, TN38 0EJ ☎ 01424 445691, ⓦ skyloninteriors.co.uk. This tiny retro design shop, selling twentieth-century and industrial designs, is worth a browse just to see what eclectic treasures they've managed to unearth: if you're on the lookout for vintage Czech laboratory glassware, or French wooden engineering moulds, this is the place. Thurs–Sat 10am–5pm.

Hastings Country Park

Visitor centre: Coastguard Lane, off Fairlight Rd · Tues–Sun 10am–4pm; closed Wed mornings Sept–June; ☎ 01424 812140, ⓦ hastingscountrypark.org.uk · Take the funicular (see p.176), or the park is a 10min climb from the Old Town; the steep steps up the cliff start from Tackleway, parallel to All Saints Street; there's parking at various locations in the park

Hastings Country Park extends three miles east from East Hill to Fairlight, a unique stretch of coastline with more than 650 acres of wild, gorse-speckled heathland, grassland, ancient woodland and dramatic sandstone cliffs. Most of the park is designated a Special Area of Conservation and a Site of Special Scientific Interest: its ancient gill (ravine) woodlands, **Fairlight Glen** and **Ecclesbourne Glen**, are home to rare liverworts and mosses, and insects found in the park include Britain's only tarantula-type spider, the purse-web. Stonechats, Dartford warblers and yellowhammers nest on the heathland, and there are spectacular migrations in spring and autumn. The woodlands are especially beautiful in the spring, when they're carpeted with bluebells and wood anemone. The **visitor centre**, at the eastern end of the park in the Firehills, has good displays on the park's wildlife and geology.

Bexhill-on-Sea

The quiet seaside town of **Bexhill-on-Sea**, five miles west of Hastings, would be off the tourist radar were it not for the De La Warr Pavilion. The **seafront** surrounding the De La Warr has recently been spruced up, with landscaped lawns, sleek new seafront shelters and free showers for beach users; it's especially good if you've got kids, with a range of play features including fountain jets and balancing beams along its length.

The De La Warr Pavilion

Marina, TN40 1DP · April Mon–Fri & Sun 10am–5pm, Sat 10am–6pm; May to mid-July & Oct Mon–Thurs & Sun 10am–5pm, Fri & Sat 10am–6pm; mid-July to Sept Mon–Thurs & Sun 10am–6pm, Fri & Sat 10am–8pm; Nov–March daily 10am–5pm · Free · ☎ 01424 229111, ⓦ dlwp.com · Bus #98 from Hastings (Mon–Sat every 30min, Sun hourly; 40min); train from Hastings (every 20min; 10min); or seafront cycle path from Hastings to Bexhill – rent bikes from Bells Bicycles (see p.180)

Bexhill-on-Sea's iconic **De La Warr Pavilion**, a sleek Modernist masterpiece overlooking the sea, was built in 1935 by architects Erich Mendelsohn and Serge Chermayeff – the first Modernist public building in the country, and the first to use a welded steel frame. It was the brainchild of the progressive 9th Earl de la Warr, local landowner and socialist, who had a vision of a free-to-all seaside pavilion for the education, entertainment and health of the masses. In its brief heyday the Pavilion flourished, but slid gradually into disrepair after World War II. After decades of hosting everything from bingo to wrestling while the building crumbled and corroded, today the Pavilion has been lovingly restored to its original glory – all crisp white lines and gleaming glass – and hosts changing **exhibitions** of contemporary art, and an eclectic mix of **live performances**, from big-name bands to comedy and film nights. Up on the first floor a **café** and restaurant offer glorious views from the floor-to-ceiling windows and balcony.

Pevensey Castle

Castle Rd, Pevensey, 12 miles west of Hastings, BN24 5LE · April–Sept daily 10am–6pm; Oct daily 10am–4pm; Nov–March Sat & Sun 10am–4pm · £4.90; EH · ☎ 01323 762604, ⓦ english-heritage.org.uk/daysout/properties/pevensey-castle

If truth be told, there isn't an awful lot left of **Pevensey Castle**, and you'll need to use your imagination – or take advantage of the excellent forty-minute audio tour – to

5

really bring the rich history of the place to life. When William the Conqueror landed here in 1066, he set up camp within the crumbling walls of an old Roman fort – one of the largest of the Saxon shore forts built on the south coast in the third century. After his victory at Battle (see box, p.187), he gave the Rape of Pevensey to his half-brother, **Robert Count of Mortain**, who built a wooden castle within the southeast corner of the Roman fort, and repaired the Roman walls for use as an outer bailey; over two-thirds of the Roman walls still remain today. Mortain's wooden castle was replaced by a sturdier stone castle in the twelfth and thirteenth centuries.

The castle survived several dramatic sieges through the centuries, but was eventually overcome – not by invading troops but by the changing coastline, which left it without access to the sea and so without a strategic purpose. By 1500 the castle was no longer in use, though it was pressed back into action again at various times when foreign invasion threatened – the Spanish Armada in 1580, Napoleon in 1805 and Hitler in 1940. The **gun emplacements** added in World War II can still be seen today.

Entry into the Roman walls is free; you only pay to cross the moat and enter the castle itself. Inside, the castle lies in ruins, but you can clamber down into the dungeons, and up a wooden staircase to the North Tower. Look out for the oubliette – a dungeon accessible only via a trapdoor in the ceiling – by the gatehouse.

Herstmonceux Castle and Observatory Science Centre

Wartling Rd, Herstmonceux, BN27 1RN **Castle, gardens & grounds** daily: April–Sept 10am–6pm; Oct 10am–5pm; castle: 2 tours between noon and 2pm • Gardens £6; castle tours £2.50, joint ticket with Observatory £12.50 • ☎ 01323 833816, ⓦ herstmonceux-castle .com **Observatory** April–Sept 10am–6pm; Jan–March, Oct & Nov 10am–5pm; last admission 2hr before • £7.80; joint ticket with castle £12.50; children over 4 £5.85/£8 • ☎ 01323 832731, ⓦ the-observatory.org

Moated **Herstmonceux Castle**, 13 miles from Hastings, was built in the fifteenth century, one of the first buildings in the south to be constructed from brick – at the time a new and fashionable building material. In 1946 the castle was sold to the Admiralty, who moved the **Royal Greenwich Observatory** to the castle grounds, away from London's lights and pollution. When the Observatory's prized Isaac Newton telescope was moved to the clearer skies of La Palma in the Canaries in 1979 it signalled the beginning of the end for the Observatory, and it was closed down in 1990, a move described by astronomer Patrick Moore – who spent much of the 1950s and 1960s here mapping the Moon's surface – as a "crack-brained idea".

The castle was subsequently bought by the **Queen's University of Canada** and is now closed to the public except on guided tours. You can still stroll round the lovely Elizabethan **walled garden** and surrounding **parklands**, but undoubtedly the best time to visit is during the annual **Medieval Festival** (see p.33), when over a thousand costumed knights, men-at-arms, jesters, minstrels and medieval traders throng the grounds.

Next door to the castle, the old observatory buildings now house the **Observatory Science Centre**, which is really two attractions in one: a fantastically well-run science centre, with over a hundred interactive exhibits, all enticingly hands-on for kids; and an observatory that's home to the historic telescopes, now fully restored to working order (telescope tours daily in school holidays and at weekends). **Star-gazing open evenings** offer you the chance to use the telescopes on selected dates in winter, spring and autumn.

Carr Taylor Vineyard

Wheel Lane, outside Westfield village, 4 miles north of Hastings, TN35 4SG • Daily 10am–5pm • Self-guided tours £1.50 per person; guided tours £16 per person, minimum group size 15 • ☎ 01424 752501, ⓦ carr-taylor.co.uk

Family-run **Carr Taylor Vineyard** is the granddaddy of the English wine scene, planted back in 1971. Not only was Carr Taylor one of the very first commercial vineyards in the country, it was also the first to produce traditional-method sparkling wine (Champagne in all but name), the real success story of English wine, and this remains one of its

5

mainstays today, together with still white wine and a variety of fruit wines. You can visit the beautiful 37-acre vineyard on a **self-guided tour**, which takes you through the vineyards, winery and bottling room, or, if there are a fair number of you, on a **guided group tour**, which will give you a bit of background on English wine, a more detailed look at the winery and bottling room, and a wine-tasting session to round things off.

Battle

The town of **BATTLE**, six miles inland of Hastings, occupies the site of the most famous land battle in British history. Here, on October 14, 1066, the invading Normans swarmed up the hillside from Senlac Moor and overcame the Anglo-Saxon army of King Harold, in what would be the last ever successful invasion of Britain (see box opposite). Battle Abbey, built by the victorious William the Conqueror in penance for the blood spilled, still dominates the town today, its impressive gatehouse looming over the southern end of the narrow, appealingly venerable **High Street**, lined with a mix of medieval timber-framed, tile-hung and Victorian buildings. Among the High Street shops, the excellent Saffron Gallery at nos. 59–60 is always worth popping into, with exhibitions featuring both local and internationally renowned artists (Mon–Sat 10am–5pm; ☎01424 772130, ⊕saffrongallery.co.uk).

Battle Abbey

At the south end of High St, TN33 0AD • April–Sept daily 10am–6pm; Oct daily 10am–4pm; Nov–March Sat & Sun 10am–4pm • £7.50; EH • ☎01424 775705, ⊕english-heritage.org.uk/daysout/properties/1066-battle-of-hastings-abbey-and-battlefield

The magnificent structure of **Battle Abbey**, founded by William in the aftermath of his victory, was ostensibly built to atone for the thousands of lives lost in the battle, but it was also a powerful symbol of Norman victory. Not for nothing did William decree that the high altar in the abbey church should be built on the exact spot where Harold met his death. The completed abbey was occupied by a fraternity of Benedictines, and over the next four hundred years grew to become one of the richest monasteries in the country, being rebuilt and extended along the way. When the Dissolution came, the land was given to King Henry VIII's friend, Sir Anthony Browne, who promptly knocked down the church and converted the abbot's lodging into a fine manor house.

The manor house still stands today, though it's out of bounds to visitors, having been occupied by Battle Abbey School since 1912. All that remains of the Norman abbey church is its outline – with the site of the high altar marked by a memorial stone – but some buildings survive from the thirteenth century, including the monks' rib-vaulted **dormitory range**. The impressive 1330s **gatehouse** houses an exhibition on medieval monastic life, but the best place to start your visit is in the modern **exhibition centre**, where a short film takes you through the background to the events of the day itself.

Audio guides (40min) take you round the site of the **battlefield**, vividly re-creating the battle and its aftermath, which local chroniclers recorded as a hellish scene – "covered in corpses, and all around the only colour to meet the gaze was blood-red". The best time to visit the abbey is during the annual **re-enactment** of the battle, held

---

THE 1066 WALK

Follow in the footsteps of the Norman invaders on the **1066 Walk**, which runs for 31 miles from William's landing place at **Pevensey** and on to the battle site at **Battle**, before continuing on to **Rye**. The waymarked, mainly low-level route takes you through beautiful villages and quiet countryside, and also passes by Herstmonceux Castle, Carr Taylor Vineyard and Winchelsea. The walk is doable in two longish days, with an overnight stop in Battle. The OS Explorer **maps** #124 and #125 cover the route.

5

on the weekend nearest to October 14, and performed by a cast of over a thousand chain-mailed soldiers, entering into their Norman and Saxon roles with gusto.

Battle Museum of Local History

The Almonry, High St, TN33 0EA • April–Oct Mon–Sat 10am–4.30pm • £1.50 • ☎ 01424 775955

At the top end of the High Street in the medieval Almonry, the small, volunteer-run **Battle Museum of Local History** contains what is believed to be the only battle-axe

---

THE BATTLE OF HASTINGS

The most famous date in English history – October 14, 1066 – and the most famous battle ever fought on English soil, the **Battle of Hastings** saw the defeat of King Harold and the end of Anglo-Saxon England.

LEAD-UP TO THE BATTLE

The roots of the battle lay in the death of Edward the Confessor in January 1066. With no children of his own, the succession was far from clear: Edward's cousin, **William, Duke of Normandy**, had reportedly been promised the Crown by Edward during a previous visit to England, fifteen years before, but it was **Harold**, Edward the Confessor's brother-in-law, whom Edward named as his successor on his deathbed. William was enraged, his sense of injustice not helped by the fact that Harold had previously sworn an oath, on holy relics no less, that he would support William's claim to the Crown.

William quickly gathered together an army and sailed for England, landing at Pevensey on September 28. Harold heard the news in Yorkshire, where he'd just been celebrating victory over another claimant to the throne – **Harold Hardrada**, King of Norway – at the Battle of Stamford Bridge on September 22. He quickly raced his troops south to meet William, but instead of giving his footsore and battle-worn army time to recuperate, he rushed to engage William in battle.

THE BATTLE

The forces met at **Senlac Hill**. Harold's army of 5000–7000 troops occupied the superior position on the brow of the hill, his soldiers forming a protective shield wall. William's Norman army – a similar size – congregated below. Statistically, the odds were in Harold's favour, but the Saxon troops made an error: when Norman soldiers made an unsuccessful charge and retreated down the hill, some of Harold's troops, instead of staying put in their unassailable hilltop position, pursued them. Separated from the rest of their army, they were surrounded by Norman soldiers and killed. William pressed his advantage, his men feigning several more retreats, each time drawing the Saxon army down the hill, only for them to be surrounded and hacked to death. It wasn't enough to defeat the English entirely, but William had two other advantages: his mounted knights, who had greater mobility in the battlefield than the Saxon foot soldiers, and his archers, who were able to breach the English line. The advantage steadily moved in William's favour, and by nightfall the battle was his, and Harold lay dead on the battlefield. The total casualties lay at around 7000, which at a time when the population of a large town was around 2500, would have been a shockingly large number.

THE BAYEUX TAPESTRY AND THE DEATH OF HAROLD

That we know so much about the battle and its lead-up is in part due to the existence of the **Bayeux Tapestry** – a 70m-long piece of embroidery created within 20 years of the battle. The most famous scene in the tapestry – the **death of Harold** – is, however, famously ambiguous. Harold's death by means of an arrow through the eye was first reported in 1080 (although it was not noted in any of the accounts written immediately after the battle), and by the following century had become an accepted fact. The scene in the tapestry seems to bear out the arrow story, but over the years scholars have variously argued that the figure with an arrow through his eye and "Harold" written above his head was not actually the king; that Harold was felled by an arrow through the eye and *then* hacked to death; and that the "arrow" through Harold's eye is just a spear he is holding, and that the fletching on it was added later in over-zealous restoration. The truth of the matter will probably never be known.

5

discovered at Battle, as well as a rare hand-coloured print of the Bayeux Tapestry, made in 1819 after a watercolour painting by Charles Stothard. The museum is also home to the oldest **Guy Fawkes** in the country, with a pearwood head dating back to the eighteenth century. Every year, on the Saturday nearest to November 5, the effigy is paraded along High Street at the head of a torch-lit procession culminating at a huge bonfire on the abbey's battlefield.

Yesterday's World

89–90 High St, TN33 0AQ • Daily: April–Oct 10am–5.30pm; Nov–March 10am–4.30pm • £7.25, children £5.25 • ☎ 01424 777226, Ⓦ yesterdaysworld.co.uk

Housed in a beautifully preserved fifteenth-century Wealden hall house, **Yesterday's World** provides a fun few hours for both kids and nostalgia buffs, consisting of forty re-created rooms, shop settings and street scenes from the eighteenth century to the 1970s, stocked with original furnishings and goods. Highlights include a Bakelite-crammed 1930s wireless shop and a Victorian kitchen kitted out with authentic accessories, while the grounds feature a 1930s tearoom and children's play area.

ARRIVAL AND INFORMATION   BATTLE

By car The car park next to Battle Abbey is the best value for stays of more than 2hr (£3.50/day; discount for EH members).

By train The train station is a well-signposted 10min walk from the High St.

Destinations Hastings (every 30min; 15min); London Charing Cross (every 30min; 1hr 30min); Tunbridge Wells (every 30min; 30min).

By bus Buses #304 and #305 run from Hastings to Battle High St (Mon–Sat hourly, Sun every 2–3hr; 15min).

Tourist information There's an unstaffed Visitor Information Point at Yesterday's World (see above).

Website Ⓦ battle-sussex.co.uk.

ACCOMMODATION AND EATING

19 Upper Lake 19 Upper Lake, TN33 0AN ☎ 01424 773104, Ⓦ 19upperlake.co.uk. Friendly B&B in a fifteenth-century house with heaps of character – beams, sloping ceilings and creakily lopsided floors – just a couple of minutes' walk from the entrance to the Abbey. Rooms are pretty and stylish, and there's a cosy sitting room kitted out with board games and books. **£85**

Battle Deli 57 High St, TN33 0EN ☎ 01424 777810. Lovely little deli crammed with delicious stuff for a picnic or an eat-in lunch – the quiches are especially good.

Mon–Sat 8.30am–5pm.

Nobles 17 High St, TN33 0AE ☎ 01424 774422, Ⓦ noblesrestaurant.co.uk. The best restaurant in town, serving delicious seasonal, local food, and with the added bonus of a small walled garden for alfresco dining in summer. Mains such as saddle of Battle-reared pork loin or local wild seabass will set you back around £15, or there's a cheaper set menu available at lunchtimes. Tues–Sat noon–2.30pm & 6pm–late.

The eastern High Weald

A feeling of remoteness characterizes the **EASTERN HIGH WEALD**, which spills over the border into neighbouring Kent (see p.144). There are no really big towns – the small market town of Heathfield is the only place of any size – and most of the landscape is given over to rolling farmland and wooded hills, peppered with quiet, sleepy villages. The two big sights in the area are **Great Dixter** – one of the country's most famous gardens – and picture-perfect **Bodiam Castle**. You can also visit **Farley Farm House**, the fascinating former home of the Surrealist artist Roland Penrose and photographer Lee Miller, which became a vibrant meeting place for leading figures in twentieth-century art, and at the other end of the scale, the house at **Bateman's**, where Rudyard Kipling quietly retreated from the outside world. Attractions for kids include the **Bentley Wildfowl and Motor Museum** and the wonderful **Wilderness Woods**.

Great Dixter

Half a mile north of Northiam, signposted from the village, TN31 6PH • April–Oct Tues–Sun & bank hol Mon: gardens 11am–5pm; house 2–5pm • House & gardens £9.50, gardens only £7.50 • ☎ 01797 252878, Ⓦ greatdixter.co.uk • Stagecoach bus #344 runs from Hastings (Mon–Sat hourly, Sun every 2hr; 50min) via Rye (20min); Stagecoach bus #340 passes through Northiam on its way from Hastings to Tenterden (Mon–Sat hourly; 45min from Hastings)

One of the best-loved gardens in the country, **Great Dixter** has come to be known above all else for bringing innovative and experimental planting to the English country garden. This exuberant, informal garden spreads around a medieval half-timbered house, which was home to the gardener and writer **Christopher Lloyd** until his death in 2005. When Lloyd's parents bought the house in 1912 there was no garden to speak of, and the **house** looked pretty different too. Lloyd's father, Nathaniel, employed a dazzling young architect, **Edwin Lutyens**, to remodel both house and garden. Lutyens promptly stripped back the fifteenth-century house to its medieval splendour, ripping out partitions and restoring the magnificent Great Hall – the largest surviving timber-framed hall in the country – to its original double-height. A new wing (to the left of the lopsided porch) was built, and another medieval house was moved piece-by-painstaking-piece from its location in nearby Bendenden and tacked on to the back of the building.

Lutyens, with Nathaniel Lloyd, also designed the **garden**, planting the hedges and topiary, incorporating old farm buildings where possible and laying the paving (recycled London pavement). As you wander round it today, through a series of intimate garden "rooms", the first thing you're struck by is its informality; all around are sweeps of wildflower-speckled meadow, and flowers spilling out of crammed, luxuriant borders. Christopher Lloyd loved change and colour, and with his head gardener **Fergus Garrett** (who continues to manage the garden today) he experimented with unusual juxtapositions and imaginative plantings, most famously ripping out his parents' rose garden to plant dahlias, bananas and other exotics. Look out, too, for occasional reminders that this was a personal garden; Lloyd's beloved dachshunds, which had a tendency to nip unwelcome visitors, are remembered in a pebble mosaic by the entrance.

MAD JACK FULLER AND THE BRIGHTLING FOLLIES

John Fuller of Brightling (1757–1834), or **"Mad Jack" Fuller** as he's affectionately known, was a true eccentric, one of the great characters of Sussex. A wealthy landowner, Fuller was a corpulent 22 stone, wore his hair in a pigtail (despite the style falling out of fashion long before), had a bellowing voice, and drove around the countryside in a heavily armed barouche. His turbulent parliamentary career ended with him hurling abuse at his fellow MPs and being expelled from the House. And yet Fuller was also a man of remarkable philanthropy, and his name crops up again and again all over Sussex: it was he who provided Eastbourne with its first lifeboat (see p.209), bought Bodiam Castle (see p.190) in 1828 to save it from demolition, and built the Belle Tout lighthouse (see p.214), saving countless lives. He was also a champion of science, founding a reference library and two professorships at the Royal Institute.

His fame endures today in the main because of the **follies** he erected around his country estate at **Brightling**, a small village five miles northeast of Battle. In true Fuller fashion each one has an outlandish tale attached to it: the **Rotunda Temple** in Brightling Park was supposedly used for gambling sessions and carousing with ladies of the night; the 35-foot-high circular **Tower**, just off the Brightling–Darwell road, was perhaps erected so that Fuller could keep an eye on the restoration work going on at nearby Bodiam Castle; and the **Sugar Loaf** (visible from the Battle–Heathfield road), was built after Fuller made a wager he could see the spire of nearby Dallington church from his estate – when it turned out he couldn't he had the tower, a replica of Dallington's church spire, built overnight so that he could win his bet. All three follies are accessible by footpath, but the easiest of Fuller's follies to visit is the incongruous blackened stone **pyramid** in the churchyard of squat-towered **Brightling church**: this is Fuller's burial place, though the story that he was interred bolt upright, dressed for dinner and with a bottle of claret on the table in front of him, has sadly been proved apocryphal.

5 Bodiam Castle

Bodiam, 9 miles north of Hastings, TN32 5UA • Mid-Feb to Oct daily 10.30am–5pm; Nov to mid-Dec Wed–Sun 11am–4pm; mid-Jan to mid-Feb Sat & Sun 11am–4pm • £6.30; NT • ☎ 01580 830196, ⓦ nationaltrust.org.uk/bodiam-castle • Bus #349 from Hastings (Mon–Sat every 2hr; 40min); steam train from Tenterden (see p.149); or boat from Newenden (April–Sept 3 daily Wed, Sat & Sun; 45min one way; £6.50 one way, £10 return; ☎ 01797 253838, ⓦ bodiamboatingstation.co.uk)

Ask a child to draw a castle and the outline of the fairytale **Bodiam Castle** would be the result: a classically stout, square block with rounded corner turrets, battlements and a wide moat. When it was built in 1385 to guard what were the lower reaches of the River Rother against the French, Bodiam was state-of-the-art military architecture, but during the Civil War, a company of Roundheads breached the fortress and removed its roof to reduce its effectiveness as a possible stronghold for the king. Over the next 250 years Bodiam fell into neglect until restoration in 1826 by "Mad" Jack Fuller (see box, p.189) and later Lord Curzon.

Inside the castle walls it's a roofless ruin, but a wonderfully atmospheric one nonetheless, with plenty of nooks and crannies to explore and steep spiral staircases leading up to the crenellated battlements. It also boasts its original portcullis – claimed to be the oldest in the country – and murder holes in the ceiling of the gatehouse, through which defenders would fire arrows or drop rocks, boiling oil, tar or scalding water on to their enemies.

The nicest way to arrive at Bodiam is on a **steam train** from Tenterden, operated by the Kent & East Sussex Railway (see p.149), or on a **boat trip** from Newenden, four miles down the River Rother.

Bateman's

Bateman's Lane, Burwash, off the A265, TN19 7DS • Mid-March to Oct Mon–Wed, Sat & Sun 11am–5pm; 2 weeks in Dec Sat & Sun 11.30am–3.30pm • £8.15; NT • ☎ 01435 882302, ⓦ nationaltrust.org.uk/batemans

Bateman's, the idyllic home of the writer and journalist **Rudyard Kipling** from 1902 until his death in 1936, lies half a mile south of **Burwash**, a pretty Sussex village of redbrick and weather-board cottages with a Norman church tower. Kipling and his wife Carrie adored the seventeenth-century manor house from the very beginning: "That's She! The Only She! Make an honest woman of her – quick!" was their reaction when they first set eyes on it. For Kipling, it was a haven from the outside world. By the turn of the century he was one of the most popular writers in the country, and he had grown heartily sick of the fame that came with his success. Bateman's gave him the seclusion that his previous home in Rottingdean (see p.262) had not. He loved the old house, all "untouched and unfaked", and the sprawling grounds with views over manicured lawns down to the river and the countryside beyond.

In his book-lined **study** – which is today laid out much as he left it, with letters, early editions of his work and mementoes from his travels on display – he wrote *Pook's Hill* and *Rewards and Fairies*, the latter containing his most famous poem, *If*. Outside in the garage you can see Kipling's beloved 1928 Rolls Royce Phantom I, which despite his childlike enthusiasm for motor cars he never drove himself, preferring to be chauffeured around the countryside. At the far end of the garden, across the stream, is a still-working **watermill** which was converted by Kipling to generate electricity; it grinds corn most Wednesdays and Saturdays at 2pm, and you can buy the stoneground flour at the mill. Special **events** run throughout the year, including occasional *Jungle Book* days and *Just So* story days for kids, and most days there's a talk on the author and a tour of the gardens.

Wilderness Woods

Hadlow Down, on the A272, TN22 4HJ • Jan–Nov Tues–Sun 10am–5.30pm, plus bank/school holiday Mons; Dec daily 9am–6pm • £4.80, children over 3 £2.95; candlelit dinner talks £35 • ☎ 01825 830509, ⓦ wildernesswood.co.uk

Just outside the village of Hadlow Down, family-run **Wilderness Woods** is a 62-acre pocket of ancient woodland that aims to give visitors a "taste of rural sustainability". It's

RUDYARD KIPLING

God gave all men all earth to love,
But, since our hearts are small,
Ordained for each one spot should prove
Beloved over all.
Each to his choice and I rejoice
The lot has fallen to me
A fair land, a fair land
Yea, Sussex by the Sea.

Sussex, by Rudyard Kipling (1902)

The reputation of **Rudyard Kipling** (1865–1936), author of *Kim*, *The Jungle Book* and the *Just So Stories*, has taken a bit of a battering over the years. In 1907, when he won the Nobel Prize for Literature, he was at the peak of his popularity, but just 35 years later George Orwell was famously writing of him: "Kipling is a jingo imperialist, he is morally insensitive and aesthetically disgusting."

Kipling was very much an author of his time. He was born in India in 1865, and after a childhood spent in England he returned aged 16 to take up a position on a small local newspaper in Lahore, where he started publishing his poems and short stories, and soaking up the sights, smells and experiences that would inform so much of his later writing. Kipling left India in 1889, travelling, writing, marrying and finally settling in Vermont, and by the time he returned to England in 1896, he had published *The Jungle Book* and its follow-up, and was famous.

In the successful years that followed he captured the mood of the nation with his poem *The White Man's Burden* (1899), a celebration of noble-spirited British empire-building that was regarded by just a small minority as imperialist propaganda. *Kim* (1901) and the *Just So Stories* (1902) followed, and Kipling's fame grew so great that he retreated to **Bateman's**, in the heart of the Sussex countryside, to escape his fans. Behind the scenes, however, all was not rosy. Kipling's beloved daughter, Josephine, had died of pneumonia in 1898 and Kipling never really recovered. When his son, John, was killed in 1915 at the Battle of Loos, having been encouraged to enlist by Kipling, he was engulfed by guilt and grief. Bateman's was indeed a haven, but it was also the place Kipling retreated to lick his wounds, and – if Orwell is to be believed – to "sulk" at the collapse of British colonialism, and perhaps his tarnished reputation too.

Despite it all, though, even Orwell admitted that Kipling could write a good line, a sentiment seemingly echoed by modern readers, who in recent years have crowned Kipling's *If* the nation's favourite poem.

a beautiful spot, crisscrossed by nature trails, and peppered with pretty woodland glades that you can rent for cookouts or camping (see p.193). Every month **candlelit dinner talks** are held, with guest speakers discussing issues relating to sustainable living. There's a full timetable of events and **activities for kids**, too – everything from bug hunts and making fairy gardens for the littlest ones through to camp-building and survival skills – and an increasing number of courses and workshops for adults, including woodworking, outdoor cooking and coppicing. A café selling seasonal, locally produced "slow food" is a great pit-stop after a stomp through the woods.

Farley Farm House

Chiddingly, Muddles Green, BN8 6HW • April–Oct Sun 10am–3.30pm, plus extra weekends during local arts festivals; entry by 50min guided tour only (every 30min); extended tours (3hr) several times a year • £9, garden only £2, extended tours £30 • ☎ 01825 872 691, ⓦ farleyfarmhouse.co.uk

Though nowhere near as well known as nearby Charleston Farmhouse (see p.221), **Farley Farm House** is just as fascinating. After World War II this redbrick house became the home of painter and biographer **Roland Penrose**, American photographer **Lee Miller** and their son, Antony, and over the next 35 years it became a meeting place for some of the leading lights of the modern art world – Picasso, Man Ray, Max Ernst and Joan Miró among them. Penrose was a key figure in the English

5

Surrealist movement, organizing the International Surrealist Exhibition of 1936, and writing biographies of Picasso, Miró, Man Ray and Tàpies. Miller, too, was best known for her Surrealist images, though she also found fame both as a portraitist and a World War II photographer; she was one of the few women war reporters to witness battle first-hand.

Tours of the house take you through the ground-floor rooms, in the main left as they were in Penrose and Miller's day, with Penrose's paintings and sketches by artist friends on the walls. Check the website for dates of the engrossing **extended tours** led by Antony Penrose, who grew up at the farmhouse and was a favourite with the visiting Picasso.

Bentley Wildfowl and Motor Museum

Halland, 7 miles northeast of Lewes, signposted from the A26, A22 & B2192, BN8 5AF • Grounds and museum: mid-March to Oct daily 10.30am–5.30pm; Nov to mid-March Sat & Sun 10.30am–4pm; Bentley House: April–Oct daily noon–5pm; miniature railway: Easter–Oct Sat, Sun & bank hols; Nov–Easter Sun & school hols • Grounds, museum & house £8, children over 3 £6; miniature railway £1 • ☎ 01825 840573, ⓦ bentley.org.uk

The **Bentley Wildfowl and Motor Museum** is tucked away along a winding country lane, and that partly explains why it never gets too busy here, making it a lovely, peaceful spot to come and while away a summer's day. The 23-acre parkland crams a lot in: there's a huge **wildfowl enclosure** of over a thousand geese, swans, ducks and flamingos; a **bluebell wood** that shelters a handful of reconstructed ancient buildings; a small **adventure playground**; and a volunteer-run **miniature railway** that connects the three. Indoor attractions include a **museum** of roped-off Edwardian and vintage motorcars and motorbikes (events are held throughout the year), and **Bentley House**, the Palladian-style mansion at the heart of the estate. To experience Bentley after the gates have closed on the last visitor, you can stay in a **shepherd's hut** (see opposite) and have the grounds to yourself.

ACCOMMODATION
THE EASTERN HIGH WEALD

The Bell High St, Ticehurst, TN5 7AS ☎ 01580 200234, ⓦ thebellinticehurst.com. The seven rooms at *The Bell* are as wonderfully quirky as the rest of this eccentric pub (see opposite). There are the unconventional room names for starters, from "Stranger than truth" to "Hush of the trees", not to mention the silver birch trees that grow up out of the floor in each room. The decor is eclectic – rough wooden headboards, tailors' dummies, safari chairs, embossed radiators and vintage clothes-horses, with fancifully tiled bathrooms boasting huge copper tubs – but thankfully eccentricity goes hand in hand with luxury, and you can also expect sublimely comfortable beds, flat-screen TVs and iPads on demand. **£110**

Dernwood Farm Wild Camping Little Dernwood Farm, Dern Lane, Waldron, near Heathfield, TN21 0PN ☎ 01435 812726, ⓦ dernwoodfarm.co.uk. Wild camping at its best: what this car-free site lacks in facilities – there are just two toilets, a cold-water sink, a standpipe and solar showers for hire – it more than makes up for in its lovely location, in a large clearing in the middle of coppiced woodland. The farm sells its own field-to-fork bacon, sausages and beef for cooking on the fire pit, plus there's campsite catering courtesy of the *Six Bells* (see opposite) in Chiddingly, who can deliver evening meals, picnic hampers and even afternoon teas. More expensive bell tents and safari tents are also available. April–Sept. Pitches (per adult) **£8**

George Inn High St, Robertsbridge, TN32 5AW ☎ 01580 880315, ⓦ thegeorgerobertsbridge.co.uk. The four comfortable, well-priced rooms in this former eighteenth-century coaching inn make a great base for the area. There's excellent food, too, sourced where possible from a thirty-mile radius of the pub, everything from Rye Bay scallops to rack of Hawkhurst lamb. In the winter there are toasty fires and mulled wine, while summer sees Pimms served in the courtyard. Tues–Sat 11am–11pm, Sun noon–8pm. **£95**

Hidden Spring Vines Cross Rd, Horam, TN21 0HG ☎ 01435 812640, ⓦ hiddenspring.co.uk. Two peaceful camping fields, overlooking orchards and fields on a 23-acre smallholding. There are just a dozen or so tent pitches, plus 10 pitches with hook-ups, a scattering of pre-erected yurts, a tipi with a romantic open fire in the centre, and an old showman's wagon. All pitches come with fire pits for campfire cookouts. Eggs, cider, apple juice and honey from the smallholding are for sale in the shop, and Redlands Farm Shop – a five-minute walk away – can take care of everything else. March–Oct. Pitches (per adult) **£9**; yurts, tipi and wagon (2-night weekend) **£140**

Original Hut Company Quarry Farm, Bodiam, TN32 5RA ☎ 01580 831856, ⓦ original-huts.co.uk. This quirky

5

glamping option has four tiny "shepherd's huts", made from recycled bits and pieces, dotted about the tranquil woodland of a working farm. It's a great location – just a fifteen-minute stroll to Bodiam Castle, the battlements of which you can see peeking up over the trees. The cosy huts come with wood-burners and their own fire pit. Three nights peak season (Fri–Sun; not school hols): **£250**

★ **The Rolling Downs** Bentley Wildfowl and Motor Museum, Halland, BN8 5AF ☎ 07941 133370, ⓦ the rollingdowns.co.uk. The best thing about a stay in the shepherd's huts on the Bentley estate (see opposite) is that once the estate closes you can have the grounds all to yourself. There are just two huts, which are rented together (the second hut, if needed, costs an additional £70 per night) and can sleep six. Inside you'll find wood-burning stoves, proper bed linen (sleeping bags for the kids), white waffle towels and bright crockery, plus board games and outdoor games. Groceries (including local sausages for the fire pit) and meals can be ordered in advance from the *Buttercup Café* (see p.231) and delivered to your hut. Mid-March to Nov. **£110**

Wilderness Woods Hadlow Down, on the A272, TN22 4HJ ☎ 01825 830509, ⓦ wildernesswood.co.uk. This lovely patch of woodland offers pretty glades for pitch-your-own camping, complete with fire pits, picnic benches and shelters. For more creature comforts there's also *The Horsebox* (April–Sept; bookable through ⓦ canopyandstars.co.uk), a converted horsebox buried away in the woods: inside they've managed to squeeze two kids' beds, a double bed, a wood-burning stove, a small kitchen and even a swanky red leather chesterfield. Pitches (per pitch; admission to woods extra) **£50**, *The Horsebox* (2 nights) **£170**

EATING AND DRINKING

★ **The Bell** High St, Ticehurst, TN5 7AS ☎ 1580 200234, ⓦ thebellinticehurst.com. There's a bit of an Alice in Wonderland feel to this recently refurbished village local: on the surface it's all old beams, wooden floors and battered sofas, but if you look a little closer you'll see bowler hat light fittings dangling from the ceiling, a pillar made from floor-to-ceiling books, and coat hooks fashioned from old cutlery; the whimsical fun even continues into the toilets where the men's urinals are upturned tubas. They also host popular monthly debate nights (last Thurs) and monthly live performance nights (last Sun). Food (mains £10–14.50) is excellent and seasonal, often featuring fish from the pub's own Fish Hut next door. Mon–Thurs noon–11pm, Fri & Sat noon–11.30pm, Sun noon–10.30pm; food served Mon–Sat noon–3pm & 6.30–9.30pm, Sun noon–4pm & 6.30–9pm.

Blackboys Inn Lewes Rd, Blackboys, TN22 5LG ☎ 01825 890283, ⓦ theblackboys.co.uk. This lovely old 1300s coaching inn comes into its own on a summer's day, when drinkers spill out onto the terrace and front lawn, where there are plenty of picnic tables under the chestnut trees. Inside there are two beamed bars, log fires and wooden floors, with Harveys and guest beers on tap. Traditional, well-priced pub food includes burgers, pies and Sussex smokies. Daily noon–11pm; food served Mon– Sat noon–2.30pm & 6–9.30pm, Sun noon–4.30pm.

★ **The Curlew** Junction Rd, Bodiam, TN32 5UY ☎ 01580 861394, ⓦ thecurlewrestaurant.co.uk. Just up the road from Bodiam, this weatherboard former coaching inn has won a Michelin star, but isn't at all stuffy. Inside it's simple and elegant, with dark grey wood-panelled walls, jolly stripy chairs and quirky plates on the wall. The short seasonal menu features dishes such as double-baked cheese soufflé (£8.50) and "chop and chips" (short rib of beef with beef-dripping chips and soused fennel; £19.50), and there's a good-value set menu Wed–Fri lunch and Wed & Thurs dinner (£18/£22 two/three courses). Wed–Sun noon–2.30pm & 6.30–9.30pm.

Six Bells The Street, Chiddingly, BN8 6HE ☎ 01825 872227. Old-fashioned and unpretentious, this well-loved pub in the tiny village of Chiddingly is a bit of a gem. A proper pub, with plenty of cosy nooks and crannies, log fires, Harveys on tap and a great atmosphere, it has stalwartly resisted the gastropub route, and the good pub grub remains excellent value. Try to catch one of the regular folk and blues nights if you can (alternate Tues nights; ⓦ 6bellsfolk.co.uk). Mon–Thurs 11am–3pm & 6–11pm, Fri & Sat 11am–midnight, Sun noon–10.30pm; food served Mon–Thurs noon–2pm & 6–9pm, Fri–Sun noon–9pm.

ROCK-CLIMBING NEAR ERIDGE GREEN

Some of the best **climbing** to be had in the Southeast is around Eridge Green, straddling the Sussex–Kent border. Two of the sites – Eridge Rocks (owned by the Sussex Wildlife Trust; ⓦ sussexwildlifetrust.org.uk) and Harrison's Rocks (owned by the British Mountaineering Council; ⓦ thebmc.co.uk) – are open access, while a third, Bowles Rocks, is owned by the Bowles Outdoor Centre (ⓦ bowles.ac). The sites are all open to experienced climbers with their own equipment, while novices can get roped up with **Nuts 4 Climbing** (☎ 01892 860670, ⓦ nuts4climbing.com), who offer taster sessions (£55), and one-day (£95) and two-day (£160) introductory courses, at Harrison's Rocks – a perfect introduction to the sport.

5

Ashdown Forest

The first thing that surprises visitors to **ASHDOWN FOREST** is how little of it is actually forest. Almost two thirds of the Forest's ten square miles is made up of high, open **heathland**, characterized by grasses, sandy soil, shrubs, bracken, gorse and heather. It's particularly lovely in late summer, when the gorse and heather flower and the heath becomes a riot of purple and yellow. It's a peculiarly un-Sussex scene, a complete departure from the rolling green hills and patchwork fields that surround it, and all the more beautiful for it, though it hasn't always been thought of this way: it was described with venom by journalist William Cobbett, as he rode through it in 1822, as "the most villainously ugly spot I ever saw in England… getting, if possible, uglier and uglier all the way".

Walking in the Forest couldn't be easier, with footpaths and bridleways striking off in every direction. Orientation can be difficult, so it's well worth picking up the excellent map (£2.50) from the Information Barn (see opposite), which marks all the trails. The Barn also has plenty of free leaflets (also downloadable from the website) describing individual walks. With one notable exception – Pooh Bridge (see box below) – the Forest never really gets too busy, and you'll generally find yourself able to enjoy the expansive views in glorious solitude, with only the odd free-wandering sheep and the shrill of a woodlark for company.

A BEAR OF VERY LITTLE BRAIN

Probably the most famous bear in the world, Pooh Bear, also known as **Winnie-the-Pooh**, was the much-loved creation of **A.A. Milne**, who wrote the classic children's books – *Winnie the Pooh* (1926) and *House at Pooh Corner* (1928) – from his weekend home at Cotchford Farmhouse near the small village of **Hartfield**, on Ashdown Forest's northeastern edge. The stories were inspired by Milne's only son, Christopher Robin, who appears in the books along with his real-life stuffed toys: Edward Bear, Piglet, Kanga, Roo, Eeyore and Tigger (Owl and Rabbit were invented for the books).

The places described in the stories were modelled closely on Ashdown Forest: the fictional **100 Aker Wood**, where the animals live with Christopher Robin, is named after the real-life Five Hundred Acre Wood; **Galleon's Leap** was inspired by the hilltop of Gills Lap; while a clump of pine trees near Gills Lap is the **Enchanted Place**, where Christopher Robin never managed to work out whether there were 63 trees or 64. The original illustrations by **E.H. Shepherd** took direct inspiration from the Forest, and perfectly capture the heathland landscape, with its distinctive hilltop clusters of pine trees.

POOH WALKS

The *Pooh Walks from Gills Lap* **leaflet**, available from the Ashdown Forest Centre (see opposite), details two short walks that take you past some of the spots featured in the book, including the Enchanted Place, the Heffalump Trap, the Sandy Pit where Roo played, and the North Pole, but by far the most popular Pooh destination is **Pooh Bridge**, where the bear-of-very-little-brain invented the game of **Poohsticks** one lazy sunny afternoon with his good friend Piglet. The bridge is so popular that sticks can be few and far between on the one-mile walk down to the bridge; pick up a few from the woods around the car park before you start. The Pooh Bridge car park is at the Forest's northern edge, just off the B2026.

POOH CORNER

The shop where real-life Christopher Robin went with his nanny to buy bulls' eyes is now **Pooh Corner**, High St, Hartfield, TN7 4AE (Mon–Sat 9am–5pm, Sun 10.30am–5pm; ☎01892 770456, ⓦpooh-country.co.uk), a small **shop and tearoom** selling a mind-boggling array of Pooh memorabilia, from soft toys, books and cross-stitch kits to tea towels, T-shirts and Sussex honey, as well as maps and guidebooks of the Forest, and a rule-book for playing Poohsticks.

Brief history

Despite its name, Ashdown Forest was never actually a forest in the modern sense of the word – "forest", from the Latin "foris", just meant "out of the jurisdiction of the common law" and signified that it was a **deer-hunting ground**. The Forest is still partly enclosed by the thirteenth-century boundary **pale** – a raised bank that enclosed the hunting ground, broken up at intervals by deer-proof gates known as hatches; no prizes for guessing that the tiny villages of Chelwood Gate, Chuck Hatch and Coleman's Hatch all once served as gateways to the forest. Its oddly fragmented shape – pockets of heathland and forest dotted here and there – is a legacy of the seventeenth century, when roughly half of it was sold off to form private enclosures. What remained became common ground, and forms the Forest boundaries today.

Habitats and wildlife

Woodland now makes up just over a third of Ashdown Forest (up from just five percent at the end of World War II), and left to its own devices it would eventually gobble up the remaining heathland, something conservationists are keen to avert. **Lowland heath** is a rare and threatened habitat, and Ashdown Forest contains one of the few remaining tracts in the country. The black Hebredean sheep you'll occasionally startle around the Forest are one of the tree-control methods the authorities have introduced to try and protect the fragile heath landscape. Other, wilder, **wildlife** you might encounter include fallow, roe and sika deer, and a wide variety of birds including woodlark, stonechat, reed bunting and nightjars.

ARRIVAL AND INFORMATION · ASHDOWN FOREST

By car There are dozens of free parking sites dotting the main roads through the forest; the Information Barn (see below) sells a map (£2.50) with parking spots marked.
By bus Metrobus #291 runs between East Grinstead and Tunbridge Wells, stopping at Forest Row, Coleman's Hatch and Hartfield (Mon–Sat hourly); #270 runs from Brighton to East Grinstead via Chelwood Gate, Wych Cross and Forest Row (Mon–Sat hourly).
Tourist information Ashdown Forest Centre Information Barn, Wych Cross (April–Oct Mon–Fri 2–5pm, Sat & Sun 11am–5pm; Nov–March Sat & Sun 11am–5pm; ☎ 01342 823583, ⓦ ashdownforest.org).

ACCOMMODATION AND EATING

Hatch Inn Colemans Hatch, TN7 4EJ ☎ 01342 822363, ⓦ hatchinn.co.uk. The nicest pub in the Forest itself is this ancient weatherboard inn, dating from 1430, which ticks all the boxes for a perfect pub lunch: a cosy, beamed interior complete with log fire, a gorgeous garden for the summer, well-kept Harveys on tap, and good, home-cooked food; at lunchtimes you can opt for a sandwich or ploughman's (£8), or more expensive mains such as steak and Guinness pie or bouillabaisse (£9–15). Mon–Fri 11.30am–2.30pm & 5.30–11pm, Sat 11.30am–11pm, Sun noon–11pm; food served Mon–Fri noon–2.15pm & 7–9pm, Sat noon–2.30pm & 7–9pm, Sun noon–2.30pm & 6.30–8.30pm.
St Ives Farm Butcherfield Lane, Hartfield, TN7 4JX ☎ 01892 770213, ⓦ stivesfarm.co.uk. This lovely low-key campsite has three shady camping fields set around a fishing lake, three miles from the nearest main road. Evening brings the crackle of campfires (firewood £4 a bag); barbecue supplies can be bought from nearby Perryhill Orchards farm shop, a twenty-minute walk away. April–Oct. Pitches (per adult) £9

The western High Weald

The **WESTERN HIGH WEALD** feels surprisingly sleepy and remote, given that it's sandwiched between sprawling Crawley and East Grinstead to the north, Horsham to the west, and Haywards Heath and Burgess Hill to the south, with the busy A23 roaring through the centre. Scattered villages and stately manor houses pepper the landscape: when the railway arrived in the mid-nineteenth century, making the area easily accessible from London, this was a popular spot for wealthy Londoners to buy or build a mansion and a slice of rural living.

5

CYCLING THE FOREST WAY

Running for just over nine miles from East Grinstead in the west to Groombridge in the east, the **Forest Way** follows the path of a disused railway line that skirts the northern fringes of Ashdown Forest. The route is flat and peaceful, shadowing the River Medway as it wriggles its way east past patchwork fields, farms, small villages and wooded hills. With dragonflies darting over the water and swallows flitting above you, it's an idyllic ride – perfect for families – and gives you a real taste of the beautiful High Weald. There are picnic benches along the track, or you can detour off to pubs at Hartfield and Withyham. A map of the route can be downloaded from ⓦ eastsussex.gov.uk.

There's **bike rental** at Future Cycles in Forest Row (Mon–Sat 9am–5.30pm, plus Sun 10am–4pm May–Sept only; ☏ 01342 822847, ⓦ futurecycles.co.uk; £20/day, £12/half-day), towards the western end of the route; for the ultimate in laidback cycling they also hire out recumbent bikes (£35/day), though the technique takes a bit of mastering.

The main draw of the area is its **gardens**: the big hitters are **Sheffield Park**, **Nymans** and **Wakehurst Place**, but **Borde Hill** and **High Beeches** come a close second, and the newly planted **Sussex Prairies** garden provides a wonderful modern counterpoint. There's another beautiful garden surrounding the Arts and Crafts house of **Standen**, though it's the house itself which is the real star, crammed full of decorative treasures by William Morris and his contemporaries. To the south lies the **Bluebell Railway**, a vintage steam railway that puffs its way north from Sheffield Park through the bluebell-speckled woodlands that gave it its name.

This part of Sussex is a real gastro hotspot, with a couple of Michelin-starred hotel restaurants, some fabulous **foodie pubs** and plenty of excellent farm shops. It's also home to the award-winning **Bolney Estate**, one of the county's top wineries.

Sheffield Park

On the A275 East Grinstead–Lewes main road, about 2 miles north of the junction with the A272, TN22 3QX • Garden daily: Jan to mid-Feb, Nov & Dec 10.30am–4pm; mid-Feb to Oct 10.30am–5.30pm; parkland dawn–dusk; garden tours May–Nov Tues & Thurs at 11am • £8.10; NT • ☏ 01825 790231, ⓦ nationaltrust.org.uk/sheffield-park-and-garden • Bus #121 from Lewes (Sat only; every 2hr; 30min); Bluebell Railway will be running from East Grinstead from spring 2013

The beautiful landscaped gardens of **Sheffield Park**, first laid out by Capability Brown in the eighteenth century, are at their very best in autumn, when they put on the most spectacularly colourful show in the Southeast. Pick a cloudless sunny day and you'll have peerless views of the brilliantly-hued foliage reflected in the mirror-like waters of the garden's five deep lakes, linked by cascades and waterfalls – though if you want to enjoy the views in relative solitude you're best off avoiding weekends and the busier, middle part of the day, when it can seem as though the whole of Sussex has turned up to see the spectacle. The 120-acre gardens are equally lovely – and much quieter – in the springtime, when daffodils and bluebells start to emerge, and in May and June when the garden is ablaze with vivid azaleas and rhododendrons.

The centrepiece of the park is a Gothic mansion built by James Wyatt, which is privately owned, although the historic, 265-acre **South Park** is open access.

The Bluebell Railway

Sheffield Park Station, on the A275 East Grinstead–Lewes main road, about 2 miles north of the junction with the A272, TN22 3QL • April–Oct daily; Nov–March Sat, Sun & school hols • Day-ticket with unlimited travel £13.50 • ☏ 01825 720800, ⓦ bluebell-railway.com • Bus #121 from Lewes (Sat only; every 2hr; 30min)

Probably the best-known vintage steam railway in the country, the **Bluebell Railway** was started by a small group of enthusiasts in 1959, just four years after the old London–Lewes line was closed, and today has blossomed into a huge operation, with more than 30 steam locos, over 100 pieces of rolling stock and more than 600 volunteers keeping the wheels rolling. The locos take around half an hour to puff the nine miles north from Sheffield Park – the southern terminus of the railway – to Kingscote, stopping off at Horsted Keynes station en route; a two-mile extension to East Grinstead is due for completion in spring 2013, and will usefully connect the line to the main train network.

All three stations have been beautifully preserved: **Horsted Keynes** in 1920s splendour, with old posters and newspaper headlines on the walls and luggage on the platforms; **Kingscote** in 1950s style; and **Sheffield Park** as a handsome 1880s station, decorated with wonderful reclaimed enamel signs proclaiming the benefits of Gold Flake cigarettes, Thorley's Food for Cattle and Virol ("anaemic girls need it"). Sheffield Park is also home to the **railway sheds** housing some of the splendid old locomotives awaiting repair, and a small **museum** which charts the development of railways from horse-drawn to electric, and also tells the story of the Bluebell Railway.

Special services run throughout the year, everything from real ale and jazz evening services to afternoon tea specials. Especially popular is the **Golden Arrow** Pullman dining train, re-creating the luxurious *Golden Arrow* which once linked London and Paris (£22 for the pullman ticket, plus £45 for dinner).

Sussex Prairies Garden

Morlands Farm, Wheatsheaf Rd, near Henfield on the B2166, BN5 9AT • June to mid-Oct daily 1–5pm • £6 • ☏ 01273 495902, Ⓦ sussexprairies.co.uk

In comparison to the grand old gardens of the Sussex Weald the **Sussex Prairies Garden** is a mere whippersnapper – it was only established in 2009 – but it's already made a bit of a name for itself. Even if you wouldn't know an aster from an acer you can't fail to enjoy the dramatic, unusual planting of this six-acre site, which features extraordinary, vibrant drifts of summer-flowering perennials and tall grasses – some thirty thousand plants in total – with pathways snaking between them. It's quite an experience weaving your way between the borders in late summer when you're dwarfed by grasses eight foot high. In winter the garden is burned to the ground, ready for it to spring into life again the following year. Every year the work of a different group of sculptors is featured, and there's also a lovely tearoom, with jolly bunting and tables outside overlooking the riot of colour.

Bolney Wine Estate

Bookers Vineyard, Foxhole Lane, Bolney, RH17 5NB • 45min taster tours Wed, Fri & Sat 10am, noon & 2.30pm; 2hr 30min cream tea tours selected weekdays and Saturdays – check the website; café Wed–Sat 8.15am–4pm • Taster tours £16, cream tea tours £25 • ☏ 01444 881894 (Mon–Fri 10am–1pm), Ⓦ bolneywineestate.co.uk

Grapes have been grown on the land that is now the **Bolney Wine Estate** since the Middle Ages, but the tradition was only reinstated in 1972, when Rodney and Janet Pratt planted their first three acres of vines. The vineyard is perhaps best known for its red wines – unusual in the UK – but it's also won awards for its sparkling wines, recently beating off the likes of Moët & Chandon, Taittinger and Heidsieck with its sparkling Chardonnay. Bolney offers a variety of tours, everything from a **taster tour**, which whisks you through the vineyard and winery and ends with a tasting session, to a more leisurely **cream tea tour**, which starts with a glass of bubbly and ends with home-made scones and jam.

Borde Hill Garden

Borde Hill Lane, near Haywards Heath, RH16 1XP • Mid-March to mid-Sept & mid- to end Oct daily 10am–6pm; mid-Sept to mid-Oct Sat & Sun 10am–6pm • £8 • ☏ 01444 450326, Ⓦ bordehill.co.uk

Beautiful **Borde Hill Garden** ranges around a handsome honey-coloured Elizabethan manor house (not open to the public) on a narrow ridge of the Sussex Weald, with

5

fantastic sweeping views all around. The gardens were planted by **Colonel Stephenson R. Clarke**, an enthusiastic naturalist, in the 1890s, from exotic trees and shrubs collected by famous plant-hunters (see box below).

The **formal gardens** closest to the house form a series of "garden rooms", ranging from a formal English rose garden and terraced Italian garden (originally the house's tennis court), to a fabulous secret, subtropical sunken dell. Further afield the estate's **woodland** is blanketed by drifts of bluebells and anemones in spring, and later ablaze with rhododendrons – a favourite of the Colonel's. By the entrance there's a small adventure playground, as well as a café and the excellent *Jeremy's Restaurant* (see p.201).

Nymans

Handcross, just off the A23, RH17 6EB • Garden daily: March–Oct 10am–5pm; Nov–Feb 10am–4pm; house March–Oct daily 11–3pm • £9; NT • ☎ 01444 405250, ⓦ nationaltrust.org.uk/nymans • Metrobus #273 (Mon–Fri every 2hr, Sat every 3hr; 1hr) from Brighton to Crawley stops in Handcross

The 30-acre gardens at **Nymans** were the work of the Messel family, who took on the estate in 1890 and set about creating one of Sussex's great **gardens**. The main draw of the garden is its plant collection – the Messels sponsored many plant-hunting expeditions that brought back rare, exotic trees and shrubs from the remotest corners of the world – and it's also a garden that prides itself on its year-round interest: daffodils, bluebells, rhododendrons and rare Himalayan magnolias in spring; stunning borders and the rose garden in full bloom in summer; autumn colour at the back of the garden; and witch hazel, winter-flowering bulbs and camellias in winter. Despite its scale, it manages to retain the friendly feel of a family garden, with intimate "garden rooms" to explore, and plenty of thought given to keeping children entertained.

The gardens are arranged around the ruins of a mock-Gothic **manor house**, which burnt down one winter shortly after World War II: the night of the fire was so cold that although fire engines arrived in plenty of time, the water was frozen solid and they were forced to stand by and watch the house burn. Only a change of wind direction spared the portion of the house that remains open to the public today: the last of the Messels, Anne, lived in these few, modest rooms until her death in 1992, and they are preserved as they were when she died, decorated with flowers from the garden.

PLANT HUNTERS AND GATHERERS: GREAT GARDENS OF THE WEALD

Some of the greatest gardens in the Southeast – **Wakehurst Place**, **Nymans**, **Borde Hill** and **High Beeches** – can be found in a pocket of sleepy Sussex countryside, all within a few miles of each other. Their proximity is no coincidence: they were established at roughly the same time, in the 1890s and the decade that followed, by men who knew and influenced each other, and who would often visit one another's gardens and exchange ideas, advice and plants.

In contrast to the prevailing Victorian fashion for orderly formal planting, the Sussex gardens share a love of **naturalism**, partly due to the influence, encouragement and advice of the great gardener **William Robinson**, whose own garden at *Gravetye Manor* – now a hotel (see p.201) – was only a stone's throw away. The other defining feature of the Sussex gardens is their **exotic planting**, which often includes rare and important trees and shrubs. The fertile acid soil and high rainfall of the Weald provided perfect conditions for experimentation with non-native species, and Messel, Stephenson R. Clarke and the Loders all helped finance the perilous **plant-hunting expeditions** around the globe, which brought back some of the rare and exotic rhododendrons, azaleas, magnolias and camellias which are today such a central feature of the gardens.

High Beeches

High Beeches Lane, near Handcross on the B2110, just off the A23, RH17 6HQ • Mid-March to Oct Mon, Tues & Thurs–Sun 1–5pm • £6.50 • ☎ 01444 400589, Ⓦ highbeeches.com

The landscaped woodland garden of **High Beeches** has a wilder feel to it than the other great Sussex gardens, with steep, meandering paths cut through long grass, tumbling streams, woodland glades, and a wildflower meadow ablaze with golden buttercups and ox-eye daisies in early summer. The 27-acre garden has beautiful displays of autumn colour, but it really comes into its own in spring, when the woodland is cloaked in bluebells, magnolias are in bloom, and early rhododendrons, followed by azaleas, set the garden aflame with splashes of red and pink.

The estate's grand house was destroyed when a stray Canadian bomber crashed into it in World War II, but the garden – much of which was created by **Colonel Giles Loder**, who ran the estate for sixty years until his death in 1966 – survived the neglect of the war. On the Colonel's death the garden was bought by another noted plant-loving family, the Boscawens, who had heard it described as the most beautiful in Sussex.

Wakehurst Place

On the B2028 between Ardingly and Turners Hill, RH17 6TN • Daily: March–Oct 10am–6pm; Nov–Feb 10am–4.30pm; Millennium Seedbank closes 1hr earlier • £11.50; NT • ☎ 01444 894066, Ⓦ kew.org/visit-wakehurst • Metrobus #82 from Haywards Heath (Mon–Sat; every 2hr; 15min)

The gardens at **Wakehurst Place** are the most visited National Trust attraction in the country, and you'll need a whole day if you want to explore the sprawling 465-acre site properly. The main appeal of Wakehurst is its diversity, from the formal gardens surrounding the Elizabethan mansion (not open to the public) near the entrance, to the wilder meadows, wetlands, steep-sided valleys and ancient woodland further afield. At the far end of the site is the **Loder Valley Nature Reserve**, a mix of meadow, woodland and wetland, with several bird hides, which allows access to a maximum of fifty people a day (no booking).

The garden was originally planted by **Sir Gerald Loder**, a member of the illustrious local family also responsible for High Beeches. Many of the exotic and rare trees Loder planted in the early twentieth century were torn down in the great storm of 1987, but Kew's **Royal Botanic Gardens** – which has managed the site since 1965, when it took on a long-term lease from the National Trust – responded with its trademark emphasis on conservation, by replanting Wakehurst with different types of woodland from around the world, re-creating endangered habitats.

The Millennium Seedbank

Wakehurst is also home to the **Millennium Seedbank**, which opened in 2010 with the aim of conserving the most endangered and important seeds from around the world. It has already collected and stored around ten percent of the world's plant species (around thirty thousand in total), including almost all of the UK's native species; the next target is 25 percent by the year 2020. The vast storage vaults are hidden underground beneath the laboratories, which you can look into from the **exhibition room**.

Standen

West Hoathly Rd, 2 miles south of East Grinstead, RH19 4NE • June–Aug daily 11am–4.30pm; March–May, Sept & Oct Wed–Sun 11am–4.30pm; mid- to end Feb, Nov & Dec Sat & Sun 11am–4.30pm; closed Jan to mid-Feb • £8.50; NT • ☎ 01342 323029, Ⓦ nationaltrust.org.uk/standen

Set in lovely countryside at the end of a long winding lane, **Standen** is a beautiful Arts and Crafts house, creaking at the seams with treasures from many of the key figures in the **Arts and Crafts movement** (see box, p.200).

The building was the creation of the architect **Philip Webb**, friend of William Morris, and a central player in the foundation of the Arts and Crafts movement. Webb was at

5

THE ARTS AND CRAFTS MOVEMENT

The **Arts and Crafts movement** started out in Britain in the nineteenth century as a reaction against the evils of mass production. There was a strong vein of socialism underpinning it – the Movement believed that mechanization threatened to dehumanize the lives of the ordinary working classes – and both John Ruskin and Alexander Pugin (see p.98) were influences.

The central ideas were a rejection of shoddy, mass-produced goods in favour of handcrafted objects; an emphasis on simple, honest design and truth to materials – in contrast to the over-elaborate showiness and artificiality of much Victorian design; and the use of nature as a source of inspiration.

The father of the Arts and Crafts movement was **William Morris**, one of the most influential designers of the nineteenth century, who in 1861 set up Morris, Marshall, Faulkner & Co (later Morris & Co), with other figures including Edward Burne-Jones, Dante Gabriel Rossetti and Philip Webb, to make and sell beautiful handcrafted objects for the home. "Have nothing in your home that you do not know to be useful or believe to be beautiful" was Morris's motto. Many of the designs that came out of Morris & Co were inspired by nature, and Morris named many of his own hand block-printed wallpapers after trees and flowers.

The Arts and Crafts movement flourished in the 1880s and 1890s but by the early twentieth century it became clear that its grand ideals were flawed; only the very wealthy could afford to buy Morris & Co's handcrafted designs, which were much more expensive to manufacture than the mass-produced items they were intended to replace.

pains to make the house functional as well as beautiful, and it was at the cutting edge of modern technology for its time, with both electricity and central heating fitted. The beautiful original light fittings – by **W.A.S. Benson**, one of Morris's protégés – can still be seen today. Webb was famed for his attention to detail, and this is evident all over the house, from the intricate fingerplates on the doors to the meticulously designed fireplaces.

The highlight, however, is Morris's exuberant **wallpapers and textiles**, deliberately offset by plain, wood-panelled walls. Look out for Morris's trellis wallpaper, his first marketed wallpaper design, in the conservatory corridor – the birds were drawn by Webb because Morris wasn't happy with his own efforts. Other gems include red lustreware and Islamic-inspired ceramic tiles by **William De Morgan** in the billiard room, and paintings and drawings by Edward Burne-Jones, Dante Gabriel Rossetti and Ford Madox Brown.

Surrounding the house are twelve acres of terraced hillside **gardens**, encompassing formal gardens and wilder areas, as well as a traditional Victorian kitchen garden.

Tulley's Farm

Turners Hill, near Crawley, RH10 4PE • Daily: farm shop 9am–5pm; tearoom 9am–4.30pm • Free; admission charged for special events (see website) • ☎ 01342 718472, ⓦ tulleysfarm.com

The excellent **farm shop** at **Tulley's Farm** operates year-round, with an in-house butcher's and deli stocking Sussex pies, local cheeses, ham on the bone and other picnic fodder. In summer the farm's strawberry and raspberry fields open for **pick-your-own**. It's all change in the school holidays, when the farm throws open its doors for a series of popular seasonal events: the **Spring Festival** features egg hunts, puppet shows, wagon rides and the like; the **Summer Maze Park** is centred on a four-acre maze with four miles of paths, with attractions such as bouncy castles, straw castles and tractor rides; **Halloween** week sees zombies and other blood-splattered creatures of the undead take over the farm for one of the largest Halloween events in the country, featuring family-friendly spooky fun in the day and properly terrifying scares for grown-ups in the evenings; and at **Christmas** things settle down again, with the living dead replaced by Santa and the annual "Vegetivity" – a nativity in vegetables.

ACCOMMODATION AND EATING   **THE WESTERN HIGH WEALD**

The Ginger Fox Muddleswood Rd, on the A281 at the junction with the B2117, near Albourne, BN6 9EA · ☎ 01273 857888, ⓦ thegingerfox.co.uk. This relaxed foodie pub is the country outpost of the Brighton-based

"Ginger" empire, and it's equally popular, with a lovely big garden and great food that might include fillet of skate with samphire or pork fillet with roasted peaches and black pudding (£12–18). Children are positively welcomed, with a play area, a treasure hunt and a special £6 two-course menu including home-made ice cream. Daily 11.30am–midnight; food served Mon–Fri noon–2pm & 6–10pm, Sat noon–3pm & 6–10pm, Sun noon–4pm & 6–10pm.

Gravetye Manor Vowels Lane, West Hoathly, RH19 4LJ ☎01342 810567, ⊕gravetyemanor.co.uk. Unashamedly old-fashioned, in a thoroughly good way, this sixteenth-century manor house nestles amid beautiful gardens planted a hundred years ago by former owner William Robinson, the pioneer of the natural-style English garden. Having free rein of the grounds is just one of the pleasures of a stay here: the 17 bedrooms – named, fittingly, after trees found on the estate – are elegantly luxurious, there's an excellent restaurant, and afternoon tea can be taken in the flower-filled garden. **£290**

★ **The Griffin Inn** Fletching, TN22 3SS ☎01825 722890, ⊕thegriffininn.co.uk. On a summer's day look no further than this fabulous country pub, which boasts what is surely the most perfect beer garden in Sussex, with views across the Weald from the huge sloping lawn. Sundays in summer see the barbecue lit, with trussed-up Rye Bay lobsters on ice by the coals, alongside fish, steak, bangers and the like, while year-round there's an excellent restaurant menu (mains £15–25) featuring produce from the Fletching market garden, meat from local farms and fish from Rye Bay. There are also 13 lovely rooms available, spread over three higgledy-piggledy old buildings. Daily 11am–midnight/1am; food served Mon–Fri noon–2.30 & 7–9.30pm, Sat noon–3pm & 7–9.30pm, Sun noon–3pm & 7–9pm. **£100**

Jeremy's Restaurant Borde Hill Gardens, Balcombe Rd, near Haywards Heath, RH16 1XP ☎01444 441102, ⊕jeremysrestaurant.com. This award-winning restaurant is a perennial favourite in this neck of the woods, especially on a summer's day when the French doors are flung open and tables are set up on the lovely terrace overlooking a Victorian walled garden. The à la carte menu (mains £15–24) might feature rump and cottage pie of Leghorn beef, or South Coast black bream with black tagliatelle, or there's a cheaper set menu (2/3 courses £15/18; available Tues–Sat lunch & Tues–Thurs dinner). Tues–Sat 12.30–2.30pm & 7–10pm, Sun 12.30–2.30pm.

Ockenden Manor Cuckfield, RH17 5LD ☎01444 416111, ⊕hshotels.co.uk. This stately Elizabethan manor house has not one but two trump cards up its sleeve: a brand-new spa, and a Michelin-starred restaurant (3 courses £53, 7-course tasting menu £75). The 28 bedrooms vary considerably: you won't get an awful lot of character or any sort of view in the cheapest rooms, but if you're willing to splash out you can enjoy one of the new glamorous open-plan spa suites (£395), which come with

roll-top baths, coffee machines and sliding doors that open on to a rooftop garden. Daily noon–2pm & 7–9pm. **£190**

The Pass South Lodge Hotel, near Lower Beeding, RH13 6PS ☎01403 892235, ⊕southlodgehotel.co.uk. Don't expect anything run-of-the-mill at this Michelin-starred hotel restaurant. All 22 seats are in the kitchen itself, allowing you to watch your food being prepared and brought to the pass for final inspection, with screens on the walls giving close-ups of the kitchen action. The focus is on "fun dining", using unusual flavours and textures, and only tasting menus are available (3, 5 or 7 courses at lunch – £25, £35 or £55; 6 or 8 courses at dinner – £60 or £70). Expect taste combinations like crab mayonnaise with chargrilled pineapple, burnt coconut and green tea. Wed–Sun noon–1.30pm & 7–8.30pm.

★ **The Royal Oak** Wineham Lane, Wineham, BN5 9AY ☎01444 881252. Everything a traditional English country pub should be, this ancient, unspoilt boozer sits on a quiet country lane, with plenty of tables on the lawn out front. Inside the thirteenth-century building it's all low beamed ceilings and uneven brick floors. Don't be thrown by the lack of hand pumps at the bar – the beer (Harveys, Dark Star and guests) is served straight from the cask. There's good, seasonal food on offer, too, including chunky ploughman's boards (£8.75), and mains such as English asparagus and broad bean risotto (£10–13). Mon–Fri 11am–3.30pm & 5.30–11pm, Sat 11am–4pm & 6–11pm, Sun noon–4.30pm & 7–10.30pm; food served Mon–Sat noon–2.30pm & 7–9pm, Sun noon–2.30pm.

★ **Sussex Prairies** Morlands Farm, Wheatsheaf Road, near Henfield on B2166, BN5 9AT ☎01273 495902, ⊕sussexprairies.co.uk. The main appeal of a stay at this B&B is the chance to enjoy the garden (see p.197) after the public has gone home; if the weather's fine you can even bring a picnic to eat amid the ornamental grasses. The three rooms have plenty of character, kitted out with knick-knacks picked up during the friendly owners' travels. Breakfast is pretty special (and about as local as you can get), featuring sausages and bacon from the owners' free-range pigs, eggs from their chickens, and honey from their hives. **£105**

★ **WOWO Wapsbourne Farm** Sheffield Park, TN22 3QS ☎01825 723414, ⊕wowo.co.uk. This lovely streamside campsite is no secret – it's a favourite of locals and Londoners alike, and with good reason. Campfires are positively encouraged, there's bags of open space for kids (plus rope swings aplenty), and on Friday nights musicians stay free if they're willing to offer up an hour's music. Home-baked bread and local meat and eggs are for sale in the shop, and buffet breakfasts (£5) are available weekend mornings. There are also a few Mongolian yurts nestled in the woods, plus a shepherd's hut and a wagon. Open year-round (woodland pitches and yurts only Nov–Feb); two-night minimum stay at weekends. Pitches (per adult) **£10**, (per car) **£5**, yurts, hut & wagon two-night weekend stay from **£136**

The Sussex Downs

THE SEVEN SISTERS

6

The Sussex Downs

The Sussex Downs form part of the South Downs, a range of gently undulating chalk hills which stretch across much of Sussex and into neighbouring Hampshire. This beautiful swathe of countryside – characterized by rolling chalk downland, and famously described by Rudyard Kipling as the "blunt, bow-headed, whale-backed downs" – is protected within the newly created South Downs National Park. Above all, this is a part of Sussex that is best appreciated on foot: over 1800 miles of footpaths and bridleways crisscross the South Downs, one of the densest networks of public rights of way in the country. Paths take you past poppy fields, dew ponds and wildflower meadows teeming with butterflies, with the song of skylarks overhead, and wonderful views all around – over patchwork fields that change colour with the seasons, sleepy villages, spired churches and distant rolling hills.

The gentle southern slopes of the South Downs slant gently down to the sea, while the steep escarpment on the northern side drops abruptly to give spectacular views over the low-lying Weald, most notably at famed beauty spots **Devil's Dyke**, **Ditchling Beacon** and **Chanctonbury Ring**. Fine old country pubs and little villages nestle beneath the hills at the foot of the scarp, among them pretty **Firle** and **Ditchling**, where over the years writers and artists have made their home, most famously the **Bloomsbury Group** at Charleston Farmhouse.

The South Downs – and the long-distance **South Downs Way** footpath, which follows the escarpment through Hampshire and Sussex – meet the sea at the **Seven Sisters**, a series of spectacular chalk cliffs, culminating in the dizzying 530-foot-high **Beachy Head**, the tallest chalk sea cliff in the country. This pristine stretch of coastline provides some of the finest scenery in the national park. The seaside town of **Eastbourne**, on the eastern side of Beachy Head, marks an end to the dramatic views, with dazzling, sheer white cliffs dropping down to an elegant promenade.

Four river valleys cut through the South Downs: from east to west, the Cuckmere, which trickles through the pretty village of **Alfriston** before meeting the sea at Cuckmere Haven by the Seven Sisters; the Ouse, which passes through the handsome county town of **Lewes**; the Adur, bypassing sleepy **Steyning**; and the Arun, which

CHARLESTON FARMHOUSE

Highlights

❶ Beachy Head and the Seven Sisters The unmissable scenic highlight of the South Downs National Park: soaring white cliffs backed by wildflower-rich chalk grassland. **See p.213**

❷ Walking the South Downs Way Some of the best walking in the Southeast can be found along this 100-mile path. **See p.213**

❸ Alfriston A contender for the title of prettiest village in Sussex, with a picturesque main street, an idyllic village green and a clutch of historic smuggling inns. **See p.217**

❹ Charleston Farmhouse The Bloomsbury Group's uniquely decorated country home gives a fascinating glimpse into the lives of Sussex's most famous bohemians. **See p.221**

❺ Paragliding on the Downs You can be up in the air in a day, in one of the country's finest paragliding destinations. **See p.224**

❻ Lewes One of Sussex's loveliest towns, with a medieval castle, a much-loved brewery, the Downs on its doorstep, and even its own currency. **See p.226**

❼ Devil's Dyke Any view described by painter John Constable as "the finest in the world" has got to be worth seeing for yourself. **See p.236**

❽ Petworth House One of the finest stately homes in the Southeast, with a magnificent haul of art, and a deer park immortalized by Turner. **See p.247**

HIGHLIGHTS ARE MARKED ON THE MAP ON PP.206–207

meaders gracefully downstream through **Arundel**, its water meadows providing scenic views of the town's magnificent castle.

West of Arundel, the Downs become more wooded on their journey into Hampshire, and the boundaries of the national park extend northward to cover the **Western Weald**, an area of woodland and heathland that after much debate was included in the Park in recognition of its outstanding natural beauty. Though not geographically part of the Sussex Downs, the Western Weald is included in this chapter as part of the national park, and counts among its highlights lovely scenery at **Black Down**, and around the market town of **Midhurst**, and a magnificent stately home at **Petworth**.

SOUTH DOWNS NATIONAL PARK ESSENTIALS

Information The South Downs National Park came into being in April 2010. Covering over six hundred square miles, it stretches for 70 miles from eastern Hampshire through to the chalk cliffs of East Sussex. The park's headquarters is in Midhurst in West Sussex, where a new South Downs Centre (see p.245) is scheduled to open in autumn 2013; further visitor centres are in East Sussex at the Seven Sisters County Park and at Beachy Head (see p.217), and there are plans to open a new visitor centre at Birling Gap (see p.217). ⓦ southdowns.gov.uk has information on public transport,

walks, mountain biking and other activities.

Getting around If travelling by public transport, the Downlander Ticket (from £10) allows a day's unlimited train and bus travel over much of the South Downs; see ⓦ southernrailwaytickets.com/downlander for details.

Walking and cycling ⓦ southdowns.gov.uk has over a dozen downloadable walks and cycle rides that start and finish at a bus stop or train station, and the National Trust – which manages some of the finest tracts of land within the

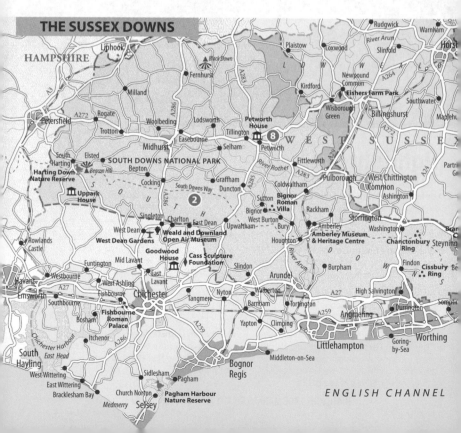

Park – also has a series of downloadable walks on its website (W nationaltrust.org.uk/visit/activities/walking). The Electric Bicycle Network (W electricbicyclenetwork.com) is at the time of writing running a pilot scheme in the western end of the national park, which may in time expand to the rest of the park.

Eastbourne

The archetypal English seaside resort, elegant **EASTBOURNE** has a certain timeless charm. A stroll along the three-mile-long prom will take you past old-fashioned ice-cream parlours, brass bands playing in the bandstand, floral displays and grand hotels offering afternoon tea. Over the years it's gained a reputation as a retirement town by the sea, derided as "God's waiting room", and "a graveyard above the ground". But Eastbourne is slowly changing, with families and creative types, priced out of Brighton, moving into the area; it even has that hallmark of seaside-town regeneration – a state-of-the-art contemporary art gallery, the Towner. Eastbourne may still lack the hipness of neighbouring Brighton, but some would say it's all the better for it.

The seafront

Eastbourne's well-conserved seafront is an elegant ribbon of Victorian terraces and villas, entirely unblemished by shops – thanks to an edict of **William Cavendish**, one of the two landowners who developed the upmarket seaside resort ("planned by

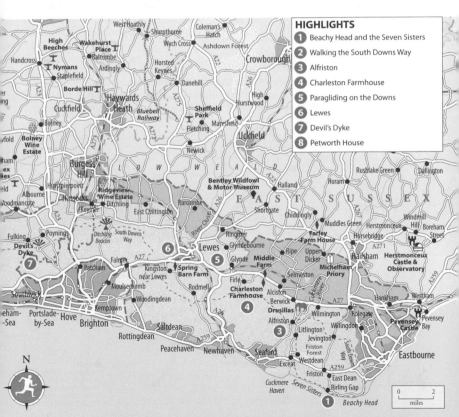

HIGHLIGHTS

1. Beachy Head and the Seven Sisters
2. Walking the South Downs Way
3. Alfriston
4. Charleston Farmhouse
5. Paragliding on the Downs
6. Lewes
7. Devil's Dyke
8. Petworth House

6

THE LIE OF THE LAND

Chalk downland is one of Britain's richest **wildlife habitats**, thanks in large part to the sheep which have been grazing the Sussex downland since the Middle Ages, keeping the turf cropped short and allowing a unique – and rare – ecosystem of slow-growing plants to develop; over forty different types of plants can grow in a single square yard, supporting an equally rich diversity of insects and small animals, including skylarks, six species of grasshopper, and the rare Adonis blue butterfly.

Chalk downland is in fact made up of a few different habitats, of which **grassland** – with its short, springy turf – is just one. Others include **scrub**, characterized by low-growing shrubs or bushes such as yellow-flowered gorse, hawthorn and blackthorn, which you'll see bent double by the wind up on Beachy Head; and **dew ponds**, man-made, clay-lined ponds built to retain rainwater for watering livestock.

Along the length of the Downs you'll see plenty of evidence, if you look closely enough, of **ancient settlements** and people, including flint mines dug by Neolithic man at Cissbury Ring; and Iron Age hillforts at Cissbury, Devil's Dyke, Chanctonbury Ring and Mount Caburn above Lewes, to name but a few. Even the footpaths that cut across the hills tell a story: many are old **drover's routes** that have been worn away through centuries of use.

---

gentlemen for gentlemen") in the nineteenth century. With its palm trees and fairy lights there's a distinct holiday vibe to it on balmy summer's evenings. The seafront strip stretches for three miles from one of Europe's largest marinas, **Sovereign Harbour** (ⓦeastbourneharbour.com), in the east, to the cliffs of **Holywell** in the west. From Holywell, paths zigzag back up to the main seafront road and the start of the footpath up to Beachy Head (see p.214). The beach is resolutely pebbly, but stretches of sand emerge at low tide.

Redoubt Fortress and Military Museum
Royal Parade, BN22 7AQ • Tues–Sun 10am–5pm • £4.50 • ☎ 01323 410300, ⓦ eastbournemuseums.co.uk

The circular **Redoubt Fortress and Military Museum**, at the eastern end of the seafront, was one of three fortresses built at the same time as the Martello towers

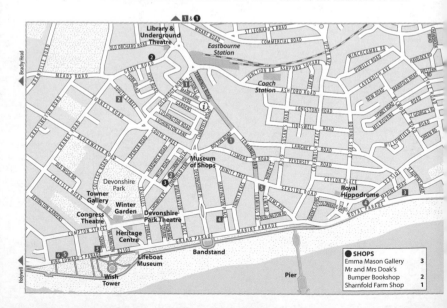

● SHOPS	
Emma Mason Gallery	3
Mr and Mrs Doak's	
Bumper Bookshop	2
Sharnfold Farm Shop	1

(see box, p.124) to counter the threat of Napoleonic invasion, and was garrisoned up until World War II. Downstairs there's an excellent museum dedicated to three regiments, including the Royal Sussex, with a collection bristling with medals, uniforms and other military paraphernalia, including a bugle rescued from the ill-fated Charge of the Light Brigade. **Events**, including living history weekends, take place throughout the year.

Eastbourne Pier and Bandstand

The focal point of the seafront is the **pier** (ⓦeastbournepier.com; free), designed by master pier-builder Eugenius Birch and opened in 1872. It was intended to match the best on the south coast, which it certainly does, with its intricate royal-blue ironwork and elegant shelters. At the end of the pier, steep steps climb up to a high dome housing a rare working **camera obscura** (mid-July to Aug daily noon–5pm, weather permitting; £2), a 360-degree Victorian projector.

The seafront's other pride and joy is the much-loved **bandstand** (ⓦeastbourneband stand.co.uk), just to the west, with a jaunty azure-blue domed roof; Sunday afternoons see traditional brass bands take to the stage (3pm; 1hr 30min; £4.50), and the bandstand also hosts big bands, tribute shows and fireworks concerts on summer evenings.

Eastbourne Lifeboat Museum

King Edward's Parade, BN21 4BY • Daily: April–Oct 10am–5pm; March, Nov & Dec 10am–4pm; Jan & Feb 10am–3pm • Free • ⓦeastbournernli.org/museum

Towards the western end of the seafront, the tiny **Eastbourne Lifeboat Museum** recounts some of the more daring rescues the town's lifeboatmen have made since 1822, when local eccentric John "Mad Jack" Fuller (see box, p.189) donated Eastbourne's first lifeboat. Cork lifejackets weren't introduced until 1854, making the bravery of those first volunteers, who generally couldn't swim, all the more astonishing. The museum is overlooked by a grassy mound topped by the **Wish Tower**, one of a series of Martello towers built along the south coast at the end of the eighteenth century.

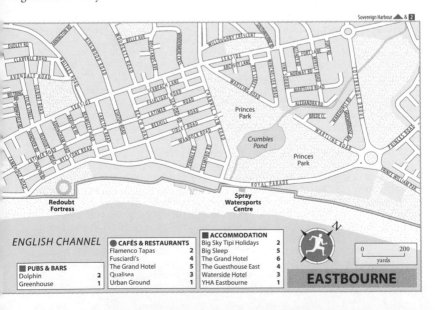

The Cultural Quarter

Eastbourne's self-styled "**Cultural Quarter**" is centred on **Devonshire Park**, dating from the 1870s. Two elegant Victorian **theatres** (see p.213) from the same period – the Devonshire Park Theatre and the Winter Garden – lie on the park's southern edge, alongside the modern Congress Theatre, but the Cultural Quarter only really gained its moniker when the **Towner Gallery** relocated in 2009.

Towner Art Gallery and Museum

Devonshire Park, BN21 4JJ • Tues–Sun 10am–6pm; tours daily at 11.30am & 2pm; tours of collection store on the last consecutive Sat & Sun of the month • Free; tours of collection store £5 • ☎ 01323 434670, ⓦ townereastbourne.org.uk

First opened in 1923, the venerable **Towner Art Gallery and Museum** was in 2009 relocated to a glamorous new home in Devonshire Park – a sleek modern edifice of glass and smooth white curves, bringing a touch of hipness to Eastbourne's Cultural Quarter. The gallery shows four or five major exhibitions a year, alongside rotating displays from its own permanent collection of modern and c ontemporary art; it's especially well-known for its modern British art, in particular the work of **Eric Ravilious** (see box below). Free **tours** of the gallery run twice daily, and tours of the collection store (showing some of the four thousand-odd works not on display at any one time) are also popular. Up on the second floor there's a **café-bar** with a small terrace overlooking the rooftops of Eastbourne to the South Downs beyond.

Eastbourne Heritage Centre

2 Carlisle Rd, BN21 4BT • April–Oct Mon, Tues & Thurs–Sat 2–5pm; Nov–March Mon & Thurs 2–4pm • £2.50 • ☎ 01323 411189, ⓦ eastbourneheritagecentre.co.uk

Housed in a striking turreted building, the displays at the **Eastbourne Heritage Centre** include old maps showing how the town grew from a few small villages into a grand Victorian resort, as well as fabulous postcards of Eastbourne in its heyday, and then-and-now photos of well-known landmarks. There's also a basement cinema showing old films of the town.

ERIC RAVILIOUS

Of all Sussex artists, **Eric Ravilious** (1903–42) – painter, wood engraver and designer – is perhaps the one who captured the local landscape the best. His beloved Sussex Downs were always a source of inspiration, whether he was painting the swelling slopes of Firle Beacon or the now-closed cement works at Asham.

Ravilious was a local lad, Sussex bred if not born: he grew up in Eastbourne, the son of a shopkeeper, and in 1919 won a scholarship to the Eastbourne College of Art. In 1922 he started at the Royal College of Art in London, where he studied under Paul Nash, became close friends with Edward Bawden and spent much of his time chatting up girls. He accepted a part-time teaching job at his old Eastbourne college in 1925, during which time he took his students sketching in Alfriston, Jevington and Wilmington, but it was only in the mid-1930s that Ravilious really rediscovered Sussex, travelling back to stay at **Furlongs**, a shepherd's cottage near Beddingham belonging to his friend and fellow artist Peggy Angus – a radical with a fondness for folk songs, home-made elderflower champagne and wild Midsummer's Eve parties. It was during these visits that Ravilious painted some of his best-known watercolours – timeless and quintessentially English evocations of prewar Sussex, where people are almost completely absent and the landscape takes centre stage.

By this point Ravilious was one of the best-known artists of the time, not only for his watercolours but also for his wood engravings – one of which, of two top-hatted cricketers, graced the front cover of *Wisden Cricketer's Almanack* from 1938 to 2002 – and ceramic designs for Wedgwood. When war broke out, Ravilious served in the Observer Corps before becoming an **Official War Artist**. In 1942 he was out on a search-and-rescue mission in Iceland when his plane came down, and his life was cut tragically short, aged just 39.

WATERSPORTS IN EASTBOURNE

If you thought tea dances were as animated as things got in Eastbourne, think again. Several outfits offer you the chance to get out and active on the water, whether exploring underwater wrecks, zipping along on RIBs or paddling more sedately in a sea kayak.

Diving charters The Sussex coast has some of the best wreck dives in the country, and a handful of charter companies offer trips from Sovereign Harbour – check out ⓦ channeldiving.com, ⓦ sussexshipwrecks.co.uk and ⓦ dive125.co.uk.

Eastbourne Kayak and Surf Hire By the Wish Tower ☎ 07917 863791, ⓦ eastbournekayakandsurf.co.uk. Sea-kayak and paddleboard hire on the beach (May Sat & Sun; June–Sept daily; £10/1hr, £15/2hr, £60/day).

Spray Watersports Centre Royal Parade ☎ 01323 417023, ⓦ eastsussx.gov.uk. Taster windsurfing and sailing lessons (£32/2hr) and longer courses. Jan–April Mon–Fri; May–Dec daily.

Sussex Voyages Lower Quayside, The Waterfront, Sovereign Harbour Marina ☎ 01293 888780, ⓦ sussexvoyages.co.uk. Popular trips in a rigid inflatable boat along the coast, including to Beachy Head and the Seven Sisters (£26/2hr).

Museum of Shops

20 Cornfield Terrace, BN21 4NS • April–Oct daily 10am–5pm; Feb, March, Nov & Dec Mon–Fri 10am–4.30pm, Sat & Sun 10am–5pm • £5 • ☎ 01323 737143

Over one hundred years of consumerism are recorded at the **"How We Lived Then" Museum of Shops**, where a range of artefacts from the 1850s to the 1970s – everything from dried egg powder to coronation cups, toys, wedding dresses, vacuum cleaners and Christmas decorations – is crammed into mock-up shops spread over four floors. It's taken the owners over fifty years to collect the over 100,000 items on display, a pretty impressive labour of love, though it's mainly of interest to those old enough to appreciate the nostalgia.

ARRIVAL AND DEPARTURE   EASTBOURNE

By car You can park for the day all along the seafront for £4.

By train Eastbourne's splendid Italianate station is a 10min walk from the seafront up Terminus Road.

Destinations Brighton (every 20min; 35min); Hastings (every 20min; 30min); Lewes (every 20min; 30min); London Victoria (Mon–Sat every 30min, Sun hourly; 1hr 35min).

By bus The coach station is on Junction Rd, right by the train station.

Destinations Brighton (every 10–15min; 1hr 15min); Hastings (Mon–Sat every 20min, Sun hourly; 1hr 10min); London Victoria (2 daily; 3–4hr); Tunbridge Wells (Mon–Sat hourly; 50min).

GETTING AROUND AND INFORMATION

City Sightseeing bus Hop-on, hop-off buses (ⓦ citysightseeing.com) run along the seafront and in a loop to Beachy Head, Birling Gap and East Dean. 10am–5pm: mid-March to mid-Nov daily; late Nov to mid-Dec Sat & Sun; every 30min; 1hr for circuit; £4, valid 24hr.

Dotto Train This land train (ⓦ stagecoachbus.com) runs along the seafront in summer, from Sovereign Harbour in the east to Holywell in the west, stopping en route at the Redoubt Fortress, the pier and the Wish Tower. April–Oct daily 10am–6pm; hourly; day-ticket unlimited travel £6.50.

Quadricycles Available from Ride'n'Joy's kiosk (☎ 07772

891152, ⓦ ride-n-joy.co.uk) at the eastern end of the seafront. April–Sept Tues & Thurs–Sun 10am–6pm; Oct–March Sat & Sun 10am–4pm; from £10/30min, £14/hr.

Taxis Call Eastbourne and Country Taxis on ☎ 01323 720720.

Tourist office 3 Cornfield Rd, just off Terminus Rd (March, April & Oct Mon–Fri 9.15am–5.30pm, Sat 9.15am–4pm; May–Sept Mon–Fri 9.15am–5.30pm, Sat 9.15am–5pm, Sun 10am–1pm; Nov–Feb Mon–Fri 9.15am–4.30pm, Sat 9.15am–1pm; ☎ 0871 663 0031, ⓦ visiteastbourne.com).

ACCOMMODATION

Big Sky Tipi Holidays Well House, Wartling Rd, Wartling, BN27 1RX ☎ 01323 832325, ⓦ bigsky tipiholidays.co.uk. Glamp in style at this lovely little site, ten miles from Eastbourne, where half a dozen authentic hand-crafted Sioux Indian tipis lie scattered around a

peaceful meadow, backed by fourteen acres of woodland. The tipis (sleeping 4–6) are cosy and well-equipped, with plenty of cushions and rugs for snugness, and fire pits outside allow for evening pow wows around the campfire. April–Sept. 2 nights **£240**

6

Big Sleep King Edward's Parade, BN21 4EB ☎01323 722676, ⓦthebigsleephotel.com. Part-owned by Hollywood actor John Malkovich, this budget boutique hotel on the seafront has a great location around the corner from the Towner, and a hip lounge and bar area featuring funky armchairs, dove-grey walls and huge chandeliers. Rooms range from no-frills doubles – great value, if you can forgive the faux-fur curtains – to more tasteful suites (£99), plus good-value family rooms. **£69**

The Grand Hotel King Edwards Parade, BN21 4EQ ☎01323 412345, ⓦgrandeastbourne.com. The best address in town is the "White Palace", a grand Victorian edifice at the western end of the seafront, which over the years has seen the great and the good pass through its doors, including Winston Churchill, Charlie Chaplin and most famously, Charles Debussy, who worked on La Mer during a stay in 1905. Standard rooms are traditional in style, and there are two excellent restaurants (see below) and an in-house spa. **£160**

The Guesthouse East 13 Hartington Place, BN21 3BS ☎01323 722774, ⓦtheguesthouseeastbourne.co.uk.

Run by a lovely couple, this award-winning boutique guesthouse, set in a Regency villa, lies moments from the pier on a quiet street. The six super-stylish self-catering suites – the larger ones great for families – come with small, well-equipped kitchenettes, but if you're feeling too lazy to cook your own eggs in the morning you can pay extra (£5–9) for a delicious breakfast delivered to your door. **£100**

Waterside Hotel 11–12 Royal Parade, BN22 7AR ☎01323 646566, ⓦwatersidehoteleastbourne.co.uk. Rooms are sleek and suitably luxurious at this boutique hotel at the eastern end of the seafront. Standard doubles (without sea view) are good value, but for a treat consider booking one of the two suites (£160), which come with freestanding baths and floor-to-ceiling windows framing a wonderful sea view, with a telescope to enjoy it with. **£90**

YHA Eastbourne 1 East Dean Rd, BN20 8ES ☎0845 371 9316, ⓔeastbourne@yha.org.uk. Modern hostel in a quiet, leafy location on the western outskirts of town, just a mile from the centre. It's 400m from the start of the South Downs Way footpath (see opposite), so a good location for walkers. Dorms **£16.40**, doubles **£43**

EATING AND DRINKING

★ **Dolphin** 14 South St, BN21 4XF ☎01323 746622, ⓦthedolphineastbourne.co.uk. This lovely, laid back Victorian pub has got everything pretty much spot on: a beautifully restored interior featuring open fires, wooden floors and comfy leather chesterfields; Harveys and Dark Star on tap; and great home-cooked food including burgers (£7.50–9.50) and fresh local fish. There's no outside space to speak of, but that's a minor quibble. Mon–Thurs 11am–11pm, Fri & Sat 11am–midnight, Sun noon–10.30pm; food served Mon & Tues noon–2.30pm & 6–9pm, Wed–Sun noon–9pm.

Flamenco Tapas 8 Cornfield Terrace, BN21 4NN ☎01323 641444, ⓦflamenco-tapas.co.uk. A little corner of Spain in Eastbourne, this traditional restaurant – with cheery red paintwork and big windows opening onto the street in summer – has over 46 different tapas dishes (most around the £5 mark), 26 Spanish wines, and live flamenco and guitar performances throughout the year. Mon & Wed 5.30–9pm, Thurs–Sat noon–3pm & 5.30–9pm.

★ **Fusciardi's** 30 Marine Parade, BN22 7AY ☎01323 722128, ⓦfusciardiicecreams.co.uk. Established in 1967, this fabulous ice-cream parlour is an Eastbourne institution, with queues out the door on summer weekends. Over 18 flavours of home-made ice cream are on offer (the honeycomb is to die for), as well as light meals and piled-high sundaes that are a work of art. Cash only. Daily 9am–7pm; June–Aug generally open until 10/10.30pm.

The Grand Hotel King Edwards Parade, BN21 4EQ ☎01323 412345, ⓦgrandeastbourne.com. Of the two restaurants at *The Grand Hotel*, the *Mirabelle* is the one to go for if you want to treat yourself, with a dining room

that's all timeless elegance and crisp white linen. Three courses at dinner cost £40 (£24 at lunch), or there's a tasting menu for £58.50, which includes dishes such as pike soufflé with sea-urchin sauce and buttered lobster. Elsewhere in the hotel, wonderful afternoon teas are served in the grand surrounds of the Great Hall (daily 2.45–6.30pm; £22.50). Tues–Sat 12.30–2pm & 7–10pm.

Greenhouse 10 Station St, BN21 4RG ☎01323 738228, ⓦthegreenhousebar.com. Cosy and mellow bare-brick basement bar, tucked away on a side street by the station. There's plenty of wine by the glass, plus cocktails and draught beers, and a courtyard out the back that comes into its own in the summer. A simple bar menu is available at lunchtime (noon–3pm). The same outfit run the *Beachouse*, a teeny café-bar with a deck right on the pebbles, between the bandstand and the Wish Tower; hours are weather-dependent, but it's generally open every day in summer. Mon–Thurs 11am–11pm, Fri 11am–1am, Sat 11am–2am, Sun 6–11pm.

Qualisea 189 Terminus Rd, BN21 3DH ☎01323 725203. The place to go for fish and chips – no frills, good value (cod and chips £5.40) and tasty, with the queues to prove it. Takeaway also available. Daily 11am–10pm.

★ **Urban Ground** 2A Bolton Rd, BN21 3JX ☎01323 410751, ⓦurbanground.co.uk. A breath of fresh air in unhip Eastbourne, this fab little independent coffee shop offers great coffee and free wi-fi in a cool, stylish interior. On the menu are sandwiches, soups, charcuterie boards (£6.50) and a assortment of spectacular cakes. It's the sort of place Brighton has in spades, but in Eastbourne it's a rare breed. Mon–Sat 7.30am–6pm, Sun 8.30am–5pm.

ENTERTAINMENT

Congress Theatre Carlisle Rd, BN21 4BP ☎01323 412000, ⓦeastbournetheatres.co.uk. Modern, large theatre with an eclectic programme of live bands, comedy, musicals, theatre, ballet, classical music and more.

Devonshire Park Theatre Compton St, BN21 4BP ☎01323 412000, ⓦeastbournetheatres.co.uk. Drama, musicals and children's theatre are the mainstays of this Victorian theatre, as well as the annual panto.

Royal Hippodrome 108–112 Seaside Rd, BN21 3PF ☎01323 412000, ⓦeastbournetheatres.co.uk. For many years the home of music hall in Eastbourne, the Hippodrome now opens for the summer season, with a long-running family show.

Underground Theatre Below Central Library, Grove Rd, BN21 4TL ⓦundergroundtheatre.org.uk. Small, independently run performance space, hosting everything from jazz or folk bands to drama and film. Tickets available on the door, from the tourist information office or from Oxboffice on ☎0845 680 1926.

Winter Garden Compton St, BN21 4BP ☎01323 412000, ⓦeastbournetheatres.co.uk. Once a skating rink, the Winter Garden now hosts comedy, children's theatre, music, tea dances and big bands.

SHOPPING

★ **Emma Mason Gallery** 3 Cornfield Terrace, BN21 4NN ☎01323 727545, ⓦemmamason.co.uk. This fab little gallery sells original prints by British printmakers, from the postwar period to the modern day, as well as books and cards. Regular exhibitions held throughout the year. Thurs–Sat 10am–5pm.

Mr and Mrs Doak's Bumper Bookshop 35 Grove Rd, BN21 4TT ☎01323 737110, ⓦbumperbookshop.co.uk. Wonderful children's bookshop with a little café at the back – all polka dots and pink milk – that's a great pit stop if you have kids in tow. Mon–Sat 9.30am–5.30pm.

Sharnfold Farm Shop Stone Cross, BN24 5BU ☎01323 768490, ⓦsharnfoldfarm.co.uk. A 10min drive from Eastbourne, this excellent farm shop sells the farm's produce, home-made bread, cheeses and chutneys; it's also one of the best pick-your-own spots in this corner of Sussex, with a huge array of soft fruit. Daily 9.30–5pm.

Beachy Head and the Seven Sisters

The glorious stretch of coast between Eastbourne and Seaford is one of the longest expanses of undeveloped coastline on the south coast, a stunning, nine-mile-long pocket of pristine shoreline, dizzying white cliffs and sweeping chalk grassland, with beautiful views at every stride. It's one of the undoubted highlights of the South Downs National Park, and far from a secret – there's always a steady stream of walkers tramping along the blowy clifftops, enjoying what is arguably the finest coastal walk in the Southeast.

Beachy Head is the tallest of the cliffs and the closest to Eastbourne; to the west of it is the tiny hamlet and pebbly beach of **Birling Gap**, and then come the gently

THE SOUTH DOWNS WAY

The glorious, long-distance **South Downs Way** rises and dips for over a hundred miles along the chalk uplands between the city of Winchester and the spectacular cliffs at Beachy Head. If undertaken in its entirety, the bridle path is best walked from west to east, taking advantage of the prevailing wind, Eastbourne's better transport and accommodation, and the psychological appeal of ending at the sea: the heart-pumping hike along the Seven Sisters and Beachy Head makes a spectacular conclusion to the trail. Steyning, the halfway point, marks a transition from predominantly wooded sections to more exposed chalk uplands.

The OS Landranger **maps** #198 and #199 cover the eastern end of the route; you'll need #185 and #197 as well to cover the lot. A **guidebook** is advised, and several are available, including the official *South Downs Way National Trail Guide* (east–west; 1:25,000 OS mapping; Aurum Press); *The South Downs Way* (either direction; 1:50,000 OS mapping; Cicerone Press); and the *South Downs Way Trailblazer Guide* (west–east; hand-drawn maps; Trailblazer). Cicerone also publish *Mountain Biking on the South Downs*, which includes the South Downs Way. For more **information**, including details on **accommodation**, see ⓦnationaltrail.co.uk/southdowns.

undulating cliffs of the **Seven Sisters**, which end at the beautiful **Cuckmere Valley**. Inland lie the pretty villages of **East Dean** and **West Dean**, the latter nestled among the beech trees of **Friston Forest**.

Beachy Head

At 530ft, majestic **Beachy Head** is the tallest chalk sea-cliff in the country, and probably the most famous, too, having been the backdrop for music videos, television dramas and films, from *Quadrophenia* to *Atonement*. Every year the cliff recedes a little further, eroded by the battering waves below – up to 1.5 feet a year, though in 1999 a record 20 feet were lost in one spectacular early-morning cliff fall, a warning to anyone tempted to stray too close to the edge. The views from the top on a clear day stretch as far as Dungeness in one direction and the Isle of Wight in the other, while down below at the foot of the cliffs is **Beachy Head lighthouse**, with its cheery red and white stripes, looking exactly as a lighthouse should. The construction of the lighthouse, completed in 1902 to replace the Belle Tout lighthouse further west (see box below), was no mean feat; 3600 tonnes of granite had to be winched down from the top of the cliff.

Beachy Head can be accessed by car or bus, but the nicest way is of course on foot, if you can manage the hefty climb up from Eastbourne; the two-mile-long path starts at the western end of the promenade, by a small café. Up on the clifftop, huddling next to each other on Beachy Head Road, are the Beachy Head Countryside Centre (see p.217) and the *Beachy Head* pub, a chain pub that's nothing special but for its lovely surroundings.

To see Beachy Head from a completely different perspective, you can head down to the beach at the base of the cliffs on a fun, organized **fossil hunt** with Discovering Fossils (3hr; £12; ⓦdiscoveringfossils.co.uk).

Birling Gap

Heading 2.5 miles west along the windswept clifftops from Beachy Head will bring you to **Birling Gap** – as its name implies, a natural dip in the cliffs. The cliff here is just 40ft high, a fraction of Beachy Head's stature, and the pebbly **beach** below can be accessed via a metal staircase. It's a wonderful, if wind-battered, spot – totally unspoilt and never really overrun, with endless rockpools and even a stretch of sand at low tide, and all with the backdrop of the Seven Sisters rearing up in the distance.

Up on the clifftop, the tiny hamlet of Birling Gap consists of little more than a few cottages, a National Trust-owned **café and bar** (see p.217) and a car park, and is set to shrink even further; the cliff is retreating by over 3ft a year – faster than anywhere else on this stretch of coastline – and the National Trust is implementing a policy of "managed retreat", which in essence means abandoning the hamlet to its inevitable fate. Of the row of eight **coastguard's cottages** built in 1878, only five remain, and in a century the whole hamlet will have vanished and Birling Gap will have reverted to grassland. The National Trust runs special **events** throughout the year, everything from rockpool rambles and fossil-hunting to guided walks and food-foraging – see ⓦnationaltrust.org.uk/birling-gap-and-the-seven-sisters for details.

BACK FROM THE BRINK: THE BELLE TOUT LIGHTHOUSE

Perched in glorious isolation on the clifftop between Beachy Head and Birling Gap, just 70ft from the crumbling edge, dumpy **Belle Tout lighthouse** was erected in 1832 and remained operational until 1902, when a more effective replacement was built at the foot of nearby Beachy Head. It hit the headlines in 1999 when its then owners, faced with the prospect of their home tumbling into the sea, had the 850-tonne building lifted up onto runners and slid back onto safer ground – an astonishing feat of engineering by any stretch of the imagination. The lighthouse has since been converted into a smart and stylish B&B (see p.217).

East Dean

A mile inland from Birling Gap, **East Dean** village is a popular starting point – or lunch stop – for walks along the Seven Sisters and Beachy Head. The old part of the village lies on and around the idyllic green, encircled by flint-walled cottages and a scattering of places to eat and drink, including the well-stocked café-deli, *Frith & Little* (see p.217), and the old, whitewashed *Tiger Inn* (see p.217), from which drinkers spill out onto the green on summer days.

Seven Sisters Sheep Centre

Gilbert's Drive, BN20 0AA • March & April daily 10.30am–5pm for lambing, plus night lambing 10pm–midnight; July & Aug daily 10.30am–5pm for shearing, plus shepherd's breakfasts Sat, Sun & school hols from 8am • £5, children £4, night lambing £25, shepherd's breakfasts £25 • ☎ 01323 423207, ⓦ sheepcentre.co.uk

A working sheep farm, the **Seven Sisters Sheep Centre** is only open for part of the year: for lambing in the spring, and for shearing in the summer. The farm has over 40 breeds of sheep, including the local Southdown, which was originally bred over two hundred years ago by John Ellman of Glynde, near Lewes. The Sheep Centre is a great place for kids, especially in the spring when there are plenty of lambs to bottle-feed; there's also a low-key playground, trailer rides, and a few goats, bunnies and chicks. In spring the centre offers **night lambing** and in summer it opens early for **shepherd's breakfasts**.

The Seven Sisters

From Birling Gap, the majestic, undulating curves of the **Seven Sisters** cliffs swoop off to the west, ending at Cuckmere Haven, where the River Cuckmere meets the sea. The three-mile walk along the springy turf of the clifftops, counting off the cliff summits – the Sisters – as you go, is exhilarating, though out-of-puff walkers beware, the "Seven" Sisters are actually eight: from east to west, Went Hill, Bailey's Hill, Flat Hill, Flagstaff Point, Brass Point, Rough Brow, Short Brow and Haven Brow. Between Flat Hill and Flagstaff Brow, the peaceful **Crowlink Valley** runs inland; there's a handy car park here, giving alternative access to the clifftops.

At the western end of the Seven Sisters, Haven Brow rewards you with a wonderful view over Cuckmere Haven, before the trail heads down to the grassy valley floor. On the far side of the estuary you can see Seaford Head and the old **coastguard's cottages** that feature in the iconic view of the Seven Sisters you'll see on all the postcards; you can't cross the river mouth here, so to climb Seaford Head and see the view for yourself you'll need to head inland for 1.5 miles and then back to the coast along the river's western bank. Seaford Head is also accessible by car from the neighbouring town of Seaford: there's a clifftop car park at South Hill Barn, though the access road to it isn't easy to find, hidden away in the suburban backstreets.

Cuckmere Haven

Beautiful **Cuckmere Haven**, the only undeveloped estuary in Sussex, is a famed beauty spot, and always busy with walkers, families and tourists ambling along the 1.5-mile-long main path that runs between the beach and the car park on the A259. Despite the steady flow of visitors it's still a gorgeous spot, with chalk downland, salt marsh and shingle habitats all encountered in a half-hour stroll. The river's much-photographed **meanders** are actually nothing more than picturesque relics – the river itself flows through an artificial arrow-straight channel to the west, and has done since the channel was built in the 1840s.

As you follow the paved path you'll notice several **pill boxes** – squat concrete forts – set into the hillsides, and the remains of a tank trap between the beach and the salt marsh – reminders of the role the valley played in **World War II**, when defences were put into place against a possible invasion. At night the valley was lit up to look like a town, in the hope that German planes would mistake the lights for Newhaven and so set their coordinates wrongly and miss their targets further north.

Friston Forest

Tranquil **FRISTON FOREST**, which covers two thousand acres north of the A259 coast road, is relatively young: it was planted last century, mainly with beech trees, interspersed with pine to provide shelter as they grew. It's a beautiful place, with sunny glades and dappled tracks crisscrossing its hilly slopes, and rare fritillary butterflies, badgers and roe deer among the wildlife. The forest is popular with **walkers** and **mountain-bikers**; a free leaflet on the main trails is available from the visitor centre at Exceat (see opposite), and bikes can be hired from the Seven Sisters Cycle Company next door (see box below).

Buried away among the trees at the forest's western edge is the tiny village of **West Dean**, with a duck pond and squat-towered Norman church, while to the east, just outside the forest boundaries, is the old flint-walled smuggler's village of **Jevington**, where the *Eight Bells* pub (see opposite) makes a good lunch stop.

ARRIVAL AND GETTING AROUND

By car Pay-and-display car parks at Beachy Head, Birling Gap (NT), Crowlink (NT), Exceat and Friston Forest (on the western side of the forest on the Litlington road; and on the eastern side at Butchershole on the Jevington road). There's also a free car park at East Dean.

BEACHY HEAD AND THE SEVEN SISTERS

By bus Buses #12 and #712 run daily every 15min between Eastbourne and Brighton, via East Dean and Exceat. Bus #13X takes a detour along the clifftops and runs between Eastbourne and Brighton via Beachy Head, Birling Gap, the Seven Sisters Sheep Centre, East Dean and Exceat

---

ACTIVITIES AT CUCKMERE HAVEN AND THE SEVEN SISTERS

While most visitors to Cuckmere Haven do little more than stroll the 3-mile round-trip down to the sea and back, there's plenty to entertain more energetic types. **Walking trails** strike off in every direction and it's easy to lose the crowds; a couple of classic walks from Exceat are suggested below (both routes marked on OS Explorer map #123). For cyclists there are excellent **mountain-bike trails** through Friston Forest, with climbs, drops and singletrack. There's even the opportunity to get out on a **canoe** on the River Cuckmere's famous meanders.

WALKING
Exceat – Seven Sisters – East Dean – Friston Forest – Exceat 8 miles. This full-day walk takes in many of the area's scenic highlights, heading down along the beautiful Cuckmere Valley before climbing up and along the Seven Sisters, turning inland just before Birling Gap. The village of East Dean makes a perfect lunch stop, before you continue north to Friston Forest, where shady trails lead back to Exceat.

Exceat – Chyngton Farm – South Hill – Hope Gap – Cuckmere River – Exceat 4.5 miles. This walk takes you up onto the other side of the Cuckmere estuary, for superlative views of the Seven Sisters. From Exceat Bridge, you follow the west bank of the Cuckmere River for 200m before heading up a gentle incline to Chyngton Farm, and then south up to South Hill. From here a trail leads down to Hope Gap – where there's beach access at low tide for rock pooling – and then along the clifftop to the coastguard's cottages overlooking Cuckmere Haven. The view from here, of

the Seven Sisters with the cottages in the foreground, is one of the finest in the Southeast. Once down at the beach, you can follow the west bank of the river upstream back to Exceat.

CYCLING
Seven Sisters Cycle Company Exceat ☎ 01323 870310, ⌨ cuckmere-cycle.co.uk. Bike hire for £10/2hr; children's bikes, baby seats and tagalongs also available, as well as maps of cycle trails along the Cuckmere Valley and through Friston Forest. Daily: April–Oct 10am–6pm; Nov–March 10am–4pm.

CANOEING
Seven Sisters Canoe Centre Exceat, at the far end of the car park ☎ 01323 870310 or ☎ 01323 491289, ⌨ eastsussex.gov.uk/leisureandtourism/sport/clubs /watersports/sevensisters. Two-hour kayaking and canoeing sessions (in a group of 8) cost £18. Prebooking only. Year-round daily.

(late April to late June Sat & Sun only; late June to mid-Sept daily; every 30min). The Cuckmere Valley Community Bus (☎01323 870032) runs hourly at weekends between Berwick Station, Alfriston, Seaford, Exceat and Wilmington.

By tour bus Hop-on, hop-off city sightseeing buses run from Eastbourne (see p.211).

INFORMATION

Seven Sisters Country Park Visitor Centre Exceat, on the A259 between Seaford and Eastbourne (March Sat & Sun 11am–4pm; April–Oct daily 10.30am–4.30pm; volunteer run, so hours can vary, especially in winter; ☎0345 608 0194, ⓦsevensisters.org.uk). Information on walks and activities in the park, plus displays and exhibitions on its history, geology and wildlife.

Beachy Head Countryside Centre Beachy Head Rd (April to mid-Oct daily 10am–4pm; mid-Oct–March Sat & Sun during school holidays only 11am–3pm ☎01323 737273, ⓦbeachyhead.org). Mainly a souvenir shop (which also sells maps and walking guides), but also has a small exhibition area on the area's plant and animal life.

Birling Gap National Trust Information Point Birling Gap (late March–Sept daily 10am–4.30pm). A new national park visitor centre is provisionally planned for the future.

ACCOMMODATION AND EATING

★ **Belle Tout Lighthouse** Beachy Head, BN20 0AE ☎01323 423185, ⓦbelletout.co.uk. Fabulous B&B in an old lighthouse (see box, p.214), perched on top of a vertiginous cliff. Most of the six smartly contemporary rooms have large picture windows making the most of the views; there's also a lounge with squishy sofas and an open fire, and a lovely breakfast room. The star of the show though is the stylishly converted lamp room, where guests can lounge on white leather banquettes and soak up the views, listening to the wind growling around the tower. **£175**

Birling Gap Café and Bar Birling Gap, BN20 0AB ☎01323 423197, ⓦnationaltrust.org.uk/birlinggap. This National Trust-owned café-bar is on borrowed time, perched as it is right on the steadily retreating clifftop, by the steps down to the beach. There's a café serving sandwiches, burgers and the like – with a few picnic tables outside – and a cosy bar offering a slightly fuller menu, plus beers from Harveys and the local Beachy Head Brewery. Daily: café March–Oct 10am–5pm; Nov–Feb 10am–4pm; bar 10am–5pm.

Eight Bells Jevington, BN26 5QB ☎01323 484442, ⓦ8bellsonline.co.uk. A proper country pub with loads of character – leaded windows, beams and inglenook fireplace – and plenty of history too: the colourful Jevington Jig, leader of the Jevington smugglers' gang (see box, p.218), was once innkeeper here. There's good home-cooked food, including dishes such as rabbit pie (£11) and sausage and mash (£10), as well as the usual sandwiches and ploughman's, but the real highlight is the lovely garden, with plenty of nooks and crannies, and great views over the Downs. Daily 11am–11pm; food served Mon–Sat noon–3pm & 6–9pm, Sun noon–9pm.

Frith & Little The Green, East Dean, BN20 0BY ☎01323 423631, ⓦfrithandlittle.com. This great little deli-café can provide everything you need for a picnic, from freshly baked pastries and bread from the Bexhill Farm bakery, to cured hams, cheeses, local ales and wines, and home-made cakes and sandwiches. A few tables are available if you want to eat in. Tues–Sat 9.30am–5pm, Sun 10am–4pm.

★ **Tiger Inn** The Green, East Dean, BN20 0DA ☎01323 423209, ⓦbeachyhead.org.uk. This quintessentially English pub, ancient and low-slung, has an idyllic location on the green in pretty East Dean. There are plenty of picnic tables outside, and inside there's a beamed main bar complete with inglenook fireplace, cosy settles, plenty of horse brasses and a stuffed tiger's head (of course). Plenty of options for ale-lovers include Harveys and a couple of brews from the local Beachy Head Brewery, while the good food ranges from ploughman's (£8) to burgers (£10.50) and slow-roasted pork belly (£13). Five understated yet luxurious rooms make a great base for the area. Mon–Thurs & Sun 11am–11pm, Fri & Sat 10.30am–midnight; food served daily noon–3pm & 6–9pm. **£95**

Alfriston and around

As the River Cuckmere draws close to the sea, the final part of its journey takes it through the lower reaches of the beautiful Cuckmere Valley, where it loops lazily through the water meadows around **ALFRISTON**, one of the prettiest villages in Sussex. Nestled beneath the Downs, the village is remarkably picturesque, its main street a handsome huddle of wonky-roofed flint cottages, narrow pavements and low-slung timber-framed and tile-hung cottages, punctuated with not one but three creaky old hostelries, each awash with history and tales of smuggling derring-do. The weathered stump of the **Market Cross** marks the High Street's northern end, while a hundred metres south a twitten cuts down to the village green, **The Tye**, and a view that's

6

SMUGGLING ON THE SOUTH COAST

In the heyday of **smuggling**, in the late eighteenth to the early nineteenth centuries, there was scarcely a community along the Sussex and Kent coast that remained untouched by it, from Chichester in the west right up to Deal in the east. Sussex and Kent were perfectly situated for the smuggling trade, just a short hop across the Channel from France, source of much of the contraband, and within easy distance of the rich consumers of London. Smuggling actually started with illegal exporting, when "owlers" smuggled wool to the continent to avoid paying wool tax. Later tobacco, brandy, tea and other luxuries were brought in from France in huge quantities; illegally imported gin was supposedly so plentiful in Kent at one point that villagers used it for cleaning their windows.

Smuggling was very much a community-wide affair, with whole villages involved in the trade, from wealthy landowners providing the capital, and members of the clergy receiving the illegal goods, to farm workers carrying and hiding the contraband. In Rottingdean near Brighton, the local vicar himself reportedly acted as a lookout.

Despite the air of romance, smuggling was often a brutal and unpleasant business, carried out by well-organized gangs with a reputation for violence. The gang leaders were often hardened criminals, and the locals who helped them generally did so through a combination of fear and extreme poverty: a farm labourer could earn a week's salary in one night as a "tubman", carrying cargo from the beach to its hiding place.

Almost every village in the area has its own infamous smuggler. At East Dean it was **James Dippery**, who managed to retain his enormous fortune by informing on his fellow smugglers. In Jevington, colourful petty criminal and innkeeper James Petit, known as **Jevington Jig**, ran a local gang that reputedly stored its ill-gotten booty in the tombs of the churchyard and the cellars of the local rectory. The Alfriston gang was led by the notorious **Stanton Collins**, and had its headquarters at *Ye Olde Smugglers Inn* – a perfect smugglers hideaway, with 21 rooms, 6 staircases, 48 doors (some of them false) and secret tunnels thought to lead as far away as Wilmington. Collins was eventually arrested in 1831, and deported for seven years, though in the end it was the less glamorous crime of sheep stealing that did for him.

The smuggling trade met little resistance from the authorities. The power of the Customs' men was limited, and they could often be bribed to turn a blind eye. Although the arrival of the **coastguards** and blockade men had some success in curtailing the smugglers' activities, it wasn't until **free trade** – and reduced import duties – was introduced in the 1840s that smuggling finally came to an end.

remained virtually unchanged for centuries, with the spire of fourteenth-century St Andrew's Church rising above a ring of trees.

The **countryside around Alfriston** is some of the most bucolic in Sussex, with dragonflies flitting across the meadows, swans gliding down the river, and winding, high-banked shady lanes passing through moss-roofed, flint-walled villages. Even if you only stroll three miles down the river to the tea gardens at nearby Litlington (see opposite), make sure you manage at least one walk from the village.

Clergy House

The Tye, BN26 5TL • Mid-March to July, Sept & Oct Mon–Wed, Sat & Sun 10.30am–5pm; Aug daily except Thurs 10.30am–5pm; Nov & Dec Mon–Wed, Sat & Sun 11am–4pm • £4.50; NT • ☎ 01323 871961, ⓦ nationaltrust.co.uk/alfriston-clergy-house

The small but perfectly formed **Clergy House**, a fourteenth-century Wealden hall house, was the very first building to be saved by the newly formed National Trust, who bought it in 1896 for the princely sum of £10 and rescued it from demolition. The thatched, timber-framed dwelling has been faithfully restored, with a large central hall and a floor made in the Sussex tradition from pounded chalk sealed with sour milk. The brick chimney was a later addition – fires would originally have been lit in the open hall in the middle of the house, with smoke rising up to escape from the eaves.

ARRIVAL AND DEPARTURE

By car The village pay-and-display car parks are on either side of the road at the northern edge of the village, but fill up very quickly.

By train and bus Berwick Station has hourly connections to Brighton, Lewes and Eastbourne. The Cuckmere Valley

ALFRISTON AND AROUND

Ramblerbus operates an hourly circular service from Berwick Station via Alfriston, Seaford, the Seven Sisters Country Park and Wilmington (April–Oct Sat, Sun & bank hols; ⓦ cuckmerebus.freeuk.com).

ACCOMMODATION AND EATING

Alfriston Village Store By the Market Cross, Alfriston, BN26 5UE ⓣ 01323 870201. This great little village store, with a well-preserved 1891 interior, has all you could possibly need for a picnic on the riverbank, including freshly baked bread and a well-stocked deli. Mon–Sat 8am–7pm, Sun 10am–5pm.

Badgers Tea House North St, Alfriston, BN26 5UG ⓣ 01323 871336, ⓦ badgersteahouse.com. Once the village bakery, this sixteenth-century cottage is now a classy tearoom with a flower-filled walled courtyard garden and a cosy, flagstone interior. Tea is served the way it should be – in silver teapots and with bone china crockery – and cakes are freshly baked on the premises. The signature cake is the gloriously artery-clogging fresh cream, gooseberry and elderflower sponge. Breakfasts, sandwiches, soups and salads are also available. Mon–Fri 9.15am–4pm, Sat & Sun 9.15am–4.30pm.

George Inn High St, Alfriston, BN26 5SY ⓣ 01323 870319, ⓦ thegeorge-alfriston.com. Instantly welcoming, this venerable timber-framed inn has a cosy interior of sloping floors, low beams hung with hops, a huge inglenook fireplace and twinkling candles on scrubbed wooden tables. The food's excellent too, ranging from platters and sandwiches (£7) through to mains (£10–17) such as rack of

South Downs lamb or monkfish in Parma ham. Out the back there's a peaceful walled garden with picnic benches. Daily 11am–11pm; food served noon–9pm.

Litlington Tea Gardens The Street, Litlington, BN26 5RB ⓣ 01323 870222, ⓦ litlingtonteagardens.co.uk. Sussex's oldest tea gardens, established in the 1800s, are a popular spot on a sunny weekend, with picnic benches and tables dotted around the lawn, and shadier seating in the surrounding summerhouses and lean-tos. Cream teas are served by waitresses in starched aprons – a nod to the tea gardens' Victorian heyday. March–Oct Tues–Sun 11am–5pm.

★ **Wingrove House** High St, Alfriston, BN26 5TD ⓣ 01323 870276, ⓦ wingrovehousealfriston.com. A stay at this stylish, colonial-style "restaurant with rooms" is a treat from start to finish. The five rooms are elegant and understated, with coir flooring and venetian blinds; it's tempting to splash out on one of the two at the front (£185), which have access to a heated wooden veranda overlooking the immaculate lawn. The restaurant is equally good, with the twin bonuses of a candlelit lounge for pre-dinner drinks and a heated terrace for alfresco dining. Seasonal produce comes from local suppliers: mains (£12–20) might include Heathfield steak with horseradish and

GUARDIAN OF THE DOWNS: THE LONG MAN OF WILMINGTON

Ancient fertility symbol or eighteenth-century folly? No one really has a clue what the **Long Man of Wilmington** is, how long he's been there or why he was carved into a Sussex hillside in the first place. This huge figure – 231ft tall, and designed to look in proportion when seen from below – is sited on the steep flank of Windover Hill, two miles northeast of Alfriston by the tiny village of Wilmington. He's one of only two human hill figures in the country (the other is the Cerne Abbas Giant in Dorset).

Various **theories** have been put forward for his origin: some believe that the figure is Roman or Anglo-Saxon; others that it is the work of a medieval monk from the nearby Wilmington priory; while recent studies have suggested that the figure may well date from the sixteenth century, perhaps the work of a landowner "marking" his land.

The Long Man was originally an indentation in the grass rather than a solid line – the pin-sharp outline you can see today was only created in 1874 when the lines were marked out in yellow bricks, replaced by concrete in 1969 (and briefly painted green during World War II, to prevent enemy planes using the landmark for navigation). The earliest known drawing of the figure, made in 1710, also suggests that it once had facial features, and a helmet-shaped head. Sadly, local folklore claiming that the Long Man once sported a penis, later removed by prudish Victorians, is probably apocryphal, though pigtails, breasts and hips were added during the filming of TV show *Undress the Nation* in 2007, much to the horror of local pagans.

A **car park** lies at the southern end of Wilmington village, from where footpaths lead up to the figure.

6

celeriac remoulade, or Firle Estate partridge bourgignon. Mon–Fri 6–9.30pm, Sat noon–2.30pm & 6–9.30pm, Sun noon–2.30pm & 6–8pm. **£100**

YHA Alfriston Frog Firle, Seaford Rd, Alfriston, BN26 5TT ☎0845 371 9101, ⓦyha.org.uk/hostel/alfriston.

Well-run hostel in a lovely sixteenth-century flint house, on the southern outskirts of Alfriston. The South Downs Way is only a five-minute stroll away, making this a great budget option for walkers. Dorms **£23.40**, twin rooms **£57**

SHOPPING

★ **Much Ado Books** 8 West St, Alfriston, BN26 5UX ☎01323 871222, ⓦmuchadobooks.com. This award-winning bookshop is the sort of place it's impossible to leave empty-handed, with a fabulous first floor that feels like someone's home, with books stacked on the mantelpiece, cushions on the floor and enticing armchairs in cosy nooks. Craft workshops and other events are held in the neighbouring barn. Wed–Sat 10am–5pm, Sun 11am–5pm.

Steamer Trading High St, Alfriston, BN26 5TY ☎01323 870055, ⓦsteamer.co.uk. A treasure-trove of kitchenware, this is the original branch of a chain that can now be found all over the Southeast. Mon–Sat 9.30am–5.30pm, Sun 11am–5pm.

The Cuckmere Valley to Lewes

There are lots of incentives to turn off the busy A27, which zips along from the Alfriston roundabout towards Lewes, shadowing the South Downs ridge. Quiet lanes strike off south towards the Downs at regular intervals, to sleepy hamlets and inviting inns, before trailing off at the bottom of the ridge. The beauty of the area drew the Bloomsbury Group here in World War I, and their fascinating country home, **Charleston Farmhouse**, can be visited today, along with the nearby church at **Berwick**, which they decorated in their own inimitable style. Further west, the estate villages of **Firle** and **Glynde** each boast grand manor houses and lovely pubs, with plenty of options for post-pub rambles into the hills. Foodies should make a point of stopping off at **Middle Farm**'s excellent farm shop and at the **English Wine Centre**, where you can pick up a few bottles of Sussex's world-class bubbly – essential if you're planning on an interval picnic on the lawns of the famous **Glyndebourne** opera house.

Drusillas Park

Alfriston Rd, BN26 5QS • Daily: March–Oct 10am–5pm; Nov–Feb 10am–4pm • Adults & children over 2 £10–16.50 depending on season • ☎01323 874100, ⓦdrusillas.co.uk

Multi-award-winning **Drusillas Park** is a sure-fire hit with kids, though it does get full to bursting in the summer holidays. There's been a zoo here since the 1930s and today it houses more than a hundred different small species, everything from lemurs to meercats, penguins to porcupines. There are plenty of other attractions alongside the animals, including a brilliant adventure playground, interactive maze, gold-panning, climbing wall, paddling pool, and a Thomas the Tank Engine train that runs around the zoo.

English Wine Centre

Alfriston Rd, by the A27, BN26 5QS • Tues–Sun 10am–5pm; wine-tasting lunches first Sat of the month • Wine-tasting lunches £39.75 • ☎01323 870164, ⓦenglishwine.co.uk

If you've not yet caught on to the success story of English wine (see box, p.28) you're in for a big surprise at the **English Wine Centre**, where a whopping 140 varieties are on sale. The shop generally has a few wines out for tasting, and also runs monthly **wine-tasting lunches** – a taster of eight wines followed by a slap-up lunch of Sussex bangers and cheeses. There's a small restaurant out the back, as well as rooms (see p.226) in a separate building for you to sleep it all off in.

Michelham Priory

Upper Dicker, BN27 3QS, signposted from the A27 and A22 • Daily: March–Oct 10.30am–5pm; Nov to mid-Dec 11am–4pm • £7.30 • ☎ 01323 844224, ⓦ sussexpast.co.uk

Venerable **Michelham Priory** has a lovely setting amid immaculate gardens and encircled by the longest water-filled moat in the country. The Augustinian priory was founded in 1229, with the medieval gatehouse and moat added at the end of the fourteenth century, but in 1537 it was dissolved and partly demolished under Henry VIII, and transformed into a private country house. Only the refectory, the undercroft (now the main entrance) and the prior's room above it remain from the original structure; the Tudor wing of the house was added in the late sixteenth century.

6

 Inside, you'll find Tudor rooms and furnishings, including a re-created kitchen complete with working spit, and a goggin, or baby cage – an early baby-walker. It's the **grounds**, though, that are the real treat, with a beautiful little kitchen garden, a medieval orchard and a moat walk giving lovely views back towards the house. Every weekend, there's have-a-go **archery** on the sweeping South Lawn (from noon), and the **watermill** mills wholemeal flour (available to buy) every afternoon from 2pm.

Berwick Church

Berwick village, off the A27, BN26 5QS • Daily 10am–dusk • Free • ⓦ berwickchurch.org.uk

From the outside, the little flint-walled **Berwick Church** looks distinctly ordinary, but step inside and you'll see why there's a steady trickle of tourists to this quiet spot. During World War II, **Duncan Grant** and his lover **Vanessa Bell** – residents of nearby Charleston Farmhouse and members of the Bloomsbury Group (see box, p.222) – were commissioned by Bishop George Bell of Chichester to decorate the church with murals, a rather enlightened move given that the couple were unmarried, not practising Christians and pacifist to boot. Bell was keen to promote the relationship between Art and the Church, and also to continue the tradition of mural painting in Sussex churches, which had come to an end after the Reformation. What resulted was a series of murals painted by the couple and Vanessa's son, **Quentin Bell**, on plasterboard panels fixed to the wall, depicting biblical events set against a backdrop of rural wartime Sussex. Sir Charles Reilly, who had recommended Grant to Bishop Bell, commented that entering the church was "like stepping out of a foggy England into Italy".

 The artists used themselves, locals and friends as models. In **The Nativity** (north side of the nave), Vanessa's daughter, Angelica, was the model for Mary, with farm workers posing as the shepherds, and the spruced-up children of Vanessa's housekeeper and gardener forming the onlookers – all set against a landscape that is unmistakeably the Downs around Berwick, with a Sussex trug full of vegetables and a local Southdown lamb at their feet. The largest painting in the church, on top of the chancel arch, is **Christ in Majesty**; here Christ is flanked on the right by the then Rector of Berwick and Bishop Bell, and on the left by three local men representing the three armed forces; the soldier, Douglas Hemming, son of the stationmaster, was later killed in action. Perhaps the most beautiful of the murals, however, are also the simplest: four roundels on the rood screen depicting the **Four Seasons**, scenes of ordinary rural life, interspersed with two panels depicting the pond at Charleston at dawn and dusk.

Charleston Farmhouse

Six miles east of Lewes, signposted off the A27, BN8 9LL • April–Oct Wed–Sat 1hr tours only 1–6pm (July & Aug from noon), Sun & bank hol Mon stewarded rooms 1–5.30pm; last entry 1hr before closing • £9.50, garden only £3.50 • ☎ 01323 811626, ⓦ charleston.org.uk

Hidden away at the end of a potholed lane under the hulking Downs, **Charleston Farmhouse** was the country home of the **Bloomsbury Group**, an informal circle of writers, artists and intellectuals who came together in the early decades of the twentieth century (see box, p.222). The house was rented by **Vanessa Bell** and the love of her life **Duncan Grant**, who moved here in 1916, in order that Grant and his lover **David Garnett** – pacifists and conscientious objectors – could work on local farms (farm labourers were exempt from military service). It was a rather unconventional household to say the least, housing not only the amicable love triangle of Vanessa, Grant and Garnett, but also Vanessa's two young sons from her marriage-in-name-only to **Clive Bell**, who himself was an intermittent visitor, until he settled permanently there in 1939.

The farmhouse became a gathering point for other members of the Bloomsbury Group, including the biographer and historian **Lytton Strachey**, the novelist **E.M. Forster**, and Vanessa's sister **Virginia Woolf**. One of the most frequent visitors was the eminent economist **John Maynard Keynes**, who insisted on wearing a suit even in the fields, and had his own room until his marriage to a Russian ballerina in 1925 saw him move to nearby Tilton House.

Vanessa's children enjoyed a childhood of almost complete liberty, and perhaps not surprisingly all grew up embracing the artistic life, her eldest son Julian becoming a poet, second son Quentin an art historian and potter, and Angelica, her daughter with Duncan Grant, a painter.

The house

Bell and Grant saw the house as a blank canvas: almost every surface is **decorated** – fireplaces, door panels, bookcases, lamp bases, screens. Many of the fabrics, lampshades and other artefacts bear the unmistakeable mark of the **Omega Workshops** (see box, p.222), the Bloomsbury equivalent of William Morris's artistic movement. In the **dining room**, the dark distempered walls with a stencilled pattern might seem commonplace to modern eyes but at the time would have been daringly modern; so too the painted circular

THE BLOOMSBURY GROUP

The group of artists, writers and thinkers that came to be known as the **Bloombury Group** had its beginnings in Cambridge, where the brother of **Virginia Woolf** and **Vanessa Bell**, Thoby, studied alongside Leonard Woolf (Virginia's future husband), Clive Bell (Vanessa's future husband), E. M. Forster, John Maynard Keynes, Roger Fry and Lytton Strachey (whose cousin, **Duncan Grant**, would later set up home with Vanessa at Charleston Farmhouse). The men graduated in 1904, the same year that Virginia and Vanessa's father died. Vanessa promptly rented a property in Gordon Square in **Bloomsbury**, painted the door a defiant red, and set up home with her siblings. Thoby's Cambridge friends began to meet at the house, sharing ideas and discussing their work with each other and the sisters, and in time, the "Bloomsbury Group" was born.

Artistically, the art critic **Roger Fry** was a huge influence on the group. It was he who brought over the first post-Impressionist exhibitions from France in 1910 and 1912, which were greeted with horror by the general public whose idea of proper art was the photorealist representation of the Victorian age. In the wake of the exhibitions, Fry, Grant and Vanessa set up the **Omega workshops** in 1913, to bring post-Impressionism to the decorative arts – furniture, ceramics, textiles and more. The idea that art did not have to be confined to a picture frame was a guiding principle behind the exuberant decorations at **Charleston Farmhouse**, where Vanessa and Grant moved in 1916.

The **values** of the Bloomsbury Group were, primarily, a loathing and rejection of Victorian conventions – its worthiness, hypocrisy, prudishness, militarism, sexism and homophobia. Instead there was a focus on individual pleasure, friendship, pacifism, and truth to oneself and one's sexuality – the last of these resulting in a bewildering amount of bed-hopping and all sorts of complicated **love triangles**: Keynes was a lover of both Strachey and Grant before he settled down with a Russian ballerina; while Vanessa, though married to Clive Bell, lived with Grant and had a child with him, **Angelica** (who was recognized by Bell to avoid scandal). Grant slept with any number of men during his years with Vanessa, among them Keynes, Strachey and writer **David Garnett**, who eventually ended up – in a move that horrified Vanessa and Grant – marrying the young Angelica.

table, signifying equality between the sexes, where women were not required to leave the table after dinner and could enter into discussions with men on an equal footing.

Around the house, the walls are hung with **paintings** by Picasso, Renoir and Augustus John, alongside the work of the markedly less talented residents. Portraits of friends and family abound, nowhere more so than in **Vanessa's bedroom**; above her bed is a large portrait of her beloved son Julian, who was killed in 1937 while working as an ambulance driver in the Spanish Civil War. Vanessa never really recovered, and when her sister committed suicide in 1941 the fun slowly ebbed out of Charleston.

Vanessa died in 1961, and Duncan Grant in 1978. The dilapidated house was bought by the Charleston Trust, restored and opened to the public, retaining the warm, lived-in feeling of a family home. The Trust puts on exhibitions throughout the year, and runs a programme of **events, talks and workshops**, including the **Charleston Festival** at the end of May.

Middle Farm

Firle, 4 miles east of Lewes on the A27, BN8 6LJ • Farm shop & cider centre daily 9.30am–5.30pm; open farm generally daily 9.30am–4pm • Open farm £4 adults and children over 3 • ☎ 01323 811411, ⓦ middlefarm.com

Opened in the 1960s, **Middle Farm** is one of the oldest farm shops in the country. There's a huge amount of produce on sale, including fresh bread, over fifty British cheeses, trugs (Sussex baskets) overflowing with wholesome fruit and veg, and home-produced beef, lamb and pork. The main draw for many, however, is the **National Collection of Cider and Perry**, a small barn crammed floor-to-ceiling with barrels housing over a hundred varieties of cider and perry; tasting glasses are provided so you can compare ciders before filling a bottle with the tipple of your choice. Elsewhere in the farm there's a restaurant and an open farm with a small playground.

The farm also hosts a couple of rollicking annual events: the boisterous **Wassail** winter celebration in January, with a ceilidh, mummers, a torchlit procession and mulled cider; and the very popular **Apple Festival** in October, featuring live bands, morris dancers, a cider bar and, of course, lots and lots of apples.

Firle

Four miles from Lewes, tiny **West Firle** – known generally as **Firle** – is a perfect Sussex village, with brick- and flint-walled cottages lining the main street, flowers cascading over low garden walls and a handsome old pub, the *Ram Inn* (see p.226), which in summer sees drinkers spilling out on to the laneside picnic tables. It's had more than its fair share of famous residents over the years – John Maynard Keynes, Katherine Mansfield and **Virginia Woolf** all lived here at one time, the last in close proximity to her sister Vanessa Bell at Charleston, a twenty-minute walk away.

Several members of the Bloomsbury set, Vanessa Bell among them, are buried in the churchyard of the village church, **St Peter's**, at the far end of The Street. Inside the church, there's a beautiful piece of modern stained glass in the organ vestry – a depiction of Blake's *Tree of Life*, designed in 1985 by English artist John Piper; look out for the Southdown sheep at the bottom of the window. Beyond the church lies **Firle Place** (☎ 01273 858307, ⓦ firle.com), built in 1473 and remodelled in the eighteenth century, probably with stone taken from the Priory ruins in nearby Lewes; the house is currently closed for refurbishment but is due to reopen in 2013 – check the website for the latest.

On the northern side of the village by the car park, the idyllically sited cricket ground, fringed by swaying oaks, is home to **Firle Cricket Club**, one of the oldest in the world, formed in 1758; check out the fixtures at ⓦ firlecc.com if you'd like to catch a match.

Glynde

Three miles east of Lewes, off the A27, the tiny estate village of **Glynde** is best known for its world-famous opera house, **Glyndebourne**, which lies just up the road. The village itself is a bit of a backwater, mainly visited by visitors to Glyndebourne and walkers taking advantage of its location at the foot of the hulking Mount Caburn.

The village was built and is still owned by the Glynde estate; the estate's manor house, **Glynde Place** (☎01273 858224, ⓦglynde.co.uk), a handsome Elizabethan affair built in Sussex flint with wonderful views across the Weald, lies at the northern fringe of the village. It's currently closed for restoration, but is due to reopen in 2013 – check the website for information. The small but perfectly formed **Meadowlands Festival** (ⓦmeadowlandsfestival.com) shatters the peace of the idyllic grounds in June, while the two-day **Food and English Wine Festival** (ⓦglyndefoodfestival.com) sets up its stalls in July, with lots of local goodies for sale, plus cookery masterclasses, foraging walks and wine tasting.

Glyndebourne

1 mile north of Glynde, BN8 5UU · ☎01273 812321, ⓦglyndebourne.com

Founded in 1934, **Glyndebourne** is one of the world's best opera houses, and Britain's only unsubsidized one. It's best known for the **Glyndebourne Festival** (mid-May to August), an indispensable part of the high-society calendar, when opera-goers in evening dress throng to the country house with hampers, blankets and candlesticks to picnic on the lawns; the operas themselves are performed in an award-winning theatre, seating 1200. It's undeniably exclusive, but the musical values are the highest in the country, using young talent rather than star names, and taking the sort of adventurous risks Covent Garden wouldn't dream of. **Tickets** for the season's six productions sell out quickly, and are eye-wateringly expensive, but there are some standing-room-only ones available at reduced prices (from £10), as well as discounts for under-30s (register first to be eligible).

ARRIVAL AND GETTING AROUND   THE CUCKMERE VALLEY TO LEWES

By train Hourly trains run from Lewes to Eastbourne via Glynde and Berwick stations.

By bus Bus #125 runs from Lewes along the A27 via Glynde, Firle and Berwick to Alfriston (Mon–Fri every 2hr).

UP, UP AND AWAY: PARAGLIDING AND GLIDING IN SUSSEX

On balmy summer's days, you can't fail to notice the colourful canopies of **paragliders** dotting the skies above Mount Caburn, floating in the thermals. Two local companies offer lessons year-round; you can be up in the air flying solo in just one day. If you'd like to have a go at the flying without the strings attached, a couple of outfits offer trial **gliding** lessons (20–30min) in dual-control gliders; it's quite an experience to be swooping silently, without power, 2500ft above the ground.

Airworks Paragliding Centre Old Station, Glynde ☎01273 434002, ⓦairworks.co.uk. Small-group courses in paragliding and paramotoring (powered paragliding). One-day introductory paragliding courses £130; five-day Elementary Pilot course £490; 30min tandem rides £140.

East Sussex Gliding Club Kitsons Field, The Broyle, Ringmer ☎01825 840347, ⓦsussexgliding.co.uk. Trial gliding lesson £99. Wed, Sat, Sun & bank hols, plus Tues April–Sept.

FlySussex paragliding On the A27, 2 miles east of Lewes, between Glynde and Firle ☎01273 858170, ⓦsussexhgpg.co.uk. The largest BHPA-approved paragliding school in the UK, with their own private flying sites. One-day introductory paragliding courses £125 (£145 weekends), five-day Elementary Pilot course £495; 30min tandem rides £130.

Southdown Gliding Club Parham Airfield, Pulborough Road, Cootham ☎01903 742137, ⓦsouthdowngliding.co.uk. Trial gliding lesson £95. Wed, Sat, Sun & bank hols, plus Fri April–Sept.

ACCOMMODATION AND EATING

★ **Cricketers' Arms** Berwick, BN26 6SP ☎ 01323 870469, ⓦ cricketersberwick.co.uk. Get here early in summer to bag one of the picnic tables in the idyllic flower-filled cottage garden of this pretty flint village pub – one of the nicest spots in the area for an alfresco pint. Food ranges from seafood platters (£13) to ham, egg and chips (£9.50), and there's well-kept Harveys on tap. Daily 11am–11pm; food served noon–9pm.

English Wine Centre Alfriston Rd, by the A27 roundabout, BN26 5QS ☎ 01323 870164, ⓦ englishwine .co.uk. The small restaurant at the English Wine Centre (see p.220) is a good place to crack open a bottle or two of England's finest and tuck into well-priced, locally sourced food, perhaps rump of Sussex lamb or sea bass with samphire (mains £11–13). Best of all, you're just a short waddle away from the five super-comfortable bedrooms in the adjoining barn – all with deep carpets, immensely fluffy duvets and luxurious bathrooms. Tues–Thurs & Sun noon–3pm, Fri & Sat noon–3pm & 6.30–9pm. **£135**

Ram Inn Firle, BN8 6NS ☎ 01273 858222, ⓦ raminn .co.uk. This sprawling pub is a corker, with a lovely walled garden and, inside, wooden floors, slate-grey walls and roaring fires in winter. The tasty food is locally sourced where possible – bread is baked in the village, and game comes from the Firle estate. Mains such as pan-fried local scallops or braised Sussex lamb shank cost £13–20, and meze and charcuterie boards are £11–15. There are four gorgeous rooms above the pub; the nicest, Bloomsbury,

has views across to the Downs and a roll-top bath. Mon–Fri 11.30am–11pm, Sat & Sun 9am–11pm; food served Mon–Fri noon–3pm & 6.30–9.30pm, Sat 9–11am, noon–3pm & 6.30–9.30pm, Sun 9–11am, noon–4pm & 6.30–9.30pm. **£110**

Rose Cottage Inn Alciston, BN26 6UW ☎ 01323 870377, ⓦ therosecottageinn.co.uk. As its name suggests, this whitewashed, creeper-clad pub was originally a cottage before being converted into the village inn in the nineteenth century, which explains its cosy, homey feel today. Inside are three small, crooked rooms with log fires, a talking African Grey parrot at the tiny bar and boxes of eggs and secondhand books for sale. There are a few tables outside on the front terrace, and good pub grub on the menu – the Jolly Posh fish pie (£11.50) is always popular. Mon–Sat 11.30am–3pm & 6.30–11pm, Sun noon–3pm & 6.30–10.30pm; food served daily noon–2pm & 6.30–9.30pm (9pm on Sun).

Tilton House Firle, BN8 6LL ☎ 01323 811570, ⓦ tiltonhouse.co.uk. This beautiful Georgian country house on the Firle estate was the former home of the late John Maynard Keynes, part of the Bloomsbury Group, and his ballerina wife Lydia Lopokova, who used to dance on the lawn in the moonlight. *Tilton House* now offers B&B, as well as popular yoga retreats and the occasional literary salon-style reading weekend in serene yet impeccably luxurious surroundings (weekend courses £300–400). **£95**

Lewes and around

East Sussex's county town, **LEWES**, couldn't be in a lovelier spot, straddling the River Ouse and with some of England's most appealing chalk downlands right on its doorstep. With a remarkably good-looking centre, a lively cultural and artistic scene, plenty of history, and a proud sense of its own identity, Lewes is one of Sussex's finest towns.

The undisputed highlight of the year for most Lewesians is **Bonfire Night**, when hundreds of elaborately costumed locals take to the streets wielding flaming torches to commemorate the burning of 17 Protestant martyrs in 1556. Anyone who's ever watched the anarchic celebrations (see box, p.230) wouldn't be surprised to learn that there's a strong streak of non conformity coursing through the veins of this pretty little Sussex town; when in 2006 Greene King decided to remove the local beer, Harveys, from the *Lewes Arms* pub, it led to a 133-day boycott by outraged locals that hit the

---

THE LEWES POUND

Created to encourage the local economy, the **Lewes pound** was launched to much fanfare and national press attention in 2008. The currency's still in circulation – though it's rare to be handed one in your change – and is available in £1, £5, £10 and £21 denominations, with the same value as sterling. It's accepted by over two hundred businesses around town, including stallholders at the farmers' markets, and is issued at various locations, among them the Town Hall, Cheese Please (see p.232) and the Harvey's Brewery Shop (see p.232). The current issue of Lewes pounds is valid until 2014. Visit ⓦ thelewespound.org to find out more.

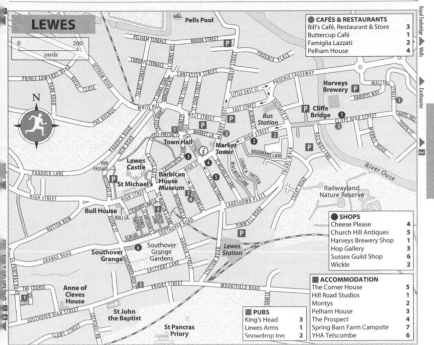

headlines around the country, before the brewer admitted defeat. Two years later, when the town proudly introduced its own currency, the **Lewes pound** (see box opposite), it was local hero Thomas Paine – revolutionary and one-time resident – whose face was chosen to adorn the notes.

Lewes Castle

169 High St • Mon & Sun 11am–5.30pm (dusk in winter), Tues–Sat 10am–5.30pm (dusk in winter); closed Mon in Jan • £6.60 • ☎ 01273 486290, Ⓦ sussexpast.co.uk

It almost comes as a surprise to stumble upon **Lewes Castle**, which is completely hidden from view on the High Street until a gap in the houses opens on to Castle Gate, and the imposing Barbican gateway. The **motte and bailey** castle was the work of William de Warenne, who was given the land by William I after the Norman Conquest. A second motte (or mound) was added when the castle was enlarged in 1100, together with a gateway and curtain walls. Castles built on two mottes were very unusual: Lewes is one of only two examples in England (Lincoln is the other). Just a single wall remains of the Norman gateway today; the majestic arrow-slitted gateway you see in front of it – the **Barbican** – was built in the early fourteenth century for added fortification. The last of the De Warennes died without heir in 1347 and the castle began its slow slide into decay, until the romantic ruins were reinvented as a tourist attraction in the eighteenth century.

The interior

Inside the complex, narrow stone steps climb up inside the Barbican to the roof, with its excellent views over the town. The best views, however, can be had from the eleventh-century **Shell Keep**, which tops one of the castle's two mottes. From here you can see the other motte, **Brack Mount**, now just a grassy hillock and closed to the public, as well as the hills to the north of town where the **Battle of Lewes** took place in 1264. The battle was the bloody culmination of a clash between Henry III and a rebel army of barons under Simon de Montfort; the king was defeated and the resulting treaty, the **Mise of Lewes**, restricted his authority and forced him to assemble a governing council – often described as the first House of Commons. Celebrations to mark the 750th anniversary of the battle will take place in 2014 – see the website for details.

Barbican House Museum

The castle ticket office is also the entrance to the **Barbican House Museum**, which has exhibits on Sussex life from the Stone Age through to medieval times. A twelve-minute film plays every half-hour, telling the history of Lewes with the help of a model of the town as it would have looked in the 1880s.

The High Street

Georgian and crooked older dwellings line Lewes's handsome **High Street**. A few minutes' walk west from the castle you'll pass **St Michael's Church**, one of the oldest in Lewes, with unusual twin towers, one wooden shingle and the other flint. On the opposite side of the road is the fifteenth-century **Bull House**, where revolutionary and pamphleteer **Thomas Paine** lived from 1768 to 1774 before emigrating to America, where he wrote *Common Sense*, the pamphlet that made his name and earned him the title "Father of the American Revolution".

On either side of the High Street, enticing narrow lanes – "twittens" – strike off into the backstreets. Blink and you'll miss tiny **Pipe Passage**, on the north side of the street; the twitten runs past the flint-and-red-brick **Round House**, an 1801-built smock windmill that once belonged to Virginia Woolf, though she never actually lived there. On the opposite side of the High Street, by the venerable timber-framed Fifteenth-Century Bookshop, the steep, cobbled and much-photographed **Keere Street** – down which the reckless Prince Regent is alleged to have driven his carriage – leads to Southover, the southern part of town.

Southover

The part of Lewes known as **Southover**, to the south of the High Street, grew up around St Pancras Priory (see opposite) and was separated from Lewes by the Winterbourne stream. The stream still trickles, sporadically, through beautiful **Southover Grange Gardens** (daily dawn–dusk), a favourite picnic spot with locals. A hole-in-the-wall kiosk (Easter–Oct) sells ice creams, sandwiches and snacks. The gardens surround **Southover Grange**, built in 1572 from the remains of nearby St Pancras Priory, and once the childhood home of the diarist John Evelyn; today the Grange serves as the local register office, but a section of it is also given over to the Sussex Guild Shop (see p.232).

Anne of Cleves House

52 Southover High St, BN7 1JA • Feb–Nov Mon & Sun 11am–5pm, Tues–Sat 10am–5pm; sometimes closed on Sat in summer for private functions – call to check • £4.70, joint ticket with the castle £9.60 • ☏ 01273 474610, ⓦ sussexpast.co.uk

Despite the name, Anne of Cleves never actually lived in the timber-framed **Anne of Cleves House**: it was one of nine Sussex properties given to her in 1540 after Henry ignominiously cast her aside after less than a year of marriage, making her one of the richest women in the country – not a bad deal considering the fate of some of Henry's other wives. The building, a Wealden hall house, was constructed in the late fifteenth century by a wealthy yeoman farmer and would originally have been open to the rafters like the Clergy House in Alfriston (see p.218). The house today is for the most part presented as it would have been in Tudor times – the highlight being a magnificent oak-beamed bedroom complete with a 400-year-old Flemish four-poster – but two rooms are given over to exhibits on the Sussex Wealden **iron industry** and the **history of Lewes**.

St Pancras Priory

Access via Cockshut Lane or Mountfield Rd • Always open • Free • Ⓦ lewespriory.org.uk

South of Southover High Street sprawl the evocative ruins of **St Pancras Priory**, founded around 1078 by William de Warenne, who also built Lewes Castle. Little remains of the priory today, but interpretive boards do an excellent job of conjuring up what the crumbling stones would have looked like in its heyday, when it was one of the largest and most powerful monasteries in England, with a church the size of Westminster Abbey and land holdings as far north as Yorkshire. Most of the priory was destroyed during the Reformation in 1538 on the orders of Henry VIII. The site became a quarry for building materials, and in the years that followed stones from here ended up being used all over Lewes. The final blow for the site was the construction of the Brighton, Lewes & Hastings Railway straight through the centre of the ruins in 1845, destroying much of what remained of the great church. Little attempt was made to safeguard the ruins, though the **caskets** containing the bones of de Warenne and his wife Gundrada were preserved, and can now be seen in the nearby **St John the Baptist church** on Southover High Street.

Cliffe

At the east end of the High Street, School Hill descends towards **Cliffe Bridge**, built in 1727 and the entrance to Cliffe, commercial centre of the medieval settlement. The riverfront here would once have been the hub of the town, but nowadays little is made of the area and you'd almost be hard pressed to notice the town has a river at all. On the far side of the bridge you can't miss the Victorian Gothic tower of **Harveys Brewery**, while semi-pedestrianized **Cliffe High Street** strikes off ahead, with antiques shops and cafés spilling out onto the pavements. At the end of the street, steep, narrow **Chapel Hill** leads straight up on to the Downs – the start of a lovely three-mile walk to the village of Glynde (see p.224) – while South Street runs south to the *Snowdrop Inn* (see p.232), named after the deadliest avalanche in British history when, in 1836, a ledge of snow fell from the cliff onto the houses below, killing eight people.

Harveys Brewery

The Bridge Wharf Brewery, BN7 2AH • ☎ 01273 480209, Ⓦ harveys.org.uk

Affectionately known locally as Lewes Cathedral, **Harveys Brewery** is the oldest brewery in Sussex. Sussex Best bitter – one of a handful of cask ales – is the most popular brew, but the brewery also produces a dozen or so seasonal ales, including Bonfire Boy, available every November, and an 8.1-percent Christmas ale which the brewery advises should be "treated with respect". The brewery **shop** on Cliffe High Street is a great place to stock up on the award-winning cask ales and bottled beers, or you can head over the road to the **brewery tap**, the *John Harvey Tavern*, to sample a pint. **Tours** are available, but with a two-year waiting list you'll have a long time to build up a thirst; see the website for details.

Pells Pool

Brook St, BN7 2PW • Mid-May to mid-Sept daily noon–7pm, sometimes until 9pm in fine weather • £4 • ☎ 01273 472334, Ⓦ pellspool.org.uk

A five-minute walk from the High Street brings you to the Pells area, where you'll find **Pells Pool**; built in 1861, it proudly holds the claim of being the oldest open-air swimming pool in the country. Fed by an icy freshwater stream, a dip in the 50-yard-long pool is certainly not for the fainthearted, but that doesn't seem to put off the locals, who throng here at summer weekends to sprawl on the shady lawn surrounding the pool. There's also a paddling pool for youngsters and a kiosk serving drinks, ice creams and snacks.

6

LEST WE FORGET: LEWES BONFIRE NIGHT

Each November 5, while the rest of the country lights small domestic bonfires or attends municipal fireworks displays to commemorate the 1605 foiled Catholic plot to blow up the Houses of Parliament, Lewes puts on a more dramatic show. Its origins lie in the deaths of the town's 17 Protestant martyrs during the Marian Persecutions of 1555–57, when Mary Tudor sentenced 288 Protestants around the country to be burned alive for their heretical views. By the end of the eighteenth century, Lewes' **Bonfire Boys** had become notorious for the boisterousness of their anti-Catholic demonstrations, in which they set off fireworks indiscriminately and dragged rolling tar barrels through the streets – a tradition still practised today, although with a little more caution.

Lewes's first **bonfire societies** were established in the 1850s to try to introduce a little more discipline into the proceedings, and in the early part of the last century they were persuaded to move their street fires to the town's perimeters. Today's tightly-knit **bonfire societies** – Borough, Cliffe, Commercial Square, Southover, South Street and Waterloo – each with its own elaborate themed costumes, colours and quasi-militaristic motto ("Death or Glory", "True to Each Other", etc), spend much of the year organizing the **Bonfire Night** shenanigans. On the night, members dress up and parade through the town, accompanied by marching bands and visiting bonfire societies, carrying flaming torches, before marching off to the outskirts of town for their society's big fire and firework display. At each of the fires, effigies of Guy Fawkes and the Pope are burned alongside the societies' annual tableaux, which generally feature contemporary, but equally reviled, figures.

The Lewes Bonfire experience is undeniably brilliant, but it does get packed, especially on years when November 5 falls on a weekend, and the official line is that it's an event for the people of Lewes only. If you do decide to come, be aware that roads into the town close from late afternoon onwards, parking is restricted, and there can be horrendously long queues at the train station at the end of the night; the event is unsuitable for children, and accommodation can get booked up more than a year in advance. If the 5th falls on a Sunday the celebrations take place on the 4th. For more, see ⓦ lewesbonfirecouncil.org.uk.

OTHER SUSSEX BONFIRE CELEBRATIONS

Although Lewes is the best known of Sussex's bonfire celebrations, many other villages and towns have their own societies which celebrate with torchlit processions and fireworks between September and the end of November, attending each other's processions, as well as the big one in Lewes. Though on a smaller scale, these events are a great way to experience the unique Sussex bonfire tradition; you can check dates with the Lewes tourist office (see opposite), or on the societies' own websites (see below). In Lewes itself, a seventh bonfire society, **Nevill Juvenile** (ⓦ njbs.co.uk), is specifically for children and holds its celebrations in October.

September Burgess Hill (ⓦ burgesshillbonfiresociety .co.uk), Mayfield (ⓦ mayfieldbonfire.co.uk).

October Eastbourne (ⓦ eastbournebonfire.co.uk), Firle (ⓦ firlebonfire.com), Hailsham (ⓦ hailshambonfire.org .uk), Hastings (ⓦ hbbs.info), Littlehampton (ⓦ little hamptonbonfire.org.uk), Newick (ⓦ newickbonfire.com), Ninfield (ⓦ ninfieldbonfire.co.uk), Rotherfield, Seaford (ⓦ seafordbonfire.co.uk), South Heighton (ⓦ south heighton.com).

November Barcombe (ⓦ barcombebonfire.co.uk), Battle (ⓦ battlebonfire.co.uk), Chailey (ⓦ chaileybonfire.co.uk), Lindfield (ⓦ lindfieldbonfiresociety.co.uk), Robertsbridge (ⓦ robertsbridgebonfiresociety.com), Rye (ⓦ ryebonfire .co.uk).

ARRIVAL AND INFORMATION

LEWES

By car There's no free parking in the centre of Lewes, and wardens are vigilant. There are plenty of car parks around town; the cheapest long-stay parking is on North St (£2/day).

By train The station lies south of High St down Station Rd; there are good connections with London and along the coast. Destinations Brighton (every 10–20min; 15min);

Eastbourne (every 20–30min; 20–30min); London Victoria (Mon–Sat every 30min, Sun hourly; 1hr 10min).

By bus The bus station is on Eastgate St, near the foot of School Hill. Destinations Brighton (Mon–Sat every 15min, Sun hourly; 30min); Tunbridge Wells (Mon–Sat every 30min, Sun hourly; 1hr 10min).

Tourist office At the junction of High St and Fisher St (April–Sept Mon–Fri 9am–5pm, Sat 9.30am–5.30pm, Sun 10am–2pm; Oct–March Mon–Fri 9am–5pm, Sat 10am–2pm; ☎ 01273 483448, ⓦ lewes.gov.uk); they hold copies of the excellent free monthly magazine *Viva Lewes* (ⓦ vivalewes.co.uk).

ACCOMMODATION

Accommodation is in very short supply in Lewes and gets booked up quickly, especially at the weekend; if you're hoping to get a room on Bonfire Night you'll generally need to book more than a year in advance. The website ⓦ lewesbandb.co.uk is a good directory of accommodation in Lewes and the surrounding area.

6

The Corner House 14 Cleve Terrace, BN7 1JJ ☎ 01273 567138, ⓦ lewescornerhouse.co.uk. There's a real home-from-home feeling about this friendly B&B, set back from Southover High Street on a quiet Edwardian terrace. The two rooms have cheery patchwork quilts on the beds, wooden floors, plenty of books, and small, immaculate bathrooms. Breakfast is served in the light-flooded kitchen-diner overlooking the garden. **£90**

Hill Road Studios 13 Hill Rd, BN7 1DB ☎ 01273 477723, ⓦ hillroadstudios.com. A twenty-minute walk from the centre of Lewes, these two stylish studios are set around the owner's home on a leafy no-through road. Each has contemporary furnishings, wooden floors and original art on the walls, as well as a small kitchenette; the more expensive Garden Studio (£115), nestled in the flower-filled garden with its own patio, is worth paying extra for. **£95**

Montys Broughton House, 16 High St, BN7 2LN ☎ 01273 476750, ⓦ montysaccommodation.co.uk. There's just one room at this boutique B&B, occupying the entire top floor of a nineteenth-century townhouse. It more than justifies its boutique tag: there's a modern oak four-poster, coffee maker, iPod dock, freestanding bath and separate state-of-the-art shower room (with bathrobes provided), plus a small kitchenette. Nice little touches such as chocolates, Sky TV and plenty of books and magazines add to the charm. **£110**

Pelham House St Andrew's Lane, BN7 1UW ☎ 01273 488600, ⓦ pelhamhouse.com. You'll need to dig deep in your pockets for a stay at this elegant townhouse hotel, with a beautiful garden dotted with sculptures and one of the best restaurants in town (see p.232). There's a huge difference in the sizes and prices of the 31 rooms: standard rooms are smart and contemporary but aren't big enough to swing even the smallest cat; while luxurious "executive" rooms (£280) come with four-posters, views over the Downs, and huge, glamorous bathrooms with free-standing baths. Midweek and low season see prices fall, and special offers can bring the rates down. **£140**

The Prospect St Martin's Lane, BN7 1UD ☎ 01273 472883, ⓦ theprospectbandb.co.uk. This lovely B&B is in a perfect spot, on a quiet twitten running down from the High Street. It's a modern, upside-down house, with two peaceful, light bedrooms (one en suite) on the ground floor, plus access to a fridge for storing picnic provisions. Breakfast features home-baked bread and is served upstairs in the fantastic breakfast room, crammed with plants, books and art, and with huge windows giving glorious views over the Downs. **£90**

Spring Barn Farm Kingston Road, BN7 3ND ☎ 01273 488450, ⓦ springbarnfarm.com. You can unzip your tent in the morning and look straight out onto the South Downs at this simple, car-free site. Campers can take advantage of half-price entry to the adjacent farm park (see p.233), making the site a great option for families, and other bonuses include the farm shop for BBQ supplies in fine weather – fire pits cost £10 per night to hire) and farm café (for rainy-day brunches). Camping (per adult) **£7**

YHA Telscombe Telscombe, BN7 3HZ ☎ 0870 770 6062, ⓦ yha.org.uk/hostel/telscombe. The nearest hostel is 6 miles south of Lewes in the peaceful little village of Telscombe, midway between Lewes and the coast (bus #123 from Lewes will get you there). There are 22 beds (five four-bed rooms and one twin) available in the characterful, converted 200-year-old flint-and-brick estate cottages. Dorms **£13**, twin room **£38**

EATING AND DRINKING

Lewes's weekly **food market** (ⓦ lewesfoodmarket.co.uk) takes place in the Market Tower on Market St every Friday morning (9.30am–1.30pm). There's a larger **farmers' market** in the shopping precinct at the bottom of the High St on the first Saturday of the month.

Bill's Café, Restaurant & Store 56 Cliffe High St, ☎ 01273 476918, ⓦ billsproducestore.co.uk. No visit to Lewes would be complete without a pit stop at this always-buzzing restaurant-cum-produce store, which started life on this spot as a greengrocer's and now has branches across the country. The "produce" side of the store has shrunk as the café-restaurant has grown in popularity, but there's still some fruit and veg for sale, as well as walls lined with colourful jars of Bill's jams and chutneys. Mains are about £9–12, and range from salads and fish-finger sandwiches to piri-piri chicken and lamb hotpot. It's always busy, so expect to queue. Mon–Thurs 8am–10.30pm, Fri & Sat 8am–11pm, Sun 9am–10.30pm.

★ **Buttercup Café** In Pastorale Antiques, 15 Malling

6

St, BN7 2RA ☎01273 477664, ⓦthebuttercupcafe
.co.uk. This friendly, quirky café is something of a hidden
gem, with a tranquil sun-trap courtyard, where half a
dozen tables sit surrounded by tubs of overflowing flowers
and the occasional antique from the neighbouring shop.
The daily-changing, seasonal food pulls off the rare feat of
being both healthy and delicious, especially the spectacular
salads (£6.50). There are generally only three or four lunch
options, which are chalked up on the board; there's also a
simple breakfast menu, and cakes and proper cream teas
are served throughout the day. Mon–Sat 9.30am–4pm.

★ **Famiglia Lazzati** 17 Market St, BN7 2NB ☎01273
479539, ⓦfamiglia-lazzati.co.uk. Bypass the pizza
chains on the High St for this proper family-run, super-
friendly Italian restaurant, where everything on the small
but perfectly formed menu (pizzas £6–10, pastas £9–11,
mains from £13) is sourced locally and cooked fresh. It's
very family friendly, too, and early evenings kids eat free
(one kids' meal per adult main course; before 6pm). Mon–
Fri noon–2.30pm & 5–10pm, Sat & Sun noon–10pm.

King's Head 9 Southover High St, BN7 1HS ☎01273
474628, ⓦthekingsheadlewes.co.uk. Terrific foodie pub,
with the added bonus of a pretty, decked beer garden with
views of the castle. Everything on the seasonally-changing
menu is pulled off to perfection, from rabbit in cider with
truffle mash (£12) to Sussex aged rib-eye with Barkham
blue butter (£19.50); good-value set menus are available
Monday to Thursday (£12 for 2 courses). Most Thursdays
there's live music (jazz, blues, Americana acoustic) – check
the website for details. Mon–Fri noon–11pm, Sat & Sun
noon–midnight; food served Mon–Fri noon–3pm &
6–10pm, Sat noon–4pm & 6–10pm, Sun noon–4pm.

★ **Lewes Arms** Mount Place, BN7 1YH ☎01273
473252, ⓦlewesarms.co.uk. One of Lewes's best-loved
locals, this frill-free, friendly pub has bags of character,

with several cosy bare-boarded rooms and a tiny bar
serving a good selection of real ales, including Harveys. The
traditional, home-cooked pub food is superb value, with
plenty on the menu under £9 (jerk chicken, burgers, home-
made pasties and more). Annual events range from
spaniel-racing and dwyle-flunking to the World Pea
Throwing Championships, held every October (the record
currently stands at over 37m). Mon–Thurs 11am–11pm,
Fri & Sat 11am–midnight, Sun noon–11pm; food
served Mon–Fri noon–8.30pm, Sat noon–9pm, Sun
noon–8pm.

Pelham House St Andrew's Lane, BN7 1UW ☎01273
488600, ⓦpelhamhouse.com. The best place in town to
treat yourself, this hotel restaurant is set in a beautiful
sixteenth-century townhouse, with a stylish little bar for
pre-dinner cocktails and a wood-panelled dining room.
Mains might include lamb with carrot and vanilla purée, or
mullet with herb blinis and fennel; two courses will set you
back £19.50, three courses £25. The restaurant is an equally
good spot for brunch or lunch (from the cheaper lounge
menu) or afternoon tea, especially on a summer's day
when you can take advantage of the terrace seating with
lovely views across to the Downs. Mon–Sat noon–
2.30pm & 6–9.30pm, Sun noon–3pm & 6–9pm.

Snowdrop Inn 119 South St, BN7 2BU ☎01273
471018, ⓦthesnowdropinn.com. This friendly, lively and
deservedly popular pub offers live music four or five nights
a week, a great range of beer (including Harveys, Dark Star,
Long Man of Wilmington and guest craft beers), and a
good-value, daily-changing menu of locally sourced food,
with lots of vegetarian options. Most mains cost £9.75
(child portions £5.75), and might include Portobello
mushroom pie with celeriac purée, Harveys sausages or
seafood paella. Daily noon–midnight; food served
noon–9pm.

SHOPPING

Cheese Please 46 High St, BN7 2DD ☎01273 481048,
ⓦcheesepleaseonline.co.uk. Award-winning shop
stocking over 100 different cheeses, mainly British, as well
as locally baked bread and chutneys. A great spot to pick up
picnic provisions. Mon–Sat 8am–5pm.

Church Hill Antiques 6 Station St, BN7 2DA ☎01273
474842, ⓦchurchhillantiques.co.uk. This antiques
centre houses more than sixty dealers selling furniture,
interiors, jewellery and more. It's one of more than a dozen
antiques shops in Lewes; also worth checking out are those
along Cliffe High St, and the Lewes Flea Market on Market
St. Mon–Sat 9.30am–5pm.

Harveys Brewery Shop 7 Cliffe High St, BN7 2AH
☎01273 480217, ⓦharveys.org.uk. The brewery shop is
crammed floor-to-ceiling with award-winning cask ales
and seasonal bottled beers, plus wines, English fruit wines
and an assortment of glasses, tankards and other Harveys-

branded merchandise. Mon–Sat 9.30am–5.30pm.

Hop Gallery Castle Ditch Lane, off Fisher St, BN7 1YJ
☎01273 487744, ⓦhopgallery.com. Well-regarded art
gallery within the eighteenth-century Star Brewery
building, with regularly changing exhibitions of
contemporary art. Check the website for exhibition
opening times.

Sussex Guild Shop Southover Grange, Southover Rd,
BN7 1TP ☎01273 479565, ⓦthesussexguild.co.uk. A
wonderful selection of textiles, prints, ceramics and
jewellery produced by Sussex craftspeople. Daily
10am–5pm.

Wickle 24 High St, BN7 2LU ☎01273 487969, ⓦwickle
.co.uk. An eclectic treasure-trove of covetable homeware,
womenswear, gifts and kids' toys and clothes, with a child-
friendly café at the back. Mon–Sat 9.30am–6pm, Sun
11am–5pm.

Spring Barn Farm

Kingston Rd, BN7 3ND • Farm park daily 9am–5.30pm; farm shop Mon–Sat 9am–5.30pm, Sun 10am–5.30pm; restaurant daily 9am–5pm • Farm park £7.50, child £6.50 • ☎ 01273 488450, ⓦ springbarnfarm.com

Spring Barn Farm, a working farm a mile south of Lewes, is idyllically situated at the foot of the Downs, with bucolic views in every direction. Its well-run farm park has plenty of stuff to keep kids entertained, from animal handling sessions to pedal go-karts, jumping pillows, a zip wire, a huge indoor play area, and tractor and trailer rides; in spring kids can help bottle-feed the lambs, and in summer there's a huge maize maze. There's a good restaurant on site, serving local Sussex produce, as well as a farm shop selling local fruit and veg, Sussex game and the farm's own beef and lamb – handy for barbecues at the onsite camping field (see p.231).

Monk's House

Rodmell, BN7 3HF • April–Oct Wed–Sun 1–5.30pm, garden open from noon; opening days may change so call ahead to check • £4; NT • ☎ 01273 474760, ⓦ nationaltrust.org.uk/monks-house

Three miles south of Lewes on the Lewes–Newhaven road, the pretty, weatherboard **Monk's House** was the home of novelist **Virginia Woolf** and her husband, Leonard. The couple moved there in 1919, with Virginia declaring "that will be our address for ever and ever"; at first it was a summer and weekend retreat, but when their London home was bombed in 1940 it became their permanent home. Like Charleston Farmhouse, where Virginia's much-loved sister Vanessa Bell lived, Monk's House hosted gatherings of the Bloomsbury Group (see box, p.222), and over the years E.M. Forster, Maynard Keynes, Vita Sackville-West, Lytton Strachey and Roger Fry all visited; informal snapshots of these guests, accompanied by Virginia's occasionally acerbic comments, are on show in the writing room in the orchard.

The chief glory of the house is the **garden**, with its beautiful views over the Ouse Valley, and paths weaving between overflowing borders. The simple **interior** of the house – of which you can see just four rooms – is unmistakeably "Bloomsbury", with painted furniture, decorated ceramics and paintings by Vanessa and her partner Duncan Grant in every room, though on a much smaller, calmer scale than at Charleston. Monk's House was for Virginia primarily a retreat, where she could work in peace.

The rural idyll was not to last, however. When World War II broke out Virginia sank into one of the deep depressions that had afflicted her throughout her life. On March 28, 1941, she wrote a letter to Leonard – "We can't go through another of those terrible times" – and walked to the River Ouse, where she filled the pockets of her coat with stones and drowned herself.

Ditchling to Steyning

From Lewes, the escarpment of the South Downs runs west in an undulating green wave, with the ribbon of the South Downs Way threading its way along the summit.

BOATING AT BARCOMBE

At **Barcombe**, four miles upstream of Lewes, you can take to the water for a gentle paddle along the **River Ouse**, one of the South's most beautiful and unspoilt waterways. The eighteenth-century *Anchor Inn* (☎ 01273 400414, ⓦ anchorinnandboating.co.uk) – actually half a mile northeast of Barcombe, but signposted from the village – hires out four- and six-seater **canoes** (£6 per person per hour) for the two-mile trip upstream past grassy banks and meadows to Fish Ladder Falls. The only building visible en route is the spire of Isfield Church, and if you're lucky you'll spot kingfisher, heron and cormorant – though on summer weekends your most likely sightings will be boatloads of other paddlers.

Some of the South Downs' most famed beauty spots, among them **Ditchling Beacon** and **Devil's Dyke**, lie along this stretch, and a blowy walk along the ridge top is by far the best way to appreciate them. Artsy **Ditchling**, huddled underneath Ditchling Beacon, and historic **Steyning**, close to the ancient hillforts at **Chanctonbury Ring** and **Cissbury Ring**, both make excellent refuelling stops.

Ditchling and around

The pretty, affluent village of **DITCHLING** lies at the foot of the Downs, overlooked by **Ditchling Beacon**, one of the highest spots on the escarpment. Handsome half-timbered and tile-hung buildings cluster around the traffic-clogged crossroads at the centre of the village, with two great lunch spots, the *Bull Inn* and *The General*, facing each other across the street (see opposite); a few steps away, the village green is overlooked by the chunky flint church of St Margaret's.

Ditchling was for many years home to a bohemian artist's commune, inspired by the Arts and Crafts movement: the typographer and sculptor **Eric Gill** (see box below) moved here in 1907, soon followed by like-minded artists and craftspeople, including printer and writer Hilary Pepler, poet and painter David Jones and calligrapher Edward Johnston, who designed the iconic London Underground font, one of the earliest sans-serif typefaces. In 1921 the deeply religious Gill, with the aim of creating "a cell of good living in the chaos of the world", co-founded the **Guild of St Joseph and St Dominic**, an experimental Catholic community of artists and craftspeople, with its own workshops, chapel and printing press on Ditchling Common just outside the village. Gill left Ditchling for Wales in 1924, but the Guild continued to flourish, only disbanding in 1989.

Ditchling Museum of Art and Craft

Church Lane, BN6 8TB · Check website for opening hours and prices · ☎ 01273 844744, ⊛ ditchling-museum.com

Some of the works of the Guild of St Joseph and St Dominic can be seen at the **Ditchling Museum of Arts and Crafts**, on the village green. Closed at the time of writing for redevelopment, the museum is due to reopen in 2013 in a stylish new complex, with vistas onto the surrounding countryside intended to link the museum to the landscape

---

ERIC GILL IN DITCHLING

One of the country's great twentieth-century artists, **Eric Gill** (1882–1940) is probably best known for his sans-serif **Gill Sans typeface**, which was famously used on the covers of the early Penguin books with their two coloured stripes. He was also a lauded sculptor, and a major influence on British sculptors such as Moore and Hepworth. His commissions included the *Stations of the Cross* at Westminster Cathedral, and *Prospero and Ariel* on the front of the BBC's Broadcasting House.

Gill was a complicated character. He was deeply religious, and had a horror of the twentieth century's mechanistic culture, despising everything that went with it, including typewriters, contraception, Bird's custard powder, and the fashion for tight trousers that constricted "man's most precious ornament". Having moved with his wife to Ditchling in 1907 he relocated in 1913 to a run-down cottage outside the village, where he and his family lived in ascetic squalor, eschewing all modern conveniences and to all outward appearances living a life of pious simplicity.

Beneath the surface, however, Gill's family set-up was anything but wholesome. When his **biography** was published in 1989, he was revealed to be an incestuous polygamist, whose unsavoury sexual proclivities would have landed him in prison today; he regularly had sex not only with two of his sisters, but also with two of his daughters, not to mention the family dog. For Gill, sex was inseparable from his deeply held religious beliefs – he believed that "sexual intercourse is the very symbol for Christ's love for his church" – but whatever bizarre morality underpinned his actions it's hard to separate the actions of the man from the achievements of the artist, and Gill's reputation has never completely recovered from the revelations.

and showcase the work of Eric Gill and his circle in the environment in which it was created. The collection includes engravings and pencil drawings by Gill, paintings by David Jones – including a beautiful *Madonna and Child* set against a lowering Sussex landscape – and weavings by Valentine KilBride and his daughter Jenny, the first woman to join the Guild in 1974. One gallery will centre on Hilary Pepler's printing press, and display some of the pamphlets, books and posters it produced; as well as being a creative outlet, it also functioned as the village's press, printing everything from beer labels to posters advertising productions by the Ditchling Dramatic Circle.

6

Ditchling Beacon

There's a National Trust car park at the summit; bus #79 from Brighton serves the car park in the summer (hourly: mid-April to mid-Sept Sat, Sun & bank hols only)

Towering above Ditchling village, 800-foot-high **Ditchling Beacon** is one of the highest points on the South Downs, and from its breezy summit there are glorious views out over the patchwork of fields, copses and tiny villages of the Weald, to the hazy outline of the North Downs beyond. The summit gained its name from its warning beacon, one of a chain of bonfire sites across the Downs lit to warn of the Spanish Armada and other invasions.

A 1.5-mile lung-busting path leads up the hill from Ditchling village, or there's a car park at the summit, from where **trails** strike off in all directions; an easy 1.5-mile stroll westwards along the ridge takes you along the South Downs Way footpath to the two **Clayton Windmills**, also known as Jack and Jill; the latter, a white wooden post mill built in 1821, is open to the public on Sunday afternoons in summer (May–Sept Sun 2–5pm; ⓦ jillwindmill.org.uk).

Ridgeview Wine Estate

Fragbarrow Lane, Ditchling Common, off the B2112, BN6 8TP • Mon–Sat 11am–4pm, closed Sat in Jan & Feb • Tours £10 • ☎ 01444 241441, ⓦ ridgeview.co.uk

It's official: the best sparkling wine in the world is produced not on the sun-kissed slopes of Champagne, but on the outskirts of the tiny village of Ditchling at the **Ridgeview Wine Estate** – well, some of it at least. The vineyard has picked up a staggering array of awards over the last ten years, including trophies for the best sparkling wine in the world in 2005, 2010 and 2011. Its sparkling whites and rosés – produced using traditional Champagne grape varieties and methods – are available nationwide, but it's much more fun to pitch up at the cellar door and taste before you buy. The vineyard also runs **tours** once or twice a month (1hr–1hr 30min) – check the website for details.

ARRIVAL AND INFORMATION

By car There's free parking in the village hall car park.

By bus Countyliner bus # 824 runs from Lewes (Mon–Fri 4

DITCHLING AND AROUND

daily; 30min).

Website ⓦ ditchling.com.

ACCOMMODATION AND EATING

★ **Blackberry Wood** Streat Lane, near Ditchling, BN6 8RS ☎ 01273 890035, ⓦ blackberrywood.com. One of the first campsites in the country to fly the "cool camping" flag, this fab little site features just twenty tent pitches in the woods, each in its own secluded glade, complete with fire pit. Those wanting a few more creature comforts can opt to stay in a separate field, where the eclectic accommodation choices include a gypsy caravan, double-decker bus and 1960s search-and-rescue helicopter. It's very popular, so book well ahead. Per person (plus £5 per tent, £25 caravan, £70 bus or helicopter) **£9**

The Bull 2 High St, Ditchling, BN6 8TA ☎ 01273 843147, ⓦ thebullditchling.com. Splendid sixteenth-century village inn, with a dark, instantly inviting interior – beamed ceilings, floorboards, huge fireplaces and the smell of wood smoke in the air. The menu changes daily, but mains (around £13) might include Harveys battered hake with home-made tartar sauce, or sesame- and sumac-seared aubergine. Upstairs are four stylish rooms with compact but sleek en-suite bathrooms: the Ruby room comes with blood-red walls, a leather day-bed and antiques from the Far East. Four additional, larger rooms are planned. Mon–Fri 11am–11pm,

Sat & Sun 8.30am–10.30pm; food served Mon–Fri noon–2.30pm & 6–9.30pm, Sat & Sun 8.30am–10.30am & noon–9pm. **£100**

The General 1 High St, Ditchling, BN6 8SY ☎ 01273 846638, ⊛ thegeneralrestaurant.com. This self-styled "open house and kitchen" combines a first-floor art gallery with a spacious café-restaurant on the ground floor. Fabulous food ranges from Tunisian dahl and chickpea roti (£9) to ciabatta with sticky Sussex bangers (£5.75) at lunch, or you could set yourself up for a day's hiking with something from the expansive breakfast menu, which covers everything from pastries, pancakes and porridge to Breakfast Trifle. Tues–Fri 11.45am–3pm & 6–11pm, Sat 8.30am–11pm, Sun 8.30am–6pm.

Hiker's Rest Saddlescombe Farm, Saddlescombe Rd, near Poynings, BN45 7DE ⊛ southdownsway-hikersrest.com. Popular with walkers, this no-frills tearoom has tables dotted around a courtyard and in an open-sided barn on National Trust-maintained Saddlescombe Farm. Simple sandwiches, soups and salads and fabulous cakes are made from local produce, much of it from the farm itself. While you're here check out the seventeenth-century donkey wheel – one of only four left in the Southeast. March–Nov Mon, Tues, Thurs & Fri 11am–4pm, Sat & Sun 11am–5pm; Dec Sat & Sun 11am–5pm.

Jolly Sportsman Chapel Lane, East Chiltington, BN7 3BA ☎ 01273 890400, ⊛ thejollysportsman.com. Well-regarded dining pub on a quiet dead-end country lane, with a large, sloping back garden and terrace looking out onto the Downs. Food is great, though pricey – mains such as slow-roasted pork belly or braised duck leg are around £16, although cheaper set menus are also available. Dark Star and Harveys are on tap, and there's also a good selection of bottled Belgian beers and over a hundred malt whiskies. Food served Mon–Thurs noon–2.30pm & 6.30–9.30pm, Fri noon–2.30pm & 6.30–10pm, Sat noon–3pm & 6.30–10pm, Sun noon–3.30pm.

Southdown Way Caravan and Camping Park Lodge Lane, Keymer, near Ditchling, BN6 8LX ☎ 01273 841877, ⊛ southdown-caravancamping.org.uk. Peaceful campsite at the foot of the Downs, with fifty tent pitches scattered around a large flat field, and eight hard pitches with hook-ups. Great views, and a good base for walks up into the Downs. April–Oct. Tent pitches **£12**, hard pitches **£22**

Devil's Dyke

On the South Downs Way, and also connected by footpath to Brighton (5 miles); bus #77 from Brighton runs on summer weekends (mid-April to mid-Sept Sat, Sun & bank hols every 30min) to the National Trust car park at the summit

One of the best-known and most-visited beauty spots on the South Downs, **Devil's Dyke** has been luring tourists for over a hundred years. A popular outing for Victorian day-trippers, it was in its heyday a positive playground of new-fangled delights, featuring swingboats, bandstands, a hotel, a funicular that brought passengers up from the village of Poynings, a single-track railway running from Hove, and most thrillingly of all, a cable car – the country's first – that took tourists across the 300-yard-wide Devil's Dyke valley. Thankfully the competing lure of cinema and other twentieth-century marvels put paid to further development, and all that remains from the beauty spot's Victorian prime are the concrete footings of the cable car's pylons.

The **views** from the grassy slopes of the summit, described by John Constable in 1824 as "the grandest view in the world", are really something special: the hill drops off steeply in front of you giving a stupendous panorama over the Weald and westwards along the grand sweep of the South Downs escarpment.

The **Dyke** itself, a steep chasm on the north side of the escarpment, is often overlooked; it lies around the other side of the *Devil's Dyke* pub and a hundred yards back along the access road. The longest, widest and deepest chalk valley in the country, it was formed by melting water in the last Ice Age – or, if you're to believe local legend, dug by the Devil to allow the sea to flood in and drown the infuriatingly pious parishioners of the Weald. The Devil was only thwarted when an old lady, hearing a noise, lit a candle to investigate and the Devil fled, fearing the light was the rising sun.

Steyning and Bramber

The great chalk escarpment of the South Downs drops down to the River Adur near **Steyning**, a pretty little town with plenty of appealingly rickety half-timbered buildings, a bustling main street and a ruined Norman castle in neighbouring **Bramber**, a one-street village that Steyning has all but swallowed up.

Steyning's oldest buildings can be found along **Church Street**, with Wealden and jettied timber-framed buildings rubbing shoulders with flint-walled cottages as the road slopes down to bulky **St Andrew's Church**, with its lofty double-height Norman nave and comparatively squat sixteenth-century tower. There are plenty of independent shops along the **High Street**, including the quirky **Cobblestone Walk** arcade at no. 74 (ⓦcobblestonewalk.com); the car park on the High Street is the location for the town's **farmers' market** on the first Saturday of the month.

Bramber Castle

Signposted from the A283, BN44 3XA • Always open • Free • ⓦ english-heritage.org.uk/daysout/properties/bramber-castle

Don't go to **Bramber Castle** expecting to clamber up the battlements: all that remains of this Norman stronghold is a section of fourteenth-century curtain wall and one tall finger of stone that once formed part of the eleventh-century gatehouse. Bramber was one of the six Rapes (districts) of Sussex established by William after the Conquest, and the castle was built here by **William de Braose** on a grassy knoll to defend the Adur gap through the South Downs. The tree-covered motte (mound) at the castle's centre, and the defensive ditch around the outer bailey, have both survived much better than the castle itself, which by 1558 was already being described as "the late castle of Bramber".

Sheltering on the hillside just below the ruins, the **Church of St Nicholas** was built at the same time as the castle and served as its chapel, making it one of the oldest Norman churches in Sussex, though in fact only the nave dates from this time.

6

ARRIVAL AND INFORMATION

STEYNING AND AROUND

By car The town's three car parks use parking discs, which are available free of charge from local shops.

By bus Bus #2A runs from Brighton via Shoreham (Mon–Fri hourly; 1hr 15min).

Website ⓦ steyningsouthdowns.co.uk.

EATING

Steyning Tea Rooms 32 High St, BN44 3YE ☎01903 810064, ⓦ steyningtearooms.co.uk. This cosy, diminutive tearoom is a real treat, with cheery floral wallpaper, scrubbed wooden tables, bunting and mismatched furniture. Great cakes, and a pear-and-stilton rarebit that's to die for, though you might have trouble squeezing out of your seat afterwards. Upstairs there's a tiny shop selling vintage gifts. No credit cards. Daily 10am–6pm.

★ **Sussex Produce Company** 88 High St, BN44 3RD ☎01903 815045, ⓦ thesussexproducecompany.co.uk. This award-winning café-cum-produce-store features heaping piles of fruit and veg, freshly baked bread, a deli counter groaning with Sussex cheeses, and Harveys on tap – while at the back of the shop there's a small, laid back café serving great breakfasts and lunches, including the "Real Ploughman's Platter" (£9), where you can choose cheeses, meats, pies and home-made sausage rolls from the deli counter. Posher meals are served on Friday and Saturday nights (mains £13–20). Mon–Thurs 8am–6pm, Fri & Sat 8am–10pm (shop closes 8.30pm), Sun 10am–4pm.

Chanctonbury Ring

Three-mile walk from Steyning to Chanctonbury, or there's a National Trust car park nearer the Ring just off the A283

The site of an Iron Age hillfort, and later two Roman-British temples, hilltop **Chanctonbury Ring** (783ft) gained its fame from the clump of beech trees planted in a circle in 1760 by **Charles Goring**, heir to the nearby Winton Estate. The hurricane of 1987 decimated the Ring, destroying much of its grandeur, and although the trees have been replanted it will take many years before the grove is fully regrown. Nothing, however, can detract from the magnificent views from the lofty hilltop lookout, stretching north across the patchwork of fields of the Weald and south towards Cissbury and the sea beyond.

Legend has it that if you run seven times anticlockwise around Chanctonbury Ring you'll conjure up the Devil, who'll offer you a bowl of soup that, if accepted, will cost you your soul. The Devil's the least of your worries if local **folklore** is to be believed: Sussex author Esther Meynell wrote in 1947 that the Ring was best avoided at midnight as "curious things are apt to happen", and over the years Chanctonbury's been the site of numerous alleged **UFO sightings**, mysterious lights and unexplained paranormal happenings, not to mention the odd black-magic ritual.

Cissbury Ring

Just above the village of Findon, a few miles west of Steyning; the National Trust car park is signposted off the A24; the Ring lies two miles off the South Downs Way, but is connected to it by footpaths

One of the biggest iron-age hillforts in the south, **Cissbury Ring** would have been a magnificent site when it was built, with a three-foot-deep ditch backed by a raised bank topped with a fifteen-foot-high timber palisade, stretching for over a mile around the hilltop. It's estimated it would have taken two hundred men over two years to complete, involving the excavation of a staggering 60,000 tonnes of chalk. Both ditch and bank can still clearly be seen today, and the half-hour stroll around the top of the earth ramparts will give you a good sense of the scale of this most massive of earthworks. At the westernmost end of the Ring, look out for bumps and hollows in the grass – the remains of **flint mines** dug by Neolithic man thousands of years before the hillfort was built. There are over two hundred mine shafts beneath the soil, some as deep as 40 feet – quite a mind-boggling feat when you consider that the miners had only antler's horns for tools.

Arundel and around

Your first view of **ARUNDEL** if you're driving in from the east is a corker, with the turrets of its fairytale castle rising up out of the trees, and the huge bulk of the Gothic cathedral towering over the rooftops. The compact town's well-preserved appearance and picturesque setting by the banks of the River Arun draw the crowds on summer weekends, but at any other time a visit reveals one of West Sussex's least spoilt old towns. The main attractions are the **castle**, seat of the dukes of Norfolk, and the **WWT Arundel Wetland Centre** on the outskirts of town, but the rest of Arundel is pleasant to wander round, with some good independent shops, cafés and restaurants on the High Street and Tarrant Street. Out of town, there are some lovely walks through the water meadows, as well as a couple of sights further afield: **Bignor Roman Villa**, containing some of the best Roman mosaics in the country, and **Amberley Museum**, a museum of industrial heritage.

Arundel Castle

Mill Rd, BN18 9AB · April–Oct Tues–Sun: keep 10am–4.30pm; Fitzalan Chapel & grounds 10am–5pm; castle rooms noon–5pm · Castle, keep, grounds & chapel £15; keep, grounds & chapel £10; grounds & chapel £8 · ☎ 01903 882173, ⓦ arundelcastle.org

Arundel's standout attraction is **Arundel Castle**, which, though pricey, has enough to keep you occupied for a whole day. Despite its romantic medieval appearance, most of what you see is little more than a century old: the original Norman castle was badly damaged in the Civil War in the seventeenth century, and was reconstructed from 1718 onwards, most extensively by the fifteenth duke at the end of the nineteenth century. Parts of the original structure still remain, notably the 100-foot-high **motte** on which it stands, constructed in 1068 by **Roger de Montgomery**. The **keep**, built in 1190, is a steep climb up 131 stairs, but rewards with wonderful views over the town and out to sea. **Events** take place throughout the year, including re-created sieges and medieval tournaments – see the website for details.

Over in the main, remodelled part of the castle, the opulent **castle rooms** provide a dramatic contrast to the medieval keep, with cold stone walls replaced by extravagantly carved woodwork, fine tapestries, ornate sixteenth-century furniture and masterpieces by Gainsborough, Holbein, Van Dyck and Canaletto. Treasures peep out from every corner, easy to miss amid the general splendour: in the **dining room**, hidden away in a small cabinet, is the gold and enamel rosary carried by Mary, Queen of Scots at her

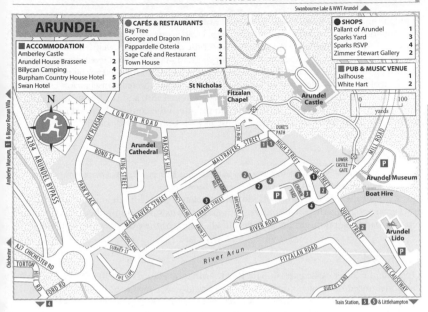

execution. Other highlights include the palatial **Barons' Hall**, the Victorian **private chapel** and the stunning Regency **library**, carved out of Honduran mahogany.

In the castle grounds, the **Collector Earl's Garden** is a playfully theatrical take on a Jacobean garden, with exotic palms and ferns, and pavilions, obelisks and urns made from green oak rather than stone. Adjacent is the beautiful fourteenth-century **Fitzalan Chapel**, burial place of the dukes of Norfolk, who have owned the castle for over 850 years in a more-or-less unbroken line. Like the castle, the chapel was badly damaged in the Civil War, when encamped Roundheads stabled their horses among the tombs, but it was restored in the late nineteenth century. Carved stone tombs are dotted around the chapel, among them the rather gruesome twin effigies of the seventh duke – one as he looked when he died and, underneath, one of his emaciated corpse.

Arundel Cathedral

Corner of Parson's Hill & London Rd, BN18 9AY • Daily 9am–6pm or dusk • Free • ☎ 01903 882297, ⓦ arundelcathedral.org

The flamboyant **Arundel Cathedral** was constructed in the 1870s over the town's former Catholic church by the fifteenth duke of Norfolk; its spire was designed by John Hansom, inventor of the hansom cab. Inside are the enshrined remains of **St Philip Howard**, the canonized thirteenth earl, who was brought up Protestant but chose to return to the Catholic faith of his birth, thereby turning his back on a life of great favour at Elizabeth I's royal court; he was sentenced to death in 1585, aged 27, when he was caught fleeing overseas, and died of dysentery in the Tower of London ten years later, refusing till the very last to renounce his faith.

St Nicholas' church

London Rd, BN18 9AT • Daily 9am–5pm • Free • ☎ 01903 882262, ⓦ stnicholas-arundel.co.uk

What you see when you walk into the fourteenth-century **church of St Nicholas** is really only half a church: behind an iron grille and glass wall lies the Fitzalan Chapel (see above), once the church's chancel but now part of Arundel Castle, and accessible only through the castle grounds. This unique state of affairs – which has resulted in a Church of England parish church and a Catholic chapel under one roof – came about in 1544 with the Dissolution, when Henry VIII sold off the chancel to the twelfth Earl, and it became the private chapel and burial place of the Earl's family. The screen has only been opened eight times in the last 35 years, most recently in 1995 for the funeral of Lavinia, Duchess of Norfolk. Elsewhere in the church, look out for the red consecration crosses on the walls, which date from the church's construction in 1380, and the beautiful carved stone **pulpit**, one of only six pre-Reformation pulpits in the country, believed to be the work of Henry Yevele, who also designed the nave in Canterbury Cathedral.

Arundel Lido

Queen St, BN18 9JG • First half of April & June–Aug daily; mid-April to end May Sat & Sun only; 10am–7pm during school hols, 12.30–7pm outside school hols • £6.50 • ☎ 01903 882404, ⓦ arundel-lido.com

Just south of the river lies **Arundel Lido**, which celebrated its fiftieth anniversary in 2010. It's a great spot for a dip on a hot day, with grassy lawns surrounding the heated pool, a separate paddling pool for kids and, best of all, a view of the castle as you swim along.

Mill Road

Opposite the lower castle gate on Mill Road, **Arundel Museum** (☎01903 885866, ⓦarundelmuseum.org.uk) is due to open in a brand-new riverside building in 2013, and will house exhibits on local history and archeology, and offer guided walks, talks and family activities. From here, **Mill Road** runs north through an avenue of trees up to **Swanbourne Lake**, an old millpond encircled by trees, with **rowing boats** for hire (March–Oct Sat, Sun & school hols from 9/10am; £3.50 per person/30min) and a tearoom. Swanbourne Lake is the entrance to the thousand-acre **Arundel Park**, which is crisscrossed with footpaths that meet up with the South Downs Way three miles away near Houghton.

WWT Arundel Wetland Centre

Mill Rd, BN18 9PB • Daily 9.30am–5.30pm; boat trips 11am–4.30pm; meadow maze April–Oct; pond-dipping sessions April–Oct Sat, Sun & school hols • £9.30, children over 4 £4.95 • ☎ 01903 883355, ⓦ wwt.org.uk/visit/arundel

The excellent **WWT Arundel Wetland Centre**, a mile out of town, is one of nine Wildfowl and Wetland Trust sites in the country, and is a great place to spend half a day, especially if you've got children in tow. The centre is home to endangered waterfowl from around the world, but a wander around the scenic 65-acre site, divided into different habitats, can also turn up sightings of native wildlife including water voles, kingfishers, sand martins, dragonflies and peregrines. Don't miss the tranquil, rustling **reedbed boardwalks** – where artist Chris Drury has created a camera obscura sculpture – or the free **boat trips**, probably your best chance of spotting water voles.

There are a couple of imaginative play areas for kids, as well as a **meadow maze** and popular **pond-dipping** sessions, where children can identify any slimy minibeasts they find under the microscope.

ARRIVAL AND INFORMATION

By car There's free parking all along Mill Rd, though spaces fill up quickly on summer weekends; failing that try the large pay-and-display car park on Mill Rd.

By train Arundel's station is half a mile south of the town centre over the river on the A27.
Destinations Brighton (Mon–Sat 2 hourly, Sun hourly; 1hr 20min); Chichester (Mon–Sat 2 hourly, Sun hourly; 20min); London Victoria (Mon–Sat every 30min, Sun hourly; 1hr 30min).

By bus Buses arrive either on the High St or River Rd.
Destinations Brighton (Mon–Fri every 30min; 2hr); Chichester (Mon–Sat every 2hr; 35min).

Tourist information An information point is scheduled to open at the new Arundel Museum (see above) in 2013; see ⓦ sussexbythesea.co.uk for the latest information.

WALKS AND BOAT TRIPS FROM ARUNDEL

Footpaths line both banks of the River Arun, and wandering even a short way up the river's reedy banks will reward you with wonderful views of Arundel Castle, rising majestically from the water meadows. Follow the **west bank** for two miles to reach the *Black Rabbit*, an idyllically sited pub that's a lovely spot for a drink, though there are better lunch options elsewhere; or head three miles up the **east bank** to reach the village of Burpham (pronounced "Burfham") and the *George and Dragon* (see below). Both routes are marked on OS Explorer **map** #121.

River-boat cruises upstream are available from the *Waterside Tea Garden and Bistro*, by the river opposite the lower castle gate on Mill Road (every 2hr; 1hr; £12; ☎01903 882609, ⑩thewatersidearundel.com), but it's more fun to have your own hand on the tiller – 4-seater self-drive **motorboats** cost £35 for an hour, which will get you a fair way up the river and back. Look out for kingfishers and herons en route.

6

ACCOMMODATION

Amberley Castle Amberley, BN18 9LT ☎01798 831992, ⑩amberleycastle.co.uk. For a real splurge, crunch up the sweeping gravel drive of this 800-year-old castle, 4 miles north of Arundel, complete with portcullis and sixty-foot curtain walls, and ensconce yourself in one of the nineteen luxurious bedrooms; many come with four-posters, and a couple even have doorways leading direct to the battlements. Outside are acres of landscaped grounds, roamed by peacocks, and a grass-covered moat that serves as a croquet lawn. **£315**

Arundel House Brasserie 11 High St, BN18 9AD ☎01903 882136, ⑩arundelhousearundel.co.uk. Rooms are smart, if a bit on the plain side, at this nineteenth-century merchant's house, with sleek bathrooms featuring walk-in rainfall showers, and welcome touches like espresso coffee machines and DVD players in all rooms. You're in a great location, at the bottom of the High Street opposite the castle, and there's a good restaurant downstairs. **£95**

★ **Billycan Camping** Manor Farm, Tortington, near Arundel, BN18 0BG ☎01903 882103, ⑩billycancamping .co.uk. You know you're onto a winner as soon as you arrive at this lovely campsite, a fifteen-minute walk from Arundel. The snug, vintage-style bell tents, tipis and yurts (available in various sizes) come decked out with bunting and fresh flowers, pathways are lit by tealights at night, and campers are welcomed with a communal stew around the campfire on

a Friday night. Bikes can be delivered to the site for £7.50/day, and massage, art classes and face painting can be pre-booked. The two-night minimum stay includes a breakfast hamper stuffed with local goodies. 4m bell tents (2 nights) **£195**, two-person tipis (3 nights) **£260**, four-person yurts (3 nights) **£360**, 5-person Airstream caravan (3 nights) **£400**

Burpham Country House Hotel The Street, Burpham, BN18 9RJ ☎01903 882160, ⑩burphamcountryhouse .com. This family-owned Georgian country-house hotel 3 miles from Arundel is a great spot to recharge the batteries, with light, tranquil rooms – many with views of the Downs – and a lovely garden with a croquet lawn, summer borders spilling onto the paths, and chickens and the two resident cats roaming free. The restaurant (Tues–Sat from 6.30pm, last orders 9.30pm) serves up bistro-style dishes featuring lots of local lamb and game, accompanied by herbs and vegetables from the garden. **£95**

Swan Hotel 27–29 High St, BN18 9AG ☎01903 882314, ⑩swanarundel.co.uk. The fifteen good-value rooms above this pub have been recently refurbished with a bit of a seaside-chic vibe, in shades of grey, cream and duck-egg blue, with coir carpet or wooden boards underfoot, white tongue-and-groove panelling, shutters, and seaside-themed photos and paintings. The cheapest rooms are on the small side, so it's worth paying an extra £15 for a superior double. Family rooms (£120) are also available. **£85**

EATING, DRINKING AND ENTERTAINMENT

Bay Tree 21 Tarrant St, BN18 9DG ☎01903 883679, ⑩thebaytreearundel.co.uk. Cosy and relaxed little restaurant squeezed into three low-beamed rooms, with windows opening out into the street in summer and a small terrace out the back. It's very popular, and justifiably so; bistro-style mains such as pheasant breast wrapped in bacon cost £16–18 at dinner; lunch features simpler dishes, including salads, paninis and jacket potatoes. Mon–Fri 11.30am–2.45pm & 6.45–9.15pm, Sat 10.30am–4pm & 6.45–9.30pm, Sun 10.30am–4pm & 6.45–9.15pm.

George and Dragon Inn Burpham, BN18 9RR

☎01903 883131, ⑩georgeanddragoninnburpham.com. Seventeenth-century foodie pub in the gorgeous village of Burpham, three miles upstream of Arundel. There's a beamed, flagstone interior, picnic tables out front and real ales from the Arundel Brewery, plus an à la carte menu that offers interesting mains (£15–20) such as maple-glazed duck breast with smoked banana purée. Simpler sandwiches and ploughman's (£5.50–7) are also available, and there's a good kids' menu. Mon–Fri noon–3pm & 6–11pm, Sat & Sun noon–11pm; food served Mon–Fri noon–2pm & 6–9pm, Sat & Sun noon–3pm & 6–9pm.

6

Jailhouse The Undercroft, Arundel Town Hall, Duke's Path, BN18 9AP ☎01903 889821, ⓦarundeljailhouse.co.uk. This underground venue puts on regular live music and comedy nights (Jailhouse Blues £5, comedy nights £10), as well as fun, monthly murder-mystery dinners (£25 including three-course buffet).

★ **Pappardelle Osteria** 41 High St, BN18 9AG ☎01903 882024, ⓦpappardelle.co.uk. This friendly café-cum-wine-bar, with its long copper communal tables, has a sociable buzz about it, with people chatting over coffee and reading papers in the daytime, and plenty of backgammon and scrabble sets on hand if you want to linger longer. In the evening there are cocktails (£6.50), over 20 different grappas, and more than 60 wines by the glass – "flites" allow you to sample three 100ml measures if you can't choose. Food is served all day, from breakfast through to antipasto plates, bruschetta, salads, *cicchetti* (Italian-style canapés) and pizza platters served with chopped preserves and fresh chillis (£17). Mon–Sat 9am–late, Sun 10am–10pm.

Sage Café and Restaurant Castle Mews, Tarrant St, BN18 9DG ☎01903 883477, ⓦsageofarundel.com. Set back from the street, with a sun-trap terrace out front, this slightly quirky café-restaurant serves up what it describes as "food for the soul" – which at dinner might be pear with Parma ham, wet salt and pure chocolate (£7.50), followed by Oolong Hills duck with clementine and spiced roots

(£16.95). It has a nice, laidback vibe, runs monthly jazz nights, and also puts on a vintage street market (11am–4pm) on the last Sunday of the month. Tues & Sun 10am–5pm, Wed–Sat 10am–11pm.

Town House 65 High St, BN18 9AJ ☎01903 883847, ⓦthetownhouse.co.uk. This Regency townhouse, overlooking the castle walls, is the grandest place to dine in town, with starched linen tablecloths, a stunning ceiling – hand-carved and gilded in Florence in the late sixteenth century – and a menu that might feature foie gras and lobster alongside local lamb or game. It's not at all stuffy, despite the grandeur, and not bad value, at £23.50 for 2 courses and £29 for 3 (£15.50/19.50 at lunch). Space is limited and it's very popular, so book ahead. Tues–Sat noon–2.30pm & 7–9.30pm.

White Hart 12 Queen St, BN18 9JG ☎01903 884422. A local favourite, this family-friendly pub has Harveys on tap and a relaxed, light interior, with white walls, big antique mirrors and fresh flowers. Food is served up by the in-house *Boca Nueva* tapas bar – small dishes start at £3 and include not only Spanish classics such as tortilla and salt-and-pepper squid but also mussels in Thai broth, tempura vegetables, and onion rings in beer batter. Mon–Thurs noon–10pm, Fri & Sat noon–11pm, Sun noon–8pm; food served Mon–Sat noon–9pm, Sun noon–4pm.

SHOPPING

Pallant of Arundel 17 High St, BN18 9AD ☎01903 882288, ⓦpallantofarundel.co.uk. Great little food shop, deli and wine merchant, with crusty bread from several local bakeries, a well-stocked cheese counter, a selection of wine, and plenty of tasty-looking home-made pork pies, Scotch eggs and the like, plus takeaway coffee. Mon–Sat 9am–6pm, Sun 10am–5pm; closes 5pm in Jan & Feb.

Sparks Yard Tarrant St, BN18 9DJ ☎01903 885588, ⓦsparksyard.com. Homeware store spread over two storeys of a handsome red brick building, stocking stylish

cookware, toiletries, toys, lighting and more. A small coffee bar on the first floor sells milkshakes, sundaes and simple soups. A second, smaller branch, Sparks RSVP, on River Rd (same hours), sells mainly stationery and gifts. Mon–Sat 10am–5pm, Sun 11am–4pm.

Zimmer Stewart Gallery 29 Tarrant St, BN18 9DG ☎01903 885867, ⓦzimmerstewart.co.uk. This excellent small gallery features contemporary painting, prints and photos, as well as ceramics and sculpture. Exhibitions change monthly. Tues–Sat 10am–5pm.

Amberley Museum and Heritage Centre

Amberley, on the B2139 between Arundel and Storrington, BN18 9LT • Mid-March to Oct Wed–Sun 10am–5pm (last entry 3.30pm); school hols also open Mon & Tues (same hours) • £9.80 • ☎01798 831370, ⓦamberleymuseum.co.uk • Amberley station is adjacent to the museum (regular trains from Littlehampton and the south coast)

If a museum dedicated to the industrial heritage of the Southeast sounds a little less than thrilling, you'll be pleasantly surprised by the excellent **Amberley Museum and Heritage Centre**. The 36-acre, open-air museum is spread around the site of the old chalk pits and lime kilns, and contains dozens of workshops, re-created shops and listed buildings (many rescued from elsewhere in Sussex), housing everything from a brickyard drying shed to a re-created 1920s bus garage. Craftspeople are on hand to demonstrate traditional skills – woodturning, pottery, stained-glass making, letterpress printing, even broom making – and hop-on, hop-off vintage green-and-yellow Southdown buses trundle regularly round the site, with a narrow-gauge train running round the perimeter. There are a few larger exhibition halls, including a Railway Hall stuffed full of old engines and wagons, and a fun Telecommunications Exhibition, with a display of telephones from 1878 onwards – an exercise in nostalgia for anyone old enough to remember the old dial telephones and the first brick-like mobiles.

Bignor Roman Villa

Bignor, RH20 1PH • Daily: March–May, Sept & Oct 10am–5pm; June–Aug 10am–6pm • £6 • ☎ 01798 869259, ⓦ bignorromanvilla.co.uk

Six miles north of Arundel, the excavated third-century ruins of the **Bignor Roman Villa** aren't on the same scale as nearby first-century Fishbourne (see p.292), but they do contain some of the best Roman mosaics in the country. The site was discovered back in 1811, when George Tupper's plough struck part of the ruins; the area was excavated, covered by thatched buildings (that still remain today), and became a popular Georgian tourist attraction. The Tupper family still own the site and farm the land around it, a beautiful spot at the bottom of the Downs scarp, just a mile or so from the South Downs Way.

Bignor started life as a farmstead and was gradually expanded over the centuries, ending up by the fourth century as a 70-room villa set in a square around a central courtyard. The western end of the north wing, and the bathhouse in the southeast corner, are all that remain today. The villa's location, for all that it seems like a sleepy backwater, was carefully chosen: **Stane Street**, one of the first paved roads in the country, passed just a few hundred yards away. Local materials were used to make the stunning **mosaics** (chalk for white, sandstone for yellow and orange, and Purbeck marble for blue and black), which increased in complexity and sophistication as the villa grew in size and wealth. Perhaps the finest mosaic is in the **winter dining room**, where the head of Venus stares out above a series of wonderful winged gladiators; adjacent to it you can see the original Roman hypocaust (underfloor heating system).

Midhurst and around

Lying as it does smack-bang in the middle of the newly created South Downs National Park, it's not surprising that **MIDHURST** has been chosen as the headquarters of the South Downs National Park Authority, and the small market town has been quick to tag itself "the heart of the national park". Ironically, Midhurst isn't actually part of the "South Downs" at all; it lies within the **Western Weald**, an area of forest and heathland that was included within the national park boundary in recognition of its exceptional beauty. The heavily wooded countryside is undeniably the main draw of the area, with hills, heathland and woodland tumbling into each other, and there are some wonderful scenic walks nearby, and a smattering of fine country pubs.

Midhurst itself has plenty of charm and a lovely location, bordered to the north and east by the wiggling, willow-fringed River Rother. The town makes a good base for exploring the area, as does nearby **Petworth**, where the magnificent Petworth House is the main draw. Northeast of here is family-friendly **Fisher's Farm Park**, while northwest, on the Surrey border, lies wild and beautiful **Black Down**, the highest point in the national park. South of Midhurst the South Downs Way threads it way along the rolling chalk downlands, past **Harting Down** nature reserve and **Uppark House** into Hampshire.

Market Square and around

Midhurst grew up around the medieval market in **Market Square**, still the most picturesque corner of town. In the centre of the Square, the **Church of St Mary Magdalene and St Denys** has Norman foundations but has been much rebuilt over the years. Further south still, on the southern slopes of the Downs, a handful of sights – Goodwood House, West Dean, Cass Sculpture and the Weald and Downland Museum – all lie within the national park and are a stone's throw from Chichester (see pp.292–293).

By the church stands the **Old Town Hall**, now *Garton's Coffee House* (see p.246), which was built in 1551 as the town's market house, originally open-sided for traders to display their goods; in 1760 the building became the town hall, with law courts on the first floor and cells below – which can still be seen in the coffee shop today. The town **stocks**, last used in 1859, sit in an alcove underneath the steps at the side of the building. Behind the Town Hall on **Edinburgh Square** you'll see a row of redbrick houses with distinctive saffron-yellow paintwork, a sign they belong to the local Cowdray Estate; the colour, now known as **"Cowdray Yellow"**, was chosen by the second Viscount Cowdray in the 1920s as a statement of his Liberal politics and has remained ever since.

North Street

Midhurst's main thoroughfare is **North Street**, which cuts through town to the west of Market Square. At the north end of the street, up by the causeway to Cowdray House, you'll see turreted **Capron House**, headquarters of the South Downs National Park Authority and site of the planned new South Downs Centre (see opposite). Further south, the Georgian-fronted *Angel Hotel* is the first of Midhurst's two splendid **coaching inns**, and was the favoured drinking hole of a certain Guy Fawkes, who masterminded his infamous plot while butler at Cowdray House. Its rival, the gloriously higgledy-piggledy *Spread Eagle* (see p.245), opposite Market Square, dates back in part to 1430.

Cowdray House

Cowdray Park, GU29 9AL; access via The Causeway from the North St car park • Mid-March to Oct Mon–Thurs & Sun 10.30am–5pm, last admission 4pm • £6.50 • ☎01730 810781, ⓦ cowdray.org.uk

The ruins of **Cowdray** have a fabulous approach, across a causeway bordered by water meadows, sidestepping brown-and-white cows. From afar the castle-like gatehouse and crenelated walls appear relatively intact, but as you draw closer jagged walls draw into view, glimpses of sky can be seen through the window frames, and the gutted, roofless shell of a once-grand Tudor house is finally revealed.

When Cowdray was built in the sixteenth century – principally by **Sir William Fitzwilliam**, friend and favoured courtier of Henry VIII – it was one of the grandest homes in the country. But in 1793 disaster struck: during renovation work a fire broke out that reduced the house to ruins. Later that year the eighth Viscount died while shooting rapids on the Rhine – a tragic coincidence that many saw as the chilling fulfillment of the **curse of Cowdray**, an imprecation supposedly put on the family back in the sixteenth century when William Fitzwilliam's heir Sir Anthony Browne pulled down Battle Abbey Church (see p.186) in the Dissolution, and the evicted monks swore his family line would perish "by fire and water". The house was left to rot, and by the nineteenth century it had become a romantic ruin, painted by Turner and Constable.

Some fragments of the house's former splendour still remain, notably the 1530s **porch**, with its intricately carved fan-vault ceiling, and the **Tudor kitchen**, which escaped unscathed thanks to its extra-thick walls, designed – ironically – to prevent any fire that might break out in the kitchen from spreading to the rest of the house. Many of the interiors were recorded in the 1780s by a Swiss artist, Samuel Grimm, and some of his pictures are reproduced on interpretive boards around the site, giving a poignant before-and-after snapshot of some of the magnificence the fire destroyed. In the vaulted **wine cellar** a fifteen-minute film tells the story of the house and its owners, who managed, despite their Catholic allegiances, to keep on the right side of the royals throughout the turbulent sixteenth century, right up until a certain **Guy Fawkes** – butler at Cowdray under the second Viscount Montague – hatched his plot in 1605; the Viscount was unaccountably absent from parliament on the planned day of the explosion, and was sentenced to forty weeks in prison for his suspected involvement in the plot.

Cowdray Estate

Farm shop Mon–Sat 9am–6pm & Sun 10am–4pm • ☎ 01730 812799, ⓦ cowdrayfarmshop.co.uk **Wildlife tours** April–Sept; 3hr • £99
• ☎ 01730 812423, ⓦ cowdray.co.uk

The **Cowdray Estate** covers 16,500 acres northeast of Midhurst, and is best known for
its **polo club** (see box below). Flanking the polo lawns is their fabulous, award-winning
farm shop at Easebourne, which sells meat, game, eggs, butter and more from the
estate; even the artisan bread is baked in-store using their own wheat. The adjacent café
(see p.246) is a great spot for lunch. In summer the estate organizes twilight wildlife-
and **badger-watching** outings in the local area.

ARRIVAL AND INFORMATION

By car There are car parks at North St and Grange Rd.

By train and bus The closest stations are at Haslemere
(bus #70 to Midhurst: Mon–Sat hourly), Petersfield (bus
#92: Mon–Sat every 1hr 30min–2hr) and Chichester (bus
#60: Mon–Sat every 30min; Sun hourly).

South Downs Centre The national park's new South
Downs Centre (ⓦ southdowns.gov.uk) is due to open in
autumn 2013 at Capron House on North St, and will include
a visitor information centre.

Midhurst tourist office At the time of writing there is a
temporary tourist information point on North St, by the car
park, but this is due to relocate during 2013, possibly into the
new South Downs Centre (see above) across the road. Call
☎ 01730 812251 or check ⓦ visitmidhurst.com for the latest.

ACCOMMODATION

Park House Bepton, near Midhurst, GU29 0JB ☎ 01730
819000, ⓦ parkhousehotel.com. This small, luxurious
country-house hotel is a gem, with glorious views, elegant
rooms (from standard rooms to suites, plus cottages in the
grounds), a croquet lawn, grass tennis courts, and an
opulent new spa – a real retreat. **£155**

Spread Eagle Hotel South St, Midhurst, GU29 9NH
☎ 01730 816911, ⓦ hshotels.co.uk. This wisteria-
covered former coaching inn, dating back in part to the
fifteenth century, oozes antiquity, from the creaking
corridors and stained-glass windows to the wonky-walled
lounge and the timber-beamed Queen's Suite (£315),
which boasts a rare, original wig closet. Standard rooms are
comfortable, and rates include use of the hotel spa. In the
dining room, look out for the pudding pots hanging from
the ceiling – a Sussex tradition whereby guests at
Christmas are given two puddings, and one is put by to
await their return the following year. **£115**

Two Rose Cottages 2 Rose Cottages, Chichester Rd,
Midhurst, GU29 9PF ☎ 01730 813804, ⓦ tworosebandb
.com. Super-friendly B&B in a Victorian cottage, in a great
central location. There are just two rooms, both en suite:
rooms are tasteful and comfy (you even get a choice of
pillows), and bathrooms come with robes, scented

THE SPORT OF KINGS: POLO AT COWDRAY PARK

Polo has been played on the lawns of **Cowdray Park** since 1910. It was introduced to the
country much earlier, in 1834, by the 10th Hussars at Aldershot, but it's Cowdray that's credited
as its spiritual home. During World War II polo had all but died out; that it didn't is due entirely
to the late **third Viscount Cowdray**, whose passion for the sport turned Cowdray into one of
the most famous polo clubs in the world and kick-started a polo renaissance around the
country. In 1956, the **Cowdray Park Gold Cup** – now also known as the Veuve Clicquot Gold
Cup – was inaugurated, and it remains the highlight of the Cowdray polo season today; the
final is one of the most glamorous events in the sporting calendar, with world-class players in
action on the field and celebrities looking on.

The **game** is fast and furious, played on horseback on a grass field 300 yards long by 160
yards wide, with two teams of four riders attempting to score goals against their opponents.
Matches are divided into seven-minute periods of play called **chukkas**, and a match will
generally be four to six chukkas long, with players changing ends after each goal. At half-time
spectators take to the field for "treading in" – stomping back the loose divots on the field.

The season at Cowdray Park runs from May to September, with **matches** most days at
one of its two grounds – the Lawns and River grounds near Midhurst, and the Ambersham
pitches between Midhurst and Petworth. To watch, all you need do is turn up with a picnic
on the day; **tickets** can be bought at the entrance gate (£5, more for the Gold Cup quarter
finals, semi-finals and final; members enclosure additional £5), and dress is smart casual.
See ⓦ cowdraypolo.co.uk for details of fixtures.

6

tealights and organic toiletries. A cosy sitting room with wood burner, private front door, great breakfasts (including kedgeree), and plenty of local maps and books, all round off a tip top B&B experience. **£80**

EATING AND DRINKING

Duke of Cumberland Fernhurst, just off the A286, GU27 3HQ ☎01428 652280, ⚲dukeofcumberland.com. This fifteenth-century pub, 5 miles north of Midhurst, has bags of character and a peerless location, perched on a hill with spectacular views all around. To see it in its full glory visit in summer and grab a table on the lovely deck or in the enormous sloping garden, complete with trout ponds (the inhabitants of which sometimes appear on the menu). The simple, rustic food is delicious but pricey: mains cost £18–22 at dinner, simpler lunch dishes £11–14. Book well ahead. Daily noon–11pm; food served Tues–Sat noon–2pm & 7–9pm, Sun & Mon noon–2pm.

Garton's Coffee House Market Square, Midhurst, GH29 9NJ ☎01730 817166, ⚲gartonscoffeehouse.co.uk. Bright and airy coffee house housed in the Old Town Hall, with floor-to-ceiling windows and tables outside on the cobbles in the summer – the nicest place in Midhurst for an alfresco cuppa. Good soups, sandwiches and salads range from £4 to £8. At the back you can still see the wooden-doored cells once used to house the town's criminals. Mon–Sat 8.30am–5pm, Sun 10am–5pm.

★ **Priory Cowdray Café** Easebourne, GU29 0AJ ☎01730 815152, ⚲cowdrayfarmshop.co.uk. What's served up at this award-winning farm-shop café will most likely have come from only a few miles away, whether steaks and burgers from the Cowdray Estate's organically reared beef, bread made from the estate's own wheat, or chips hand-cut from potatoes grown two fields away. Mains such as beef and bacon pie or lamb burger cost £10–13, but sandwiches (£5–6) are also on offer. Popular set-menu suppers (£35) run once a month. Daily 9am–5pm.

Three Horseshoes Elsted, GU29 0JX ☎01730 825746. For peerless views of the South Downs you can't beat the garden of this pretty, white-painted, sixteenth-century inn, which looks out across fields and woodland to Harting Down. Inside there's plenty of character (flagstone floors, real fires in winter and beams aplenty), and a good selection of beer served straight from the cask. The food's good too (mains £10–18) – make sure you save room for the crowd-pleasing puds. Mon–Sat 11am–2.30pm & 6–11pm, Sun noon–3pm & 7–10.30pm; food served noon–2pm & 6–9pm, Sun 7–8.30pm.

Petworth

The honey-coloured, high stone walls of Petworth House loom over the handsome little town of **PETWORTH**, seven miles east of Midhurst. The town owes its existence to the great house and its estate: for centuries the Leconfield Estate employed virtually everyone in the town, and reminders of its importance can be seen in the

WALKS AROUND MIDHURST

There are some fabulous walks to be had in the countryside around Midhurst. The **South Downs Way** (see p.213) can be joined two miles south of town, accessed from the village of Cocking at the foot of the scarp (bus #60 from Midhurst; Mon–Sat every 30min, Sun hourly). From Cocking you can head east along the Way towards Upwaltham or west towards Harting Down (see p.249). The walks below are marked on OS Explorer **maps** #133 and #120.

Midhurst River Walk This three-mile peaceful riverine path (waymarked Rother Walk) runs west from Midhurst's North Bridge Weir along the River Rother to Woolbeding, where you can visit the lovely National Trust-owned Woolbeding Gardens (Thurs and Fri; pre-booking only; ☎01730 716304, ⚲nationaltrust.org.uk/woolbeding-gardens). For a circular walk take the waymarked trail heading east just before you hit the A272, which will take you back through Midhurst to your starting point.

Chalk Stones Trail This five-mile self-guided trail cuts through the heart of the Downs, from Cocking in the north to West Dean in the south, following the trail of thirteen snowball-like chalk sculptures by artist Andy Goldsworthy.

The huge chalk balls started off 6–7ft in diameter, but have slowly eroded since they were put in place in 2002; some are half-hidden in hedgerows, others in plain view. Download a trail map from the National Trail website (⚲nationaltrail.co.uk/southdowns/uploads/Chalk%20Stones%20leaflet.pdf). Bus #60 runs from West Dean back to Midhurst (Mon–Sat every 30min, Sun hourly).

Harting Down circular This four-mile route takes you east along the ridgetop South Downs Way, with panoramic views across the Weald, before cutting south around the lower slopes of Beacon Hill, and then heading back to your starting point through a cool, dark yew wood and up onto Harting Hill.

brown-painted doors of the hundreds of estate cottages built in the mid-nineteenth century (and numbered according to when they first appeared in the rent records). Even today, it's the great house that brings in the tourists, and most visitors, justifiably, make a beeline straight for it; the rest of town, though, is a bit of a gem, if you can ignore the constant rumble of heavy traffic, with some good independent shops and a thriving **antiques trade** – a map of the thirty-plus antiques shops can be picked up at any antiques shop, or downloaded from ⓦpaada.com.

Market Square and around

The centre of town is **Market Square**, site of the town's marketplace since at least 1541. In the centre of the square is **Leconfield Hall**, built in 1794 as a courthouse; the old fire bells, which once served as the town's fire alarm, can be seen up on the pediment above the clock. The hall is one of the venues for July's **Petworth Festival** (ⓦpetworthfestival .org.uk), a two-week-long arts festival.

From Market Square, cobbled **Lombard Street** – once the town's busiest thoroughfare and still its prettiest – climbs north to Church Street and the **Church of St Mary's**; to the left of the church is the entrance to Petworth House, while to the right you'll see a fantastically elaborate iron **streetlamp**, designed by Charles Barry (of Houses of Parliament fame) and erected by the townspeople in 1851 as a token of thanks to Lord Leconsfield for installing gas lighting in the town.

Petworth House

Petworth, GU28 9LR • House mid-March to Oct Mon–Wed, Sat & Sun 11am–5pm, also Thurs 11am–5pm for 20min snapshot tours only; Pleasure Ground mid-Jan to mid-March Mon–Wed, Sat & Sun 10.30am–3.30pm; mid-March to Oct daily 10.30am–5pm; Nov to mid-Dec Mon–Wed, Sat & Sun 10.30am–3.30pm; park daily 8am–dusk • House £12, snapshot tours £5, Pleasure Ground and park free; NT • ☎01798 342207, ⓦ nationaltrust.org.uk/petworth

Petworth House, built in the late seventeenth century, is one of the Southeast's most impressive stately homes. The grounds alone are worth the visit: seven hundred acres of stunning parkland, ponds and woodland, roamed by the largest herd of fallow deer in the country and dotted with ancient oaks. The park – containing the 30-acre woodland garden known as the **Pleasure Ground** – was landscaped by Capability Brown and is considered one of his finest achievements, but it was **Turner** who made the sweeping vistas famous, immortalizing the park in several of his paintings.

Nineteen of Turner's paintings are on view in the house, and form just part of Petworth's outstanding **art collection**, with works by Van Dyck, Titian, Gainsborough, Bosch, Reynolds and Blake. Other treasures include the **Molyneux globe**, dating from 1592 and believed to be the earliest terrestrial globe in existence, and the **Leconfield Chaucer** manuscript, one of the earliest surviving editions of the *Canterbury Tales*.

The opulent **decor** is equally jaw-dropping. Highlights are Louis Laguerre's murals around the **Grand Staircase**, which trace the myth of Prometheus and Pandora, and the dazzling **Carved Room**, where flowers, fruit, vines, musical instruments and birds have been carved in joyfully extravagant detail by master woodcarver Grinling Gibbons.

The **servants' quarters**, connected by a tunnel to the main house, contain an impressive series of kitchens bearing the latest kitchenware of the 1870s, and a copper batterie de cuisine of more than a thousand pieces – all polished by a team of strong-elbowed volunteers every winter.

Petworth Cottage Museum

346 High St, GU28 0AU • April–Oct Tues–Sat & bank hols 2–4.30pm • £3 • ☎01798 342100, ⓦ petworthcottagemuseum.co.uk

For an alternative and intriguing view of the life of one of the great house's former employees, **Petworth Cottage Museum** is well worth a visit. Seamstress Mary Cummings lived in this gas-lit abode, which has been restored using her own possessions to show how it would have looked in 1910, with family photos on the wall, the washing-up by the sink and the kettle on the range.

6

By car There's a large car park in the centre of town and another at Petworth House (£2 to non-NT members).

By train and bus The closest stations are Haslemere (no bus connection) and Pulborough (bus #1: Mon–Sat hourly,

Sun every 2hr; 15min). Bus #1 also connects Petworth with Midhurst (15min).

Website ⓦ visitpetworth.com.

ACCOMMODATION AND EATING

★ **Horse Guards Inn** Upperton Rd, Tillington, GU28 9AF ☏ 01798 342332, ⓦ thehorseguardsinn.co.uk. Fabulous, friendly little gastropub 2 miles west of Petworth, decked out with informal, shabby-chic panache. In winter there are four fires on the go in the cosy, stripped-floor interior (Harveys and guest ales on tap), while in summer you can escape to the gorgeous garden, an idyllic little haven with bunting, hay-bale seating, deckchairs and a hammock. The menu is small and seasonal; mains (around £15) might include Selsey crab with sea vegetable salad in summer, or pheasant with hawthorn jelly in winter. The pub also has three serene, pretty B&B rooms. Daily noon–11pm; food served Mon–Sat noon–2.30pm & 6.30–9pm, Sun 12.30–3.30pm (two sittings at 12.30pm & 2.30pm) & 6.30–9pm. £85

Hungry Guest Lombard St, GU28 0AG ☏ 01798 344564, ⓦ thehungryguest.com. This hip café, with geometric wallpaper and funky lighting, is an unlikely but happy find on olde-worlde, cobbled Lombard Street. It's a particularly good spot for brunch, and the afternoon tea is a steal at £7. It's also open in the evenings at weekends, serving dishes such as nettle and spinach risotto cakes (£9) and lamb koftas (£8.50). Mon–Wed & Sun 8.30am–5pm, Thurs–Sat 8.30am–11pm.

Hungry Guest Bakery and Food Shop Middle St,

GU29 0BE ☏ 01798 342803, ⓦ thehungryguest.com. This excellent produce store bakes its own bread, pastries and brownies, and sells local Wobblegate apple juice, a good selection of charcuterie, and cheese from a dedicated cheese room – all you need for a picnic at Petworth Park. Mon–Fri 10am–6pm, Sat 9am–6pm, Sun 10am–4pm.

★ **Old Railway Station** 2 miles south of Petworth on the A285, GU28 0JF ☏ 01798 342346, ⓦ old-station.co.uk. Petworth's former railway station (1892) has been converted into a smart, colonial-style B&B, with breakfast and afternoon tea served in the high-ceilinged old waiting room; in summer there are tables out on the platform. The largest rooms are upstairs in the station house, but for sheer character they can't compete with the rooms in the stylishly converted Pullman carriages on the platform. £160

Woodland Yurting Tittlesford, near Petworth, RH14 9BG ☏ 01403 824057, ⓦ woodlandyurting.com. Seven simple yurts – three big enough for families – tucked away in a peaceful meadow backed by traditionally managed woodland. The emphasis is on getting back to nature, with fire bowls for cooking, composting toilets and alfresco solar-powered showers. Bushcraft taster sessions, holistic massages and organic hampers are available for an extra charge. April–Sept. 2-person yurts (2-night weekend) £140

Fishers Farm Park

Newpound Lane, Wisborough Green, RH14 0EG • Daily 10am–5pm • £8.25/11.25/14.25 low/mid-peak season, children £6.50/8.50/10.50, under-2s free • ☏ 01403 700063, ⓦ fishersfarmpark.co.uk

If you've got kids aged between 2 and 10 you really can't go wrong with the award-winning **Fishers Farm Park** – the farm park to end all farm parks. There are all the usual animals on show, ready for petting, bottle-feeding and riding, plus fun pig and sheep races and the Shetland Grand National. The 10-acre adventure play area is fantastic, featuring everything from swingboats, slides and sandpits to pedal karts, bumper boats, jumping pillows, tree houses and climbing walls, with a few scare-free "rides" thrown in for good measure. It's not cheap, but it's friendly and well run, jam-packed with things to do, and once you're through the doors everything's included.

Black Down

Black Down (917ft), up near the Surrey border, is the highest point in the national park – a wild and rich landscape of heathland, ancient woodland, bogs and wildflower meadows, crisscrossed by trails. **Tennyson** lived here for almost a quarter of century before his death, and immortalized the beautiful view from his study in a poem: "You came, and looked and loved the view/Long-known and loved by me/Green Sussex fading into blue/With one gray glimpse of sea." To capture the view for yourself, park at the free car park on Tennyson Lane (southeast of Haslemere) and follow the footpath for a mile to the **Temple of the Winds**, one of the finest viewpoints in Sussex, where the ground falls away before you and miles of patchwork fields and copses stretch into the distance, backed by the blue-green smudge of the South Downs; on a clear day you can glimpse the sea, forty miles away. Black Down is also one of the best **star-gazing** destinations in the country: see ⓦnationaltrust.org.uk/black-down for a downloadable star-gazing walk.

Harting Down

Wonderful views, wild flowers, butterflies and skylarks abound at the National Trust-run **Harting Down Nature Reserve**, where there are plenty of options for circular walks (see box, p.246) – walkers thin out the further you get from the hilltop car park. The highest point is steep-sided **Beacon Hill** (794ft), site of an Iron Age hillfort and home to the remains of a Napoleonic War telegraph station.

Uppark House

South Harting, Petersfield, GU31 5QR • House mid-March to Oct Mon–Thurs & Sun 12.30–4.30pm, open for guided tours only 11am–12.30pm; mid-Nov to mid-Dec Sun 12.30–4.30pm, open for guided tours only 11am–12.30pm; garden mid-March to Oct Mon–Thurs & Sun 11am–5pm; mid-Nov to mid-Dec Sun 11am–3pm • £8.40, garden only £4.20; NT • ☎01730 825857, ⓦnationaltrust.org.uk/uppark

Handsome **Uppark House** sits, as it has done for centuries, perched high up on the Downs, with no hint that things might have been very different. For in 1989, while the house was undergoing restoration work, a fire caused by workman's blowtorch started a blaze that virtually reduced it to ruin. The house was open at the time, and National Trust staff, volunteers and members of the family managed to carry much of the house's art and furniture collection to safety. The decision was made to restore the house as it would have been on the day before the fire broke out, and this kicked into action a £20-million restoration, involving hundreds of craftsmen, many of whom had to relearn skills that had been lost for decades. The house finally reopened in 1995.

Even before the fire, the house had seen its fair share of excitement. It was built in 1690, and bought some fifty years later by **Sir Matthew Fetherstonhaugh**, who lavished some of his huge fortune on furnishing the house with treasures acquired on the Continent. When he died, his playboy son **Sir Harry** took up the reins with some relish, installing the teenage Emma Hart (the future Lady Hamilton, Nelson's mistress) as his live-in lover in the house, where she would reportedly dance naked on the dining-room table. Harry certainly knew how to enjoy himself: at the ripe old age of 70 he scandalized Sussex society by marrying his 21-year-old dairymaid, Mary Ann Bullock.

The elegant Georgian **interior** is crammed with treasures from Sir Matthew's Grand Tour; highlights include the sumptuous gold and white Saloon, and an eighteenth-century doll's house with tiny hallmarked silverware. The **servants' quarters** are presented as they would have been in the late nineteenth century when the mother of **H.G. Wells** was housekeeper here.

Uppark's beautiful **gardens** have lovely views over the Downs, and contain the elegant Georgian dairy where Mary Anne Bullock's singing first caught the roving Sir Harry's attention.

6

Brighton

BRIGHTON PAVILION

Brighton

Sandwiched between the sea and the South Downs, Brighton (or Brighton and Hove to give it its official name) is the jewel of the south coast – colourful and creative, quirky and cool. On a summer's day, with the tang of the sea in the air, the screech of seagulls overhead and the crowds of day-trippers streaming down to the beach, there's a real holiday feel to the city. Vibrant, friendly and tolerant, this is a city that knows how to have fun. The essence of Brighton's appeal is its bohemian vitality – a buzz that comes from its artists, writers, musicians and other creatives, its thriving gay community, and an energetic local student population from the art college and two universities. Despite the middle-class gentrification that's transformed the city over the last decade, it still retains the appealingly seedy edge that led Keith Waterhouse to famously describe it as a town that always looks as if it's helping police with their enquiries.

A visit to Brighton inevitably begins with a visit to its two most famous landmarks – the exuberant **Royal Pavilion** and the wonderfully tacky **Brighton Pier**, a few minutes away – followed by a stroll along the seafront promenade or the pebbly beach, with its beachfront bars and shops. Just as fun, though, is an unhurried meander around some of Brighton's distinct neighbourhoods: the car-free **Lanes**, a maze of narrow alleys marking the old town, crammed with restaurants, jewellery shops and boutiques; the more bohemian **North Laine**, where you'll find the city's greatest concentration of independent shops, and some fabulous cafés and coffee shops; **Kemptown** village, the heart of Brighton's gay community, with antiques shops and some cool little cafés; and **Hove**, with an elegant beachfront and some great restaurants.

Brighton's other great joy is its fantastically vibrant and eclectic **cultural life**: on any given night of the week there'll be live music, comedy gigs, plays, concerts, talks and films, so whether you want to catch a big-name band in an intimate venue, a free acoustic gig in a pub or a string quartet in a concert hall, see subversive theatre or a family-friendly mainstream show, you'll find something to entertain you. The city's packed **festival calendar** partly accounts for this, with festivals devoted to film, literature, music and comedy taking place throughout the year, as well as the Brighton Festival – the country's largest arts festival after Edinburgh – which runs for three weeks in May.

Brief history

Recorded as the tiny village of Brithelmeston in the Domesday Book, Brighton remained an undistinguished fishing town until the mid-eighteenth century, when the new trend for **sea bathing** established it as a resort. The fad received royal approval in the 1780s, after the decadent **Prince Regent** (the future George IV) began patronizing the town in the company of his mistress, thus setting a precedent for the "dirty

Highlights

❶ Royal Pavilion This extraordinary Oriental-style palace is the city's must-see sight, with jaw-dropping, no-expense-spared opulence courtesy of the profligate Prince Regent. See p.254

❷ North Laine Brighton at its bohemian, buzzy best, with hip coffee shops, cafés spilling out on to the streets and plenty of quirky independent shops for browsing. See p.257

❸ Beach sports The beach may be pebbly but you can still feel the sand between your toes at the seafront's beach volleyball courts. See p.259

❹ Brighton Festival and Fringe The biggest arts festival in England is an all-singing, all-dancing three week culture-fest of art, dance, music, comedy and theatre, with hundreds of shows and performances to choose from. See p.263

❺ Eating out From Jack *and Linda's* takeaway mackerel rolls on the beach, to *Riddle and Finns'* champagne and oysters, Brighton's eating scene covers all budgets and tastes. See p.268

❻ Komedia You're spoilt for choice when it comes to nights out in the city, but make sure at least one of them is spent here, at this great arts venue that puts on comedy, cabaret, film, live music and club nights. See p.275

HIGHLIGHTS ARE MARKED ON THE MAP ON PP.254–255

weekend", Brighton's major contribution to the English collective consciousness. By the end of the 1700s the town was the most fashionable resort in the country, visited by the great and good of high society – though the arrival of the train in 1841 soon put paid to that, kickstarting mass tourism and a popularity with day-trippers from the capital that's continued unabated to this day.

Royal Pavilion

4/5 Pavilion Buildings • Daily: April–Sept 9.30am–5.45pm; Oct–March 10am–5.15pm; last entry 45min before closing • £9.80 • ☎ 0300 290900, ⓦ brighton-hove-rpml.org.uk

In any survey to find Britain's most loved building, there's always a bucketful of votes for Brighton's exotic extravaganza, the **Royal Pavilion**, which flaunts itself in the middle of the Old Steine, the main thoroughfare along which most of the seafront-bound road traffic gets funnelled. Commissioned by the fun-loving **Prince Regent** (see box, p.256) in 1815, the Pavilion was the design of **John Nash**, architect of

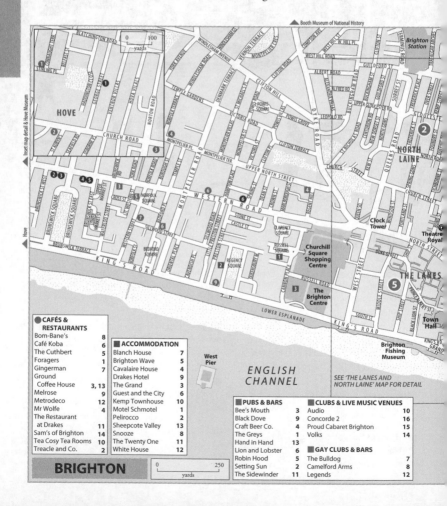

BRIGHTON

● CAFÉS & RESTAURANTS

Bom-Bane's	8
Café Koba	6
The Cuthbert	5
Foragers	1
Gingerman	7
Ground Coffee House	3, 13
Melrose	9
Metrodeco	12
Mr Wolfe	4
The Restaurant at Drakes	11
Sam's of Brighton	14
Tea Cosy Tea Rooms	10
Treacle and Co.	2

■ ACCOMMODATION

Blanch House	7
Brighton Wave	5
Cavalaire House	4
Drakes Hotel	9
The Grand	3
Guest and the City	6
Kemp Townhouse	10
Motel Schmotel	1
Pelirocco	2
Sheepcote Valley	13
Snooze	8
The Twenty One	11
White House	12

■ PUBS & BARS

Bee's Mouth	3
Black Dove	9
Craft Beer Co.	4
The Greys	1
Hand in Hand	13
Lion and Lobster	6
Robin Hood	5
Setting Sun	2
The Sidewinder	11

■ CLUBS & LIVE MUSIC VENUES

Audio	10
Concorde 2	16
Proud Cabaret Brighton	15
Volks	14

■ GAY CLUBS & BARS

The Bulldog	7
Camelford Arms	8
Legends	12

London's Regent Street. What Nash came up with was an extraordinary confection of slender minarets, twirling domes, pagodas, balconies and miscellaneous motifs imported from India and China, all supported on an innovative cast-iron frame, creating an exterior profile that defines a genre of its own – Oriental-Gothic.

Inside, one highlight – approached via the restrained Long Gallery – is the **Banqueting Room**, which erupts with ornate splendour and is dominated by a one-tonne chandelier hung from the jaws of a massive dragon cowering in a plantain tree. Next door, the huge, high-ceilinged **kitchen**, fitted with the most modern appliances of its time, has iron columns disguised as palm trees. The stunning **Music Room**, the first sight of which reduced George to tears of joy, has a huge dome lined with more than twenty-six thousand individually gilded scales and hung with exquisite umbrella-like glass lamps. After climbing the famous cast-iron staircase with its bamboo-look banisters, you can go into Victoria's sober and seldom-used bedroom and the **North Gallery** where the king's portrait hangs, along with a selection of satirical cartoons. More notable, though, is the **South Gallery**, decorated in sky-blue with trompe l'oeil bamboo trellises and a carpet that appears to be strewn with flowers.

7

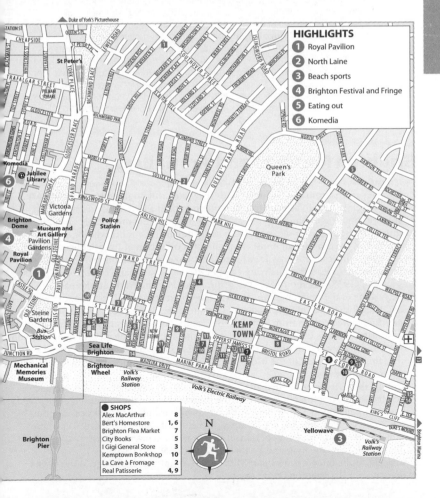

HIGHLIGHTS
1 Royal Pavilion
2 North Laine
3 Beach sports
4 Brighton Festival and Fringe
5 Eating out
6 Komedia

● **SHOPS**

Alex MacArthur	8
Bert's Homestore	1, 6
Brighton Flea Market	7
City Books	5
I Gigi General Store	3
Kemptown Bookshop	10
La Cave à Fromage	2
Real Patisserie	4, 9

THE FIRST GENTLEMAN OF ENGLAND: GEORGE IV

Born on August 12, 1762, **George, Prince of Wales**, was the eldest son of George III and Queen Charlotte, and a constant source of disappointment to his straight-laced father. He was vain, indolent and profligate, with a life devoted almost entirely to pleasure – gambling, heavy drinking, dining, mistresses, racing and fine clothes.

George's love affair with Brighton started in 1783, when on the advice of his physicians he visited the small seaside town – by that stage already a popular health resort. He liked it so much that he rented a farmhouse, which he later transformed into a lavishly furnished villa. His presence over the next forty or so years was instrumental in the town's meteoric transformation into a fashionable and slightly racy "London by the sea". George had the time of his life there, building up unspeakably large debts (running to tens of millions of pounds in today's money), and spending his days in the pursuit of pleasure – promenading, horseriding, partying, and frolicking with his mistress, **Mrs Maria Fitzherbert**, whom he secretly – and illegally – married in 1785, and installed in a house on the west side of the Old Steine. A twice-widowed commoner, and Roman Catholic to boot, Fitzherbert couldn't have been a more unsuitable partner.

In 1795 George's disapproving father forced a marriage with **Princess Caroline of Brunswick**. It was not a success. Caroline had as much contempt for her portly husband as his father did, and George continued his dissolute lifestyle unrepentant, with the couple separating soon after the birth of their only child the following year.

In 1811, George became **Prince Regent** after his father was declared insane, and within a few years he hired John Nash to transform his villa into the extravagant palace that stands today. When his father died in 1820 he was crowned **King George IV** – by this time morbidly obese, suffering from gout and digestive problems, and frequently caricatured in the national press as being completely out of touch with a nation reeling from famine and unemployment in the aftermath of the Napoleonic Wars. When George died in 1830, aged 68, his passing was neatly summed up by *The Times*: "There never was an individual less regretted by his fellow-creatures than this deceased king."

Brighton Museum and Art Gallery

Royal Pavilion Gardens, BN1 1EE • Tues–Sun 10am–5pm • Free • ☎ 03000 290900, ⓦ www.brighton-hove-rpml.org.uk

Across the gardens from the Pavilion stands the wonderful **Brighton Museum and Art Gallery**, which houses an eclectic mix of modern fashion and design, archeology, art and local history in a grand building that used to form part of the royal stable block. It's free to enter, and there's lots to see, so you can easily dip in and out of it during a stay.

Downstairs, the central hall houses the museum's collection of **twentieth-century art and design**, a procession of classic Art Deco, Art Nouveau and modern furniture that includes Thomas Heatherwick's witty "Keep Off The Glass" chair (2004/5) and Dalí's famous sofa (1938) based on Mae West's lips. Next door the **World Stories** gallery displays some of the museum's top-class 13,000-object ethnographic collection, while across the hall the **Ancient Egypt** galleries contain some mummified animals and wonderful painted coffins from 945–715 BC, courtesy of famous Egyptologist – and Brightonian – Francis Llewellyn Griffith. Two other rooms on the ground floor take you through the **history of Brighton**, covering everything from the rise of the dirty weekend to the famous 1964 clash of the Mods and Rockers on Brighton seafront that inspired the film *Quadrophenia*.

Upstairs there's a room themed around "The Body" and another on "Performance", which has some fantastic **puppets** from the museum's world art collection, alongside a willow-and-paper model from Brighton's very own Burning the Clocks celebrations (see p.263). The **Costume gallery** includes garments belonging to George IV, whose love of fashion (and his own appearance) led his wife to comment rather sniffily "I ought to have been the man and he the woman to wear petticoats."

Adjacent to the museum, and part of the same complex of buildings, is the town's main concert hall, **Brighton Dome** (see p.275).

BRIGHTON GALLERIES

It's no surprise that creative, bohemian Brighton has a thriving arts scene. These two contemporary galleries both put on several exhibitions a year.

Fabrica 40 Duke St, BN1 1AG ☏ 01273 778646, ⓦ fabrica.org.uk. Visual arts organization with a contemporary art gallery housed in an old church on the edge of The Lanes. Three main shows a year, often featuring installations (free). Wed, Fri & Sat noon–5pm, Thurs noon–7pm, Sun 2–5pm.

Phoenix Brighton 10–14 Waterloo Place, BN2 9NB ☏ 01273 603700, ⓦ phoenixarts.org. Arts organization housed in a huge building opposite St Peter's church, with over a hundred studio spaces, plus a gallery putting on half-a-dozen shows a year (free). Hours vary.

The Lanes

Tucked between the Pavilion and the seafront is a warren of narrow, pedestrianized alleyways known as **the Lanes** – the core of the old fishing village from which Brighton evolved. It's a great place to wander, with some excellent cafés and restaurants, and plenty of interesting independent shops and boutiques, including the long-established jeweller's shops for which the area's known. At the northern fringes of the Lanes, on Duke Street, make sure you pop your head into the **Fabrica** contemporary art gallery (see box above) to see if there's a show on.

North Laine

If you're looking for the Brighton that's bohemian, hip and slightly alternative, you'll find it in **North Laine**, which spreads north of North Street as far as Trafalgar Street, bordered by Queens Road to the west and the A23 to the east. What used to be the city's slums is now its most vibrant neighbourhood, packed with coffee shops and pavement cafés, cool boutiques and quirky independent shops selling everything from vintage clothing and vinyl to Afghan rugs and bonsai trees. Several streets are pedestrianized, while others become temporarily car-free at the weekend, when the crowds descend en masse and café tables and stalls spill out on to the streets. The North Laine **website** (ⓦ northlaine.co.uk) features a downloadable map, as well as reasonably comprehensive listings for the many shops and eating places.

The seafront

Every visitor to Brighton will find their way down to Brighton's **seafront** at some point, and in summer it certainly feels that way, with crowds of holidaymakers and Brightonians soaking up the sun in the beachfront cafés, or crunching their way over the pebbly beach to find an unoccupied spot.

The section of seafront between the two piers is where most of the action takes place. Here, down beneath the street-level prom with its distinctive turquoise-blue railings, the **Lower Esplanade** runs west from Brighton Pier along to its ruined counterpart in Hove, lined for much of its length by bars, clubs, cafés, galleries (ⓦ theartistquarter .co.uk) and gift shops, many snuggled into the old redbrick **fisherman's arches**, and with stalls or tables out by the pebbles. Soon after passing the derelict West Pier, you reach the wide grassy lawns and quieter seafront of **Hove Lawns**, a stretch of beach where evening barbecues are allowed.

East of Brighton Pier, the venerable Volk's Railway trundles along for a mile to the **naturist beach** – the first public naturist beach in the country, and usually the preserve of just a few thick-skinned souls – and then on to Brighton Marina.

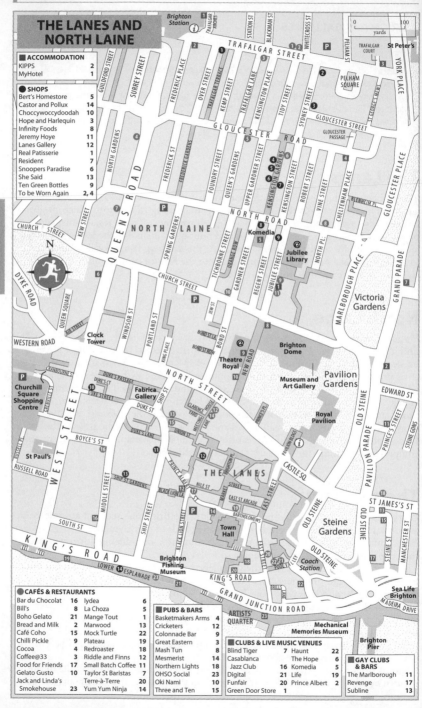

Brighton Pier

Madeira Drive, BN2 1TW • Daily 10am–11pm, rides and sideshows Mon–Fri noon–6pm, Sat 11am–10pm, Sun 11am–11pm •
☎ 01273 609361, Ⓦ brightonpier.co.uk

To soak up the tackier side of Brighton, take a stroll along **Brighton Pier**. Opened in 1899, its every inch is devoted to fun and money-making, from the side stalls and two cacophonous amusement arcades, to the **fairground rides** at the end of the pier, which range from the traditional (helter-skelter, carousel and dodgems) to the downright terrifying (the Booster, which lifts you 40ft in the air, leaving you dangling over the sea).

Mechanical Memories Museum

250 King's Road Arches, on the Lower Esplanade (at beach level) 100yd west of Brighton Pier, BN1 1NB • Sat, Sun & school hols noon–6pm, weather permitting during winter months • Free • Ⓦ mechanicalmemoriesmuseum.co.uk

The country's oldest established vintage penny arcade, the tiny **Mechanical Memories Museum** houses around fifty antique penny slot machines – Fortune Tellers, clunky moving models, games of skill, saucy What The Butler Saw peep-shows, and more – from the early 1900s to the 1960s. You can buy big pre-decimal pennies at the counter to play the machines – a wonderfully old-fashioned antidote to the screeching, flashing modern-day arcades on the pier next door.

LIFE'S A BEACH

It's not quite California, but there's a definite beachfront buzz about Brighton, and there's no better way to experience it than to spend the morning stretching your muscles, whether catching a wave on an SUP, playing a game of beach volleyball or peddling leisurely along the seafront.

BEACH SPORTS

★ **Yellowave** 299 Madeira Drive, BN2 1EN ☎ 01273 672222, Ⓦ yellowave.co.uk. The country's only year-round beach sports venue is a brilliant spot, with all manner of sports on offer on the six sand courts, from beach soccer to ultimate frisbee, although the main focus is beach volleyball (court rental including a ball £20/hr; beginners' coaching sessions £5). Even if you don't want to play it's a great place to hang out and soak up the laidback beach vibe, with a bouldering wall and sandpit to keep youngsters happy, and a lively, bare-boards café with great food and plenty of tables outside. May–Sept Mon–Fri 10am–10pm, Sat & Sun 10am–8pm; Oct–April Tues–Thurs 11am–9pm, Fri 11am–5pm, Sat & Sun 10am–5pm.

Lower Esplanade beach volleyball There's a council-run, beach volleyball court on the Lower Esplanade between the piers (May–Sept; £22/hr; ☎ 01273 292716).

WATERSPORTS

Brighton Dive Centre 37 The Waterfront, Marina Village, Brighton Marina, BN2 5WA ☎ 01273 606068, Ⓦ thebrightondivecentre.co.uk. PADI courses and boat/shore dives (from £45).

Brighton Watersports 185 King's Road Arches, on the Lower Esplanade, BN1 1NB ☎ 01273 323160,

Ⓦ thebrightonwatersports.co.uk. Right down by the pebbles, this well-established outfit offers stand-up paddleboarding (SUP; board rental £10/hr; 2hr 30min introductory lesson £40); kayaking (kayak rental £10/person/hr; 3hr lesson £40); wakeboarding (£20/20min or £40/40min); and scuba diving (pier dives £30, or £50 with kit rental). If it all sounds too much like hard work, they also have towable ringos (£20/20min).

Lagoon Watersports Hove Lagoon, BN3 4LX ☎ 01273 424842, Ⓦ lagoon.co.uk/hove-lagoon. This sheltered beachfront lagoon offers windsurfing (2hr taster session £50); stand-up paddleboarding (2hr introductory lesson £40); and cable wakeboarding (2hr beginners' course £50). Their sailing school based at Brighton Marina offers longer dinghy sailing courses (2 days/£200) and high-speed powerboat rides (30min/£25).

Ross Boat Trips Pontoon 5, West Jetty, Brighton Marina, BN2 5WA ☎ 07958 246414 & ☎ 07836 262717, Ⓦ watertours.co.uk. Mackerel fishing trips (March–Nov; 90min/£20); powerboat rides (25min/£15); and sea cruises (45min; £8.50).

CYCLING

Cycling A cycle path runs the length of Brighton seafront, meeting up just east of the Marina with the Undercliff Walk (see p.262) – note that cyclists must give way to pedestrians here. Bike rental available (see p.264).

7

Brighton Fishing Museum

201 King's Road Arches, Lower Esplanade (at beach level), BN1 1NB • Daily 9am–6pm • Free • ⓦ brightonfishingmuseum.org.uk

The golden days of Brighton's local fishing industry are revisited at the **Brighton Fishing Museum**, which displays old photos, video footage and memorabilia, and houses a large Sussex clinker, a boat once common on Brighton beach. Before Brighton's rise as a fashionable resort it was the most important fishing town in Sussex, with four out of every five men working as fishermen; the rise of tourism led to the decline of the fishing fleet, leading some resourceful fishermen to turn to tourism instead, offering pleasure cruises or becoming dippers or bathers for Brighton's bathing machines.

The surrounding area is known as the **Fishing Quarter**. There's a good fishmonger here, with a stall opposite selling jellied eels, roll mops and the like, as well as the wonderful *Jack and Linda's Smokehouse* (see p.268) a few doors down.

West Pier and i360

7

At the western end of the seafront, all that remains of the once-grand **West Pier**, built in 1866 by Eugenius Birch, is a blackened skeleton no longer connected to the mainland. The pier was once one of the finest in the country – and the first to be Grade I-listed – but after decades of neglect it was all but destroyed by storms and two separate fires in 2002/2003. Today the rusting carcass has become an iconic sight, especially in winter, when the skies above the pier are filled at dusk with swirling clouds of **starlings**.

At the site of the former entrance to the pier, a slender 475ft-tall viewing mast, the **i360** (ⓦ brightoni360.co.uk), is scheduled to open in 2015. Designed by the architects of the London Eye, the mast will feature a flying saucer-shaped observation pod, which will whisk visitors 460ft up for views over the city.

Brighton Bandstand

King's Rd, BN1 2FN • Concerts June–Aug Sun 2–4pm • Free • ⓦ brighton-hove.gov.uk

Brighton's beautiful Victorian **bandstand** – also known as The Birdcage – is the only one to survive of eight that once graced the seafront. During summer it puts on free Sunday afternoon concerts, which range from traditional brass bands to indie bands.

Brighton Wheel

Madeira Drive, BN2 1TB • Daily: June–Sept 10am–11pm; Oct–May 10am–8pm • £8 • ☎ 01273 722822, ⓦ brightonwheel.com

Just east of Brighton Pier is Brighton's London-Eye-in-miniature, the **Brighton Wheel**, which is due to remain on its seafront spot until 2016. Your ticket buys you three speedy revolutions, accompanied by a fun commentary by comedian Steve Coogan, a Brighton resident. Don't go expecting spectacular views (the wheel's just 165ft above sea level), but it's a fun fifteen-minute spin nonetheless.

Sea Life Brighton

Marine Parade, BN2 1TB • Daily 10am–4/5/6pm depending on season, day of week and weather • £16.20, children over 3 £11.40; discounts available online; glass-bottomed boat £3, behind-scenes tour £3, boat & tour £5 • ☎ 01273 604234, ⓦ visitsealife.com/Brighton

Sea Life Brighton is the world's oldest operating aquarium, opened in 1872. The atmospheric main aquarium hall still looks largely as it would have done in Victorian times, lined with tanks and with a wonderful vaulted ceiling, and is the real star of the show. Elsewhere there's a short tunnel leading you through a tank populated by sharks and stately giant turtles, and a small, dark room of jellyfish floating mesmerically in glowing, colour-changing tubes. Talks and feeding sessions take place throughout the day, as well as rockpool handling sessions, but even allowing for these you'll be hard pressed to fill more than two hours, and at well over £50 for a family of four it's not cheap.

BEST OF BRIGHTON FOR KIDS

Brighton Pier A surefire hit with most ages, with arcade games, stalls, scary rollercoasters and gentler rides. Plus doughnuts. See p.259

Yellowave This beach sports venue is a great spot for kids, and you can take an old electric train along the seafront to get to it. See p.259

Biking along the prom Rent bikes at the seafront and you can cycle for miles along the promenade; the quieter end around Hove Lawns is best for smaller cyclists. See box, p.259

Gelaterias Ice cream is bound to feature in your stay – just make sure it's from one of the city's fab *gelaterias*. See p.272

Komedia Voted best family-friendly theatre in the South, this venue puts on shows for kids several times a month. See p.275

Volk's Electric Railway

March–Sept Mon–Fri 10.15am–5pm, Sat & Sun 10.15am–6pm • Every 15min • £1.20 single to halfway station, £2 single to Black Rock (for the Marina), £3.10 return to Black Rock • ⓦ volkselectricrailway.co.uk

Just east of Brighton Pier, the antiquated locomotives of **Volk's Electric Railway** – the first electric train in the country, dating back to 1883 – trundle eastward for just over a mile to Black Rock, by the Marina, stopping off halfway near the excellent Yellowave beach sports venue (see box, p.259). The railway was built by **Magnus Volk**, a nineteenth-century inventor and engineer, who was also responsible for setting up the first telephone line in the city and installing its first electric lighting.

Brighton Marina

BN2 5UF • ⓦ brightonmarina.co.uk

Brighton Marina – the largest in Europe – is a rather soulless concrete sprawl of factory outlet shops, a cinema, bowling alley, casino, superstore, as well as a clutch of chain restaurants that do at least make the most of their waterfront location, with pleasant outdoor seating looking over the bobbing, clanking boats. Various **watersports** outfits and boat operators operate out of the Marina (see box, p.259).

Hove

Although it forms a continuous conurbation with Brighton – and to most visitors' eyes is just another neighbourhood – **Hove** was, until quite recently, a completely separate town. It grew up as the resort of Brunswick Town in the 1820s, separated from Brighton by open fields, and it was only in 1997 that it was merged with its flashier neighbour to form the borough of Brighton and Hove, which achieved city status three years later.

Hove has always been rather protective of its separate identity: its tongue-in-cheek slogan, "Hove, actually", originates from the sniffy response of local residents to outsiders asking if they live in Brighton. It definitely has a calmer, less raffish air to it, with handsome Regency architecture around the **Brunswick area**, an elegant lawn-backed **seafront** – where the division between Brighton and Hove is marked by the **Peace Statue** – and plenty of good cafés and restaurants along and around the main drag, Western Road, which changes into Church Road just west of Palmeira Square.

Hove Museum

19 New Church Rd, BN3 4AB • Mon, Tues & Thurs–Sat 10am–5pm, Sun & bank holiday Mon 2–5pm • Free • ☎ 03000 290900, ⓦ brighton-hove-rpml.org.uk • Bus #1, #1A, #6, #49 or #49A from North St or Churchill Square

Like its sister museum in Brighton, **Hove Museum** is a bit of an eclectic treasure-trove. Its single most prized possession is the 3500-year-old **Hove amber cup** – discovered nearby in 1856 and considered to be one of Britain's most important Bronze Age finds

7

THE UNDERCLIFF WALK

Built between 1928 and 1935 to provide sea defences for the crumbling cliffs, the **Undercliff Walk** stretches 3.5 miles from Brighton Marina east to Saltdean. It's one of Brighton's lesser-known treasures, and makes a wonderful day-trip from the city if combined with a wander around the pretty village of Rottingdean or a swim in Saltdean's Art Deco lido. The walk is lovely on a summer's day at low tide, when you can drop down to the beach to poke around the rockpools, but it's definitely best – and most exhilarating – in stormy weather, when at high tide the wind carries the spray right over the sea wall on to the promenade.

If you're walking the route in one direction, you can catch **buses** #12, #13, #14, #27 or #47 back to Brighton (every 10–15min) from bus stops on the coast road at Rottingdean or Saltdean.

ROTTINGDEAN

Two and a half miles along the Undercliff Walk you'll come to the Gap – a natural break in the cliffs, which allows access to the little village of **Rottingdean**. Cross over the busy coast road and head up the High Street to reach The Green, the picturesque, leafy hub of the village. It was here that Pre-Raphaelite painter **Edward Burne-Jones** and his nephew **Rudyard Kipling** made their home in the late nineteenth century: the Burne-Jones' former holiday house, North End House, sits on the western side, just a stone's throw from Kipling's house, The Elms, on the village green itself. Neither building is open to the public today, but you can wander through the peaceful flint-walled **Kipling's Gardens** (daily until dusk; free) beside his old home.

Kipling wrote many of his best-known works while in Rottingdean, including some of his *Just So* stories, but eventually he lost patience with tourists coming to gawp at him and removed himself to a more secluded haven at Bateman's near Burwash (see p.190). Burne-Jones remained in Rottingdean until his death in 1898 and is buried at the flint-walled thirteenth-century **church of St Margaret's** on the northeastern corner of The Green, which contains some wonderful **stained-glass windows** created by him in collaboration with William Morris. Just south past the duck pond the **Grange Museum and Art Gallery** (Mon, Tues & Thurs–Sat 10am–4pm, Sun 2–4pm; ☎01273 301004, ⓦrottingdeanpreservationsociety.org.uk), originally the vicarage, has plenty of material dedicated to its two famous residents.

SALTDEAN LIDO

A mile further on from Rottingdean, you'll come to **Saltdean** with its wonderful **Art Deco lido**, designed by architect Richard Jones and opened in 1938; with its two curved wings swooping away from a main block, topped by sun terraces – a design intended to emulate the bridge of an ocean liner – it's a real gem, and the only Grade II* listed lido in the country. After the lido was threatened with permanent closure, a victorious campaign by local residents saw it taken back into council ownership in 2012, and at the time of writing it is closed pending a decision about tendering and redevelopment; see ⓦsaltdeanlido.co.uk for the latest news.

– but it's equally known for its wonderful **contemporary crafts collection**, one of the finest in the country, comprising over two hundred pieces of ceramics, textiles, metalwork and other crafts by local and international makers. You also shouldn't miss the **Film Galleries**, which record Hove's important role in the early silent film industry, and show some of the wonderful films made, in a tiny six-seat cinema.

Elsewhere there's an interesting display on the **history and architecture** of Hove, with some great pictures of the earliest stages of development, with a ribbon of grand seafront crescents and squares backed by open fields. For kids, the **Wizard's Attic**, an imaginatively interactive room stuffed full of antique toys, is a sure-fire hit, while the museum **café** is surely the most cultured place for a cuppa in town, with tables surrounded by cabinets of exquisite pottery from Wedgwood and other big names.

Out of the centre

Most of Brighton's sights are very central, but there are a few a little further afield that are well worth seeking out. Remember also that Brighton sits on the edge of some stunning countryside, which is easily accessible: the **Breeze up the Downs** bus network connects it in the summer to beauty spots Devil's Dyke (see p.236) and Ditchling Beacon (see p.235), both just a twenty-minute ride away.

Preston Manor

Preston Drove, just off the A23, BN1 6SD • April–Sept Tues–Sat 10am–5pm, Sun 2–5pm • £6, Haunted House Experience £28 • ☎ 03000 290900, ⓦ brighton-hove-rpml.org.uk • A 5min walk from Preston Park train station, or bus #5, #5A, #17, #40, #40X or #273

Two miles north of Brighton, pretty **Preston Manor** dates from 1738, though it was extensively remodelled in 1905 by the Stanford family, who lived there for 138 years before gifting it to the city of Brighton in 1932. Its series of period interiors engagingly evokes the life of the Edwardian gentry, from the servants' quarters downstairs to the luxury nursery upstairs; the Stanfords were ferocious entertainers, counting Rudyard Kipling and Queen Victoria's daughters among their regular visitors.

Preston Manor is known for its ghostly sightings and supernatural activity, earning itself the moniker "**Brighton's most haunted house**" when LivingTV's *Most Haunted!* programme visited. Ghost hunters have claimed all sorts of spooky happenings – everything from disembodied hands turning doorknobs to lights turning off by themselves; those of a stalwart disposition can join one of the regular **Haunted House evenings**.

Booth Museum

194 Dyke Rd, BN1 5AA, 1 mile from the centre of town • Mon–Wed, Fri & Sat 10am–5pm, Sun 2–5pm • Free • ☎ 0300 290900, ⓦ brighton-hove-rpml.org.uk • Bus #14, #27, #27A or #27B

A half-hour walk from the city centre, the **Booth Museum of Natural History** is a wonderfully fusty old Victorian museum with beetles, birds, butterflies and animal skeletons galore. The museum was purpose-built by nineteenth-century natural historian and eccentric Edward Thomas Booth to house his prodigious collection of stuffed birds – one of the largest in the country, accumulated through a lifetime of obsessive bird-hunting; rumour had it that Booth kept a locomotive under steam at Brighton station so that he could be ready to set off in pursuit of a rare species at a moment's notice. Booth's technique of mounting birds in a diorama of their natural habitat, rather than on a simple wooden perch, was completely new, and copied around the world.

BRIGHTON'S BEST FESTIVALS AND EVENTS

Scarcely a week passes in Brighton without a festival or event taking place. We've picked out the best below, but there are many more (see pp.32–33), or check out ⓦ visitbrighton.co.uk.

Brighton Festival ☎ 01273 709709, ⓦ brighton festival.org. The biggie, taking place over three weeks in May at various venues. England's largest arts festival, it includes over 200 events, including exhibitions, street theatre, talks, dance and concerts. Guest artistic directors have included Anish Kapoor, Aung San Suu Kyi and Vanessa Redgrave.

Brighton and Hove Fringe Festival ☎ 01273 709709, ⓦ brightonfestivalfringe.org.uk. Running at the same time as the Brighton Festival, the open-access Fringe stages over 700 events, everything from live music and drama to literature readings and comedy nights, as well as the Artists' Open Houses Festival (ⓦ aoh.org.uk), when hundreds of homes open their

doors to show the work of local artists and craftspeople.

London to Brighton Veteran Car Run ⓦ lbvcr .com. Taking place on a Sunday in early November, this long-established event (which first took place in 1896) sees up to 550 venerable old crocks – all built before 1905 – attempt the sixty-mile route from London's Hyde Park to Brighton's Madeira Drive.

Burning the Clocks ⓦ burningtheclocks.co.uk. This festival to mark the winter solstice on December 23 sees hundreds of beautiful paper and willow lanterns – everything from small lanterns to incredible sculptures – carried through the streets, before they are thrown onto a huge bonfire on the beach, accompanied by a fireworks display.

ARRIVAL AND DEPARTURE   BRIGHTON

BY CAR
The main A23 road into Brighton often suffers from traffic jams at weekends in summer, and once you're in the centre free on-street parking is extremely limited, so consider avoiding driving in.

Park-and-ride Free at Withdean Stadium (BN1 5JD, signposted from the A23); bus #27 runs into town every 15min Mon–Sat, every 30min Sun; a City Saver bus ticket costs £4.40 (see below).

Parking Pay-and-display parking in central Brighton costs £3.50/1hr, £6/2hr and £10/4hr (max stay). Seafront parking charges drop outside the central zone (east of Yellowave, and west of Hove St), and allow longer stays (£5/11hr). The cheapest long-stay multistorey car parks are Regency Square and Trafalgar St (both £12/24hr); you can park for free at Brighton Marina and walk or take the bus into town. Brighton and Hove Council's website ⓦ journeyon.co.uk has a useful car parking map.

BY TRAIN
Brighton station At the top of Queen's Rd, which descends to the Clocktower and then becomes West St, eventually leading to the seafront, a 10min walk away.
Destinations Arundel (Mon–Sat every 30min, Sun hourly; 1hr 20min); Bognor (every 30min; 45min); Chichester (every 30min; 45–55min); Eastbourne (every 20min;

35min); Hastings (every 30min; 1hr 5min); Lewes (every 10–20min; 15min); Littlehampton (every 30min; 45min); London Bridge (Mon–Sat 4 hourly, Sun 2 hourly; 1hr); London King's Cross (2–4 hourly; 1hr 15min); London Victoria (1–2 hourly; 55min–1hr 20min); Shoreham-by-Sea (every 30min; 15min); Worthing (every 30min; 25min).

Hove station Much smaller and quieter than Brighton, it is at the top of Goldstone Villas; it's a 10min walk south along Goldstone Villas and then George St to reach Church Road, the main drag.
Destinations Arundel (1–2 hourly; 1hr 5min); Chichester (every 30min; 45min); Littlehampton (every 15min; 35–45min); London Victoria (1–2 hourly; 1hr 10min); Shoreham-by-Sea (every 15min; 10min); Worthing (every 10min; 15–20min).

BY BUS
The bus station is just in from the seafront on the south side of the Old Steine.
Destinations Arundel (Mon–Fri every 30min; 2hr); Chichester via Bognor, Littlehampton, Worthing & Shoreham-by-Sea (Mon–Sat every 15min, Sun every 30min; 1hr 45min); Eastbourne (every 10–15min; 1hr 15min); Lewes (Mon–Sat every 15min, Sun hourly; 30min); London Victoria (hourly; 2hr 20min); Tunbridge Wells (Mon–Sat every 30min, Sun hourly; 1hr 35min).

GETTING AROUND

PUBLIC TRANSPORT
The website ⓦ journeyon.co.uk is a great resource, with a journey planner. Most of the city is walkable, but buses can be useful for west Hove and some further-flung sights.
Tickets The City Saver gives you one day's unlimited travel for £4.40 (£4 if bought in advance from shops). Short-hop journeys cost £1.50.

TAXIS
The main taxi ranks are at Brighton and Hove stations, East St, Queens Square near the Clock Tower, outside St Peter's church and outside Hove Town Hall.
Brighton and Hove Streamline Taxis ☏ 01273 202020.
Brighton and Hove Radio cabs ☏ 01273 204060.

BY BIKE
The ⓦ journeyon.co.uk website has a downloadable cycling map of the city and information on bike rental and bike parking.
Amsterdammers Unit 8, under the station, off Trafalgar St (Mon–Fri 9am–6pm, Sat 9.30am–5pm, Sun & bank hols 10am–4pm; ☏ 01273 571 555, ⓦ brightoncyclehire.com). Bikes cost £7/3hr, £10 /24hr.
Brighton Beach Bike Hire Madeira Drive, by Yellowave ☏ 07917 753794, ⓦ brightonsports.co.uk. May–Sept Mon–Fri 11am–6pm, Sat & Sun 10am–6pm; Oct–April hours vary – check website or call for details. Californian beach-cruiser-type bikes cost £12/3hr, £16/4hr+.

INFORMATION

Tourist office Accessed through the Royal Pavilion shop at 4–5 Pavilion Buildings (Daily: April–Sept 9.30am–5.15pm; Oct–March 10am–5pm; ☏ 01273 290337, ⓦ visitbrighton.com). There are also information points at Brighton Pier and the Brighton Toy and Model Museum, 1min from the station at 52–55 Trafalgar St (Tues–Fri 10am–5pm, Sat 11am–5pm). The main office sells bus tickets, tickets for the Pavilion and Sea Life Centre,

and has free city maps. The accommodation booking service costs £3 if booked by phone on ☏ 01273 290337, or £1.50 per adult in person at the main tourist office.
Apps, magazines and websites VisitBrighton produces a free app for smartphones – search for "Brighton official city guide". The best listing magazine is *Source Magazine* (ⓦ brightonsource.co.uk), but *XYZ* (ⓦ xyzmagazine.co.uk) and *BN1* (ⓦ bn1magazine.co.uk) are also worth a look.

7

CITY TOURS

In addition to the recommended tours below, you can also download half a dozen **podcasts** and a similar number of **PDF walking tours** from the ⓦ visitbrighton.co.uk website. The website also allows you to book a free two-hour tour with the **Brighton Greeters** scheme, which pairs up visitors with a volunteer Brighton resident tour guide.

Brighton City Walks ☎07941 256148, ⓦ brightoncitywalks.com. Runs the Brighton Story (Tues, Thurs, Sat & Sun 2pm; no booking required; 90min; £5), a general tour of the city, plus two other private tours: "Brighton Rock", which follows in the footsteps of the 1930s Graham Greene novel; and "Lost cinemas of Brighton".

Brighton Sewer Tours ☎01903 272606, ⓦ sewertours.southernwater.co.uk. Brighton's famous, award-winning tours of its Victorian sewers are much more fun than they sound, taking you through narrow corridors and up and down metal ladders to see the still-working legacy of the Victorians, and filling you in on lots of interesting stuff about the city along the way (May Tues & Thurs 6.30pm, Sat 9.30am & 11am; June–Sept Wed 6.30pm, Sat 9.30am & 11am; 1hr; £12).

Brighton Walks ☎01273 302100, ⓦ brightonwalks .com. Runs Brighton Breezy (March–Nov Sat 11am; April–Sept also Thurs 11am; 1hr; no booking required; £5), a general tour of Brighton, plus monthly ghost tours

(last Sat of month 7.30pm) and murder and mystery tours (second Sat of month; 7.30pm).

Only in Brighton ☎07954 482112, ⓦ onlyinbrighton .co.uk. Equally popular with locals and visitors, this quirky tour answers all the important questions about Brighton life: how did a song performed at the Brighton Dome help trigger the Portuguese Revolution? Why did the Prince Regent need a stiff brandy when he met his future wife? And just what connects Mount Everest and the Hove branch of Tesco? The same guide runs "Piers and Queers" tours (on request), exploring the city's LGBT history (most Fri & Sat at 7pm, plus some Sat at 2pm – check website for dates; no booking required; 80min; £7).

Sightseeing bus Hop-on, hop-off buses (March & April Sat & Sun 10am–4pm; May to mid-Sept daily 10am–6pm; mid-Sept to end Sept Sat & Sun 10am–6pm; every 30min–1hr; 50min for whole circuit; £10, valid 24hr; ⓦ city-sightseeing.com) run around the city's main sights, including the Royal Pavilion, pier and Hove Lawns, connecting with the station.

ACCOMMODATION

There's no two ways about it: accommodation is pricey in Brighton; the prices we give are weekend, high-season rates, but if you're visiting out of summer, and especially during the week, these rates can fall dramatically, so it pays to check out a few options online. Year-round, you'll be required to stay a minimum of two nights at the weekend. Some of the nicest, most characterful B&Bs are in **Kemptown**, on the eastern side of the city; with some excellent cafés, restaurants and antique shops up at the "village" end of Kemptown, this can be a great place to base yourself.

CENTRAL BRIGHTON

The Grand 97–99 King's Rd, BN1 2FW ☎01273 224300, ⓦ devere-hotel.co.uk; map pp.254–255. This grand Victorian edifice, with its impressively pompous plasterwork, is the most iconic hotel in the city – most famous as the scene of the IRA's attempted assassination of the Conservative Cabinet in October 1984. Rooms are resolutely traditional, common areas are opulent, plus there's a spa, two restaurants, and a lounge serving the finest afternoon tea in town (Mon–Fri 3–6pm, Sat & Sun 2pm & 4.30pm sittings). The price of a stay can be surprisingly reasonable, especially when special offers or last-minute bargains bring the rates down. **£115**

KIPPS 76 Grand Parade, BN2 9JA ☎01273 604182, ⓦ kipps-brighton.co.uk; map p.258. This hostel – an antidote to the party hostels of Brighton – feels more like a small hotel, and has an unbeatable location opposite the Royal Pavilion. Rooms and dorms are plain but comfy, plus there's a licensed bar, low-key events every evening (Wii,

cocktails, pizza), and excellent-value breakfasts (£2 for dorms, included for rooms). Dorms **£24.50**; rooms **£76**

Motel Schmotel 37 Russell Square, BN1 2EF ☎01273 326129, ⓦ motelschmotel.co.uk; map pp.254–255. If you're willing to snuggle up, this friendly, super-central B&B, just moments from Churchill Square and the sea, offers some of the best-value rooms in the city – the smallest rooms really *are* small, but remain bright and cheerful, with art on the walls and fun patterned headboards and cushions. Breakfasts run from fish finger sarnies on home-baked bread to boiled eggs with smiley faces drawn on, and can be served in bed on request. **£90**

MyHotel 17 Jubilee St, BN1 1GE ☎01273 900300, ⓦ myhotels.com/my-hotel-brighton/; map p.258. This hip, fun contemporary hotel has a brilliant location, right in the heart of North Laine, and incorporates not only one of the city's best restaurants, *Chilli Pickle* (see p.269), but also one of its best coffee shops, *The Small Batch Coffee Co* (see p.271). The rooms have been designed along feng shui lines, so you'll find curved walls inset with crystals, vibrant colour and spiritual artwork. Rates vary according to demand, and can drop as low as £60 out of peak times, so check online for bargains. **£120**

★ **Pelirocco** 10 Regency Square, BN1 2FG ☎01273 327055, ⓦhotelpelirocco.co.ukk; map pp.254–255. "England's most rock'n'roll hotel" is a real one-off, featuring extravagantly themed rooms inspired by pop culture and pin-ups. There's a Fifties-style boudoir, a Pop Art "Modrophenia" room featuring bedside tables made from scooters, and a "Play room" that comes with a circular bed with a mirrored canopy and a pole-dancing pole in the corner of the room; you can even add an erotic hamper from the She Said boutique (see p.276) for the ultimate dirty weekend. **£115**

KEMPTOWN

Blanch House 17 Atlingworth St, BN2 1PL ☎01273 603504, ⓦblanchhouse.co.ukk; map pp.254–255. Brighton's original boutique hotel is still going strong, with a mix of styles and prices across its twelve rooms. The main draw though is the wonderful high-ceilinged champagne and cocktail bar down on the ground floor – the perfect start to a night on the town. **£125**

Brighton Wave 10 Madeira Place, BN2 1TN ☎01273 676794, ⓦbrightonwave.comk; map pp.254–255. This friendly B&B has a lovely relaxed feel, with a bright and cheery breakfast room that features art for sale on the walls, fairy lights in the fireplaces and newspapers spread out on the table by the sofas. Rooms are smart and contemporary, with en-suite showers, and welcome extra touches include a large DVD library and breakfast served until 10.30am at weekends. **£110**

Cavalaire House 34 Upper Rock Gardens, BN2 1QF ☎01273 696899, ⓦcavalaire.co.ukk; map pp.254–255. Warm and welcoming B&B with plenty of charm and character – artwork from Brighton artists on the walls, fresh flowers in the cheery breakfast room, and a friendly resident dog. There's a range of rooms, from cosy, traditionally styled standard doubles through to larger, more boutiquey deluxe rooms. **£99**

Drakes Hotel 33–34 Marine Parade, BN2 1PE ☎01273 696934, ⓦdrakesofbrighton.comk; map pp.254–255. The unbeatable seafront location is the big draw at this chic, minimalist boutique hotel, which boasts the best sea views in town. All the luxuries you'd expect are there, and the most expensive rooms come with freestanding baths by floor-to-ceiling windows looking out over the twinkling lights of the pier. The excellent in-house restaurant (see p.268) is one of Brighton's best. **£145**

★ **Guest and the City** 2 Broad St, BN2 1TJ ☎01273 698289, ⓦguestandthecity.co.uk; map pp.254–255. A great central location, super-friendly hosts, burlesque-themed wallpaper in the hallway and stylish rooms featuring retro furniture and sweets – what's not to love? It's worth spending a tiny bit more to bag one of the two

nicest rooms (£140), which feature wonderful stained-glass windows of classic Brighton scenes and a covered balconette. The owners couldn't be more helpful – guests even get armed with a specially printed map of the city featuring eating and shopping recommendations, complete with accompanying discount card. **£120**

★ **Kemp Townhouse** 21 Atlingworth St, BN2 1PL ☎01273 681400, ⓦkemptownhouse.com; map pp.254–255. Sophisticated, stylish and very friendly, this Regency townhouse – the city's only five-star B&B – has nine lovely rooms decorated in muted tones, with black-and-white prints of Brighton or the sea up on the walls, subway-tiled wet rooms, iPod docks and carafes of complimentary port. If you're not too fussed about space, the cosy double (£115) is a bit of a bargain. **£145**

★ **Snooze** 25 St George's Terrace, BN2 1JJ ☎01273 605797, ⓦsnoozebrighton.com; map pp.254–255. This cool and quirky B&B in the heart of Kemptown is crammed with fun touches, from the graffiti-style re-creation of the Sistine Chapel in the breakfast room, to the mismatched vintage cups and saucers that hold your morning coffee. The six en-suite rooms are styled with a hotchpotch of vintage furnishings – ranging from a full-on, eyepopping 1960s room, to a dark red boudoir plastered with old black-and-white photos of scantily clad damsels – plus there are two über-cool 1970s-style suites (£155). Rates drop substantially during the week. **£130**

★ **The Twenty One** 21 Charlotte St, BN2 1AG ☎01273 686450, ⓦthetwentyone.co.uk; map pp.254–255. This Regency townhouse is a super-friendly home from home, with stylish rooms – chandeliers, fluffy cushions and cream linens – immaculate bathrooms, a DVD library, iPads, bathrobes and a positively indecent amount of baked treats and retro sweets awaiting you in your room – you'll never have seen a tea tray quite like it before. The lovely owners and their attention to detail make it very popular. **£109**

White House 6 Bedford St, BN2 1AN ☎01273 626266, ⓦwhitehousebrighton.com; map pp.254–255. Set back from the road slightly, and facing south, this lovely townhouse B&B seems flooded with light. The serene rooms are sunny and bright, with sisal flooring and cocooning shades of cream and sage on the walls – impeccably tasteful, and a real haven from the bustle of Brighton. The rooms at the front even boast that elusive thing in Brighton – a proper sea view. **£110**

CAMPING

Sheepcote Valley Wilson Ave, BN2 5TS ☎01273 626546, ⓦcaravanclub.co.uk; bus #1 or #1A to Wilson Ave; map pp.254–255. Brighton's leafy campsite lies a mile or so inland from Brighton Marina, on the far side of Kemptown, a 40min walk into the centre. The site is mainly for caravans, but there are 80 tent pitches. Pitches (for 2 adult) **£31.60**

7

EATING

As you'd expect from cool, cosmopolitan "London-by-the-sea", there's a thriving café culture in Brighton, with hip little **cafés and coffee shops** sprouting up all over the city, but especially concentrated around the lively North Laine area; sitting over a flat white and watching Brighton life go by is an essential box to tick on any trip to the city. Brighton also boasts the greatest concentration of **restaurants** in the Southeast after London, among them some long-established gems including, appropriately enough for a town that embraced lentils and tofu long before they became mainstream, one of the country's best vegetarian restaurants.

THE SEAFRONT

★ **Jack and Linda's Smokehouse** 197 King's Road Arches; map p.258. This tiny beachfront takeaway is run by a lovely couple who've been traditionally smoking fish here for over a decade – the diminutive black-painted smokehouse is on the pebbles just across from Jack and Linda's arch. Grab a fresh crab sandwich or hot mackerel roll (£3–4) to eat on the beach for a perfect summer lunch. April–Sept daily 10am–5pm; Oct Fri, Sat & Sun 10am–5pm.

Melrose 132 King's Rd, BN1 2HH ☎ 01273 326520, ⓦ melroserestaurant.co.uk; map pp.254–255. Along with the *Regency* next door, this traditional seafront establishment is a bit of a Brighton institution – it's been dishing up tasty, excellent-value fish and chips (£6.75), shellfish platters (£46 for two), local crab and lobster, roasts and custard-covered puddings for over forty years. Daily 11.30am–10.30pm.

The Restaurant at Drakes 33–34 Marine Parade, BN2 1PE ☎ 01273 696934, ⓦ therestaurantatdrakes.com; map pp.254–255. The stylish restaurant in the basement of one of Brighton's best hotels serves locally sourced, beautifully presented food that might include roasted Kent partridge with fondant potato and cobnuts, or pan-fried local cod with cockle sauce (two courses £30, three courses £40). To make a real occasion of it arrive early for a pre-dinner drink in the cocktail bar, with its wonderful views out to sea. Daily 12.30–2pm & 7–9.45pm.

CITY CENTRE

Café Koba 135 Western Rd, BN1 2LA ☎ 01273 720059, ⓦ koba-uk.com; map pp.254–255. By day a buzzy café, by night a low-lit cocktail bar and bistro, this three-level place on busy Western Rd manages to cover all the bases. Drop in first-thing for coffee and crumpets with blackberry

butter, or stop by later for well-executed bistro fare – salads, burgers, steaks, fishcakes and the like (£7–14). Sundays see award-winning roasts added to the menu, featuring lamb shank, pork belly and sirloin steak (£12.50). And the cocktails are ace, too. Café Mon–Fri 8am–5.30pm, Sat 8am–6.30pm, Sun 10am–7pm; bar and bistro Mon–Wed 6–11pm, Thurs 6pm–midnight, Fri 6pm–late, Sat 7pm–late, Sun (bar only) 7–11pm.

Gingerman 21A Norfolk Square, BN1 2PD ☎ 01273 326688, ⓦ gingermanrestaurant.com; map pp.254–255. You can't spend long in Brighton without stumbling on one of the foodie outposts of the Ginger empire – there's a *Ginger Pig* in Hove, a *Ginger Dog* in Kemptown, and a *Ginger Fox* (see p.200) in nearby Albourne – but this one-room restaurant was where it all started. It still serves up some of the best food in Brighton: at lunch there's a weekly-changing short menu with a choice of two for each course (two or three courses £15/18; Tues–Sat), while at dinner the menu, and price tag, enlarges (two/three courses £30/35). Tues–Sun 12.30–2pm & 7–10pm.

THE LANES

Bar du Chocolat 27 Middle St, BN1 1AL ☎ 01273 732232, ⓦ choccywoccydoodah.com; map p.258. The café outpost of Choccywoccydoodah (see p.276) is every bit as decadent as the shop: gorge yourself on a feast of chocolatey delights – proper hot chocolate, milkshakes, cakes, chocolate dipping pots and sundaes – in the red-walled front room with its oversized tasselled lampshades hanging low over the tables, or in the opulent "choccywockyboudoir" out the back, where you'll be surrounded by extravagant murals of voluptuous nudes. Mon–Sat 10am–6pm, Sun 11am–5pm; sometimes closed for special functions.

Food for Friends 18 Prince Albert St, BN1 1HF ☎ 01273

BEST PLACES FOR …

Brunch *Bill's* (see opposite), *Café Coho* (see p.271), *Café Koba* (see above), *Mange Tout* (see p.270), *Plateau* (see opposite).

Afternoon tea *The Grand* (see p.266), *Metrodeco* (see p.270), *Mock Turtle* (see opposite), *Tea Cosy Tea Rooms* (see p.270), *Terre-à-Terre* (see opposite), *Treacle & Co* (see p.270).

Quirky Brighton *Bom-Bane's* (see p.270), *Marwood* (see p.271), *Metrodeco* (see p.270), *Tea Cosy Tea Rooms* (see p.270).

Treating yourself *Chilli Pickle* (see opposite), *Gingerman* (see above), *The Restaurant at Drakes* (see above), *Riddle and Finns* (see opposite).

Veggies *Food for Friends* (see above), *Iydea* (see opposite), *Terre-à-Terre* (see opposite).

202310, ⓦfoodforfriends.com; map p.258. Brighton's original vegetarian restaurant has been going strong for over thirty years, though it's come a long way from its original cheap-and-cheerful hippie roots: today it pulls in the crowds for its sophisticated, seasonal veggie cooking, which is imaginative enough to please die-hard meat-eaters too. Mains such as spicy Asian tofu salad, or Portobello mushroom with feta and tomato stuffing served on roast onion *boulangère*, cost £12–14, less at lunch, or there's a seasonal, three-course set menu for £20. Mon–Thurs & Sun noon–1pm, Fri & Sat noon–10.30pm.

Mock Turtle 4 Pool Valley, BN1 1NJ ☎01273 327380; map p.258. If you're after an antidote to Brighton's hip coffee shops, look no further than this old-fashioned teashop, which has been here for donkey's years and is always packed to the rafters. The traditional menu offers loose-leaf teas, inexpensive home-made cakes, giant doughnuts filled with home-made jam, and an excellent cream tea featuring amply proportioned scones, served warm with lashings of cream. Tues–Sun 9am–6pm.

Plateau 1 Bartholomews, BN1 1HG ☎01273 733085, ⓦfacebook.com/plateaubrighton; map p.258. "Wine, beats and bites" is the tagline of this buzzy, laidback little restaurant-cum-wine-bar just opposite the Town Hall. There's a good selection of classic cocktails (£7 and up), organic beers and organic and biodynamic wines (some from Sussex producers) running alongside a well-executed, inventive menu which includes sharing platters (the "plateau" of the name; £14/15) of charcuterie and fish, small "bites" (ranging from black pudding with pickles, to seared scallops; £5–8), and bigger *plats* (from £11), allowing you to drop in for a glass of wine and a nibble or settle down for a full three-course feast. Mon–Thurs 9am–10pm, Fri & Sat 9am–11pm, Sun 10am–11pm.

★ **Riddle and Finns** 12B Meeting House Lane, BN1 1HB ☎01273 328008, ⓦriddleandfinns.co.uk; map p.258. This bustling champagne and oyster bar has established itself as one of the city's most popular restaurants. As well as oysters (served with a choice of ten hot and cold sauces) there's a huge range of shellfish and fish on offer (mains £12–18), served at communal marble-topped tables in a white-tiled, candlelit dining room. It's very popular, and they don't take bookings, so expect a wait at busy times. Mon–Thurs & Sun noon–10pm, Fri & Sat noon–11pm, plus Sat & Sun 9–11.30am.

★ **Terre-à-Terre** 71 East St, BN1 1HQ ☎01273 729051, ⓦterreaterre.co.uk; map p.258. One of the best vegetarian restaurants in the country, this multi-award-winning place is famed for its fabulously inventive global veggie cuisine (mains around £14/15). The taster tapas plate for two (£23) is a good place to start if you're befuddled by the weird and wonderful creations on offer, everything from Black Bean Cellophane Frisbee to Arepas Chilli Candy. The imaginative afternoon tea (3–6pm) is also worth a special mention: £10

buys you a platter of creative puds and treats accompanied by tea, coffee or lashings of ginger beer. Mon–Fri noon–10.30pm, Sat 11am–11pm, Sun 11am–10pm.

Yum Yum Ninja 15–18 Meeting House Lane, BN1 1HB ☎01273 326330, ⓦyumyumninja.com; map p.258. Pan Asian tapas is the thing at this sleek, slick restaurant. Start off with a glass of sake or an Asian-inspired cocktail at the glamorous blue-lit *izakaya* (bar) upstairs, and then head down to take a seat at one of the communal benches in the restaurant, or at a table in the courtyard hung with glowing red Chinese lanterns. You could happily spend a small fortune, but if you stick to dim sum (£3–4) and the cheaper tapas (from £5.50) it's more affordable, and there are also good-value bento box meals (£10 Mon–Thurs until 7pm & Fri lunch) plus all-you-can-eat dim sum Sundays (£19.50). Mon–Thurs noon–10.30pm, Fri & Sat noon–11.30pm, Sun 1–9pm.

NORTH LAINE

Bill's The Depot, 100 North Rd, BN1 1YE ☎01273 692894, ⓦbills-website.co.uk; map p.258. Housed in an old bus depot, this cavernous café-restaurant – part of the *Bill's* empire which started in Lewes (see p.231) – is always heaving. Scrubbed wooden tables are surrounded by tall shelves lined with colourful jars of *Bill's* chutneys and jams, with blackboards chalked up with the day's specials. It's open from breakfast (one of the best in town) through to dinner, with mains (£8–12) ranging from fishfinger sandwiches to Thai green prawn curry. Mon–Sat 8am–11pm, Sun 9am–10.30pm.

★ **Chilli Pickle** 17 Jubilee St, BN1 1GE ☎01273 900383, ⓦthechillipickle.com; map p.258. You really can't go wrong with a meal at this stylish Indian restaurant in North Laine – recently voted one of the best restaurants in the country. The food is sophisticated, authentic and innovative: in the evenings you'll find everything from masala dosas to Chennai seafood stew on the menu (mains £9–17), while at lunchtimes it offers a range of thalis (£11–12), as well as small portions (£3.50–8) of utterly delicious street food for sharing. Daily noon–3pm & 6–10.30pm.

Cocoa 48 Queens Rd, BN1 3XB ☎01273 777412, ⓦcocoabrighton.co.uk; map p.258. This little French patisserie on scruffy Queens Rd isn't anything special in the interior design stakes, but no matter: it's the glorious patisserie creations of chef Julien Plumart – trained by Raymond Blanc – that take centre stage. Choose from exquisite tarts (£2.50–3.50), classic pastries or jewel-like macaroons, which come in over a dozen flavours (£1.25 each), with a new flavour added every week on "Macaron Friday". Mon–Fri 8am–7pm, Sat & Sun 8.30am–7pm.

Iydea 17 Kensington Gardens, BN1 4AL ☎01273 667992, ⓦiydea.co.uk; map p.258. The idea at *Iydea* is good-value, wholesome and delicious veggie food served up cafeteria-style, and it's certainly been a popular one, with the café picking up several awards and plenty of loyal

7

custom. What's on offer changes every day, but there tends to always be a quiche, a lasagne, a curry and enchiladas, alongside half a dozen other dishes; pick one main, add two vegetable dishes or salads, and two toppings and you're away (£4.70–7.70). Mon–Thurs 9am–4.30pm, Fri & Sat 9am–5pm, Sun 9.30am–4.30pm.

La Choza 36 Gloucester Rd, BN1 4AQ ☎01273 945926, ⓦlachoza.co.uk; map p.258. Step into this fab little Mexican street-food restaurant and you're greeted by a colourful riot of pink walls, jewelled skulls, Mexican wrestling masks and seats covered in vivid floral vinyl. The food is equally cheering, with snacks (around the £5–6) ranging from calamari with lime and chipotle mayo to slow-cooked beef and pit-smoked pulled pork. Burritos, quesadillas and tostadas (£5–7) can be washed down with a mean margarita. Tues & Wed 11.30am–6pm, Thurs–Sat 11.30am–9.30pm, Sun 11.30am–4.30pm.

Mange Tout 81 Trafalgar St, BN1 4EB ☎01273 607270; map p.258. There's a lovely relaxed vibe at this classic bistro, which has big windows, pot plants, and a steady stream of regulars stopping by. The menu features French classics – *escargots*, *moules*, *tartines* and *l'entrecôte* (£5.50–17) – alongside sharing platters and a long list of specials chalked up on the board, perhaps seared venison with black cabbage, or halibut with crispy fishcake and braised fennel. It's a popular spot for brunch, with breakfast served until the eminently civilized hour of 4pm. Mon–Wed & Sun 9am–6pm, Thurs–Sat 9am–9.30pm.

HOVE

Foragers 3 Stirling Place, BN3 3YU ☎01273 733134, ⓦtheforagerspub.co.uk; map pp.254–255. Relaxed and unpretentious, this pub on a quiet Hove side-street is both a proper, friendly local and an award-winning foodie hotspot. The food, as the pub's name suggests, is ultra seasonal and local, with greens and herbs foraged locally, and meat and fish sourced from Sussex and Kent suppliers. Mains are around £12–15, or there's an excellent-value £12 for two courses deal at lunch (not Sun) and during the evening Mon–Wed. Mon–Thurs & Sun noon–11pm, Fri & Sat noon–midnight; food served Mon–Fri noon–3pm & 6–10pm, Sat noon–4pm & 6–10pm, Sun noon–4pm.

★ **Treacle & Co** 164 Church Rd, BN3 2DL ☎01273 933695, ⓦtreacleandco.co.uk; map pp.254–255. This lovely little café is a mishmash of quirky, eclectic style – antique mirrors hang on utilitarian tiled walls, and flowers in milk bottles sit next to plastic animal lamps. There's a simple menu (welsh rarebit, pies, sandwiches and the like), but the main draw are the stupendously good cakes and tarts, all baked here, and piled high on a wooden counter – everything from meringues the size of melons to multi-storey cream-laden confections, gooey salt caramel tarts and (equally good) gluten-free loaf cakes. Mon–Fri 8.30am–5.30pm, Sat 9am–5.30pm, Sun noon–5pm.

KEMPTOWN AND HANOVER

★ **Bom-Bane's** 24 George St, BN2 1RH ☎01273 606400, ⓦbom-banes.co.uk; map pp.254–255. Fabulous, eccentric café-restaurant run by musician Jane Bom-Bane, a model of whom graces the exterior of the building wearing one of her extraordinary mechanical hats. The decor is decidedly quirky, with each of the tables – from the TurnTable to the Twenty Seven Chimes Table – holding a surprise in store. Food runs from salads and sandwiches to the trademark *stoemp* (Belgian mash) and sausage (£10.25), plus there are film (Wed) and occasional live music (Tues & Thurs) nights. Tues 5–11pm, Wed–Sat 12.30–11.30pm.

The Cuthbert 136 Freshfield Rd, BN2 0BR ☎01273 699693, ⓦthecuthbertpubandkitchen.co.uk; map pp.254–255. The food at this gastropub is a real cut above. Lunch and dinner mains (£10–16) might include roast venison or Moroccan spiced lamb pie, plus there's a weekday set lunch menu, which at £14 for two courses plus a glass of wine or a pint is a steal. The pub's very child friendly, with a children's menu (£5), and there's a large garden – a rarity in Brighton. Mon–Sun 11.30am–11pm; food served Mon–Sat noon–3pm & 6–10pm, Sun noon–4.30pm.

Metrodeco 38 Upper St James's St, BN2 1JN ⓦmetrodeco.com; map pp.254–255. This self-styled 1930s Parisian-style tearoom is a real one-off: you drink your tea (over 20 blends) amid elegant Art Deco and twentieth-century furniture, most of which is for sale; there's also a showroom downstairs. It's built up a reputation, too, for its canine-friendliness, and has hosted all sorts of doggie events, from tea parties to dog weddings. Even if you're not an Art Deco loving dog owner it's still a great spot, with top breakfasts, lunches, and afternoon teas featuring dainty sandwiches, scones and fancies (£16 Mon–Fri, £18 weekend). Daily 9.30am–6.30pm.

Sam's of Brighton 1 Paston Place, BN2 1HA ☎01273 676222, ⓦsamsofbrighton.co.uk; map pp.254–255. This cosy bistro has a loyal following for its friendliness and consistently excellent food – the menu changes daily, but might include Southdown lamb rump with spiced aubergine, or South Coast fish risotto (mains £12–18); at lunch or early evening there's an excellent-value set menu (two courses £12.50, three for £15; Tues–Sat noon–3pm & Tues–Fri 6–7pm). Tues–Fri noon–3pm & 6–10pm, Sat 10am–3pm & 6–10.30pm, Sun 10am–4pm.

Tea Cosy Tea Rooms 3 George St ⓦtheteacosy.co.uk; map pp.254–255. Taking quirky to a whole new level, this kitsch tearoom is decked from head to foot in royal memorabilia, and serves afternoon teas named after members of the royal family: opt for the Prince Harry Tea and you'll get boiled eggs and soldiers (£4), or you could go the whole hog and order the Queen Elizabeth Coronation High Tea (£24). A strict code of etiquette forbids the dunking of biscuits on pain of removal from the premises. Cash only. Wed–Fri & Sun noon–5pm, Sat noon–6pm.

COFFEE CULTURE: BRIGHTON'S BEST COFFEE SHOPS

Brighton has properly embraced coffee culture and you don't need to go far to find an independent café serving a seriously good cup of coffee. We list some of the best below.

CITY CENTRE

Mr Wolfe 15 Montpelier Place, BN1 3BF ⓦmrwolfe .co.uk; map pp.254–255. A bit of a hidden gem, there are just a handful of tables in this tiny, perfectly formed coffee shop, with charcoal-painted floors and walls. Excellent Monmouth coffee is available to drink in or take away, alongside own-baked cakes and delicious sandwiches and toasties made from artisan bread. Mon–Fri 8am–5pm, Sat 9am–5pm, Sun 10am–5pm.

THE LANES

Café Coho 53 Ship St, BN1 1AF ☎01273 747777, ⓦcafecoho.co.uk; map p.258. This award-winning coffee shop and café looks a treat – stone floors, an exposed brick wall and a long wooden counter piled high with pastries and deli-style sandwiches. The coffee is Union's Revelation blend, and excellent; the café's also licensed, so you can accompany your breakfast eggs Benedict with a Bloody Mary. At the weekend the café stays open late serving tapas, and cheese and charcuterie plates. Mon–Thurs 8am–6.30pm, Fri 8am–late, Sat 9am–late, Sun 9am–6.30pm.

Marwood 52 Ship St BN1 1AF ☎01273 382063, ⓦthemarwood.com; map p.258. A real one-off, this relaxed coffee shop's eclectic, cluttered decor includes Action Men abseiling from the ceiling and a jumble of skateboards, cassette decks, framed photos and a stuffed cat decorating the walls. The coffee (Mozzo) is "kick arse", plus there are great cakes and a simple menu (mains around £7) that runs from hangover breakfast burritos to "Kenn Dodds Dads Dogs Dinner". Mon & Tues 8am–8pm, Wed–Fri 8am–11pm, Sat 9am–11pm, Sun 10am–8pm.

NORTH LAINE

Bread and Milk 82 Trafalgar St, BN1 4EB ☎01273 674432, ⓦbreadandmilk.co.uk; map p.258. White tiled walls and industrial-style light fittings greet you at this beautifully styled coffee shop, which has a few tables inside, plus a bench outside for sunny-day people-watching. The coffee is 100 percent arabica, plus there are good-value toasted sandwiches and pitta pockets, to eat-in or take-away. Mon–Fri 7am–6pm, Sat 8am–6pm, Sun 9am–5pm.

Coffee@33 33 Trafalgar St, BN1 4ED; map p.258. This small, friendly, white-walls-and-bare-boards coffee shop has just a handful of seats – grab a spot by the window seat, with its coffee bean sack cushions, and enjoy what's regularly described as some of the best coffee in the city; Monmouth and changing guest blends feature, alongside home-made sandwiches, flapjacks and pastries. Mon–Fri 7.30am–6pm, Sat 9am–6pm, Sun 10am–5pm.

Small Batch Coffee 17 Jubilee St, BN1 1GE ☎01273 697597, ⓦsmallbatchcoffee.co.uk; map p.258. With its own roastery in Hove, this Brighton-based coffee chain has one up on its competitors. There are five branches around the city but the sleek flagship shop is here, in the ground floor of *Myhotel*. Coffee lovers can choose from espresso, cold-brew (brewed for five hours to create a delicate flavour), pour-over (filter), or a brewed coffee at the syphon bar. Beans change seasonally. Mon–Sat 7am–7pm, Sun 8am–6pm.

Taylor St Baristas 130 Queens Rd, BN1 3WB ☎01273 735466, ⓦtaylor-st.com; map p.258. This laidback Antipodean-owned coffee shop – with branches around the country – really knows its stuff: their bespoke Rogue espresso blend changes seasonally, plus there's a weekly changing guest espresso and guest filter coffee. Tasting notes are chalked up on the blackboard, and you can opt for espresso, pour-over or Aeropress. It's also a good spot for brunch (served till 3pm) or lunch (mains all around the £6 mark). Mon–Fri 7.30am–5.30pm, Sat 8am–5.30pm, Sun 10am–5pm.

KEMPTOWN

Ground Coffee House 36 St Georges Rd, BN2 1ED & 84 Church Rd, Hove, BN3 2EB ☎01273 696 441, ⓦgroundcoffeehouses.com; map pp.254–255. This excellent coffee shop – featuring cork ceiling, wooden floor, arty magazines, eclectic music, and a stylish wooden counter piled high with sandwiches, cakes and pastries – operates an ethical direct-trade model, and serves up some of the finest coffee in the city; the house blend is Union, but they also use Square Mile, Extracts and Origin. Mon–Fri 7am–6pm, Sat 8am–6pm, Sun 8am–5pm.

Redroaster 1D St James's St, BN2 1RE ☎01273 686668, ⓦredroaster.co.uk; map p.258. At the bottom end of St James's St, this refreshingly plain and slightly scruffy coffee house was one of the first to fly the coffee flag in the city. They have an in-house micro-roastery where they roast all their own beans, and serve over twenty different cups of coffee, from the usual lattes and espressos to *bombóns* (espresso layered over condensed milk). The properly thick hot chocolate is legendary. Mon–Sat 7am–7pm, Sun 8am–6.30pm.

7

GLORIOUS GELATO

Happily for ice-cream lovers, a couple of top-class *gelaterias* have opened in Brighton in the last few years. With flavours such as Pier Doughnut, Liquorice, and Bacon and Maple Syrup just begging to be tasted, there's simply no excuse for spending money on an inferior soft scoop.

Boho Gelato 6 Pool Valley, BN1 1NJ ☎01273 727205; map p.258. Join the queue and try out one of the 24 weird and wonderful ever-changing flavours at this wonderful little *gelateria*. The *gelato* is all made on-site, and in the past has included Brighton Rock, Gorgonzola and Rosemary, Squirrel Nuts and Bourbon and Bourbon (biscuits and whiskey). Daily 11.30am–7/8pm in summer, 5.30pm in winter.

Gelato Gusto 2 Gardner St, BN1 1UP ☎01273 673402, ⓦgelatogusto.com; map p.258. The flavours aren't as wacky here, but the ice cream's just as good: flavours change regularly, but might include Sea Salt Caramel or Arundel Ales Sussex Gold *sorbetto*, alongside the classics. There are a few tables, where you can enjoy fantastic sundaes. Mon–Fri 11.30am–6.30pm, Sat 11am–6.30pm, Sun 11am–6pm.

DRINKING

7

Brighton has an illustrious history of catering to drinkers and partygoers: in 1860 the town boasted 479 **pubs** and **beer shops** – more than the combined number of all the other local shops. Though drinking establishments no longer make up the majority of the town's businesses, the perfect venue and tipple can still be found for all comers, from traditional boozers to quirky indie hangouts, and sleek and chic **cocktail bars**.

THE SEAFRONT

OHSO Social 250A King's Road Arches, BN1 1NB ☎01273 746067, ⓦohsosocial.co.uk; map p.258. The main draw of this beachfront bar is the fantastic location; tucked in next to the pier, it has great views from its large open-air terrace. Though alfresco eating and drinking is what this bar is all about, the interior decor is cool, with illuminated signs on the wall and diner-esque leather booths. Mon–Thurs 10am–late, Fri–Sun 10am–2am.

CITY CENTRE

★ **Craft Beer Co.** 22–23 Upper North St, BN1 3FG ⓦthecraftbeerco.com; map pp.254–255. A must for beer aficionados, this pub boasts an incredible range of nine cask ales changing daily, 21 keg taps dispensing beer from around the world, and 200 bottled varieties on offer at any one time. Staff are super friendly, keen to talk about the beers, and offer free tasters. Prices can be on the high side, but their house Craft Pale Ale, brewed for them by Kent Brewery, is £2.95 a pint. Mon–Fri noon–11pm, Sat 11am–11pm, Sun noon–10.30pm.

★ **Lion and Lobster** 24 Sillwood St, BN1 2PS ☎01273 327299, ⓦthelionandlobster.co.uk; map pp.254–255. One of the best pubs in Brighton, the *Lion and Lobster* manages to pull off a series of impressive paradoxes. The framed prints and pictures, patterned carpet and velvet seats give the pub a traditional feel but the atmosphere is young and fun. Though usually busy, various booths offer privacy, and screens showing the football are visible from most seats, but don't dominate. Good food is served until late, and on Monday nights participants in the pub quiz are even served free pizza. Mon–Thurs 11am–1am, Fri & Sat 11am–2am, Sun 11am–midnight.

THE LANES

Cricketers 15 Black Lion St, BN1 1ND ☎01273 329472, ⓦcricketersbrighton.co.uk; map p.258. Brighton's oldest pub – all red velvet and gilt – has been immortalized both in print and on stage, in Graham Greene's *Brighton Rock*, and more recently in the National Theatre's *One Man Two Guv'nors*. Mon–Thurs 11am–midnight. Fri & Sat 11am–1am, Sun 11am–11pm.

Colonnade Bar 10 New Rd, BN1 1UF ☎01273 328728, ⓦgoldenliongroup.co.uk/bars-and-pubs/colonnade-bar; map p.258. Right next to the Theatre Royal, the *Colonnade Bar* has an appropriately traditional look, with plenty of tasselled velvet, and black-and-white headshots of actors who have graced the boards next door. "Willie", the 120-year-old automaton doffing his top hat, greets patrons from the window, and there's outdoor seating overlooking the Pavilion Gardens. Mon–Thurs noon–11pm, Fri & Sat noon–midnight, Sun noon–10.30pm.

Mash Tun 1 Church St, BN1 1UE ☎01273 684951; map p.258. This very popular student-y pub is often heaving, particularly at the weekend. The inside is fairly basic, but cool tunes, trendy bar staff and a "celebrity wall of death" sweepstake contribute to the young and lively atmosphere. The location is conveniently central, and drinks are quite reasonably priced. Standard pub food is served every day. Mon–Thurs & Sun noon–2am, Fri & Sat noon–3am.

Mesmerist 1–3 Prince Albert St, BN1 1HE ☎01273 328542, ⓦdrinkinbrighton.co.uk/mesmerist; map p.258. Describing itself as "a twenty-first-century gin palace", this large bar attracts a diverse clientele. Cheap drinks deals appeal to the younger punters, but the welcoming atmosphere brings in all ages, dancing to the classic rock'n'roll and swing tunes. Free entry makes it the perfect stopping point between bar and club – it's casual enough for a drink but dance-y enough to get the party started. Live music events are often held during the week. Mon–Thurs & Sun noon–1am, Fri & Sat noon–2am.

Northern Lights 6 Little East St, BN1 1HT ☎01273 747096, ⓦnorthernlightsbrighton.co.uk; map p.258. This cosy, laidback bar is a real Brighton institution. The Scandinavian theme is very apparent in the drinks and food: there are over twenty flavoured vodkas (including an amazing tar flavour), plus aquavit and a selection of Swedish flavoured ciders, plus a menu featuring reindeer and herring. Mon–Thurs 5pm–midnight, Fri 3pm–2am, Sat noon–2am, Sun 3pm–midnight.

Oki Nami 6 New Rd, BN1 1UF ☎01273 773777, ⓦokinami.com; map p.258. This cocktail bar is the upstairs part of an establishment also housing a Japanese restaurant, co-owned by Norman Cook (aka Fatboy Slim). Consisting of a single small room and balcony overlooking New Road, the draw is the interesting cocktails list (many £3.50 5–8pm) and the excellent people-watching. Bar snacks come from the kitchen downstairs, so you can nibble on sushi or prawn crackers with your cocktail. Mon–Thurs & Sun 5pm–midnight, Fri & Sat 5pm–1am.

NORTH LAINE

Basketmakers Arms 12 Gloucester Rd, BN1 4AD ☎01273 689006, ⓦbasket-makers-brighton.co.uk; map p.258. A cosy, traditional boozer, serving a wide selection of real ales. Vintage ephemera cover the walls, including a selection of tin boxes – open them to find hidden messages from previous punters inside. The only downside is that the pub is more popular than it is spacious; at the weekend it can be difficult to find a seat. Mon–Thurs & Sun 11am–11pm, Fri & Sat 11am–midnight.

Great Eastern 103 Trafalgar St, BN1 4ER ☎01273 685681; map p.258. This cosy pub at the bottom of Trafalgar St eschews TV screens and fruit machines in favour of bookshelves stocked with well-thumbed books and board games. The wooden furniture and bare boards create a cosy feel, accentuated by candlelight in the evenings. The Sunday roast and the impressive array of whiskies on offer make it a local fave. Mon–Thurs & Sun noon–midnight, Fri & Sat noon–1am.

HOVE

Bee's Mouth 10 Western Rd, BN3 1AE ☎01273 770083; map pp.254–255. Stepping into this dimly-lit, surreal pub midway along Western Rd is a little like falling down the rabbit hole. The well-stocked bar offers a fantastic range of bottled beers, including some unusual flavoured lagers. While floorspace is limited, the pub descends three floors and on any given night the subterranean levels host life-drawing classes and film nights, as well as a diverse schedule of live music (particularly jazz) and DJs. Mon–Thurs 4.30pm–1am, Fri 4.30pm–2am, Sat 3.30pm–2am, Sun 3.30pm–1am.

Robin Hood 13 Norfolk Place, BN1 2FP ☎01273 325645; map pp.254–255. Not accidentally named, this fab place just off Western Rd is Britain's first not-for-profit pub: after staff and overheads have been paid, all profits go to charities and local causes. Not only is the establishment run on such heartwarming principles, it's a lovely, cosy pub in-and-of itself. There's a great range of drinks, from ales to flavoured vodkas, a pianist plays every Sunday afternoon and there's a large selection of board games to play. Tasty, reasonably priced home-made pizza is served all day. Mon–Thurs & Sun noon–11pm, Fri & Sat noon–1am.

KEMPTOWN AND HANOVER

Black Dove 74 St James's St, BN2 1PA ☎01273 671119, ⓦblackdovebrighton.com; map pp.254–255. This trendy, justifiably popular bar at the top of St James's St has a cool, speakeasy vibe, with lots of dark wood and antiques, plus a decent cocktail list and a wide selection of bottled beers and ciders. The downstairs lounge feels like an opium den with palm-frond fans and very low lighting. On Fridays and Saturdays DJs play tunes that run from soul to rock'n'roll, roots, jazz and afrobeats. Mon–Thurs 4pm–midnight, Fri & Sat 4pm–1am, Sun 4pm–11pm.

The Greys 105 Southover St, BN2 9US ☎01273 680734, ⓦgreyspub.com; map pp.254–255. There seems to be a pub on every street in this part of Hanover, but *The Greys* is particularly nice. During the day the chilled-out atmosphere and cosy decor make it feel like you've stumbled into Hanover's communal living room, with locals chatting to one another. In the evenings the pub often plays host to various talks, comedy and musical events, with a particular emphasis on country, bluegrass and Americana; check their website for listings. Mon–Wed 4–11pm, Thurs 4–11.30pm, Fri 4pm–12.30am, Sat noon–12.30am, Sun noon–11pm.

Hand in Hand 33 Upper St James's St, BN2 1JN ☎01273 699595; map pp.254–255. This tiny, eccentric brew-pub is the downstairs room of a yellow-and-red building which also houses the Kemptown Brewery (established in 1989). The ale made upstairs is sold downstairs, along with a wide selection of other interesting beers. A handwritten newsletter informs customers of the musical events being held throughout the month. Mon–Sat noon–midnight, Sun noon–11.30pm.

Setting Sun 1 Windmill St, BN2 0GN ☎01273 626192; map pp.254–255. The name of this hilltop pub sums up what makes it such a popular destination, in spite of the hike required to reach it. It has fantastic views over Brighton – particularly impressive at sunset – which can be enjoyed from the decking in warm weather or from the conservatory in winter. Inside is relaxed and understated, with lots of bare wood and candlelight; there's also good-value food (mains £9–14). Mon–Wed & Sun noon–11pm, Thurs–Sat noon–midnight.

7

The Sidewinder 65 St James's St, BN2 1JN ☎01273 679927, ⓦdrinkinbrighton.co.uk/sidewinder; map pp.254–255. This large, comfortable pub has a lot going for it, not least the two enormous beer gardens. During the day the atmosphere is relaxed, while several evenings a week the pub hosts DJs, and at the weekends the atmosphere gets particularly lively. Mon–Thurs & Sun noon–1am, Fri & Sat noon–2am.

Three and Ten 10 Steine St, BN2 1TE ☎01273 609777, ⓦthreeandten.co.uk; map p.258.This titchy pub, and theatre venue (see opposite), tucked away near the bottom of St James's St isn't very easy to find, but is worth seeking out. The ground floor houses the pub part, decked out with a cosy, dark wood decor, wood fire and central bar. In winter it's particularly snug, and serves a selection of hot alcoholic drinks. Another big draw is the late opening hours, offering a more chilled out alternative to the rest of the area's bars and clubs. Mon–Thurs & Sun 4pm–1am, Fri & Sat 4pm–3am.

CLUBS AND LIVE MUSIC

Brighton is renowned for its vibrant nightlife which, reflecting the city's personality, comes in various flavours. From the kiss-me-quick, stag and hen, messy hedonism of West St, right through to a flourishing alternative and live music scene, the party never stops. Many clubs are concentrated in the arches along the **Lower Esplanade beachfront**, which offers dependable, mainstream clubbing, but some of the more interesting nights are in small, quirky venues throughout the city.

THE SEAFRONT

Audio 10 Marine Parade, BN2 1TL ☎01273 606 906, ⓦaudiobrighton.com; map pp.254–255. Trendy seafront venue set on two floors. Watch the sunset from the laidback, upstairs cocktail bar and terrace, then move downstairs to the small, unpretentious club. The broad range of nights cover rock and indie, hip-hop, drum'n'bass, house, techno and more. Entry £3–8; free before midnight on Sat.

Concorde 2 Madeira Shelter Hall, Madeira Drive, BN2 1EN ☎01273 673311, ⓦconcorde2.co.uk; map pp.254–255. It's worth the walk along the seafront to get to this slightly out-of-the-way live venue and club. Housed in a high-ceilinged Victorian building, it feels intimate but not cramped, and has a much better atmosphere than the city's larger live venues. The line-up ranges from big-name live acts, to up-and-coming musicians and varied club nights.

Digital 187–193 King's Road Arches, BN1 1NB ☎01273 227767, ⓦyourfutureisdigital.com; map p.258. The first-rate sound and lighting system at this mid-sized seafront club no doubt helps its pulling power, frequently attracting big-name DJs, particularly at weekends. Midweek nights offer reliable, student-y fun, covering r'n'b, indie and electro. Drinks prices are moderate. Entry £1–15.

Funfair 12–15 King's Rd, BN1 1 NE ☎01273 757447; map p.258.This kitsch, vintage funfair-themed club has a lot of fun quirks, including a ball pit, seaside face holes, distortion mirrors and themed booths available for private hire. Exotic performers such as snake charmers and sword swallowers entertain punters, and the music is a fun, accessible mix of Motown, rock'n'roll, soul, pop, disco and 90s. Entry £5–7.

Life 159–161 King's Road Arches, BN1 1NB ☎01273 770505, ⓦlifebrighton.com; map p.258. Another seafront venue that morphs from its daytime guise as a chilled-out beach bar to a popular nightclub. A mix of electro, r'n'b and commercial bass, plus inexpensive door prices, attract a young clientele. Entry free–£8.

Volks 3 The Colonnade, Madeira Drive, BN2 1PS ☎01273 682828, ⓦvolksclub.co.uk; map pp.254–255. This small, long-running club peddles all things bass, with a schedule chock-full of dubstep, drum'n'bass, reggae, jungle and breaks. The venue is appropriately dark and sweaty, and has some of the latest opening hours of any Brighton clubs, often keeping the party going until 7am. Entry £3–8.

THE LANES

Casablanca Jazz Club 3 Middle St, BN1 1AL ☎01273 321817, ⓦcasablancajazzclub.com; map p.258. Established in 1980, this Brighton stalwart has ensured its longevity with a dependable mix of jazz, funk, latin and disco, washed down with cheap drinks. Head downstairs for live bands and to salsa 'til you sweat. Entry £3–7.

Haunt 10 Pool Valley, BN1 1NJ ⓦthehauntbrighton .co.uk; map p.258. Set in a converted booth, this club and music venue is a great space, with a dancefloor and raised stage overlooked by a balcony. Club nights are on-trend electro and indie, and retro 80s and 90s. Also regularly hosts up-and-coming live acts. Club entry £3–6, gigs vary.

NORTH LAINE AND AROUND

Blind Tiger 52–54 Grand Parade, BN2 9QA ⓦplay groupbrighton.org; map p.258. Smallish café-bar/live venue with a laidback artsy vibe. Run by local event organizers Playgroup, whose stock-in-trade is madcap musical mischief and merriment, the venue maintains the festival feeling with live music and DJ nights ranging from funk, reggae, gypsy swing, spoken word and rock 'n' roll to jungle, folk and more.

★ **Green Door Store** Trafalgar Arches, Lower Goods Yard, BN1 4FQ ⓦthegreendoorstore.co.uk; map p.258. Hip young things dance the night away in this über-cool club and live music venue in the arches under the train station. Bare brickwork and an alternative array of music that covers anything from psych, blues, punk, rock'n'roll to powerdisco make it eye-wateringly trendy but still good fun. Best of all, the bar is always free entry. Gig entry varies.

The Hope 11 Queens Rd, BN1 3WA ☎01273 325793, Ⓦdrinkinbrighton.co.uk/hope; map p.258. This cool indie music pub – featuring Chesterfields, wooden tables and funky wallpaper – puts on free acoustic gigs in the bar, while upstairs a 100-person capacity venue showcases mainly rock and indie bands, and weekend club nights.

★ **Komedia** 44–47 Gardner St, BN1 1UN ☎0845 293 8480, Ⓦkomedia.co.uk/brighton/; map p.258. This top-notch arts venue (see below) also hosts live music and fun, unpretentious and frequently retro-themed club nights, playing rock'n'roll, 60s, and alternative 80s. Devoted punters of all ages turn up in era-appropriate attire. Club entry £4–6.

Prince Albert 48 Trafalgar St, BN1 4ED ☎01273 730499; map p.258. Another Brighton institution, this pub-cum-music venue is immediately recognizable from the Banksy kissing policemen and graffiti portrait commemorating John Peel emblazoned on the building's side wall. The ground floor is a spacious pub, while upstairs a small venue hosts alternative live acts of various stripes.

KEMPTOWN

Proud Cabaret Brighton 83 St Georges Rd, BN2 1EF ☎01273 605789, Ⓦbrightoncabaret.com; map pp.254–255. This ballroom venue takes its identity seriously, and following a lavish refurbishment, the interior feels suitably decadent, with glitzy chandeliers and a glass-domed ceiling. Evenings kick off with a dinner and cabaret show, before the tables are cleared away and the dancing commences. Dinner, show and club £34.50 (booking required); show and club £4; club only £2.

THEATRE, COMEDY AND CINEMA

The Basement 24 Kensington St, BN1 4AJ ☎01273 699733, Ⓦthebasement.uk.com. Quirky performance and theatre venue with an emphasis on the experimental, innovative and subversive. The regular Supper Club night contains a mix of performances that could include everything from music, art, poetry, comedy to video art, often involving audience interaction.

Brighton Dome 29 New Rd, BN1 1UG ☎01273 709709, Ⓦbrightondome.org. The Royal Pavilion's former stables is home to three venues – Pavilion Theatre, Concert Hall and Corn Exchange – offering mainstream theatre, concerts, dance and performance.

Brighton Little Theatre 9 Clarence Gardens, BN1 2EG ☎01273 777748, Ⓦbrightonlittletheatre.com. Amateur theatre company that's been going since 1940 and stages around a dozen productions a year at its little 71 seat theatre.

★ **Duke of Yorks Picturehouse** Preston Circus, BN1 4NA ☎0871 704 2056, Ⓦpicturehouses.co.uk. Grade II-listed cinema – one of the oldest still-functioning cinemas in the country, opened in 1910 – with buckets of character, velvet seats and a licensed bar. The programme is a great mix of art-house, independent and classic films, alongside live streamed opera and ballet, all-nighters and themed evenings.

★ **Komedia** 44–47 Gardner St, BN1 1UN ☎0845 293 8480, Ⓦkomedia.co.uk/brighton/. A Brighton institution set across three floors, this fantastic arts venue hosts comedy, cabaret and spoken word events, as well as live music and club nights (see above). The Duke of York's cinema (see above) has three screens upstairs.

New Venture Theatre Bedford Place, BN1 2PT ☎01273 746118, Ⓦnewventure.org.uk. Community theatre that's been going for over sixty years, putting on amateur productions of popular dramas and original work.

Nightingale Theatre 29–30 Surrey St, above Grand Central Bar by Brighton station, BN1 3PA Ⓦ01273 702563, Ⓦnightingaletheatre.co.uk. Well-regarded venue offering an eclectic programme of theatre, talks and readings, installations, music, cabaret and dance in the intimate surrounds of the station's old hotel.

The Old Market (TOM) 11A Upper Market St, Hove, BN3 1AS ☎01273 201801, Ⓦtheoldmarket.com. Theatre, comedy, live music and cabaret all feature on the programme of this stylish performing arts venue and exhibition space on the borders of Hove.

Theatre Royal New Rd, BN1 1SD ☎01273 764400, Ⓦambassadortickets.com/theatreroyal. One of the oldest working theatres in the country, offering predominantly mainstream plays, opera and musicals.

Upstairs at Three and Ten 10 Steine St, BN2 1TE ☎07800 983290, Ⓦupstairsatthreeandten.co.uk. Tiny venue hosting live music, innovative theatre and regular comedy nights.

SHOPPING

Brighton's a great shopping destination, with plenty of interesting independent shops. The places to head for are the **Lanes** and (especially) **North Laine** (Ⓦnorthlaine.co.uk), though for antiques shops you'll need to head out to **Kemptown**, where a wander along the main drag – which changes name from Upper St James's St to Bristol Rd to St Georges Rd – will uncover lots of gems; pick up a copy of the *Antiques in Kemptown* leaflet and map. For work by some of Brighton's thriving population of artists and makers, there are galleries scattered throughout town but the best– and most fun – time to buy is during the biannual **Artists Open Houses** events (May & Dec; Ⓦaoh.org.uk), when you can visit the artists in their homes. Brighton's high-street chains are around **Churchill Square**, with higher-end chains concentrated on **East St** at the bottom end of the Lanes.

7

7

THE SEAFRONT

★ **Castor and Pollux** 165 King's Road Arches, Lower Promenade, BN1 1NB ☎01273 773776, ⓦcastor andpollux.co.uk; map p.258. This great beachfront gallery sells limited edition prints (by Rob Ryan, Mark Hearld, Angie Lewin and others), alongside posters, art and design books, jewellery, pottery, stationery and more – a positive treasure-trove of cool, covetable decorative items. Hours vary but generally summer daily 10am–6pm; winter Sat & Sun 11am–4pm; closed Jan.

THE LANES AND AROUND

Choccywoccydoodah 24 Duke St, BN1 1AG ☎01273 329462, ⓦchoccywoccydoodah.com; map p.258. Make sure you check out the seasonally changing window display of this fantastic chocolaterie, whose fantastical creations – cakes shaped like fairytale castles, mermaids or giant stags – are all made from solid chocolate. Inside you can buy smaller-scale chocolatey treats. Down the road at no. 15 there's another great Sussex chocolate company, Montezumas. Mon–Sat 10am–6pm, Sun 11am–5pm.

Jeremy Hoye 22A Ship St, ☎0845 094 3175, ⓦjeremy -hoye.com; map p.258. A favourite of the fashion press, this contemporary jeweller has an impressive following for its silver charms, which feature Brighton landmarks among them – a deckchair, Brighton Pavilion and more (from £50). Mon–Sat 10am–6pm, Sun 11am–5pm.

Lanes Gallery 32 Meeting House Lane, BN1 1HB ☎01273 734347, ⓦthelanesgallery.co.uk; map p.258. This lovely little gallery sells paintings and prints alongside ceramics, jewellery, cushions and other crafts. Mon–Sat 10.30am–5pm, Sun 11am–4pm.

She Said 11 Ship St Gardens, BN1 1AJ ☎01273 777811, ⓦshesaidboutique.com; map p.258. As you'd expect from the home of the dirty weekend, Brighton has its fair share of erotic emporiums, but this one, tucked away on a quiet, non-seedy side street, is a touch above the rest: it's even been featured in *Vogue*. The ground floor is largely devoted to lacey undies and silk corsets, with the saucier stuff kept downstairs. Mon & Sun noon–5pm, Tues–Sat 11am–6pm.

NORTH LAINE

Bert's Homestore 10 Kensington Gardens, BN1 4AL ☎01273 675 536; map p.258; 155–156 Western Rd, BN1 2DA ☎01273 774212; map pp.254–255; 33 George St, Hove, BN3 3YB ☎01273 732 770; map pp.254–255; ⓦbertshomestore.co.uk. Fabulous kitchenware and homeware, featuring polka dots, floral prints and bright primary colours. Mon–Sat 9–6pm, Sun 11am–5pm.

Hope and Harlequin 31 Sydney St, BN1 4EP ☎01273 675222, ⓦhopeandharlequin.com; map p.258. This beautifully presented vintage shop has the feel of an upmarket boutique, and stocks vintage clothing and modern collectables from the late 1800s to the 1970s,

though it's especially strong on the 1930s and '40s. Mon–Sat 10.30am–6pm, Sun 11am–5pm.

Infinity Foods 25 North Rd, BN1 1YA; map p.258. This organic vegetarian and vegan store – run as a workers' co-operative – has been going for over forty years, and sells seasonal fruit and veg, fresh bread (from the on-site bakery), natural bodycare products and more. Mon–Sat 9.30–6pm, Sun 11am–5pm.

Real Patisserie 43 Trafalgar St, BN1 4ED ☎01273 457019; map p.258; 34 St Georges Rd, Kemptown, BN2 1ED ☎01273 609655; map pp.254–255; 25 Western Rd, Hove, BN3 1AF ☎01273 457018; map pp.254–255; ⓦrealpatisserie.co.uk. Brighton-based bakery and patisserie – with three branches in the city – selling fantastic artisan bread, pastries and tarts. Trafalgar St Mon–Sat 7am–5.30pm; St Georges Rd Mon–Sat 7.30am–5.30pm; Western Rd Mon–Sun 8am–6pm.

Resident 28 Kensington Gardens, BN1 4AL ☎01273 606312, ⓦresident-music.com; map p.258. This award-winning independent record shop often has limited editions and indie exclusives, and also sells tickets for local venues. Mon–Sat 9am–6.30pm, Sun 10am–6pm.

★ **Snoopers Paradise** 7–8 Kensington Gardens, BN1 4AL ☎01273 602558; map p.258. This labyrinthine flea market, with its salmon-pink paintwork, is a Brighton institution, featuring ninety stalls over two floors, selling vintage clothes, furniture and jewellery, birdcages and old cameras. Mon–Sat 10–6pm, Sun 11am–4pm.

Ten Green Bottles 9 Jubilee St, BN1 1GE ☎01273 567176, ⓦtengreenbottles.com; map p.258. Pay £5 corkage and you can drink your bottle there and then in this cool little wine-shop-cum-bar, which has a great selection, including local Sussex fizz. It also sells wines by the glass and runs private wine-tasting events (£15/head). Mon & Tues 11am–10pm, Wed & Thurs 11am–11pm, Fri & Sat 11am–midnight, Sun noon–9pm.

To be Worn Again 12 Sydney St, BN1 4EN ☎01273 680296; 12 Kensington Gardens, BN1 4AL ☎01273 687811; ⓦtobewornagain.co.uk; map p.258. Brighton's biggest vintage and second hand clothing company, selling mainly 60s to 80s gear, has two shops in North Laine, both crammed with clothes and decked out with appropriately retro memorabilia. Mon–Sun 10am–6pm.

HOVE

City Books 23 Western Rd, BN3 1AF ☎01273 725306, ⓦcity-books.co.uk; map pp.254–255. Brighton's largest independent bookshop is a thriving and much-loved fixture in the city, organizing big-name literary talks and readings. Mon–Sat 9.30am–6pm, Sun 11am–4.30pm.

★ **I Gigi General Store** 31A Western Rd, BN3 1AF ☎01273 775257, ⓦigigigeneralstore.com; map pp.254–255. Beautifully styled little shop stocking homeware and gifts – pottery, hand-blown glassware, antique linen tablecloths, scented candles, bangles and more, all in muted, earthy shades. Upstairs there's an equally chic café, a serene space with floor-to-ceiling windows – great for a breather from shopping – while the stylish I Gigi Women's Boutique is a few doors along at no. 37. Mon–Sat 10am–5pm, Sun 11am–4.30pm.

La Cave à Fromage 34–35 Western Rd, BN3 1AF ☏01273 725500, ⓦla-cave.co.uk; map pp.254–255. There are over 200 cheeses – plus 30 types of cured meats and 50 wines – on sale at this cheese emporium. There are also a few tables where you can sit and feast on cheese platters (£10) and other *fromage*-focused delights. Mon & Tues 10am–7pm, Wed 10am–9pm, Thurs–Sat 10am–10pm, Sun 11am–6pm.

KEMPTOWN

Alex MacArthur 101 St Georges Rd, BN2 1EA ☏01273

607533, ⓦalexmacarthur.co.uk; map pp.254–255. Stylish antiques shop, with pieces spanning the centuries. The owner's four-storey Regency home, five minutes away, doubles as a private showroom, with every item for sale. Thurs–Sat 10.30am–5.30pm, or by appointment.

Brighton Flea Market 31A Upper St James's St, BN2 1JN ☏01273 624006, ⓦflea-markets.co.uk; map pp.254–255. The unmissable pink facade of this long-established flea market houses over a hundred stalls and cabinets on two levels, selling everything from furniture, bric-a-brac and jewellery to stuffed ferrets. Mon–Sat 10am–5.30pm, Sun 10.30am–5pm.

Kemptown Bookshop 91 St Georges Rd, BN2 1EE ☏01273 682110, ⓦkemptownbookshop.co.uk; map pp.254–255. Award-winning independent bookshop, with a good selection of cards, prints and book-related gifts. Mon–Sat 9am–5.30pm.

7

GAY BRIGHTON

As you would expect from a city as synonymous with gay life as Brighton, the nightlife here doesn't disappoint. Radiating outwards from St James's St in **Kemptown** the scene is surprisingly compact but varied. **Brighton Pride** (date varies each summer; ⓦpridebrighton.org) is an LGBT Pride parade and ticketed party in Preston Park. In recent years Pride has diversified to include more fringe theatre and cultural events alongside the alcohol-fuelled celebrations.

INFORMATION AND TOURS

Brighton and Hove LGBT Switchboard ⓦswitchboard.org.uk. Running since 1975, the switchboard provides information about the Brighton scene, support and advice and a counselling service.

GScene Magazine ⓦgscene.com. LGBT lifestyle, listings and community magazine for the local area.

Piers and Queers tour ☏07954 482112, ⓦonlyinbrighton.co.uk. Fun, illuminating 80min private walking tour for groups of 2–25, looking at the city's LGBT history, personalities and stories.

Zhoosh ⓦzhooshbrighton.co.uk. An online LGBTQ community, with events directory and community news.

BARS AND CLUBS

The Bulldog 31 St James's St, BN2 1RF ⓦbulldogbrighton .com; map pp.254–255. Unpretentious and earthy, Brighton's longest-running gay bar pulls off the difficult trick of being both cruisey and welcoming. With the best-value drinks prices on the scene, it's packed at weekends, and is popular as a post-club spot as it's open right through till morning. Mon–Wed 11am–2am, Thurs 11am–3am, Fri & Sat 11am–5.30am, Sun midday–2am.

Camelford Arms 30–31 Camelford St, BN2 1TQ ⓦcamelfordarmsbrighton.co.uk; map pp.254–255. This cosy community pub, with a welcoming atmosphere and excellent food, is a popular first-stop on weekends for a crowd that includes plenty of bears, otters and their admirers. Mon–Wed & Sun noon–11.30pm, Thurs noon–midnight, Fri & Sat noon–1am.

Legends 31–34 Marine Parade, BN2 1TR ⓦlegendsbrighton.com; map pp.254–255. Comprised of the ground-floor *Legends Bar* with terrace overlooking the sea, and the free-entry *Basement Club*, this venue has a friendly, mixed crowd. Downstairs the music runs from chart pop to dance; upstairs the bar hosts cabaret nights with local drag stars. Opening times vary; check website.

The Marlborough 4 Princes St, BN2 1RD ⓦdrinkinbrighton.co.uk/marlborough; map p.258. One of only a handful of lesbian venues on the scene, *The Marlborough* has a loyal clientele who enjoy the pub's pool table, popular bar menu, DJs every weekend and regular open-mic nights. Upstairs in the sixty-seat theatre, local LGBT company Pink Fringe regularly programme provocative and entertaining queer theatre and performance art.

Revenge 32–34 Old Steine, BN1 1EL ☏01273 606064, ⓦrevenge.co.uk; map p.258. A leading presence on the city's gay scene and a key player in Brighton Pride, with a young studenty crowd regularly packing out the two floors and roof terrace. Nights include foam parties and themed events around bank holidays. Weekly lesbian night Girls on Top is a particular highlight, with great pop from the club's DJs. Free entry–£10. Opening times vary; check website.

Subline 129 St James's St, BN2 1TH ⓦsublinebrighton .co.uk; map p.258. *Subline* is Brighton's only men-only cruise bar. Dark and subterranean, with industrial decor, the bar runs theme nights including leather, underwear-only and foam parties. Members only but you can join on your first visit (£10). Wed & Thurs 9pm–1.30am, Fri & Sat 9pm–4am, Sun 8pm–2am.

The West Sussex coast

WEST WITTERING BEACH

The West Sussex coast

The West Sussex coast, which stretches for 35 miles from the outskirts of Brighton west to Chichester Harbour, for the most part lacks the scenic splendours of the Downs that border it to the north, but rewards in other ways, with low-key seaside towns and quiet shingle beaches that are a refreshing antidote to the bustle of flamboyant Brighton. The undoubted highlight of the coastal plain is the Manhood Peninsula, particularly its western coastline, which abuts the beautiful estuarine landscapes of Chichester Harbour – the one part of the coast that really does hold its own scenically. To the north, the lovely cathedral city of Chichester makes the perfect base from which to explore it.

The easternmost stretch of coast, from Brighton to Bognor, is a more-or-less unbroken ribbon of development, with the fringes of one seaside town merging into another, and only the odd pocket here and there of undeveloped coastline holding off against the sprawl. First up is the low-key port and town of **Shoreham-by-Sea** on the banks of the River Adur, while further west lies a trio of seaside towns, part of a wave of resorts which grew up along the south coast in the eighteenth century, hoping to emulate the success of royally favoured Brighton. Sedate, humdrum **Worthing** is followed by spruced-up **Littlehampton**, by far the nicest of the bunch, with a great setting on the River Arun and two good beaches, each backed by a cool café. Brash buckets-and-Butlins resort **Bognor** lies eight miles further on. The **beaches** along this stretch are all pebbly, with sand at low tide; none see the crowds you get at Brighton, and at their best – at the nature reserves at Shoreham-by-Sea, Littlehampton's West Beach and nearby Climping – they possess a wild, windswept beauty, with rare vegetated shingle that bursts into flower in summer.

Just west of Bognor lies the flat **Manhood Peninsula**, with the beautiful creeks and tidal mudflats of **Chichester Harbour** on its far western edge. There are plenty of opportunities here for watersports, walks and cycling, or you can simply kick back on a leisurely boat trip. The undisputed jewel in the crown of the peninsula is pristine, dune-backed **West Wittering Beach** – one of only two sandy beaches in Sussex, and consequently besieged by windbreak-toting holidaymakers in summer.

Inland lies **Chichester**, a pocket-sized, culture-rich city surrounded by some great foodie pubs and with an unbeatable location sandwiched between the sea, sand and sails of Chichester Harbour to the south, and the South Downs National Park stretching towards Midhurst (see p.243) to the north: with the city as your base it's perfectly possible to be tramping the Downs in the morning, and basking on the beach by the afternoon.

Shoreham-by-Sea to Bognor

The first stretch of the seafront A259, which runs west along the coast from Brighton, isn't pretty: Hove's elegant seafront squares gradually give way to industrial estates, retail parks and a huge cargo port complete with power station, before winding up at

The Downs Link and the South Coast
   Cycle Route p.283
Boat trips from Littlehampton p.285
The International Bognor Birdman p.286

Glorious, glorious Goodwood p.294
Walks, watersports and two wheels on
   the Manhood Peninsula p.296
Chichester Harbour boat trips p.298

CHICHESTER CATHEDRAL

Highlights

❶ Littlehampton Traditional seaside fun goes happily hand-in-hand with stylish beach-café culture at this low-key seaside town. **See p.284**

❷ Chichester Cathedral Chichester's great medieval cathedral is as well known for its modern devotional art as for its more ancient treasures. **See p.288**

❸ Pallant House Gallery This modern art gallery is Chichester's pride and joy: a roll call of the great and the good in twentieth-century British art. **See p.288**

❹ Fishbourne Roman Palace One of the country's most important collections of Roman remains, and the biggest Roman dwelling ever discovered north of the Alps. **See p.292**

❺ Cass Sculpture Foundation The home of twenty-first-century British sculpture, with arresting large-scale works tucked away in peaceful woodland. **See p.293**

❻ Cycling the Manhood Peninsula With flat countryside, canalside towpaths and sparkling coastal views, the Manhood Peninsula is a great place to explore by bike. **See p.296**

❼ West Wittering Beach Even the summertime crowds that flock to this undeveloped sandy beach can't quite dispel its magic. **See p.296**

❽ Chichester Harbour The stunning watery landscapes of Chichester Harbour are best enjoyed on a boat trip. **See p.297**

HIGHLIGHTS ARE MARKED ON THE MAP ON P.282

THE WEST SUSSEX COAST

N

0 2

ENGLISH CHANNEL

Selsey Bill

SOUTH DOWNS NATIONAL PARK

HAMPSHIRE

Worthing
Shoreham-by-Sea
Southwick
Littlehampton
Bognor Regis
Chichester
Selsey
Midhurst
Petworth
Pulborough
Storrington
Arundel

Wineham
Partridge Green
Henfield
Woodmancote
Fulking
Upper Beeding
Steyning
Bramber Castle
Chanctonbury Ring
Cissbury Ring
Washington
Findon
High Salvington
Durrington
Sompting
Lancing
Goring-by-Sea
Ashington
West Chiltington Common
Amberley Museum & Heritage Centre
Rackham
Amberley
Burpham
Angmering
Houghton
West Burton
Bury
Bignor Roman Villa
Bignor
Sutton
Coldwaltham
Fittleworth
Duncton
Graffham
Selham
Upwaltham
Slindon
Tortington
Walberton
Barnham
Yapton
Middleton-on-Sea
Climping
Nyton
Tangmere
East Dean
Charlton
Singleton
Weald and Downland Open Air Museum
West Dean Gardens
Goodwood House
Cass Sculpture Foundation
Mid Lavant
East Lavant
Pagham
Pagham Harbour Nature Reserve
Church Norton
Nyetimber
Sidlesham
Bepton
Cocking
Elsted
Beacon Hill
South Harting
Harting Down Nature Reserve
Uppark House
Rowlands Castle
Rogate
Funtington
West Ashling
Fishbourne
Fishbourne Roman Palace
Bosham
Westbourne
Southbourne
Emsworth
Havant
West Itchenor
Itchenor
Birdham
Medmerry
Bracklesham Bay
East Wittering
West Wittering
East Head
Chichester Harbour
South Hayling
Manhood Peninsula
Rowlands Castle

River Adur
River Arun
River Rother

South Downs Way

A283
A27
A24
A280
A259
A29
A286
A285
A272
A286
A29
A27
B2141
B2146
B2145
B2179
A259

the low-key port and town of **Shoreham-by-Sea** on the banks of the River Adur. Further west, past the genteel seaside town of **Worthing**, lies **Littlehampton**, a lovely little resort with good beaches and some great places to stay and eat, and finally gaudy **Bognor**, the south-coast home of Butlin's.

GETTING AROUND AND INFORMATION   SHOREHAM TO BOGNOR

By train Southern run trains along the coast from Brighton to Shoreham-by-Sea, Worthing, Littlehampton and Bognor (every 30min); you'll need to change for Littlehampton and Bognor.

By bus Stagecoach Coastliner bus #700 runs along the coast from Brighton to Chichester via Shoreham-by-Sea, Worthing, Littlehampton and Bognor every 15min.

Websites For information about Shoreham and Worthing, visit ⑩ visitworthing.co.uk; Littlehampton and Bognor are both covered by ⑩ sussexbythesea.co.uk.

Shoreham-by-Sea

The shabby little town and port of **Shoreham-by-Sea** probably won't be top of anyone's list of Sussex must-sees, but you might well pass through to pick up the Downs Link cycle trail (see box below), take in a comedy or music gig at the excellent Ropetackle Centre (⑩ ropetacklecentre.co.uk), or visit the excellent **Farmers' and Artisans' Market** (second Sat of the month 9am–1pm), selling arts, crafts and local produce.

Once in town it's worth poking around a little further to find a couple of gems dating back to the twelfth century: the church of **St Mary de Haura**, set in a peaceful square along Church Street; and the diminutive, chequerboard **Marlipins Museum** of local history on the High Street (May–Oct Tues–Sat 10.30am–4.30pm; £2; ☎ 01273 462994, ⑩ sussexpast.co.uk). Shoreham's other draw is its **beach**, a nature reserve with vegetated shingle habitat above the high-tide mark and a good sweep of sand at low tide.

Just west of town, across the River Adur, Shoreham's fabulous Art Deco airport – the oldest licensed airfield in the country – is the base for Brighton Scenic's **sightseeing flights** (20min–1hr 15min; £58–118; ☎ 07918 902721, ⑩ brightonscenic.co.uk), which range east to Brighton and the Seven Sisters, inland to Arundel, and west as far as the Isle of Wight.

Worthing

The seaside town of **Worthing** was, like Brighton, once a fishing village until the fashion for sea bathing took off in the eighteenth century. When the Prince Regent's younger sister, Amelia, was sent here to recover from tuberculosis in 1798 (Brighton being deemed too racy), Worthing's smart, respectable reputation was sealed. While Brighton has blossomed over the years into a brash, beautiful London-by-the-Sea,

---

THE DOWNS LINK AND THE SOUTH COAST CYCLE ROUTE

Shoreham lies at the southern end of the **Downs Link** long-distance bridleway and cycle route, which runs along a disused railway line and, as the name suggests, links the North Downs to the South Downs. The route starts on the North Downs Way near Guildford, and stretches south for 37 miles through woodland, heathland and farmland to meet the South Downs Way just south of Bramber at Botolphs; the final stretch follows the River Adur valley down to Shoreham. **M's Cycles** on Shoreham High St (Tues–Sat 9am–6pm, Sun 10am–4pm; ☎ 01273 567591, ⑩ mscycles.co.uk) rents bikes (£25/day; 48hr notice required), and you can download a **map and route guide** at ⑩ westsussex.gov.uk/downslink.

Shoreham also lies along National Cycle Network Route 2 – also known as the **South Coast Cycle Route**. The five-mile stretch from Shoreham town centre to Worthing is mainly traffic-free, and once you've hit Shoreham beach it follows the coast all the way, ending up at the excellent *Coast Café* (see p.284) in Worthing; download a route map from ⑩ sustrans.org.uk.

Worthing has struggled to throw off its rather staid reputation – it is the headquarters of the English Bowling Association, after all. That said, its low-key charms make a welcome breather from the frenetic pace of Brighton: the pebbly **beach**, backed by five miles of prom, never gets too busy, and the seafront boasts an elegant Art Deco pier and one of the oldest working **cinemas** in the country, the Dome (ⓦworthingdome .com), opened in 1911. Down at **Splash Point**, there's a fun, interactive water-play area for kids, and a great café, *Coast Café* (see below), as well as the adjacent **Worthing Sand Courts** (£10/hr), where you can kick off your shoes and have a go at beach volleyball, beach tennis or sand soccer.

EATING AND DRINKING

WORTHING

Coast Café West Kiosk, Brighton Rd, BN11 2ES ☎01903 216 937, ⓦcoastcafe-worthing.co.uk. This lovely, laid-back beach café is flanked by artists' studios, has a deck right out on the pebbles, and puts on occasional live music, cabaret and beach parties. The good, simple food runs from burgers to mixed fish meze. Easter to mid-Oct Mon–

Thurs & Sun 9.30am–5pm, Fri & Sat 9.30am–10pm.
Macaris Restaurant and Café 24–25 Marine Parade, next to the Dome ☎01903 532753, ⓦmacaris restaurant.co.uk. A Worthing institution that's been serving up ice creams to holidaymakers since 1959. Mon–Fri 9am–5.30pm, Sat & Sun 9am–5.45pm.

Littlehampton

Rather improbably, the best-known tourist attraction in the little seaside town of **LITTLEHAMPTON** is a small seafront café. When the daringly stylish *East Beach Café* opened its doors in 2006, it was to a fanfare of media attention: *Vogue* magazine breathlessly dubbed the town the "coolest British seaside resort" – to the bewilderment of the locals. The café did, however, help kick-start some regeneration, and today Littlehampton makes a great day-trip or base for a longer stay, with a lovely setting by the River Arun, good beaches, excellent-value accommodation and, as you'd expect of any self-respecting seaside town, plenty of traditional entertainment on tap.

The seafront and East Bank

Littlehampton's seafront is an attractive affair, with lawns backing onto the promenade, and a shingle **beach** that at low tide reveals large swathes of sand. Along the prom runs **Britain's longest bench**, a funky ribbon of candy-coloured reclaimed slats that twists and loops its way for 350 yards along the seafront, bending around bins and lampposts, disappearing into the ground at points, and rising up to form two giant, sculptural shelters. The bench ends near the iconic *East Beach Café* (see opposite), with its rippling, rusted steel shell; the multi-award-winning design of the café was the work of design supremo Thomas Heatherwick.

Adjacent are Norfolk Gardens, from where the **Littlehampton Miniature Railway** (ⓦlittlehamptonrailway.co.uk) trundles along in summertime to nearby **Mewsbrook Park**, where there's a large boating lake with pedalos and kayaks for rent. At the other, western, end of the seafront is **Harbour Park** (ⓦharbourpark.com), a small-scale, run-of-the-mill amusement park that's been pulling in holidaymakers ever since Billy Butlin started operating the first rides here in 1932.

Littlehampton prom comes to an abrupt halt at its western end as it meets the **River Arun** – one of the fastest-flowing rivers in the country – which rushes out to sea in a dead-straight channel. A riverside walkway leads up the east bank of the river, past fish-and-chip shops, bobbing boats and kids waiting patiently with crabbing lines, to the smart, pedestrianized **East Bank Riverside Development**.

Look and Sea Visitor Centre

63–65 Surrey St, BN17 5AW • Daily 9am–5pm • £2 • ☎01903 718984, ⓦlookandsea.co.uk

Along the East Bank you can't miss the **Look and Sea Visitor Centre**, with a viewing tower up on the third floor giving fabulous 360-degree views over the town and inland

---

BOAT TRIPS FROM LITTLEHAMPTON

Action Boat, at the Harbour Office on Pier Rd (daily 10am–5pm; ☎0844 870 9794, ⓦactionboat
.co.uk), offer **harbour tours** (April–Oct daily at 2pm; 30min; £5) and **powerboat rides**
(April–Oct Sat, Sun, bank hols & school hols 10am–5pm; 20min; £10), as well as charters. There's
a possibility that a service to and from Arundel might start up in 2013 – check the website for
the latest.

---

to Arundel Castle and Chanctonbury Ring; lower floors cover the town's history, taking
you through its trading and shipbuilding past, and its subsequent rise (and fall) as a
holiday resort, with plenty of interactive elements to keep kids entertained.

West Beach

Cross the pedestrian bridge a quarter of a mile upstream of the Look and Sea Visitor Centre, then follow Rope Walk down the western bank
of the river, around a 20min walk; or take the ferry south of the Visitor Centre by the Harbour Board office (April–Oct daily 10am–5pm;
£1); there's also a car park at West Beach, but it's a long detour inland to get to it

Over on the west bank of the River Arun, Littlehampton's wild and windswept **West
Beach**, backed by sand dunes flecked with marram grass, feels a world away from the
mini-golf and boating lakes of the town. The *East Beach Café* has a sister café here, the
diminutive but similarly stylish *West Beach Café* (see below), with huge doors that open
to the elements. Follow the beach westwards for 1.5 miles to reach **Climping Beach**,
which together with West Beach is protected as a Site of Special Scientific Interest, for
its dunes, rare vegetated shingle and sand flats.

8

GETTING AROUND AND INFORMATION

LITTLEHAMPTON

By bike There's bike rental at Dutch Bike Shop, 46A Pier Rd
(Mon–Sat 9am–5pm; ☎01903 730089, ⓦdutchbikeshop
.co.uk). Bikes £6/hr, £10/half-day, £20/day.

Tourist information In the Look and Sea Visitor Centre,
63–65 Surrey St (daily: July–Sept 10am–5pm; Oct–June
10am–4pm; ☎01903 721866, ⓦsussexbythesea.com).

ACCOMMODATION AND EATING

Bailiffscourt Hotel Climping St, Climping, BN17
5RW ☎01903 723511, ⓦhshotels.co.uk. With its
flagstone floors, mullioned windows and weathered
stonework, *Bailiffscourt Hotel* looks like it's been in this
spot for centuries, but it was in fact only built in 1927. The
39 luxurious rooms vary hugely in size, price and decor –
some are traditional, some full-blown medieval, others
more contemporary. There's also an excellent spa, 30
acres of parkland roamed by peacocks and, best of all,
wild and all-but-deserted Climping Beach right on your
doorstep. **£250**

★ **East Beach Café** East Beach, BN17 5NZ ☎01903
731903, ⓦeastbeachcafe.co.uk. The food in this
striking seafront café is every bit as good as the award-
winning architecture: the standard menu – burgers, fish
and chips, risotto, ploughman's – runs alongside daily
fish specials, perhaps panfried sardines with beetroot, or
whole roasted mackerel (£8–18). The clean-lined, cave-
like interior, with its rippling ceiling, has wonderful
floor-to-ceiling views out to sea, and there are also
plenty of tables outside. It gets busy, so book ahead.
June to mid-Sept daily 10am–5pm (lunch served
Mon–Fri noon–2.30pm, Sat & Sun noon–3pm) &
6–9pm; mid-Sept to May daily 10am–5pm (lunch

served Mon–Fri noon–2pm, Sat & Sun noon–
2.30pm), Fri & Sat also open 6–9pm.

★ **Regency Guest House** 85 South Terrace, BN17 5LJ
☎01903 717707, ⓦtheregencyguesthouse.co.uk.
Stylish, super-friendly and brilliant value, this B&B
opposite the beach is a little gem. Rooms are decked out
with funky wallpaper and fabrics, bathrooms are sleek and
glamorous, and thoughtful added extras include beach
towels supplied in Cath Kidston bags, and fresh-baked
muffins on arrival. The breakfasts – featuring not only
home-made bread and jam but also home-made brown
sauce and ketchup – are a real treat. **£85**

★ **West Beach Café** Rope Walk, BN17 5DL ☎01903
718153, ⓦwestbeachcafe.co.uk. Less showy than its
sister café across the river, this small-but-perfect café has
an unbeatable location on unspoilt West Beach, and big
blue floor-to-ceiling windows that are flung open in good
weather. The short menu features fish and chips, Thai fish
cakes, fried smelts, scampi and the like, which you can eat
in or take away down to the beach with a bottle of wine or
local Wobblegate cider. Home-made ice cream rounds off
the perfect beach-café experience. April–Sept Mon–Fri &
Sun 10am–5pm, Sat 10am–7pm; Oct Sat & Sun
10am–5pm; stays open later in fine weather.

THE INTERNATIONAL BOGNOR BIRDMAN

Brilliantly bonkers and quintessentially British, the **International Bognor Birdman competition** (ⓦbirdman.org.uk) sees hundreds of daredevils strap themselves into human-powered flying machines and fling themselves off the end of Bognor pier in an attempt to fly 100 metres and gain the prized Birdman Trophy.

The event started back in 1971 in nearby Selsey, but moved to Bognor in 1978 and over the next decade started to gather interest internationally, with TV crews and competitors arriving from around the world. Health and safety concerns in 2008 saw the event move to nearby **Worthing**, and when two years later the competition returned to Bognor, Worthing decided to carry on staging its own contest (ⓦworthingbirdman.co.uk); the two separate competitions generally now take place a few weeks apart in August.

There's a (semi-) serious contingent who take part – the Condor Class is for standard hang-gliders, while the Leonardo da Vinci Class is for self-designed and -built flying machines – but what the competition's best known for are the fancy-dress **"fun flyers"** taking the plunge for charity; over the years flying doughnuts, vampires, pantomime horses, a Dr Who tardis and a chicken-and-mushroom pie have all tipped themselves over the edge.

The **current record** for Bognor stands at 89.2m, set in 1992, while in Worthing the 100m target was missed by a (controversial) whisker in 2009, when Steve Elkins managed a whopping 99.86 metres.

YHA Littlehampton Surrey St, BN17 5AW ☎0845 371 9670, ⓦyha.org.uk. This modern, 32-bed hostel is in a great location, right next to the Look and Sea Visitor Centre, a five-minute stroll from the beach. Self-catering only. Dorms __£15__, doubles __£30__

Bognor Regis

"Oh, bugger Bognor!", George V famously exclaimed of the little seaside town, and the words have stuck – perhaps a little unfairly. Despite its royal associations ("Regis" was added to its name after the king's visit in 1929), **Bognor Regis** is best known today for a slightly lower-brow connection – Billy Butlin of holiday-camp fame – and for its traditional, unpretentious seaside entertainments. Behind the Blue Flag pebble-and-sand beach you'll find tacky amusements aplenty, crazy golf, a miniature railway, boating lake, and fish-and-chip shops at every turn.

Butlin's

Upper Bognor Rd, PO21 1JJ • Funfair and indoor water park: mid-Feb to Oct selected days including school hols 10am–8pm, water park from noon • Day-ticket £25/17 peak/off-peak, children £15/8.50 • ☎0845 070 4754, ⓦbutlins.com

The flagship **Butlin's camp**, which first opened here in 1960 and now boasts a couple of funky hotels alongside the more basic chalets, sits at the eastern end of the seafront; you can visit its funfair and indoor water park on a day-ticket – a good option for kids on a rainy day.

Chichester and around

The handsome market town of **CHICHESTER** has plenty to recommend it: a splendid twelfth-century cathedral, a thriving cultural scene centred on its highly regarded Festival Theatre (see p.291), and one of the finest collections of modern British art anywhere in the country at the Pallant House Gallery. There are some excellent attractions within just a few miles of the city, too: the Roman ruins at **Fishbourne**; beautiful **West Dean Gardens**; the **Weald and Downland Open-Air Museum**, which contains more than fifty reconstructed historic buildings; the **Cass Sculpture Park**, home of contemporary British sculpture; and finally, the dashing **Goodwood Estate**, host to three big annual events.

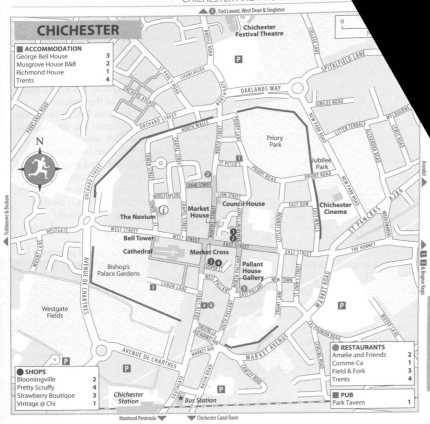

CHICHESTER

■ ACCOMMODATION

George Bell House	3
Musgrove House B&B	2
Richmond House	1
Trents	4

● SHOPS

Bloomingville	2
Pretty Scruffy	4
Strawberry Boutique	3
Vintage @ Chi	1

● RESTAURANTS

Amelie and Friends	2
Comme Ca	1
Field & Fork	3
Trents	4

■ PUB

Park Tavern	1

8

Market Cross and around

The centre of Chichester is marked by its splendid Gothic **Market Cross**, an octagonal rotunda topped by ornate finials and a crown lantern spire, built in 1501 to provide shelter for the market traders. The buzz of commerce still dominates the surrounding area today, with the four main thoroughfares leading off from the Cross – North, East, South and West streets – each lined with shops, and a **farmers' market** setting up its stalls on the first and third Friday of the month (9am–2pm). There are several fine buildings up North Street, including the dinky little **Market House** (also known as the Butter Market), built by Nash in 1807 and fronted by a Doric colonnade; a tiny flint **Saxon church** with a diminutive wooden shingled spire; and the redbrick **Council House**, built in 1731, with Ionic columns on its facade.

The city walls

The centre's cruciform street plan, and the **city walls** that encircle it, are a legacy of Chichester's Roman beginnings. The city started life as the settlement of Noviomagus Reginorum, connected to London by the arrow-straight Stane Street. The **Roman city walls** were built in the third century, and large sections (much restored over the years) still stand today, though the ancient gateways are long gone. Pavement markers, signposts and interpretive boards guide you round the 1.5-mile circuit; for much of the route there's a footpath on top of the walls, and it's a fun way to see the city, hopping on and off at various points to visit Chichester's other sights.

er Cathedral

RP • Daily: mid-April to mid-Oct 7.15am–7pm; mid-Oct to mid-April 7.15am–6pm; dr
.30pm • Free • ☎ 01243 782595, Ⓦ chichestercathedral.org.uk

ester's splendid **cathedral** has stood at the heart of the city fo
. Building began in 1076, after the Norman conquerors move
ey, ten miles away. The cathedral was consecrated by Bishop Lu
out 1300 has only been minimally modified, with the exception
reestanding fifteenth-century bell tower and the slender spire; the la
after it came spectacularly crashing down in 1861 when the choir sc

The interior is renowned for its prestigious **modern devotional a**
font of smooth Bodmin stone and beaten copper by **John Skelton**
entrance; an enormous altar-screen tapestry by **John Piper**; and a st
– an exuberant blaze of ruby-red – by **Marc Chagall** nearby. Perhaps
greatest artistic treasures, however, are its oldest: in the south aisle,
you'll see a pair of exquisite Romanesque carvings – the **Chichester**
around 1125, and showing the raising of Lazarus. Notable for the wo
expressive faces of the figures, the reliefs would once have been brigh
semiprecious stones set in the eyes.

Elsewhere you can see a couple of enormous **Renaissance wooden pan**
Lambert Barnard – depicting the past bishops of Chichester (north transept), and
Henry VIII confirming the Chichester bishopric (south transept) – as well as the
fourteenth-century **Fitzalan tomb** of Richard Fitzalan, thirteenth earl of Arundel. The
earl's stone effigy, lying sweetly hand-in-hand with his countess, inspired Philip Larkin's
poem *An Arundel Tomb*, which famously concludes "What will survive of us is love."

Behind the cathedral, Canon Lane leads to the fourteenth-century gateway to the
Bishop's Palace; the Palace itself is not open to the public, but the beautiful **Bishop's
Palace Gardens** (daily 8am–dusk; free) are one of the city's hidden gems and a perfect
picnic spot, with expansive lawns, great views of the cathedral, a Tudor walled garden
and sections of Roman wall.

Pallant House Gallery

9 North Pallant, PO19 1TJ • Tues, Wed, Fri & Sat 10am–5pm, Thurs 10am–8pm, Sun & bank hols 11am–5pm; highlights tours Sat 2pm,
themed tours Thurs 5.15pm • £9, Tues £4.50, Thurs 5–8pm free (£4.50 for exhibitions) • ☎ 01243 774557, Ⓦ pallant.org.uk

Hidden away off South Street, in the well-preserved Georgian quadrant of the city
known as the Pallants, is the wonderful **Pallant House Gallery**, Chichester's answer to
Tate Modern. The gallery contains one of the most important collections of modern
British art in the country, with works by almost every notable British artist of the last
hundred years, including Moore, Freud, Sickert, Hepworth, Blake, Piper, Hodgkin,
Sutherland and Caulfield. The collection started with the bequest of **Walter Hussey**, the
dean of Chichester Cathedral – who commissioned much of the modern art in the
cathedral including the Piper tapestry and the Chagall window (see above) – and has
grown with future bequests to become an eclectic "collection of collections",
encompassing paintings, ceramics, furniture, sculpture and more.

The guiding principle is that art of different periods sits side by side, so as you wander
through the creaky-floored rooms of the handsome Queen Anne townhouse that
houses the rotating **permanent collection**, you might find a *Hearth Stone* by Andy
Goldsworthy nestled in a fireplace beneath an eighteenth-century portrait, or a
four-poster bed sharing a room with a ball gown made from pink metallic balloons.
Installations often take over the sweeping stairwell of the townhouse, and the gallery
holds several excellent **temporary exhibitions** each year in its award-winning
contemporary extension, where there's also a designated room for **prints and drawings**.
A free **tour** of the collection's highlights runs on Saturdays, while themed tours take
place on Thursdays; other events are organized throughout the year.

The Novium

Tower St, PO19 1QH • April–Oct Mon–Sat 10am–5pm, Sun 10am–4pm; Nov–March Wed–Sat 10am–5pm, Sun 10am–4pm • £7 •
📞 01243 775888, 🌐 thenovium.org

The city's sleek new museum of local history – the **Novium** – is housed in a state-of-the-art building a stone's throw from the cathedral. The first sight that greets you as you walk in is the recently excavated **Roman bath house**, which stood on this site nearly two thousand years ago; after its discovery in the 1970s it was buried under a car park for safekeeping until the Novium build allowed it to see the light of day once again. If you've seen the wonderful remains at Bignor (see p.243) and Fishbourne (see p.292) you might be a bit underwhelmed, but a film projected onto the wall behind does a good job of bringing the excavation to life. Also here are the incomplete but beautiful **Chilgrove mosaic**, discovered in the Chilgrove valley nearby, and the **Jupiter Stone** statue base, unearthed during excavations in West Street.

The other two floors hold thematically arranged **exhibitions** of local objects from the museum's huge, eclectic collection – over 350,000 artefacts in all – which runs from prehistoric stone tools and a mammoth's shoulder bone to the old toll board and weighing scales once used at the Butter Market. From the top-floor foyer there are great views of the cathedral.

Chichester Ship Canal

Canal Basin, Canal Wharf, just outside the city walls, PO19 8DT • Boat trips Feb half-term 2 trips daily at 11am & 1.45pm; mid-March to
early Nov 4 trips daily at 10.15am, noon, 1.45pm & 3.30pm; 1hr 15min return • Boat trips £5.50, rowing boats £6 for first 30min, £3/hr
thereafter • 📞 01243 771363, 🌐 chichestercanal.org.uk

Just outside the southern city walls, Chichester Canal Basin is the start of the **Chichester Ship Canal**, which skirts the outskirts of the city before flowing lazily through flat countryside to Chichester Marina at Birdham, four miles away. The canal opened in 1822 to carry cargo between the sea and the city, but it was never a commercial success and was abandoned in 1928. Today the Chichester Canal Trust hires out **rowing boats** and runs **boat trips** aboard a twelve-seat narrowboat, the *Egremont*, as far as the Crosbie Bridge at Donnington two miles away. A **towpath** runs the length of the canal down to the marina – part of the long-distance Lipchis Way (see box, p.296). Whether on foot or on the river the canal makes a lovely, peaceful outing from the city, with wildflowers speckling the riverbanks in summer, dragonflies flashing above the water, and swans and mallards gliding along; you also get great views back across the meadows to the cathedral, a view immortalized by Turner in 1829.

ARRIVAL AND DEPARTURE

CHICHESTER AND AROUND

By car Chichester has plenty of long-stay (3hr-plus) car parks – at Cattle Market, Westgate, Northgate, Basin Rd and Avenue de Chartres – all signposted from the city's approach roads.

By train The station, on Stockbridge Rd, is a ten-minute walk north to the Market Cross.

Destinations Arundel (Mon–Sat 2 hourly, Sun hourly; 20–30min); Brighton (2 hourly; 45–55min); London Victoria (2 hourly; 1hr 35min).

By bus The bus station lies across the road from the train station on Southgate.

Destinations Arundel (Mon–Sat hourly; 30min); Brighton via Bognor, Littlehampton, Worthing & Shoreham-by-Sea (Mon–Sat every 15min, Sun 2 hourly; 1hr 45min).

GETTING AROUND AND INFORMATION

By bike There's bike rental at Barreg Cycles, 2 miles from the centre in Fishbourne (15/day; 📞 01243 786104, 🌐 barreg .co.uk). In the Witterings, *Stubcroft Farm* (see p.299) rents bikes for £10/day. West Wittering Cycle Hire (£18/day; 📞 07973 489019, 🌐 westwitteringcyclingholidays.co.uk) will also deliver bikes; its daily rate includes a route map.

On foot Guided city walks run throughout the year,

bookable through the tourist office (April–Sept Tues & Wed at 11am, Sat at 2pm; Oct–March Tues at 11am, Sat at 2pm; £4).

By taxi Chichester Taxis (📞 01243 330015).

Tourist office At the Novium, Tower St (Mon–Sat 10am–5pm, Sun 10am–4pm; 📞 01243 775888, 🌐 visit chichester.org).

8

ACCOMMODATION

There's generally no problem finding a place to stay in or around Chichester other than during **Goodwood**'s three big annual events (see box, p.294), when the most popular accommodation can fill up more than a year in advance. Note that the prices below exclude the Goodwood periods, when rates rise across the board.

IN TOWN

George Bell House 4 Canon Lane, PO19 1PX ☎01243 813586, ⓦchichestercathedral.org.uk. What makes a stay here special is the location: this eight-bedroom Victorian house, once home to the Archdeacon of Chichester, is owned by the cathedral and located in the grounds, just by the Bishop's Palace gateway. The rooms are big, comfortable and tranquil, if a little bland; two come with baths, the others showers. An added bonus is the top-notch art on the walls, which is lent by the Pallant House Gallery. Breakfast costs extra (£8.90). **£99**

★ **Musgrove House B&B** 63 Oving Rd, PO19 7EN ☎01243 790179, ⓦmusgrovehouse.co.uk. This friendly, stylish boutique B&B, just a short walk from the centre, is a real bargain. The three lovely rooms are all impeccably tasteful, decked out in cocooning shades of grey, with shutters on the windows, super-comfy beds with silk duvets, and fun high-tech touches like bathroom mirrors you can light up with a wave of your hand. The prints on the wall are all for sale, so you can take some of the style home with you. **£75**

★ **Richmond House** 230 Oving Rd ☎01243 771464, ⓦrichmondhousechichester.co.uk. This fab boutique B&B, set in a period house a 10min walk from the centre, is incredibly warm and welcoming: you feel at home from the moment you arrive. The three serene, stylish rooms are all slightly different, but might feature Liberty-print furnishings or antique mirrors, and all come with fresh flowers and spotless, luxurious bathrooms equipped with Molton Brown toiletries. Room Three (£125), with its free-standing bath flanked by stone angels, is worth splashing out on if you want to treat yourself. **£90**

Trents 50 South St, PO19 1DS ☎01243 773714, ⓦtrentschichester.co.uk. As long as you don't want an early night, the five rooms above this popular restaurant-bar are a good bet – you're right in the thick of things, and the rooms are modern and well appointed. Things quieten down after closing time, and there's no rush to get up early the following morning, with breakfast (not included; £2.25–7.25) served until 11.30am. **£110**

OUT OF TOWN

Goodwood Hotel Goodwood Estate, 3 miles from Chichester, PO18 0QB ☎01243 775537, ⓦgoodwood .co.uk. The Goodwood Estate's country-house hotel isn't cheap, but you're not just paying for the rooms – which are suitably deluxe – but for the whole Goodwood experience. A night here gives you access to the health club and spa, two golf courses, and a couple of excellent restaurants supplied in part from the estate's own farm. If you're feeling flush you could even take a pleasure flight from Goodwood aerodrome, or go for a spin around the famed motor-racing circuit (see p.294). **£170**

Richmond Arms Mill Rd, West Ashling, PO18 8EA ☎01243 572046, ⓦtherichmondarms.co.uk. There are just two B&B rooms above this excellent pub (see opposite) in the pretty village of West Ashling, a five-minute drive from Chichester. Rooms are smart and luxurious, with bathrooms featuring polished wooden floors, roll-top baths and walk-in showers; the larger room (£110) comes with a sofa bed, so is a good option for families. The real selling point, however, is the great food on offer downstairs, though bear in mind the restaurant's not open every day so you're best off avoiding Sun–Tues nights if you want to really make the most of a stay. **£95**

Royal Oak Pook Lane, East Lavant, 3 miles from Chichester, PO18 0AX ☎01243 527434, ⓦroyaloakeast lavant.co.uk. This lovely dining pub (see opposite), set on a quiet lane just north of Chichester, offers a range of gorgeous, stylish rooms – four above the pub, two in an adjacent barn backing on to fields, a suite in a two-storey flint cottage, and more across the lane. All come kitted out with DVD players, plump down duvets and L'Occitane toiletries; room rates even include newspapers for the ultimate lazy lie-in. **£145**

EATING AND DRINKING

IN TOWN

★ **Amelie and Friends** 31 North St, PO19 1LY ☎01243 771444, ⓦamelieandfriends.com. This stylish, buzzy little restaurant has a beautiful walled garden out the back, and a striking main dining room sporting polished boards, wooden tables, Eames Eiffel chairs and industrial-style aluminium light fittings running along the walls. The menu changes every few weeks, but lunch (mains £7.50–13) might feature burgers with home-made beetroot chutney, or pork belly sandwich with peanut and chilli relish, while evening dishes (£13–15) run from bream with aubergine caviar to trio of pork belly, pork cheek and black pudding. Mon–Sat 10am–11pm (food served until 9pm), Sun 10am–4pm.

Comme Ca 67 Broyle Rd, PO19 6BD ☎01243 788724, ⓦcommeca.co.uk. The decor is a little bizarre but the food's a winner at this authentic French restaurant just up the road from the Festival Theatre – and the terrace garden couldn't be lovelier, dripping with plants, vines and hanging baskets. You've a choice of two set menus: the Monet (2/3 courses £22/25), or the push-the-boat-out Versailles (2/3 courses £30/35), featuring the likes of foie gras, Selsey lobster and Dover sole. It's worth booking ahead at pre- and post-theatre times. Tues 5.30–9.30pm, Wed & Thurs noon–2pm & 5.30–9.30pm, Fri & Sat noon–2pm & 5.30–10.30pm, Sun noon–2pm.

Field & Fork Pallant House Gallery, 9 North Pallant (entrance in East Pallant), PO19 1TJ ☎01243 770827, ⊚fieldandfork.co.uk. Owned by former *Kensington Place* head chef, Sam Mahoney, the small but perfectly formed restaurant inside the Pallant House Gallery is one of the best places to eat in the city, serving up imaginative, locally sourced food (mains £14–17), with fruit and vegetables supplied from their own glasshouse. Also worth a mention are the delectable afternoon teas (3–5pm; £15; book in advance), which come with lime and basil pannacotta and rosé wine and orange jelly. Tues, Wed & Sun 10am–5pm, Thurs–Sat 10am–10pm.

Park Tavern 11 Priory Rd, PO19 1NS ☎01243 785057, ⊚parktavernchichester.co.uk. A proper pub with a great atmosphere and plenty of eclectic, quirky knick-knacks, overlooking Priory Park. The food is seasonal, home-made and great value – the menu features sandwiches and ploughman's (£6/7), plus mains around the £10 mark; superior bar snacks (£4–5) include gourmet Scotch eggs, whitebait and pork belly with apple sauce. Fuller's ales on tap, plus a guest beer. Mon–Sat 11am–11pm, Sun noon–10.30pm; food served Mon, Wed & Sun noon–3pm, Tues & Thurs–Sat noon–9pm.

Trents 50 South St, PO19 1DS ☎01243 773714, ⊚trentschichester.co.uk. This laid back restaurant-bar is one of the city's most popular places to while away an evening. The Mediterranean-inspired menu changes seasonally, but might feature pan-fried sea bass or tomato-and-parmesan *arancini* (£12–16), alongside sandwiches and salads (£8–12); there's also a monthly-changing set menu (2/3 courses £13.95/15.95). The *Shed Bar* has an outdoor heated terrace and puts on occasional live-music nights. Mon–Sat 7.30am–11pm (food until 10pm), Sun 8.30am–10.30pm (food until 9.30pm).

OUT OF TOWN

Earl of March Lavant Rd, 3 miles from Chichester, PO18 0BQ ☎01243 533993, ⊚theearlofmarch.com. This renowned foodie pub is run by the former executive head chef of the *Ritz*, Giles Thompson, so it's no surprise that the food is excellent: mains cost £16–25, though lighter lunches (£6–11.50, including sandwiches, salads and Scotch eggs with home-made piccalilli) are also available,

and there's a good-value set lunch (2/3 courses £18.50/21.50). On a fine day reserve a table in the terrace garden, which backs right onto the surrounding fields and has fabulous views across to the Downs. Daily 11am–11pm; food served Mon–Sat noon–2.30pm & 5.30–9.30pm, Sun noon–3pm & 6–9pm.

Fox Goes Free Charlton, near Goodwood, PO18 0HU ☎01243 811461, ⊚thefoxgoesfree.com. This seventeenth-century flint country pub oozes character – well-worn brick floors, sagging beams and inglenook fireplaces – and history: back in the 1600s William III used to drop in to refresh his hunting party here. The large garden is the crowning glory, with picnic tables under the apple trees and beautiful views of the Downs. Food is traditional and home-made, and runs from sandwiches to pie and chips (mains £10.50–16). Mon–Sat 11am–11pm, Sun noon–10.30pm; food served Mon–Fri noon–2.30pm & 6.30–10pm, Sat & Sun noon–10pm.

★ **Richmond Arms** Mill Rd, West Ashling, PO18 8EA ☎01243 572046, ⊚therichmondarms.co.uk. Just down the road from the picturesque village duck pond, West Ashling's small pub looks nothing special from the outside but the food (mains £15–22) is fantastic: a lip-smackingly good meal here might start with hot and runny chorizo Scotch egg with shaved fennel and saffron aioli, followed by barbecued Cornish squid with spicy coleslaw and a peanut poppadom, and finish with peanut-butter brûlée with home-made sour cherry and salted caramel ice cream. Even the bar snacks are great, featuring crunchy smoky sardines, gremolata-coated halloumi fries, and Serrano ham cut to order on the glossy red slicing machine by the door. Wed–Sat noon–3pm (food until 2.30pm) & 6–11pm (food until 9pm), Sun noon–3pm (food orders until 2.30pm).

Royal Oak Pook Lane, East Lavant, 3 miles from Chichester, PO18 0AX ☎01243 427434, ⊚royaloakeastlavant.co.uk. Two-hundred-year-old, vine-covered coaching inn in a pretty village just outside Chichester, with bags of character and style and a lovely terrace, with more tables out the front overlooking the quiet village lane. The food is great, sourced from local suppliers where possible: mains (£15–22) might include rump of Southdown lamb, wild local sea bass or monkfish wrapped in nori seaweed. Daily 8am–11pm; food served Mon–Fri noon–2pm & 6–9pm, Sat noon–2.30pm & 6–9.30pm, Sun noon–3pm & 6.30–9pm.

ENTERTAINMENT

Chichester Cinema New Park Rd, PO19 7XY ☎01243 786650, ⊚chichestercinema.org. Chichester's excellent art-house cinema screens up to five films a day.

Chichester Festival Theatre Oaklands Park, PO19 6AP ☎01243 781312, ⊚cft.org.uk. One of the best regional theatres in the country, opened in 1962 when it

was the very first thrust-stage theatre, with Laurence Olivier as artistic director. Today, many productions from the theatre's annual season (roughly Easter–Oct) move on to the West End and Broadway; in winter it hosts touring shows.

8

SHOPPING

Bloomingville 1 St Martin's St, PO19 1NP ☎01243 527257. This chic Danish store stocks a tempting array of homeware and furniture, with many items sourced directly from Southeast Asia and Africa; pieces for sale might include vintage Indian saris made into throws, funky light fittings and hand-block-printed crockery. Mon–Sat 9.30am–5.30pm.

Pretty Scruffy 1 Cooper St, PO19 1EB ☎01243 779715, ⓦprettyscruffy.com. "Happiness is handmade" is the slogan of this little shop-cum-gallery, which stocks exclusively hand made, mostly local, arts and crafts, everything from jewellery, fabrics, pottery and buttons to cards and leather notebooks. The tiny gallery upstairs features changing exhibitions. Mon–Sat 10am–5.30pm.

Strawberry Boutique 1 Cooper St, PO19 1EB ☎01243 773700, ⓦstrawberryboutique.co.uk. This quirky independent boutique stocks funky brands such as Odd Molly, American Vintage, Minkpink, Superdry and Mais il est où le Soleil?, plus jewellery and accessories. Mon–Sat 10am–5.30pm.

Vintage @ Chi 2 Jays Walk, St Martin's St, PO19 1NP ☎01243 773644, ⓦvintagechi.com. For good-quality vintage clothing look no further than this tiny shop, crammed with great pieces, and with the feel of an upmarket boutique. Mon–Sat 10am–5pm.

Fishbourne Roman Palace

Salthill Rd, Fishbourne, PO19 3QR • Jan Sat & Sun 10am–4pm; Feb, Nov to mid-Dec daily 10am–4pm; March–Oct daily 10am–5pm • £8.20 • ☎01243 789829, ⓦsussexpast.co.uk • Train from Chichester to Fishbourne (hourly; 3min)

Fishbourne Roman Palace, two miles west of Chichester, is the largest and best-preserved Roman dwelling in the country, and the largest north of the Alps. Roman relics have long been turning up in Fishbourne, and in 1960 a workman unearthed their source – the site of a depot constructed by the invading Romans in 43 AD, which is thought later to have become the vast palace of the Romanized king of a local tribe, Cogidubnus. The palace was built around 75–80 AD, on a huge scale, with around a hundred rooms, 160 columns, 43,000 roof tiles and up to two miles of masonry walls. The one surviving wing – the **north wing** – represents just a quarter of the site; a large part of the complex lies buried beneath Fishbourne village.

Fishbourne has the largest collection of in-situ **mosaics** in the country, and some of the earliest too. When the palace was built craftsmen laid the black-and-white geometric mosaics that were popular in Rome at the time, but as tastes changed, from the early second century onwards, these were supplanted by polychrome mosaics, which featured a central panel surrounded by a large border – the dolphin-riding cupid being Fishbourne's most famous example. Nearby Bignor Roman Villa (see p.243) has some stunning polychrome mosaics, and makes a fascinating follow-on visit.

An **audiovisual programme** gives a fuller picture of the palace as it would have been in Roman times, and the extensive **gardens** attempt to re-create the palace grounds – which might well have been the earliest formal gardens in the country – with new planting in the original bedding trenches. There is at least one **guided tour** a day, as well as occasional handling sessions, and special events take place throughout the year.

West Dean Gardens

West Dean, PO18 0RX • Daily: March–Oct 10.30am–5pm; Nov–Feb 10.30am–4pm • £8.10 March–Oct, £5 Nov–Feb • ☎01243 818210, ⓦwestdean.org.uk • Stagecoach Coastline bus #60 from Chichester or Midhurst (Mon–Sat 2 hourly, Sun hourly)

With wildflower meadows, sweeping lawns, flower gardens and fruit orchards, all set against a backdrop of the South Downs, **West Dean Gardens** are among the loveliest in Sussex. You could happily spend half a day or more exploring: highlights include the walled **Kitchen Garden** – one of the most perfect examples you'll see anywhere, with neat, white-painted Victorian glasshouses, fruit trees trained into sculptural shapes, and supernaturally neat rows of flawless vegetables – and the pretty **Spring Garden**, where you'll find dinky flint bridges spanning the crystal-clear River Lavant, and two Surrealist fibreglass **tree sculptures**. The sculptures were created by poet and writer **Edward James**, who once owned the West Dean Estate and is best known for his early support and patronage of Surrealist art; Salvador Dalí's iconic *Mae West Lips Sofa* and

Lobster Telephone were both created in collaboration with James. James is buried up in the 50-acre **arboretum**, half a mile or so uphill across sloping parkland dotted with grazing sheep; it's at its most beautiful in spring, when rhododendrons and azaleas daub the pathways with splashes of red and pink.

Edward James's mansion, at the centre of the gardens, operates as **West Dean College**, an internationally renowned residential college dedicated to arts and crafts. To get a taster, you can enrol on one of the thirty or so **day courses**, which span everything from stained-glass making and woodcarving to garden design and digital photography.

Weald & Downland Open Air Museum

Singleton, PO18 0EU · Jan to mid-Feb Wed, Sat & Sun 10.30am–4pm; mid-Feb to mid-March, Nov & Dec daily 10.30am–4pm; mid-March to Oct daily 10.30am–6pm; Downland Gridshell tour daily at 1.30pm · £10 · ☎ 01243 811363, ⊛ wealddown.co.uk · Stagecoach Coastline bus #60 from Chichester or Midhurst (Mon–Sat 2 hourly, Sun hourly)

Five miles north of Chichester, the **Weald & Downland Open Air Museum** is a brilliantly engaging rural museum. More than fifty buildings from the last seven hundred years – everything from a medieval farmstead to a Tudor market hall to a pair of Victorian labourer's cottages – have been dismantled from sites around the Southeast and reconstructed at the fifty-acre site. None would have survived without the museum's intervention: some were virtually tumbledown, while others were due to be demolished to make way for development, such as Longport Farmhouse, the museum's entrance and shop, which was moved from the site of the Eurotunnel terminal in Folkestone.

Many of the buildings have been decked out as they would have been originally, using replica furniture and artefacts. In the working Tudor kitchen in sixteenth-century **Winkhurst Farm** you can even taste some of the food of the period – handmade butter and cheese, griddle bread and pottage. Stewards inside the buildings are on hand to talk about what life would have been like for those who lived there, and there are regular **demonstrations** – different every day – of rural crafts and trades. There's a daily tour of the modern, innovative **Downland Gridshell** building, the museum's vast workshop and store, as well as numerous events and activities throughout the year.

Cass Sculpture Foundation

Goodwood, 5 miles north of Chichester, PO19 0QP · April–Oct Tues–Sun & bank holiday Mon 10.30am–4.30pm · £10 · ☎ 01243 538449, ⊛ sculpture.org.uk

The magical **Cass Sculpture Foundation** is an absolute must for anyone interested in contemporary art, with more than eighty large-scale works nestled among the trees in a beautiful 26-acre woodland setting. Uniquely, all of the sculptures are for sale – ranging in price from a few thousand pounds to well over a million – meaning that the pieces on display change from year to year as they are sold. The dynamo behind the operation is retired businessman **Wilfred Cass**, whose own Modernist house lies hidden among the trees. Plenty of big names have been on show over the years – Tony Cragg, Antony Gormley, Thomas Heatherwick, Eduardo Paolozzi, Andy Goldsworthy, Rachel Whiteread and more – but the Foundation also commissions sculpture from lesser-known British talent, meeting the cost of the materials and then taking a share of the profits when the piece is sold, before ploughing the money back into the Foundation.

The Goodwood Estate

Goodwood, 4 miles north of Chichester, PO18 0PX · **Farm shop** Mon–Sat 9am–6pm, Sun 10am–4pm · ☎ 01243 755154 **Motor Circuit** Track Days April–Oct · £165 half-day, £320 full day **Aerodrome** 30min flight £122, 45min £183, 1hr £245

Goodwood's name is synonymous with glamorous sporting pursuits, and its three big annual events – **Glorious Goodwood**, the **Festival of Speed** and the **Goodwood Revival** (see box, p.294) – draw spectators from around the world. At the centre of the estate is

8

GLORIOUS, GLORIOUS GOODWOOD

Goodwood's three big **events** are all incredibly popular. Book your accommodation as far in advance as you can – many hotels and B&Bs are booked up more than a year in advance – and be prepared for **accommodation** prices to soar. For exact dates and further details, see ⓦ goodwood.co.uk.

Festival of Speed 4 days in late June/early July. This long weekend of vintage and special cars – featuring everything from Formula One racers and supercars to motorbikes, rally cars and classics – bills itself as "the largest motoring garden party in the world", and is held in the grounds of Goodwood House, attracting around 150,000 petrolheads. The 1.16-mile hill climb is the main event of the weekend (Sat & Sun), but there's plenty of other stuff going on, and the public can wander around the paddocks and get up close to the cars and the stars. Tickets cost £20 (Thurs), £39 (Fri) or £55 (Sat or Sun), or you can buy a four-day pass for £120.

Glorious Goodwood 5 days in late July. One of *the* events of the social and racing year, as much about celeb-spotting, champagne and fashion as it is about the horse racing – Edward VII famously described it as "a garden party with racing tacked on". More than 100,000 race-goers attend over the five days, but if you miss the glamorous main event, there are plenty of other meetings from May to October. Ticket prices depend on which enclosure you're in: cheapest is the Lennox Enclosure (£16); then comes the Gordon Enclosure (from £38); the Richmond Enclosure is members-only.

Goodwood Revival 3 days in mid-Sept. This nostalgic motor-race meeting relives the glory days of the Goodwood Motor Circuit, welcoming the cars and motorbikes that would have competed during the 1940s, 1950s and 1960s. Many cars are driven by famous names from the past and present, and the entire event is staged in an authentic period setting, with staff – and most of the 100,000 spectators – dressing up in period garb. Tickets cost £36 (Fri) or £56 (Sat or Sun), or you can buy a three-day pass for £117.

the magnificent **Goodwood House** (see below); surrounding it are a famous **racecourse** high up on the Downs, which has hosted horse racing since 1802; a celebrated **motor-racing circuit**; an **aerodrome**; two **golf courses** (one ranked in the top 100 in the country); a hotel (see p.290); a **farm shop**; and a members-only **sporting club**, The Kennels, built in 1787 to house the third Duke of Richmond's hounds and huntsman – the prized dogs apparently had central heating in their quarters a hundred years before it was installed in the main house.

If you've got deep pockets, all of the above is yours to be enjoyed: you can drive your car round the historic Goodwood Motor Circuit on a **Track Day**; take the controls of an aircraft on a short flight from the aerodrome; or play a round of golf on the Park Course (the more prestigious Downs Course is reserved for members and hotel guests). A day at the races is a positive bargain by comparison, with the cheapest tickets a snip at £8, or come for one of the evening races in summer; see ⓦ goodwood.co.uk for fixtures.

Goodwood House

Late March to mid-Oct most Sun & Mon 1–5pm; most of Aug open Mon–Thurs & Sun; check website for exact dates • 1hr guided tours March–July every 30min; stewarded rooms Aug–Oct • £9.50 • ☎ 01243 755055, ⓦ goodwood.co.uk

Seat of the Dukes of Richmond, Lennox, Gordon and Aubigny, **Goodwood House** is every bit as splendid as the rest of the estate. When the first Duke of Richmond – the illegitimate son of Charles II and his French mistress – bought the house in 1697 it was little more than a hunting lodge, but over the years successive generations improved and enlarged it into what you see today. The Earl and Countess of March live in the house, so only the **staterooms** are open to the public, and those only on certain days of the week for parts of the year. The rooms are furnished in opulent Regency style, a fitting home for the family's stellar art collection which includes Sèvres porcelain and paintings by Stubbs, Reynolds, Van Dyck and Canaletto. Each year, an **exhibition** (August to mid-October) highlights a different aspect of the house's history; previous exhibitions have focused on the Horse, the House Party and Royal Goodwood.

The Manhood Peninsula

South of Chichester, the **MANHOOD PENSINULA** is bordered by Chichester Harbour in the west and Bognor Regis in the east, with Selsey Bill – the southernmost point of Sussex – at its tip. Its rather wonderful name probably comes from the Old English *maene-wudu*, meaning "men's wood" or common land, though no woodland to speak of remains today, with the peninsula mainly given over to agriculture. Inland the landscape is flat and featureless (most of it no more than six metres above sea level, making it easy cycling territory), but the main appeal of the area is around the coast, where you'll find some of the last remaining stretches of undeveloped coastline in Sussex. The best way to enjoy the peninsula, known locally as "God's pocket" for its benevolent microclimate, is to make the most of the great outdoors, whether by taking a boat trip, enrolling in a watersports taster course or simply striking off on a coastal footpath.

Pagham Harbour RSPB Nature Reserve

Nature Reserve Open access **Visitor centre** Selsey Rd, 1 mile south of Sidlesham, PO20 7NE • Mon–Fri 10am–4pm, Sat & Sun 10am–4.30pm • ☎ 01243 641508, ⓦ rspb.org.uk/reserves/guide/p/paghamharbour • Car parks at visitor centre, Pagham Beach & Church Norton; bus #51 from Chichester (20min); cycle route #88 (Bill Way) from Chichester Canal Basin

On the east side of the Manhood Peninsula, **Pagham Harbour Nature Reserve** feels blissfully remote – you wouldn't think that brash Bognor lies just five miles away along the coast. The bay at the heart of the reserve is intertidal, and the landscape transforms dramatically throughout the day: at high water it's filled by the sea, while low tide sees the water ebb away to reveal expanses of mudflats and saltmarsh, picked over by wading birds. Surrounding the bay is a patchwork of meadow, farmland, copses, lagoons, reed beds and, on either side of the harbour mouth, two long shingle spits that are speckled with sea kale and yellow horned poppies in early summer.

The reserve is an important wetland site for wildlife, with the tidal mudflats attracting scores of **bird** species throughout the year, including thousands of Brent geese in winter; there are hides at Pagham Beach and Church Norton, with a third near the **visitor centre** just south of Sidlesham. The visitor centre is also the starting point for the circular 1.5-mile **Sidlesham Nature Trail**, which takes you along the edge of Pagham Harbour as far as Sidlesham, home to the excellent *Crab and Lobster* pub (see p.299). Beyond Sidlesham, a footpath continues around the bay, hugging the shoreline all the way to Pagham Beach. The RSPB, which manages the reserve, runs **guided walks** and activities.

A few miles southwest of Pagham Harbour, a new intertidal area the size of three hundred football pitches is being created at **Medmerry**, between Selsey at the southernmost tip of the peninsula, and Bracklesham Bay to the west. The scheme – designed to reduce flood risk – will create new wildlife habitats, footpaths, cycle ways and viewing areas, and is expected to be complete in 2013, though the habitat will take several years to develop.

Bracklesham Bay and East Wittering

Along the southwest coast of the Manhood Peninsula, the seaside villages of **Bracklesham Bay** and **East Wittering** merge together in an unremarkable modern sprawl of bungalows and shops. The beach along this stretch lacks the wow-factor of famous West Wittering further west; it's pebbly for a start (though there's plenty of sand at low tide) and is backed by modern residential blocks in place of West Wittering's grass-flecked dunes. It is, however, one of the best stretches of coast for **fossil-hunting**, in particular around Bracklesham Bay, where every day at low tide hundreds of fossils including bivalve shells, shark's teeth and corals are washed up on the sand – the easiest fossil-hunting going, and perfect for families. The best hunting ground is around

8

WALKS, WATERSPORTS AND TWO WHEELS ON THE MANHOOD PENINSULA

The great outdoors is what the Manhood Peninsula does best. The area is very well set up for walkers and cyclists, with miles of footpaths and cycle paths criss crossing the peninsula – bikes can be rented in the Witterings (see p.289). If you want to get out on the water virtually every watersport you can think of, and possibly one or two you haven't, is on offer around the coast.

WATERSPORTS

Mulberry Divers 9 Orchard Parade, East Beach, Selsey (☎ 01243 601000, ⓦ mulberrydivers.co.uk). Shore and boat dives exploring the wrecks and reefs off the peninsula leave several times a day at weekends (£23–30).

Wittering Surf Shop 11–13 Shore Rd, East Wittering (Mon–Fri 9am–5pm, Sat 9am–5.30pm, Sun 10am–4pm; ☎ 01243 672292, ⓦ witteringsurfshop.co.uk). Surfboard hire costs £6/half-day, £8/full day; wetsuits are £5/7.

X-Train West Wittering Beach (daily 9am–5.30pm; ☎ 01243 513077, ⓦ x-train.co.uk). This well-established outfit is the only one on the sands of West Wittering. Taster sessions are on offer for most watersports, with longer sessions/courses available: windsurfing (2hr/£48); kitesurfing (2 days/£225); powerkiting (2hr/£37); surfing (2hr/£37); stand-up paddle surfing (2hr/£48).

CYCLING

Bill Way Signposted route from Chichester Canal Basin to Pagham Nature Reserve along a canalside path and minor roads. See ⓦ selseycyclenetwork.org.uk for a basic route map of this and other cycle routes on the peninsula.

Chichester–Itchenor–Bosham–Chichester circular This circular route follows the Salterns Way (see below) as far as Chichester Marina, then continues to Itchenor, where you can pick up the (summer-only) ferry across to Bosham Hoe. The route then leads up through Bosham and Fishbourne before returning to Chichester. See ⓦ conservancy.co.uk/page/on-your-bike/424 for a route map.

Salterns Way This signposted route runs for 11 miles from the Market Cross in Chichester to the dunes of East Head, partly on cycle paths, partly on country lanes and roads. See ⓦ conservancy.co.uk/page/cycling/346 for a route map.

WALKING

Chichester Harbour Walks There are lots of downloadable walks on the Chichester Harbour Conservancy website, including a lovely 4-mile low-tide circular walk around West Wittering and East Head – see ⓦ conservancy.co.uk/assets/assets/waks_easthead.pdf.

Lipchis Way This long-distance north-to-south footpath (ⓦ newlipchisway.co.uk) runs from Liphook in Hampshire via Chichester to West Wittering. The latter part of the walk runs from Chichester along Chichester Ship Canal, past Itchenor and along the coast to West Wittering (10 miles), where you can pick up bus #52 or #53 back to Chichester (Mon–Sat every 15min, Sun hourly).

Bracklesham Bay car park and the few hundred yards east towards Selsey; see ⓦ westsussexgeology.co.uk for details of organized fossil hunts.

East Wittering is a popular location for **surfing**; you can hire boards and wetsuits from the Wittering Surf Shop (see box above).

West Wittering Beach

Beach Daily: mid-March to mid-Oct 6.30am–8.30pm; mid-Oct to mid-March 7am–6pm **Café** Mid-March to mid-Oct daily 9am–6pm; mid-Oct to mid-March Fri, Sat & Sun 10am–4pm • Parking £1–7.50 depending on season, day & time • ☎ 01243 514143 (Estate Office), ⓦ westwitteringbeach.co.uk

The wonderful thing about unspoilt **West Wittering Beach** is what *isn't* there: no amusement arcades, caravan parks or lines of shops selling garish seaside paraphernalia. Instead you'll find acres of soft white sand dimpled by shallow pools at low tide, a line of candy-coloured beach huts, grassy dunes, a modest shop and café – and that's about it. It could all have been so different, had a band of foresighted locals not scraped together £20,546 in the 1950s to buy the land and prevent it being turned into a Butlin's holiday camp; the West Wittering Estate is now managed as a conservation company, with parking fees paying for the maintenance of the beach and surrounding area.

The big grass field behind the beach serves as the car park; at its eastern end by the entrance you'll find a small cabin housing X-Train, which offers **watersports** sessions (see box opposite); and at its western end is National Trust-owned East Head (see below). **West Wittering village** – which counts among its residents Rolling Stones guitarist Keith Richards – lies less than a mile inland.

The beach gets incredibly busy on summer weekends, when as many as 15,000 holidaymakers can descend in a day. Queues on the access road can snake back for miles; if you're staying in Chichester and don't want to spend an hour or two in traffic your best bet is to hire a bike and cruise past the jams on the Salterns Way cycle route (see box opposite).

Chichester Harbour

Chichester Harbour is the Southeast's smallest Area of Outstanding Natural Beauty, a glorious estuarine landscape of inlets and tidal mudflats, pretty creekside villages and hamlets, big skies, and sparkling water dotted with sails. One of Sussex's few remaining tracts of undeveloped coastline, the harbour shelters a rich diversity of habitats – shingle banks, saltmarsh, mudflats, sand dunes and ancient woodland – and wildlife; over 50,000 birds use the harbour every year, making it a top site for bird watching, especially in winter. Exploring is easy: boat trips (see box, p.298) run all year, and 28 miles of footpaths wiggle around the coastline. **Chichester Harbour Conservancy** (ⓦconservancy.co.uk), which manages and conserves the harbour, also runs an excellent programme of **activities**, everything from nature walks, foraging and stream-dipping to kids' activities, bird watching and art events.

8

East Head

At the mouth of Chichester Harbour, National Trust-managed **East Head** is a pristine salt-and-shingle spit that's prized for its rare sand dune and saltmarsh habitats. It's connected to the western end of West Wittering Beach by a narrow strip of land known as "The Hinge", and covers around ten hectares – you can walk its length in just fifteen minutes, but despite its proximity to the beach's hordes it never really gets too busy. On the spit's western (seaward) side there's a **beach** of fine sand backed by constantly shifting dunes knitted together with clumps of shaggy marram grass; on its eastern side is a large area of salt marsh which fills and empties with each tide – a popular **birdwatching** site, especially in winter. Boardwalks snake across the spit, protecting the fragile dune system; at the far northern end you'll often see boats anchored in the summer, and, in winter, the occasional seal basking on the beach.

From The Hinge, a footpath runs north for a quarter of a mile to a specially constructed **crabbing pool**, and on to the village of Itchenor, 3.5 miles away, skirting the shoreline all the way, with flat farmland on one side, beautiful views across the water on the other.

Itchenor

The long, winding country lane leading to the quiet sailing village of **Itchenor** ends at the slipway, with lovely views across to Bosham Hoe on the far side of the creek across a sea of masts and sails. There's a viewing platform next to the slipway, a lovely place to sit and watch the bobbing, clinking boats, but most people come to Itchenor to get out on the water themselves (see box, p.298): **boat trips** run throughout the year, and from spring to autumn a small **passenger ferry** shuttles across the creek to Bosham Hoe, a thirty-minute walk from picturesque Bosham. Just by the slipway, the office of the **Chichester Harbour Conservancy** (Mon–Fri 9am–5pm, plus Easter–Sept Sat 9am–1pm; ☏01243 513275, ⓦconservancy.co.uk) has plenty of information on the harbour, boat trips, walks and other activities. While you're waiting for your boat you can grab a drink at the *Ship Inn* up the lane (see p.299).

8

CHICHESTER HARBOUR BOAT TRIPS

The best way to appreciate gloriously scenic Chichester Harbour is on the water. The harbour is one of the most popular boating waters in the country, with over 12,500 craft using it annually, and there are several ways you can join in.

HARBOUR TOURS

Chichester Harbour Conservancy ☎ 01243 513275, ⓦ conservancy.co.uk. The Conservancy runs boat trips on two vessels. The *Solar Heritage* is a solar-powered catamaran, with virtually silent engines that allow it to glide peacefully along the inlets and creeks, getting up close to wildlife; various cruises are available, including the standard "harbour discovery" tour, evening cruises, nature tours, family-friendly I-spy and smuggling-themed cruises, and winter-only bird watching cruises. Departures are from Itchenor (1hr 30min; £7.50; advance booking only) throughout the year, apart from mid-July to early September, when the catamaran departs from Emsworth (1hr; £6; pay in cash on the day), just over the border in Hampshire. The Conservancy's other boat is the *Terror*, a traditional open-decked sailing boat that's the last remaining vessel of the oyster fleet that once operated out of Emsworth; trips run from May to September, departing from Emsworth (2hr; £12.50).

Chichester Harbour Water Tours ☎ 01243 670504, ⓦ chichesterharbourwatertours.co.uk. Boat trips around the harbour leave from Itchenor up to four times a day during high summer, daily during spring and autumn, and weekends only during April and October (1hr 30min; £7.50).

BOAT HIRE

Itchenor Boat Hire ☎ 01243 513345, ⓦ itchenor boathire.co.uk. Offers self-drive, small-boat hire to those with prior experience, by the day or half-day (April–Oct only). A four-person dory costs £60–70/half-day, £105–115/day.

ITCHENOR–BOSHAM FERRY

Itchenor Ferry ⓦ itchenorferry.co.uk. Runs from the end of the jetty at Itchenor across the channel to Smugglers Lane at Bosham Hoe (mid-May to Sept daily 9am–6pm; April to mid-May & Oct Sat & Sun 9am–6pm; £2, bikes 50p).

Bosham

One of the prettiest, and certainly the most popular village on the harbour is historic, creekside **Bosham** (pronounced "Bozzum"). The village's appearance changes dramatically throughout the day as the tidal creek fills and empties: at low tide it's surrounded by green- and dun-coloured mudflats and marooned boats, while at high tide the water comes slapping right up against the back walls of the buildings along waterfront Shore Road. Despite warning signs, and tell-tale seaweed on the road, you still get the odd hapless parked car caught out by the tide; pop into the village pub, the *Anchor Bleu* (see opposite), and you'll see photos up on the walls of cars in various sorry states of submersion.

Fittingly, Bosham is one of the places put forward as the possible location of **King Canute**'s (994–1035) failed attempt to turn back the tide – a deliberate display to show the limits of his power to his fawning courtiers. Canute's young daughter is said to be buried in pretty, shingle-spired **Bosham Church**, parts of which date back to Saxon times. Look out for the reproduction of a scene from the **Bayeux Tapestry** in the north aisle, which depicts Harold, the Earl of Wessex and soon-to-be last Saxon King of England, praying in the church in 1064 before sailing off to Normandy to settle the matter of the English throne's succession with his rival, William of Normandy.

Beyond the church, over the millpond stream, lies National Trust-managed **Quay Meadow**, with **Bosham Quay** at its southern end; in summer it's a popular picnic spot, with good crabbing from the quay wall at high tide.

ARRIVAL AND GETTING AROUND | THE MANHOOD PENINSULA

By car If you're travelling to West Wittering be aware there can be daily traffic jams to and from the beach in summer. Get there early, or consider hiring a bike (see p.289).

By bike Bike routes crisscross the Manhood Peninsula (see box, p.296).

By bus Stagecoach bus #52 or #53 to Bracklesham, East

Wittering and West Wittering (Mon–Sat every 15min, Sun hourly), and #56 to Old Bosham (Mon–Sat every 1hr 15min, Sun 3 daily). Compass Travel bus #150 runs between

Itchenor, East Wittering, Bracklesham, Sidlesham & Selsey (Mon, Wed & Fri 3 daily).

ACCOMMODATION AND EATING

Anchor Bleu Bosham High St, Bosham, PO18 8LS ☎01243 573956, ⓦanchorbleu.org. The back terrace of this whitewashed eighteenth-century inn is the perfect spot to sit and watch the tide turn; at high water the sea laps right up against the terrace wall. Inside there are low, beamed ceilings and flagstone floors; the food is classic, well-done seasidey pub grub – baguettes and ploughman's (£5–9), fish and chips (£12), fresh dressed crab (£9) and the like at lunch, plus proper, satisfying puds like spotted dick and treacle sponge. Mon–Thurs 11am–11pm, Fri & Sat 11am–11.30pm, Sun noon–10.30pm; food served noon–3pm & 6.30–9pm (except Sun eve Oct–April).

Beach House B&B Rookwood Rd, West Wittering, PO20 8LT ☎01243 514800, ⓦbeachhse.co.uk. Your best option if you want to stay close to West Wittering Beach is this friendly, family-run B&B with attached restaurant; it's just a fifteen-minute walk from the beach in the heart of West Wittering village. Rooms are functional rather than luxurious, with a nautical vibe that's carried through to the bright, airy restaurant. Food is available throughout the day, from breakfast onwards: the lunch menu features salads, burgers, toasties and ciabattas, with mains (£10–16) such as Southdown leg of lamb at dinner. April–Sept daily 8am–8.15pm; Oct–March Wed, Thurs & Sun 8am–3pm, Fri & Sat 8am–8.15pm. **£90**

Crab & Lobster Mill Lane, Sidlesham, PO20 7NB ☎01243 641233, ⓦcrab-lobster.co.uk. If you want to treat yourself, this classy sixteenth-century inn on the edge of Pagham Harbour is the place: the rooms are effortlessly stylish, and the restaurant has an upmarket menu (mains £15–23) focused on seasonal, local produce – fish from Selsey, meat from local farmers, and honey from beekeepers in Sidlesham. At the back of the pub there's a peaceful terrace and beer garden with lovely views over the countryside. Mon–Thurs noon–2.30pm & 6–9.30pm, Fri noon–2.30pm & 6–10pm, Sat noon–10pm, Sun noon–9pm. **£160**

Drift-In Surf Café 11–13 Shore Rd, East Wittering, PO20 8DY ☎01243 672292, ⓦdriftinsurfcafe.co.uk. As you might expect from a café that's connected to a surf shop, this place has a laidback vibe, with vintage surfboards on the walls, surf magazines on the coffee table, and old coffee-bean sacks serving as tablecloths. The menu is perfect energy fodder after a morning catching waves – smoothies, shakes, hot chocolate, wraps and pancakes. Mon–Sat 9am–5pm, Sun 10am–4pm; hours vary in winter.

The Landing Pound House, Pound Rd, West Wittering, PO20 8AJ ☎01243 513757, ⓦthelanding.co.uk. This tiny coffee shop brings a dash of style to West Wittering, with its bare boards, Eames chairs and Plumen lighting. It's a lovely, sunny spot for breakfast or lunch, with big windows, a few tables on the front terrace, and a couple more out back by the herb patch. On the menu you'll find great coffee, wine and beer, sandwiches and Minghella artisan ice cream. There's also a small deli, with freshly baked bread for sale – perfect for beach picnics. Tues–Fri 8am–5pm, Sat & Sun 9am–5pm, sometimes later in summer.

★ **Samphire English Kitchen** 57 Shore Rd, East Wittering, PO20 8DY ☎01243 672754, ⓦsamphireeast wittering.co.uk. The Witterings' culinary star is this tiny weatherboard restaurant with a passion for fresh produce: its menu changes daily to make the most of the best local ingredients, including fish from the beach 100m away. Outside, the place has an appealingly ramshackle air, with distressed paintwork and rusted light fittings; inside it's cosy and intimate, with a jumble of pictures on the walls and mismatched furniture. A typical meal might start with a trio of mackerel – pan-fried, pâté and pickled (£7.50) – followed by fish stew (£17); there's also a set lunch menu (2/3 courses £13/16), which is an absolute bargain even without the accompanying glass of wine. Mon–Sat 11am–2pm & 6–9pm.

Ship Inn The Street, Itchenor, PO20 7AH ☎01243 512284, ⓦtheshipinnitchenor.co.uk. Just up the lane from Itchenor's slipway, this redbrick pub is always busy in summer with boaties and tourists, and the picnic tables out front are a fine spot to settle down with a pint. Food is decent pub grub (sausages, burgers, fresh fish, steaks; £9–17), and there are Sussex-brewed beers and guest ales on tap. Daily 11am–11pm; food served noon–2.30pm & 6.30–9.30pm; no food Sun eve in winter.

Stubcroft Farm Stubcroft Lane, East Wittering, PO20 8PJ ☎01243 671469, ⓦstubcroft.com. This no-frills, eco- and wildlife-friendly campsite is the nicest place to camp on the Manhood Peninsula, and very popular, so book ahead in summer. The slightly cramped pitches are spread over three paddocks on a working sheep farm; BBQs are allowed, there's a small shop, and as an added bonus you can help bottle-feed the lambs in spring. The nearest beaches (East Wittering and Bracklesham Bay) are a twenty-minute walk away, but the campsite also hires out bikes (£10/day) so it's equally easy to cycle to sandy West Wittering. The farmhouse also has a few good-value B&B rooms. Camping (per adult) **£7**, doubles **£85**

8

Surrey

RHS WISLEY

Surrey

Often unfairly dismissed as a well-heeled swathe of suburbia, Surrey has much to recommend it, particularly for ramblers. Carpeted with woodlands, the county is bisected laterally by the chalk escarpment of the North Downs, which rise west of Guildford, peak around Box Hill near Dorking, and continue east into Kent. Within the Downs lies the Surrey Hills, an Area of Outstanding Natural Beauty, where two gentle, long-distance paths set off on their way – in the north, the North Downs Way, which starts at Farnham and follows ancient pilgrims' routes to finish in Dover; further south, the Greensand Way leads from Haslemere to Hamstreet, near Ashford. These, along with countless shorter footpaths and hedge-tangled bridleways, lead you within a hiking-boot's throw of ancient bluebell woods, gently undulating fields, butterfly-speckled chalk grasslands, and sleepy little villages that have dozed here since medieval times.

Surrey's wealth dates largely from the sixteenth and seventeenth centuries, when farming and the local paper, gunpowder and iron industries were booming; later industrialization effectively passed Surrey by, and the county remained largely rural until the coming of the railways. You'll see many fine examples of **Arts and Crafts** architecture: architect **Edwin Lutyens** and his gardening partner **Gertrude Jekyll** hailed from here, inspired by Surrey's vernacular architecture and its pre-industrial feel – before rampant road- and suburb-building of the early twentieth century changed its aspect forever.

Most of the key attractions are in the **Surrey Hills**, where a number of grand estates, among them the Edwardian **Polesden Lacey,** and beauty spots, primarily **Box Hill** and **Leith Hill**, offer sweeping views over pristine countryside. These chalky slopes provide perfect conditions for viniculture, with **Denbies**, currently the largest vineyard in England, offering tours. The market towns of **Guildford** and **Dorking** provide restaurants, hotels and train connections, but it's far nicer, if you are planning a longer visit, to stay out in the countryside, kicking back in peace and quiet just a handful of miles from the capital. In the pretty cluster of villages between Guildford and Dorking, **Shere**, **Abinger** and **Peaslake** offer laidback, chocolate-box appeal and excellent local walks.

In the **west**, Surrey has a different flavour. Here protected areas of wild lowland heath dominate, with the eerie natural amphitheatre of the **Devil's Punch Bowl** making a dramatic destination in the **Greensand Hills**. North Surrey, cut through by the roaring **M25** orbital motorway, is far less rural, though beyond the collection of satellite towns and light industrial installations are a few attractions, chiefly **Wisley**, the Royal Horticultural Society's flagship garden.

Farnham and around

The attractive market town of **FARNHAM** lies tucked into Surrey's southwestern corner on its border with Hampshire. Notwithstanding its thousand-year history, its most striking buildings date from the eighteenth century, when hop farming boomed hereabouts. The Georgian architecture is at its best along **Castle Street**, which links the

BOX HILL

Highlights

① Devil's Punch Bowl Swathed in myth, this dramatic natural amphitheatre has a wild, raw beauty unseen elsewhere in the county. **See p.304**

② The Watts Gallery Arts and Crafts gallery in a country village, displaying the works of one of the leading lights of British nineteenth-century art. **See p.306**

③ Box Hill Hikers, cyclists and Sunday strollers make a beeline for this popular beauty spot – as featured in Jane Austen's Emma – near Dorking. **See p.309**

④ Polesden Lacey The immaculate, extensive estate, crisscrossed with walks, and the quirky Edwardian house give Polesden Lacey the edge over many stately homes. **See p.309**

⑤ Hannah Peschar Sculpture Garden Wander through another world in this magical, artistic spot. **See p.310**

HIGHLIGHTS ARE MARKED ON THE MAP ON P.305

9

centre with the castle – the castle's small motte-and-shell **keep** gives good views across to the Downs (Feb–Dec Mon–Fri 9am–5pm; Sat & Sun 10am–4pm; free; EH; Ⓦenglish-heritage.org.uk). Meanwhile, in the former home of a wealthy hop merchant, the quirky **Museum of Farnham**, 38 West St (Tues–Sat 10am–5pm; free; Ⓦwaverley.gov.uk/museumoffarnham), offers a lively jog through local history. The long-distance **North Downs Way** starts at Farnham, signposted from the railway station (see below).

Devil's Punch Bowl

London Rd, Hindhead, GU26 6AB • Daily dawn–dusk; café April–Oct Mon–Fri 9am–5pm, Sat & Sun 9am–6pm; Nov–March daily 9am–4pm • Free; parking £3; NT • ☎ 01428 681050, Ⓦ nationaltrust.org.uk/hindhead-and-devils-punchbowl • Haslemere station (on the line from Guildford) is 3 miles south

A large natural depression, created by subterranean springs eroding the clay soil from below, the **Devil's Punch Bowl**, some nine miles south of Farnham, offers a startling counterpoint to the softer countryside elsewhere in Surrey. Its wild heathland slopes carpeted with heather and gorse, surrounded by ancient woodlands, the Bowl is a daunting, occasionally eerie vision, offering long walks around the rim and down into the valley. No one knows for sure how it got its name, though many folk tales ascribe it to the devil's handiwork – one story suggests the bowl was created when he flung clods of earth at the god Thor. Since the 2012 rerouting of the busy A3 – which used to run around the rim of the Bowl – into a tunnel, the Punch Bowl now segues seamlessly into neighbouring **Hindhead Common**, where Sir Arthur Conan Doyle, who lived for ten years in the village of Hindhead, was inspired to write *Hound of the Baskervilles*. Accessible on the Greensand Way, the Punch Bowl and common are crisscrossed by bridleways and walking paths, including three NT trails that strike off from the café.

ARRIVAL AND INFORMATION

FARNHAM AND AROUND

By train Farnham station, on Station Hill, across the River Wey in the south of town, is a 10min walk from the centre. There are connections with London Waterloo (every 30min; 1hr) and Woking (every 30min; 23min).

Tourist office South St, midway between the station and the centre (Mon–Thurs 9am–5pm, Fri 9am–4.30pm; ☎ 01252 712667, Ⓦ www.farnham.gov.uk).

ACCOMMODATION AND EATING

The Crown Inn The Green, Petworth Rd, Chiddingfold, GU8 4TX ☎ 01428 682255, Ⓦ thecrownchiddingfold.com. You can enjoy good real ales and top-notch gastropub grub in a smart oak-panelled dining room or the more casual bar at this sixteenth-century country inn around 20min drive from the Devil's Punchbowl. Mains – venison burgers, bouillabaisse, chargrilled steak – start at £14.50, with a few simpler choices at £10, and sharing platters (including seafood, Camembert or roast duck) from £6.50 per person. The veggie choices, though few, are creative. They also offer eight swanky bedrooms. Daily noon–11pm; food served Mon–Sat noon–2.30pm & 6.30–10pm, Sun noon–3pm. **£150**

Dovecote B&B Pickhurst Rd, Chiddingfold, GU8 4TS ☎ 01428 682920, Ⓦ bedandbreakfastchiddingfold .co.uk. Pretty three-room B&B in a sixteenth-century house, convenient for the Devil's Punchbowl, with a lush garden, complete with clucking hens, and a cosy, beamed guest lounge with a real fire. The best room, a large double, is en suite, while another double and twin share a bathroom with a clawfoot tub. **£105**

★ **Farnham Maltings** Bridge Square, Farnham, GU9 7QR ☎ 01252 745444, Ⓦ farnhammaltings.com. Farnham's excellent community arts centre, which hosts live music, theatre and movies, along with crafts workshops, has a riverside café with books to browse, good coffee and cakes, breakfasts and simple home-made food, including sandwiches, noodles, soups and salad, all at around £5–7. Mon & Tues 9.30am–5pm, Wed–Fri 9.30am–9pm (5pm in summer), Sat 10am–4pm.

YHA Hindhead Devil's Punch Bowl, off A3/Portsmouth Rd, GU8 6NS ☎ 0845 371 9022, Ⓦ yha.org.uk/hostel /hindhead. Though it's only open to individuals and families in the Easter and summer holidays (pre-booked groups have the run of the place for the rest of the year) it is well worth booking in advance at this tiny, very simple YHA, a tranquil self-catering hideaway in a beamed cottage, with neck-cricklingly low ceilings, on the floor of the Punch Bowl. Whole hostel (sleeps 12) **£519**, dorm **£18**, twin room **£40**

9

Guildford and around

GUILDFORD, with its cobbled high street lined with half-timbered buildings, is an attractive county town, set on the River Wey and with lovely views across the surrounding countryside. To get a broad panorama, walk up to the medieval **Guildford Castle** (April–Sept daily 10am–5pm; March & Oct Sat & Sun 11am–4pm; £3; ⓦ www.guildford.gov .uk/GuildfordCastle), which has a viewing platform in the tower. Otherwise, formal sights are few, though the **Guildford House Gallery** (May–Sept Mon–Sat 10am–4.45pm, Sun 11am–4pm; Oct–March Mon–Sat 10am–4.45pm; free; ⓦ guildford.gov.uk/gallery), occupying one of the high street's handsome seventeenth-century townhouses, at no. 155, stages arts and crafts exhibitions and has a peaceful courtyard **café**.

The Watts Gallery

Down Lane, Compton, GU3 1DQ • Tues–Sat 11am–5pm, Sun 1–5pm • £6.50 • ⓣ 01483 810235, ⓦ wattsgallery.org.uk • #46 bus (hourly Mon–Sat) from Guildford town centre

The country village of **Compton**, a ten-minute drive from Guildford, may seem an unexpected spot for a nationally important art gallery. A century ago, however, its presence was not so incongruous: Surrey played a key role in the Arts and Crafts movement (see box, p.200), and influential Victorian painter George Frederic Watts and his wife Mary – also an accomplished artist, who designed the local cemetery chapel and established a pottery nearby – had lived in Compton since 1891. Applying the Arts and Crafts principles that art should be available to all, Watts commissioned a simple building to display his work. Today the **Watts Gallery** reveals much about this experimental figure, its vibrant crimson and turquoise walls displaying his huge range – from light-infused metaphysical landscapes to allegories, socially conscious portraits and breathtakingly vigorous sculpture. The **tearoom** serves tempting cakes and light lunches, on crockery based on Mary Watts' Compton pottery.

Clandon Park

West Clandon, GU4 7RQ • Mid-March to July, Sept & Oct Tues–Thurs & Sun 11am–5pm; Aug Mon–Thurs & Sun 11am–5pm • £8.30; NT • ⓣ 01483 222482, ⓦ nationaltrust.org.uk/clandon-park • Clandon station is 1 mile north

Three miles northeast of Guildford, the beautifully proportioned Palladian mansion **Clandon House**, built in 1720 by Venetian architect Giacomo Leoni – also responsible for Lyme Park, in Cheshire – features a stunning two-storey white **Marble Hall**, an elegant wedding cake of a room with an elaborate stucco ceiling depicting mythological scenes and ornamental fireplaces sculpted by John Michael Rysbrack. The house is filled with eighteenth-century furnishings, Meissen porcelain and textiles; rather more incongruous, in the formal seven-acre gardens, is the nineteenth-century **Maori meeting house**, brought here by a previous owner of Clandon after his stint as Governor of New Zealand.

Winkworth Arboretum

Hascombe Rd, Godalming, GU8 4AD • Daily: Nov–Jan 10am–4pm; Feb & March 10am–5pm; April–Oct 10am–6pm • £5.90; NT • ⓣ 01483 208477, ⓦ nationaltrust.org.uk/winkworth-arboretum • Godalming station is 2 miles northwest

Leafy Surrey doesn't get much prettier than at **Winkworth Arboretum**, a dazzling hillside ensemble of trees seven miles south of Guildford. It is particularly spectacular in **autumn**, when the views down the steep wooded slopes into the valley below blaze with reds and oranges; but spring, when the haze of bluebells, cherry blossom and azaleas bring a different aspect to the woods, is also stunning. The arboretum was the creation of Dr Wilfred Fox, who in the 1930s and 1940s planted more than a thousand exotic and rare trees among the existing oak and hazel woods. Take a look in the old boathouse by the tranquil lake, where a little exhibition reveals intriguing historical snippets.

Vann Garden

Vann Lane, off the A283 near Hambledon, GU8 4EF • Occasional dates April–July, as part of the National Gardens Scheme (NGS), or by appointment • £5; guided tours £6 • ☎ 01428 683413, ⓦ vanngarden.co.uk • Witley station is 3 miles west

Attached to the privately owned Vann house, the **Vann Garden** was designed in 1911 by genius garden designer **Gertrude Jekyll** (1843–1932), a leading light in the Arts and Crafts movement. A series of ponds linked by a waterfall and crisscrossed by pathways and bridges, the garden is a typically lush and generous Jekyll creation, with large, bold and wild-looking plantings creating a dramatic, romantic palette. It's one of the few Jekyll gardens open for visits, and well worth working your schedule around it.

Shere and around

SHERE, its half-beamed and rough-plastered cottages clustered around the River Tillingbourne – more of a stream, really, populated with ducks and with a tree-shaded green alongside – must be Surrey's prettiest village. It's been used as a location in countless movies, from *The Railway Children* to *Bullitt*, and was covered with a picturesque frosting of snow in *The Holiday*, starring Cameron Diaz and Kate Winslet. The likeable **Shere Museum**, Gomshall Lane (April–Oct Tues & Thurs 10am–3pm, Sat & Sun 1–5pm; Nov–March Sat & Sun 1–5pm; free; ☎ 01483 202769), presents two intriguing rooms packed with local curiosities, while walks and biking trails shoot off in all directions. A mile northwest, the tranquil **Silent Pool**, a clear spring-fed lake surrounded by box trees, is a lovely picnic spot; look out for the vivid blue flash of kingfishers.

Other appealing villages nearby include **Abinger Hammer** – once home to author E.M. Forster – and the laidback, quiet hamlet of **Peaslake**, whose surrounding woodlands and hills are perfect for rambles and mountain biking; on fair weekends the village centre, with its one pub, fills up with super-keen cyclists.

ARRIVAL AND INFORMATION

GUILDFORD AND AROUND

By train Guildford station is a mile west of the centre, across the River Wey.

Destinations Clandon (every 15–25min; 12min); Godalming (every 15–35min; 8min); Gomshall (for Shere; every 1–2hr; 15min); Haslemere (every 10–20min; 15min); London Waterloo (every 15–25min; 33min); Witley (every 30min–1hr; 15min).

Tourist office 155 High St (May–Oct Mon–Sat 9.30am–5pm, Sun 11am–4pm; Nov–April closed Sun; ☎ 01483 444333, ⓦ guildford.gov.uk/visitguildford).

ACCOMMODATION

★ **Leylands Farm** Leylands Lane, Abinger Common, RH5 6JU ☎ 01306 730115, ⓦ leylandsfarm.co.uk. Luxurious, peaceful B&B in your own self-contained, two-storey barn conversion – complete with living/dining room with a toasty woodburner – next to a rustic farmhouse. Minimum two nights April–Sept. **£80**

Radisson Blu Edwardian High St, Guildford, GU1 3DA ☎ 0800 374411, ⓦ radissonblu-edwardian.com. Upmarket business hotel with high-concept design

aspirations, with a gym, a pool and a swish British restaurant, *Relish*, and cocktail bar, *MKB*. **£120**

★ **Rookery Nook** The Square, Shere, GU5 9HG ☎ 01483 209399, ⓦ rookerynook.info. In the centre of Shere, this cute half-timbered fifteenth-century cottage offers comfortable B&B in two clean, quiet rooms, one with North Downs views, with shared bath. The friendly owners, keen walkers and cyclists, offer secure bike storage. **£85**

EATING AND DRINKING

GUILDFORD

The Keystone 3 Portsmouth Rd, GU2 4BL ☎ 01483 575089, ⓦ thekeystone.co.uk. Tucked away off the high street, this is a warmhearted pub with community events, from science debates to live folk music, cider festivals and art exhibitions. The pub grub (mains from £8) is hearty, with great pies, including game, fish and veggie versions – perfect with a real ale. Mon–Thurs noon–11pm, Fri & Sat

noon–midnight, Sun noon–5pm; food served Mon–Sat noon–3pm & 6–9pm, Sun noon–3pm.

GODALMING AND AROUND

Bel & The Dragon Old Church, Bridge St, Godalming ☎ 01483 527333, ⓦ belandthedragon-godalming.co.uk. Sleek restaurant-bar converted from a church. Food (mains from £16) is classic British with a twist, listing partridge, plaice and slow-cooked shoulder of lamb alongside rotisserie suckling pig and chargrilled lobster (£25), and the wine list is long. Mon–Fri 8.30am–11pm, Sat 9am–11.30pm, Sun 9am–10.30pm; food served Mon–Sat noon–3pm & 6–10pm, Sun noon–3.30pm & 6–9.30pm.

Dog and Pheasant Haslemere Rd, Brook, GU8 5UJ ☎01428 682763, ⊛dogandpheasant.com. Out in the countryside near Godalming, this unpretentious old pub, opposite a pretty village green and with a big garden, is popular for its interesting real ales and food. Dishes put a twist on British classics – the fish, from pan-seared scallops to daily specials, is particularly good. Mains from £11. Book ahead. Food served Mon–Fri noon–2.30pm & 6–9.30pm, Sat noon–9.30pm, Sun noon–8pm.

★ **The White Horse at Hascombe** The Street, Hascombe, GU8 4JA ☎01483 208258, ⊛whitehorse hascombe.co.uk. Lovely old pub, five miles south of Godalming, warmed in winter by a woodburning stove and with a large garden. You can drink real ales and eat delicious, locally sourced food in the large garden or in the dining room; the daily changing menu (mains from £10) offers upmarket gastropub treats, so you might see excellent home-made burgers or a posh ploughman's with focaccia. Mon–Thurs 11am–11pm, Fri & Sat 11am–midnight, Sun noon–10.30pm; food served noon–3pm & 6–10pm.

SHERE AND AROUND

★ **The Abinger Hatch** Abinger Lane, Abinger Common, RH5 6HZ ☎01306 730737, ⊛theabingerhatch.com. This comfortable pub offers excellent, good-value and locally sourced food in a peaceful setting. Dog- and family-friendly (with a large play area for kids), it's popular with walkers and cyclists, and on Sundays for its roasts, but worth visiting any time, whether you fancy bangers and mash, pheasant pie or a tasty macaroni cheese with herb salad. They can even prepare you a picnic to eat on the grass, with rugs provided. Mains from £8.50. Mon–Sat 11am–11pm, Sun 11am–11pm; food served Mon–Sat noon–10pm, Sun noon–9pm.

Hurtwood Inn Walking Bottom, Peaslake, GU5 9RR ☎01306 730851, ⊛hurtwoodinnhotel.com. At the heart of Peaslake, this large, friendly 1920s inn makes a good base for cycling and walking breaks, with comfortable rooms in the main building and basic, motel-like "garden rooms" at the back. The pub serves real ales and cider, Modern European bar snacks (£6–8) and mains – sausage and mash, calves' liver, pies, pasta – from £11. **£95**

Kinghams Gomshall Lane, Shere, GU5 9HE ☎01483 202168, ⊛kinghams-restaurant.co.uk. *Kinghams*, in a seventeenth-century building surrounded by a gorgeous cottage garden, offers upscale dining in cosy surroundings. The menu offers creative takes on classic British and French cuisine, from spice-marinated Gressingham duck breast on pak choi to ling with crab and spring onion crust. Mains from £16, though there's a two-course set menu for £16.95 (Tues–Thurs lunch & dinner, Fri & Sat lunch). Book ahead. Tues–Sat noon–3pm & 7–10pm, Sun noon–3pm.

The William Bray Shere Lane, Shere, GU5 9HS ☎01483 202044, ⊛thewilliambray.co.uk. Large, pub – owned by The Stig of *Top Gear* fame – where you can eat Modern British gastropub food in a smart dining room, buzzy bar area or on a terrace. The locally sourced food (mains from £14) is full of robust flavours – goat's cheese and beetroot tart, maybe, or oven-roasted sea trout with thyme rosti and samphire. Mon–Sat 11am–11pm, Sun 11am–8pm; food served Mon–Sat noon–10pm, Sun noon–8pm.

Dorking and around

Set at the mouth of a gap carved by the River Mole through the North Downs, the historic market town of **DORKING** is famed for its **antique stores** – nearly twenty of them on the handsome sixteenth-century **West Street** alone (⊛www.dorkingantiques .com) – and is also surrounded by some of the Surrey Hills' biggest sights. **Box Hill**, on a chalk escarpment above the River Mole north of Dorking, draws streams of walkers and keen cyclists at the weekend; you can also take walks around the nearby **Leith Hill**, in the grounds of **Polesden Lacey**, and even through the vineyards at **Denbies**, which also offers tours. Further south, the idiosyncratic **Hannah Peschar Sculpture Garden** is a glorious spot, hidden in the woods towards Sussex.

Denbies Wine Estate

London Rd, RH5 6AA • April–Oct Mon–Sat 9.30am–5.30pm, Sun 10am–5.30pm; Nov–March closes 5pm; tours April–Nov daily hourly (except 1pm) 11am–4pm; Dec–March Mon–Fri noon, 2pm & 3pm, Sat & Sun hourly (except 1pm) 11am–4pm • Free; indoor tours £9.50, £12 with sparkling wines, £14 with food; "train" tours £5.50 • ☎01306 876616, ⊛denbies.co.uk • 15min walk north from Dorking train station

With 265 acres of vines, planted on the sunny south-facing slopes of a sheltered valley, **Denbies** is currently the largest privately owned vineyard in England. The chalky soil and the microclimate in this area, very similar to the Champagne region of France, are ideal for wine production – indeed, the Romans grew grapes just 300 yards away – and nineteen varieties are now planted here. Denbies specializes in traditionally produced sparkling wines – champagne in all but name – including the delicious sparkling Greenfields, but they also offer around a dozen whites (among them the Surrey Gold, a very drinkable blend of Müller-Thurgau, Ortega and Bacchus), some solid reds, and the dry, light Chalk Ridge rosé.

This is a big, very commercial operation centring on a busy restaurant and shop. Indoor tours lead you through the winery, explaining the process, with tastings at the end. Even nicer, especially on a sunny summer's day, is to ride the little "train" through the vineyards, which are part of a much larger estate, dipping in and out of beautiful dappled woodland and affording wonderful views over the slopes to Box Hill, Dorking and Leith Hill. You can also walk through the estate on public footpaths.

Box Hill

Box Hill Rd, KT20 7LB • Daily dawn to dusk • Free; NT • ☎ 01306 885502, ⓦ nationaltrust.org.uk/box-hill • Box Hill & Westhumble train station is 0.5 miles west

It's a stiff cycle ride up the zigzagging path to the top of **Box Hill**, a mile from the North Downs Way, where a variety of walks and paths lead you through woodlands of rare wild box trees, yew, oak and beech, and across chalk grasslands designated as a Site of Special Scientific Interest and scattered with wild flowers and fluttering with butterflies. NT trails include an adventurous "natural play trail" for kids, the two-mile Stepping Stones walk along the River Mole, and some longer, more strenuous options. Brilliant views abound, most famously from the **Salomons' Memorial** viewpoint near the café, where on a clear day you can see across the Weald to the South Downs.

Polesden Lacey

Near Great Bookham, RH5 6BD • **House** Jan & Feb guided tours only Sat & Sun 11am–3.30pm; March–Dec Wed–Sun 11am–5pm; last entry 30min before close • £10.80 with gardens; NT • **Gardens** Jan to mid-Feb daily 10am–4pm; mid-Feb to Dec daily 10am–5pm • £6.66 • ☎ 01372 452048, ⓦ nationaltrust.org.uk/polesden-lacey • Boxhill & Westhumble station is 3 miles east

Four miles from Dorking, and minutes from the North Downs Way, the grand Edwardian estate of **Polesden Lacey** practically begs you to while away the day with a picnic. On the velvety lawn of the South Terrace, you'll find deckchairs, rugs, and on summer weekends a stall serving jugs of Pimms that you can quaff while enjoying uninterrupted views of the Surrey Hills. If you're feeling more active, take a wander around the gardens, which include a hop field, orchard and an old walled rose garden and the 1400-acre surrounding estate – in summer you can even play croquet.

Though some rooms are yet to be restored, the **house** – remodelled from a nineteenth-century building by the architects of the *Ritz* – is worth a look. It's largely set up to appear as it might have been in 1906, when owned by the wealthy socialite Margaret Greville (1863–1942), and while filled with priceless artworks, it's the human details that linger. A wireless burbles in the library, the dining room has touchscreen tablets filling you in on the luminaries who ate here – among them Edward VII and his lover Alice Keppel, Camilla Parker-Bowles' great-grandmother – and in the billiards room you can take a quick shot to the accompaniment of 78s on the wind-up Vitrola.

Leith Hill

Near Coldharbour, Dorking • Tower April–Oct Fri–Sun 10am–5pm; Nov–March Sat & Sun 10am–3.30pm • £1.30; NT • ☎ 01306 712711, ⓦ nationaltrust.org.uk/leith-hill

Reaching the lofty heights of 967ft, **Leith Hill** is the highest point in the Southeast, topped with a neo-Gothic eighteenth-century tower, a folly from the top of which you

9

can peer through a telescope to see the sprawling mass of London in the north and the Channel to the south. A number of trails wind through open heathlands and through the woods, particularly lovely in spring, when drifts of bluebells shimmer across the floor, and the rhododendrons burst into colour.

Hannah Peschar Sculpture Garden

Standon Lane, near Ockley, RH5 5QR • May–Oct Fri & Sat 11am–6pm, Sun 2–5pm • £10 • ☎ 01306 627269, ⓦ hannahpescharsculpture .com • Ockley station is 3 miles northeast

Tucked away off a hedgerow-tangled lane outside the hamlet of Ockley, a twenty-minute drive south of Dorking, the **Hannah Peschar Sculpture Garden** has a fairytale feel. Owned by an artist/landscape designer couple, the setting is a work of art in itself – a secret forest of lofty mature trees, giant ferns and towering broadleaf plants. A vision of impossibly green lushness, dappled with light, it's all amazingly peaceful, silent other than the burble of rushing streams and the rat-a-tat of distant woodpeckers. Follow winding, mossy paths and cross honeysuckle-tangled footbridges to discover modern sculptures among the giant ferns, dangling from branches, or standing alone in glades. Some, made of weather-battered wood, or cool green and brown marble, look as if they have grown from the soil, while others, constructed from steel, cement and fibreglass, make a striking contrast with the organic world around them.

ARRIVAL AND INFORMATION

DORKING AND AROUND

By train The station is 1.5 miles north of the centre. Destinations Box Hill & Westhumble (every 30min–1hr; 2min); London Victoria (every 30min; 1hr); London Waterloo (every 30min; 50min); Ockley (every 30min–1hr; 11min).

Website ⓦ visitdorking.com.

ACCOMMODATION

Denbies Farmhouse London Rd, Dorking, RH5 6AA ☎ 01306 876777, ⓦ denbies.co.uk. With a rather special setting on the Denbies estate, right at the edge of the vineyards, the farmhouse offers seven simple en-suite B&B rooms and a peaceful front garden where you can sit and enjoy a glass of something good. Bike rental £5/day. **£105**
Garden Cottage Polesden Lacey, nr Great Bookham, RH5 6BD ☎ 0844 800 2070, ⓦ nationaltrustcottages.co.uk. This handsome, ivy-strewn National Trust property – somewhat larger than a cottage – is in a gorgeous spot next to the Polesden Lacey rose garden, with an outdoor seating area and a real fire in winter. Three smart bedrooms sleep six.

Minimum stay two nights. Two nights **£990**
★ **YHA Tanners Hatch** Off Ranmore Common Rd, nr Dorking, RH5 6BE ☎ 0845 371 9542, ⓦ yha.org.uk /hostel/tanners-hatch. Deep in the woods, well off the beaten track (it's a 15min walk from the nearest car park), this cute-as-can-be seventeenth-century cottage, surrounded by an old English garden, is on the Polesden Lacey estate, with wonderful views. Inside is simple, snug and cosy, with low-beamed ceilings, creaky narrow stairs and a real fire. It's self-catering, and hostellers and campers alike can make campfires and stoke up barbecues in the woods. The toilet/shower block is outside. Dorms **£18**; camping per person **£11**

EATING AND DRINKING

Bryce's Fish The Old School House, Stane St, Ockley, RH5 5TH ☎ 01306 627430, ⓦ bryces.co.uk. Proudly ungastrified, this pub-restaurant is a friendly spot to dine on fresh fish and seafood. The restaurant is quite pricey, with two-/three-course menus at £29/34, but it's just as nice to eat in the old-fashioned bar area, all carpets and beams, where mains, including a delicious smoked haddock with spring onion mash and poached egg, start at £13. Bar snacks and light bites (perhaps Cullen skink or grilled sardines) are cheaper still, with rock oysters at £2 a go. There's also an above-average veggie selection. Daily noon–10pm; food served daily noon–2pm & 6.30–9pm (2.30pm/9.30pm in the bar); closed Sun night & Mon in winter.

Running Horses Old London Rd, Mickleham, RH5 6DU ☎ 01372 372279, ⓦ www.therunninghorses.co.uk. An upmarket sixteenth-century inn near Box Hill, serving excellent Modern British food. It's not cheap, with even the simplest dishes like roasted butternut squash risotto, a classic fish pie, or a grilled halloumi salad at around £14, but the three-course menu for £34 is good value, including the likes of crispy confit duck with wasabi potatoes. They also offer five B&B rooms. Food served Mon–Fri noon–2.30pm & 7–9.30pm, Sat noon–3pm & 7–9.30pm, Sun noon–3pm & 6–9pm. **£110**
Two to Four 2–4 West St, Dorking, RH4 1BL ☎ 01306 889923, ⓦ 2to4.co.uk. The best restaurant in Dorking,

with seasonal, locally sourced mains from £18 and good-value set menus (two/three-course lunch £12/16 Tues–Sat; two-course dinner £15 Tues–Fri). Typical dishes include roasted cod with crushed potatoes and pea shoots, or courgette, lemon and chilli risotto. Tues–Sat noon–2.30pm & 6.30–10.30pm.

North Surrey

North Surrey, straggling out beyond the Greater London borders, lacks the rural atmosphere that defines the hills and heaths to the south, but there are a few key attractions here, including the **Epsom Downs racecourse**, home of the Derby (ⓦepsomderby.co.uk) since 1780, and **RHS Wisley**, a dream-come-true real-life catalogue for keen gardeners.

RHS Wisley

4 miles east of Woking, GU23 6QB • March–Oct Mon–Fri 10am–6pm, Sat & Sun 9am–6pm (glasshouse from 10am); Nov–Feb Mon–Fri 10am–4.30pm, Sat & Sun 9am–4.30pm (glasshouse from 10am) • £10.50; free parking • ☎ 0845 260 9000, ⓦ rhs.org.uk/gardens/wisley

Established in Victorian times to cultivate "difficult" plants, **RHS Wisley** is still a working and demonstration garden, constantly experimenting with new plants and cultivation techniques. Its sheer size – 240 acres – means it remains blessedly uncrowded even in high summer (though the glasshouse can fill up); it is also, with its trails, woodlands and lakes, the kind of garden that even non-gardeners can enjoy.

The crowd-pleaser is the vast, 40ft-high **glasshouse**, with three climatic zones teeming with rare and exotic plants, planted around waterfalls and pools. It's particularly popular during the **butterfly show** in the first months of the year, when thirty species of butterfly flutter by like something from a dream. Elsewhere, don't miss the **wild garden**, an abundant woodland featuring giant lilies, poppies, magnolia and bamboo – it's bright with azaleas and wisteria in spring and even boasts camellias in winter. **Battleston Hill** comes into its own in late spring when you might catch not only the bluebells but also the firework display of rhododendrons and azaleas; you'll also see exquisite wisteria, tumbling through the branches of a stand of silver birch, and, in autumn, the unusual, purple-spotted toad lily. From the **orchard**, planted with hundreds of old fruit trees, to the **pinetum**, with its mighty redwoods, Wisley's trees are as fascinating as its smaller plants. If you're here in October, make for the **Seven Acres**, where the broad-leaved Wisley Bonfire tree turns a breathtaking burnt gold.

ACCOMMODATION AND EATING   NORTH SURREY

143 The Canopy 143 High St, Epsom, KT19 8EH ☎01372 745330, ⓦ143thecanopy.com. Good-looking restaurant in Epsom, with reliable British cooking and the odd creative surprise: Cajun salmon with black-eye beans, sweet potato hash and fried plantains, for example. Lunchtime sees sandwiches and light bites (smoked mackerel pâté; savoury tarts) from £5.50, and they offer two-/three-course menus (lunch Tues–Sat: £12.95/£15.95; dinner Tues–Thurs: £16/£20). Tues–Sat 10am–4.30pm & 6.30–9.30pm, Sun (except last in month) noon–3pm.

Hamiltons 23 Windsor St, Chertsey, KT16 8AY ☎01932 560745, ⓦhamiltons23.com. A friendly restaurant with rooms, where you can eat classy Modern European dishes – black-legged chicken with thyme gnocchi; warm salad of wood pigeon with caramelized walnuts – before retiring upstairs to your bed. Restaurant Tues–Thurs 4–10pm, Fri & Sat 4–10.30pm, Sun noon–4pm. __£95__

Swallow Barn Milford Green, Chobham, GU24 8AU ☎01276 856030, ⓦswallow-barn.co.uk. Set in four acres of gardens, with an outdoor swimming pool, *Swallow Barn* offers three comfortable double/twin B&B rooms in a quiet spot near Wisley. __£90__

Drake's High St, Ripley, GU23 6AQ ☎01483 224777, ⓦdrakesrestaurant.co.uk. The booking system is a little precious, but the amazing food and friendly service make up for it at this Michelin-starred restaurant near Wisley. Beautifully executed, it's all about the robust flavours, which are fresh and intriguing, with dishes described as a list of ingredients (pea, egg, broad beans, grapefruit, lamb sweetbreads, for example). It can get pricey, with a six-course "flavour journey" (£39.50), and a "flavour discovery" (£80), both for the whole table only, but the three-course set-lunch menu is great value at £28. Tues 7pm & 9pm; Wed–Sat noon, 2pm, 7pm & 9pm.

CARVED VAULTING, CANTERBURY CATHEDRAL CLOISTERS

Contexts

History

As the part of the country closest to mainland Europe, the southeast corner of England has played an important part in British history. It was here that Caesar landed his troops in the Roman invasion of Britain in 55 BC, and here too, over a millennium later in 1066, that William of Normandy defeated King Harold in the last successful invasion of Britain. Over the years the coastline of Kent and Sussex has been at the frontline of potential invasion, facing off threats from Napoleon and Hitler among others, with the coast's iconic White Cliffs standing as a symbolic, and practical, bulwark against would-be invaders.

Prehistory

The southeast corner of England has been inhabited, intermittently at least, for half a million years or more. For much of this period it was covered by snow during successive ice ages, but a land bridge to continental Europe allowed early man to come and go. The earliest hominid remains so far discovered in Britain – a shinbone and two teeth, alongside worked flint implements – were unearthed at **Boxgrove**, near Chichester in West Sussex, and date back between 524,000 and 478,000 years. "Boxgrove Man" was a nomadic hunter, over 5ft 10in tall, who roamed the shoreline, hunting large mammals using worked flint tools.

The last spell of intense cold began about 17,000 years ago, and it was the final thawing of this last Ice Age around 7000 years ago that caused Britain to separate from the European mainland, with the warmer temperatures allowing natural woodland to cloak the land. The earliest farmers appeared about 4000 BC. These tribes were the first to make some impact on the environment, clearing forests, enclosing fields, constructing defensive ditches around their villages and digging mines to obtain flint used for tools and weapons. The **flint mines** in Sussex are among the oldest in England: they were begun around 4000 BC and continued until 2800 BC, with the resulting flint axes being used for barter and trade along the South Downs. At Cissbury Ring in West Sussex (see p.238) you can still see the bumps in the grass from the network of shafts, some 40ft deep.

The transition from the Neolithic to the **Bronze Age** began around 2000 BC with the importation from northern Europe of artefacts attributed to the **Beaker Culture** – named for the distinctive cups found at many burial sites. The 3500-year-old **Hove amber cup** – considered to be one of Britain's most important Bronze Age finds – is on show at Hove Museum in Brighton (see p.261). The spread of the Beaker Culture along European trade routes helped stimulate the development of a comparatively well-organized social structure with an established aristocracy. Large numbers of earthwork forts and round barrow, or burial mounds, were constructed in this period, with settlements across the Southeast, including just outside Eastbourne underneath Shinewater Park – thought to be one of the largest Bronze Age villages in Europe, though it remains unexcavated.

c.500,000 BC	4000 BC	2000 BC	500 BC
Boxgrove Man roams the shore around present-day Chichester.	Farming and the mining of flint for trade begins.	The start of the Bronze Age; earthwork forts and villages are built.	The Iron Age sees a network of hillforts established across the Downs.

THE PILTDOWN HOAX

The skull of "**Piltdown Man**" was discovered in a gravel pit in Piltdown in East Sussex in 1912 by **Charles Dawson**, a respected lawyer and amateur geologist, and sensationally hailed as the missing link between apes and humans, a paleontological find of immense significance. As the years went by, and more ancient hominid fossils were unearthed around the globe, it became increasingly clear that Piltdown Man was a bit of an anomaly that didn't quite fit with other discoveries. It took more than 40 years, however, until 1953, to unearth the truth: what had been presented as a 500,000-million-year-old skull had in fact been cleverly assembled from a medieval skull and an orang-utan jaw, and the Piltdown hoax passed into history as one of the greatest archeological hoaxes ever perpetrated.

The Iron Age and the Romans

By 500 BC, the Southeast was inhabited by a number of different Celtic tribes, each with a sophisticated farming economy and social hierarchy. Familiar with Mediterranean artefacts through their far-flung trade routes, they gradually developed better methods of metal-working, ones that favoured **iron** rather than bronze, from which they forged not just weapons but also coins and ornamental works. Their principal contribution to the landscape was a network of hillforts and other defensive works, among them the **hillforts** of Mount Caburn near Lewes, Cissbury Ring (see p.238), Chanctonbury Ring (see p.237), the Trundle near Chichester, and Oldbury near Ightham.

The Roman invasion of Britain began hesitantly, with small cross-Channel incursions in 55 and 54 BC led by **Julius Caesar**, who landed near Deal in Kent. Almost one hundred years later, the death of the king of southeast England, Cunobelin (Shakespeare's Cymbeline), presented **Emperor Claudius** with a golden opportunity and in August 43 AD, a substantial Roman force landed, though the jury is still out on precisely where – possibly at Richborough (see p.106) in Kent, possibly further west beyond Chichester. The Roman army quickly fanned out, conquering the southern half of Britain and subsuming it into the Roman Empire.

Roman rule lasted nearly four centuries. Commerce flourished, cities such as Canterbury and Chichester prospered, and Roman civilization left its mark all over the Southeast: in coastal forts at Richborough and Pevensey (see p.184), a clifftop lighthouse at Dover (see p.114), arrow-straight roads, city walls still standing in Chichester, which also retains the original Roman cruciform street plan (see p.287), and wealthy **Roman villas** at Lullingstone in Kent (see p.153), and Bignor (see p.243) and Fishbourne (see p.292) in Sussex – the last of these the largest and best-preserved Roman dwelling in the country.

The Anglo-Saxons

From the late third century, Roman England was subject to **raids** by **Saxons**, leading to the eventual withdrawal of the Roman armies at the begining of the fifth century. This gave the Saxons free rein to begin settling the country, which they did throughout the sixth and seventh centuries, with the **Jutes** from Jutland establishing themselves in eastern Kent. The southeast corner of England was divided into the **Anglo-Saxon kingdoms of Kent, Sussex and Wessex** – the last of these stretching west into Somerset

55 and 54 BC	43 AD	410
Julius Caesar's first incursions into Britain.	The Romans invade under Emperor Claudius, and rule for nearly four centuries.	The Romans withdraw from Britain, leaving the Saxons and Jutes to settle the Southeast and establish the Anglo-Saxon kingdoms of Kent, Sussex and Wessex.

and Dorset – with power and territory fluctuating and passing hands among them over the centuries that followed. The Anglo-Saxons all but eliminated Romano-British culture, with the old economy collapsing and urban centres emptying.

The early Anglo-Saxon period saw the countrywide revival of Christianity, which was driven mainly by **St Augustine** (see box, p.50), who was despatched by Pope Gregory I and landed on the Kent coast in 597, accompanied by forty monks. Ethelbert, the king of the Kingdom of Kent and the most powerful Anglo-Saxon overlord of the time, received the missionaries and gave Augustine permission to found a monastery at **Canterbury**, where the king himself was then baptized. The ruins of Augustine's abbey, including the remains of its seventh-century St Pancras church, can still be visited today (see p.49).

By the end of the ninth century the Kingdom of Wessex had established supremacy over the Southeast, with the formidable and exceptionally talented **Alfred the Great** recognized as overlord by several southern kingdoms. His successor, **Edward the Elder**, capitalized on his efforts to become the de facto overlord of all England. The relative calm continued under Edward's son, Athelstan, and his son **Edgar**, who became the first ruler to be crowned **King of England** in 973.

After a brief period of Danish rule – most famously under the shrewd and gifted **Canute**, who famously failed to turn back the tide at Bosham (see p.298) – the Saxons regained the initiative, installing **Edward the Confessor** on the throne in 1042. On Edward's death, **Harold** was confirmed as king, ignoring several rival claims including that of William, Duke of Normandy. William wasted no time: he assembled an army, set sail for England and famously routed the Saxons at the **Battle of Hastings** in 1066 (see box, p.187). On Christmas Day, **William the Conqueror** was installed as king in Westminster Abbey.

The Middle Ages

William I swiftly imposed a Norman aristocracy on his new subjects, reinforcing his rule with a series of strongholds. The strategically important kingdom of Sussex was divided into five **rapes** (administrative divisions), each with a newly built **castle** at its centre, controlled by one of William's most loyal supporters: Robert, Count of Eu, in Hastings (see p.178); Robert, Count of Mortain, in Pevensey (see p.184); William de Warrene in Lewes (see p.227); William de Braose in Bramber (see p.237); and Roger of Montgomery in Chichester and Arundel (see p.238). In Surrey castles sprang up at Guildford (see p.306) and Farnham (see p.304), and in Kent at Canterbury, Rochester, one of the best-preserved Norman fortresses in the country (see p.70), Leeds (see p.158) near Maidstone, and Dover (see p.112), although Kent itself retained some autonomy under Norman rule, possibly because of the resistance it put up against its invaders; the county motto, "Invicta", meaning undefeated, was adopted after the Conquest, and the "Man of Kent" term (see box, p.316) may also date from this time. The earliest Norman castles were motte-and-bailey earth-and-timber constructions, later replaced with more permanent stone castles.

Alongside the castles, mighty stone-built **cathedrals, abbeys and churches** were erected. William raised the great Benedictine Battle Abbey (see p.186) on the site of his famous victory and in Lewes, William de Warrene founded **St Pancras Priory** (see p.229), which was to become one of the largest and most powerful monasteries in England. The Saxon See at Selsey was moved to Chichester, where the mighty

597	973	1066
St Augustine lands on the Kent coast to spread Christianity around the country.	Edgar becomes the first king of England.	The Battle of Hastings sees William the Conqueror from Normandy defeat King Harold, marking the end of Anglo-Saxon England.

KENTISH MEN AND MAIDS OF KENT

To call oneself a **Kentish Man (or Maid)**, or a **Maid (or Man) of Kent**, would seem at first to be simply a matter of semantics. However, these proudly held labels in fact refer to geographical areas: although the division is generally taken to be the River Medway, strictly speaking **Kentish Men** are born west of a line that cuts through a point just east of Gillingham, and **Men of Kent** in the more rural area to the east. Some believe that this east–west division may date back to the fifth century, when, following the departure of the Romans, **Saxons** moved into the west of the region, while the **Jutes**, who called themselves Kentings, or "Men of Kent", settled in the east. Others say that "Men of Kent" only became an accepted term after the **Norman invasion**, when people of East Kent resisted William the Conqueror with more force than those in the west, were granted certain privileges because of it, and were bestowed with the name as a form of unofficial honour.

Chichester cathedral (see p.288) was founded, and up in northern Kent, Rochester cathedral was built on the site of an Anglo-Saxon place of worship. In Canterbury the Norman archbishop Lanfranc rebuilt the existing cathedral in 1070 following a huge fire, and the Normans established a Benedictine abbey on the site of the Saxon St Augustine's Abbey. A hundred years later the cathedral became an important pilgrimage site – second only to Rome – when the murder of Archbishop **Thomas à Becket** ended up with Becket's canonization (see box, p.43).

In 1264, the countryside around Lewes in East Sussex saw one of just two major battles to have taken place in the Southeast (the other was at Battle in 1066). The **Battle of Lewes** was the bloody culmination of a clash between Henry III and a rebel army of barons under Simon de Montfort; the king was defeated and the resulting treaty, the **Mise of Lewes**, restricted his authority and forced him to assemble a governing council – often described as the first House of Commons. De Montfort's role as de facto ruler of England was short-lived; the following year Henry III's son Edward (later Edward I) routed the barons' army at the battle of Evesham in Worcestershire in 1265, killing De Montfort in the process.

The outbreak of the **Black Death** came in 1349. The plague claimed about a third of the country's population – and the scarcity of labour that followed gave the peasantry more economic clout than they had ever had before; for the first time dwellings such as the Clergy House in Alfriston (see p.218) were erected by wealthy yeoman farmers. Predictably, the landowners attempted to restrict the accompanying rise in wages, thereby provoking the widespread rioting that culminated in the abortive **Peasants' Revolt** of 1381, led by **Wat Tyler** of Kent. Another popular uprising, this time organized by Kentish man **Jack Cade**, took place in 1450, with Cade leading an army of five thousand to London, where he listed the grievances of the common people and demanded reform from the King; the rebellion was quickly crushed and the fleeing Cade was caught and killed while hiding in a garden in Lewes.

The Tudors and the Stuarts

The start of the **Tudor** period saw the country begin to assume the status of a major European power. Henry VIII – best remembered for his multiple wives, whose former

1170	1264	1349	1381
Canterbury Cathedral becomes one of Christendom's greatest pilgrim shrines when Archbishop Thomas à Becket is murdered on the orders of Henry II.	The Battle of Lewes is fought between Henry III and Simon de Montfort's army of rebel barons.	Black Death decimates the region.	Wat Tyler leads the Peasants' Revolt.

homes can be found scattered all over the region, from Anne Boleyn's childhood home of Hever Castle (see p.155), to the various properties settled on Anne of Cleves in her divorce settlement – built coastal fortresses at Deal and Walmer (see p.110), designed to scare off the Spanish and the French, and around 1570 he founded the vast **Chatham Historic Dockyard** (see p.72), which quickly became the major base of the Royal Navy. This effectively spelled the end of the **Cinque Port federation** (see box, p.105), which had been established in 1278 and granted trading privileges to the south-coast ports of Dover, Hythe, Sandwich, Romney and Hastings in return for their providing maritime support in times of war – though their demise was only a matter of time anyway, with the shifting coastline leaving many of them stranded high and dry miles inland.

Henry VIII also presided over the establishment of the **Church of England** and the **Dissolution of the Monasteries**, which conveniently gave both king and nobles the chance to get their hands on valuable monastic property in the late 1530s, and reduced the monasteries at Battle, Lewes and elsewhere to ruin. In 1553 Henry's daughter Mary, a fervent Catholic, ascended the throne and returned England to the papacy. Her oppression of Protestants during the **Marian Persecutions** of 1555–57, when seventeen Protestants in the Sussex town of Lewes were condemned to be burned alive (along with 271 others around the country) is at the root of the Sussex town's riotous bonfire celebrations today (see p.230).

The country reverted to Protestantism with Elizabeth I, but tensions between Protestants and Catholics remained, and Protestants' worst fears were confirmed in 1605 when **Guy Fawkes** – butler at Cowdray House in West Sussex (see p.244) – and a group of Catholic conspirators were discovered preparing to blow up King and Parliament in the so-called **Gunpowder Plot**. During the ensuing hue and cry, many Catholics met an untimely end and Fawkes himself was hanged, drawn and quartered.

In the turbulent years of the **English Civil War** (1642–51), the Southeast, which remained almost entirely Parliamentarian, saw little serious fighting – though the castle at Arundel was reduced to rubble when it was held under siege first by Royalists and then by Parliamentarian troops. For the next eleven years England was a **Commonwealth** – at first a true republic, then, after 1653, a **Protectorate** with Cromwell as the Lord Protector and commander-in-chief. The turmoil of the Civil War unleashed a furious legal, theological and political debate, and spawned a host of leftist sects, the most notable of whom were the **Levellers**, who demanded wholesale constitutional reform and whose first manifesto was drafted at Guildford in Surrey, and the more radical Surrey-based **Diggers**, who proposed common ownership of all land. Cromwell died in 1658 to be succeeded by his son **Richard**, who ruled briefly and ineffectually, leaving the army unpaid while one of its more ambitious commanders, General Monk, conspired to restore the monarchy. Charles II, the exiled son of the previous king, entered London in triumph in May 1660. For the next 150 years the Southeast was to remain largely untroubled by conflict.

The Georgian era

The next serious threat to the region's peace came in the form of the most daunting of enemies, **Napoleon**. "All my thoughts are directed towards England. I want only for a favourable wind to plant the Imperial Eagle on the Tower of London," Napoleon

1450	1509	1555–57
Jack Cade marches an army to London, demanding reform for the common people.	Henry VIII comes to the throne: he founds the Chatham Historic Dockyard and orders the Dissolution of the Monasteries.	The Marian Persecutions of Mary I sees hundreds of Protestants burned alive around the country, including at Lewes and Canterbury.

THE WEALDEN IRON INDUSTRY

Little evidence remains today of the great furnaces of the **Wealden iron industry** that once roared and blazed in the ancient forests of Kent, Sussex and Surrey. During the Tudor and early Stuart periods timber and iron production had made the Weald the most important iron-producing centre in Britain: wood from the forest was used not only for **shipbuilding** (Sussex oak was especially prized) but also to cheaply power the furnaces of the Weald's great **iron ore mines** – with the iron used not just to produce domestic firebacks and the like, but also the cannons and weaponry for the great Tudor and Stuart navies. By the mid-sixteenth century there were fifty **furnaces** and forges, double that number 25 years later. **Ironmasters' houses** sprang up in the Weald, among them Gravetye Manor (see p.201) and Bateman's (see p.190).

The good times couldn't last forever; iron ore supplies started to dwindle, prices were undercut by foreign imports and production elsewhere in the country, and by 1717 the number of furnaces had dropped to fourteen. The ironworks at Hoathly near Lamberhurst in Kent lingered on until 1784, and those at Ashburnham in Sussex until 1796, but they simply couldn't compete with the great coke-fired factories of the North with its vast coalfields.

threatened. Henry VIII's coastal fortresses were garrisoned once again; a thirty-mile canal – the Royal Military Canal (see p.30) – was dug between Hythe and Winchelsea in Kent, with a raised northern bank forming a parapet; and more than a hundred squat Martello towers (see box, p.124) were erected along the south coast, stretching from Suffolk all the way round to Sussex. In the event, by the time the fortifications were completed – the canal in 1809, the Martello towers by 1812 – the threat of invasion was long past, with Nelson's decisive victory over **Napoleon** at **Trafalgar** in 1805 helping to put paid to his plans for invasion. Final defeat for the French emperor came ten years later by the Duke of Wellington at **Waterloo**, signalling the end of the Napoleonic Wars (1803–15).

England's triumph over Napoleon was underpinned by its financial strength, which was itself born of the **Industrial Revolution**, the switch from an agricultural to a manufacturing economy that changed the face of the country in the space of a hundred years – though it barely scratched the surface of life in the rural Southeast. By the time James Watt patented his **steam engine** in 1781, Sussex and Kent's industrial era had already been and gone, with the collapse both of the great **Wealden iron industry** (see box above) and of the **Wealden cloth industry** which had been centred around Cranbrook in Kent and had all but disappeared by 1700. Surrey's great **paper and gunpowder mills**, at their peak in the seventeenth century, fared a little better, clinging on until the late nineteenth and early twentieth centuries. The Southeast thus remained largely agricultural throughout the Industrial Revolution – with Kent in particular relying heavily on its thriving **hop-growing** industry, which peaked in the late nineteenth century – and retained its rural landscape of small towns and villages, escaping the urban industrial sprawl of the North.

While the landed gentry spent their money on splendid country estates, life for **agricultural labourers** was hard: low wages, high rents, soaring bread prices thanks to the Corn Laws, and the introduction of labour-displacing agricultural machinery all contributed to widespread discontent, and it was in Kent that the **Swing Riots** began in 1830, with peasants rising up to destroy the much-hated threshing machines, and

1642–51	1736	1783–1826
The Southeast escapes relatively unscathed from the English Civil War, though Arundel Castle is reduced to rubble.	The first seawater baths open at Margate, Britain's first seaside resort.	George IV patronizes the small seaside town of Brighton, helping it become the south coast's most fashionable resort.

unrest spreading throughout the whole of southern England and into East Anglia. It was really little wonder that **smuggling** (see box, p.218) was such an attractive proposition to the rural communities along the Sussex and Kent coasts: a desperately poor farm labourer could earn a week's salary in one lucrative night as a tubman, carrying contraband cargo. Smuggling reached its peak in the late eighteenth and early nineteenth centuries, and only really died out with the introduction of free-trade policies after 1840.

A series of judicious parliamentary acts made small improvements to the lot of the rural labourer: the **Reform Act** of 1832 established the principle (if not actually the practice) of popular representation; the **Poor Law** of 1834 did something to alleviate the condition of the most destitute; and the repeal of the Corn Laws in 1846 cut the cost of bread. Significant sections of the middle classes were just as eager to see progressive reform as the working classes, as evidenced by the immense popularity of **Charles Dickens** (1812–70), whose novels – many set in and around his native town of Rochester (see box, p.70) – railed against poverty and injustice.

The general sense of inequity felt by the rural poor can't have been helped by the antics of their future monarch, **George IV** (see box, p.256), along the coast at **Brighton**, where he was living the high life with his mistress, helping turn the little fishing town into the most fashionable resort on the south coast. The town's transformation had begun in the second half of the eighteenth century when Dr Russell of Lewes began to recommend sea-bathing as an alternative to "taking the cure" at spa towns such as fashionable **Tunbridge Wells** (see p.134). Brighton was one of the earliest **seaside resorts** in the country, but it was not the first: that honour goes to Margate (see p.89) on the North Kent coast, where the first seawater baths opened in 1736. It was only in the Victorian era, however, that the phenomenon of the seaside town really took off.

The Victorian era

In 1837 **Victoria** came to the throne. Her long reign witnessed the zenith of British power: the British trading fleet was easily the mightiest in the world and it underpinned an empire upon which, in that famous phrase of the time, "the sun never set". Sussex-based author Rudyard Kipling (see box, p.191) became the poet of the English empire, coining such phrases as "the white man's burden"; wealthy landowners thought nothing of dispatching plant hunters to scour the globe searching for exotic specimens to populate their great Wealden gardens (see box, p.198); and Victorian explorers proudly displayed their hunting trophies in museums such as the Powell-Cotton Museum in Margate (see p.92). There were extraordinary intellectual achievements too – as typified by the publication of *On the Origin of Species* in 1859, written by Charles Darwin from his home in Kent (see p.154).

Perhaps the biggest change the Victorian era brought to the Southeast was the **arrival of the railway** between the 1830s and 1860s, which at one stroke opened up the region to Londoners, both commuters and holiday makers alike. The world's first scheduled steam passenger service, the **Canterbury & Whitstable Railway**, began puffing its way between cathedral town and coast in 1830, carrying day-trippers to the beach and back.

Newcomers built villas and country houses in the Weald, settlements grew up along the railway routes – the start of the **commuter belt** – and the **seaside town**

1803–15	1796	1830
Defences are erected along the south coast during the Napoleonic Wars, which end with the defeat of Napoleon at Waterloo.	The last furnace of the great Wealden iron industry closes its doors, just as the Industrial Revolution is gathering steam elsewhere in the country.	Agricultural labourers rise up in the Swing Riots, which start in Kent and spread across the south.

boomed. All along the Sussex coast the resorts expanded rapidly: the population of Hastings grew from 3175 in 1801 to 17,621 in 1851, to a staggering 65,000 by the end of the century. The fishing industry in many towns dwindled, as tourism became a major source of income, and piers and bandstands sprang up all along the coast. In Kent, Herne Bay, Margate, Broadstairs and Ramsgate all thrived, as the train replaced the slower, weather-dependent steamboats. Kent also saw another phenomenon on the rise, as thousands of **hoppers** from London's East End migrated down to the hop fields of Kent every autumn to pick up casual work during the hop harvest (see box, p.137).

The World Wars

The outbreak of **World War I** in 1914 saw an ever-present threat of invasion hang over the southeast corner of the country. In Dover Castle you can visit a fire command post with a chart room – its broad table spread with maps, charts and tin mugs of tea – and an observation room, where binoculars and telescopes were used to keep a 24-hour watch on the harbour and the Straits.

The war dragged on for four miserable years, its key engagements fought in the trenches that zigzagged across northern France and west Belgium. Britain and her allies eventually prevailed, but the number of dead beggared belief. The Royal Sussex Regiment alone lost nearly seven thousand men. The number of men enlisting caused a severe shortage of agricultural labourers, and conscientious objectors moved to the countryside to work the land, thus exempting themselves from military service; among them were Duncan Grant and his lover David Garnett, who with Vanessa Bell set up house at Charleston, marking the beginning of Sussex's famous connection with the **Bloomsbury Group** (see box, p.222).

When **World War II** broke out in September 1939, the Southeast was once more at the frontline: the Nazis' **Operation Sea Lion** had gone so far as to identify Camber Sands, Winchelsea, Bexhill and Cuckmere Haven in Sussex as potential invasion points. Barbed wire was strung up along the coast, pill boxes and anti-tank obstacles put in place, the Martello towers, built in Napoleonic times, re-employed and the Home Guard mobilized. The Cuckmere Valley – where you can still see tank traps and crumbling pill boxes today (see p.215) – was lit up at night to look like the nearby port of Newhaven to confuse enemy planes, while the nearby Long Man of Wilmington hill figure was temporarily painted green so it could not be used for navigation. Idealized posters of the Sussex Downs ("Your Britain – Fight For It Now") were used in propaganda, and Dame Vera Lynn sang the iconic (*There'll be Bluebirds Over*) *The White Cliffs of Dover* (see box, p.117).

Kent in particular played a crucial role in the war. It was from here in 1940 that **Operation Dynamo** – the rescue of around 300,000 troops stranded at Dunkirk by a flotilla of large and little boats – was masterminded from secret underground tunnels beneath Dover Castle (see p.113). That same summer saw the **Battle of Britain** fought in the skies above Kent – a famous victory that put paid to Hitler's invasion plans and led charismatic prime minister **Winston Churchill**, who had his own home in Kent at Chartwell (see p.152), to famously dub it the nation's "finest hour". Today, the Battle of Britain memorial (see p.124) sits on the famous white cliffs between Dover and Folkestone.

As the war continued, both Kent and Sussex suffered heavily from **bombing raids**. In June 1942 a Luftwaffe raid on Canterbury left whole streets and hundreds of houses

1837	1859	1830–60	1914–1918
Victoria comes to the throne.	Charles Darwin publishes *On the Origin of Species*, much of which was written from his home in Kent.	The railway arrives in Kent and Sussex, and seaside resorts boom all along the coast.	World War I leaves 7000 men of the Royal Sussex Regiment dead, and the Bloomsbury Set arrives at Charleston Farmhouse in Sussex.

destroyed, though amazingly the cathedral came through unscathed. The ports of Ramsgate, Dover and Folkestone all took a battering too, from shells fired from German boats in the Channel. In the summer of 1944, 1500 doodlebug bombs fell on Kent on their way to London, bestowing the unenviable nickname of "**doodlebug alley**" on the beleaguered county. At the end of the war, nearly one in three of all the houses in the nation had been destroyed or damaged, nearly a quarter of a million members of the British armed forces and over 58,000 civilians had lost their lives.

To the modern day

A very different **landscape** emerged from the end of World War II, particularly in Sussex, where there had been widespread ploughing up of the Downs' chalkland turf for wartime grain production – a change from the traditional mixed "sheep and corn" farming that was practised before the war. The ploughing up of grassland continued after the war, leading to an enormous loss of biodiversity that is only recently being reversed. Some estimate that during this period the percentage of chalk grassland on the eastern Downs fell from 50 percent to just 3–4 percent. As early as 1929 there had been calls for the South Downs to be protected as a national park, to guard against the urban sprawl fast swallowing up the countryside, but instead after World War II the government opted to give the Sussex Downs partial protection as an AONB (Area of Outstanding Natural Beauty), with the High Weald AONB following soon after. It was only in 2010 that the South Downs finally gained full **national park** status and protection.

Elsewhere in the region, the **transport** infrastructure improved dramatically, making the Southeast even busier, and cementing its status as affluent, prime commuting territory. Motorway building took off in the 1960s and 1970s; Gatwick Airport saw its first flights to the continent in 1949 and became Britain's second largest airport in 1988 when the North Terminal opened; and the Channel Tunnel opened in 1994. The Local Government Act of 1972 saw Sussex divided into the separate counties of **East** and **West Sussex** in 1974, spelling an end, on paper at least, of the ancient Saxon kingdom of Sussex.

Alongside the expansion there was also decline. By the 1960s, the **hop-farming industry** was on its last legs, as machines replaced hop-pickers and cheaper hops were imported from abroad. Elsewhere in Kent, the county's **coal mines** – discovered near Dover in 1890 but beset by difficulties from the very beginning – were closed by the National Coal Board in the 1980s; Kent miners were among the most vocal in the year-long **miners' strike** (1984–85), and were the only miners in the country who voted to continue striking at the conference that opted to end the strike in 1985.

Around the coast, the traditional **seaside towns** were suffering too. The rise of the package holiday (and later budget airlines) saw holidaymakers abandon the traditional train-served resorts in droves in the 1960s and 1970s. By the end of the century, seaside towns such as Margate had become sorry shadows of their former selves, with boarded-up shop fronts and derelict seafront attractions, and areas of huge social deprivation.

The new century, however, has brought about a decided sea change at the seafront. Margate's spanking new contemporary art gallery, retro shops and hip galleries have breathed new life into the town, a story that's been repeated around the coast at Folkestone, Hastings and elsewhere (see box, p.6). The seaside is back in fashion.

1939–1945	1974	2010	2011
The Southeast suffers from heavy bomb damage in World War II; the Dunkirk rescue operation is coordinated from Dover Castle; and the Battle of Britain is fought in the skies above Kent.	Sussex is divided into the separate counties of East Sussex and West Sussex.	The South Downs National Park is created.	Turner Contemporary opens in Margate.

Books

Many writers have lived or worked in Kent, Sussex and Surrey, using real-life historical incidents, people and locations to inspire them. The list below is necessarily selective – we've marked our very favourites with the ★ symbol.

FICTION AND POETRY

★ **Daisy Ashford** *The Young Visiters*. Written in 1890 by a 9-year-old girl from Lewes, Daisy Ashford, this warm and witty tale of Victorian love was first published in 1919 – complete with wonderfully idiosyncratic spelling – and has never been out of print since.

★ **Jane Austen** *Emma*. Austen's slyly witty novel about a misguided matchmaker was written while the author was living in Surrey; the famous picnic scene, in which Emma attempts to enjoy a fashionable alfresco foray that all goes horribly wrong, is set on Box Hill.

★ **H.E. Bates** *The Pop Larkin Chronicles*. Made into a hugely popular TV series, *The Darling Buds of May*, Bates's stories of the ever-optimistic Larkin family, with their earthy, often transgressive ways, are splendid examples of storytelling, portraying Kent as a land, in many ways, unto itself – both deeply conservative and rumbustuously independent.

E. F. Benson *Mapp and Lucia*. Comic novel – one of a series – set between the wars following snobbish rivals Emmeline Lucas and Elizabeth Mapp, each vying for social supremacy in the fictional town of Tilling, which was modelled very closely on Benson's home town of Rye; fans of the books can head to Rye to join tours of *Mapp and Lucia's* Tilling (see p.169).

A. S. Byatt *The Children's Book*. Covering the period from 1895 to 1919, Byatt's complex, wordy novel – which gives more than a nod to the real lives of writer E. Nesbit and artist Eric Gill – tells the story of a tangled set of bohemian families tussling with their creative, and procreative, urges. While the characters can be too narcissistic to be likeable, and the historical context occasionally heavy-handed, the sense of time and place – Romney Marsh and around – is striking and original.

Nick Cave *The Death of Bunny Monroe*. Rock musician Cave's Brighton-based novel follows Bunny Munro – travelling salesman, sex addict and all-round loser – as he takes to the road with his son after the death of his wife. Funny, sad and downright filthy in equal measure, and as the title suggests, there's no happy ending.

Geoffrey Chaucer *The Canterbury Tales*. Chaucer's great work of poetry, written in the mid-fifteenth century, takes the form of a series of yarns recounted by a motley crew of pilgrims heading from Southwark to Canterbury (see box, p.47). Full of wit and deftly drawn characters, it changed

English literature forever and remains an entertaining read today. Various translations into modern English, including versions from Penguin Classics and Oxford World Classics, are available, but it's a rewarding challenge to encounter it in the original, too.

★ **Charles Dickens** *David Copperfield*; *Great Expectations*; *The Mystery of Edwin Drood*; *Nicholas Nickleby*; *Pickwick Papers*. Dickens, who spent much of his childhood in and around Rochester, frequently used North Kent locations in his books – including the opening pages of *Great Expectations*, which rank among the most atmospheric passages in English literature. The author's last and unfinished novel, *Edwin Drood*, is a complex and engaging mystery largely set in Rochester, while *David Copperfield's* Miss Trotwood – and the donkeys that so infuriated her – were inspired by a real person, and a real house, in Broadstairs. Of course, Dickens hopped about all over southern England, with Surrey locations included in *Nicholas Nickleby* (Devil's Punchbowl) and *Pickwick Papers* (Dorking).

★ **T.S. Eliot** *Murder in the Cathedral*. Spare, visceral, overwrought and intellectual, Eliot's short play (see box, p.44), which tells the story of the assassination of Thomas à Becket in Canterbury cathedral, is a beautiful piece of writing, shedding light on the man whose violent death made the city one of the most important pilgrimage sites in the world.

E.M. Forster *A Room with a View*. The second part of Forster's Edwardian romance has his heroine, Lucy, return to life in Surrey after a tumultuous Grand Tour of Europe; inevitably, however, she's driven to reject the respectable civility of the Home Counties for something rather more passionate.

Stella Gibbons *Cold Comfort Farm*. First published in 1932, this comic classic is a merciless parody of the rural melodramas popular at the time. The orphaned, no-nonsense Flora Poste descends on her crazy, gloomy relatives, the Starkadders, in deepest rural Sussex, and sets about tidying their lives up.

★ **Graham Greene** *Brighton Rock*. Melancholic thriller with heavy Catholic overtones, set in the criminal underworld of 1930s Brighton and featuring anti-hero Pinkie Brown, teenage sociopath and gangster, who is hunted down by middle-aged avenging angel Ida, representing the force of justice.

★ **Patrick Hamilton** *Hangover Square.* Hamilton's 1941 masterpiece, set in seedy 1930s London, Brighton and Maidenhead, tells the dark story of lonely, schizophrenic George Harvey Bone and his obsession with greedy, unscrupulous Netta, a failed actress, whose cruel rejection of him ultimately leads to tragedy.

★ **Russell Hoban** *Riddley Walker.* Cult sci-fi fantasy set in a loosely disguised, post-apocalyptic Kent – with towns including Ram Gut, Sam's Itch and Horny Boy – thousands of years after a nuclear holocaust. Told in a futuristic pidgin English, it's a compelling and hugely affecting read.

Peter James *Dead Simple.* The first title in a series of bestselling crime thrillers featuring Brighton-based detective superintendent Roy Grace, with the seaside city and the surrounding area looming large on the covers and in the storylines.

Rudyard Kipling *The Collected Poems.* Collection of poems by Sussex-based poet and author Kipling, which includes the wonderful *Smuggler's Song*, as well as *Sussex*, his poem in praise of his adopted county: "God gave all men all earth to love,/But, since our hearts are small/Ordained for each one spot should prove/Beloved over all. . ./Each to his choice, and I rejoice/The lot has fallen to me/In a fair ground–in a fair ground –/Yea, Sussex by the sea!"

Marina Lewycka *Two Caravans.* Lewycka's follow-up to the wildly popular *A Short History of Tractors in Ukrainian* sees a young Ukrainian woman, Irina, working as a seasonal fruit-picker in a less-than-bucolic contemporary Kent, along with a ragged band of overseas workers dreaming of a better life. The word play, and humour, are as sharp as in the first novel, though the issues are dark.

W. Somerset Maugham *Of Human Bondage; Cakes and Ale.* As a youth Maugham lived in the fishing village of Whitstable with his aunt and taciturn uncle, a vicar. He writes about it, disguised as "Blackstable", near the cathedral town of "Tercanbury", in these two novels. The first, written in 1915, portrays the Kent coast as a lonely and rather bleak place, while the second, from 1930, is a little cheerier.

★ **Melanie McGrath** *Hopping.* The title is a little misleading – while the annual "hop", in which the main characters decamp from the East End to East Kent to work on the hop harvest, is key to this compelling family saga, the novel's scope reaches far beyond that, offering a detailed history of how London's East End changed through the course of the twentieth century.

★ **A.A. Milne** *Winnie the Pooh* and *The House at Pooh Corner.* Milne's much-loved children's classics, beautifully illustrated by E.H. Shepherd, were written from his home in Ashdown Forest, with many of the Forest's real-life locations appearing in the books (see box, p.194).

George Orwell *A Clergyman's Daughter.* Written in 1935, Orwell's short novel tells the story of a young country woman who suffers a mysterious bout of amnesia and finds herself lost in London. The chapter in which she hooks up with a group of hop-pickers and travels to Kent draws heavily on Orwell's own hopping seasons. Unsurprisingly, he reveals a bleaker side to the whole business than is usually described, conveying in detail the poor conditions and pay suffered by the transient workers.

Julian Rathbone *The Last English King.* Fictionalized account of the 1066 invasion seen through the eyes of Walt, the last surviving of King Harold's bodyguards. A lively, gripping story, and one that vividly brings to life the events of that most tumultuous, momentous year in English history.

★ **Vita Sackville-West** *The Edwardians.* This mischievous dig at the English upper classes, published in 1930 but set during the final years of the Edwardian era, is Sackville-West's most popular novel. On one level a coming-of-age tale about siblings Sebastian and Viola, who together create an amalgam of Vita herself, it's also an expression of the author's tortured ambivalence about her background – her passion for her childhood home (the vast Knole estate in Kent); her bitter disappointment at not being able to inherit, despite being an only child; her shame at enjoying privilege based upon a feudal system. Above all, however, *The Edwardians* is a paean to Knole itself, as strong a character as any in the book and described in vivid and romantic detail.

★ **Graham Swift** *Last Orders.* Beautifully written, moving account of a group of ageing men on an expedition from London to Margate, where their recently deceased friend has asked them to scatter his ashes. Stop offs include Rochester, Canterbury and a hopping farm, with the poignant climax taking place on the bleak, windy Harbour Arm at Margate.

Russell Thorndike *Doctor Syn* novels. Swashbuckling adventures of the wonderfully named vicar whose wife's betrayal turns him to revenge, piracy, murder and smuggling. The books, published between 1915 and 1945, take us from the sleepy Kentish village of Dymchurch in the Romney Marsh, via the high seas and the American colonies and back again.

Robert Tressell *The Ragged Trousered Philanthropists.* Published posthumously in 1914, Tressell (real name Robert Noonan) based his classic socialist novel on his own experiences of poverty and hardship while working as a decorator in Hastings, which appears in the book as Mugsborough. His impassioned Marxist critique of capitalism in the workplace, where the "philanthropists" of the title are the workers who help line the pockets of their bosses, has over the years been dramatized for stage, TV and radio.

Sarah Waters *Tipping the Velvet.* Waters' debut, alive with the author's now-familiar storytelling genius and deft characterization, follows the fortunes of Nan, an oyster girl from Victorian Whitstable, who after encountering a charismatic male impersonator sets off on a picaresque journey through the London lesbian demi-monde. The Whitstable oysters' potential for erotic metaphor is, as you might expect, exploited with verve.

H.G. Wells *Kipps; The History of Mr Polly; Tono-Bungay*. Wells conveys a convincing sense of place – including Romney Marsh and Folkestone – in *Kipps*, his 1905 comic novel of an ordinary man, trapped in a stultifyingly lower-middle-class life, whose fortunes change with a huge inheritance. *Mr Polly* (1910), much of which is set around "Fishbourne" – based on Sandgate, near Folkestone, where Wells lived for a while – has many of the same themes, though a slightly darker edge. Well's semi autobiographical novel, *Tono-Bungay* (1909), tells the tale of George, an apprentice chemist (like Wells), whose uncle's fictitious medicine becomes a spectacular success despite having no medical benefits whatsoever. The first part of the book describes George's life as a servant's child at Bladesover House, modelled on Wells' own experiences at Uppark House, where his mother was housekeeper.

Virginia Woolf *Orlando; Between the Acts*. Nigel Nicolson, Vita Sackville-West's son, called *Orlando* the "longest and most charming love letter in literature". It's an astonishing gift from Woolf to Sackville-West, with whom she had an affair, and who in this book lives for three centuries, changes sexes, and muses on the nature of life, love, art and history. Mercurial, mischievous and cerebral, the book is populated with thinly disguised characters and real-life photos; at the heart of it, though, is Knole, the grand Kentish estate that Sackville-West was never able to inherit (see p.151). *Between the Acts* was Woolf's final novel, published in 1941 shortly before her suicide, and follows the staging of a play at Pointz Hall, an Elizabethan manor house inspired by real-life Firle Place and Glynde Place near Woolf's home at Rodmell.

Helen Zahari *Dirty Weekend*. Provocative and disturbing, this novel follows young Brighton girl Bella who, having been terrorized by a neighbour, "woke up one morning and realized she'd had enough". Over the next 48 hours – the "dirty weekend" of the title – she sets off to exact her violent vigilante revenge on him and others like him. The book garnered reviews from each end of the spectrum when it was published, hailed as "brave, brilliant and beautiful" by one reviewer, dismissed as "more offensive than pornography" by another, and the subsequent film adaptation by Michael Winner proved equally controversial.

HISTORY, BIOGRAPHY AND TRAVELOGUE

Peter Brandon *Sussex*. Authoritative and encyclopedic, this illustrated book traces the history of Sussex from its earliest peoples to the modern day, taking in wildlife, artists and writers, history, folklore, geology, castles, gardens, market towns and cities along the way.

Julie Burchill and Daniel Raven *Made in Brighton*. The controversial journalist and her husband take a look at Britain through the lens of Brighton, interspersing personal stories of their lives in the city with wider observations on everything from the Labour party to former glamour model (and fellow Brightonian) Jordan.

William Cobbett *Rural Rides*. Written between 1821 and 1832, journalist and political reformer Cobbett's account of his travels on horseback through southern England bemoans the death of the old rural England and its customs, while decrying both the growth of cities and the iniquities suffered by the exploited poor. A page-turner it's not, but nonetheless it's a fascinating snapshot of the region in the early nineteenth century.

Sophie Collins *A Sussex Miscellany*. Quirky dip-in-and-out-of collection of Sussex trivia – one of a series of beautifully produced and illustrated books on Sussex published by Sussex-based Snake River Press (ⓦ snakeriverpress.co.uk). Other titles in the series include books on Sussex wildlife, writers and artists, food and drink, landscape, gardens (see opposite) and walks.

Richard Filmer *Hops and Hop Picking*. Written in 1982, this slim volume offers a deft historical account of the hopping industry in Britain, taking it from its Roman roots to its demise in the late twentieth century, with lots of clearly written technical detail and intriguing historic photos.

David Howarth *1066: The Year of the Conquest*; **Frank McLynn** *1066: The Year of the Three Battles*; **Peter Rex** *1066: A New History of the Norman Conquest*. Three excellent books on the Norman Conquest of 1066. Howarth's book puts the invasion in the context of the year it took place; McLynn overturns some of the myths about the battle and takes a closer look at Harold Hardrada, whom Harold defeated at Stamford Bridge before his own defeat at the hands of William; and Rex covers not only the background to the Norman invasion but also continues the story to the final crushing of lingering English resistance in 1076.

★ **Olivia Laing** *To the River*. This acclaimed account of the author's midsummer walk along the River Ouse from source to sea is beautifully written and observed, interweaving nature writing, history and folklore, with plenty on Virginia Woolf, who drowned herself in the river in 1941.

Terence Lawson & David Killingray (eds) *An Historical Atlas of Kent*. This intriguing, comprehensive history, sponsored by the Kent Archaeological Society, uses around 250 maps and short essays to illustrate everything from Anglo-Saxon churches to medieval almshouses, breweries to suburban sprawl.

Philip MacDougal *Chatham Dockyard: The Rise and Fall of a Military Industrial Complex*. A lengthy account, published in 2012, of the great royal dockyard, which, founded in the late sixteenth century, built hundreds of warships for the Royal Navy before being wound down in the 1980s. It's a good read even if you're not wild about ships, putting the docks into a broader historical context.

★ **Judith Mackrell** *The Bloomsbury Ballerina*. Engrossing account of one of the fringe members of the Bloomsbury

Group – Lydia Lopokova, the larger-than-life Russian ballet star who became the much-adored wife of sober economist, Bloomsburyite (and former homosexual) John Maynard Keynes – much to the disgust of Vanessa Bell, Virginia Woolf and Lytton Strachey, who bitchily dismissed her as a "half-witted canary". A fascinating portrait of a woman whose life included encounters with Nijinsky, Stravinsky and Picasso, and ended at Tilton House in Sussex, where you can now stay overnight (see p.226).

Adam Nicolson *Sissinghurst: An Unfinished History.* Fascinating book by the grandson of Vita Sackville-West and Harold Nicolson about his struggles with the National Trust to revitalize the estate around Sissinghurst in Kent, with a broader, personal and lively history of both the estate and Kent itself thrown in.

Richard Platt *Smuggling in the British Isles.* A good introduction to the smuggling trade that operated up and down the coastline of Britain in the eighteenth and early nineteenth centuries; Kent and Sussex's smuggling outfits – including the notorious Hawkhurst Gang – had the most fearsome reputation of the lot.

Vita Sackville-West *Pepita.* Sackville-West's biography of her grandmother, a half-Gypsy Spanish dancer, and her mother, the illegitimate, volatile Victoria, who is catapulted into the aristocracy to become mistress of the Knole estate in Kent, reads like a rollicking melodrama and is all the more compelling for being entirely true.

ART

Quentin Bell and Virginia Nicholson *Charleston: a Bloomsbury House and Garden.* This fascinating account of the Bloomsbury Group's country home – written by Vanessa Bell's son and Quentin Bell's daughter – gives an insider's view of life in the bohemian household. With plenty of photographs of the farmhouse's inimitable decorative style, as well as snapshots from the family album, it's the perfect souvenir after a visit.

Ruth Cribb and Joe Cribb *Eric Gill: Lust for Letter and Line.* A great introduction – with plenty of illustrations – to the late, great artist, typographer, sculptor and wood engraver Eric Gill (see box, p.234), whose controversial

personal life and sexual predilections have received as much attention in recent years as his art. Fiona MacCarthy's authoritative, fascinating biography, *Eric Gill*, is equally recommended; her commendably non-judgemental book was the first to reveal Gill's sexual improprieties.

★ **James Russell** *Ravilious in Pictures: Sussex and the Downs.* Twenty-two colour plates of Eric Ravilious's beautiful watercolour landscapes of the Sussex Downs, painted in the 1930s before his death in World War II. Social historian James Russell's accompanying short essays provide the background on Ravilious's life (see box, p.210) and the quintessentially English scenes he painted.

GARDENS

Jane Brown *Sissinghurst: Portrait of a Garden.* Lavishly illustrated coffee-table book that brings the ebullience and abundance of Sackville-West's garden to life, as well as providing a good chunk of history about the estate itself.

★ **Lorraine Harrison** *20 Sussex Gardens.* A succinct, well-written tour of twenty of the best Sussex gardens, taking in various different historical periods and horticultural styles, from the excellent Sussex-based publisher Snake River Press. A sister title, *Inspiring Sussex Gardeners*, focuses on the designers and plant hunters behind the gardens.

★ **Derek Jarman** *Derek Jarman's Garden.* A poignant diary, illustrated with arty photos, recording the last year of Jarman's life as he created his shingle garden in Dungeness. Bittersweet, poetic and full of simple joy, much like the garden itself. The preface is by Keith Collins, Jarman's friend and current inhabitant of Prospect Cottage, where the

garden can still be seen.

Stephen Lacey *Gardens of the National Trust.* Lavishly photographed volume on the National Trust's expansive national collection of gardens, which includes some of the finest gardens in Sussex, Kent and Surrey.

★ **Judith Tankard** *Gertrude Jekyll and the Country House Garden.* Using a wealth of luscious photos from *Country Life* magazine, for whom Jekyll was the gardening correspondent, this stunning coffee-table book celebrates the work of the influential Surrey-based garden designer, both with collaborators, including her great friend the architect Edwin Lutyens, and on her own.

Various *Essays on the Life of a Working Amateur 1843–1932.* A highly readable compendium of personal essays about Gertrude Jekyll, written by members of her family and various experts, covering a broad range of Jekyll's work – including interior design – beyond her garden design.

FOOD AND DRINK

★ **Mandy Bruce** *The Oyster Seekers.* Charmingly illustrated tome, produced in association with *Wheelers Oyster Bar* in Whitstable, which works as both an excellent recipe book and a lively, nostalgic history of the oyster industry and fishing on the east coast.

Bill Collison *Bill's The Cookbook: Cook, Eat, Smile.* Seasonally inspired cookbook championing British produce from the man whose original grocer's shop in Lewes (see p.231) has grown to become a highly successful chain of restaurants across London and the South.

★ **Amanda Powley and Phil Taylor** *Terre à Terre: the Vegetarian Cookbook*. Innovative, exciting recipes – from Dunkin Doughnuts (parmesan and porcini-dust doughnuts served with chestnut soup) to No Cocky, Big Leeky (sausages and mash) – from Brighton's multi-award-winning vegetarian restaurant (see p.269), which is regularly voted among the best in the country.

WALKING AND CYCLING

AA *40 Short Walks in Kent; 40 Short Walks in Sussex; 40 Short Walks in Surrey*. Easy-to-follow routes spanning anything from one to four miles, with good, concise background on local history, wildlife and landscape. They also include useful details for dog-owners, include refreshment-break and public-toilet information, and suggest more detailed maps.

Deirdre Huston and Marina Bullivant *Cycling in Sussex*. Twenty bike rides, from 4km to 28km, on off-road trails or quiet roads in Sussex, with routes divided into "family", "easy", "medium" and "hard", plus coverage of the county's seafront cycle routes and trails along old railway lines. Huston's *Cycling Days Out: South East England* covers Sussex, Kent, Surrey and Hampshire, with half a dozen or so rides suggested for each county.

Pathfinder Walks Series of excellent practical walking guides with maps and route descriptions. Titles include *East Sussex and the South Downs*; *West Sussex and the South Downs*; *Surrey and Sussex*; *Kent*; and *Surrey*. Produced by the Ordnance Survey.

Helena Smith *The Rough Guide to Walks in London and Southeast England*. Handy, pocket-sized book covering walks for all abilities around the Southeast, all starting and finishing at train stations. Each walk features recommendations for places to stop off for lunch or a pint, and there's plenty of background information on everything from Sussex smugglers to stone circles. It's especially useful for Londoners, as it covers walks within the capital too.

Small print and index

A ROUGH GUIDE TO ROUGH GUIDES

Published in 1982, the first Rough Guide – to Greece – was a student scheme that became a publishing phenomenon. Mark Ellingham, a recent graduate in English from Bristol University, had been travelling in Greece the previous summer and couldn't find the right guidebook. With a small group of friends he wrote his own guide, combining a highly contemporary, journalistic style with a thoroughly practical approach to travellers' needs.

The immediate success of the book spawned a series that rapidly covered dozens of destinations. And, in addition to impecunious backpackers, Rough Guides soon acquired a much broader readership that relished the guides' wit and inquisitiveness as much as their enthusiastic, critical approach and value-for-money ethos.

These days, Rough Guides include recommendations from budget to luxury and cover more than 200 destinations around the globe, as well as producing an ever-growing range of eBooks and apps.

Visit **roughguides.com** to see our latest publications.

Rough Guide credits

Editors: Natasha Foges and Alice Park
Layout: Umesh Aggarwal
Cartography: Ed Wright
Picture editors: Rhiannon Furbear and Marta Bescos
Proofreader: Diane Margolis
Managing editor: Mani Ramaswamy
Assistant editor: Prema Dutta
Photographer: Chris Christoforou
Production: Charlotte Cade
Cover design: Nicole Newman, Umesh Aggarwal

Editorial assistant: Olivia Rawes
Senior pre-press designer: Dan May
Design director: Scott Stickland
Travel publisher: Joanna Kirby
Digital travel publisher: Peter Buckley
Operations coordinator: Helen Blount
Publishing director (Travel): Clare Currie
Commercial manager: Gino Magnotta
Managing director: John Duhigg

Publishing information

This 1st edition published May 2013 by
Rough Guides Ltd,
80 Strand, London WC2R 0RL
11, Community Centre, Panchsheel Park,
New Delhi 110017, India
Distributed by the Penguin Group
Penguin Books Ltd,
80 Strand, London WC2R 0RL
Penguin Group (USA)
345 Hudson Street, NY 10014, USA
Penguin Group (Australia)
250 Camberwell Road, Camberwell,
Victoria 3124, Australia
Penguin Group (NZ)
67 Apollo Drive, Mairangi Bay, Auckland 1310,
New Zealand
Penguin Group (South Africa)
Block D, Rosebank Office Park, 181 Jan Smuts Avenue,
Parktown North, Gauteng, South Africa 2193
Rough Guides is represented in Canada by Tourmaline
Editions Inc. 662 King Street West, Suite 304, Toronto,
Ontario M5V 1M7
Printed in Malaysia by Vivar Printing Sdn Bhd

MIX
Paper from
responsible sources
FSC   www.fsc.org   FSC™ C018179

Help us update

We've gone to a lot of effort to ensure that the first edition of **The Rough Guide to Kent, Sussex and Surrey** is accurate and up-to-date. However, things change – places get "discovered", opening hours are notoriously fickle, restaurants and rooms raise prices or lower standards. If you feel we've got it wrong or left something out, we'd like to know, and if you can remember the address, the price, the hours, the phone number, so much the better.

Please send your comments with the subject line "**Rough Guide Kent, Sussex and Surrey Update**" to ✉ mail@uk.roughguides.com. We'll credit all contributions and send a copy of the next edition (or any other Rough Guide if you prefer) for the very best emails.

Find more travel information, connect with fellow travellers and book your trip on ⊕ roughguides.com

Photo credits

All photos © Rough Guides except the following:
(Key: t-top; c-centre; b-bottom; l-left; r-right)

p.3 Corbis, John Miller
p.7 Alamy, Lenscap (tr); Howard Taylor (tl); AWL
Images, Travel Pix Collection (b)
p.9 Alamy, Peter Gates (tr); PCJones (cr); Getty Images, Dan
Kitwood (br)
p.11 Alamy, Derek Croucher (b); Visit Kent Limited (tl)
p.12 Alamy, David Baker (b)
p.13 arcblue.com, Peter Durant (bl)
p.14 Visit Kent Limited (br)
p.16 Alamy, Tony Watson (b)
p.17 Alamy, Robert Bird (bl); Getty Images, Laurie Noble (br)
p.18 Getty Images, Lyn Holly (t)
p.55 Browns Coffeehouse (br)

p.64–65 Corbis, Arcaid/Robert Greshoff
p.67 Visit Kent Limited
p.132–133 SuperStock, Nelly Boyd
p.135 Visit Kent Limited
p.147 SuperStock, EWA Stock (tr); Visit Kent Limited (b)
p. 253 Alamy Travel Pictures
p.300–301 Corbis, Martyn Goddard
p.303 Corbis, John Miller

Front cover View of the Seven Sisters cliffs and Lighthouse
at Beachy Head © 4Corners: SIME / Riccardo Spila
Back cover Sussex Downs, Dover Castle, The Pavilion
gardens, Brighton; all © Rough Guides, Chris Christoforou

ABOUT THE AUTHORS

Claire Saunders grew up in Brighton, which wasn't anywhere near as cool then as it is now. After almost ten years of working as an editor and then Managing Editor at Rough Guides in London, she moved back down to Sussex, where she now lives in Lewes and works as a freelance writer and editor. She researched and wrote the Sussex chapters for this book.

Samantha Cook is a London-based writer and editor. She's worked for Rough Guides for many years, writing about the USA, New Orleans, Paris, Cult Movies and Chick Flicks, among other subjects. In the last few years she has returned to her roots, co-authoring *The Best Places to Stay in Britain on a Budget* and the *Rough Guide to Vintage London*. A longtime fan of the southeast coast, she was delighted to be able to spend a year exploring the length and breadth of Kent and Surrey for this brand new guide.

Acknowledgements

Thanks to Georgia Amson-Bradshaw, who wrote the "Drinking" and "Clubs and live music" sections of the Brighton chapter, and Danny Weddup, who wrote "Gay Brighton".

At Rough Guides, Claire and Sam give huge thanks to Mani Ramaswamy for the initial phone call, and to dream-team editors Natasha Foges and Alice Park, each of whom was a pleasure to work with, steering the book (and us!) with calm, efficiency and aplomb. Thanks too to Ed Wright, who wrought his usual magic with the maps, Rhiannon Furbear and Marta Bescos for the lovely pictures, and to Umesh Aggarwal for the splendid layout.
Samantha Cook: I couldn't have hoped for a lovelier co-author than Claire Saunders, whose generosity, elegant turn of phrase, enviable efficiency and brilliant sense of humour played a huge part in making this book such a happy experience. Thanks, too, to Amy Carey at the *Hotel du Vin*, Tunbridge Wells; Gavin Oakley at the *White Cliffs Hotel*, St Margaret's-at-Cliffe; Dominic Parker at the *Salutation* in Sandwich; Anna Deacon at the arthouse, Canterbury; George Shaw at Avocado PR; Clare Elson, *Castaway Cottage*, Whitstable; Jane Bishop at the *Walpole Bay Hotel*, Margate; the team at the Ambrette, Margate; everyone at the *Minnis Bay Restaurant*; Tamsin Leigh at Penshurst Place; Denbies Wine Estate; the staff of the National Trust and English Heritage; Visit Britain; Eleanor Aldridge, Katie Bennett and Natasha Foges for canny dining tips, and Andy Turner for directing me towards some very nice pubs; Claire Spooner for Folkestone thoughts; Adrian Ward for Surrey snippets; Ally Scott, Matt Anstee, Satch and Jem for road-testing Diggerland; Pam Cook for lots of lovely garden tours and inspiring road trips, and Jim Cook and Ulli Sieglohr who so kindly whisked us off somewhere else entirely. Above all, as ever, love to Greg Ward, who doubles the fun and halves the stress, and without whose support – on so many levels – writing this book just wouldn't have been possible.
Claire Saunders would like to thank: Heather and Bryan Allen, Robin and Jane Field, Javed Khan, Dev Biswal, George Shaw, Jane Ellis, Jo Gaukrodger, Jo Glynde, Margaret Murphy, Corinne Rhoades, Hilary Williams and all the others who have helped me in my research. A special thank you to Georgia for her great reviews of Brighton's pubs and nightlife, which saved me from setting foot in a club for the first time in fifteen years; to Danny for his excellent round-up of the Brighton LGBT scene; and of course to Sam, the perfect co-author in every respect. Most of all, a huge thanks to Ian for uncomplaining support and patience; to Christine, Terry, mum and dad for heroic childcare duties; to mum for advice, support and company on the road; and to Tom and Mia, who've endured a long summer of their mum unaccountably choosing to sit in a darkened room in front of a computer rather than play ninjas with them.
Chris Christoforou I would like to say a very special thank you to Rhiannon Furbear for giving me the fantastic opportunity to work on and produce the photos for another wonderful Rough Guides book, and a very big thank you to all the angels who assisted me along the magical way in beautiful Sussex, Kent and Surrey.

Index

Maps are marked in **grey**

C

D

E

F

G

Map symbols

The symbols below are used on maps throughout the book

-----	Road	⧫	Point of interest	⌂	Observatory	✛	Hospital
▬▬	Pedestrianized/restricted access road	⚲	Museum	✈	Airport	⚓	Swimming pool
///////	Steps	♜	Castle	✗	Minor airport/airfield	⊙	Statue
=○=	Railway & station	🏛	Stately home	𝔐	Rock formation	⚑	Golf course
==○==	Private/tourist railway & station	⌂	Abbey	ᗡᗡᗡ	Cliffs		Building
+++++	Funicular railway	♈	Gardens	★	Bus stop/bus station	⚑	Church
)(	Bridge/tunnel entrance	⸪	Ruins/archeological site	ⓘ	Tourist office		South Downs National Park
→	One-way street	▲	Peak	Ⓟ	Parking		Park/forest
- - - -	North Downs Way	⚜	Viewpoint	✉	Post office	+└	Cemetery
- - - -	South Downs Way	🐘	Zoo/wildlife park	@	Internet access		Beach
- - - -	Saxon Shore Way	🦃	Nature reserve	Ⓣ	Public toilets		Marshland
- - - -	Greensand Way	🍇	Vineyard/wine estate	⊠	Gate		Tidal flats
- - - -	Other footpath/cycling route	🕎	Lighthouse	▬	Wall		Shingle

Listings key

- ■ Accommodation
- ● Shop
- ● Café/restaurant
- ■ Bar/pub/club/live music